HISTORY OF WOMEN IN THE UNITED STATES

HISTORY OF WOMEN IN THE UNITED STATES

Historical Articles on Women's Lives and Activities

Edited by Nancy F. Cott

Series ISBN 3-598-41454-4

1. Theory and Method in Women's History
   ISBN 3-598-41455-2 Part 1
   ISBN 3-598-41477-3 Part 2

2. Household Constitution and Family Relationships
   ISBN 3-598-41456-0

3. Domestic Relations and Law
   ISBN 3-598-41457-9

4. Domestic Ideology and Domestic Work
   ISBN 3-598-41458-7 Part 1
   ISBN 3-598-41475-7 Part 2

5. The Intersection of Work and Family Life
   ISBN 3-598-41459-5 Part 1
   ISBN 3-598-41476-5 Part 2

6. Working on the Land
   ISBN 3-598-41460-9

7. Industrial Wage Work
   ISBN 3-598-41461-7 Part 1
   ISBN 3-598-41693-8 Part 2

8. Professional and White-Collar Employments
   ISBN 3-598-41462-5 Part 1
   ISBN 3-598-41694-6 Part 2

9. Prostitution
   ISBN 3-598-41463-3

10. Sexuality and Sexual Behavior
    ISBN 3-598-41464-1

11. Women's Bodies: Health and Childbirth
    ISBN 3-598-41465-X

12. Education
    ISBN 3-598-41466-8

13. Religion
    ISBN 3-598-41467-6

14. Intercultural and Interracial Relations
    ISBN 3-598-41468-4

15. Women and War
    ISBN 3-598-41469-2

16. Women Together: Organizational Life
    ISBN 3-598-41470-6

17. Social and Moral Reform
    ISBN 3-598-41471-4 Part 1
    ISBN 3-598-41695-4 Part 2

18. Women and Politics
    ISBN 3-598-41472-2 Part 1
    ISBN 3-598-41697-0 Part 2

19. Woman Suffrage
    ISBN 3-598-41473-0 Part 1
    ISBN 3-598-41696-2 Part 2

20. Feminist Struggles for Sex Equality
    ISBN 3-598-41474-9

HISTORY OF WOMEN IN THE UNITED STATES

Historical Articles on Women's Lives and Activities

20. Feminist Struggles for Sex Equality

Edited with an Introduction by

Nancy F. Cott
Yale University

K · G · Saur
Munich · New Providence · London · Paris · 1994

Publisher's Note
The articles and chapters which comprise this collection originally appeared in a wide variety of publications and are reproduced here in facsimile from the highest quality offprints and photocopies available. The reader will notice some occasional marginal shading and text-curl common to photocopying from tightly bound volumes. Every attempt has been made to either correct or minimize this effect.

Copyright information for articles reproduced in this collection appears at the end of this volume.

Library of Congress Cataloging-in-Publication Data
History of women in the United States : historical articles on
women's lives and activities / edited with
an introduction by Nancy F. Cott.
p. cm.
Includes bibliographical references and indexes.
Contents: 1. Theory and method in women's history -- 2. Household constitution and family relationships -- 3. Domestic relations and law -- 4. Domestic ideology and domestic work -- 5. The intersection of work and family life -- 6. Working on the land -- 7. Industrial wage work -- 8. Professional and white-collar employments -- 9. Prostitution -- 10. Sexuality and sexual behavior -- 11. Women's bodies -- 12. Education -- 13. Religion -- 14. Intercultural and interracial relations -- 15. Women and war -- 16. Women together -- 17. Social and moral reform -- 18. Women and politics -- 19. Woman suffrage -- 20. Feminist struggles for sex equality.
ISBN 3-598-41454-4 (set)
1. Women--United States--History. 2. Women--United States--Social conditions. I. Cott, Nancy F.
HQ1410.H57 1992
305.4'0973--dc20 92-16765
CIP

Die Deutsche Bibliothek - CIP - Einheitsaufnahme

History of Women in the United States: historical articles
on women's lives and activities / ed. with an introd. by Nancy F. Cott.
- Munich ; New Providence ; London ; Paris : Saur.
ISBN 3-598-41454-4
NE: Cott, Nancy F. (Hrsg.)
Vol. 20. feminist struggles for sex equality - (1994)
ISBN 3-598-41474-9

Printed on acid-free paper/Gedruckt auf säurefreiem Papier

A Reed Reference Publishing Company

Printed in the United States of America
Printed/Bound by Edwards Brothers Incorporated, Ann Arbor

ISBN 3-598-41474-9 (vol. 20)
ISBN 3-598-41454-4 (series)

Contents

Series Preface ix
Introduction xi

Feminist Friends: Agrarian Quakers and the Emergence of Woman's Rights in America
NANCY A. HEWITT 3

Women's Rights and the Wrongs of Marriage in Mid-Nineteenth-Century America
FRANÇOISE BASCH 26

Labor's True Woman: Domesticity and Equal Rights in the Knights of Labor
SUSAN LEVINE 49

Sisters of the Grange: Rural Feminism in the Late Nineteenth Century
DONALD B. MARTI 66

Populism and Feminism in a Newspaper by and for Women of the Kansas Farmers' Alliance, 1891-1894
MARILYN DELL BRADY 81

The Anarchist-Feminist Response to the "Woman Question" in Late Nineteenth-Century America
MARGARET S. MARSH 107

Feminist Responses to "Crimes against Women," 1868-1896
ELIZABETH PLECK 122

Charlotte Perkins Gilman: A Feminist's Struggle with Womanhood
MARY A. HILL 142

The Women's Trade Union League and American Feminism
ROBIN MILLER JACOBY 166

Creating a Feminist Alliance: Sisterhood and Class Conflict in the New York Women's Trade Union League, 1903-1914
NANCY SCHROM DYE 181

CONTENTS

Feminism as Life-Process: The Life and Career of Lucy Sprague Mitchell
JOYCE ANTLER 196

Feminist Politics in the 1920s: The National Woman's Party
NANCY F. COTT 220

The National Woman's Party and the Origins of the Equal Rights Amendment, 1920-1923
PETER GEIDEL 246

Feminist against Feminist: The First Phase of the Equal Rights Amendment Debate, 1923-1963
JUDITH SEALANDER 272

Organized Women in Mississippi: The Clash over Legal Disabilities in the 1920's
MARTHA H. SWAIN 287

Challenging "Woman's Place": Feminism, the Left, and Industrial Unionism in the 1930s
SHARON HARTMAN STROM 299

Humor and Gender Roles: The "Funny" Feminism of the Post-World War II Suburbs
NANCY WALKER 327

The Woman's Community in the National Woman's Party, 1945 to the 1960s
LEILA J. RUPP 343

Women Activists, Southern Conservatives, and the Prohibition of Sex Discrimination in Title VII of the 1964 Civil Rights Act
CARL M. BRAUER 369

The Origins of the Women's Liberation Movement
SARA M. EVANS 389

CONTENTS

Race, Class, and Gender: Prospects for an All-Inclusive Sisterhood
BONNIE THORNTON DILL 401

The Rise and Fall of Feminist Organizations in the 1970s: Dayton as a Case Study
JUDITH SEALANDER and DOROTHY SMITH 421

Feminism and the Contemporary Family
BARBARA EASTON..442

A Response to Inequality: Black Women, Racism, and Sexism
DIANE K. LEWIS..468

Copyright Information 491

Index...495

Series Preface

In the space of one generation, women's history has become the fastest-growing area of scholarship in U.S. history. Since the resurgence of feminism in the late 1960s and 1970s, insistent questions about the historical meanings of "woman's place" have sowed and reaped a garden of scholarship. Where scholarly works used to be bare of mention of women, academic enterprise has now produced a vigorous growth of books and articles, bringing to light diverse women of every region, race, class and age. This research is marked by a renovating intent that refuses to accept as "human" history a history of men. Interest is lively and debate is stimulating and sought after: attendance at the Berkshire Conference on the History of Women rivals the size of the annual convention of the American Historical Association.

While books in women's history are daily increasing in numbers and strength, as in any fast-developing field the scholarly literature in the form of articles is most expansive and up-to-the-minute. All the history journals now publish articles on women's work, domestic settings, family relations, household matters, female politics and organizations and so forth, and new journals have sprung into being to concentrate on such topics. Women's historians publish in numerous regional and thematic history journals as well as in feminist outlets and in journals of other social science disciplines. This series brings together a collection of outstanding articles from the field, almost all written in the past twenty years and more than half published during the 1980s. It brings together, in volumes organized by topic, essays otherwise widely dispersed. These volumes reprint only articles that originally appeared in journals, not chapters of books; review articles are not included. Articles have been chosen for overall quality and for range. Each one was chosen for one or more of the following reasons: because it is the standard authority on its subject matter; represents an important statement on a topic by a recognized scholar; presages an important book to come; provides a first look at new evidence or new methods; or opens an untapped area or new controversy. Older articles have been reprinted if their data or interpretation have not been surpassed or if they marked an important stage in the historiography, even if since superseded.

The historical coverage of the series extends from the Revolutionary era to the 1960s. The articles themselves are dated from the 1940s through 1988. Volumes are organized by topic rather than time period. Within each volume, the articles are ordered chronologically (with respect to substance), so that the whole can be read as an historical overview. The only exception to this ordering principle is Volume One, on Theory and Method, in which the contents are arranged in order of publication. Within each volume there is an attempt to include articles on as diverse kinds of women as possible. None of the volume topics is regionally or racially defined; rather, all volumes are topically designed so as to afford views of women's work, family lives, and public activities which cut across races and regions. Any volume in the series stands on its own, supplying as full a treatment of a designated subject matter as the scholarly literature will provide. Several groupings of volumes also make sense; that is, volumes two through five all center around domestic and family matters; volumes five through nine consider other varieties of women's work; volumes nine through eleven concern uses and abuses of women's bodies; volumes twelve through fourteen look at major aspects of socialization; and volumes fifteen through twenty include organizational and political efforts of many sorts.

As a whole, the series displays in all its range the vitality of the field of women's history. Aside from imbuing U.S. history with new vision, scholarship in this area has informed, and should continue to inform, current public debate on issues from parental leave to the nuclear freeze. By bringing historical articles together under topical headings, these volumes both represent accurately the shape of historical controversy (or consensus) on given issues and make historians' findings most conveniently available for current reference.

Introduction

The term feminism has presented problems for historians. Feminism is only one word, and historians have used it to cover many varieties of ways that women have asserted themselves individually or as a group. It has been used, certainly, to describe explicit movements for women's rights or the ballot. Often it has been used in connection with reform activities, where women's efforts on behalf of others (whether women needier than themselves, or children, or the poor, or slaves, or the unchurched) has been seen in terms of the reformers' intent to advance their own stature and status. Some overgeneralize the word, applying it to all the notable things women have done, even to all women's public activities. To escape this pitfall, on the other hand, historians may go to the other extreme of specifying very precise requirements to warrant use of the word. In contemporary usage, the word feminism is regularly used and abused, encompassing a wide range of understandings and distortions.

In the most literal sense, descriptions of "feminism" or "feminists" are necessarily present-minded. These terms were not in use in the United States before the twentieth century. "Feminism" came into the English language from the French. *Feminisme* seems to have been coined in the 1880s by Hubertine Auclert, a determined advocate of political rights for women and the founder of the first woman suffrage society in France. By the 1890s French women's groups were hesitantly using the term, and it migrated to England, where it was used (usually surrounded by quotation marks) more by detractors than by advocates. The word feminism occasionally appeared in American publications in the first decade of the twentieth century, usually to refer to developments in Europe. Between 1910 and 1913, however, as the woman suffrage movement blossomed with new energies, and political rebellions of many sorts were appearing in the U.S., women seized the word feminism to refer to their heightened expectations, their expanded protests against male domination and efforts to redefine the hierarchy of gender.

The claim to feminism was thus a consciously modern claim: the women who so defined themselves saw their intents as breaking away from the established "woman movement" of the nineteenth century. They went beyond the demand for the ballot and claimed economic independence, full political participation, individual and sexual expression. They sought to eliminate a unitary definition of womanhood and to make room for full individuality among women.[1] Feminism thus has a visible beginning, if the term itself is taken as a guide. The early twentieth-century women who embraced the word saw themselves as part of a tradition of advocacy, however, going back at least to Mary Wollstonecraft, the English woman who penned *A Vindication of the Rights of Woman* in 1792. Their intents comprised a new phase rather than emerging *de novo*.

When the authoritative Oxford English Dictionary first included the word feminism—not until the 1933 supplement—it defined it, without chronological beginning or end points, as "the opinions and principles of the advocates of the extended recognition of the achievements and claims of women; advocacy of women's rights." Now that the term feminism is established, the convenience of applying it farther back than the twentieth century, to refer to the tradition of protest against male domination and for the establishment of women's rights, cannot be denied. But at the same time it is crucial to recognize that that tradition is internally variegated, proposed by more than one kind of person, displaying more than one rationale and approach. If feminism is to be viewed retrospectively and inclusively, what characterizes its tenets are three principles: opposition to categorical sex hierarchy; understanding that women's condition is socially constructed (that is, historically shaped by human social usage rather than divinely or naturally ordained); and awareness that women, although individuals, as individuals share a group definition as women. As historian Linda Gordon's recent pithy statement put it, "Feminism is a critique of male supremacy, formed and offered in the light of a will to change it, which in turn assumes a conviction that it is changeable."[2]

Given this kind of overarching definition, many and diverse kinds of women's activities in the past can be seen to have feminist aspects. Indeed, it can be fairly said that the story of women's struggles for rights and prerogatives equal to men's has been the central narrative in women's history. The series of campaigns for women's legal rights and the vote are usually pictured as the core of feminist matters, and there is sense to that arrangement. In this series of volumes, however, articles on women's legal "disabilities" and efforts to eliminate sex discrimination in property, marriage and divorce are in volume III (*Domestic Relations and Law*). Articles focusing on the history of woman suffrage campaigns are located in the volume just preceding this one (XIX). And in the prior volumes, (XVI, XVII, XVIII), covering women's organizational lives, their endeavors in social and moral reform, and political participation, there are many topics and historians' treatment also pertaining to the history of feminist struggles for sex equality. It is not a simple or clear-cut matter—nor is it necessarily historically accurate—to separate feminist struggles from other forms and goals of women's politics. Therefore many overlapping and intersecting themes crop up in volumes XVI through XX. What this volume concentrates on are ideas, intents and manifestations of women's rights advocates and feminist activists so far as these have been perceived and treated by historians apart from suffrage campaigns. Most of these topics and treatments involve women working together in voluntary organizations, but as distinct from volumes XVI and XVII, the focus in these articles is on the feminist aspect of the association. The coverage moves from antebellum agrarian Quakers through Populists, anarchists, labor-union women and individualists to the inventors of the

Equal Rights Amendment and the women's liberation movement of the 1960s. Therefore the volume offers superb opportunity to test, examine and compare the core values and varieties of feminism over a century and a half of expression.

Notes

[1] See Nancy F. Cott, *The Grounding of Modern Feminism* (New Haven, CT, Yale Univ. Press, 1987).

[2] *Oxford English Dictionary . . . Supplement* (Oxford [England], Oxford Univ. Press, 1933), 362-63; Linda Gordon, "What's New in Women's History," in *Feminist Studies/Critical Studies*, Teresa de Lauretis, ed. (Bloomington, IN, Indiana U. Press, 1985), 29.

Feminist Struggles for Sex Equality

FEMINIST FRIENDS: AGRARIAN QUAKERS AND THE EMERGENCE OF WOMAN'S RIGHTS IN AMERICA

NANCY A. HEWITT

Historian Nancy Cott captured the paradox of women's status in early-nineteenth-century America by identifying "two seemingly contradictory visions of women's relation to society: the ideology of domesticity, which gave women a sex-specific role to play, primarily in the home; and feminism, which attempted to remove sex-specific limits on women's opportunities and capacities." Cott argues that historically the emergence of feminism "depended on" the slightly earlier "subtle changes in women's view of the domestic role."[1] What was essential about that new domestic experience was the sex-consciousness it fostered, a sex-consciousness most forcefully depicted by Carroll Smith-Rosenberg. The "female world of love and ritual" that she discovered in the private interstices of middle-class life revealed the domestic circle as a seedbed not only of sex-conciousness, but also of sex solidarity.[2] Suddenly, women's separation from productive labor and relegation to the private sphere appeared less restrictive and isolating; rather, it provided the necessary resources for women's reemergence as public arbiters of moral and social order.

Numerous other historians have sought the roots of feminism first in extensions of women's domestic roles through missionary and charitable societies and then in elaborations of evangelical theology. Female neighbors, kin, and coworshipers served as agents of evangelical revivals and had their own sisterly bonds strengthened through the conversion experience. It was these tightly knit circles of women who joined forces to eradicate prostitution, intemperance, and enslavement. In these latter campaigns, women met barriers to their public efforts based solely on sex,

Feminist Studies 12, no. 1 (Spring 1986). © by Feminist Studies, Inc.

leading some to claim rights for themselves as a precondition for aiding others.[3]

It is this last step in the scenario, from moral crusades to feminism, that proved the most difficult, for both the women who took it and the historians who attempted to explain it. Conventional evangelical Protestantism, which initially liberated women from the domestic circle, nonetheless proved a barrier to overt feminism. Blanche Glassman Hersh, for example, notes that "emancipation from religious orthodoxy was a crucial element in the development of a feminist leadership." Of the fifty-one feminist abolitionist leaders Hersh studied, twenty-one grew up in Quaker, Unitarian, or Universalist families. Of the twenty-seven who were raised in orthodox or evangelical faiths, nine rejected these youthful affiliations to become Unitarians, Universalists, or Quakers; and nine others "deconverted" to join radical religious sects or to join no sect at all. Nonetheless, Hersh claims that the ideology her feminist abolitionists bequeathed to later generations was rooted in the doctrine of sexual spheres and in the belief in female moral and spiritual superiority, that is, in the social and cultural mores of middle-class evangelicals.[4] Thus, the existing historical literature suggests that the birth of feminism was a two-step process – from domesticity to humanitarian reform via evangelical religion, and from evangelical crusades to feminism via a second conversion to unconventional Prostestantism.[5]

This article puts this scenario to the test by examining the origins of the woman's rights movement in early nineteenth-century Rochester, New York. In Rochester, boom-town growth, the development of a market economy, the building of the Erie Canal, and the appearance of evangelical ministers nurtured a large number of charitable and reform associations in the 1820s and 1830s, several of which were founded and directed by women. Many Rochester women, then, did take the first step from domesticity to reform. They were aided, moreover, by the preachings of Charles Grandison Finney and his local evangelical counterparts, who convinced the wives of lawyers, land speculators, artisans, and merchants to shift their emphasis from amelioration to the wholesale eradication of society's vices. As I have demonstrated elsewhere, however, neither boom-town benevolence nor evangelically inspired perfectionism proved adequate to transform these female activists into feminist advocates. When national and local clergymen and editors began to balk at women's expanding role in the public domain, Rochester's evangelical women listened to their paternal censors, and retreated.[6] Most either discontinued their activist careers during the 1840s or redirected their energies to church and charitable efforts. The reasons for this self-imposed detour from the feminist path were complex, but they included the internalization of the tenets of "true womanhood" – piety, purity, domesticity, and submissiveness – combined with the ritual humiliation before God demanded in the conversion experience and with upward economic and social mobility.[7]

Those few Rochester women who did accept Elizabeth Cady Stanton's call to attend the first woman's rights convention in Seneca Falls, New York, in July 1848, and who organized an even more radical gathering in Rochester that August took an alternate path to the public platform. They were among the large contingent of Quakers who gathered for the convention from Waterloo and Auburn, New York, and Philadelphia as well as from Rochester. At least one-fourth of the one hundred signers of the Declaration of Sentiments drafted at the 1848 meeting were members of the Society of Friends. Frederick Douglass, the lone black participant, was the only non-Quaker among five Rochester signers. These feminist Friends did not perhaps answer Stanton's call at all. Rather they answered the call of American Quakerism's leading spokeswoman, Lucretia Mott, and of her three coreligionists – Mary Ann McClintock, Jane Hunt, and Martha Wright – who helped Stanton organize the historic event in Seneca Falls.[8]

The Quaker women who attended the 1848 meetings had bypassed, for most of their lives, the basic elements of the new urban bourgeois gender system – the separation of spheres, the sex-consciousness of domesticity, and the ideology of female moral and spiritual superiority. Instead they worked alongside husbands in downstate and central New York farming communities; imbibed a group consciousness rooted in religious persecution; proclaimed woman's equality before God and in the religious "meeting"; and viewed change, both personal and social, as a gradual unfolding of the Divine presence. These agrarian Quakers were active before 1848 as advocates of Indian rights, communitarianism, temperance, and abolition, but not alongside urban evangelicals. Within Quaker meetings and within "popular" associations dominated by Quakers, women and men shared public labors. Accused of being extremists, this group of agrarian Quakers lived up to its detractors' fears and extended its critiques to the land monopoly, capital punishment, and gender roles.

Radical Quakers' uniqueness within the nineteenth-century reform community is best exemplified by their justification for women's entrance into the public realm. Rejecting claims for separate spheres or female superiority, they argued for women's natural right to equality. Thomas Paine, Charles Fourier, and Mary Wollstonecraft, along with a pantheon of Quaker pietists, were their theoretical guides. This ideological divergence from dominant definitions of woman's place was directly related to the group's agrarian Quaker heritage. The social relations of production and politics in native villages, combined with a supportive brand of sectarian theology, allowed some female Friends to resist the attractions of true womanhood and to view equality as a sounder basis for progress than moral superiority.[9]

The path to Rochester and to woman's rights originated for feminist Friends in Jericho, Westbury, Milton, Farmington, Scipio, and similar villages in New York, New Jersey, Pennsylvania, and western Massachusetts. Within these communities, work, worship, and social welfare were defined by a greater diffusion of power and equality of status than were to be found in commercial New England towns. Following "quietistic ideals" developed in the eighteenth century, the residents of Quaker villages dwelt "upon withdrawal from contact with the world," isolating themselves from the cultural and social as well as the economic and political developments that shaped the lives of other female activists.[10]

The demand for labor on family farms assured that women's work would be visible and that, at least during planting and harvesting, women and men would work side-by-side. At the same time, religious precepts promoting social duties and condemning finery and display limited the elaboration of domesticity within Quaker households. Even in urban Philadelphia, Lucretia Mott ordered her domestic life so that no "excess duties," including "unnecessary stitching" or "ornamental work" on clothes would take time away from reading, meditation, and community work.[11] Quaker farm women, further removed from the accoutrements of the new domesticity, would have had less time or use for the fancy dress, abundant furnishings, or lavish social entertainments that characterized affluent urbanites and those who sought to emulate them. Plainness, according to Quaker doctrine, was "the surest way to avoid 'those gaieties which tend to divert and alienate the mind from the simplicity and gravity of the Truth' and as a garrison against 'fashion-mongers.'" Regular "family visits" by those appointed by the meeting increased conformity to these general principles.[12]

In the 1820s, when Rochester's future feminists made their marital choices, they applauded each other on finding "kind, affectionate husbands, ready to share with us whatever may attend us through life."[13] Thus, as romantic love entered the fantasies of urban, middle-class daughters, Quaker farm girls continued to follow the model of their parents' generation, combining mutual respect and affection with hard work. Courtship was to unfold gradually within circles of families and friends, and women were to play a specific role in the courtship process.[14] Marriage proposals were laid before the women's and men's meetings by the couple, accompanied by both sets of parents and by two female and two male friends. Committees from both meetings were then appointed to "consider the proposal" and to report on the "life and conversation" of the concerned couple. When approved, the marriage would be solemnized a month later at a regular midweek meeting during which the bride and groom rose, exchanged identical promises, and received a certificate of marriage from an elderly Friend.

Newlyweds were admonished to "take care of one another" so as to become an "invaluable companion" and "friend."[15] Young brides simultaneously urged each other to maintain social contacts and community activities. Thus Elizabeth Mott wrote to her sister Amy Kirby that she "fear[ed] that the domestic concerns of life will become all" and sought "more substance for the mental power to act upon" so that "they will be occupied with something of a higher nature than patching [one] thing and making another."[16] Many married Quaker women found such substance by serving as ministers, caring for orphans, visiting prisoners or Indians, and attending to religious and social duties. Even in their domestic labors, they were rarely as isolated as their urban, middle-class counterparts. A constant flow of relatives, as visitors and boarders, joined in household and farm labor, while the major burdens—spring housecleaning, farm chores, and painting and repairs—were shared by household members of all ages and both sexes.[17] This is not to suggest that there were no distinctions of tasks by gender in agrarian Quaker families, but rather that those distinctions were less rigid and more frequently abandoned than in the households of the new urban middle class.

Indeed, for Quaker farm daughters, young men's desire to attain middle-class status by heading to the rich farmlands or urban centers to the west necessitated a renewed concern with self-sufficiency that limited the appeal of true womanhood ideals. In 1823, Amy Willis wrote to her friend Amy Kirby that their native village of Jericho would "be quite stripped of beaus" within a year.[18] One friend, rather than fearing spinsterhood, feared that her lot would be "cast in a distant land" with a pioneering husband, and another noted that she would feel "lonely and dejected. . . without one female to whom I could unbosom my feelings."[19] A few who had earlier achieved the status of frontier wives were already returning home as widows, "severed" as one proclaimed "from the friend to whom her heart was most dear."[20]

Amy Kirby, who was born in Jericho, New York, in 1802 and moved to Rochester in 1836, became that city's leading feminist activist in the 1840s. In the early 1820s, her older sister Hannah moved to central New York upon her marriage to Isaac Post. Hannah soon wrote Amy, begging that she visit in order to alleviate her isolation and to assist in farm and household chores. Having spent several months with Hannah in 1823 and 1824, Amy planned to move permanently to central New York upon her marriage to a Quaker youth in a neighboring town. Her plans were abruptly foreclosed, however, when the young man died just months before the wedding. While mourning his loss, Amy heard that a close friend, newly married and living on an isolated homestead, was languishing with a terminal illness; she died the same year. The husband of another childhood friend was jailed for drunkenness and wife abuse. A year and a half later Hannah died, and Amy left her childhood home for good to care for the grieving Isaac and his two young children. Finally, in 1829, at age twenty-seven, Amy agreed to give up her role as nursemaid to her niece and nephew in order to become their stepmother. She thus entered the wifely role, having already labored side-by-side with Isaac and knowing, as one friend reminded the new couple, that "connubial happiness" and "domestic felicity" could be short-lived.[21]

The experiences of Amy Kirby Post were not unlike those of

many of her Quaker sisters who surrounded her on Long Island, in central New York, and later in Rochester. Of the two dozen Quaker women who led woman's rights efforts in Rochester, one-half were single or widowed during the early years of their activism. Four others married widowers with children prior to joining public campaigns. Several wrote of female relatives or friends who suffered abuse or abandonment at the hands of husbands. At least fourteen of the twenty-four feminist Friends helped support their families, either by providing labor on family farms or by pursuing jobs as teachers, seamstresses, nurses, or lecturers. A far smaller proportion of Rochester's nonfeminist female activists experienced spinsterhood, widowhood, or wage labor; and those who did did not have the tradition of female self-sufficiency that gave independent women and women's work status in agrarian Quaker communities.[22]

Agrarian Quakers were a mobile lot in the nineteenth century, but only when they moved to urban centers like Rochester did geographical change mean significant experiential change. The entry of the Posts, DeGarmos, Fishes, Burtises, Anthonys, and other agrarian Quaker families into the heterogeneous, dynamic, and non-Quaker environs of Rochester forced them to confront new economic, political, and cultural options. The power of communal norms was diminished at the same time that extended kinship networks were disrupted. Opportunities in shopkeeping and manufacturing drew Quaker men toward urban lifestyles and Yankee ethics of individualism while the cult of true womanhood encouraged Quaker farm wives to retreat to domesticity.

Isaac Post, for instance, opened a butcher shop upon his arrival in the city, then within a few years shifted to the cleaner and more respectable occupation of pharmacist. Each of these moves took his work farther from home and Amy's involvement. Some of his coreligionists entered the commercial arena by cultivating cherry or apple orchards and developing nurseries. Others turned to selling drygoods or establishing woolen manufactories. A few entered artisanal ranks as stonecutters, jewelers, or tailors as well as butchers, defying the general trend among that class of workers by enjoying some financial success. As these ex-farmers looked around them, they saw Rochester's earliest Quaker settlers, who had arrived two decades earlier, leading prosperous lives as merchants, manufacturers, and professionals.

The wives of Rochester's pioneer Quaker families had already accepted the accoutrements of domesticity. As urban economic and political institutions diminished women's access to power in the community, pioneer Quaker women accepted the double-edged sword of glorification in the private and subordination in the public domain. The availability of manufactured goods, such as clothing, shoes, and medicine, added weight to the argument that women should trade productive for consumptive roles, public labors for privatized domesticity. Those Quaker women who wished to maintain some influence in civic affairs could do so by joining one of the existing female benevolent or reform organizations. Societies to aid the sick, poor, orphans, homeless women, and slaves – all single sex, all asserting female moral superiority, and all justifying their efforts on religious grounds – offered female Friends an acceptable mode of public activism, one based on female separation and subordination. In addition, the Quaker meeting still offered women an opportunity to assert their influence within their own religious community.

The female migrants of the 1830s and 1840s were encouraged to follow the paths of their Quaker forerunners. Their husbands sought upward mobility, often in occupations that required less labor from wives outside the domestic circle. The women were invited to support local benevolent efforts, and some, like Amy Post and Sarah Fish, briefly joined the Female Charitable Society, contributed to the orphanage fund, and affixed their signatures to petitions circulated by the evangelically inspired Female Anti-Slavery Society. Even relatives who remained in Quaker farm villages on Long Island or in central New York may have unwittingly pushed their newly urbanized sisters to adopt domesticity. As Mary Post complained to her sister-in-law Amy, she expected more letters and visits from her since "retirement from farm life must give you more leisure time."[23]

Yet several dozen of the newly arrived Friends ultimately rejected the options offered them and instead forged a new style of public activism and a new set of associations through which to pursue their goals while retaining their "woman's right" within the family, the meeting, and the community.[24] Some of these women would join male kin and coworshipers in efforts to revitalize the Society of Friends, some would move on to worldly activism in campaigns to abolish slavery, and a smaller number would press forward with demands for economic and racial equality and woman's rights.

The women who forged this new path had gained the bottom rungs of Rochester's emerging bourgeoisie, but they retained some distance from their more fully urbanized neighbors both geographically and ideologically. A few of these families, such as the Anthonys, continued to survive by agriculture; others, like the Posts, returned to that pursuit during hard times. All of them retained strong ties to agrarian Quakers in their native communities as well as to those who migrated further west. Most of the women also continued to assume some productive roles, whether married or single. Their male kin, moreover, did not enter existing political parties but remained, like their wives and daughters, self-conscious nonparticipants in the electoral system.

This circle of Quaker families attempted to maintain or re-create strong kinship networks and extended community ties by living in close proximity and by hosting newly arrived kin, newly married or widowed children, and itinerant Quaker preachers and reformers. By the early 1840s, for instance, Amy and Isaac Post, their daughter Mary and her husband William Hallowell, Amy's sister Sarah and her husband Jeffries Hallowell, Isaac's nephew Edmund Willis, and at least five other Post relatives lived within a ten-block area of the city's First Ward. Another cluster of Fish relatives, numbering at least ten persons, lived in a single large house in the Second Ward, while the Anthonys, their cousins the Burtises, and the DeGarmos inhabited neighboring farms in the northwest corner of the city. A number of these families temporarily moved to Sodus Bay together in the mid-1840s to join a Fourierist phalanx and then returned to one of the existing Quaker enclaves by the late 1840s. These families visited regularly, held religious and reform meetings in their homes, traveled together to other parts of the state, sent their children to live in each other's houses, and joined forces to reform society.

One final factor that divided these new Rochester Quakers from the pioneer Friends and from some of their fellow migrants was religion itself. The structure of the Society of Friends and its role in reforming the world as well as the role of women in the Society became sources of bitter dispute in the 1820s and again in the 1840s. By the late eighteenth century, some broad guidelines, officially written into the *Rules of Discipline* and accepted by all Quaker meetings, defined women's role in the Society and Society's role in the world. In general, women and men sat in separate meetings, each having responsibility for the care and discipline of its own sex. The women's meeting often had greater responsibility for the "oversight of marriages" while they had to gain the concurrence of men to discipline, disown, admit, or reinstate women members and to approve women ministers. The men's meeting did not necessarily have to seek such concurrence from the women. Still, as traveling ministers or speakers within their home meeting, women held absolutely equal rights with men and were similarly acclaimed or criticized for the theological soundness and clarity of their presentations.[25] In politics, the religious proscription against the "deceitful spirit of party" equalized women's and men's participation in the electoral process.[26] Views on political issues were expressed, but generally through religious testimonies which necessitated the consent of both the women's and men's meetings. Itinerant ministers also articulated such testimonies, including such notable women as Rachel Hicks, Priscilla Cadwallader, and Lucretia Mott.

As the numbers of Quakers expanded and as the concerns of the meeting became more complicated, most Quaker groups came to depend on a core of leaders known as the ministers and elders. They initiated testimonies and sanctioned ministers as well as administered the affairs of the monthly, quarterly, and yearly meetings. By the 1810s and 1820s, the ministers and elders were implementing most major policies and programs of the Society of Friends. Women had the right to serve in this select group, but, as with other hierarchical institutions, men tended to dominate in the upper echelons of the administrative structure. Despite this, even some men were disturbed at the increasingly "churchly" structure of their Society.

In 1828, protracted debates within the Society over increasing bureaucratization, the role of the Society in worldly reform, and the proper interpretation of early Quaker texts led to the group's division into Orthodox and Hicksite branches. The latter attracted most of the agrarian and reform-minded members. They followed the teachings of Elias Hicks, who emphasized the revelatory power of "Inner Light" over any laws or principles provided in "external aids," including the Bible. Women and men were equally endowed with this Light. In addition, Hicksites rejected Original

Sin, asserting that women and men could use their rational powers to "rise above that innocent state" in which they were "created, to the exalted state of virtue and glory."[27] They also rejected churchly structures and sought to return to the simplified and democratic forms of worship advocated by the Society's founders.

It was at the time of the Hicksite separation that the Society of Friends began its most rapid expansion into western New York, an expansion in which Hicksites predominated.[28] By 1834, a sufficient number of Hicksites resided in central and western New York to form a Yearly Meeting, the boundaries of which extended north to Ontario, Canada, and westward into Michigan. Future feminists were prominent in the early deliberations of this Genesee Yearly Meeting, and they often invited Lucretia Mott to their annual gatherings to address the membership on any of the reform issues of the day. In 1836, several of Rochester's most reform-minded women and men were appointed to consider changes in the Society's *Rules of Discipline*. The issues they raised – women's full equality in the Society, the role of Quakers in the antislavery cause, and the reemergence of ministers and elders – initiated a decade-long series of debates that ultimately led to the division of the Hicksites.[29]

Although the Yearly Meeting did not act quickly on the reform proposals, many of those who advocated changes in the *Rules of Discipline* did begin to act. In 1837, Phebe Post Willis of Long Island had written Amy and Isaac Post asking, "How is it that you tell us nothing about abolition movements in Rochester? I should scarcely suppose you were members of that society by your silence on the subject."[30] That silence diminished as the Yearly Meeting proved intractable in furthering the antislavery cause. First dissenting Hicksites began holding "numerous little abolition meetings" in their homes. Soon the Posts began wondering why they should "exclude all who do not happen to be included within the pale of our religious faith" from such associations and, with a Long Island Friend, concluded that "our light (if we have any) would be more likely to shine where it would do good by uniting with all without distinction of Sect or creed."[31] Then in 1842, when ex-Quaker antislavery lecturer Abby Kelley appeared at Rochester's Washington Street Presbyterian Church, a large body of disaffected Hicksites were in attendance. At least twenty were among the first thirty-four officers of the Western New York Anti-

Slavery Society (WNYASS) founded there. The WNYASS, which extended membership equally to both women and men, attracted no evangelical women to its roster and only a few of their male relatives. One of the latter, Samuel D. Porter, served as the first WNYASS president, but he feared being lumped unjustly with "agrarians, disorganizers, infidels, & fanatics" and withdrew from the society in 1844. After that year, the WNYASS consisted solely of self-styled "fanatics."[32]

Throughout this period, disowned and disaffected Hicksites asserted ever more radical positions on woman's rights. In some cases this meant putting into practice existing principles of equality. It also meant that women themselves labored against a heritage of quietist ideals in order to claim the rights they sought. Women called their own "free meetings" to discuss "subjects of Social and Pecuniary interest" and trained themselves as speakers, pamphleteers, healers, and ministers.[33] Their actions began to take effect and as early as 1845, Boston abolitionist Jeremiah Sanderson wrote to Amy Post: "Woman is rising, becoming free. The progress manifest at present of the idea of Woman's Rights in the public mind" demonstrates "what a few years comparatively may effect."[34] By 1846, Amy Post and her female coworkers were selling copies of Samuel J. Mays's "Sermon on the Rights of Women" at their WNYASS fair and complaining openly when the "Lords of Creation" in their own midst refused to recognize women as equals.[35]

Even the most radical Hicksite women still performed some gender-specific tasks within antislavery organizations, but unlike other female activists, they claimed the right to equality with men in the decision-making bodies of such associations.[36] WNYASS women were not yet the equals of men in officeholding, policy-making, or public speaking, but they advanced their position considerably during the 1840s. By this time, the causes they advocated and women's place in them aroused the kind of vociferous opposition once visited upon evangelical women, but Hicksite women refused to retreat. Rather, they extended and intensified their efforts. "Cold looks, unyielding purse strings, and repelling voices and actions" could not "dishearten" the antislavery sisters, but instead "inspir[ed] them with courage for fresh victories."[37] Indeed, condemnation was viewed as a badge of honor, a sign that one had been "more faithful in the cause of the downtrodden." "Blessed are they who are persecuted for righteousness's sake," wrote one Hicksite, "for theirs is the kingdom of Heaven."[38]

In 1843, the Genesee Yearly Meeting began aiding radicals seeking the kingdom of heaven, such as Isaac and Amy Post, Mary Hallowell, and Lewis Burtis, by releasing them from membership. Within a few years, the efforts of local meetings in Rochester and Michigan to increase women's role and diminish the power of the ministers and elders shattered the fragile consensus that had been built on years of postponing action. On June 6, 1848, the Genesee Yearly Meeting disowned a large group of dissidents for their disregard of the "injunctions of the discipline and the authority of the church."[39] They were followed out of the meetinghouse by those like-minded Friends who had escaped formal censure. Still wishing to create a religious association based on the principles of equality and free thought, these rebel Quakers called a meeting at Waterloo, New York, for June 14 and 15 to form a new society, the Yearly Meeting of Congregational Friends. Lucretia Mott, who observed the proceedings at the Genesee gathering, was invited to participate as were all who sought a Society in which there would be no ministers and elders, no rules of admission or disownment, no limits on worldly activity, and no tolerance for racial or sexual discrimination.[40] Satisfied after two days' labor that they had created the basis for a new and better form of religious association, the Congregational Friends adjourned with a call for a second and larger gathering in October.

Lucretia Mott remained in upstate New York after the dramatic events of June to visit her sister, Martha Wright. It was when the two sisters returned to Waterloo in July to visit Congregational Friends Thomas and Mary Ann McClintock that Mott was reunited with Elizabeth Cady Stanton, and the two put into effect the plan for a woman's rights convention they had devised at the World Anti-Slavery Convention in 1840. For the recently formed Congregationalists this was the perfect opportunity to extend the attack on religious tyranny and sexual oppression. Thus, the call went out for the Seneca Falls Woman's Rights Convention.[41] The event attracted a wide range of participants, one hundred of whom, including Rochesterian Amy Post and four neighbors, signed the final Declaration of Sentiments that declared "woman is man's equal." At the end of the meeting, believing that "there were still many new points for discussion, and that the gift of tongues had been vouchsafed to them," the audience "adjourned, to meet in Rochester in two weeks." Amy Post, Mary Hallowell, Sarah Fish, and Sarah C. Owen were appointed the local arrangements committee for this second gathering.[42]

The Rochester Woman's Rights Convention, held August 2, 1848, was dominated by Congregational Friends. Among the officers, however, were two women who were not Quakers and yet illustrate the tenuous relationship between evangelical Protestantism and feminism. Abigail Bush was raised in the orthodox First Presbyterian Church and joined her mother in charitable works at a young age. In 1831, she experienced conversion and became a "Brick church perfectionist" in the midst of Finney's revival fervor.[43] A few years later, she married abolitionist Henry Bush and spent the next decade bearing and rearing five children. She reemerged in the public domain in 1843 as a member of the WNYASS, but only after withdrawing from the Brick Presbyterian Church. Another Brick church member turned feminist was Sarah C. Owen. She moved to Rochester in the mid-1830s and was soon active in the Female Moral Reform Society. However, in 1840, as evangelical women retreated from their critiques of the sexual double standard and their advocacy of abolition, Owen, like Bush, joined forces with Quaker dissidents. In doing so, Owen brought upon herself the condemnation of her congregation and was excommunicated in 1845.

These ex-evangelicals were never able to convert others among their former coworshipers to feminism, and they remained active themselves only a few years. Both Owen and Bush moved west in the 1850s, losing their circle of Congregational coworkers and finding it impossible to forge a new network. They did not lose their interest in radical causes. Yet without the support of those Quaker women whose experience and ideology provided the preconditions for feminism, these evangelical women were left alone with their unorthodox views and their memories of earlier campaigns.[44]

The highpoint of Owen's and Bush's activist careers was the Rochester Woman's Rights Convention. The meeting was a direct outgrowth of the Seneca Falls' gathering, yet it differed from it in two crucial ways. First, the earlier convention was called to discuss the "social, civil, and religious condition and rights of women"; the Rochester meeting was called to consider the "Rights of women, Politically, Socially, Religiously, and Industrially." The greater emphasis on rights, and on economic rights in particular, showed the influence of women well practiced in public pursuits and productive labor. Unlike at Seneca Falls, a woman, Abigail Bush, served as president of the Rochester meeting, for these seasoned activists had come to realize that woman could only be redeemed from her "degraded position" by "the most strenuous and unremitting effort" to "claim an equal right to act."[45] At the opening session, Elizabeth Stanton and Lucretia Mott proclaimed it "a most hazardous experiment to have a woman President and stoutly opposed it. . . . They were on the verge of leaving the Convention in disgust" when Amy Post "assured them that by the same power by which they had resolved, declared, and debated, they could also preside at a public meeting."[46] The audience, filled with Amy's kin and coworkers, approved the proposed slate. Here the grass roots experiences of local Friends put them in advance of their more prominent national leaders.

The presentation of the agenda by the female officers revealed a bold and broad conception of woman's rights. The elective franchise, the ninth of eleven proposals at Seneca Falls and the one that received the most opposition, topped the Rochester agenda. Yet political rights were only a small portion of the demands of the Rochester organizers. Their own experience in relatively egalitarian families, joint-sex religious meetings, paid labor, and public service made them sensitive to women's relative deprivation in many domains of modern urban life. The leaders of the convention urged "women no longer to promise obedience in the marriage covenant" and to allow "the strongest *will* or the superior intellect" to "govern the household." They beseeched women to claim equal authority "on all subjects that interest the human family," one of the most important of which was women's economic status. Many women were plying "the needle by day and by night, to procure a scanty pittance for [their] dependent famil[ies]." The husband's "legal right to hire out his wife for service" and "collect her wages" was labeled "a hideous custom" that reduced woman "almost to the condition of a slave."[47]

The committee of arrangements appointed women to investigate the wrongs of the laboring classes and "to invite the oppressed portion of the community to attend the meetings of the convention and take part in its deliberations."[48] At the convention, Owen read an address on "woman's place and pay in the world of work" which was elaborated upon by Mrs. Roberts, who reported on the "average price of labor for sempstresses." Mrs. Galloy "corroborated the statement, having herself experienced some of the oppression of this portion of our citizens." For participants who were in more secure economic circumstances, the conveners noted that "those who believe the laboring classes of women are oppressed" should do "all in their power to raise their wages."[49]

Moreover, Rochester's feminists predicated woman's political, familial, and economic rights on historical proofs of her capacity for equality. "From Semiramis to Victoria," declared one speaker, "we have found the Women of History equal to the emergency before them!" Recognizing that most women failed to match the achievements of such historical role models, feminists reminded their audience that "only by faithful perseverance in the practical exercise of those talents so long 'wrapped in a napkin and buried under the earth'" would woman "regain her long-lost equality with man." This mytho-historical perspective on women's oppression and the possibilities of its overthrow was combined with a sensitivity to socialization. The speakers granted that "woman's intellect is feeble," but claimed it was so "because she has been so long crushed. . . . Let her arise and demand her rights and in a few years we shall see a different mental development." Here, they compared women with slaves of the South and saw foreshadowed woman's rise in the "progress [made] within the past few years" by escaped slaves resettled in the free environs of the North.[50]

By arguing that history and education, custom and deprivation, were the key forces in the oppression of women, Rochester's feminists rejected the argument of separate spheres and separate natures that dominated the discussion of women's role in nineteenth-century America. Lucretia Mott voiced the sentiments of her Congregational sisters when she objected to the very "language of flattering compliment" that portrayed women as more devoted, spiritual, and altruistic than men. These mid-nineteenth-century feminists did not seek a matriarchate that would replace the domination of men by that of women, nor did they make special pleadings based on woman's nature. Rather, they proclaimed it the "duty of woman, whatever her complexion, to assume, as soon as possible, her true position of equality in the social circle, the Church, and the State."[51]

Immediately after the Rochester Woman's Rights Convention and for the next six decades, Congregational Friends worked to achieve equality in their own lives and in the lives of all women. Amy Post and Sarah Owen helped organize a Working Woman's Protective Union in August 1848, declaring that women were entitled "equally with men to the products of their labor or its equivalent."[52] They and their coworkers assisted their working-class sisters by providing jobs, temporary housing, and childcare to black women escaping from the South and to white women escaping from intemperate or abusive husbands.[53] In 1853, Sarah Burtis opened new job opportunities for local women by becoming the first female store clerk in Rochester, though she was married and had several children.[54] Within their own families, these same women sought to provide models of egalitarian relations. Owen went so far as to declare that if a man sought to dominate her, "I would let him know that I *could* live without him."[55] Already-married women sought to share decision-making; to provide equal educations to sons and daughters; and to assert their right to travel, speak, and act independently of even the most beloved spouses.[56]

This concern with model behavior derived in part from feminists' belief that the personal was political and in part from their economic circumstances. Hicksite abolitionists had resolved in 1843 that they should apply "their principles in all their social, political, and religious relations"; in the following years they frequently provoked public condemnation by so doing. Women in particular faced verbal and physical harassment for traveling and socializing in racially mixed company, for speaking before mixed-sex audiences, for wearing turkish trousers instead of long skirts, and for casting ballots in the 1872 presidential election, almost a half century before women gained the "right" to vote.[57] These and similar badges of radicalism were the most accessible forms of social commentary for those with limited resources. The choice then was both pragmatic and ideological. Political statements that were expressed through the events of everyday life required no hierarchy of administration, allowed for independent and decentralized action, and were equally available to all.

The blueprint for social change lived out by feminist Friends was most often debated at the annual meetings of the Congregational Friends, where the campaign for woman's rights was placed in the larger context of a "thorough re-organization of Society."[58] Meeting just two months after the Rochester convention, the Congregational Friends proclaimed: "When we speak of the Rights of Woman, we speak of Human Rights." They rejected innate sexual differences and declared instead for "common natures, common rights, and a common destiny" for women and men.[59] They may have been unique among their contemporaries, including other activists and other Quakers, in extending this belief in human equality across the color line: "Every member of the human family," they asserted, "without regard to color or sex, possess potentially the same faculties and powers, capable of like cultivation and development and consequently has the same rights, interests, and destiny."[60]

Most feminist Friends sustained their arguments into the post-Civil War period despite the pressure of changing circumstances. When William Lloyd Garrison and other abolitionist leaders concluded that their goals had been achieved, members of the WYNASS were among the dissenters who formed the Equal Rights Association. Its first annual meeting was held in Rochester in 1866, but when president Wendell Phillips proclaimed it was the "Negro's hour," several local feminists disagreed, believing that it was possible to obtain votes for women and blacks simultaneously. They maintained this position after joining the National Woman Suffrage Association whose leaders gave female suffrage primacy.[61] Rochester's feminist Friends also gave a feminist presence to other progressive organizations, such as the National Liberal League, which mounted campaigns for the reorganization of government along social scientific lines and against Victorian sexual standards. In the league's proposed "Liberal compact for government," Amy Post discovered a critical omission – "that omission was the word *woman*." She cautioned her "thoughtful and conscientious" colleagues not to "forget that we – Women – are the long downtroden [*sic*] class of National Citizens."[62] Finally, as a wider range of women entered women's rights campaigns, reshaping the goals and strategies of the movement, feminist Friends remained adamant in rejecting any basis for woman's rights except their natural equality of condition.

A few feminist Friends continued to fight for their goals into the twentieth century, although they could not maintain control of the movement. Instead the goals were narrowed, almost exclusively to suffrage, to gain a mass following, and arguments were adopted that were rooted in the cults of domesticity and true womanhood. Although this mass movement rejected the ideology of its radical foremothers, it was nonetheless born from their agitations. Only after several decades of public advocacy of absolute equality between the sexes was it possible for large numbers of women and men to accept women's equal access to the ballot as a reasonable, even moderate, proposal. Thus, feminist Friends provided the preconditions for the later suffrage victories even as the suffragists themselves rejected their fundamental beliefs.

In the same way, the evangelical environment of Rochester that radical Quakers rejected provided the preconditions for a feminist rebellion. For only when women raised in the relatively egalitarian enclave of Quaker farm villages moved into a heterogeneous urban arena, where women's and men's roles were increasingly distinct and unequal, were they provoked to reconsider the very nature of sex roles. Because the first feminists remained economically, residentially, and culturally marginal to the emerging bourgeoisie, they were able to elaborate a wholly different concept of gender roles. Believing that "corrupt customs," a "perverted application of the Scriptures," exclusion from education and occupations, and women's own self-effacement had limited their development, the feminist sought to "move in the enlarged sphere which her great Creator" had "assigned her," opening up new avenues for women at large and thereby "freeing the entire human family from thraldom both physical and moral."[63] Feminists did not achieve this final goal, but they did illuminate the path along which later generations of women could seek their own emancipation.

NOTES

The author wishes to thank Mary Huth, Marcus Rediker, Steven F. Lawson, and especially Judith Wellman and Mary P. Ryan, for their many and various contributions to this article.

1. Nancy F. Cott, *The Bonds of Womanhood: "Woman's Sphere" in New England, 1780-1835* (New Haven: Yale University Press, 1977), 5; also 197-206 generally.
2. Carroll Smith-Rosenberg, "The Female World of Love and Ritual: Relations between Women in Nineteenth-Century America," *Signs* 1 (Autumn 1975): 1-29.

3. The earliest versions of this interpretation appeared in Eleanor Flexner, *Century of Struggle: The Women's Rights Movement in the United States* (Cambridge: Harvard University Press, 1959); Andrew Sinclair, *The Emancipation of the American Woman* (New York: Harper & Row, 1965); and Alice Rossi, ed., *The Feminist Papers: From Adams to de Beauvoir* (New York: Columbia University Press, 1973).
4. Blanche Glassman Hersh, *The Slavery of Sex: Feminist-Abolitionists in America* (Chicago: University of Illinois Press, 1978), ix, 136-39, 204-9.
5. In addition to Hersh, see Cott, 204; Carroll Smith-Rosenberg, "The Cross and the Pedestal: Anti-Ritualism, Liminality, and the Emergence of the American Bourgeoisie," in *The Rising Tide of Evangelical Religion*, ed. Leonard I Sweet (Mercer, Ga.: Mercer University Press, 1984): 199-231; and Ellen DuBois, *Feminism and Suffage: The Emergence of an Independent Women's Movement in America, 1848-1869* (Ithaca, N.Y.: Cornell University Press, 1978). This interpretation has been reinforced by historians' reliance on Elizabeth Cady Stanton's account of her own transition to feminism in *Eighty Years and More: Reminiscences, 1815-1897* (1898; reprint, New York: Schocken Books, 1971), esp. 127-48.
6. See Nancy A. Hewitt, *Women's Activism and Social Change: Rochester, New York, 1822-1872* (Ithaca, N.Y.: Cornell University Press, 1984), chaps. 4 and 5; and "Yankee Evangelicals and Agrarian Quakers: Gender, Religion, and Class in the Formation of a Feminist Consciousness in Nineteenth-Century Rochester, New York," *Radical History Review*, nos. 28-29-30 (1984): 327-42.
7. Barbara Welter, "The Cult of True Womanhood, 1820-1860," *American Quarterly* 18 (Summer 1966): 151-64, 171-74; Smith-Rosenberg, "The Cross and the Pedestal"; and Hewitt, *Women's Activism*, 59-60, 123-24.
8. Seneca Falls residents who attended the first convention included Wesleyan Methodists, Baptists, Episcopalians, and at least one Catholic. Unlike the Quaker participants, the more diverse group from Seneca Falls did not remain active in feminist causes beyond this first meeting. Judith Wellman has generously shared with me both her statistics and her insights from her forthcoming study of the Seneca Falls convention.
9. Mary Kirby and Sarah Hallowell to Amy Post, 20 Feb. 1838; and Amy Post to Frederick Douglass, 13 Feb. 1860, Isaac and Amy Post Family Papers (hereafter cited as IAPFP), University of Rochester, Rochester, New York; the *Phalanx*, 4 Nov. 1843, and 5 Jan., 4 May, 15 June, and 9 Dec. 1844; "Address to Reformers," from the Yearly Meeting of Congregational Friends, in *Liberator* 19 (6 July 1849); Isaac Post, *Voices of the Spirit World* (Rochester, N.Y.: Charles H. McDonnell, 1852); and Anna Davis Hallowell, ed., *James and Lucretia Mott, Life and Letters* (Boston: Houghton Mifflin, 1884), 186-87. Although a high percentage of early feminists were Quakers, only a small percentage of Quakers were feminists. Those Quakers most likely to become feminists moved from rural to urban areas, were economically marginal to the new bourgeoisie, maintained strong ties with agrarian Quakers, sought reforms within the Society of Friends, advocated the abolition of slavery, and experienced many of the uncertainties of women's lot in their youth.
10. Rufus M. Jones, *Later Periods of Quakerism*, 2 vols. (1921; reprint, Westport, Conn.: Greenwood Press, 1970), 1:101.
11. Hallowell, 251.
12. Jones, 1:175.
13. Maria Willetts to Hannah Kirby Post, 18 Apr. 1823, IAPFP.
14. See in IAPFP, Mary W. Willis to Amy Kirby, 182-; Mary W. Willis to Hannah Kirby Post, 1 July 182-; Amy Willis to Amy Kirby, 8 Dec. 1822; and Abbey Gifford to Amy Kirby, 16 May 1823.
15. Mary Kirby to Hannah Kirby Post, 2 June 182-; and Amy Willis to Amy Kirby, 30 Aug. 1823, IAPFP.

16. Elizabeth Mott to Amy Post, 17 June 183-, IAPFP.
17. Amy Kirby to Mother, 24 May 1823; Phebe Kirby to Amy Kirby, 26 May 1823; Sarah Hallowell to Amy Post, 5 May 1841; and Susanna Hallowell to Sarah Hallowell, 8 June 1847, IAPFP.
18. Amy Willis to Amy Kirby, 30 Aug. 1823, IAPFP.
19. Hannah Kirby Post to Amy Kirby, 182-; and Amy Willis to Amy Kirby, 30 Aug. 1823, IAPFP.
20. Amy Willis to Amy Kirby, 30 Aug. 1823, IAPFP.
21. John Ketcham to Isaac and Amy Post, 20 Jan. 1829, IAPFP.
22. In contrast, very few of the sorts of problems noted among Quaker feminists in the IAPFP are discussed in the correspondence of evangelical women activitists. Either their circumstances were sufficiently more secure to minimize such difficulties, or they did not feel such problems should be discussed, even in private correspondence.
23. Mary W. Post to Amy Post, 183-, IAPFP.
24. Isaac Post to Amy Post, n.d., IAPFP.
25. Jones, 1:186-7; *Rules of Discipline of the Yearly Meeting of Friends held in Philadelphia* (Philadelphia: J. Mortimer, 1828), 114-17. Also, Mary Robbins Post to Amy Post, Nov. 183-; Jane Johnson to Priscilla Cadwallader, 4 Jan. 1833; Noah Haines to Isaac Post, 10 Feb. 1834; and Phebe Post Willis to Isaac and Amy Post, 4 May 1837, IAPFP.
26. *Rules of Discipline*, 109.
27. Jones, 1:453.
28. See A. Day Bradley, "Progressive Friends in Michigan and New York," *Quaker History* 52 (1963): 95-103; and Carlisle G. Davidson, "A Profile of Hicksite Quakerism in Michigan, 1830-1860," *Quaker History* 59 (1970): 106-12.
29. Genesee Yearly Meeting of Women Friends (hereafter (GYMWF), Minutes, June 1835, June 1836, June 1837, June 1838, June 1839, and June 1840, Haviland Records Room, New York City.
30. Phebe Post Willis to Isaac and Amy Post, 5 Apr. 1837, IAPFP.
31. John Ketcham to Isaac and Amy Post, 11 Mar. 1841, IAPFP. See also, Ida Husted Harper, *The Life and Work of Susan B. Anthony*, 3 vols. (Indianapolis: Bowen-Merrill Company, 1899), 1:48.
32. Samuel D. Porter to Abby Kelley, 16 Sept. 1842, Abby Kelley Foster Papers, American Antiquarian Society, Worcester, Massachusetts; "American Anti-Slavery Society" report on Rochester meeting, *Liberator* 13 (6 Jan. 1843); "First Annual Meeting of the Western New York Anti-Slavery Society," *Liberator* 14 (5 Jan. 1844); "Second Annual Meeting of the Western New York Anti-Slavery Society," *National Anti-Slavery Standard* 5 (6 Mar. 1845).
33. Notice of a Free Meeting, n.d., IAPFP.
34. Jeremiah Burke Sanderson to Amy Post, 8 May 1845, IAPFP.
35. Samuel J. May to Isaac Post, 20 Dec. 1846. On controversies with men in the WNYASS, see William C. Nell to Amy Post, 11 Aug. 1849, IAPFP.
36. For a comparison of evangelical and Hicksite forms of activism, see Nancy A. Hewitt, "Yankee Evangelicals and Agrarian Quakers"; and "The Social Origins of Women's Antislavery Politics in Western New York," in *Crusaders and Compromisers: Essays on the Relationship of the Antislavery Struggle to the Antebellum Party System*, ed. Alan M. Kraut (Westport, Conn.: Greenwood Press, 1983): 205-33.
37. "Anti-Slavery Bazaar," *Rochester North Star* 11 (7 Jan. 1848).
38. Nathaniel Potter to Isaac Post, 18 Sept. 1845, IAPFP.
39. GYMWF, June 1847 and June 1848. These Minutes indicate no dissension over the issues discussed. For a more conflict-filled version, see Yearly Meeting of Congregational Friends (hereafter YMCF), *Proceedings of the Yearly Meeting of Congregational Friends, Held at Waterloo, N.Y., from the Fourth to the Sixth of the Sixth Month, Inclusive, 1849* (Auburn, N.Y.: Oliphant's Press, 1849), 32-35. Those who withdrew voluntarily in-

cluded feminist activists Sarah A. Burtis, Rhoda DeGarmo, and Sarah Fish.

40. "Basis of Religious Association," in YMCF, *1849 Proceedings*, appendix.

41. Existing studies of the convention rely heavily on Stanton's *Eighty Years and More*, and on Stanton, Susan B. Anthony, and Matilda Joslyn Gage, *A History of Woman Suffrage*, 4 vols. (New York: Fowler and Wells, 1881). These works do not note the importance of the Hicksite-Congregational Friends as a group. Judith Wellman's work in progress does contain significant information on this circle of activists.

42. Rochester Woman's Rights Convention (hereafter RWRC), "Proceedings," in *The Concise History of Woman Suffrage*, ed. Mari Jo Buhle and Paul Buhle (Chicago: University of Illinois Press, 1978), 99.

43. William Channing Gannett thus identified Abigail Bush in his speech for the Fiftieth Anniversary of the RWRC, 1898, Unitarian Society of Rochester Records, University of Rochester.

44. See Abigail Bush to Amy Post, 185-; and Sarah C. Owen to Amy Post, 12 Feb. 1850 and 24 Sept. 185-, IAPFP.

45. *Report of the Woman's Rights Convention, Held at Seneca Falls, N.Y., July Nineteenth and Twentieth, 1848* (Rochester: John Dick, 1848), 3; RWRC, Minutes, 2 Aug. 1848, Phebe Post Willis Papers, University of Rochester. Because the Seneca Falls Convention had already provoked considerable criticism, the choice of more radical language seems particularly noteworthy.

46. RWRC, "Proceedings," 99. For the disappointed response of one agrarian Quaker to Lucretia Mott's role in the RWRC, see Mary Robbins Post to Amy Post, 2 Sept. 1848, IAPFP.

47. RWRC, Minutes; and RWRC, "Proceedings," 102.

48. *Rochester Daily Advertiser*, 3 Aug. 1848.

49. RWRC, "Proceedings," 102.

50. RWRC, Minutes.

51. Ibid.

52. "Women's Protective Union," *Rochester North Star* 1 (15 Sept. 1848).

53. For example, see Linda Brent, *Incidents in the Life of a Slave Girl* (Boston, 1861), written by Harriet Brent Jacobs, an escaped slave who lived with the Posts from about 1849 to 1851. Also Nancy Hassey to ______, n.d.; E. Bowen to Amy Post, 19 Nov. 1857; and Jenny Dods to Amy Post, n.d., IAPFP; and Lucy N. Colman, *Reminiscences* (Buffalo: H.L. Green, 1891), 85.

54. Blake McKelvey, *Rochester: The Water-Power City, 1812-1854* (Cambridge: Harvard University Press, 1945), 349.

55. Sarah C. Owen to Amy Post, 185-, IAPFP. At the same time, Owen praised the Post's marriage, based as it was on the "principles of equal rights" (Sarah C. Owen to Amy Post, 31 July 185-, IAPFP).

56. Sarah E. Thayer to Amy Post, 9 Mar. 1853 and 1 Aug. 1857; Jacob Post to Amy Post, 4 May 1858; Sarah Hallowell Willis to Amy Post, 6 Mar. 1852, IAPFP; and Coleman, *Reminiscences*, 3, 20-41.

57. *Liberator* 13 (6 Jan. 1843). See also Mary Robbins Post to Isaac and Amy Post, 184-; Rebecca M.C. Capron to Amy Post, 1 Apr. 1850; and Sarah Thayer to Amy Post, 1 Aug. 1857, IAPFP; WNYASS, Fair Report, n.d. IAPFP; and Harper, *Life and Work of Susan B. Anthony*, 1:423-39; and *Rochester Democrat and Chronicle*, 1 Nov. 1872.

58. YMCF, *1849 Proceedings*, 6.

59. YMCF, *Proceedings of the Yearly Meeting of Congregational Friends, Held at Waterloo, N.Y., from the Third to the Fifth of the Sixth Month, Inclusive, 1850* (Auburn, N.Y.: Henry Oliphant, 1850), 14, 15.

60. YMCF, *Proceedings of the Yearly Meeting of Congregational Friends, Held at Waterloo, N.Y., on the Fifth, Sixth, and Seventh of the Sixth Month, 1853* (Auburn, N.Y.: Knapp &

Peck, 1853), 6.
61. DuBois, 56-64. On Rochesterians specifically, see Amy Post to Aaron M. Powell, 186-, IAPFP.
62. Amy Post to A.L. Rawson, 9 Sept. 1879, IAPFP. See also William Leach, *True Love and Perfect Union: The Feminist Reform of Sex and Society* (New York: Basic Books, 1982), 137-38, 293.
63. *Seneca Falls Report*, 5; and YMCF, *1850 Proceedings*, 6.

Courtesy, American Antiquarian Society

Ernestine Rose

Women's Rights and the Wrongs of Marriage in Mid-Nineteenth-Century America

by Françoise Basch

INTRODUCTION

In the nineteenth century the oppression of women appeared starkly in the marriage relation: wedding bells rang in major inequalities between bride and bridegroom and sternly prescribed different gender roles. In spite of the reform of married women's property laws beginning in mid-century, the act of marriage, both legal and religious, sanctioned a rigidly patriarchal relationship. Throughout the century, the official discourse on women, denigrating the relatively autonomous 'spinster' and exalting the powerless wife and mother, imposed an inverted image of reality.

Imbedded in the 'reform' discourse of ante bellum America, strictures on marriage appeared in such disparate trends as temperance, anti-slavery, spiritualism, and utopianism. Their arguments followed two main diverging lines, one directed against the repression of sex and of the individual, the other against the subjection of women. This essay focuses on the critique of marriage, expressed and conceptualized by the early American women's rights movement, in the context of wide ranging political, intellectual, and religious ferment.

The women's rights advocates, from their very origins, had addressed the slavery of wifehood, making it the paradigm of female oppression, and the battlecry of emancipation. Indeed the battle for the improved legal and social status of married women broadened into the fight for political rights, so that marriage appeared as a metaphor for the complexities of both the public and private spheres.

The women's rights movement undertook a major onslaught on marriage, but similar ideas and aspirations circulated freely among the reformers, especially the Spiritualists and the Utopian socialists. Since these two groups made the critique of marriage central to their philosophy, and began officially at approximately the same time (1848), and in the same area (New York State), they deserve a brief mention in this study.

From the 1840s, Spiritualism in ante bellum America expressed a longing for individual freedom against hierarchies of all kinds, and a denial of sin and damnation. In a period of acute social anxiety, the belief in the communication with the spirits of the dead served to assuage the terrors of death and of final separation. Within this context, some spiritualists rebelled against the constraints of marriage and a minority even rallied to the cry of 'free love', a term which implied a variety of positions, ranging from support for divorce, to bolder and more imaginative forms of sexual union, and which included the emancipation of women.

Utopian communities were inspired by Enlightenment rationalism and belief in progress, as well as by the millenarian philosophy of the Revivalist movement which spread in the eastern United States in the late eighteenth and early nineteenth century. These alternative societies evolved models of total chastity (Shakers), rigid systems of 'complex marriage' (Oneida), or of complete individual freedom (Modern Times). In one form or another, marriage was questioned, and the oppression of women recognized. At the same time, these pioneers strove to transform the conjugal cell, the 'isolated home,' incorporating it into a larger community. In this pursuit of a freer and more equal marriage relationship, Spiritualists and Utopians shared some of the aspirations of the women's rights movement.

Two main preoccupations run through this paper. One concerns the discourse on marriage in the women's rights movement, its ideological origins, impact and coherence. The other examines the scope and depth of the feminist attacks on marriage. Were they launched as reforms to repair defective institutions? Or did their proponents, either deliberately or unconsciously, set out to totally subvert the dominant order and patriarchal values?

• • • •

Most feminist historians have downplayed the issue of marriage in the women's rights movement and have seen the suffragists' attitude as reformist and basically domestically oriented, or, as Nancy Cott put it, 'at one with esteem for home and the family.'[1] Blanche Glasman Hersh interprets nineteenth-century feminist ideology as 'the basic acceptance of marriage and the family as central social institutions.'[2] Ellen DuBois shifts the discussion; to her the real boldness of the movement lay in the passage from the traditionally 'feminine' private sphere to the public arena, previously exclusively male.[3] In the pages that follow, I wish to qualify these perspectives. To be sure, marriage and the family were not the only targets of the new suffragist movement, and the private domain still held most women in its thrall. But we should not understate the militants' growing ambivalence about the notion of 'Woman's sphere'. While transcending 'public' and 'private' they saw them as intimately connected.[4] In order to shed more light on these questions and suggest a revaluation, I propose taking a closer look at the underpinnings of the suffragist critique, their strategies, their emotional and ideological discourse.

Ante bellum America was teeming with crusades, causes, reforms and philanthropical schemes. Among them, the Temperance and the Anti slavery movements played a crucial role in the history of American women. The two main ideological inspirations at work in this reform effervescence were the evangelical movement, kindled by religious Revivals, and the philosophy of the Rights of Man. Within this bipolar framework, women claimed the right to define both their specific sphere of action and their political and social emancipation. In the mid nineteenth century the institutions of marriage and the family were undergoing a major shift and the Women's Rights critique fed into an already powerful stream. Views differ as to the effects of these upheavals on the family and on the status of women. Some hold that, as industrial capitalism pushed production out of the home in the first half of the century, the fabric of the family loosened and its members, including women, became more independent of and less subservient to the patriarchal authority. Others argue that industrialization increased the subjection of women. Whatever the reasons, there were substantial changes in American marriage and family law in the nineteenth century, affecting both the relationship of husband and wife and of the married couple with the outside world. One manifestation of these shifting attitudes was the modification of the marital property system which started in the 1830s. This process of reform[5] originated not only with partisans of women's rights and reform eccentrics, but with practical minded mainstream politicians, eager to eradicate the legal and financial absurdities surviving from the past.[6]

The women's rights leaders presented a fairly homogeneous ethnic, class, religious and national identity. As daughters of farmers, sea captains, or merchants, of Universalist, Congregational, or Presbyterian clergymen, they shared a predominantly white, American, middle class and Protestant background. Only Ernestine Rose's Polish Jewish origins set her apart from the others.[7] Mainstream American, the women's rights movement did not include cranks or marginal personalities. (Mary Gove Nichols' and Victoria Woodhull's connections with the Movement were episodic.)[8] They conceived their objective, the emancipation of women, within the dominant nineteenth century cultural intellectual framework, the ideals of the American Revolution and the ethics of evangelicalism. Although they could not vote and remained outside parties, their strategies and tactics followed normal American methods of political agitation. In this respect the women's rights group moved within the same power network as the establishment it attacked and, like Her Majesty's opposition, aimed mostly at reforming it.

OPPRESSION

Marriage, a subject of public discussion and struggle, appeared for many suffragists as a private preoccupation and anxiety. 'I am so well aware that society stands over a heaving volcano . . . that I am afraid to speak or think on the subject [of reforming marriage]', wrote Lydia Maria Child.[9] For Elizabeth Cady Stanton, too, the urgency and scope of the marriage question seemed self evident.[10] 'How this marriage question grows on me. It lies at the very foundation of all progress.' she wrote to Susan B. Anthony in June 1860.[11] In women's rights speeches woman's oppression, built into 'man made' marriage, was a recurring theme. Explicitly more interested in reform than in disruption, women's rights activists claimed not to attack marriage in and of itself but, 'man made marriage which makes man master, woman slave,'[12] 'I hate and repudiate that phrase, and the promiscuous relations that it seems to indicate . . .' Stanton declared, against the accusation that she supported 'easy divorce.'[13] But the passionate tone and emotional metaphors of much of her writing on marriage create a different impression. Stanton's speech before the tenth National Women's Convention on May 10 and 11 1860 is a case in point. An experienced orator, familiar with rhetorical effects, she painted a terrifying fresco of marriage and the family: in this hell on earth, man sacrificed his victims on pagan altars, his wife 'the mother of the race' and his innocent children. In our time, said Stanton, the family, 'this great conservator of national virtue and strength, had become the scene of "debauchery and violence." '[14] '. . . The marriage relation is nought but a Pandora's box of woes unutterable.'[15] The male brute's degenerate children, the tortured wife dying in India on her husband's funeral pyre, or more slowly in America from unwanted pregnancies, those were the actors of this modern tragedy.

Stanton was reinforced in her convictions by the poignant interest the marriage question, unlike that of suffrage, aroused among women.[16] 'How the women flock to me with their sorrows . . .'[17] she remarked when they packed the halls where she spoke, making an indirect comment on how most women failed to relate political equality with personal oppression.

The emotionally explosive symbol of the slave summarized best the subjection of women, and the parallel haunted these feminists, many of whom had discovered their own oppression through anti-slavery struggle. Woman is a slave, Stanton, Henry Blackwell, and Lucy Stone repeated, hardly different from southern Negroes;[18] like them, she lost her name and must take on that of her owner; like them, she was sold to the highest bidder; like them she lost all her rights with marriage. Her dependence was in some ways worse, for she suffered 'the triple bondage of man, priest and law . . .'[19] When only male ex-slaves were later given the right to vote with the Fifteenth Amendment, this reinforced male domination. Whatever the color, whatever the class, women lost everything through gender; and men gained everything their class allowed them. In 1859, well before the polemics on the Fifteenth Amendment, Stanton humorously remarked that this was not a good time to be a Negro or a woman. And, when she imagined Peter asking her where she wanted to sit in paradise, she would answer, 'Anywhere so I am neither a Negro nor a woman. Confer on me, good angel, the glory of white manhood, so that henceforth, sitting or standing, sitting up or lying down, I may enjoy the most unlimited freedom.'[20]

Among all the accusations against marriage, the most significant and devastating was the wife's deprivation of her social identity. 'From the cradle to the grave she is another's . . . let us first obtain *ourselves*. Give us ourselves and all that belongs to us will follow', Ernestine Rose demanded.[21] Losing her own name, for her oppressor's, another similarity with the slave, was seen as the sharpest symbol of the loss of not only identity but social and legal existence. Without a name the woman and the slave were only chattels. 'Ask your coloured brethren if there is nothing in a name. Why are the slaves nameless until they take that of their masters'? Simply because they have no independent existence.'[22]

Rose and Stanton did not merely describe the different aspects of women's oppression, but analysed the patriarchal order responsible for this state of things. 'It must strike every careful thinker that an immense difference lies in the fact that man has made the laws . . .' said Stanton.[23] Their acute consciousness of the political privileges of one gender group led them to consider women's political participation as a priority.

In order to demonstrate married women's specific oppression (single women were legally almost autonomous), partisans of the Cause referred to esoteric law treatises and used Latin quotations in their impassioned speeches.[24] Briefly, this is how they depicted women's status in the middle of the 19th century: the law makes the woman *femme covert sub potestate viri* or, in the terse eloquent phrase of the British lawyer, Blackstone, '. . . the husband and wife are one, and that one is the husband . . .' Married woman's total alienation – 'she is nameless, purseless, childless' –

was relentlessly analyzed and denounced.[25] Because of her legal non-existence, she could not sue or be sued, own any property, whether earned or brought into marriage, or have any rights in her children. Widows did not fare any better and the dead husband's property went to the children. Marriage, a system of 'legalized robbery', stripped all women, whether rich or poor.

Suffragist speakers displayed astonishing rhetorical skills in their brief against the condition of married women. Ernestine Rose, who looked at the condition of widows as exemplifying women's oppression, commented on their pathetic status with biting irony and an abundance of sordid details.

> . . . the law kindly allows her her own wearing apparel, her own ornaments . . . one bed with appurtenances for the same, a stove, a Bible, family pictures . . . and also spinning wheels and weaving looms, one table, six chairs, ten cups and saucers, one tea pot . . . (much laughter). But the law does not inform us whether they are to be tea or table spoons; . . . The law allows the widow something more. She is allowed one cow, all sheep to the number of ten, with the fleeces . . . two swine and the pork therefrom.[26]

Such a satirical inventory no doubt provided some comic relief but aimed primarily at arousing righteous indignation against cruel and absurd laws. At the same convention, Lucy Stone evoked the same theme in angry tones when she described the agony of a woman sequestered for three years by her husband. In view of all the 'bitter, bitter suffering of thousands of your sisters', prematurely white hair and lined faces, it would be more appropriate, Lucy Stone said, to speak of A Woman's Wrongs rather than of A Woman's Rights Movement. Not everybody in the audience sympathized, and the speeches seemed to have received a mixed response. 'Hiss-s-s! Bow-ow-ow! Men, women and bloomers! Pantalooned mob as aforesaid: Oh! dry up!'[27]

Often activists also questioned the contemporary ideal of the scene of marriage, the Home. 'Sheerest humbug',[28] said one woman who denounced it as another verbal masquerade designed to gloss over the domestic and social aspects of woman's slavery. 'The last stronghold of woman's degradation . . . is the sacred enclosure of the Home', declared Stanton.[29] The suffragists discussed domestic slavery in terms suited to different milieux. They insisted on the overt degradation and brutality among the poorer classes and ridiculed the glorification of the middle class wife and mother. Stanton called the housewife 'the satellite of the dinner-pot; the presiding genius of the bath tub; . . . the gay butterfly of fashion; the femme covert of the law . . .'[30] She, like other suffragists, protested vehemently against the waste of energy and talent resulting from the stultifying life of the 'fairy of the Home', made worse by the 'spaniel wife' mentality and the deplorable repression widespread among women.[31] Stanton herself chafed against the confinement and drudgery of her own life. Ambivalent as she was about public life and conventions, she nonetheless expressed her distress at being homebound.[32] And, by contrast, her husband's independence aroused her obvious resentment. 'As I contrast his freedom with my bondage, I feel that because of the false position of women, I have been compelled to hold all my noblest aspirations in abeyance in order to be a wife, a mother, a cook, a household drudge.'[33] Stanton's husband implied that her hostile feelings about married life included the procreative function. 'You must not frighten her half to death, by telling her constantly what a "horrid affair" it is. You must remind her of the royal courage of Victoria . . .' he warned her, referring to a friend.[34]

In Stanton's analysis, the slavery of women's domestic life was bitterly enhanced by the accepted code of hypocritical male courtesies to women. Nothing more ridiculous and inappropriate, she wrote humorously, than 'this walking to dinner two by two as did the animals in Noah's ark . . .' If men wanted to help, let them share the chores, '. . . help us get dinner, pick and prepare vegetables, . . . crack ice, etc. . . .'[35] The discourse of chivalry struck her as a mere masquerade.

The legal and domestic subjection of women in marriage which the feminists so passionately denounced proceeded mainly from what Stanton called 'the Husband's right of property in the wife . . .'[36] But the phrase included an explosive element, the husband's right of property to his wife's body and the control of procreation.[37] The subject of sexual slavery, which did surface in women's rights meetings, was discussed more openly in female temperance circles. The temperance movement focused on the horror of poverty-stricken families victimized by the sinful intemperance of improvident husbands, or the worse horror of degenerate offspring conceived by alcoholic parents. Stanton had joined the movement in the early 1850s and became president of the New York section in 1852.[38] In her temperance speeches, she stigmatized the sexual and reproductive consequences of alcoholism more than the 'vice' itself, and she constantly exhorted woman to fulfil both duties to herself and to mankind by denying her husband access to her body.[39] Woman militants generally denounced the husband's right in the property in the wife's body both as an outrage that inflicted unwanted offspring on the wives[40] and as a system of 'legalized prostitution'[41] which deeply offended woman's purity as well as the dictates of romantic love.

Though rarely expressed directly, the woman's claim to control her body, under the slogan 'voluntary motherhood', became a suffragist demand, less loud than the insistence on the vote but no less imperative and quite clear by the 1870s.[42] Before the emergence of moral reform in the 1870s, feminists could see no other way of dealing with man's 'gross animal nature' than trying to resist sexual advances or living separately. In the 1850s and 1860s the women who approached the problem expressed such a distaste for man's physical nature, 'drunk with wine and passion', that the possibility of asking men to control their sexual urge seemed remote.[43]

RESISTANCE: PERSONAL AND COLLECTIVE

The discourse of protest against marriage originated in middle-class educated circles, among women unusually active in contemporary social movements, and in a context of unusual male comprehension and sympathy. They were certainly not representative of the rank and file of the women's rights movement, and much less of women in general. Yet their introduction of new symbols into accepted rituals, breaking away from the dominant discourse, was a significant step in the formulation of emancipation.

In a culture dominated by the domestic ideal, only a few voiced hostile comments on the married condition. The experience of those women's rights advocates known to have made a personal protest in their own lives is significant. Both Lucy Stone and Abby Kelley, engaged to be married to men they appreciated and loved, waited several years before finally taking the fateful step. Kelley's hesitations originated in her realistic fear of having to terminate her political activities after marriage. Public opinion, she feared, would impose on her the wife's traditional role, and, happy to get rid of a cumbersome abolitionist, push her into the home: '. . . they would say that I was *under obligation to take care of your public constitution and nurse you* . . .' Conservative opinion had already interfered in her life and accused her of neglecting her mother.[44] When Abby Kelley, aged thirty-five, and Stephen Foster finally married, in 1845, it was in the simple Quaker style, 'priestless, cakeless, wineless', declaring 'their purposes to perform faithfully all the relative duties of husband and wife.'[45] Lucy Stone was thirty-seven when she married and her ambivalence sounded more like terror, with its attendant symptoms of panic and depression. Like Abby Kelley, an anti-slavery and suffragist militant, she understandably feared having to renounce her political activities. But the nature of her feelings appeared more complex and painful. She loathed the idea of losing the single woman's independence. 'I have planned and executed without counsel and without control. I have shared thought, and feeling and life with myself alone.'[46] A deep-seated anxiety coloured by sexual overtones, 'deep revulsion of feeling', increased her malaise. Henry Blackwell's 'feminism' made Stone's resistance appear more paradoxical. For not only had he decided to wait for her almost as long as Jacob for Rachel, fourteen years at least, but he promised her complete freedom as a wife. 'You are your own mistress and will always remain so.' Moreover, he legally guaranteed her her own property and earnings, and the exclusive right to decide 'where and how often you shall become a mother'. They married on May 1, 1855 and instead of the marriage service they read the famous 'protest', in which Blackwell disavowed his privileges as a husband. He was thus fulfilling his earlier promise: 'I wish, as a husband, to renounce all the privileges which the law confers upon me, which are not strictly *mutual* . . . '

Like Olympia Brown and other suffragists, Lucy Stone decided to keep her own name, asking people to call her 'Mrs. Lucy Stone' and signing legal documents, 'Lucy Stone, wife of Henry Blackwell'.[47] But this was no easy step, encountered much resistance and branded one for life in the eyes of friends and foes. Many years later, when she chose to belong to the more traditional American Woman Suffrage Association rather than to the National, somebody would periodically bring up her former stand against the slavery of married women and contrast it with her present conformity.[48] Claiming her own name for a woman, and in some cases, her first name, was an affirmation of her identity and represented an important symbolic protest, enhanced by the analogy with slavery. 'When a slave escapes from a Southern plantation, he at once takes a name as the first step in liberty – the first assertion in individual identity. A woman's dignity is equally involved in a life-long name, to mark her individuality', Stanton wrote.[49] She herself was extremely sensitive on the use or omission of her first name.[50] Little did she expect that, to Anthony's consternation, her own daughter would introduce herself the day after her wedding in 1878 as 'Mrs. Eugene Lawrence', thus taking on not only one new male surname but also a male Christian name.[51] The rebellion against traditional marriage also took the form of changing the marriage service, either by rewriting it or by omitting the word 'obey'.[52]

Apart from these individual escapes, militant women voiced their criticism of marriage in organized political action. The two public campaigns directly related to the status of the wife demanded 'property rights for women' and the liberalization of divorce. The first aimed at securing married women their property, whether inherited or acquired. The campaign started in 1836, twelve years before Seneca Falls, with Ernestine Rose and Paulina Wright as the main fighters. After two defeats in 1836 and 1840, and eight more years of strenuous but more collective efforts, the first Married Women's Property Act was voted on April 1848 in New York State. It gave wives control over the property they owned at the time of their marriage. But they had to wait until 1860 for the Earnings Act and the Act on Rights and Liabilities of Husband and Wife to grant them financial and legal autonomy, as well as equal rights over their children.[53]

The campaign for the liberalization of divorce involved a more radical stand, based as it was on the questioning of key principles of the dominant marriage ideology. Deeply opposed to the intrusion of religion into public and private life, the supporters of divorce in the mid-19th century (coming from suffragist, spiritualist and utopian socialist circles) viewed marriage as a contract that could be dissolved, and not as a religious life-binding commitment. Unlike spiritualists and utopians, whose ideas centered on the rejection of dogma and hierarchy, such questioning of authority played little part in the concerns of the woman's rights movement and challenged deep-seated cultural habits. Only a few leaders – Stanton, Rose, Anthony, and Stone – spoke out clearly for divorce reform. Stanton's concern with this question persisted long after the main agitation in the 1860s.[54] The McFarland case, for instance, in which a man convicted of murder was granted custody of his child, confirmed her determination to put all her energy towards 'the entire revision of the laws of New York on marriage and divorce . . .'[55] Even if, on the other hand, the more subtle task of teaching 'women her duties to herself in the home . . .' also appeared urgent.[56]

The imperious necessity of divorce dawned on Stanton during her temperance days in the 1850s.[57] Early on, she declared her intention to struggle towards making drunkenness grounds for divorce, thus linking the two battles, temperance and women's rights. In a six point program, she drew up a drastic plan of ostracizing drunks, particularly within the family. 'Let no woman remain in relation of wife with the confirmed drunkard. Let no drunk be the father of her children, etc.'[58] The evil of male drunkenness, 'rum-maddened husbands and fathers', 'brutal drunkards', exacerbated by women's helplessness, haunted Stanton and others. Strategically, the theme of male intemperance, whether outlined as a social disease, or evidence of the male's evil nature, served as powerful ammunition for divorce reform among liberals and traditionalists as well. And the image of the woman brutalized by her drunk husband, a powerful paradigm of the female predicament, served several purposes: a call to rescue victimized females and to save such middle class values as the ethic of work, self control, abstinence, family; it justified middle class women in reprimanding the men in the lower classes; elicited the support of poor women; and generally aroused female militancy.

Beyond the responsibility of individual men, Stanton, as well as Rose and Stone, held that the church's indiscriminate opposition to divorce was responsible for the social disaster of the drunken husband which ruined families, brutalized wives, and produced degenerate children. 'Their God sanctions violence, oppression, and wine-bibbing, and winks at gross moral delinquencies . . .' ranted Stanton somewhat confusedly.[59] Opposition to religion and to the church was woven into suffragist ideology and practice. Early on, the Garrisonian abolitionists had denounced the nefarious effects of clerical authority on women; and the conflict remained an issue for the women's movement until the Civil War. Stanton recounts dramatically how Garrison, 'in a few bold strokes of the hammer of his truth . . .' had freed her from 'spiritual bondage'.[60]

The issue of divorce came up in full force at the 1860 National Woman's Rights Convention, where, encouraged by the impending discussion of a new bill, Stanton decided to raise the question and to present ten resolutions to support it. In terms of success the issue appeared premature. The same year the New York Legislature repealed the bill in an atmosphere of hatred and anger, and, torn apart, the Woman's Rights convention rejected Stanton's resolutions.[61] In fact, Stanton's decision to broach the problem at a Woman's Convention was only approved by her closest supporters, and aroused considerable and unexpected hostility. Even Lucy Stone proved extremely ambivalent, first uttering doubts as to the appropriateness of the subject for a woman's meeting, then, later, just before the event, expressing guarded encouragement, and finally joining the anti-divorce camp at the convention.[62] The divorce partisans had not expected such fierce opposition, but after the fact, Stanton reflected '. . . we have thrown our bombshell into the center of woman's degradation and of course we have raised a rumpus.'[63]

The debate on divorce at the 1860 Convention revealed the ideological poles within feminism. On the conservative side, the Reverend Antoinette Brown made an eloquent plea against divorce based on arguments such as the nature of the indissoluble marriage tie, and woman's duty to sacrifice herself and accomplish a moral and religious mission.[64] 'I must seek first to regenerate him, the nearest and dearest to me . . .' Her model of true womanhood conformed to tradition. In addition, the opponents of divorce denied the inadequacy of marriage and, even in this suffragist stronghold, ignored the oppression of woman. For when Wendell Phillips, William Lloyd Garrison and others argued at the 1860 Convention that this topic should not be discussed at a women's gathering, because marriage concerned men and women equally, they denied the fundamental principle of the feminist analysis, the inequality between the conditions of the sexes.[65] 'Marriage has ever been a one sided matter resting most unequally between the sexes. By it man gains all – woman loses all; . . . By law . . . woman has never been thought of other than a piece of property . . . She must accept marriage as man proffers it or not at all, . . .' Anthony wrote.[66]

Stanton and Rose were not at a loss for arguments to debunk the so-called holiness of marriage. The stark tragic facts, mismatched partners, strife within families, martyrdom of wives, wretchedness and despair everywhere proved the depressingly human character of the institution.[67] Besides, Rose argued, because the main objective of marriage consisted in '. . . the happiness of the parties . . . concerned and secondly the welfare of society . . .' why consider it as eternal, why not dissolve it in cases of incompatibility, brutality, drunkenness, etc?[68] Both Rose and Stanton insisted on the necessity of divorce as opposed to separation, which maintained the divorce taboo and prevented the spouses from remarrying. The right to remarry affirmed the potential right of individuals to happiness in this world.

Not only did the opponents of divorce consider any attempt at reforming marriage as the open door to sin, a Pandora's box of vice and immorality, not only did the convention reject the pro divorce resolutions, but the press added insult to defeat by accusing the suffragists of propagating free love. 'I began to feel as if I had inadvertently taken out the underpinning from the social system', said Stanton.[69] Indeed, public opinion responded to the demand for divorce as if it were a bomb intended to blow up society at large, blurring in their indignation the complex ideological fabric of the pro divorce discourse, with its three main strands: the romantic longing for 'a union of soul to soul', the demand for equality in marriage, and a global if implicit attack against male power, biologically based and culturally constructed.

FREE LOVE

The accusation of free love was hurled against any attempt at marriage reform, whether articulated by woman's rights advocates or by any other Reformer. 'Free love was casually associated both with Woman's Rights and with socialism,' Mari Jo Buhle writes.[70] Free Lovers did generally support woman's emancipation in ante bellum America. Woman reformers did not escape this thinly-veiled accusation of promiscuousness and immorality which regularly came up in the press.[71] The women's rights movement responded negatively to these accusations and partisans of free love were rare among them. Even a bold critic of marriage like Ernestine Rose did not approve of free love. She viewed divorce not only as an escape for women from bad marriage, from 'legalized prostitution', but as a means of avoiding the 'crimes and immoralities' of free love, a sensible *via media* between woman's slavery and a frightening outlaw territory.[72] In no way did she condone or aspire to total freedom in personal and sexual relationships. But in spite of her relatively clear position, Rose did not escape the stigma of free love. At the 'Free Convention of the Friends of Human Progress' in Rutland, Vermont, in 1858, a picturesque gathering of reformers, her name was associated with that of a certain Julia Branch. In fiery oratory, Branch had irrevocably condemned the institution of marriage and the family, which she decried as particularly destructive among the poorer classes, and defended the right of 'women to choose the father of their children'.[73] Rose supported a different resolution, drafted by Stephen Foster, which defended 'exclusive conjugal love based on perfect equality between one man and one woman . . . the only true home . . . the isolated home . . .' and explicitly dissociated herself from Branch's anarchic and free love overtones.[74] Still the *New York Times* reports referred to both women as free lovers. And Rose never quite lost that stigma.[75] Beyond Rose's personal reputation and her interest in Utopian socialist communities, the accusation of free love clearly aimed at discrediting the woman's rights and the reform movements.

The fear of free love, as myth and reality, in suffragist circles, was illustrated by two incidents involving the anarchist free lover, Stephen

Pearl Andrews. At the 1853 Woman's Convention in New York, he introduced himself to suffragist Clarina I. H. Nichols as the founder of 'Modern Times' (a free love community on Long Island) and asked permission to discuss his ideas 'with the leading advocates of the movement with a view to co-operation.'[76] Nichols, 'shocked out of all courteous circumlocution . . .', rejected his ideas out of hand, and she did not feel any better disposed towards him when he developed his views further.[77] Andrews attended another convention in 1858. According to a *New York Times* report, his attempt at launching a discussion on 'the right (of woman) to change and experiment' was not taken up, drowned in Anthony's and Rose's strategically vague remarks.[78] Clearly, free love had no place in the public image of a movement in search of mass support and legal change.

While not suited to the needs and tolerance of the rank and file, free love as a paradigm of freedom represented a tempting intellectual challenge to an unconventional personality like Elizabeth Cady Stanton, one who 'reached beyond the accepted beliefs of her contemporaries to investigate daring, often heretical ideas . . .'[79] In an undated letter where she drew up a list of the current accusatory terms catalyzing fear and hostility, she included the phrase 'Free love', together with 'woman infidel', 'strong-minded woman', 'blue stocking', etc.[80] But in a speech given in 1869 in New York City, she dealt openly and at some length with the subject.[81] Like all free lovers and some feminists, she protested against the interference of religion and law in private life, stating with quasi anarchist optimism that laws were unnecessary except for bad people. Thus she seemed to support unequivocally total freedom in relationships outside any constraint or model. Choosing a partner for life, for example, was part of this new found freedom, she explained paradoxically. But Stanton ventured further into subtler areas of psychology and dwelt on the possibility of mutual oppression, 'through the right of ownership over the other'.[82] This vehement attack against the possessiveness and dependence, which structured most monogamous relationships in or outside marriage, seemed to carry a personal echo, and beyond the parameters of reform and struggle, pointed to the necessity of redefining human relationships towards more individual freedom.

The substance of Stanton's message as well as the metaphors she used indicate that she fully realized the hazards of such a voyage into the unknown. 'Think twice' she said to those who decided to embark on the ship of freedom, for this was only a first step. 'The next better thing is wisdom.' Her obvious excitement at novelty and risk-taking suggests her vision of feminism as a sweeping revolutionary force.[83] Quoting the well known spiritualist, Andrew Jackson Davis, she humorously warned against the snares of fad diets and non-conformity: 'If anybody began with bran bread, he was sure to end up with infidelity'.[84] No one could calculate or predict the consequences of the woman's struggle. But one thing was certain: equality for women would 'revolutionize' the family and spread further. For, in a society in which man, according to John Stuart Mill, was not prepared to live with an equal in private or in political life, real female equality could only be achieved at the price of a revolution. (Stanton, of course, rarely indulged such apocalyptic vision in public speaking, for neither the discourse on sexual freedom nor the call for revolutionary upheaval suited her audience at large.[85])

The Woodhull episode further illustrates the woman's rights leaders' attitude towards free love. During the brief but significant idyll between the Suffragists and Victoria Woodhull, it became increasingly clear that the former would not and could not endorse extreme views on marriage or free love. The suffragists worked with Woodhull as long as she was useful to the Cause, notwithstanding her notorious reputation, her stand on sexual freedom, and her radicalism. They used her insight into the Constitution and her aura of fascinating newcomer on the suffrage scene. But before long, her controversial views and way of life, which fed the righteous wrath of the other suffragist camp, The American Woman's Suffrage Association, rang the death knell of their association. And largely under Susan B. Anthony's strong arm and sense of strategy, Woodhull was put aside. Not unexpectedly, Stanton was the only suffragist to continue for a time to support and defend Woodhull.

IDEOLOGY

We need at this stage to tease out the ideological strands that run through the discourse of the suffragist critique of marriage and define its intellectual heritage. Structured around two main trends, the feminists' thinking on the subject pointed on the one hand to the philosophy of the 'natural rights of man', derived from the principles of the American Revolution and the eighteenth century Enlightenment tradition. On the other, it drew its inspiration from the evangelical creed which preached the conversion of sinners and salvation, and posited the moral superiority and the redeeming mission of the 'mothers of the race'.[86]

Ernestine Rose, the most articulate advocate of the natural rights theory, equated the three concepts, 'natural', 'human', and 'man' as found in the American Declaration of Independence. Nothing therefore, she and Paulina Wright Davis argued, could justify excluding women from the principles 'that all men are created free and equal . . .'[87] Women, 'one half of the people of this Republic', had arbitrarily been stripped of their natural rights and, like the slaves, had to be freed from crushing tyranny.[88]

Rose added a distinctly European grist to the rationalist mill. Born in a Jewish ghetto, in Russian-dominated Poland, she had experienced political and racial oppression. The struggle for the emancipation of women represented for her one episode of the warfare against 'the despotism of kings and the bigotry of priests'.[89] Unique in the suffragist movement, her anticlericalism and revolutionary rhetoric came out in full force at the Worcester Convention of October 1851. In her spoken reply to the letter of congratulations written by Jeanne Deroin and Pauline Roland to their American sisters,[90] she lamented the new French rulers' betrayal of the principles of 'liberté, egalité, fraternité'.[91]

Rose loathed and abhorred the church as the main instrument of women's oppression. Countering Antoinette Brown at the 1852 convention, she refuted both her attempts at legitimating woman's emancipation through the Bible and the principle of authority itself.[92] The oppressed, she argued, have to fight for their freedom, not wait for the oppressor to grant it. 'When the inhabitants of Boston converted their harbour into a teapot rather than submit to unjust taxes, they did not go to the Bible for their authority . . .'[93] A self styled 'infidel', Rose's anticlericalism and to some extent her foreign origin, had not only aroused fierce hostility at many of her public appearances but isolated her within a still largely Christian woman's movement. 'Mrs. Rose is not appreciated, nor can be by this age . . .' wrote Anthony, who, for all her sympathy and admiration, failed to understand Rose's bitterness.[94]

It followed logically from the 'natural rights' idea that both men and women belonged to one human nature. 'Humanity recognizes no sex; mind recognizes no sex; virtue and vice, pleasure and pain, happiness and misery, life and death recognize no sex.' stated Rose.[95] Rose consistently and Stanton sometimes viewed the difference between the sexes as an artificial construct designed to justify selfish male interests. To prove her point, Rose quoted a statement from Roebuck, an English MP, cynically explaining his opposition to women's political activity by his need for the 'perfect, soothing, gentle peace' at home, indispensable to him after a day 'sullied by politics'.[96] Men had invented an idea of woman's nature designed to serve their own ends, said Stanton. 'What is man's idea of womanliness? It is to have a manner which pleases him – quiet, deferential, submissive, approaching him as a subject does a master.'[97]

The rationalist approach to women's rights implied definite strategies and priorities in the struggle. Even though Stanton sometimes expressed doubts and was tempted to deal with the 'social' first (meaning domestic and personal), the movement's consensus placed top priority on the demand for the vote. Faithful to the liberal democratic tradition, they trusted political institutions and believed that the vote for women would change and improve the private as well as the public sphere.[98] 'The ballot box is the focus of all other rights . . .' Rose wrote.[99] The more far sighted militants did not see the quest for political rights as an end in itself but as the thrust which would burst open the prison of the home and revolutionize marriage, if not abolish it.

The idea of woman's innate superiority competed and intermixed with the human rights view of men and women. According to Mary Ryan the idea of the superior and specific nature of woman began to evolve in the

1840s, as many women joined in the romantic and Victorian worship of exquisitely sensitive and morally exceptional womanhood.[100] The domestic novels stressed the difference between the sexes in terms of complementarity, but the militant women's discourse asserted female superiority in more aggressive terms. Within this cult of true womanhood many questions were asked: did these differences between the sexes originate from biology or culture, were they permanent or temporary?[101] Answers varied of course. Harriot Hunt maintained that, whatever the differences between the sexes, it would be absurd to exacerbate them by inculcating boys and girls with different habits.[102] You should no more teach them differently than feed them differently. Rose demanded equality between the sexes, with or without difference,[103] whereas Antoinette Brown used her belief in the physical and mental difference between the sexes to argue that men were constitutionally unable to represent women. So whether in doubt or in certainty about the problem, they all concurred in the demand for equality.

Over the years Stanton expressed contradictory opinions on the subject. Much of her analysis went to show that society, i.e. men, had a vested interest in constructing a model of female-specific nature that would justify their hegemony. She leaned therefore towards a cultural model of gender difference. But more often, she explicitly and implicitly set off women's perfection against the abysmal inferiority of the male race, thus suggesting an innate difference between the sexes. Masculine nature seemed to be the target of her assault on the male animal appetites that inevitably aroused female revulsion: '. . . her whole soul revolting at such gross association! Her flesh shivering at the contamination of that embrace!'[104]

In the sweeping accusations combining moral censure and physical distaste, she included men of her own class, equally given to intemperance, equally afflicted with a repulsive appearance, betraying their animal nature.[105] In May 1852, she wrote:

> I have no desire to sit in council with vulgar, rum-drinking, wine-bibbing, tobacco-chewing men, with thick-lipped voluptuaries, gourmands and licentiates . . . who resort to fist-cuffing, drinking and duelling . . . to state nice questions of honor and statesmanship.[106]

Her obsession with men's grossness, expressed in the tone and the metaphors, such as drunken brutes and thick-lipped louts, suggested strong overtones of physical violence and rape. When she wrote 'Woman's degradation is man's idea of his sexual rights', she showed her ability to distance herself from her emotional outburst.[107] But whether emotional or analytical, her message stated the moral and physical incompatibility between the sexes. Totally undesirable, the apes should definitely be removed to their own planet.[108]

The theme of innate or acquired male brutality persisted through several decades in the women's rights movement. Elizabeth Pleck convincingly argues that Stanton and Anthony's preoccupation with crimes against women began in the 1850s with their activity in the Temperance Movement at the same time as Stanton's attempt to make cruelty and 'habitual drunkenness' grounds for divorce. It increased in the 1860s as Stanton and Anthony became involved in some famous criminal cases on behalf of female victims. Even though in the 1870s the fight against violence to women merged with that of social purity, for Stanton and Anthony the victimization of women, routinely associated with slavery, remained closely connected with inequality in the family and the abuses of marriage.[109] The 'conservative feminists', Lucy Stone and Henry Blackwell, held similar views and railed against the 'hydra-headed monster' of intemperance and male licentiousness.[110] Both radical and conservative feminists advocated extreme punishment for wife beaters and rapists.

Outside women's circles, Robert Dale Owen expressed a similar tension between masculine baseness and female purity in his remarks on divorce. The overtones of marital rape are clear in his contrast between the 'pure, gentle, blameless Christian wife' and the 'bloated wretch', the 'Caliban' and in the equation of masculinity with animality: 'The bedchamber is his; the bed is the beast's own lair.'[111] In a recent article on the exchange of ideas between two feminist writers, Anna Jameson in England and Sarah Grimke in the US, during the 1850s, Gerda Lerner identifies contemporary attacks against male sexuality and 'the horrors of forced maternity' as unmistakable 'euphemisms for marital rape.'[112]

So the passionate rhetoric against men, tormenters of women, both in upper and lower classes, was in the air. Stanton's heavy handed attack on masculinity expressed not only her own feelings but embodied a collective value judgment that had originated in Temperance circles and was later echoed in campaigns from various parts of the women's movement.

The contemporaneous discourse on the family encouraged a Manichean view of the world which condemned men and idealized women. Stanton had her moments of ambivalence towards the idea of woman's superiority and proved quite capable of contradicting herself. But on the whole, she idealized women as excessively as she had reviled men. Not only did she endow them with perfection as mothers, teachers, and organizers, but she believed women had the ability to learn any profession they chose.[113] Moreover, in the best Victorian tradition she assigned to them the special mission of abolishing male violence by female peace and justice. Like many of her contemporaries, she saw women as divine instruments of salvation of mankind.[114] Only through woman's glorious mission (Sarah Grimke), 'her superior power' (Frances Gage) did man stand a very slim chance of redemption.

The idea of woman's mission and social responsibility seemed to originate obscurely from her maternal function.[115] 'As mothers of the race, there is a spiritual insight, a divine creative power that belongs to women' wrote Stanton.[116] Whatever the exact nature of this mission, it prescribed the preservation of the race as the imperative duty of 'scientific mothers'.[117] Stanton's eugenic preoccupation with 'enlightened motherhood' sometimes took on alarming proportions: 'A High sense of justice will restrain the nervous, the feeble, the diseased from entailing their weaknesses from other generations. In China they whip the Father for the child's short-comings . . .'[118] However alarming the implications of the eugenic crusade, one can read in it the demand for women's right to their bodies, the refusal of access or control of procreation, in the context of a respectable scientific pursuit.

Woman's superiority, man's baseness, woman's oppression, male tyranny, these contrasts couched in many different ways already structured women's rights thinking in the early days. As early as 1848, Gerda Lerner detects a 'polarized view of the sexes' in the 'Declaration of Sentiments', and in Sarah Grimke's 'Sense of her Own Selfhood'.[119] The impossibility of communication between men and women, other than in terms of oppression of violence, emerged early as a leitmotiv in feminist discourse and continued as a part of it for several decades. How could one imagine a common future in a heterosocial order? How could such a damning appraisal fail to suggest a separatist solution? Avoiding marriage was a step in the right direction. Without the possibility of divorce, warned Stanton, 'beware of putting your head into [the marriage] noose'.[120] Others suggested alternatives to marriage. Convinced that attitudes lagged far behind reforms, Anthony predicted that 'an epoch of single women' would provide a necessary transition between man-made marriage and a new more egalitarian relationship. Her community was a place where independent women, blissfully free from the marriage obsession, met men as equals: 'Lovely white cottages wreathed in vines, nestled midst gardens of vegetables and flowers . . . each a little Paradise save the presence of the historic Adam'.[121] Earlier, an article in *The Una* voiced a similar desire to make single life both attractive and even financially profitable for unmarried women in a mixture of utopia and realism. Women in this communal framework could both invest their savings and enjoy freedom from domestic chores. 'If a sufficient number of such women join, all the domestic work would be divided among them . . . it seems to me that a good many ladies of small means, or discontented life and wasting it without objects, might make themselves homes in Rarity Bay'.[122]

'We shall be our own lawyers and our own judges . . . our own jury too', Ernestine Rose had said in 1853.[123] In her universalist philosophy this statement pointed to a temporary stage before the glorious times to come, when humanity, justice and universal love would abolish class and sex barriers. As early as 1852 Stanton had contrasted more categorically the radically diverging interests of men and women. 'Let us have separate purses, separate schools and a new code of laws for our special benefit'.

This sounded like a boycott of a government, which denying the right of half of the human race, had waged 'war on the helpless nations, to enslave the helpless Africans, or hunt to death the red man of the soil . . . We consent not that one tithe of our money shall go to support such abominations.'

Viewed as a temporary or a lasting solution, a separate women's world was alluring to the early suffragists, and the separatist message rang loud and clear.[124]

CONCLUSION

This survey of the women's rights discourse on marriage reveals views of the oppression of women, of the strategies of resistance, of gender differences and incompatibility, which explode far beyond the confines of a few piecemeal social reforms. Through the content of their arguments and the emotional power conveyed by tone, metaphor and symbols, these women boldly challenged the prevailing value system. Whether arguing from a 'natural rights' or from a 'true womanhood' position, they struck at the roots of Victorian patriarchy. Both these ideological trends made extreme and unattainable demands for the total overthrow of male dominated culture and politics, and for a radical change in human nature, based on the innate superiority of women and the inferiority of men. Feminists found the oppression of women by men so inextricably built into the social fabric, that the first basic step towards equality, the enfranchisement of women, implied no less than a major upheaval. So, while assuming that woman's vote would revolutionize public and private life, they also realized that entrenched male supremacy ruled out the whole undertaking. In this double message, confident radicalism alternated with realistic pessimism.

The theme of gender incompatibility naturally raised the question of the separation of the sexes. We hear the voices of these women, incensed by male tyranny, repelled by male grossness, suggesting a separate world of woman-identified women. Meanwhile, a few others evoked the remote possibility of harmonious relations between men and women, in a mood of utopian longing and wishful thinking. Upheaval, separatism, and revolution were sometimes heard in full in the suffragists' discourse, sometimes read between the lines as a definite, if blurred, subversive message.

Subversion, however, did not define the identity of the women's rights movement as a political force within the framework of reform. The suffragists had taken a major step in moving from the private to the public sphere, thus challenging conventional roles and basic Victorian assumptions about sexuality. Their approach differed, however, from that of other reformers. To the Spiritualists and Utopians, the fight against women's oppression was only one cause in their comprehensive alternative scheme which defended individual freedom, opposed clericalism, explored the spirit world and the psychic unknown, constructed Heaven on earth and experimented with new forms of family life. Casting their net more widely, they experimented in a marginal and controversial terrain. The women's rights advocates, on the other hand, who effectively questioned dominant nineteenth-century values through their critique of marriage, used traditional methods of agitation, spoke the same language as their opponents and moved within an intricate network of institutions and in permanent dialogue with them. Reformers in their unique ideological and strategic terms, they inserted the critique of marriage into their fundamental challenge of the contemporary power structure.

NOTES

ACKNOWLEDGEMENTS
I want to thank the Pembroke Center for Teaching and Research on Women (Brown University) for making the research for this article possible. My thanks too to the American Antiquarian Society, Worcester, Mass. for immensely facilitating my work. I am also grateful to Claudia Koonz, Mari-Jo Buhle and Joan Scott for valuable comments.

1 Nancy Cott, *The Bonds of Womanhood*, New Haven, 1977, p. 205.

2 B. Glasman Hersh, *The Slavery of Sex*, Chicago, 1978, p. 201.

3 Ellen Carol DuBois, 'The Radicalism of the Woman Suffrage Movement', *Feminist Studies*, vol. 3, no. 1/2, 1975, pp. 63–71.

4 The campaign for the legal reform of marriage in the 19th century was one demonstration, among many others, of the connection between the two domains. See Norma Basch, *In the Eyes of the Law*, Ithaca, 1981, pp. 162–163. On the same subject, see Susan Kent, 'Sex, Power and Politics', Ph.D. thesis, Brown University, 1984, p. 101.

5 The struggle for the Married Women's Property Acts in the State of New York started in 1836 and ended twenty four years later with the Earnings Act of 1860.

6 Basch, *In the Eyes of the Law*, p. 113.

7 Ernestine Rose (1810–1892). Jewish. Born in Poland. Rabbi father. Reformer, suffragist, and free thinker. Mary Gove Nichols (1810–1884). Born in New Hampshire; free thinking and universalist parents. Women's rights and health reformer. Edited health journals and ran a water cure establishment. Novelist. In 1848, married her second husband, Thomas L. Nichols. Both turned to spiritualism and Catholicism.

8 Victoria Claflin Woodhull (1838–1927) began as a Wall Street broker. In 1870, she ran for president of the United States. She belonged to Marx's International Working Men's Association, later fought for woman's suffrage with the National Woman's Suffrage Association. A defender of free love, she was involved in the Beecher Tilton adultery case. Arrested and jailed, she became an outcast in the U.S. and spent the latter part of her life in England. Working hard at disowning her past, she married a banker in 1883.

9 Letter to Lydia Maria Child, 1856, quoted in Kirk Jeffrey, 'Marriage, Careers and Feminine Ideology in 19th century America', *Feminist Studies*, vol. 2, no. 2/3, 1975, p. 123. Lydia Maria Child (1802–1880), woman of letters, wrote for the causes of abolitionism and woman's emancipation. A Unitarian, she lived mostly in Boston.

10 Elizabeth Cady Stanton (1815–1902). Born in Johnstown, N.Y. Father a judge. Presbyterian family. Woman's rights leader and writer.

11 T. Stanton and H. Stanton Blatch, *Elizabeth Cady Stanton as Revealed in her Letters, Diaries and Reminiscences*, New York, 1969, vol. 2, p. 82.

12 *The Revolution*, 19 May 1870.

13 *The Revolution*, 17 and 24 February 1870.

14 *History of Women's Suffrage* (Hereafter referred to as HWS), New York, 1881, I, pp. 718–719.
15 'Home Life', *Elizabeth Cady Stanton Papers*, The Library of Congress, August 1875, reel 4.
16 Stanton, *The Revolution*, 14 April 1870.
17 Stanton, *Letters, Diaries* . . . II, p. 127.
18 Lucy Stone (1818–1893). Born in Massachusetts. Suffragist and abolitionist. School teacher. Studied at Oberlin College. Married Henry Blackwell in 1855.
19 *Proceedings of the Seventh National Convention of Women's Rights*, New York, 1856, p. 88 (hereafter referred to as *Proceedings*) and Hersh, *The Slavery of Sex*, p. 197–198.
20 23 Dec. 1859, Stanton, *Letters, Diaries* . . . II, p. 75.
21 *Proceedings*, October 1853, New York, p. 41.
22 Stanton *Letters, Diaries* . . . II, p. 16.
23 Stanton, *The Revolution*, 15 October 1868.
24 'Legal Rights of Women', *The Una*, April 1854, p. 244. Rose, *Proceedings*, New York, October 1853, p. 49.
25 *The Revolution*, 15 October, 1853.
26 *Proceedings*, October 1853, New York, p. 49.
27 *Ibid.*
28 *Proceedings*, p. 52, October 1850, Worcester, p. 52.
29 *Stanton Papers*, Address before the 1st National Convention of Women's Suffrage, 1869, reel 3.
30 *Proceedings*, September 1852, Syracuse, p. 30.
31 Stanton, *Letters, Diaries* . . . II, 1 May, 1859, p. 73.
32 *Letters, Diaries* . . . II, 20 June, 1853, p. 51.
33 Lois Banner, *Elizabeth Cady Stanton*, Boston, 1980, p. 34.
34 *Stanton Papers*, reel 1, 1834, Library of Congress.
35 Stanton, *The Lily*, August 1851.
36 Speech to the McFarland-Richardson protest meeting, May 1869 in Ellen DuBois (ed.), *Elizabeth Cady Stanton/Susan B. Anthony Correspondence, Writings, Speeches*, New York, 1981, p. 127.
37 Linda Gordon, *Woman's Body, Woman's Right*, London, 1980, p. 90.
38 Banner, *Stanton*, p. 54.
39 'Marriage and Divorce', *The Revolution*, 22 October 1868 and *HWS*, I, p. 719.
40 *The Revolution*, 8 July, 1869.
41 Stanton, *HWS*, I, p. 719 and Rose, *HWS*, I, p. 731.
42 Banner, *Stanton*, 82. Gordon, *Woman's Body*, p. 90.
43 *Ibid.*, p. 83.
44 *Abigail Kelley Foster Papers*, 30 July 1843, American Antiquarian Society, Worcester, Mass. Abby Kelley Foster (1810–1887). Born in Pelham, Mass. Quaker background, farmer father. Abolitionist and woman's rights lecturer. Married Stephen Foster, a radical abolitionist, in 1845.
45 Jane H. Pease, *The Freshness of Fanaticism, Abby Kelley Foster, an Essay in Reform*, Ph.D. thesis, University of Rochester, N.Y. 1969, p. 83.
46 The source for this and the following quotations of the Stone-Blackwell correspondence is Leslie Wheeler (ed.), *Loving Warriors*, New York, 1981, pp. 73, 80, 109, 136 and 115.
47 Olympia Brown (1835–1926) was a women's rights advocate and a Universalist minister.
48 Some examples: S. B. Anthony at the Convention of the American Woman Suffrage Association in Cleveland, 22–23 November 1870. *The Revolution*, December 1 1870. In October 1870, a woman from Vineland, N.J. wondered at 'the strong attack' on *The Revolution*, from *The Woman's Journal* 'whose two principal proprietors . . . shocked the whole world . . . by creating a new and radical marriage service, and by refusing to be called by one another's name.' *The Revolution*, October 27 1870. In the *Woodhull and Claflin Weekly*, 16 December 1871, Stanton, in one of her articles written in support of Victoria Woodhull, also wondered at Lucy Stone's inconsistency.
49 *HWS*, I, 2 August 1848, p. 80.
50 Stanton, *Letters, Diaries* . . . II, p. 84 and p. 117.
51 Susan B. Anthony (1820–1906). Born in Mass. Quaker family. Mill owner father.

Woman suffrage leader, temperance and abolitionist militant. *Anthony Papers*, Diary, October 2, 1878, reel 2, Library of Congress.

52 *Letters, Diaries* . . . I, p. 68 and *The Revolution*, March 24, 1870.

53 *HWS*, I, pp. 686–687. (This act gave a wife control over her earnings and she became joint guardian of her children.)

54 Stanton, *Letters, Diaries* . . . I, p. 185.

55 Speech to the McFarland-Richardson protest meeting, May 1868, in DuBois, *Stanton/Anthony*, p. 127. Found guilty of murdering his ex-wife's lover, McFarland was acquitted on grounds of insanity, yet entrusted with their son's custody.

56 *Ibid.*, and *The Revolution*, 14 April, 1870.

57 Banner, *Stanton*, p. 54.

58 *HWS*, I, pp. 482, 494.

59 *HWS*, I, p. 496.

60 Ellen DuBois, *Feminism and Suffrage 1848–1869*, New York, 1980, p. 34.

61 'The Tribune thundered every morning in its editorial its loudest peals which reverberated through the state . . .' Stanton, *Letters, Diaries* . . . I, p. 184.

62 Lucy Stone to E. C. Stanton, April 16, 1859, reel 1, *Stanton Papers*; Alma Lutz, *Created Equal*, New York, 1940, p. 113.

63 *Stanton*, Letters, Diaries . . . II, 81.

64 *HWS*, I, p. 725. Antoinette Brown Blackwell (Reverend) (1825–1921). Born in Henrietta, N.Y. revival country. Congregational and Unitarian minister. Studied theology in Oberlin College. Lecturer on woman's rights, anti slavery, temperance.

65 *HWS*, I, p. 732.

66 *HWS*, I, 735.

67 *HWS*, I, 719.

68 *HWS*, I, 731.

69 Stanton, *Letters, Diaries* . . . I, p. 190.

70 'Feminism and Socialism', Ph.D. thesis, Wisconsin, 1974, p. 45.

71 On September 8, 1855, fot example, the *New York Times* made some acid remarks about 'free lovers' and 'reformers' within feminism.

72 *HWS*, I, p. 131.

73 *Banner of Light*, 10 July, 1858.

74 *Proceedings* from the Free Convention held at Rutland, 25, 26, 27 July 1853, Boston, 1858, 56.

75 N.Y. *Daily Times*, 2 July, 1858 and E. Suhl, *Ernestine Rose and the Battle for Human Rights*, 1959, New York, p. 195.

76 Clarina Irene Howard Nichols (1810–1885). Born in Vermont. Baptist family. Newspaper editor, woman's rights leader. Active in campaign for women's property rights in 1847.

77 *S. B. Anthony Papers*, 1880, Schlesinger Library, Cambridge, Mass. reel M 42 (1).

78 *New York Daily Times*, 14 May, 1858.

79 Ellen DuBois, 'On Labor and Free Love: Two unpublished speeches of Elizabeth Cady Stanton', *Signs*, Autumn, 1975, p. 257.

80 *Stanton Papers*, 'Speech to the Young Men Suffrage Association, 1870, reel 3.

81 'On Labor and Free Love', *Signs*, p. 265 and 'Address to a Club of Men and Women in New York City about 1869', *Stanton Papers*, reel 3.

82 *Stanton Papers*, 'Address to a Club of Men . . .' reel 3, p. 5.

83 'Address . . .' and 'Home Life', 1875, reel 4.

84 DuBois, 'On Labor and Free Love', p. 268. Andrew Jackson Davis (1826–1910). Shoemaker's son. The Poughkeepsie seer was a renowned healer and mesmerizer. Author of works on the occult, mysticism and science. Twice married. First wife died in 1853. Two years later, married Mary Robinson Love, who like his first wife was a divorcee.

85 DuBois, 'On Labor and Free Love'.

86 See William Leach, *True Love and Perfect Union*, New York, 1980, p. 8, and Mary Ryan, 'The Empire of Mothers', *Women and History*, Summer/Fall 1982.

87 *Proceedings*, Syracuse, 1852, p. 56 and *Ibid.*, New York, 1853, p. 33.

88 *HWS*, I, p. 675 and Paulina Wright Davis (1813–1876). Born in Bloomfield, N.Y. reformer, suffragist, anti slavery and temperance lecturer. *HWS*, I, 57.

89 *Proceedings*, New York, 1853, p. 45.

90 Two French feminist socialists jailed after the failure of the 1848 revolution.

91 *HWS*, I, p. 237.
92 Suhl, *Ernestine Rose* . . . p. 128.
93 *Proceedings*, Syracuse, 1852, p. 69 and p. 129.
94 *Anthony Papers*, Diary, April 1854 in DuBois, *Stanton/Anthony*, p. 75.
95 *Proceedings*, Worcester, October 1851.
96 Suhl, *E. Rose*, p. 130–1.
97 *HWS*, IV, p. 165–166.
98 Stanton, 'Home Life', in DuBois, *Stanton/Anthony*, p. 132.
99 *Proceedings*, November 1856, New York, p. 74.
100 Ryan, 'The Empire of Mothers', p. 80 and p. 37.
101 Barbara Welter, 'The Cult of True Womanhood: 1820–1860', *The American Quarterly* XVIII:2, part 1 (1966), pp. 151–174.
102 Harriot Hunt, *Glances and Glimpses*, Boston, 1856, pp. 393–395. Harriot Hunt (1805–1875) was born in Boston in Universalist family. Physician and reformer, she practised alternative medicine based on good nursing, natural diet and bathing.
103 *Proceedings*, September 1852, Syracuse, p. 21, 22.
104 Stanton, 'Marriage and Divorce', *The Revolution*, 22 October 1868.
105 *Stanton Papers*, 'The Subjection of Women', 1876, reel 4.
106 *The Lily*, May 1852.
107 Stanton, *Letters, Diaries* . . . II, p. 82.
108 In their article, 'Seeking Ecstasy in the Battlefield', in Carol Vance (ed.), *Pleasure and Danger*, New York, 1984, Ellen DuBois and Linda Gordon relate the two symbols of sexual danger to women, prostitution and rape, respectively to the 19th and 20th centuries. They also find among 19th century feminists 'an avoidance of criticizing men and marriage directly', (p. 35). These statements need qualification. For we find substantial evidence of strong reaction against male brutality in the family on the part of both liberal and conservative suffragists. And the rhetoric of Temperance, shot through with the fear of male sexual violence often suggesting rape, influenced feminists at large.
109 Elizabeth Pleck, 'Feminist Responses to "Crimes Against Women", 1868–1896', *Signs*, vol. 8, no. 3, Spring 1983, p. 458.
110 Pleck, p. 459.
111 Horace Greeley, *Recollections from a Busy Life*, New York, 1869, p. 576.
112 Gerda Lerner, 'Comment on Lerner's "Sarah Grimke's *Sisters of Charity*",' *Signs*, Summer 1985, p. 814.
113 *Stanton Papers*, 'Self Government', reel 4.
114 *The Lily*, May 1852, p. 40.
115 Cott, *Bonds of Womanhood*, p. 148.
116 Banner, *Stanton*, p. 76.
117 *Stanton Papers*, undated, untitled.
118 *Ibid.*
119 Lerner, p. 813.
120 *Stanton Papers*, 'Home Life', August 1883, Providence, reel 4.
121 Anthony, 'Homes for Single Women', October 1877, DuBois, *Stanton/Anthony*, p. 146.
122 Letter in *The Una*, April 1853.
123 *Proceedings*, September 1853, New York, p. 48.
124 *The Lily*, May 1852.

Labor's True Woman: Domesticity and Equal Rights in the Knights of Labor

Susan Levine

The language of domesticity with its sentimental attachment to hearth and home and its strict and limiting definition of the feminine sphere was a dominant feature of nineteenth-century American culture. But we must look more closely at the rhetoric of domesticity in the context of nineteenth-century women's lives to see just what the words meant to particular groups of women, especially those outside the middle class. In what way did the cult of domesticity enter the lives of working-class women? Did it simply trickle down into their consciousness making their lives a never ending struggle for middle-class respectability? Or did working-class women take up the rhetoric of domesticity on their own terms? It seems likely that the language of home, family, and femininity had special meanings for working-class women, particularly those whose experiences were shaped by the labor and reform movements of the Gilded Age. For an earlier era Ellen DuBois has convincingly related the very emergence of the women's rights movement to the development of a distinct woman's sphere. Recent work on the Women's Christian Temperance Union (WCTU) likewise demonstrates that Frances Willard harnessed contemporary domestic imagery to build a broad-based reform movement that ultimately challenged the assumptions of the domestic ideology itself. Domesticity, family, and womanhood are therefore not static, universal, or unchanging categories. This paper argues that the experience of working-class women in the Gilded Age labor movement allowed them to use the language of domesticity to criticize the competitive capitalist system that they saw encroaching upon their traditional rights, dignity, and comforts. Ideologically as far removed from modern-day feminism as from the Victorian cult of ladyhood, these late-nineteenth century women discovered a source of cultural support and political opportunity in the labor movement of their day.[1]

Susan Levine is visiting assistant professor at Duke University.

[1] On "true womanhood" and woman's sphere in the nineteenth century, see Barbara Welter, "The Cult of True Womanhood: 1820–1860," *American Quarterly*, 18 (Summer 1966), 151–74; Nancy F. Cott, *The Bonds of Womanhood: "Woman's Sphere" in New England, 1780–1835* (New Haven, 1977), 160–206; Carroll Smith-Rosenberg, "The Female World of Love and Ritual:

The Noble and Holy Order of the Knights of Labor, in particular, provided a powerful alternative to the growing popular image of true womanhood. Begun in 1869 as a secret trade union, the Knights emerged ten years later as the largest and most encompassing labor organization of the century. During the mid-1880s the Knights extended trade unionism and a tradition of republican egalitarian reform to the growing mass of immigrant, unskilled industrial laborers. Their compelling vision juxtaposed a cooperative, moral industrial order against the ravages of the competitive wage system. This system, it seemed, had only recently enveloped vast new numbers of American women.[2]

By the 1880s wage work for many women was a fact of life. From 1870 to 1910 the proportion of women "engaged in gainful occupations" steadily increased from 14 percent to over 20 percent. This general figure, however, masked the specific importance of women's work for particular communities or industries. In some areas, few if any women worked outside their own homes, while elsewhere the figures far exceeded the national average. In 1880, for example, women constituted 26 percent of Philadelphia's workers, 34 percent of the workers in Fall River, Massachusetts, and 35 percent of the work force in Atlanta, Georgia. Women's work-force participation depended largely on local employment opportunities. Areas with major concentrations of textile mills or clothing industries employed the largest numbers of women. In Philadelphia women made up 46 percent of the city's textile industry while in Fall River the figure approached 50 percent. Except for two textile cities, Lowell and Lawrence, Massachusetts, Atlanta had the highest percentage of employed women because of exceptional numbers of domestic servants, most of whom probably were black. In contrast, centers of heavy industry such as Chicago or Pittsburgh held fewer opportunities for women's employment. In Chicago women constituted only 19 percent of the work force, 42 percent of them working as servants and another 34 percent in the clothing industry. Clearly the significance of women's work varied according to local circumstances. Nonetheless, in particular communities and specific industries, women's wage work had become a central feature of Gilded Age life.[3]

Relations between Women in Nineteenth-Century America," *Signs*, 1 (Autumn 1975), 1–29. On the relationship of this ideology to women's politics in the nineteenth century, see Ellen Carol DuBois, *Feminism and Suffrage: The Emergence of an Independent Women's Movement in America, 1848–1869* (Ithaca, 1978), 15–52; Barbara Leslie Epstein, *The Politics of Domesticity: Women, Evangelism, and Temperance in Nineteenth-Century America* (Middletown, Conn., 1981); and Mari Jo Buhle, *Women and American Socialism 1870–1920* (Urbana, Ill., 1981), 49–103. For a recent discussion of domestic ideology and women's work, see Alice Kessler-Harris, *Out to Work: A History of Wage-Earning Women in the United States* (New York, 1982), 45–72.

[2] On the Knights of Labor, see Norman J. Ware, *The Labor Movement in the United States, 1860–1895: A Study in Democracy* (New York, 1929); Gerald N. Grob, *Workers and Utopia: A Study of Ideological Conflict in the American Labor Movement, 1865–1900* (Chicago, 1969), 11–78; and Leon Fink, *Workingmen's Democracy: The Knights of Labor and American Politics* (Champaign, Ill., 1983).

[3] U.S. Department of the Interior, Census Office, *Compendium of the Ninth Census of the United States* (Washington, 1872), 594; U.S. Bureau of the Census, *Thirteenth Census of the United States Taken in the Year 1910*, vol. IV: *Population, 1910: Occupation Statistics* (Washington, 1914), 37; U.S. Department of the Interior, Census Office, *Tenth Census of the United States: 1880*, vol. I: *Statistics of the Population* (Washington, 1883), 862, 870, 877, 894, 895.

When the Knights of Labor reached out to a mass constitutency during the late 1870s and early 1880s female factory workers readily responded. The Knights' open principles of organization, their commitment to unskilled as well as skilled workers, and their early pledge to support both equal pay for equal work and women's suffrage made their organization particularly appealing to women. In 1881 when the organization officially opened its doors to women, they found many already organized into local unions or fledgling Knights' assemblies.[4] By 1883 one labor editor observed, "In almost every city where the Knights of Labor have an organization the women who work for wages have banned together and formed an assembly."[5]

Between 1881 and 1890 women formed a small but significant force within the labor movement. In 1887 Leonora M. Barry, the Knights' general investigator for women's work, estimated that about 65,000 women belonged to the order. This figure represented about 10 percent of the Knights' total membership, just under the percentage of women in the work force generally. During the 1880s the Knights chartered over four hundred local assemblies that included women. Of these, two-thirds were "ladies' locals," while the others were mixed assemblies of men and women. Women also chartered both mixed-trade and single-trade assemblies.[6] For example, all the operatives in the Helping Hand Assembly worked in the Haverhill, Massachusetts, shoe factories, while Leonora M. Barry's Amsterdam, New York, assembly included "all female employees in the city; carpet and hosiery operatives, dressmakers, milliners and music teachers." The Zanesville, Ohio, Ladies of Labor invited "all who labor at any useful employment and especially . . . the ranks of those who earn their own livelihood" to join their assembly.[7]

The scope of women's activities within the order and the widespread support for their endeavors, including strikes, hint at both the significance of women for the order and the importance of the movement for the women themselves. During the 1880s women in mills and factories across the country spontaneously engaged in collective action in strikes, boycotts, and informal protests. The Knights and the labor press enthusiastically reported on the progress of organization among women. Many of the Knights' major industrial actions, including the great Mohawk Valley knit-goods strike in 1885 and the nationwide carpet weavers' strike lasting from 1884 until 1886, were initiated and organized by young women workers.[8] One labor editor praised the work

[4] For an extended discussion of women's role in the Knights of Labor, see Susan Beth Levine, "Their Own Sphere: Women's Work, the Knights of Labor and the Transformation of the Carpet Trade, 1870–1890" (Ph.D. diss., City University of New York, 1979), 179–238.

[5] *New York Voice of the People*, Feb. 11, 1883. See also *John Swinton's Paper*, April 11, 1886.

[6] Leonora M. Barry's estimate appeared in *Detroit Advance and Labor Leaf*, Dec. 11, 1888. Information on female membership in the Knights of Labor is based on Jonathan Garlock and N. C. Builder, "Knights of Labor Data Bank: Users' Manual and Index to Local Assemblies," manuscript, 1973 (in Susan Levine's possession); John B. Andrews and W. D. P. Bliss, *A History of Women in Trade Unions* (Washington, 1911), 118–22; and an exhaustive list of women's and mixed-sex assemblies compiled from labor newspapers. For estimates of the Knights' total membership, see Ware, *Labor Movement in the United States*, 66.

[7] *Journal of United Labor*, July 16, 1889.

[8] See Levine, "Their Own Sphere," 50–114, 179–238.

being done by women and said "they are the best men in the Order."[9] Kansas Knight, Hugh Cameron, the "Bard of the Bluff" dedicated one of his poems to women in the movement:

Her faith and patient industry
  as willing, useful worker,
Will strengthen earnest workingmen,
  check doubter, growler, shirker,
Here she's her brother's equal quite,
  she votes as well as he,
Therefore our Order's rightly blessed,
  with much prosperity.[10]

Cooperative production combined with industrial action provided a strategic focus for women in the Knights movement. Because women had traditionally been excluded from trade unions, cooperatives represented an especially important form of protection from the wage system. By taking seriously the Knights' goal of cooperation, women hoped not only to avoid the exploitation of "wage slavery" but also to alleviate the terrible conditions under which so many worked.[11] The blacklisted garment workers who founded Chicago's "Our Girls Co-Op" in 1886 wrote, "We, as wage workers, have been in the workshop for years . . . and not wishing to be dependent upon a wage system we have formed a cooperative society." Under the banner of "CO-OP OR STARVE," their venture maintained itself for about two years.[12] In Indianapolis the Martha Washington Assembly initiated a cooperative underwear factory to "give employment to unemployed women and also to give to the laborers the profit of their labor."[13] Women's cooperatives were widespread although generally short lived. Lady Knights in Danville, Massachusetts, for example formed a cooperative underwear factory and urged men in the order to "help the noble women on to success." Massachusetts shoe stitchers formed a cooperative stitching room, as did their sisters in Philadelphia and in Binghamton, New York. In addition, Knights in many neighborhoods and towns formed consumer cooperatives designed to help members keep down the cost of living.[14]

The Knights viewed women activists in a fundamentally different way than did the middle-class press of the day. Local newspapers often referred to trade union women as "amazons" and questioned their right to the title of "lady."[15]

[9] *John Swinton's Paper*, April 26, 1885.

[10] *Richmond Whig*, Oct. 6, 1866.

[11] On cooperation in the Knights, see Ware, *Labor Movement in the United States*, 320–33. See also Clare A. Horner, "The Knights of Labor and Producers' Cooperation," typescript, 1979 (in Levine's possession).

[12] *Chicago Knights of Labor*, Dec. 11, 1886; *John Swinton's Paper*, Jan. 9, 1887.

[13] Catherine F. Kirn and Mary E. Armstead to Terence V. Powderly, Jan. 20, 1887, microfilm reel 20, Terence V. Powderly Papers (Catholic University of America Library, Washington).

[14] See, for example, *Haverhill Laborer*, April 30, 1886; *Boston Labor Leader*, Jan. 1, 1887; *Philadelphia Inquirer*, Sept. 3, 1884; announcement for the Fannie Allyn Cooperative Fair sponsored by Cincinnati, Ohio, Local Assembly No. 4457, Feb. 28, 1886, microfilm reel 14, Powderly Papers.

[15] *John Swinton's Paper*, June 27, 1886.

During the 1885 Yonkers, New York, carpet weavers' strike, the local editor cautioned the women "to go to Sunday School and be good girls" so that they might "yet get good husbands and become honored members of society."[16] These same women were highly honored members of the labor movement's "society." The labor press praised them for their "strength and dedication as unionists." Popular editor John Swinton bestowed the women with silver medals of honor and extolled them for their "self-denial in behalf of womanhood."[17]

Through their range of activity in the Knights' movement, women were encouraged to become informed and "improving" citizens. Women's columns in the labor press combined news of women's strikes and industrial conditions with lessons in cooperation, suggestions for self-education, and advice on domestic concerns. The "Labor Book News Agency" printed in every local labor newspaper recommended reading for local assemblies and offered books at discount rates, particularly to locals desiring to establish libraries or book exchanges. For women, the lists and libraries represented a crucial link to the Knights' movement, which expected them to be as educated in the "questions of the day" as their brothers. Mrs. L. Wright warned her sister readers: "Don't let your natural love for 'nice things' prevent you from sparing a little for books and papers from which to study the social and labor questions. A great deal of reading may be enjoyed for a small sum by exchanging with each other and will be a preparation for you to assist in the work which needs the united efforts of all earnest, thoughtful men and women—the emancipation of the workers from the thraldom of wage slavery."[18]

The Knights' lists included books on the woman question, such as August Bebel's *Women and Socialism*, Margaret Fuller's *Woman in the Nineteenth Century*, and the feminist lectures of Lillie Devereux Blake. The lists also suggested readings in political economy, science, and literature. Among the recommended authors were Karl Marx, Ferdinand LaSalle, Charles Darwin, George Eliot, and Samuel Taylor Coleridge.[19] One woman encouraged the readers of *John Swinton's Paper* to take their education seriously. "Human misery must be cured and not diminished," she wrote, "but in order to cure, one must know the cause of the malady. Think then, think hard, working girl! To find out the *cause*, and when you have done so, new duties, new obligations towards yourself and society are in store for you."[20]

[16] *Yonkers Statesman*, May 29, 1885.

[17] *John Swinton's Paper*, June 6, June 14, 1885.

[18] *Ibid.*, Dec. 12, 1885.

[19] See, for example, *Philadelphia Tocsin*, Aug. 7, 1886. This issue advertised the "Knights of Labor Library," including "32 separate works by 28 authors" to be sent at the reduced price of five dollars to Knights of Labor local assemblies and other libraries. The list included works by August Bebel, Charles Darwin, Henry George, John Swinton, Marie Howland, and others. In *John Swinton's Paper*, March 2, 1884, the editor advertised "Swinton's Storyteller." A subscription of one dollar per year would yield the reader the works of Mark Twain and Edgar Allan Poe among others. In *John Swinton's Paper*, July 5, 1885, Swinton announced the "New York Labor Lyceum and Circulating Library." Included among the books offered were Margaret Fuller's *Woman in the Nineteenth Century* (1845), Lillie Devereux Blake's *Woman's Place Today* (1883), assorted works of fiction, dictionaires, and copies of the Constitution of the United States.

[20] *John Swinton's Paper*, March 1, 1885.

The order's literary overtures lessened the isolation of women in the home and brought them into contact with contemporary political and cultural trends. Domestic advice in the columns of the labor press served a similar end. Suggestions on "Food for Hard Workers" were interspersed with reminders that "to organize is justly one of women's rights."[21] Another note informed women: "Fourteen states now grant the right to women to vote in school board elections. Demand this in your state." Lists of famous women appeared side by side with articles on painless childbirth, comments on food adulteration, and advice on child-rearing.[22]

By addressing housewives as well as wage earners, the Knights opened important options for working-class women. "Ladies' locals" encompassed both housewives and employed women—sometimes together, sometimes in distinct assemblies—and possessed full rights and privileges within the organization. Defining productive toil by a moral rather than a strictly economic yardstick, the Knights thus offered women a role in the movement not directly dependent upon their status in the labor market. One female correspondent to *John Swinton's Paper* referred to "the housekeeping wives of laboring men" as a "class of people." The conditions of this class—long hours, subsistence standard of living—were no better, she claimed, than that of female wage earners.[23] Another woman informed Chicago's Knights, "The wives of nine out of ten laboring men work more hours per day than you do."[24] Still another noted, "Housework is not mere physical labor, it requires as much hard work to keep a house successfully as to build a house successfully."[25]

A similar logic led the Knights to extend their efforts to domestic servants. For the first time women's major arena of employment was taken seriously within the ranks of the labor movement. Domestic workers—housewives, servants and housekeepers—represented fully one-quarter of all women's local assemblies.[26] Cooks, parlor maids, laundresses, and housekeepers as well as housewives joined the organization. In 1883 Shawnee, Ohio, housekeepers formed the Good Will Assembly, and in 1886 their counterparts in Wabash, Indiana, chartered the Martha Washington Assembly. Cooks in Georgia, black parlor maids in Arkansas, the housekeepers in Illinois all became lady Knights.[27] The order's recognition of work within the home as a vital part of the community's total production leo them, in short, to a dramatic upgrading of women's role in the labor movement.

[21] *Ibid.*, Dec. 13, 1885.

[22] See, for example, *Journal of United Labor*, May 22, Nov. 25, 1887.

[23] *John Swinton's Paper*, Dec. 19, 1886.

[24] *Chicago Knights of Labor*, Sept. 11, 1886; see also *Detroit Labor Leaf*, Oct. 7, 1885; and *Journal of United Labor*, Oct. 8, 1887.

[25] *Journal of United Labor*, Jan. 10, 1885.

[26] For a detailed description of women's local assemblies, see Levine, "Their Own Sphere," 179–238.

[27] *Ibid.* In my estimate of women's membership in the order, housewives, boardinghouse keepers, housekeepers, servants, laundresses, cooks, and parlor maids were all considered domestic workes. The Knights organization of black women was practically unique in the history of the American labor movement.

The Knights did not, however, reject the home as the proper sphere of women's activities. In fact, they hoped that by reforming the wage system they would elevate and, in some sense, extend that sphere. Some women in the organization did offer tentative proposals for reform within the domestic sphere that echoed the values of cooperative production. "Only cooperation," wrote one woman, "offers escape for the overtired housekeeper." She assured her readers that "there are many ways in which housemothers can help one another that will serve to lighten daily toil and increase happiness." One cooperative scheme called simply for "neighborly neighbors to work together: Let their bread making all be done one day and let them take turns at baking it, even including the making of it. One doing it one week, the other the next. It entails upon the one extra work for that week, but she finds compensation in being exempt from this duty the succeeding two, three or four weeks."[28] Following this suggestion, Toledo's Joan of Arc Assembly formed a home-baked-goods cooperative, and New York tenement women pooled their incomes to buy supplies in bulk. The New York women reported a saving of nearly 50 percent in their weekly budgets. "Why should there be as now," they asked, "in one block of dwellings from thirty to forty cooks with attending waste of materials and physical strength?"[29] In their discussions of cooperative housekeeping the women reflected the influence of many contemporary feminist writers.[30] Although the actual number of cooperative housekeeping ventures is impossible to determine, the principle formed part of an overall critique of the wage system and the beginnings of a critique of domestic arrangements within it.

The local assembly, the basic unit of Knights' organization, provided a crucial test site for the order's principles as they applied to women. Women were encouraged to attend local assembly meetings and even to bring their children. A Michigan Knight commented that in his area "the sisters had enough sense to take their babies along with them, thereby not being detained from the meeting."[31] A woman addressing the readers of the *Journal of United Labor* told women their presence in the local assembly would "tone up the meetings," and another encouraged women to join the movement "because it is a striving for a noble equality, join to help protect the chastity of the home."[32] George Bennie, an Erie, Pennsylvania, Knight, worried that if his wife joined the movement, she would be forced to "sit amongst a lot of men from half past seven until eleven in the evening." But General Master Terence Powderly assured him, "She does not unsex herself by going where her father,

[28] *Journal of United Labor*, Dec. 24, 1887.

[29] *Ibid.*, April 2, 1887.

[30] See, for example, William Leach, *True Love and Perfect Union: The Feminist Reform of Sex and Society* (New York, 1980), 202–12. See also Dolores Hayden, "Redesigning the Domestic Workplace," *Chrysalis*, 1 (1977), 19–29; Dolores Hayden, "Two Utopian Feminists and Their Campaigns for Kitchenless Houses," *Signs*, 4 (Winter 1978), 274–90.

[31] *Journal of United Labor*, July 25, 1885.

[32] *Ibid.*, Oct. 15, 1887.

brother or lover goes in the evening. If the assembly is a bad place for a woman to go it is a bad place for the man to go."[33]

As a self-conscious microcosm of the society it was trying to build, the order ultimately extended its educational claims to the entire family. During the mid-1880s a number of labor newspapers that had been carrying women's columns initiated children's pages as well. The columns included games and stories as well as practical advice. The *Detroit Labor Leaf* advised all boys and girls, "Recollect when you hear of a strike that somebody's father is trying to make things easier for you and always remember to be honorable to union men and women."[34] The Knights' moral code strongly condemned any abuse of home or family. Along with embezzlement and slander, the Knights counted desertion, drunkenness, or wife beating as grounds for expulsion.[35]

The ideal of hearth and home provided a powerful ideological symbol for the Knights' movement. The *Journal of United Labor* approvingly quoted orator and free thinker Robert Ingersoll, who observed: "The family is the heart of all society. If we have no family we can have no community, no township, no state, no nation. The greatest patriots are those who seek to preserve the family intact; the most unpatriotic are those who disintegrate the family by compelling women and children to toil for scanty subsistence."[36] The Knights shared Ingersoll's concern for the family. To save it, however, would require reshaping of both work and community life. In the process family life itself would be significantly altered by becoming a more integral part of the public trust.

The Knights' ideal of equal rights within the movement and within the working-class community generally operated in tenuous balance with their romantic and sentimental domestic vision. A movement poet, A. M. Sheridan, expressed the combination of expectations for women in a poem dedicated to the striking Philadelphia carpet weavers.

We ask not your pity, we charity scorn,
We ask but the rights to which we were born.
For the flag of freedom has waved o'er our land,
We justice and equality claim and demand.

Then strive for your rights, O, sisters dear,
And ever remember in your own sphere,
You may aid the cause of all mankind,
And be the true women that God designed.[37]

The Knights' commitment to equal rights inherently challenged conventional notions of domesticity and woman's sphere. Yet the Knights simultaneously asserted industrial reform and social renewal in the name of domestic

[33] George Bennie to Powderly, Jan. 24, 1887, microfilm reel 20, Powderly Papers; Powderly to Bennie, Jan. 28, 1887, *ibid*.

[34] *Detroit Labor Leaf*, Oct. 7, 1885.

[35] See, for example, list of grounds for expulsion from the Order, 1882, microfilm reel 5, Powderly Papers.

[36] *Journal of United Labor*, March 10, 1885.

[37] *Ibid.*, Jan. 10, 1885.

idealism. The order held two seemingly contradictory goals. One was the elimination of wage work for women—in Powderly's words, "to secure homes for the women."[38] "We place women on the same plane as men," he wrote, "we would exalt them even higher."[39] At the same time the order asserted its aim "to protect and elevate the laboring class irrespective of sex."[40] "The rights of the sexes are co-equal," Powderly said, "their privileges should be the same and I can see no reason why women should not be entitled to giving to the world its products as well as men . . . the working women of America do not ask for the cooperation of men . . . as a favor but as a right to which they are entitled by reason of the nobility of toil no matter by whom performed."[41]

Two women nationally prominent in the Knights' movement symbolized in their own lives and in their oganizational roles the twin aspects of labor's "true woman." Leonora M. Barry, a knit-goods worker from Amsterdam, New York, who was the only woman to hold national office in the order, and Elizabeth Rodgers, a Chicago housewife who headed the organization's largest district assembly, each in her own way reflected the tension between the Knights' commitment to equal rights and its domestic idealism.

Elizabeth Rodgers represented the Knights' domestic ideal when she charmed the 1886 Richmond convention with her two-week-old daughter, her tenth child. She recalled, "I was the first woman in Chicago to join the Knights. They offered us the chance, and I said to myself, 'There must be a first one, and so I'll go forward.'"[42] The wife of an iron molder and labor activist, Elizabeth Rodgers was involved with the labor movement from a young age. Irish-born like many of her fellow Knights, she came to North America at the age of six, settling with her mother in London, Ontario. During the 1850s she grew up amidst an active labor community where she met and married union organizer George Rodgers. The two of them were blacklisted "all over this western country," and for six years the couple was constantly on the move. Wherever they settled, Elizabeth Rodgers kept boarders in order to supplement or at times to provide the family income. Simultaneous commitment to the labor movement and to her family required great sacrifice from Elizabeth Rodgers. Several times during her married life she was forced to "sell all her furniture" and uproot her home and children. Beginning her own labor career during the severe depression of the early 1870s when the family settled permanently in Chicago, she became the presiding officer of the "first women's union." In 1877 she was elected one of the few female delegates to the Illinois state trades assembly. Despite the burden of housework and a growing number of children, she continued her labor activities and in 1882 became master workman of Chicago's Local Assembly No. 1789. She represented that body in the city's fifty-thousand-member District Assembly No.

[38] Terence Powderly, "Report of the General Master Workman," Nov. 1888, p. 12, microfilm reel 67, Powderly Papers.

[39] Powderly to Bennie, Jan. 28, 1887, microfilm reel 20, *ibid.*

[40] *New York Voice of the People*, Feb. 11, 1883.

[41] Powderly, "Report of the General Master Workman," 13.

[42] Frances E. Willard, *Glimpses of Fifty Years: The Autobiography of an American Woman* (Chicago, 1889), 523.

24. In 1885 Powderly chartered her as a regular organizer, and in 1886 when the district master workman died, Elizabeth Rodgers took over the office as the order's first female district master workman.[43]

Elizabeth Rodgers displayed an undeviating commitment to both family and political concerns. When her husband once suggested that she resign her labor activities to concentrate on the family, she reminded him, "Women should do anything they liked that was good and which they could do well."[44] Her decision to remain active was an easy one, she said. "Knowing my duty to my sex I thought it was an opportunity to show our brothers how false the theories are that women are not good for anything."[45] Indeed, her public commitments went beyond the labor movement. She was active in Irish affairs and temperance politics as well. Perhaps the most striking feature of her career was her consistent devotion to family life. She bore twelve children, raised ten, and kept house for a workingman. She said proudly, "I do, and always have done, all my own work." Even when pregnant or nursing, she presided over regular meetings of three hundred or more and spent many hours at Knights of Labor duties. Temperance leader Willard once visited Elizabeth Rodgers in her "small, but comfortable, . . . house." Willard was greeted at the door by "a woman . . . with sleeves rolled up and babe in arms." Her "healthful" complexion and "honest gray" eyes combined with a "round, clear voice, gentle and womanly," showed Willard a person with "her mental faculties . . . thoroughly well in hand." This warm and motherly woman defied the strictures on nineteenth-century womanhood by becoming an important figure in the public world.[46]

If Elizabeth Rodgers represented the Knights' domestic ideal by combining hearth and home with a commitment to the labor movement, Barry represented the order's ideal wage-earning woman. Barry was forced into wage work by necessity but immediately joined the Knights in an effort to ameliorate her condition. Barry was also more typical of later female labor activists. During her four-year tenure as general investigator, she devoted her life entirely to the labor movement.

A "tall commanding figure" with a "warm voice," Barry came to the labor movement late in her life.[47] She was born in Ireland in 1849 and settled with her family in upstate New York during the 1850s. There she became a rural school teacher. In 1871 she married William E. Barry, an itinerant painter and musician. The couple moved from town to town for ten years, during which time they had three children. In 1881 Barry lost both her husband and her only daughter to one of the persistent fevers of the time. Left to support herself and

[43] This account of Elizabeth Rodgers's life is taken from a detailed biography that appeared in the *Detroit Labor Leaf*, Dec. 29, 1886.

[44] Willard, *Glimpses of Fifty Years*, 523.

[45] *Chicago Knights of Labor*, March 5, 1887.

[46] Willard, *Glimpses of Fifty Years*, 522–23. For additional information on Rodgers, see Edward T. James, Janet Wilson James, and Paul S. Boyer, eds., *Notable American Women, 1607–1950: A Biographical Dictionary* (3 vols., Cambridge, Mass., 1971), III, 187–88; and *Journal of United Labor*, Jan. 8, 1886.

[47] *Detroit Advance and Labor Leaf*, Dec. 15, 1888.

two boys, she attempted to maintain domestic life by taking in sewing but found the strain too great on her eyes. Living in Amsterdam, New York, the center of the nation's knit-goods industry, Barry then sought employment in one of the local mills.[48]

Barry's labor career began soon after she entered the factory. Women in Amsterdam had organized the Victory Assembly in early 1883, and within a year it claimed fifteen hundred members. Barry joined the local in 1884 and soon became master workman. The next year she went as a delegate to the district assembly, and in 1886 she joined Elizabeth Rodgers at the Knights' Richmond General Assembly, where she was elected general investigator for women's work.[49] In her acceptance speech Barry promised to "investigate the condition of working women, instruct and educate them in the Order, and organize female locals when it will not conflict with more important work."[50] She set up subcommittees in every district assembly and encourged all lady Knights to "acquire a thorough knowledge of the condition of working women within their jurisdiction." Barry assured the women that "any abuse existing which a female local would be delicate in mentioning to the General Executive Board may be communicated to the president of the Committee on Women's Work."[51]

During her four years as general investigator, Barry effectively lived without a home. She spent most of those years on the road visiting local assemblies in almost every part of the country. Barry traveled all but two weeks of the year, staying in hotels or with friendly Knights of Labor families. She entered one son in a Philadelphia convent school and placed the other with her sister-in-law. Like many women who turned to labor activism, Barry found that the movement demanded a difficult choice between more traditional feminine concerns and a significant role in public life.[52]

The problems of organizing women became apparent during Barry's first year in office. She was charged with "investigation" but had no legal authority to enter factories or to act on violations she saw. In her first annual report she said, "I was obliged to refrain from going through establishments where the owners were opposed to our Order lest some of our members be victimized."[53] She did accompany various state factory inspectors and gave the Knights' General Assembly detailed reports on the condition of working women throughout the country. Her reports always emphasized the need for orga-

[48] James, James, and Boyer, eds., *Notable American Women*, I, 101–02.

[49] *Journal of United Labor*, July 16, 1889.

[50] Mary Hanifin, "Report of the Committee on Women's Work," Oct. 1886, p. 287, microfilm reel 67, Powderly Papers.

[51] *Ibid.*

[52] James, James, and Boyer, eds., *Notable American Women*, I, 101–02. Barry chronicled her travels and work schedule in her annual reports to the Knights' General Assembly. See, for example, Leonora M. Barry, "Report of the General Investigator," in *Proceedings of the General Assembly of the Knights of Labor of America, Eleventh Regular Session, Held at Minneapolis, Minnesota, October 4 to 19, 1887* (n.p., 1887), 1581–88. On the strains between union activism and personal life for women, see Alice Kessler-Harris, "Organizing the Unorganizable: Three Jewish Women and Their Union," *Labor History*, 17 (Winter 1976), 5–23.

[53] Barry, "Report of the General Investigator" (1887), 1581.

nization and protection through the Knights. But recognizing the limits of this route, Barry also became a strong advocate of state and federal protective legislation.

Unable to act on her investigative experience, Barry turned increasingly toward organizing through the order's educational activities. She became one of the Knights' most popular lecturers at public meetings as well as at private Knights' gatherings. She was "to the women of the Order," wrote one labor editor, "what Terence V. Powderly is to the men."[54] Barry made it her duty to publicize and raise funds for women's strikes around the country. She encouraged a wide range of women's activities, including educational sessions and cooperatives. In 1888 Barry delivered a Fourth of July speech to over three thousand people in Rockford, Illinois. In her honor the women's local there renamed the holiday "Foremothers' Day."[55]

Barry's annual reports outlined two major obstacles facing women in their organizing efforts. The first was the undeniable persistence of male hostility to women in their organization. The second was women's own reluctance to take advantage of the movement. "While the cause of [women's] lack of interest in organized labor is largely due to their own ignorance of the importance of this step," she said, "yet much blame can be attached to the neglect and indifference of their brother toilers . . . who seem to lose sight of one important fact, that organization can never do the work it was intended to do until every competitor in the labor market can be taught its principles."[56] Barry warned the Knights, "If those who pledged themselves to the support of [equal pay] do not resolve to trample under foot their selfish personal ambition and for a time turn their attention to the poor down-trodden white slave, as represented by the women wage-workers of this country, then let us here and now withdraw the twenty-second plank out of our platform, and no longer make a farce of one of the grandest principles of our Order."[57]

In Barry's thought, as in her life experience, changing realities had forced a revision, albeit a reluctant one, of the premises of women's sphere. Equal rights, with all it implied for active citizenship, offered the crucial safeguard for women in a changing world of wage labor and disrupted households. When she retired as general investigator in 1889, Barry told the assembled Knights, "If it were possible, I wish that it were not necessary for women to learn any trade but that of domestic duties, as I believe it was intended that man should be the bread-winner." "But," she added, "as that is impossible under present conditions, I believe women should have every opportunity to become proficient in whatever vocation they choose or find themselves best fitted for."[58] Her most difficult task, she reflected, had been acquainting woman

[54] *Detroit Advance and Labor Leaf*, Dec. 15, 1888.

[55] Leonora M. Barry, "Report of the General Investigator of Women's Work," Nov. 1888, p. 6, microfilm reel 67, Powderly Papers.

[56] Barry, "Report of the General Investigator" (1887), 1587.

[57] *Ibid.*, 1581. The twenty-second plank called for equal pay for equal work for both sexes.

[58] Leonora M. Barry, "Report of the General Instructor and Director of Woman's Work," in *Proceedings of the Thirteenth Regular Session of the General Assembly Held at Atlanta, Ga., 1889* (n.p., n.d.), 1. It is generally assumed that Barry's speech reflected her own motivation for retiring

"with her own values and the important part she plays in the industrial and social welfare of our nation, and encouraging her in demanding and securing that which is her just right."[59] Barry warned women who "foolishly imagin[e] that with marriage their connection with and interest in labor matters end" that they would only find the "struggle" harder when forced to "work for two instead of one."[60] Another woman echoed Barry's cautions when she told the lady Knights, "as you doubtlessly have already or will soon pledge yourself to the man you love for better or worse, let me tell you that if you do not join him in his efforts to organize labor it will be all 'worse' and no 'better.'"[61]

Elizabeth Rodgers and Barry continued to be active in reform politics even after the Knights' decline in the late 1880s. Elizabeth Rodgers retired from the labor movement to take up Catholic reform work and temperance. She helped to organize the Women's Catholic Order of Foresters, a fraternal, insurance society, and she served as its head until 1908.[62] Barry quit the labor movement in 1890 and married Obadiah Read Lake, a St. Louis printer. She too remained active in Catholic charity work, temperance, and suffrage politics. During the 1890s she campaigned for suffrage in Colorado, worked for the WCTU, and served as an officer of the Catholic Total Abstinence Union of America. She became a widely sought speaker on the Chautauqua circuit and a lecturer for the famous agency of Redpath and Slayton. Sometimes known as "Mother Lake," Barry continued her dedication to labor reform, one of her most popular speeches being "The Dignity of Labor."[63] For these women as for numerous others, the Knights served as a crucial political and philosophical training ground.

Many early-twentieth-century labor and reform activists testified to the importance of the Knights in their early education. Mary Harris Jones ("Mother Jones"), the "Miners' Angel" who remained active until her death in the 1930s, recalled her experience in the order's early days. "The Knights of Labor was the labor organization of those days," she wrote. "I used to spend my evenings at their meetings, listening to splendid speakers."[64] Mary Elizabeth

from the Knights when she remarried in 1890. There is evidence, however, that Barry was forced to retire her position and disband the women's committee under financial pressure from Terence V. Powderly. In July 1888 Barry wrote a "strictly confidential" letter to Charles Lichtman, saying: "I have this day received a positive yes . . . from our GMW to retire from the lecture field. Of course he knows best and I obey. When my voice is lifted for the K of L again it will be under different circumstances than now exist." Lichtman replied: "I sympathize with you fully in what I know are your feelings. It seems to me that economy may be practical in other directions without clipping the only work being done in behalf of women." Lichtman then added: "The time will come when we can speak with perfect freedom and satisfy our consciences at the same time. But more of this when we meet." Although this communication reveals some underlying tension between Barry and Powderly, in public she remained a Powderly supporter. Leonora Barry to Charles Lichtman, July 1888, microfilm reel 27, Powderly Papers; Lichtman to Barry, July 1888, *ibid.*

[59] Barry, "Report of the General investigator of Women's Work" (1888), 15.

[60] Barry, "Report of the General Instructor and Director of Woman's Work," 2.

[61] *Journal of United Labor*, Oct. 15, 1887.

[62] James, James, and Boyer, eds., *Notable American Women*, III, 187–88.

[63] *Ibid.*, I, 101–02.

[64] Mary Harris Jones, *The Autobiography of Mother Jones*, ed. Mary Field Parton (Chicago, 1976), 14; James, James, and Boyer, eds., *Notable American Women*, II, 287. Mary Harris Jones

Lease, the well-known Populist organizer, began her career as a Knights' lecturer and in 1887 became master workman of one of Kansas's largest local assemblies.[65] Leonora O'Reilly, who served on the board of the Women's Trade Union League, recalled joining the Knights in 1886. She had accompanied her mother to "labor and radical meetings" and then turned to the Knights.[66] Agnes Nestor, also active in the Women's Trade Union League, was too young to join the order, but her father, a staunch Knight of Labor, taught her trade union principles.[67] Alzina P. Stevens, a "bright and brainy little woman" who taught herself the printing trade and became the first woman member of Toledo's Typographical Union No. 63, also used her experience in the Knights to become an active labor reformer and trade union advocate throughout the Populist era and into the twentieth century. Stevens joined the order during the early 1880s. She became master workman of Toledo's Joan of Arc Assembly No. 2341 and in 1886 was elected district master workman of the city's populous District Assembly No. 72. In 1890 Stevens was nominated to succeed Barry as general investigator, but by that time the Knights' movement was seriously on the wane. Stevens declined the nomination and turned instead to factory reform and Populist politics. During the 1890s Stevens became assistant factory inspector for the state of Illinois. She later joined Jane Addams at Hull House and became active in social work and juvenile reform.[68] Although scant records of lady Knights survive, those that we have attest to the impact of the order among working-class women of the Gilded Age and to the important part the Knights played in contributing to a wide range of reform concerns.

The career of Mrs. E. C. Williams Patterson, a Knights' organizer, reveals the broad range of issues that informed the experiences of women in the order. Born in the "burnt-over" district near Seneca Falls, New York, Patterson was one of fourteen children. Her French mother and Scottish father held an uncharacteristic belief in education for their daughters and sent her to a country school and a ladies' academy. When her schooling was completed, Patterson moved, probably with her new husband, to California, where she lived on a farm for several years. As a member of the Universalist church, Patterson began her lecturing career with speeches on spiritualism. She soon broadened her range to include temperance, suffrage, and "all kindred topics." She considered herself a "progressive spiritualist" and joined the Theanthropic Society, under whose auspices she embarked on the professional lecture circuit. In 1885 Patterson joined San Francisco's Local Assembly No. 2999 and turned her energies to the labor movement. Her first lecture topic for the

claims to have sought refuge in the Knights of Labor hall during the 1871 Chicago fire and to have joined the order shortly after, even though women were not officially granted membership for another decade.

[65] James, James, and Boyer, eds., *Notable American Women*, II, 380–81; Henry Perry to Powderly, Feb. 7, 1888, microfilm reel 25, Powderly Papers.

[66] James, James, and Boyer, eds., *Notable American Women*, II, 651–53.

[67] *Ibid.*, 616.

[68] *Ibid.*, III, 368; see also *Detroit Labor Leaf*, Dec. 22, 1886.

Knights was "Woman's Position as Related to the Labor Movement." This topic was "enthusiastically received," and she became one of the order's most widely sought speakers. Patterson reportedly delivered 129 lectures in two months' time and "held as many assembly talks." One newspaper claimed in 1886, "She has done more than any other woman in Illinois to organize factory girls and thus pave the way for them to receive equal pay for equal work with men." Patterson always considered herself a "firm believer in evolution." She was committed to women's rights as much as to the labor question and felt the order allowed her to be "free and frank to avow her belief upon any topic, claiming for her sex equal rights to every opportunity and condemning fearlessly every wrong action which debars her sex of these rights."[69]

The Knights of Labor supported women's rights in a broad sense and forged what might be termed a labor feminism. Women in the Knights insisted upon full equality with men, including equal pay, equal rights within the organization, and equal respect for their productive work whether in the home or factory. The lady Knights did not challenge the notion of a domestic sphere for women. Rather, like many nineteenth-century feminists, they believed in a particularly feminine sensibility, one that upheld the values of hearth and home and that could at the same time infuse the public world with a more moral, humane, and cooperative character. The broad reform vision of the Knights provided women with a link between their industrial concerns and the issues addressed by the contemporary women's movements, most notably suffrage and temperance.[70]

The Knights vocally supported women's suffrage and frequently welcomed suffrage speakers to their local assemblies and lecture platforms. "If women cannot be entrusted with the vote," wrote one lady Knight, "they cannot be trusted to raise boys who are future law makers."[71] Despite their support for the principle of suffrage, the lady Knights differed with the suffrage movement in important ways. Women in the order, like many trade union activists later, tended to see industrial problems as their major concerns, while the suffrage movement increasingly focused on the vote as the key to women's equality. In 1886 the Knights' Committee on Women's Work said there was "more important work for women to do before they are prepared to vote in the affairs of the nation."[72] A few months later the *Journal of United Labor* told its readers, "The enfranchisement of woman means much more than the ballot, and while this advance step is imperatively called for, there are other reforms that rest on woman herself and need not wait for legislation, indeed, legislation can do little toward their accomplishment." The *Journal* focused on the central problem for working women when it observed, "In the matter of the individual relation of woman to her employer, while the ballot would doubt-

[69] The account of Mrs. E. C. Williams Patterson is based on a biographical sketch that appeared in the *Dubuque Industrial Leader*, Aug. 13, 1887, clipping, microfilm reel 24, Powderly Papers.

[70] For a discussion of nineteenth-century feminism, see Leach, *True Love and Perfect Union*, 133–212; and Buhle, *Women and American Socialism*, 214–87.

[71] *Journal of United Labor*, June 11, 1887.

[72] Hanifin, "Report of the Committee on Women's Work," 288.

less make her an important factor in social and political economics, it does not touch the more important business relations."[73]

The issue that most clearly united lady Knights with the Gilded Age women's movement was temperance. The order enthusiastically embraced the temperance cause. The notions of sobriety and respectability easily complemented their vision of domesticity in a cooperative industrial community. Leading women from the temperance movement, most notably Willard of the WCTU, often spoke at Knights' events drawing the links between industrial reform and the issue of drink. Willard praised the order's stand on equal pay and temperance and observed: "I see that the Knights of Labor are also the Knights of the new chivalry. Who knows but these men shall bring in the new republic?"[74] For Gilded Age women the temperance movement represented the most inclusive critique of social and domestic arrangements. The organization of the WCTU, in particular, afforded women of varying class and ethnic backgrounds an opportunity for independent political action. Infused with the energy and vision of Willard's "do everything" strategy, the WCTU became perhaps the most significant women's movement of the century.[75]

For working-class women the issue of temperance held special importance. In many working-class communities the saloon was the traditional meeting place for trade unions as well as for political organizations. Lady Knights, and a significant number of men, argued that using the saloon as a meeting place not only gave support to the monopolistic brewing interests but also encouraged division within the family by separating the husband from his wife and children. The Knights proposed their own local assemblies as alternatives to saloon culture and posed their movement as the alternative focus for working-class community life.[76] Willard noted the success of this effort, saying, "The Local Assembly in every town and village draws young men away from the saloon, its debates help to make them better citizens, and that the mighty Labor movement has, by outlawing the saloon socially, done more for temperance than we who devote our lives to its propaganda have been able to achieve in the same period."[77]

The Gilded Age labor movement sought to define a working-class culture in opposition to the prevailing currents of individualist morality and corporate power. Domestic harmony, a cooperative workplace, and an active democratic citizenry defined an alternative industrial society for both women and men. The domestic ideal fundamentally motivated industrial reform and collective action. Yet the organization of women and their experiences within the move-

[73] *Journal of United Labor*, Nov. 25, 1886. See also Gregory S. Kealey, *Toronto Workers Respond to Industrial Capitalism, 1867–1892* (Toronto, 1980), 188. For a critical discussion of feminism, suffrage, and the labor movement, see DuBois, *Feminism and Suffrage*, 105–61.

[74] *Enterprise* (Kans.) *Anti-Monopolist*, April 28, 1887.

[75] See, for example, Epstein, *Politics of Domesticity*, 89–146. For a discussion of the Knights' attitudes on temperance see David Brundage, "The Producing Classes and the Saloon: Denver in the 1880s," typescript, 1979 (in Levine's possession).

[76] *Journal of United Labor*, Sept. 6, 1888.

[77] Willard, *Glimpses of Fifty Years*, 525.

ment implicitly and sometimes explicitly challenged the notion of woman's sphere. The Knights' commitment to equal rights upheld women's role as citizens.

But the extension of the domestic sphere was only possible within the context of a movement open to all and committed to broad social reform—one that within its own ranks sought to create a new social order. With the decline of the Knights' movement after 1890, the contours of domesticity for working-class women changed. Where the Knights had attempted to include women's concerns as integral to building the cooperative movement, the trade union movement afterwards assigned those concerns, and the women who held them, to an essentially auxiliary role. Domesticity, in short, returned to the kitchen, to the impoverishment of both home and union hall.

DONALD B. MARTI

SISTERS OF THE GRANGE: RURAL FEMINISM IN THE LATE NINETEENTH CENTURY

Mrs. Eliza C. Gifford told the 1894 meeting of the New York State Grange that it belonged to the "greatest equality club the world has ever known." That was an informed opinion, based on long service to the W.C.T.U., the New York State Woman Suffrage Association, and the Grange itself.[1] It was also something of an exaggeration, though hardly different on that score from what historians have been saying about the Order of the Patrons of Husbandry, or Grange, ever since. Dennis Sven Nordin, for example, writes that the Order "never wavered on the question of extending suffrage and equal rights to the fairer sex."[2] In fact, the Order's record on those matters was more complex than Gifford or Nordin recognized. It began with a cautiously limited commitment to uplift farm women, and came to support equal suffrage only when feminist members artfully reinterpreted that commitment. By the 1890s Grange feminists had done their work so effectively that they could portray the Order as the rural arm of the women's rights movement. They exaggerated, but Grange writers, astute observers such as Susan B. Anthony, and later historians took them seriously.[3] They really had brought the Order close enough to their own views to make large claims convincing.

The Order's first cautious responses to the vexed "woman question" were virtually forced by the fact that it grew up among aspiring, middle-

DONALD B. MARTI is Associate Professor of History, Indiana University at South Bend.

[1] Mrs. Eliza C. Gifford, address to the New York State Grange, February 1894, MS. in the Patterson Library and Art Center, Westfield, New York; *The Centennial History of Chautauqua County* (Jamestown, New York: Chautauqua History Co., 1904), 2:290–91.

[2] D. Sven Nordin, *Rich Harvest: A History of the Grange, 1867–1900* (Jackson: The University Press of Mississippi, 1974), 193. The Order's own historian says much the same, though he recognizes some shifts in its position on suffrage. See Charles M. Gardner, *The Grange—Friend of the Farmer* (Washington: National Grange, 1949), 198–99.

[3] Susan B. Anthony and Ida Husted Harper, eds., *History of Woman Suffrage* (New York: Arno Press, 1969), 4:327; Gardner, *The Grange*, 194.

class Protestant folk in the years just after the Civil War. Women of that kind were then giving more attention to the equal suffrage issue than they ever had before, and many of them were taking a vocal new part in the temperance crusade. The Independent Order of Good Templars, which was the only pre-Civil War temperance organization that was growing immediately after the conflict, included women as fully equal members. It was probably the first fraternal organization to do that, though Grangers later claimed priority for themselves.[4] Then, in the 1870s, Frances Willard and the W.C.T.U. made large new assertions about women's capabilities and the social duties encompassed by "Home Protection." The Grange could hardly ignore their claims; too many of its own sisters were also members of the W.C.T.U., or at least admirers of Frances Willard. The Poplar Ridge, New York, woman who observed of her Grange that nearly "all the ladies are also W.C.T.U.'s" described a common situation. It forbade the Grange to ignore women, or to treat them as guests and cooks, as earlier agricultural societies and farmers' clubs had done.[5]

The Order's first professions of interest in women also owed something to a few of them who gave practical help in founding the Grange. Those women brought equalitarian views to the Order, along with work and money. Mrs. Elizabeth Thompson, for example, helped her friend William Saunders "in circulating literature" to promote the Grange. Mrs. Thompson was a wealthy New York City widow who regularly gave to organizations designed to educate working people, both urban and rural. In 1879, when her interest in the Grange had passed, she cooperated with the equally disaffected Saunders to promote the American Workers' Alliance. It was to admit both genders on equal terms, as did the Grange. Apparently that was a general characteristic of the good causes which Mrs. Thompson chose to assist.[6]

Another helpful woman, who actually joined the Grange and took an energetic part in its early activity, was Marie Stevens Howland. A thorough radical, who advocated communal living and related sex reforms,

[4]Eleanor Flexner, *Century of Struggle* (New York: Atheneum, 1971), part 2; John Kobler, *Ardent Spirits: The Rise and Fall of Prohibition* (New York: G. P. Putnam's, 1973), 96; Gerald L. Prescott, "Wisconsin Farm Leaders in the Gilded Age," *Agricultural History* 44 (April 1970): 183–99; Prescott, "Farm Gentry vs. the Grangers: Conflict in Rural California," *California Historical Quarterly* 56 (Winter 1977/1978). Lee Benson portrays rather wealthier Grange leaders in *Merchants, Farmers and Railroads* (Cambridge, Mass.: Harvard University Press, 1955).

[5]Ruth Bordin, *Woman and Temperance: The Quest for Power and Liberty, 1873–1900* (Philadelphia: Temple University Press, 1981); *The Husbandman* 17 (8 October 1890):2.

[6]Frances E. Willard and Mary A. Livermore, eds., *American Women* (New York, Chicago, and Springfield, Ohio, 1897), 2:712; *Washington Post*, 1 May 1879; clipping from "D.C.: A National Republic" in National Grange Records, and "Prospectus of the American Workers' Alliance" in William Saunders scrapbooks, both in Cornell University Archives, Ithaca, New York.

all broadly inspired by Fourierist doctrine, Mrs. Howland lived with her husband on a farm near Hammonton, New Jersey. Their home was a bucolic, radical salon, well-decorated with Fourierist slogans, and a center of New Jersey Grange activity as well. Both Howlands were delegates to the 1874 National Grange. The *Proceedings* of that session show that Mrs. Howland proposed that men and women pay equal dues (sisters then and later paid less than male members) and her husband later recalled that she "surprised members by sitting at the same table as the men rather than on a separate set of benches for women at the side of the room."[7] The Grange could hardly forget about women when the surprising Mrs. Howland was present.

The most widely acknowledged of the women who made themselves helpful to the early Grange was Miss Caroline Hall of Boston, Washington, and sometimes Minnesota. Her uncle, Oliver Hudson Kelly, consulted her about his first, tentative plans for the Order. She then suggested that it ought to admit both men and women members, rather than following the exclusively male pattern of earlier farm organizations. Apparently Miss Hall thought that the farm women whom she had seen while teaching in rural Minnesota needed the social opportunities that the Grange could provide. She also guessed that women would make the Order stable by doing much of its routine work. She herself did a great deal of the drudgery required to organize the first state Grange, which was in Minnesota partly because she lived there at the time, and she also served as lady assistant steward of the National Grange through its first several years. Finally, she helped the Order financially at moments when it might otherwise have failed. Because of her ideas, work, and money the National Grange of 1893 recognized her as a founder of the Order, along with her uncle and six other men usually so honored. A year later Mrs. Eliza Gifford called Miss Hall the real founder of equality in the Grange. There was opposition to the principle at first, Mrs. Gifford recalled, but Miss Hall's "insistence conquered."[8]

In fact there was opposition. Cautious men feared that admitting women to the Grange on terms of equality might encourage feminist excesses, which they identified with equal suffrage advocacy. Some male Grangers in the South thought that the Order was all too likely to be pulled in that direction because of the large role it assigned to the sis-

[7]Dolores Hayden, *The Grand Domestic Revolution: A History of Feminist Designs for American Homes, Neighborhoods, and Cities* (Cambridge Mass.: MIT Press, 1981), 91–101; Ray Reynolds, *Cat's Paw Utopia* (El Cajon, Calif.: The Author, 1972), 37–39; *Proceedings of the Seventh Session of the National Grange*, 1874, p. 35.

[8]Oliver Hudson Kelly, *Origin and Progress of the Order of the Patrons of Husbandry in the United States* (Philadelphia, 1875), 15; *The National Grange Monthly*, March 1919, clipping in National Grange Records; Mrs. Eliza C. Gifford, address to the New York State Grange, February 1894.

ters.[9] And like-minded brothers in Vermont warned that "if women were allowed a part in running the organization, pretty soon some fool would advocate that they vote in general elections."[10] But more optimistic spirits prevailed. Believing that women could enjoy equality in the Order without untoward consequences outside of it, Grangers admitted women to full membership, reserved four offices for them while excluding them from none of the others, and refused to charter state organizations where those rules were not followed. At the same time the Order flattered the sisters with fulsome rhetoric about their special virtues and claims to dignity.[11]

One illustrative example of such rhetoric was the statement at the end of the National Grange's 1874 Declaration of Purposes. It said that the Grange meant "to inculcate a proper appreciation of the abilities and sphere of woman." That came after more specific statements about "our business interests," and may not have represented the most intense concern of delegates other than Mrs. Howland. Still, it was a clear and substantial statement for those who understood its terms. Unhappily, the Declaration implied, some people did not understand them. Correct "appreciation of the abilities and sphere of woman" had to be taught to such folk by the Grange.[12]

The ignorant, who needed Grange instruction, were farmers, both men and women. Farm men were widely accused of forcing their wives to work so hard that they lacked energy and leisure to cultivate their lofty, feminine qualities. In 1862, for example, a physician reported to the U.S. Commissioner of Agriculture that the typical farm wife was a "laboring drudge." Her typical husband forgot that she was "not a machine, and therefore needs rest, recreation, and change." The doctor guessed that three-fourths of farm wives were kept from developing their highest potentialities by such tyranny.[13]

Grangers were usually less harsh in their criticisms of brutal farmers and stultified wives than was that physician, but they found many ways of saying that farmers should treat their wives considerately, so that they

[9] Robert Arnold Calvert, "The Southern Grange: The Farmers' Search for Identity in the Gilded Age" (Ph.D. diss., University of Texas, 1969), 147–48.

[10] Guy B. Horton, *History of the Grange in Vermont* (Montpelier: State Grange, 1926), 52.

[11] Gardner, *The Grange*, 191. Mrs. Eliza C. Gifford cited Grange praise of women, and turned it to feminist purposes, in New York State Grange Greeting to the National Woman Suffrage Association, February 1898, MS. in Patterson Library and Art Center, Westfield, New York.

[12] *Proceedings of the Seventh Session of the National Grange*, 1874, p. 60; conventional ideas about the "sphere" appropriate to women are summarized in Barbara Welter, "The Cult of True Womanhood" in *Dimity Convictions: The American Woman in the Nineteenth Century* (Athens: Ohio University Press, 1976).

[13] W. W. Hall, "Hardships of Farmers' Wives," *U.S. Commissioner of Agriculture Annual Report for 1862*, 462–70.

could rise to the full dignity of women's sphere. Not surprisingly, many of those expressions came from Grange sisters who could be very specific about ways in which their menfolk needed to advance. An Indiana woman summarized the required improvements by describing the ideal farmer of the coming twentieth century. He would treat his wife as a partner; his home would be a "model of beauty, luxury, and art" where womanly virtues would find their true sphere. That ideal, readers might have inferred, was some distance from Hoosier reality.[14]

The Order's 1874 statement about women was a laconic summary of substantial ideas. Its meaning would be explained — and enlarged — by enthusiastic female exegetes. It stirred little obvious interest among male Grangers, however. The only important person of that description who said much about sex roles was the Reverend Aaron Grosh, first chaplain of the National Grange. Author of much Grange ritual and rhetoric, Grosh devoted a chapter of his 1876 book, *Mentor in the Granges and Homes of Patrons of Husbandry*, to the place of women in the Order. It said that the Grange needed women, not just because they did much of its work, but because they elevated its tone. Woman's "gentle influence, her instinctive perceptions of righteousness and purity — all these are needed in the Grange, and also in society at large." Grosh wanted the Order to be a channel through which women's ennobling influence would be released from the "seclusion" of their rural homes into the world. If it became that, society at large might rise to the Order's own high standard of gentility.[15]

Grosh stipulated that releasing feminine virtues into the world did not require such unnatural innovations as "'Woman Suffrage' and 'Women's Rights.'" He made that explicit. The first subtitle in his chapter on "Woman in the Grange" is "Not there politically." Hostile critics accused the Grange of fostering political ambitions among its female members, but Grosh refuted that convincingly. The Order, as he accurately reported, had taken no position on equal suffrage when he published his book. Further, there was no risk that women who were accustomed to voting and leadership in the Grange would try to extend that into public life. There was a sharply drawn line between the Grange, which was supposed to be an extension of the farm home, and politics. The Grange was domestic and so a legitimate part of women's sphere; politics belonged to the rough, male world. Voting in the Grange, therefore, had no more to do with the political franchise than did "voting for officers or for resolutions in a sewing circle."[16]

[14] *American Grange Bulletin and Scientific Farmer* 21 (28 May 1896): 10.

[15] Rev. A. B. Grosh, *Mentor in the Granges and Homes of Patrons of Husbandry* (New York, 1876), chap. 6.

[16] Ibid., 119–20.

Grosh assured his readers that the Grange would not tempt women to desert their sphere. It would simply help farm women to enjoy its full dimensions, and discharge its highest duties, rather than being confined to its lowest parts. Farm women needed that, Grosh thought, because they were terribly confined. While their men got out among neighbors to enjoy the society of equal minds, women stayed in "the heated, steaming kitchen, among children and domestics only." Ceaseless, stultifying drudgery sent a "startling disproportion of farmers' wives to the lunatic asylums," ruined the health of many more, and deprived almost all of the knowledge that they needed to instruct their children. How, Grosh asked, could a woman "be the proper and efficient educator of the young, without being liberated in part from her confining pursuits?"[17]

The Grange offered partial liberation. That began with membership. Women joined the Grange, usually with their husbands, though single women such as Miss Hall also belonged, and progressed through their own hierarchy of degrees, which paralleled that of the men. Fourth-degree members conducted the ritual of their local Granges, and four of the places in that ritual had to be occupied by women. No Grange could open properly without women, though women could conduct a perfectly legal meeting without men. The offices that absolutely required women were lady assistant steward, Pomona, Flora, and Ceres. They were generally innocuous and ornamental, though a New York State newspaper once professed to be shocked that Christian women were disporting themselves as pagan goddesses. That provoked a Grange woman to write a long, learned poem defending Pomona, Flora, Ceres, and ancient culture generally.[18]

Women could hold mortal offices, too. They were local Grange lecturers, commonly enough, which meant that they arranged programs. Women who served as state Grange lecturers or assistants sometimes traveled widely in their own states and beyond. Less prominent women served as secretaries, treasurers, and chaplains. But they rarely became masters, overseers, or members of executive committees. The New York State Grange journal actually warned against electing women to such responsible positions in 1875, when its editor thought that the National Grange might be about to forbid it. That did not happen, but the unwritten bar was strong until the 1880s. It weakened severely in 1893,

[17] Ibid., 121–24.

[18] Nordin, *Rich Harvest*, 10; minutes of the St. Lawrence, New York, Grange record that none of the male officers appeared on 16 September 1893. A sister took the master's chair and conducted a discussion that mostly concerned Grange suppers. New York Grange Records, Cornell University Archives; *The Husbandman* 1 (23 June 1875): 2.

when Mrs. Sarah E. Baird began her long service as master of the Minnesota State Grange.[19]

Women mostly held secondary Grange offices, but they spoke out at Grange meetings and regularly contributed essays, poems, and other effusions to Grange publications. Highly literate and thoughtful women arose throughout the Order to express views on many subjects connected with the place of women in rural society. The Grange gave those women forums, in meetings and print, to make themselves known among their sisters. Some forfeited part of the opportunity by publishing under pseudonyms, as "Matron," "Floy," "Filbert," and so on, but others used their ordinary names and garnered a little fame. Probably Mrs. Mary Ann Mayo was most notable among the women who found an audience through the Grange. Others, such as Mrs. Eliza C. Gifford, cut conspicuous figures in women's organizations, too, but certainly owed part of their renown to the Order.[20]

Less articulate or less confident women, who did not become famous beyond their neighborhoods, also used the Grange to make a little sound in the world. The sisters of Delphi Grange in New York, for example, could not bring themselves to write whole speeches, so they each wrote little statements which they pieced together, quilt fashion, into essays. Their discourse on "Home," which one of them called "the dearest spot in the world," was published in the New York State Grange journal.[21] The Grange provided such meek spirits with opportunities for self-expression and solidarity with other women.

Everyone recognized that women had favorite subjects to express themselves about. Texas Grange leaders, for example, observed that women stayed away from discussions of cooperatives, but were just as reliably attracted by any program or activity having to do with children. They were vitally interested in persuading children to succeed them in the Order and in farming. Texas State Grange responded to that feminine inter-

[19] *The Grange Visitor* 1 (March 1876): 5; *Journal of Proceedings Seventeenth Annual Session of the New Hampshire State Grange*, 1891, pp. 81–83, includes an estimate that almost 40 percent of N.H. Grange lecturers and secretaries were women, and the complaint that higher offices were denied to them; *The Husbandman* 1 (31 March 1875): 4; *State Grange of Minnesota Seventy-Fifth Anniversary Observance* (St. Paul: State Grange, 1947), 11.

[20] *The Grange Visitor, The Husbandman*, and the *American Grange Bulletin and Scientific Farmer* are rich with examples of women's writing, which often originated as program presentations at Grange meetings. Much of it is well-written and informed, suggesting that the authors frequently enjoyed secondary education as did Mary Ann Mayo and Eliza C. Gifford. Mrs. Mayo's Grange career is described in Donald B. Marti, "Woman's Work in the Grange," *Agricultural History* 56 (April 1982): 439–52; The use of pseudonyms came under explicit discussion in *The Grange Visitor* 5 (15 January 1879): 7. Mrs. M.J. Spencer, who identified herself as "Aunt Margaret," said that pseudonyms reflected the "modesty that pervades a woman's mind."

[21] *The Husbandman* 12 (3 March 1886): 2.

est in 1879 by fostering "juvenile granges," which were later promoted nationally. That response was occasioned in large part by the decline of Texas's formerly strong Grange movement, and its leaders' conviction that women would have to be stirred to keep the Order alive.[22]

Eastern Grangers, who were increasingly dominant in the Order after 1880, also agreed that women had distinctive interests. A historian of Maine and New Hampshire granges reports that they increasingly stressed social and intellectual matters, which were considered especially interesting to women, at the expense of economic issues, which were thought not to interest them at all.[23] Some women denied that they were indifferent to business, but their infrequent pronouncements on farming were limited to poultry and dairying, which came within women's sphere, apparently, as other agricultural matters did not. Despite their occasional protestations, women really did seem to have their own interests in the Grange, which were different from their brothers' concerns.[24]

One of their most intense interests, which men were not supposed to share, was "Household Economy." Grange women had much to tell each other about laundry, cleaning windows, making dusters out of turkey feathers, and cookery. Women knew those things as men knew field crops, and they were proud of being "experts in this art." Domestic skills were absolutely essential to proper womanhood; neglecting cookery, a sister wrote, was an "outrage on woman's nature." Occasional recipes and household hints from "Bach," a male New Yorker, were treated with utter contempt. A sister guessed that the interloper must have learned the domestic arts from his mother, and judged that boys who sought such instruction were "not generally the stuff of which our staunch men are made." The boundaries of women's sphere were to be vigilantly guarded.[25]

At the same time, some Grange sisters argued that women should limit their investments in housework and cooking lest they fall into mindless drudgery The really important part of women's sphere was motherhood. One sister called it "the highest function of the female life." In "the perfectly organized human female," motherhood was the "product of love founded upon reason and religion." It was all spiritual and intellectual. It was also a heavy responsibility. Mothers shaped their

[22]Calvert, "The Southern Grange," 148, 150, 156; Gardner, *The Grange*, 196; Nordin, *Rich Harvest*, 40.

[23]Ralph Booth Sherman, "The Grange in Maine and New Hampshire" (Ph.D. diss., Boston University, 1973), 70.

[24]*The Husbandman* 10 (5 March 1884): 2; 8 (20 August 1881): 2.

[25]Marti, "Woman's Work in the Grange," 444–45; minutes of Magee's Corners Grange, 29 March 1880; Reading Centre Grange, 19 January 1878; Clymer Grange, 11 September 1875; all in New York Grange Records; *The Husbandman* 6 (10 December 1879): 2; 6 (31 March 1880): 2; 8 (25 January 1882): 2.

children's characters, the sisters generally assumed, with very little help from their male partners.[26]

In fact the only real importance of men was negative. They were the family members most likely to bring the contagions of the world into the home. Mary Mayo, for example, warned mothers that older boys ranged out into society where they found bad things to read and drink.[27] Another Grange woman made the same point with a cautionary tale about a really cultivated woman who suffused her surroundings with love and beauty. Then, as her happy children gathered around her one tranquil evening, their father's "clumsey feet" were heard to "stumble over the door-step." The brutal man had been drinking. He destroyed the harmony that his wife had created.[28] The point of the story, and of Mrs. Mayo's warning, was clear. Women might do their duty in the home only to be defeated by evils transmitted through their men. Little could be done about the men, but women could try to protect their homes by cleansing the world around them.

That was just what Frances Willard was teaching women through the W.C.T.U. The great contagion in society, though certainly not the only one, was alcohol. It threatened every woman's home. Women, therefore, could not fully perform their domestic duty without facing that social evil. Grazing the edge of paradox, Willard told them that they had to act in society because of their domestic responsibility. In 1876 she began to tell them publicly that they needed the vote because men, voting alone, would never prohibit liquor. A real political genius, Willard made a case for women's suffrage grounded on the same idea of separate spheres which taught Rev. Aaron Grosh that women had no place in politics.[29]

Grangers wrestled with the suffrage issue from the 1870s onward. In 1876, for example, the master of the New Hampshire State Grange assured members that "we are not the direct advocates of equal suffrage," but obliquely recognized that equality within the Grange might finally have repercussions in political life. By voting and holding offices within the Grange, "woman may show herself capable of many things heretofore considered, even by most members of her own sex, as entirely unfitted."[30] A year earlier the Wisconsin State Grange had taken a cautious step toward extending equality into politics by recommending that women be eligible for local school offices. Several states were then en-

[26]*The Husbandman* 1 (13 January 1875): 3.
[27]*The Grange Visitor* 6 (1 November 1880): 6; 17 (1 September 1892): 6.
[28]*The Husbandman* 4 (22 August 1877): 2.
[29]Bordin, *Woman and Temperance*, 56.
[30]*Proceedings of the New Hampshire State Grange*, 1876, p. 4

franchising women for school purposes; that was considered an appropriate extension of maternal duty.[31]

Neither the National Grange nor any State Grange advocated woman suffrage more generally in the 1870s. Then the Indiana State Grange adopted straightforward equal suffrage resolutions in both 1881 and 1882, apparently because the sisters present in those sessions were united in their support. The 1881 *Proceedings* report that the Indiana Grange supported equal suffrage without opposition.[32] If that was literally true, it was altogether extraordinary. Other states had long, hard debates over equal suffrage. New York Grangers fought a particularly long battle which *The Husbandman*, the State Grange newspaper, recorded in exhaustive detail.

New Yorkers began to debate equal suffrage in 1875 when the Ladies' Committee, consisting of all the sisters present in the State Grange of that year, issued a special report on the status of women in the Order. They began by expressing fulsome appreciation for all that the Grange was doing to expand the social and intellectual opportunities of farm women. Then they urged the brothers to "increase the opportunities of woman outside the Grange as well as in."[33] If that was a guarded call for equal suffrage, as seems likely, it may have provided the occasion for a closely subsequent flurry of antisuffrage pronouncements by male Grangers. A local master, for example, denounced "strong-minded ladies" who sought to "violate" female character by enfranchising women. The Grange, in wholesome contrast to such harpies, was uplifting women in ways that harmonized with their distinctive virtues.[34] Then a writer in *The Husbandman* asserted that overworked farm women, whom he described with palpable sympathy, would get no benefit from voting. That only interested a pampered elite. Moreover, he reminded women that "to all men Ruth is the sweetest type of womanhood, and it is their desire to have you remain so forever."[35] That demand for submissiveness provoked a distinctly "strong-minded" response from Mrs. Ella C. Goodell of Canastota, New York. Mrs.

[31] *Proceedings of the Wisconsin State Grange*, 1875, p. 84; Elizabeth Cady Stanton, Susan B. Anthony, and Matilda Joslyn Gage, *History of Woman Suffrage* (New York: Arno Press, 1969), 3:288, 515, 530, and numerous other entries.

[32] *Proceedings of the Eleventh Annual Session of the Indiana State Grange*, 1881, p. 29; *Proceedings of the Twelfth Annual Session of the Indiana State Grange*, 1882, pp. 29, 39; Nordin, *Rich Harvest*, 193, provides a long list of state Grange actions in favor of equal suffrage. The only two which predate the Indiana resolution of 1881 are the New Hampshire master's speech and the Wisconsin resolution concerning school offices, both cited immediately above.

[33] *The Husbandman* 1 (20 January 1875): 1.

[34] Ibid. (17 February 1875): 5.

[35] Ibid. (2 October 1875): 5.

Goodell's acerbic and often elegant writing enlivened the journal into the 1880s.

Mrs. Goodell argued from a clear understanding and entire acceptance of women's sphere. Woman, she wrote, should be "the priestess of the home." At the same time, her "broad charity" should "embrace the world and all its duties."[36] That was not exactly Frances Willard's doctrine of "Home Protection," which held that women had to act on the world in order to prevent its evils from engulfing their homes. Mrs. Goodell argued, a little more simply and positively, that women's duty centered on the home, but extended into the world beyond. That was a common enough idea, popularized most effectively in John Ruskin's *Sesame and Lilies.* In its second part Ruskin taught that "woman has a personal work and duty relating to her home, and a public work and duty which is also the expansion of that." *The Husbandman* quoted that passage, accurately and approvingly, a few years later.[37]

Referring directly to the male writer's desire that women be like the biblical Ruth, "the sweetest type of womanhood," Mrs. Goodell argued that women were not obliged to be what men desired. Woman was not "made for man, created to minister to his passions and desires." Women's sphere was coordinate to man's, and fully equal to it. Finally, she argued that voting really would benefit overworked farm women. It would inspire them to read and think, which would equip them to fulfill the entirety of women's sphere.[38]

A little later Mrs. Goodell wrote in answer to a woman who had spoken against equal suffrage at the Wayne County Grange Council. The speech, printed in *The Husbandman,* argued that women needed no rights that the "noble, generous nature" of men had not already granted. As for voting, the speaker had three votes — those of her husband and two grown sons. Mrs.Goodell responded first by suggesting that the three men might "have each a mind of their own." Further, she asked who voted for unmarried women, who owned no franchised citizens. That may have been a little facetious, but Mrs. Goodell was dead earnest when she asserted that prohibition could never be enacted by male votes. Temperance required equal suffrage, just as Frances Willard said.[39]

That began an intense argument in 1876. The lady Mrs. Goodell at-

[36]Ibid. (10 November 1875): 2.

[37]John Ruskin's *Sesame and Lilies* began as a pair of lectures in 1864, and then became what the *DNB* calls his most popular book. Its first American edition appeared in 1865. The quotation is taken from the 1890 Dana, Estes and Company edition, 99. It also appears in *The Husbandman* 18 (24 February 1892): 2.

[38]*The Husbandman* 2 (10 November 1875): 2.

[39]Ibid. (22 December 1875): 5; (2 February 1876): 4–5.

tacked wrote that men should not have their own minds when moral issues are at stake. She would never "consent that my husband or son should be on the wrong side, neither could I rest until their convictions coincided with my own."[40] That illustrated the common view that women's existing influence was stronger than their votes could be. Other women advanced the even more common idea that voting would taint female purity. One conceded that women's votes might be needed to win prohibition, and that laws in general would be better if women had a voice in making them. But still she insisted that the cost to women themselves would be excessive. The only way to work for temperance without sacrificing purity was to pray for it.[41]

The antisuffrage views expressed in New York persisted among Grangers throughout the country. Some Grangers, particularly women, rejected equal suffrage long after the Order went on record in its favor. But the Order did go on record, at various times in various units, because two equal suffrage arguments were persuasive to its members. In the first place, the argument that prohibition required equal suffrage was powerful because a great many Grangers favored prohibition. A report of the Michigan State Grange in 1883 illustrated the point by observing that "the temperance question created almost as much interest as though the meeting had been one of Good Templars instead of Patrons of Husbandry." The Michigan Grange then passed a resolution calling temperance "one of the essential principles upon which our Order is founded," and criticizing the legislature for not pushing onward to prohibition.[42] The Illinois public official who complained that "these d—d grangers are all prohibitionists" certainly exaggerated, but prohibitory sentiment was widespread in the Grange, and furnished a compelling argument for equal suffrage.[43]

Grange women also found an argument in the Order's professions of respect for women's sphere. By using Willard's or Ruskin's formula to define that sphere as including some kind of social outreach, women persuaded Grangers that equal suffrage was consistent with the Order's original commitments to them. Mrs. Gifford recalled in 1894 that "the prejudice of ignorance" at first kept Grangers from seeing that their commitments to women required them to support equal suffrage, but logical explication of Grange principles demonstrated the connection beyond any doubt.[44] Of course the women who made that explication

[40] Ibid. (1 March 1876): 2.
[41] Ibid. 3(21 February 1877): 2.
[42] *The Grange Visitor* 9 (15 December 1883): 2.
[43] Nordin, *Rich Harvest*, 191.
[44] Mrs. Eliza C. Gifford, address to the New York State Grange, February 1894.

had to ignore the early Grangers' careful distinction of their sort of appropriate equality from the inappropriate kind represented by equal suffrage, but they did that blithely enough. Grange principles, as they reinterpreted them, included support for equal suffrage.

Mrs. Gifford tested the force of that argument in the New York State Grange of 1881. She submitted resolutions asking the Grange to declare for equal suffrage as an expression of "one of its fundamental principles," which was the equality of men and women. She prevailed, but not without opposition. A large minority voted against equal suffrage on the declared grounds that voting and fighting should go together, and that only bad women would want to vote anyway. A slight majority accepted equal suffrage on the strength of Mrs. Gifford's argument that they were already committed to it by the Order's equalitarian principle.[45]

The National Grange lagged behind Indiana and New York, though it considered equal suffrage in 1879. A Colorado sister introduced the issue that year and chaired the special committee of three men and three women which was appointed for its consideration. The committee recommended against equal suffrage, leaving its chair to present a minority report of her own in its favor. She argued that women were being taxed without representation, that many of them were ignorant of government and needed the "ballot as an educator," and that the Grange principle of equality implied support for equal suffrage. Her motion to have the minority report adopted received nine votes to twenty-four against its adoption. Women members voted eight to four against it.[46]

The issue arose again in the National Grange of 1885. One of a long series of resolutions adopted that year announced that the Grange would "hail with delight any advancement in the legal status of woman, which may give to her the full right of the ballot-box, and an equal condition of citizenship." The resolution called that an implication of the principle of equality which Gangers had always accepted. It passed by twenty-eight votes to eighteen. Apparently the Order had taken a firm, clear stand.[47]

But it changed just a year later, in 1886, when it responded to a greeting from the Nebraska Woman Suffrage Association with gingerly caution. Sister Rhone of Pennsylvania, who chaired the committee that wrote the response, held that the suffrage issue should be addressed in each state, that it was inappropriate for the National Grange because it

[45] Ibid.

[46] *Journal of Proceedings of the Tenth Session of the National Grange*, 1876, pp. 94, 121, 169–71.

[47] *Journal of Proceedings of the Nineteenth Session of the National Grange*, 1885, pp. 105–7.

was not a national issue. The National Grange acted on that view by striking a clause favoring equal suffrage from the report of its committee on agriculture.[48]

The 1886 actions angered feminist sisters. The women of the San Jose, California, Grange expressed "sorrow and indignation" because blacks could vote, women could not, and the Grange did nothing to right the wrong.[49] In the absence of National Grange action, several state units, including California, Michigan, Illinois, Ohio, New Jersey, and Iowa endorsed equal suffrage over the next few years. New York State Grange reaffirmed its commitment to equal suffrage in 1891. By that time it was actively cooperating with the New York State Woman Suffrage Association and the W.C.T.U.'s suffrage campaign.[50]

Then a New York Grange woman moved to renew National Grange support of equal suffrage. Mrs. Eliza C. Gifford, whose husband was then master of the New York State Grange, introduced an equal suffrage resolution at the National Grange of 1891. Then, and again in 1892, the National Grange referred the issue to the states. Finally, in 1893, the body approved a resolution submitted by its committee on education. It simply said that the Grange "is in favor of granting to women the same privileges at the ballot-box as are granted to men." Grange feminists took that as the conclusion of their long struggle, but it was not. Later, in 1914, the National Grange returned to saying that suffrage was a state issue. Then, in 1915, it endorsed an equal suffrage amendment to the United States Constitution. Certainly the Order was not "unwavering" in its support of equal suffrage, despite its best historian's belief.[51] Wavering was perhaps the most consistent aspect of its posture.

Still, feminists who observed the Order's position in the 1890s professed understandable satisfaction. Mrs. Gifford called it the world's greatest equality club and Dr. Mary Walker, M.D., came before the New York State Grange, dressed in her usual "neat broadcloth (gentlemen's) suit," to praise it just as fulsomely.[52] Perhaps best of all, Susan B. An-

[48]*Journal of Proceedings of the Twentieth Session of the National Grange*, 1886, pp. 139, 144–45; Gardner, *The Grange*, 198.

[49]*The Grange Visitor* 12 (15 April 1887): 5.

[50]Nordin, *Rich Harvest*, 193n; Fred Trump, *The Grange in Michigan* (Grand Rapids: The Author, 1963), 42; *Journal of Proceedings of the Eighteenth Annual Session of the California State Grange*, 1890, p. 98; *Journal of Proceedings of the Twentieth Session of the Illinois State Grange*, 1891, p. 58; *Twenty-Second Session of the Iowa State Grange*, 1892, p. 23; *Twentieth Session of the Iowa State Grange*, 1890, pp. 19, 26; *Journal of Proceedings of the Eighteenth Annual Session of the New York State Grange*, 1891, pp. 128–30.

[51]*Journal of Proceedings of the Twenty-Fifth Annual Session of the National Grange*, 1891, pp. 39, 130; *Journal of Proceedings of the Twenty-Sixth Annual Session of the National Grange*, 1892, pp. 168–69; *Journal of Proceedings of the Twenty-Seventh Annual Session of the National Grange*, 1893, p. 89; Gardner, *The Grange*, 198.

[52]*Journal of Proceedings of the Nineteenth Annual Session of the New York State Grange*, 1892, pp. 33–34.

thony told the National American Woman Suffrage Association that the Grange was its great rural ally. She said that from the "first recognition of women in the early Granger days" she had been able to tell a "Granger woman as far off as I could see her, because of her air of feeling herself as good as a man."[53] With that the Grange was fully accredited as the rural arm of organized feminism.

The kind sisters exaggerated the Order's support for their cause, but they were entitled to be impressed by the contrast between its first, cautious espousals of equality and the things they had persuaded it to say and hear by the 1890s. The brothers who warned early Grangers that equality between the sexes could not be safely confined within the Order were right. Optimists such as the Reverend Grosh, who thought that a clear line could be drawn, that equality could be kept on the domestic side, where the Grange belonged, and kept off the political side, turned out to be wrong. They underestimated what their feminist sisters would do with a little equality.

[53] Anthony and Harper, eds., *History of Woman Suffrage*, 4: 327.

Populism and Feminism in a Newspaper by and for Women of the Kansas Farmers' Alliance, 1891–1894

by Marilyn Dell Brady

THE EMERGENCE of the Farmers' Alliance movement in the 1880s brought new hope and a new sense of power to many farmers throughout the West and the South. Appearing first in Texas in the 1870s, the Alliance created cooperatives for buying and selling farm products. Its members published newspapers and held meetings to teach others the organization's new and potentially radical message that farmers could unite and gain control over forces they viewed as oppressive. Initially the Alliance avoided political involvement, but as the cooperatives and the mass meetings grew they laid the groundwork for effective political power. By 1890, the Populist party developed as the political arm of the movement, gradually overshadowing its other concerns.[1]

Kansas farmers began to flock to the banner of the Farmers' Alliance after land prices collapsed in 1887 and drought struck in 1888. Plagued with large mortgages and falling prices for their goods, they were ready to listen to the innovative solutions being put

1. Lawrence Goodwyn, *Democratic Promise: The Populist Movement in America* (New York: Oxford University Press, 1976).

forth by the Farmers' Alliance. As in other states, at first efforts of the Kansas Alliance went into organizing cooperatives, publishing newspapers, and holding mass meetings. By 1890, the Kansas Alliance claimed to have 100,000 members, and it had laid the foundation for a successful challenge of the traditional Republican monopoly of state government. Like the successes of the cooperatives that had preceded them, the victories won by the Kansas Populist party in 1890 offered Kansas farmers new avenues of power.[2]

For women as well as men the Farmers' Alliance promised hope and expanded opportunities for expression. While few women achieved the national prominence of Annie L. Diggs and Mary Elizabeth Lease, numerous others spoke, wrote, and organized for the movement. The *Farmer's Wife*, a monthly newspaper published in Topeka, Kansas, from 1891 to 1894, provides a record of their activities and their viewpoints.[3]

The *Farmer's Wife* was an Alliance newspaper by and for Alliance women. Its pages document that women were deeply involved in the Alliance movement in ways that have generally escaped the notice of histo-

2. Robert C. McMath, Jr., "Preface to Populism: The Origin and Economic Development of the 'Southern' Farmers' Alliance in Kansas," *Kansas Historical Quarterly* 42 (Spring 1976): 55–65, and Peter H. Argersinger, "Road to a Republican Waterloo: The Farmers' Alliance and the Election of 1890 in Kansas," *Kansas Historical Quarterly* 33 (Winter 1967): 443–69. For general discussion of Populism in Kansas see O. Gene Clanton, *Kansas Populism: Ideas and Men* (Lawrence: University Press of Kansas, 1969) and Walter Nugent, *The Tolerant Populists* (Chicago: University of Chicago Press, 1963).

3. *Farmer's Wife*, Topeka, Kansas State Historical Society.

ians.[4] The paper indicates that for some women the Alliance provided opportunities for political activities and public self-expression, but that such opportunities were limited by resistance from men within the movement and from other women outside of it. The paper also reveals the ongoing interest of its contributors in domestic affairs. It also shows their somewhat confused and contradictory attempts to interweave private and public concerns for women and to envision women, as mothers, holding powerful positions in both their families and in society at large. Its articles demonstrate how, in their achievements, their frustrations, and their rhetoric, the women who wrote for the

4. Julie Roy Jeffrey, "Women in the Southern Farmers' Alliance," *Feminist Studies* 3 (1975): 72–91, discusses the letters that women wrote to a North Carolina paper that was edited by Alliance men. The women whom she describes were less interested in pushing their own political causes than those who wrote for the *Farmer's Wife*. Biographical information of leaders can be found in Pauline Adams and Emma S. Thornton, *A Populist Assault: Sarah E. Van De Vort Emery on American Democracy* (Bowling Green, OH: Bowling Green State University Popular Press, 1982); Douglas A. Bakken, ed., "Luna E. Kellie and the Farmers' Alliance," *Nebraska History* 50 (Summer 1969): 185–206; Betty Lou Taylor, "Mary Elizabeth Lease" (Master's thesis, Municipal University of Wichita, 1951); Dorothy Rose Blumberg, "Mary Elizabeth Lease, Populist Orator: A Profile," *Kansas History* 1 (Spring 1978): 3–15; and the following biographies in *Notable American Women, 1607–1950*, 3 vols. (Cambridge: Belknap Press of Harvard University Press, 1971): Ross E. Paulson, "Annie Le Porte Diggs," 1:481–82; Russel B. Nye, "Sarah Elizabeth Van De Vort Emery," 1:582–83; Ross E. Paulson, "Mary Elizabeth Clyens Lease," 2:380–82; and Paul L. Murphy, "Marion Marsh Todd," 3:469–71. Limited discussion of the woman suffrage issue in Kansas Populism can be found in Clanton, *Kansas Populism: Ideas and Men*, 92–95, 100–101, 151–62; Nugent, *Tolerant Populists*, 50–52, 73, 123–24, 130, 158–62, 183–84; and Wilda M. Smith, "A Half Century of Struggle: Gaining Woman Suffrage in Kansas," *Kansas History* 4 (Summer 1981): 74–95. Jack Blocker, "The Politics of Reform: Populists, Prohibition, and Woman Suffrage, 1891–1892," *Historian* 34 (August 1972): 614–32, discusses national debates.

Farmer's Wife had much in common with other activist women of the late nineteenth century.[5]

The women whose writings appeared in the *Farmer's Wife* were a diverse group, ranging from the famous to the obscure. The major contributors to the paper and the driving force behind its production seem to have been Emma D. Pack, editor and co-owner of the paper; Bina Otis, wife of Populist Congressman John Otis; and Fannie McCormick, the foreman of the Kansas Knights of Labor. More well-known contributors included popular Alliance orators Annie Diggs and Mary Lease and national Woman's Christian Temperance Union officers Mary Livermore and Frances Willard. However, over half of the approximately thirty women whose original articles and poems appeared in the *Farmer's Wife* could not be iden-

5. For discussion of other women activists whose experiences are comparable, see Dolores Hayden, *The Grand Domestic Revolution* (Cambridge: Massachusetts Institute of Technology, 1981); Mari Jo Buhle, *Women and American Socialism, 1870–1920* (Urbana: University of Illinois Press, 1981); Margaret Marsh, *Anarchist Women* (Philadelphia: Temple University Press, 1981); Ellen Carol DuBois, *Feminism and Suffrage: The Emergence of an Independent Women's Movement in America, 1848–1869* (Ithaca: Cornell University Press, 1978); and Marilyn J. Boxer and Jean H. Quateart, eds., *Socialist Women: European Socialist Feminism in the Nineteenth and Early Twentieth Centuries* (New York: Elsevier, 1978).

Annie L. Diggs, noted as a Populist orator and political organizer, was a prominent contributor to the Farmer's Wife. *Born in Canada in 1848, she had moved to Kansas in 1873, where she was involved in temperance, woman suffrage, and a variety of other reform movements.*

tified, making generalizations about the contributors and their motivations hazardous.[6]

Actual ownership and publishing responsibility for the *Farmer's Wife* rested with Emma Pack and her husband Ira, both of whom had been involved previously in Kansas newspapers. From 1884 to 1890, Ira Pack

6. Biographical information on national leaders was found in the sources cited above. Additional information came from the *Farmer's Wife* itself and from the biographical files, vertical file index, and the Kansas card catalog in the Library, Kansas State Historical Society. Material was not found on the other contributors in these sources.

had published the *City and Farm Record*, a Topeka paper devoted to real estate and land sales. In 1890, he began advocating the Alliance cause, changed the name of his paper, and moved it to Burlington, Kansas. Meanwhile, Emma Pack was editing *Villa Range: Ladies' Home Journal*, Topeka, which consisted largely of reprinted fiction, fashion news, and domestic advice. By 1891, the Packs had both terminated their other papers and merged their resources into the *Farmer's Wife*. Ira edited the first three issues before turning the duties over to Emma, who continued to edit the paper for its three-year existence.[7]

No publication or distribution statistics are available for the *Farmer's Wife*, and there is no evidence that the paper had a large or widespread readership. Information about the social and economic status of the women who wrote for the paper is scanty, but there is no reason to believe that they were themselves poverty-stricken farm women. Articles about the difficulties of getting good servants indicate that they had some financial security. The women who wrote most frequently for the paper seem to have lived in the Topeka area, and events taking place there received major coverage. Some speeches and letters by women from around Kansas were published, often from traveling lecturers or old friends. Although the *Farmer's Wife* aspired to be a national publication, the major contributors from outside Kansas were women active nationally in the prohibition movement and Emma Ghent Curtis, wife of a Colorado rancher. In the opening issue of the paper, Annie Diggs felt the need to respond to the charge that farmers' wives were not directly responsible for publishing the paper. Her position was that

7. Kansas State Historical Society and Department of Archives, *History of Kansas Newspapers* (Topeka: Kansas State Printing Plant, 1916); *City and Farm Record*, Topeka; and *Villa-Range: Ladies' Home Journal*, Topeka; biographical clipping on I. W. Pack, Haskell County Clippings, 1:7, Library, Kansas State Historical Society.

Emma D. Pack, editor of the Farmer's Wife, *was born in Pennsylvania and graduated in 1869 from the Elmira Female College in Elmira, New York. She and her husband had a small fruit farm in Iowa before moving to Topeka in 1880.*

men who published farm journals were not actual farmers, and that no farmer or his wife would ever have time to edit a paper.[8]

The ideological position of the women who wrote for the *Farmer's Wife* is somewhat easier to identify than

8. *Farmer's Wife*, July 1891, 1.

their social position. These women clearly belonged to the more radical group within the Kansas Alliance movement. Like some of their male counterparts, they were more interested in cooperative ventures than in winning political elections or organizing as a party. Their commitment to urban workers and their advocacy of prohibition and woman suffrage set them off from those in their party who were ready and willing to accept fusion with the Democrats. The issues that most concerned the women of the *Farmer's Wife* were ones that divided the Populist party in Kansas in the 1890s.[9]

Three types of articles predominated in the pages of the *Farmer's Wife*: political, domestic, and those that sought to combine political and domestic themes. The explicitly political articles attempted to further the Alliance cause and described women's involvement in that movement. Some of these were written by local women, and others were reprinted from other Alliance papers. The vast majority of the articles by men in the *Farmer's Wife* fell into this latter category. The women responsible for the paper were also deeply concerned with the domestic problems of rural women. Convinced that farmers' wives lived lives of drudgery and isolation, they deliberately wrote articles trying to be cheerful and helpful. Most domestic articles, however, were reprinted from eastern magazines. In addition, local women constantly sought to interweave political and domestic concerns around the image of responsible motherhood. By using such rhetoric, they were able to justify political activities for themselves and for other women and to argue that women had critical roles to perform in both the home and in government.

The political articles in the *Farmer's Wife* give abundant evidence that women did play an active role in the Alliance movement, a more active one than has been recognized generally by historians. Women were reported serving as local officers in Alliance organiza-

9. The divisions among the Kansas Populists are major themes in the works on that topic by Clanton and Nugent, cited above.

Fannie McCormick, shown here in a portrait from the Farmer's Wife, *was the first president of the National Women's Alliance. She lived on a farm near Great Bend and had been a candidate for state superintendent of public instruction on the 1890 Populist ticket.*

tions and speaking at Alliance meetings throughout Kansas. Accounts and letters of women who were traveling as lecturers for the Alliance cause were printed regularly in the *Farmer's Wife*. The paper also listed the women who held public offices in the state in 1892 and claimed that over twenty Alliance newspapers were edited by women.[10] In the opinion of Maud E.

10. *Farmer's Wife*, January 1893, 1; August 1891, 8.

Pack, daughter of the paper's editor and herself a stenographer for the Populist governor of Kansas, "The great influx of women in the Farmers' Alliance and Industrial Union and kindred organizations in Kansas proves conclusively that they are the power behind the throne."[11]

While many of the articles in the *Farmer's Wife* reprinted or repeated standard Alliance rhetoric, the paper also allowed its contributors to express their own political views. Repeatedly, the women writing for the *Farmer's Wife* directed their remarks to other women and urged them to become active in supporting the Alliance cause. The wives of male leaders were often directly addressed. At the same time, contributors to the *Farmer's Wife* wanted to secure a place for themselves within the movement, and they consistently sought to placate any fears Alliance men might have about their participation.

The *Farmer's Wife* is full of examples of the way in which women authors made clear that they did not intend to attack the men when urging greater women's participation in the Alliance. An article by Bina Otis in the first issue is typical of their approach. Otis asked pointedly, "Is it because our husbands love us less that they do not surround us with as many comforts [as rich women have]?" With glowing optimism, Otis described what the Alliance could do for homes and, therefore, for women. Claiming that the Alliance movement was "for the protection of our homes," she asked, "Who can be more interested in the homes of the country than the American woman?" She argued that homes and women were essential to the political good of the country because "our homes are the hope of our nation, the nurseries of patriotism, the fortress of freedom, the center of national strength . . . ." In addition, she enumerated how the Alliance provided women with new opportunities for education and self-improvement, and she set forth the need for each woman to take a wifely, nonthreatening interest in the

11. Ibid., July 1891, 3.

movement. "[We believe] that the highest ambition of every true wife is to be the helpmeet and companion of her husband . . . and that woman's duties, in reform, as well as elsewhere, should be identical with man's. Our husbands are beginning in this struggle and need our assistance."[12]

Such rhetoric was continually published in the *Farmer's Wife*, but it was supplemented by more explicit, more controversial statements. By the second issue of the newspaper, contributors had moved beyond a defense of their own work in the movement to the advocacy of woman suffrage, the cause that came to dominate their paper. In the reprint of her Fourth of July address at Manhattan, Fannie McCormick placed the issue of suffrage in the context of her general statements about the need for patriotism and for the Alliance movement. Noting the presence of women in her audience, she stated:

> The ladies are here because in this grand republic woman has been accorded more rights and privileges, and is more nearly on political equality with man, than in any nation on earth They still remind their brothers, however, that "taxation without representation" is not justice, and threaten to throw "the tea overboard" if full suffrage is not given them.[13]

Mrs. M. E. Clark, speaking before the Shawnee County Alliance, linked the cause of suffrage to women's importance both in the Alliance movement and in the home. She praised Alliance men for wanting to "save our homes and our country," but she claimed that they also needed "to recognize the fact that the wife and mother were as much interested in the movement as they." She urged them to realize that just as a woman's "counsels [*sic*] were sought and obtained on all matters of importance in the home, so also should she have a voice" in the movement. After elaborating how "the Alliance owed its success largely to its women,"

12. Ibid., 1.
13. Ibid., August 1891, 1.

Clark went on to ask pointedly, "But does it not seem strange, that knowing her true heart and wisdom, pertaining to the governing of the home, the rearing and moulding of the life and minds of their children, that she should still be deprived a voice in the governing of our country?"[14]

During the fall of 1891, contributors to the *Farmer's Wife* proposed an ambitious plan for using the national Alliance movement to increase women's political impact. Emma Pack, Bina Otis, and Fannie McCormick were involved in organizing a group called the National Women's Alliance (NWA), which they envisioned as uniting rural and urban women behind a broad program of reforms. The *Farmer's Wife* was to be the group's official publication. Wives of other Populist leaders were included in the incorporation of the organization, and vice-presidents representing twenty-five states and the District of Columbia were chosen.

The paper claimed that the National Women's Alliance was "composed of farmers wives and the women of trades unions and wage workers" and listed women's groups who were joining behind its banner. These included the Ladies' Christian Alliance of Sulphur Springs, Texas, the Illinois Womens' Alliance, several local South Carolina organizations, the Alliance Womens' Association of Kansas, the Factory Girls' Union, the Women Wage Earners' branch of the Alliance, the Womens' Labor Union, and the Alliance Kindergarten. It was predicted that the NWA would soon become "the leading organization of women in the United States, surpassing the currently popular suffrage and temperance clubs."[15]

Identifying themselves as "we, the industrial women of America," the NWA published a statement of goals which clearly indicated an awareness of issues

14. Ibid.
15. Ibid., September 1891, 4; November 1891, 8.

being debated within the Alliance movement and a willingness to support its more radical segments:

> 1st. To study all questions relating to the structure of human society, in the full light of modern invention, discovery and thought.
>
> 2d. To carry out into practical life the precepts of the golden rule.
>
> 3d. To recognize the full political equality of the sexes.
>
> 4th. To aid in carrying out the principle of cooperation in every department of human life to its fullest extent.
>
> 5th. To secure the utmost harmony and unity of action among the Sisterhood, in all sections of our country.
>
> 6th. To teach the principles of international arbitration and, if possible, to prevent war.
>
> 7th. To discourage in every way possible the use of all alcoholic liquors as a beverage, or the habitual use of tobacco or other narcotics injurious to the human system.[16]

In the hope of furthering these goals, a national conference of the NWA was planned coinciding with the National Farmers' Alliance meeting scheduled for St. Louis in February 1892, where the diverse priorities of the movement were to be debated.

Nettie S. Nutt explained to the readers of the *Farmer's Wife* the reason the new organization was needed and the hope it held for women. Despite the fact the "women are far greater slaves to wage tyranny than men," Nutt complained that "working women have been too much neglected by the founders and advocates of labor organizations." She stressed the need for women to organize in their own behalf. Nutt proclaimed that if a woman "toils with man in his daily occupations, justice demands for her equal pay . . . ." Optimistic about the gains she believed women had made in recent years, Nutt had faith in their ability to choose between being independent and being "a slave

16. Ibid., November 1891, 8.

to the needle or the loom." Victory for women was assured, she said, "if every advocate of female suffrage would join issues with every great political reform element, enrolling the nation's toilers under its banner . . . ."[17]

In December, the *Farmer's Wife* reported the formation of more women's alliances and the endorsement of the NWA by the male leaders of the movement. This endorsement, however, differed significantly from the aggressive statements of purpose put out by the NWA. The men stated:

> *Resolved*, That we endorse most heartily the educational bureau recently established, known as the National Woman's [*sic*] Alliance, which has for its objects the education of women of economic questions and of placing reform literature within reach of all the people.[18]

The national Alliance meeting in February 1892 proved a disappointment to the National Women's Alliance. Woman suffrage was buried and temperance defeated as delegates sought to bridge the differences between northern and southern elements in the movement.[19] Frances Willard, who had worked actively and unsuccessfully to unite the Populists and the Prohibitionists, angrily described events for the *Farmer's Wife*, placing the blame on the "liquor wing and the conservatives of our southern brethren in the People's Party."[20] Emma D. Pack editorialized about the convention's failure to adopt suffrage, plaintively remarking, "Brother, we only ask for the power to help you make the grand movement a success . . . woe be to anyone who shall say that the dear old flag does not mean liberty for the mothers of this land."[21] Emma Ghent Curtis addressed a poem "to A Colored Brother at the Conference" in which she called his opposition to woman suffrage particularly unfair because of women's efforts to end slavery.[22]

17. Ibid., 1.
18. Ibid., December 1891, 3.
19. Blocker, "Politics of Reform," 614–32.
20. *Farmer's Wife*, April 1892, 1.
21. Ibid., March 1892, 3.
22. Ibid., 1.

A number of noted reformers were represented in the pages of the Farmer's Wife, *including Frances E. Willard, the famed temperance advocate and national WCTU president from 1879 until her death in 1898.*

Curtis's poem drew an angry response from Mrs. J. T. Kellie. In a poem of her own, Kellie spoke for the black male delegates who opposed the woman suffrage plank. While admitting the justice of women's right to suffrage, the black man in her poem stated that to advocate it now would be fatally divisive for the labor movement. Without unity, he maintained that the right of suffrage was useless.

> For I stood there a living example
> Of wrongs years of votes failed to right,
> And long years to come yet will fail to,
> Unless all the toilers unite.

Through her black male narrator, Kellie described black wives and daughters, agreeing that, since all wrongs could not be corrected immediately, woman suffrage should take second place to those issues about which laboring people could agree.[23]

Like women in other movements for social change, the Alliance women were told — and were telling each other — that continued work for woman suffrage was fatally divisive. And like women in other movements, the Alliance women who favored suffrage began to look outside their own movement for projects and allies. Although the *Farmer's Wife* continued to print the officers and bylaws of the NWA for another year, Emma Pack, Bina Otis, and Fannie McCormick abandoned efforts to work with men in the national Alliance movement and, instead, focused their attention on Kansas struggles. Along with urging the election of Mary Lease as senator, they aligned themselves with other woman suffrage advocates and pushed for the passage of equal suffrage in the state.

These new projects also encountered difficulties. Lease's campaign came to nought, and the relationship between the Alliance women and other Kansas woman suffrage campaigners was stormy. In December 1891, the *Farmer's Wife* carried a story about the annual Kansas Equal Suffrage Association meeting, claiming that almost half of those present were Alliance women whom a speaker had insulted by calling "calamity howlers." In the course of the meeting, he was "properly rebuked," and a Populist woman was chosen as an officer of the group.[24] The next year Populist women again were reported as being involved in the organization.

23. Ibid., April 1892, 1.
24. Ibid., December 1891, 1.

Bina A. Otis, president of the Woman's Progressive Political League, was also the first treasurer of the National Women's Alliance. Born on a farm in New York State, she had lived in Kansas since the 1860s.

Emma Pack and Bina Otis were not content to work solely within the Kansas Equal Suffrage Association, however. In the spring of 1893, they reported the formation of another women's organization, the Woman's Progressive Political Club of Topeka. Seventy-five women, many of them unfamiliar to readers of the *Farmer's Wife*, attended the first meeting. The reasons given for the club's formation were said to be the pending vote on a state equal suffrage amendment and the rise of the Populist party which, the women claimed, needed the "molding influences of the patriotic and progressive women." The club planned to "carry on a vigorous campaign of education along the lines of political economy, industrial co-operation and domestic science." In addition to woman suffrage, the women hoped to ensure that "the politics of our state and nation [would] be made more than a mad scramble for office, or muddy whirlpool of corruption." The women argued for "equitable distribution and economic consumption, . . . that land ought not to be monopolized," and "that labor is the most important factor in creating wealth." They also proclaimed that war should be abolished and maintained that the open saloon, the "mortgage fiend," the "tax gatherer," and the "railroad king" were evils that must be destroyed. "All sisters for reform" were encouraged to join. Local clubs in other towns were told to organize and send delegates to a state meeting. A future national organization was envisioned but never achieved.[25]

Although the Populist women showed increased willingness to work with other prosuffrage women, they frequently reiterated that they had not given up their old loyalties. They repeated their allegiance to the Omaha Platform and their opposition to war and referred to themselves as "an auxiliary of the People's Party."[26] Bina Otis insisted that the Woman's Progressive Political League, as the group came to be called, was "not a 'suffrage association'" but "a political club that endorses equal suffrage and temperance."[27]

As Kansas moved toward a vote on the equal suffrage amendment in 1894, the suffrage issue began to predominate in the pages of the *Farmer's Wife*, gradually squeezing out other materials. Prosuffrage articles and speeches were regularly printed, along with refutation of various antisuffrage positions. The visits of national suffrage leaders to Kansas were reported. When the state leaders of the Populist party endorsed suffrage in June 1894, their action was lauded, and no indication was given of the fierce struggle which had

25. Ibid., April 1893, 4; May 1893, 3.
26. Ibid., August 1893, 1.
27. Ibid., May 1893, 1.

KANSAS WOMEN!

THE THIRD STAR OF THE WEST: **Wyoming, Colorado and Kansas.**

The Great Amendment Campaign Now Open.

The question of Equal Suffrage to be settled November, 1894, when Kansas, like Wyoming and Colorado, will give full enfranchisement to women.

The "FARMER'S WIFE" the Leading Exponent.

The Editor and Publisher has sufficient income to support themselves. The FARMER'S WIFE pays no salaries. EVERY DOLLAR received will go towards carrying the

AMENDMENT To a Successful Issue.

GET US A CLUB! And help the cause along. Don't delay. Get the FARMER'S WIFE in every family at once. Send for Subscription Blanks and Club rates.

☞ Single Subscriptions, 50 cents a year.

EMMA D. PACK,

TOPEKA, - - - KANSAS.

ensued over the passage of the issue. Following the failure of Kansans to pass the equal suffrage amendment in November 1894 and the poor showing of the Populist party in that year, the *Farmer's Wife* ended its three years of publication. Although the newspaper had proven to be a vehicle that allowed women a new opportunity to express their political priorities and to further their own political goals, none of the causes dearest to the hearts of the contributors had been won. Suffrage, temperance, and pacifism remained unpopular among the majority of Populist men.[28]

On the other hand, the contributors to the *Farmer's Wife* did not seem to share many of the goals generally considered significant by Populist men and by historians. The free silver issue and specific candidates' election campaigns seldom appeared in the *Farmer's Wife* except in occasional reprints from other papers. Even the dramatic incidents of the "legislative war" between Republicans and Populists received only passing attention. According to the evidence of the *Farmer's Wife*, women found space to act and to express themselves within the movement, but they and their concerns were never fully integrated into it. Their attempts to form a "woman's movement" within the Alliance movement failed.

Domestic as well as political concerns were regularly addressed in the *Farmer's Wife*, but again the women were not successful in achieving their goals. Contributors to the newspaper frequently expressed sympathy for what they saw as the wretchedness of rural women's lives. Maudlin stories by local women frequently told of sweet, weak, eastern women destroyed on Kansas farms. According to a typical description by Frances Garside, at thirty a farm woman was old and tired of her lot and her life.[29] Annie Diggs claimed that large numbers of farm women were found in mental

28. Both Nugent, *Tolerant Populists*, 161, 183–84, and Clanton, *Kansas Populism: Ideas and Men*, 168, maintain that woman suffrage was a critical factor in the losses of the Populists in Kansas in 1894.
29. *Farmer's Wife*, January 1893, 3.

institutions and hoped that "possibly if the monotony of work and thought were more frequently broken by the reading of something not seen and learned in the daily round of farm life the proportion of mentally worn out farmers' wives might not be so large."[30] Drudgery was a common theme. In her article "The Cook-Stove and Wash-Tub," Bina Otis described a combination which she believed made "farmers' wives prematurely old, and serfs instead of the joyous queen . . . ."[31] Fannie McCormick complained that although "new machinery has done much to lighten and lessen the work of men on the farm . . . dishwashing, cooking, scrubbing and ironing, like perpetual motion, seem beyond the skill of inventors."[32]

The *Farmer's Wife* was seldom able to offer concrete suggestions for alleviating such conditions. Certainly, the paper did provide farm women with varied reading material about new topics. Fiction for both women and children was regularly reprinted from eastern papers and magazines. Many advice columns addressed problems of rural living. With no sex stereotyping, articles offered suggestions on such topics as how to raise pigs and build milking stools. Other columns explicitly addressed problems of childrearing and housekeeping. Much of the reprinted material, however, seems to have had no relation to the lives women were actually living on Kansas farms.

Frequent articles described exotic places or told of fashionable living in eastern cities and resorts. Pictures and articles featured elaborately dressed women and children with tiny waists, lace, and frills hardly suitable for farm life. Suggested menus and advice for the hostesses also were far removed from the actual conditions farmers' wives faced. Such reading may have introduced a welcome element of novelty for rural

30. Ibid., July 1891, 1.
31. Ibid., September 1891, 1.
32. Ibid. McCormick's article in the *Farmer's Wife* was reprinted as part of her novel, *A Kansas Farm on the Promised Land* (New York: John Alden, 1892). Evidence does not support the dire picture of the insanity of farm wives created by Diggs and other contributors to the *Farmer's Wife*.

women, but it did little to help them envision viable alternatives. In fact, these articles reinforced an upper-middle-class image of women as dependent and decorative rather than advocating radical changes in either women's roles or in the social and economic power structure.

Local contributors occasionally sought to address the concrete needs of farm women. Emily E. Lathrop published several articles that gave explicit advice to women on how to raise and educate their children. In her eyes, the home was the best place to educate children and "the greatest work of the Woman's Auxiliary to the Alliance . . . is to study the means of making and preserving the Home and Nursery as the basis of good society and a just Government."[33] In order to do this, she proposed an organization called the National Children's Home Kindergarten and Industrial Alliance. She intended to print and distribute a series of leaflets that would aid women in educating their children in proper religious and economic views. Her sample questions, printed in the *Farmer's Wife*, stressed people's right to have debt-free, permanent homes. She criticized two kinds of people who she believed lived off the work of others: those who were "ignorant, vile savages, and lazy, poor vagabonds" and those who were "learned, greedy, civilized, and idle rich hypocrites." Her vision of the future was "to unite all families together into one National Cooperative Union."[34]

While Lathrop devoted herself solely to educational programs, Bina Otis offered the readers of the *Farmer's Wife* a somewhat more sweeping social vision of what women's lives could be like in the future. Assuming that women would always "live for the coming generation," she announced that "our highest ambition is to provide for our children, that they may develope [*sic*] into full manhood and womanhood, physically, mentally and morally." She believed it would be

33. *Farmer's Wife*, January 1892, 4.

34. Ibid., December 1891, 5; January 1892, 1; June 1893, 4. Lathrop and her husband James were engaged in a wide variety of religious and political reform activities, including the publication of the *Voice of True Reform*, Topeka, which reported on the *Farmer's Wife* and the National Women's Alliance.

Entitled "Watering Place Toilets," this drawing in the September 1891 issue portrayed a way of life far removed from that of the typical Farmer's Wife *reader.*

possible to reorganize society so that "every able-bodied person can labor one-third of the time, rest one-third, and spend the remaining third in study and recreation." Technological change was critical in achieving this goal. "Electricity will, eventually, assist us to reach the co-operative laundry and kitchen." Then, Otis believed, "the mother of the coming time will be able to give to her children what she can not do while the present conditions of society exists, but is what they most need: that is, more of her time."[35]

The alternatives being put forth by Lathrop, Otis, and other local women often implicitly contradicted the alternatives suggested in the reprinted stories and advice columns. But even Lathrop and Otis did not challenge traditional ideas of womanhood and offered no consistent analysis of the domestic problems of rural life. The connecting theme that does appear throughout the paper is an image of women exercising power both in their homes and in their communities. For the contributors to the *Farmer's Wife*, as for other women activists of the era, the problems that both women and society faced were to be overcome by women assuming power in both the private world of the family and the public world of politics.

For this reason, whether the topic of discussion centered on political or domestic issues, the women who wrote for the *Farmer's Wife* constantly invoked the ideal of motherhood. Authors repeatedly claimed that women's duties to their families required them to become involved in political affairs. The words of Frances F. Allen were typical:

> Mothers, what assurance have you that the dear little ones you feed and nurture so tenderly to-day will not help swell the numbers of hungry ones in the years to come, unless something is done to wrest the power

35. *Farmer's Wife*, September 1891, 1. A cooperative kitchen in existence in Junction City, Kansas, was described in the *Farmer's Wife*, February 1892, 4, and in Mary A. Humphrey, "An Experiment in Co-operative Cooking," *Agora* 2 (July 1892): 23–26. Congressman John Otis seems to have shared his wife's commitment to cooperatives. Nugent, *Tolerant Populists*, 78–79, and Clanton, *Kansas Populism: Ideas and Men*, 80–82.

> from the merciless few . . . . Mothers, would it not be well to ponder over this pathetic story of fallen women? . . . in the fate of the thousands of women wage-earners of to-day, might possibly be mirrored the lives of your darling girls, unless there is a radical change . . . .[36]

A mother's responsibility in educating her children was frequently a theme in the paper. As Nettie S. Nutt expressed it, "Educate and ennoble the mother and the result will be a nation of powerful intellects, wise, just and human laws and a prosperous, contented people, dwelling in the light of knowledge and liberty."[37] Mamie M. Bruner instructed mothers to "educate your daughters against this one great sin" of gossiping about "fallen women" and instead to help such women to live better lives. She believed that girls should be taught "that intellectual and spiritual attainments are higher and nobler than a silk gown or a new spring bonnet." In her eyes, as women became "womanly," by self-education and self-reform, the country would become a better place, and "the light, gentle, quick steps of women's feet" shall be heard in the halls of Congress.[38] More specifically, contributors to the *Farmer's Wife* maintained that women had special responsibility to educate coming generations to the equality of the sexes. Nutt urged, "Let every woman join the ranks of educators, and in the glow of the closing era mould the minds that shall govern the future, to the recognition of women as the equal of man, and the mothers of the nation."[39]

Women's motherly responsibility went beyond their own children, however, to encompass all the needy of the world. To again quote Nettie Nutt, "It is given to woman to guide the childlike, uplift the fallen and encourage the weak." The cooperation of women would

36. *Farmer's Wife*, October 1891, 1.
37. Ibid., February 1892, 1.
38. Ibid., November 1891, 1.
39. Ibid., February 1892, 1.

aid "the convulsions of mother earth as she travails in the birthpains of earth's crowning era. which shall restore perfect manhood and place woman in her rightful place as the beauty and glory of the human race . . . ."[40]

The *Farmer's Wife* and the women who contributed to it cannot be said to have achieved their goals in either the political or the domestic sphere. Their efforts generally reveal their own confusion and ambivalence as well as the opposition they encountered in these areas. Nonetheless, the paper gives evidence that there were women within the Alliance movement speaking out in their own behalf and the behalf of other women. Like women in other movements, the women of the Alliance movement were working to improve women's lot by seeking to gain a political voice, by addressing the domestic problems of women, and by trying to bring the private and the public spheres of their lives into closer harmony around images of responsible motherhood.

Marilyn Dell Brady *is currently historian in residence in Kansas City, Kansas, working on a project sponsored by the Wyandotte County Museum and the Kansas City Kansas Community College and funded by the Kansas Committee for the Humanities. She has a B.A. degree and an M.A. in library science from the University of Oklahoma and an M.A. in history from Texas Christian University. She is currently completing her doctoral dissertation in American history at the University of Kansas, where she has taught courses in history and women's studies.*

40. Ibid., August 1891, 5.

THE ANARCHIST-FEMINIST RESPONSE TO THE "WOMAN QUESTION" IN LATE NINETEENTH-CENTURY AMERICA

MARGARET S. MARSH
Stockton State College

IN THE POPULAR PRESS, THE FEMINIST MOVEMENT IN LATE NINETEENTH-century America was often regarded not as a set of coherent beliefs and demands but as the rather nebulous and disconcerting "Woman Question." The very phrase evokes a sense of uncertainty, an inability to describe precisely the nature or motives animating the demands for sexual equality. The "woman question" was indeed both vexing and puzzling, not only for contemporaries but also for scholars attempting to cope with the complex phenomenon of nineteenth century feminism—a phenomenon which cannot be subsumed, as it was so conveniently after the ratification of the Nineteenth Amendment, in the demand for woman suffrage.

In an effort to explore the whole range of concerns embodied in the "woman question," historians in the last decade have been examining the political perspectives and the attitudes of those women whose concerns differed markedly from the legal and political interests which by the early 1880s had come to characterize the organized women's rights movement. Among those "other" women were the anarchist-feminists, who launched a stinging attack on prevailing cultural mores and social norms—an attack which rested on an ideology significantly at variance from the precepts that had come to dominate mainstream feminism. Interestingly, very little scholarly attention has been focused on anarchist women, with the exception of Emma Goldman, who was not fully representative of them.

Despite their differences, some common theoretical territory united all feminists in nineteenth-century America. They believed that American society had institutionalized certain inequities for women, inequities which required remedy. As Kathryn Kish Sklar noted in her biography of Catharine Beecher, feminists agreed that women had a right to participate in and to influence society. Beyond that agreement, however, lay a dilemma which was articulated as early as the 1830s and which continues to plague feminists: should women exercise their power by emphasizing their differences from men, or their common humanity? Increasingly in the nineteenth century, the organized feminist movement resolved the dilemma by arguing that, while women had a right to equal access to the political, legal, and educational institutions, they also, by reason of their maternal and reproductive roles, differed from men intellectually, psychologically, and physically.[1]

By the last quarter of the nineteenth century, mainstream feminism, in which I include the suffrage organizations, the women's clubs, and reform groups such as the Women's Christian Temperance Union, had chosen to exploit the idea of inherent differences between women and men as a justification for granting women civic and legal equality. Many feminists adopted the Social Purity crusade which swept the nation in the mid-70s, contending that if women were allowed to express their superior moral sense at the ballot-box, they would be able to alleviate social evils like drunkenness and prostitution. In other words, reform-minded feminists argued, women would extend their nurturing role from the domestic circle to the larger society. The capitulation to what William O'Neill has referred to as the Maternal Mystique reflected a growing desire on the part of feminists to win the support of the larger society by suggesting that feminism did not, after all, threaten cultural foundations. Accordingly, mainstream feminist leaders (with the exception of the aging Elizabeth Cady Stanton and the younger Charlotte Perkins Gilman) muted the earlier criticisms of sexual and familial relationships and concentrated on legal and political issues. Whether they shifted their emphasis because of ideological considerations or as a tactical move does not concern us here; in the eyes of its own rank-and-file and the larger society the movement as a whole became less radical, less threatening, and hence less likely to result in fundamental changes.[2]

The anarchist-feminists refused to accept this solution. Rejecting outright any notion of significant inherent intellectual or psychological differences between the sexes, they continued to insist on equality based on

[1] Kathryn Kish Sklar, *Catharine Beecher: A Study in American Domesticity* (New Haven: Yale Univ. Press, 1973), 137; Robin Miller Jacoby, "Feminism and Class Consciousness in the British and American Trade Union Leagues, 1890–1925," in Bernice Carroll, ed., *Liberating Women's History* (Urbana: Univ. of Illinois Press, 1976), 137–38.

[2] William O'Neill, *Everyone was Brave* (New York: Quadrangle, 1969), 5–7, 31–38; Aileen Kraditor, *Ideas of the Woman Suffrage Movement* (New York: Columbia Univ. Press, 1965), 56–74.

a shared humanity. This approach had the strength of continuing to confront the vexing questions of domestic and economic equality; however, those were questions which an increasingly family-centered society was unwilling or unable to answer.

* * *

Anarchism in late nineteenth-century America was a complex philosophical and political movement which does not lend itself to succinct definition. It is necessary therefore to confine the discussion of anarchist theory to those aspects which relate directly to the development of anarchist-feminism. In terms of its social and political implications, which were the major concern of the anarchist-feminists, the most important precept of American anarchism was the belief that not only government but all forms of coercive external authority must be abolished to implement the ideal of personal liberty. To paraphrase the often-quoted anarchist poet John MacKay, anarchists wished neither to rule nor to be ruled. Two distinct anarchist philosophies competed for followers in the United States—the individualist and the communist. For both groups, individual freedom, limited only by the proscription against interference with the liberty of others, was of primary importance; the principal point of controversy involved the means of attaining that goal. At its simplest level, the individualist argument contended that while government as well as all other forms of nonvoluntary authority must be abolished, some form of private property system was essential to individual liberty. The communist-anarchists, on the other hand, in part reflecting the Marxist influence which had significantly affected European anarchism, insisted on the elimination of private property as well, with the substitution of small, noncoercive, cooperative communities as a foundation for a new society.[3]

Together, the two factions of American anarchism may have claimed some 50,000 adherents at the peak of their strength in 1884 through 1886, before the Haymarket riot, although since anarchists tended to eschew formal organization exact numbers are unobtainable. While anarchism never reached the status of a mass movement, it was highly visible, partly as a result of its urban orientation. Chicago was the headquarters of communist-anarchism until the early twentieth century; the individualists looked to Boston for leadership. Philadelphia and New

[3] James J. Martin, *Men Against the State* (Colorado Springs: Ralph Myles, 1970); Eunice Minette Schuster, *Native American Anarchists: Smith College Studies in History*, 17 (Oct. 1931–July 1932); Terry M. Perlin, "Anarchist-Communism in America, 1890–1914," (Diss. Brandeis Univ. 1970). MacKay's poem can be found in Emma Goldman, *Anarchism and Other Essays* (New York: Dover, 1969), 47.

York both contained active and vocal movements, and smaller cities such as Denver served as regional centers. Anarchists occasionally established rural communes, but these were exceptions to the general rule.[4]

Headquartered in urban centers and creating a powerful media impact, anarchism appeared to be a much more ominous force than it actually was. The anarchists, including the anarchist-feminists, also were convinced that theirs was an ultimately irresistible movement. Anarchist-feminists felt a responsibility to articulate and to practice a set of principles consonant both with anarchist theory and with their view of equality. Anarchist-feminism, therefore, developed directly from the cornerstone of anarchist philosophy—the primacy of complete individual liberty. This individualistic premise led directly to the contention that the most important source of woman's inequality was her dependence on men, particularly within the family structure. If they had stopped at that point, the anarchist-feminists would have sounded very similar to the women at Seneca Falls; but the anarchists contended that within the existing institutional framework equality was impossible. If women truly intended to achieve equality, the first step must be a declaration of independence from men and from male-dominated institutions, beginning with marriage. This emphasis on "free love" was not unique to the feminists within the anarchist movement. However, while nonfeminist anarchists hoped for the replacement of state-controlled marriage by consensual "free unions," they intended no substantial changes in the way households were organized. Anarchist-feminists, on the other hand, wanted very much to tamper with household organization; they universally believed that women should always be self-supporting. Many individualists argued that only when women began to maintain "independent" homes, apart from their male companions, would complete liberation become possible.[5]

[4] George Woodcock, *Anarchism* (Cleveland: World, 1962), 462 estimates the numbers of anarchists living in Chicago at about 30,000. Several contemporary essays attempted to assess the class, ethnic, and geographical patterns of anarchism; see especially R. Warren Conant, "Anarchism at Close Quarters," *Arena*, 28 (Oct. 1902), 338–45; R. Heber Newton, "Political, Economic, and Religious Causes of Anarchism," *Arena*, 27 (Feb. 1902), 113–15; Washington Gladden, "The Philosophy of Anarchism," *Outlook*, 69 (Oct. 1901), 449–54.

[5] Linda Gordon, "Voluntary Motherhood: The Beginnings of Feminist Birth Control Ideas in the United States," in Mary Hartman and Lois Banner, eds., *Clio's Consciousness Raised* (New York: Harper and Row, 1974), 67; Herbert Osgood, "Scientific Anarchism," *Political Science Quarterly*, 4 (Mar. 1889), 21; *Liberty*, 4 (Sept. 15, 1888), 6–7; Voltairine de Cleyre, "Those Who Marry Do Ill," *Mother Earth*, 2 (Jan. 1908), 500–11. The *absolute* rejection of marriage distinguished anarchist-feminists from the critics of the *existing* marriage system, as analyzed by Sondra P. Herman, "Loving Courtship or the Marriage Market: The Ideal and Its Critics, 1871–1911," *American Quarterly*, 25 (May 1973), 235-52.

Like mainstream feminists, anarchist-feminists decried the sexual double standard. While the former dealt with the prevailing sexual norms by attempting to "raise" the moral standards of men, the latter demanded equality of sexual freedom. Many argued in favor of "varietism"—that is, nonexclusive sexual relationships—on the grounds that exclusivity implied that lovers held property rights over one another. The twin issues of independent homes and sexual varietism surely posed important questions regarding childrearing. This is one area in which attitudes seemed sharply divided. One viewpoint held that, whether or not parents lived together, each parent was equally responsible for the welfare of the children, arguing that if women held the sole responsibility they were unfairly burdened, creating a condition of inequality. Others offered the view that children should reside with the mother, who would therefore be their primary caretaker. On the face of it this seems to demonstrate that the maternal mystique, which so severely hampered the mainstream feminist movement, also affected the ideas of the anarchist-feminists. However, although there were some elements of that attitude, for the most part anarchist-feminists were convinced that once anarchism had come to prevail children would not be cared for primarily by parents themselves, but by adults who chose child-care as their careers.[6]

The question of childrearing in anarchist-feminist ideology remains a difficult one for the historian, because evidence concerning actual parent-child relationships is so meager. The theories by themselves seem vague and contradictory. In the pages of *Liberty,* the principal organ of the individualists, one group argued that in anarchist theory neither parent was obligated to care for the children. While such a theoretical position does demonstrate that the freedom of the adult was clearly more important than the welfare of the child, those same writers also argued that parents would instinctively care for their children out of love. The whole question of parent-child relationships was apparently a trying one for the anarchist-feminists, who were unable to develop a satisfactory solution.

Whether the anarchist-feminists insisted on separate homes or argued for a communal existence in the belief that such a mode of living left women freer, the chief requisite for domestic independence was economic freedom. The following quote from *Liberty* columnist Florence Finch Kelly indicates the inseparability of the two goals:

> I cannot see that much advance toward individualism in the relations between men and women is possible until the economic freedom of women shall have become an established fact . . . Not until woman becomes a self-supporting,

[6] *Liberty,* 5 (May 1888); *Liberty,* 6 (Jan. 18, 1889); *Liberty,* 6 (Sept. 15, 1888); *Liberty,* 5 (June 23, 1888).

> independent creature who has ceased to beg alms of [man] and who can and does support herself as easily and with as much comfort as he does, will he respect her as an equal and lose the last remnants of that old spirit of tyranny which made him get everything under his thumb that he could.[7]

And Marie Louise, prominent individualist and former member of the faction-ridden First International, echoed that sentiment. What women needed, she argued, was "Liberty to act; Liberty to work; Liberty to live; Liberty to feel that our own acquired emancipation and happiness are not soiled by the aid of jealous proxies."[8]

* * *

The majority of the anarchist-feminists who created this ideology were largely anonymous women who wrote articles for, or correspondence to, the English-language anarchist periodicals of the late nineteenth century, particularly *Liberty* and *Lucifer*. To the extent that such ideas appear to have been widely shared by women anarchists of the rank-and-file, anarchist-feminism may be said to have been a grass roots phenomenon. Unfortunately, beyond a few articles or letters, we know very little about most of these women. It is possible, however, to use the admittedly less than ample data to present a tenative analysis of the socioeconomic backgrounds and ideological concerns of some of the women who became anarchist-feminists.[9]

During the late nineteenth and early twentieth centuries, anarchist-feminism attracted supporters from among both native Americans and the foreign-born. Anarchist-communist women were either immigrants themselves or the children of immigrants; a substantial proportion were Jews from Russia or eastern Europe. Their fathers worked as poorly paid manual laborers or kept small shops, while their mothers often took in piecework. Anarchist-communist women rarely attended school for more than a few years, economic necessity cutting off their opportunities. After leaving school, most of them remained in the large cities in which they had been reared, finding work in factories, sweatshops, or domestic service.

On the surface, the individualists seemed rather different from the communists; they were predominantly native-born Americans of varied socioeconomic backgrounds. Despite such differences, the two groups bore striking similarities. The individualists, although attaining higher levels of education, were usually unable to maintain a comfortable income; they

[7] *Liberty*, 5 (Feb. 25, 1888).
[8] *Liberty*, 5 (May 12, 1888).
[9] The following observations are based on a preliminary analysis of data from the anarchist subsample (N = 10) of a systematically gathered sample of mainstream feminists, socialists, anarchists, and labor activists (N = 40).

often eked out wages as country school teachers, itinerant lecturers, or private tutors. Thus the insistence of both groups of anarchist women on the coupling of financial independence and control over other aspects of their lives appeared to stem from their own occupational experiences.

Although most of the anarchist-feminists whose backgrounds I have been able to trace participated in the anarchist movement for a period of two or more years, not all of them were long-term activists. Some of the women became disillusioned when the movement failed to resolve the personal difficulties which had led to their initial involvement. Others, for whom anarchism was a manifestation of youthful rebelliousness, outgrew their commitments and came to terms with conventional society. Finally, for some women anarchist ideology was an intellectual fad, later abandoned for more fashionable philosophies.

The most important differences between the short-term radicals and those who remained in the movement are not found in an analysis of class, ethnicity, or educational background. Rather, the distinctions rested on the nature of their involvement. Those who were lifetime activists, or who adopted the ideology as mature adults, appear to have developed an intellectual framework which emphasized the interrelationships of anarchist theory, the psychological needs of individuals, and a sense of social responsibility. The short-term activists, on the other hand, tended to view anarchism primarily as a personal answer to their dissatisfactions with conventional society.

In order to underscore and expand upon the discussion of anarchist-feminism, I have chosen to emphasize the career of Voltairine de Cleyre (1866-1912). While her name is hardly familiar today, during her lifetime her influence among the anarchists was exceeded only by that of Emma Goldman. Her prominance in the movement rested chiefly on her position as one of the two native American anarchists who successfully bridged the distance between the native-born, English-speaking individualists and the predominantly foreign-born communist-anarchists. (The other was her mentor, Dyer D. Lum.) She began her career as an individualist, gradually developing an ideology which offered a practical, if somewhat theoretically inconsistent, amalgam of the two approaches. Because she was not fully at home in either camp, yet was influential in both, she offers a particularly felicitous illustration of the anarchist-feminist perspective.[10]

[10] For published information on de Cleyre see Shuster, *Native American Anarchism*, 88, 160–61, 167; Terry Perlin, "Anarchism and Idealism," *Labor History*, 14 (Fall 1973), 506–20; Emma Goldman, *Voltairine de Cleyre* (New York: Oriole Press, 1932); and Paul Avrich, *An American Anarchist: The Life of Voltairine de Cleyre* (Princeton: Princeton Univ. Press, 1978).

Born in Leslie, Michigan, on November 17, 1866, de Cleyre was the youngest of three daughters of Hector Auguste and Harriet De Claire, an itinerant tailor and a seamstress. Her parents separated early in her childhood, and she lived with each of them at various periods. Her father, having recognized her intellectual abilities, somehow financed an expensive convent education for her, despite his relative poverty. After graduation from high school, she restlessly moved from Michigan to western Pennsylvania and then to Kansas before she finally settled in Philadelphia, where she lived throughout most of her life. In a pattern similar to other American anarchists, de Cleyre gravitated from the free thought movement through socialism before adopting anarchism in 1888.[11]

My primary concern in this essay is to analyze those aspects of de Cleyre's anarchism that are directly related to her feminist viewpoint. I do not, however, suggest that those aspects are divorced from her total philosophy. In fact, de Cleyre's anarchism appears to be inextricably tied to her ideas about the "Woman Question." Moreover, it is probable that her conversion to anarchism resulted from a belief that the anarchist philosophy offered the best hope for the achievement of sexual equality. It is at least clear that her feminism preceded her anarchism. Although it may be exaggerated to contend that her anarchism was merely a by-product of that feminism, nonetheless in choosing a political ideology one of her chief concerns was the position it offered to women. Suggestive of her early preoccupation with the role of women is the fact that when she first began to publish her poems and articles she adopted the pseudonym "Fannie Fern," after a recently deceased novelist of that name who had been noted (and sometimes castigated) for her independence both in her novels and her personal life. Later, in 1890, de Cleyre was one of the founding members of an apparently short-lived "freethought" feminist organization, The Woman's National Liberal Union, under the direction of Matilda Joslyn Gage.[12]

The principal indication of the close interrelatedness of de Cleyre's feminism and anarchism can be found in her own explanation of her advocacy of anarchism. In part, she became an anarchist because of her "anger at the institutions set up by men obstensibly to preserve . . . female purity, really working out to make [a woman] a baby, an irresponsible

[11] Agnes Inglis, "Notes for a Biography of Voltairine de Cleyre," c. 1934 (typewritten). Letter from Adelaide Thayer (de Cleyre's sister) to Joseph Ishill, Feb. 3, 1935.

[12] On the original Fanny Fern, see Ann D. Wood, "The 'Scribbling Women' and Fanny Fern," *American Quarterly*, 23 (Spring 1971), 4–24. Matilda Joslyn Gage, ed., *Women's National Liberal Union: Report of the Convention for Organization* (Syracuse, N.Y.: Master's and Stone, 1890).

doll of a creature not to be trusted outside her 'doll's house.'" Further her "disgust with the cramped, subordinated circle provided for women" in art and literature led her to conclude that there was no chance for women to improve their status in existing society. Finally, claiming that existence was intolerable where women (and men) were imprisoned in rigidly defined social roles, she experienced "a wild craving after freedom from conventional dress, speech, and custom, an indignation at the repression of one's real sentiments, and the repetition of formal hypocrisies." Only anarchism, she concluded, provided her with a philosophy which satisfied both her political and psychological needs.[13]

In two essays, published in 1891 and 1896, de Cleyre systematized the anarchist-feminist perspective. In the first essay de Cleyre insisted that the prerequisite for the achievement of sexual equality was woman's *"freedom to control her own person"* (italized in original). That control precluded marriage, which for de Cleyre as for most anarchists was equivalent to prostitution. "Remember," she admonished women who were contemplating marriage, "what the contract means: the sale of the control of your person in return for 'protection and support.'" She warned members of her sex not put any faith in suffrage: "The ballot hasn't made men free and it won't make us free." To a significant extent, her prescriptions for the achievement of equality were based on standard anarchist economic remedies; for example, she advocated "the destruction of any and every barrier, the abolition of every law by which the sources of wealth are held out of use:—in other words . . . the complete liberation of land and capital." But she went beyond anarchist doctrine as enunciated by its theorists (who were all men) and insisted on a direct relationship between feminism and anarchism. Women must insist "on a new code of ethics founded on . . . equal freedom; a code recognizing the complete individuality of women." In the final analysis, women must free themselves, by "making rebels whenever we can. By ourselves living our beliefs."[14]

De Cleyre's conviction that women must themselves take the initiative through individual rebellion against prevailing attitudes and behavior patterns was characteristic of anarchist-feminism. However, such an attitude ought not to be viewed as an indication of insensitivity to the

[13] Voltairine de Cleyre, "Why I Am an Anarchist," *Mother Earth*, 3 (March 1908), 16–21; "Sex Slavery," *Selected Works of Voltairine de Cleyre* (New York: Mother Earth, 1914), 344–51.

[14] De Cleyre, "The Gates of Freedom," *Lucifer* (1891). This essay is located in a clipping file in the Joseph Ishill Collection at Houghton Library, Harvard University. The exact dates are not on the clipping. De Cleyre, "The Case of Woman vs. Orthodoxy," *Boston Investigator* (Sept. 18, 1896).

social context of woman's position. In the second of the two articles, for the freethought periodical, *The Boston Investigator*, she conceded that "material conditions determine the social relations of men and women"; therefore, in her view, the emancipation of women had become possible only with the dominance of industrialization in nineteenth-century America. Nevertheless, she continued to stress the significance of the individual act of rebellion: "The first and best of praise is due to the 'voice crying in the wilderness'. . . . Those who call for the breaking of the barriers will always precede the general action of the masses; but I add that were it not for the compulsion of material necessity the preaching would be barren."

De Cleyre deplored the legalistic and political emphases of the woman's rights movement of her own day, as the above quotes suggest. Intellectually, she was far more compatible with such isolated rebels as Mary Wollstonecraft, in honor of whom she wrote poetry and delivered lectures. Her stress on the necessity of personal liberation became even more pronounced as the mainstream feminists concentrated more intensively on group action. Until her death in 1912 she continued to insist on the importance of individual refusal to conform. Her opposition to marriage, in which she included "free unions," intensified as she remained convinced, both ideologically and personally, that women would never be free until they declared their economic and emotional independence from men.[15]

* * *

Despite the conviction that anarchism was the only philosophy which promised the possibility of a society based on economic, social, and sexual freedom, none of the anarchist-feminists believed that their male corevolutionaries viewed the "Woman Question" seriously enough. De Cleyre castigated anarchist men publicly for their ambivalence and outright indifference to women's equality. Florence Finch Kelly noted in *Liberty* that "man is still a little bit tyrannical. Even the best of men and the most imbued with a desire for justice and equity . . .—even these still have something of the tyrant in their feelings toward and their treatment of women."[16]

My research suggests that while most anarchist men assumed that once anarchism had been achieved equality would follow, very few agreed

[15] De Cleyre's Wollstonecraft poem is in her *Selected Works*, 49; for her attitude on marriage in her later years, see "Those Who Marry Do Ill," *Mother Earth*, 2 (Jan. 1908).

[16] De Cleyre, "Sex Slavery," 349; *Liberty*, 5 (Feb. 25, 1888), 2.

with the anarchist-feminists that immediate action was feasible, or even desirable. They joined in urging that the "Woman Question" be subordinated to the other economic and political goals of anarchism. More important, anarchist men apparently anticipated no fundamental alteration in the relationship between the sexes even after the triumph of anarchist principles. An illuminating series of essays on the issue of sexual equality appeared in *Liberty* in 1888, in which Victor Yarros contended that women, if they expected to attain personal independence in the future, must sacrifice the issue of equality in the present. Rather, each woman should "join her strength to that of man . . . in *his* effort to establish proper relations between labor and capital. And only after the material foundations of the new social order have been successfully built, will the Woman Question proper loom up and claim attention." A "new social order" notwithstanding, Yarros expected domestic arrangements to remain substantially as they were, with the exception that either party would be free to terminate any unsatisfactory partnership. "When I speak of a man's and a woman's making a home, I mean that he is to provide the means and she is to take care of the domestic affairs." Yarros' viewpoint was typical. Most anarchist men, despite their advocacy of free love, retained a rather traditional attitude on woman's place in the family structure. Linda Gordon's contention about free lovers in general, that "they did not challenge conventional conceptions of woman's passivity and limited sphere of concern," applies to most anarchist men.[17]

Even in their core demand of economic independence, anarchist-feminists met with resistance from their male comrades. Georgia Replogle, by trade a compositor, by political affiliation an anarchist, and co-editor of the periodical *Egoism*, argued in an editorial which appeared in her journal that women deserved equal pay for equal work. Nonsense, retorted Benjamin Tucker, editor of *Liberty* and the leader of the individualists. "Apart from the special inferiority of woman as printer . . . there exists the general inferiority of woman as worker. . . ." Even skilled women, he argued, demonstrated "a lack of ambition, of self-reliance, of a sense of . . . responsibility."[18]

[17] *Liberty*, 5 (May 12, 1888). Some anarchist-communists believed that once anarchism became established women's role would change. See Henry Addis, "Essays on the Social Problem," *Free Society*, 6 (June 1898), 19–20; *Liberty*, 5 (Sept. 15, 1888), 7; Linda Gordon. "Voluntary Motherhood," 67.

[18] *Liberty*, 8 (Nov. 21, 1891), 1; Emma Goldman, *Living My Life* (New York: AMS Press, 1970), esp. 34–35. See also Joseph Labadie's letter in *Liberty*, 5 (Feb. 23, 1889); and Hutchins Hapgood, *A Victorian in the Modern World* (New York: Harcourt, Brace and World, 1939), 330–31, as well as his *An Anarchist Woman* (New York: Duffield, 1909), for explorations into the relationships between men and women among the communist-anarchists.

The above paragraphs suggest that the individualists, at least, despite their assertions that at some point in the future the issue of sexual equality would "loom up and claim attention," were unwilling to question their own conventional conceptions of woman's role either in the economic or domestic sphere. Since the anarchist-feminists averred that immediate changes were necessary in just those areas, a meeting of the minds was at best unlikely. Sexual egalitarianism appears to have been almost as rare among the communists. Certainly the position of Johann Most, the preeminent figure among communist-anarchists in the United States, tended toward outright misogyny. The rank-and-file of both sides of the movement agreed that woman's equality was an issue not worthy of immediate consideration.

The principal exception to this view was Moses Harman, who transcended conventional attitudes towards women's roles. Harman edited the journal *Lucifer*, dedicating it to "the emancipation of women from sex slavery." During the 1890s *Lucifer* was the only male-edited anarchist journal which consistently denounced the oppression of women. Perhaps inevitably, neither *Lucifer* nor Harman was taken seriously by anarchist men.[19]

Like the male former abolitionists who in the late 1860s stood firmly behind the suffrage amendment which enfranchised black men only, and like the socalist men of the early twentieth century who urged patience upon women comrades who wished to make an issue of sexual inequality, anarchist men persisted in believing that masculine concerns were by their very nature universal concerns, while the demands of the women were at worst selfish and at best of secondary importance. The abolitionist men, pleading that it was "the Negro's hour," perhaps forgot that half the former slaves were women, doubly cursed by their race and sex. Socialist men proclaimed adherence to the ideal of sexual equality but allowed women little power within the party; in many cases they were more traditional in their domestic arrangements than the most ardent capitalist.

Because the abolitionists were reformers and not critics of the entire American social and political system, their inability to surrender their assumption of the preeminence of masculine goals is understandable. That the socialist and anarchist men were similarly incapacitated, despite their radical philosophies, indicates that the premise of female subordination extended even to those men who scorned conventional society. Just as anarchist women had been unable to free themselves completely from

[19] Letter from Dyer D. Lum to Voltairine de Cleyre, Jan. 9, 1891.

the concept of the Maternal Mystique, anarchist men were incapable of ridding themselves of the notion of distinct spheres of concern for men and women, with women confined to the domestic and personal, hence less important, sphere.

* * *

Despite the fact that some feminists who were not anarchists would have agreed in part with the major contention of anarchist-feminists—that economic dependence subordinated women to men—the ideology of anarchist-feminism as a whole elicited little serious attention outside the anarchist movement during the late nineteenth and early twentieth centuries. It appealed neither to mainstream feminists nor to most women radicals, who turned instead to an equally unsatisfactory socialist movement. The reasons for this rejection lie partly in the changing nature of both anarchism and feminism during this period, and partly in the inappropriateness of an individualistic ethos in an organizational age.

Until the 1870s, the anarchist movement in the United States consisted of small groups of intellectuals who traced their abhorrence of government partially to the doctrines of the French philosopher Pierre Joseph Proudhon and partially to the American nonresistants of the antebellum era. For the most part, these anarchists were peaceful philosophers who, although considered eccentric on social and sexual questions, were not viewed as a threat to the fabric of society. Thus it was possible for them to ally with various other "reform" groups, including feminists, to promote specific issues. In fact, as late as the early 1870s there remained an organizational tie between the anarchists and feminists, when Elizabeth Cady Stanton served as vice-president of the anarchist-dominated American Labor Reform League.[20]

Even such tenuous connections had been severed by the end of the seventies, however. Feminism became more respectable, while anarchism, in the form of the development of communist-anarchism, was perceived as becoming more radical. Partly because of the rhetoric of the German-born Johann Most and his followers, partly because of antiforeign sentiment, the anarchist came to be viewed as a symbol of irrational violence. The public image of the anarchist was that of a wild-eyed, bomb-throwing fanatic. Alliances between anarchists and reform groups grew more difficult to achieve. As anarchism became more revolutionary, and as feminists became ever more determined that working within the existing legal and political framework offered their best hope for achieving equality, any community of interest between the two groups vanished.

[20] Martin, *Men Against the State*, 115–17, 203; O'Neill, *Everyone was Brave*, 34, 29.

Although the negative public image of anarchism, particularly after the Haymarket Riot of 1886, may have prevented some potential adherents from even an investigation of the ideology of the anarchist-feminists, that seems an insufficient explanation for its failure. The primary reasons behind the failure appear to lie in the nature of the ideology itself. The anarchists' goal of complete personal freedom, limited only by the proscription against interfering with the liberty of others, precluded organization, except in the most informal sense. Although there was widespread agreement on the answers to the "Woman Question" among anarchist-feminists, there was little coordination in promoting their ideas, and they worked mostly as isolated individuals. Their writings were scattered, almost haphazardly, throughout the anarchist press. The only anarchist journal concentrating on the subject of women was *Lucifer*, which increasingly after 1895 dealt almost exclusively with issues of sexuality. With the exceptions of the *Egoist* and *Clothed with the Sun*, two small eccentric papers with tiny circulations, no anarchist paper was edited or published by a woman until Emma Goldman began *Mother Earth* in 1906, too late to exert any influence for changes in the by now pragmatic, almost totally suffrage-oriented feminist movement. Even at the more personal level of intellectual interaction among peers, the anarchist-feminists do not appear to have developed any social forms comparable to the homosocial interpersonal relationships which were so successful in providing a support network for both suffragists and social feminists.

In an organizational age, the insistence on the part of the anarchist-feminists that equality was based on individual refusal to participate in an unjust society seemed anachronistic, even to many radical women. Their conviction that personal independence was necessarily connected to a rejection of marriage and the nuclear family structure further alienated them even from those who may have adhered to other aspects of the anarchist tradition. As Richard Sennett has pointed out in *Families Against the City*, the last quarter of the nineteenth century was an infelicitous period for attacks on family structure. Such attacks threatened the emergent belief that the family offered the most secure refuge from a chaotic, unstable, constantly changing industrial society. Further, the anarchist-feminist contention that one of woman's first steps toward equality should be complete self-support not only offered even greater insecurity, but also contravened a growing national trend toward sentimentality about the family. Women who were dissatisfied with contemporary economic or social conditions had other choices, particularly socialism, which did not threaten the existing family structure. In fact, much American socialist literature insisted that socialism would purify marriage.[21] As a result, anarchist-feminists could not hope to gain the support of even most radical women.

Despite its inability to influence the direction of mainstream feminism in late nineteenth- and early twentieth-century America, anarchist-feminism was not simply a *divertissement* in the struggle for sexual equality. Significant in their own right, the anarchist-feminists offer the historian the opportunity to study the interplay between cultural and physical determinants of social roles, such as class and sex, and the development of ideology. To a certain extent, the anarchist-feminists appear to have been almost reactionary. They were undaunted individualists in an organizational age; they were antifamily in an era of family romanticism. Nevertheless, the developments in twentieth-century attitudes about women's roles may suggest to us their particular strengths. Their insistence that the roots of inequality lay in the domestic relationship has resurfaced as modern feminists realize the inability of legal and political reform to assure complete equality. The equalization of relationships is one of the principal problems bequeathed to the feminists of the late twentieth century. Finally, they refused to be shaken in their belief that what was most important about men and women was not their difference from each other, but their common humanity. This premise, a truism for the early feminists, appeared to have been left behind by a generation of pragmatic suffragists and social feminists who used their womanhood as a tactic in their drive for political and legal rights. In the short run, the organized feminists seemed to have been following the most assured path to equality. In the long run, however, American society still struggles with the issues abandoned by the organized feminists but kept alive by the unsuccessful, unpragmatic anarchist-feminists.

[21] Richard Sennett, *Families Against the City* (New York: Random House, 1974), esp. 116–19. For the working class family, see David Walkowitz, "Working Class Women in the Gilded Age: Factory, Community, and Family Life among Cohoes, New York Cotton Workers," *Journal of Social History*, 5 (Summer 1972), 464–90. On women and socialism, see Olive M. Johnson, "Woman and the Socialist Movement," (New York: Socialist Labor Party, 1919), a pamphlet first published in 1907. Jeanneth D. Pearl, "Women in Society," *Unity*, 1 (Jan. 1911), 6–8; R. B. Tobias and Mary Marcy, *Women as Sex Vendors* (Chicago: Chas. H. Kerr, 1918).

Feminist Responses to "Crimes against Women," 1868–1896

Elizabeth Pleck

American feminists have long responded to "crimes against women" by providing local support services for victims, lobbying for legislative reform, and exposing the social origins of women's oppression. In one generation, for example, women initiated the following activities:

> A separatist women's religious group established a commune in rural Texas for battered wives and wives of alcoholics.
>
> The San Diego women's movement opened a shelter for battered wives.
>
> Chicago feminists provided legal aid for victims of incest, rape, and wife beating; appeared in court along with rape victims to encourage them to testify; and lobbied the state legislature to pass stiffer criminal penalties against rapists and perpetrators of incest.

At the same time, women activists across the nation demanded compensation for battered wives. Some lobbied for the passage of new laws, while others drew attention to the courtroom trials of women victims. Concerned about the relationship between sex and violence, women writers and organizers denounced pornography and male sadomasochism, and began to concern themselves with the lives of prostitutes. A well-known novelist caused a sensation when she published a book charging a famous male novelist with incest. Believing that all women are enslaved by the fear of rape, a leader of the women's movement called for self-defense training for women and stiffer penalties for convicted rapists. A feminist intellectual published her treatise on "crimes against women," in which she denounced the Christian religion and the state as

The author has benefited from the criticisms of this paper by Estelle Freedman, Linda Gordon, and Sonia Michel.

[*Signs: Journal of Women in Culture and Society* 1983, vol. 8, no. 3]

sources of women's degradation. More conservative women hoped that the passage of a national constitutional amendment would offer the ultimate remedy for the problem of wife beating.

This catalog of feminist interest, which appears so contemporary, represents instead the activities of American women's organizations between 1868 and 1896. This range of responses to what nineteenth-century feminists termed "crimes against women" disproves the assumption that the earlier women's movement, preoccupied with the suffrage question, ignored concerns such as violence against women. This essay explores the origins and decline of nineteenth-century feminist responses to crimes against women by analyzing the beliefs and actions of four sets of reformers and organizations: liberal feminists Susan B. Anthony and Elizabeth Cady Stanton; conservative feminists Lucy Stone and Henry Blackwell; the Women's Christian Temperance Union (WCTU); and Chicago's Protective Agency for Women and Children. These reformers—some primarily intellectuals, others mainly activists—differed in the degree to which they gave sustained attention to crimes against women, but their shared goal was increased protection for women and stiffer criminal penalties for male offenders. All identified the roots of such crimes in the nature of the family, male sexuality, and intemperance.

Some assigned greater weight to one cause over another, however, and some feminists were more vigorous in their critique of the family. To understand their responses, it is crucial to keep in mind that these reformers perceived crimes against women through the rhetoric and social thought of an earlier age. It is tempting to criticize them for overemphasizing women's victimization, eliding types of victimization that were quite distinct, or oversimplifying and even confusing the issue in their arguments. Indeed, their understanding of the issue was at times simplistic, and they often advocated severe punishments, although not with as much vehemence or meanness of spirit as the male reformers of their day. But these limitations must be understood in historical context: nineteenth-century feminists were trying to gain the attention of a society at best indifferent and at worst hostile to any public discussion of violence against women. Their rhetorical excesses and mistakes serve as warnings for the women's movement today, but their courage and concern for the suffering of other women also serve as examples of commitment in the face of social conservatism and public indifference.

Liberal Feminists

Elizabeth Cady Stanton, Susan B. Anthony, and their less well-known colleague Matilda Joslyn Gage first became interested in crimes against women in the 1850s as a result of their involvement in the women's temperance crusade. They demanded that wives of drunkards, who were often beaten, should have the right to divorce their husbands on grounds of cruelty or habitual drunkenness. For the next nine years they campaigned unsuccessfully to reform New York's divorce law. Both Stanton and Anthony knew many women victims, and Anthony had aided one New York woman who fled with her daughter from an abusive husband.[1] The Civil War and then the postbellum campaign for woman's suffrage preempted this early interest. Between 1868 and 1870, however, Stanton and Anthony actively wrote, spoke, and demonstrated on behalf of women who were victims of violence or sexual exploitation. They championed the cause of Hester Vaughn, a servant accused of infanticide; called for the conviction of Albert McFarland, a wife beater who murdered his ex-wife's fiancé; and demanded the death penalty for rape.[2]

Although Stanton believed that rape and wife beating occurred mainly among the poor and "refined sensualism" was common mainly among wealthy men,[3] those implicated in these cases were not poor and immigrant men, but men of property and education. McFarland was a New York lawyer, and Vaughn's seducer was her wealthy Philadelphia employer. Stanton aided an abused ex-wife of a Massachusetts senator, and before the Civil War she spoke out about many cases of "aggravated cruelty" among the Dutch aristocracy in New York.[4] Feminists charged that the law had treated these men too leniently; they cried out against the double standard by which Hester Vaughn was sentenced to death for infanticide, "which could not be proved against her . . . while he who betrayed her walks this green earth in freedom."[5]

Just after the end of the Civil War, when Stanton and Anthony became involved in these cases, Victorian silence about this double standard was beginning to give way to public discussion of health, sexuality, prostitution, and marriage. Advocates of free love wanted to bring out into the open "the secret sexual practices" of moral hypocrites, and Stanton sought to expose the secrecy upon which traditional marriage

1. Ida Husted Harper, *The Life and Work of Susan B. Anthony*, 2 vols. (Indianapolis: Hollenbeck, 1898), 1:204.

2. Ellen DuBois, *Feminism and Suffrage: The Emergence of an Independent Women's Movement in America, 1848–1869* (Ithaca, N.Y.: Cornell University Press, 1978), pp. 145–47.

3. Lois W. Banner, *Elizabeth Cady Stanton: A Radical for Woman's Rights* (Boston: Little, Brown & Co., 1980), p. 73.

4. Elizabeth Cady Stanton, *Eighty Years and More: Reminiscences, 1815–1897* (1898; reprint ed., New York: Schocken Books, 1981), p. 215.

5. *The Revolution* (New York) (January 14, 1869), pp. 24–25, reprinted in Ellen Carol DuBois, ed., *Elizabeth Cady Stanton, Susan B. Anthony: Correspondence, Writings, Speeches* (New York: Schocken Books, 1981), p. 123.

rested.[6] At the same time, the popular press contributed to the heady atmosphere by feeding its audience a steady diet of stories involving sensational divorces, scandalous courtroom trials, and brutal family crimes. Indeed, the few criminal statistics available on husband-wife murder suggest that domestic violence may have been increasing as part of a general crime wave attributed to postwar economic and social tensions.[7] The increase in violent crimes, however, did not lead to the discovery of female victimization, since Stanton and Anthony had been pointing out instances of it as early as the 1850s. But the combination of a more open cultural atmosphere, sensationalized press reports, and fears of a crime wave may have made the public more willing to listen to their arguments and may have abetted the perception that such "outrages" were increasing.

As former abolitionists, Stanton and Anthony frequently relied on the analogy with slavery when they discussed crimes against women. Denied personal liberty, a wife was subjected to the authority of a master, whose commands she was forced to obey. They referred to married women who had to flee their abusive husbands as "fugitive wives" running to Indiana and Connecticut divorce mills "like slaves to their Canada, from marriages worse than plantation slavery."[8] Stanton and Anthony's concern was not only for married women, but for the treatment of women in general. They never devised a single term to describe the forms of woman's victimization, but relied instead on the repetition of specific examples: "the prosecutions in our courts for breach of promise, divorce, adultery, bigamy, seduction, rape; the newspaper reports every day of every year of scandal and outrages, of wife murders

6. William Leach notes this post–Civil War change in atmosphere but not the distinct chill in the air that resulted from the discovery of the Beecher-Tilton affair. William Leach, *True Love and Perfect Union: The Feminist Reform of Sex and Society* (New York: Basic Books, 1980), pp. 118–19.

7. Edwin Powell's figures for police arrests in Buffalo show that murder and assault rates increased dramatically at the end of the Civil War. These increases could not have been due only to an increased willingness of police to make arrests, since the arrest rate for violent crimes grew twice as fast as the total arrest rate. See Edwin H. Powell, "Crime as a Function of Anomie," *Journal of Criminal Law, Criminology, and Police Science* 57, no. 2 (June 1956): 161–71. Similarly, the rate of major crime in Boston grew by 21 percent between 1867 and 1874, even though the number of police in Boston increased only 10 percent. See Theodore N. Ferdinand, "The Criminal Patterns of Boston since 1849," *American Journal of Sociology* 73, no. 1 (July 1967): 84–99. Only a small proportion of incidents of family violence ever appear in police records, though murder between spouses is well recorded. In Philadelphia the rate of husband-wife murders increased dramatically from 1 per 1 million persons between 1839 and 1845 to 4.1 per 1 million between 1874 and 1880, then vacillated slightly before declining at the end of the century. Manuscript Docket Books, Court of Quarter Sessions, Philadelphia, City Archives of Philadelphia.

8. Paulina Wright Davis, *A History of the National Woman's Rights Movement* (New York. Journeymen Printers Cooperative, 1871), p. 66.

and paramour shootings, or abortions and infanticide."[9] The single common denominator in these crimes was not so much male violence as male sexual privilege and aggression.

What these feminists were interested in, then, was "social purity." Social purity reformers advocated a single standard of sexual morality, and, since the 1860s, British feminists had waged political campaigns based on these beliefs. Led by Josephine Butler, these women fought to repeal the Contagious Diseases Acts that required the medical inspection of prostitutes. Social purity activists opposed the acts in part because they facilitated men's use of prostitutes by reducing the risk of venereal disease, and in part because they identified with the plight of prostitutes forced to undergo inspection. After the defeat of the acts, advocates of social purity pressed for the complete abolition of prostitution. Reformers in the United States also fought the medical regulation of prostitution when the idea was introduced in the 1860s and 1870s. Many of the American social purity activists were advocates of temperance and woman's suffrage as well; Stanton and Anthony, for example, successfully opposed inspection laws when they were introduced in the New York State legislature.[10]

Stanton and Anthony were also influenced by two works published in 1869 that incorporated social purity ideas: John Stuart Mill's *Subjection of Women* and Harriet Beecher Stowe's *Lady Byron Vindicated.*[11] Mill characterized sexual intercourse as merely an "animal function"—as the worst form of degradation when an unwilling wife became the object of her husband's animalism. Mill was as fond of the analogy between slavery and marriage as were Stanton and Anthony. He did not deny that many marriages operated tolerably under a system of absolutism on one side and loving submission on the other, but he believed that as long as husbands possessed unlimited power in marriage, brutal men could commit violence against their wives and children. Mill, like Stanton and Anthony, rejected the ideal of family stability, and favored divorce for wives on grounds of cruelty.

Mill's *Subjection of Women* also helped inspire Harriet Beecher Stowe to publish *Lady Byron Vindicated,* a denunciation of the English romantic poet for having committed incest with his half-sister. Stowe, an old friend of Lady Byron, defended the estranged wife of the poet against

9. Susan B. Anthony, "Social Purity," in Aileen S. Kraditor, ed., *Up from the Pedestal: Selected Writings in the History of Feminism* (Chicago: Quadrangle Books, 1970), p. 160.

10. David Pivar, *Purity Crusade: Sexual Morality and Social Control, 1868–1900* (Westport, Conn.: Greenwood Press, 1973), p. 51.

11. John Stuart Mill, "The Subjection of Women," reprinted in *Essays on Sex Equality: John Stuart Mill and Harriet Taylor Mill,* ed. Alice S. Rossi (Chicago: University of Chicago Press, 1970); and Harriet Beecher Stowe, *Lady Byron Vindicated: A History of the Byron Controversy* (Boston: Fields, Osgood & Co., 1870).

an attack by her husband's mistress, whose memoirs had been published that year. Lady Byron had confided to Stowe that her husband had fathered a child by his half-sister before they were married, and that the affair continued after she married him. Stowe implied that Lady Byron also had been beaten by her husband when he was drunk. Public reaction ran against Stowe for defaming Lord Byron and for discussing in print a subject that was not to be mentioned in polite society. But Elizabeth Cady Stanton compared the book favorably with John Stuart Mill's *Subjection of Women:* "Our present civilization is marked with as hideous outrages on the mothers of the race, in marriage, and out of it, as has ever blackened the pages of history at any period of the world."[12] She added "incest in high places" to the other outrages she described before a women's rights convention in 1870.[13]

Although Stanton and Anthony directly credited many of their ideas to the writings of Mill and Stowe, they were more circumspect about the influence of their colleague Matilda Joslyn Gage. Active in the women's rights movement since the 1850s, Gage became president of the National Woman Suffrage Association in 1879. She published her major work, *Woman, Church and State*, in 1891.[14] In it she traced the historical origins of state and legal oppression of women in West European and American history, and linked these dual sources of oppression with diverse forms of women's victimization, from wife beating to polygamy and witchcraft. When canon law gained ascendancy over civil law, she argued, many of the punishments for crimes against women were eliminated. Canon law also embedded in the law a view of woman as the property of her husband, a view that was later incorporated in common law. Gage had worked out this argument by the time the first volume of the *History of Woman Suffrage*, which she coauthored with Stanton and Anthony, appeared in 1881. The volume included Gage's essay "Woman, Church and State," in which she also exposed the legal and religious sources of women's oppression. Likewise, Stanton argued that "men abuse wives, taught by law and gospel that they own them as property."[15] It is difficult to say whether this idea originated with Stanton or with Gage.

Stanton and Anthony never hewed entirely to Gage's analysis, but often combined it with arguments about social purity. Indeed the "hideous outrage" of marital rape (always referred to through euphemism) appeared to confirm both perspectives. Because the wife was her husband's property, he had the right to sexual intercourse with her at his pleasure. They also combined their belief in social purity with a call for

12. Leach (n. 6 above), pp. 118–19.

13. Davis (n. 8 above), p. 68.

14. Matilda Joslyn Gage, *Woman, Church and State* (1891; reprint ed., Watertown, Mass.: Persephone Press, 1981).

15. Davis (n. 8 above), p. 72.

temperance. Thus, in an address before a social purity convention, Anthony singled out the "twin vices" of "drunkenness and licentiousness" committed by "the bloated drunkard" and "the diseased libertine" (a reference to the communication of venereal disease to wives by their husbands).[16]

Their solution to the problem of women's slavery in marriage was to reform the institution of marriage or to emancipate the wife through divorce. Stanton argued that she was not seeking to destroy the family, but to create a marriage of equals, based on companionship and spiritual union as well as physical attraction and concern for children. No marriage could be equal, however, until the wife had the right of "voluntary motherhood," the right to refuse her husband intercourse. For the wife trapped in a "discordant marriage," Stanton advocated full divorce with the right of remarriage, and held that the mother should be given special consideration in the award of child custody. For Stanton, marriage was not a sacrament but rather a contractual relationship that either party should be free to dissolve.

After 1870, Stanton and Anthony held no further dramatic protest meetings against crimes against women. In their journal, *The Revolution*, stories of infanticide and of sons murdering their mothers were buried amidst reports of the fight for suffrage. Stanton continued to advocate divorce, but she was less specific about the reasons for it. Her 1870 speech on "Marriage and Divorce" mentioned that abuse of children and wives arose out of man's ownership of women as property. Five years later, her standard public lecture still called for liberalized divorce and even decried male domination in the family, but did not mention the abuse of wives or children.[17]

Stanton's self-censorship can be explained in several ways. For one, she had lost suffragist support as a result of her impassioned attack on marriage, stemming from the McFarland-Richardson trial in 1869. In addition, the passage in 1873 of the Comstock Law, which banned dissemination through the mails of birth control information and pornography, helped to end open discussion of such topics as rape and incest. Radical ideas about labor or homesteads for ex-slaves were generally subdued by a conservative climate, while many liberal divorce laws dating from the antebellum period were removed from the statute books. Then came the Beecher-Tilton scandal, brought about by Victoria Woodhull's exposure of Henry Ward Beecher's adultery with one of his female parishioners. Stanton and Anthony, friends of both the accused

16. Anthony, p. 159; and Elizabeth Cady Stanton, "'Speech to the McFarland-Richardson Protest Meeting,' May, 1869," in DuBois, ed. (n. 5 above), p. 127.

17. Contrast the speech she gave at the annual convention of the National Woman Suffrage Association in 1870 with her favorite speech for the lecture circuit, "Home Life." See Judith Papachristou, *Women Together* (New York: Alfred A. Knopf, 1976), p. 62; Elizabeth Cady Stanton, "Home Life," in DuBois, ed. (n. 5 above), pp. 131–38.

and his accuser, were tarnished by their association with known advocates of free love and presumed adulterers. On the lecture circuit, they responded to the hisses and boos of their audiences by muting their rhetoric so as not to alienate their listeners further.

Stanton and Anthony had never regarded women's victimization as a separate issue, but rather as a means of dramatizing the need for voluntary motherhood, woman's right to divorce, temperance, and social purity. They used instances of wife beating and incest, for example, to strengthen their claim for a woman's right to divorce, but they believed that the solution, divorce, was more important than the problem, domestic violence. They had risked violating cultural standards of propriety by attacking the family and advocating divorce, but after being associated with several sex scandals they could no longer afford to do so. Nineteenth-century feminists could either do battle against specific domestic outrages without attacking the institution of the family (as did the advocates of temperance), or they could attack the family and champion divorce while remaining vague about the circumstances that required it (as did Stanton and Anthony); they could not do both.

Conservative Feminists

As leaders of the American Woman Suffrage Association, Lucy Stone and her husband Henry Blackwell have been regarded as the conservatives of the nineteenth-century women's movement. They viewed the question of marriage and divorce as peripheral to the suffrage movement; divorce, they argued, was not a woman's issue. They even helped pass a resolution at a national suffrage convention "that the ballot for woman means stability for the marriage relation, stability for the home, and stability for our republican government."[18] Stone's reputation as a conservative also arose because of the split in suffrage ranks regarding acceptance of the Fourteenth Amendment. Stone and Blackwell, who worked to include woman's suffrage as part of the amendment, were willing to accept the enfranchisement of only black men, whereas Stanton and Anthony opposed the introduction of male-only suffrage into the U.S. Constitution. Lucy Stone held conservative views on other issues as well. She did not favor general strikes, and she was unsympathetic when labor unrest led to violence. She and her husband also maintained a dignified silence about Harriet Beecher Stowe's denunciation of Lord Byron, and she found the involvement of Stanton and Anthony with the Beecher-Tilton scandal and their association with Victoria Woodhull an embarrassment.

Before Stone and Blackwell became editors of the *Woman's Journal*

18. *Woman's Journal* (Boston) (December 3, 1870).

in 1872, the journal featured articles that called divorce for women "an escape out of tyranny into freedom." Under their editorship, such articles quickly disappeared. During those first years they seemed deliberately to avoid controversial issues in order to concentrate on women's rights. In 1876, however, Stone announced her intention of publishing a weekly catalog of crimes against women. As justification she cited the appearance of newspaper reports that indicated an increasing incidence of "crimes against women." Such reports compelled her to overlook "standards of propriety" in detailing torture, maiming, and brutality against women.[19] Beneath the headline of "crimes against women," readers of the *Woman's Journal* found stories of wife murder, rape, incest, and wife beating; a mutual suicide agreed upon in a love pact; physical assaults by boys against girls; and even crimes committed by women, such as infanticide or crimes of passion where women had responded to seduction, rape, or male violence.

Although Stone and Blackwell were regarded as the conservatives of the women's rights movement, their analysis of crimes against women was virtually identical with that of Stanton and Anthony. They, too, believed that abuse of wives grew out of a husband's ownership of his wife as a form of property—"domestic tyranny," as they sometimes called it. They believed in social purity, and Stone campaigned for the punishment of male pimps and procurers rather than prostitutes. Indeed, Henry Blackwell argued that "the most oppressed and abused class of women in society" was not the assaulted wife, who could still cling to a mantle of respectability, but instead that class of woman "which associates with men outside of the legal sanctions of marriage" (i.e., prostitutes).[20] They also railed against the "hydra-headed monster" of intemperance and of male licentiousness, and gave special attention to the status of married women, although they recognized that crimes against women were committed whether the victims were "living in or out of the marriage relation."[21] And though they knew that wife beating occurred in every class and ethnic group, they held that "a large majority of such crimes" occurred among immigrants, because women were held in low regard in the countries from which the immigrants came.[22]

The most marked difference between Stanton and Anthony, on one hand, and Stone and Blackwell, on the other, was in the solutions they emphasized. In 1879 Stone introduced a bill in the Massachusetts legislature to protect the assaulted wife whose husband had been convicted of criminally assaulting her.[23] The proposed bill gave an assaulted wife the

19. Ibid. (January 28, 1877).
20. Ibid.
21. Ibid.
22. Ibid. (May 15, 1875).
23. Wife beating had been a crime under Massachusetts law since the colonial period—as early as 1641. Any remaining doubt about the legal status of wife beating was

right to apply at a neighborhood police court for a legal separation, an order requiring her husband to pay support for her and her children, and the award of custody over her children. Three times she introduced this legislation—in 1879, 1883, and 1891—and three times it failed.

The idea for this bill came from the prominent English suffragist Frances Power Cobbe, who had sent Stone a copy of the protection bill she helped pass in Parliament. Cobbe's article, "Wife Torture in England," published in the *Contemporary Review* in 1879, had shocked the English public with tales of atrocities and helped attract popular support for her bill. More sophisticated than most Americans, Cobbe acknowledged that the assaulted wife was not always innocent or defenseless; sometimes she fought back or even initiated violence. She herself learned about this issue when members of Parliament unsuccessfully attempted to pass a law requiring the flogging of convicted wife beaters. Cobbe opposed the legislation because she believed that a husband who had been beaten would retaliate against his wife. She favored a protection bill as a more suitable alternative, especially for working-class women, among whom assaults "were tenfold as numerous and twenty times more cruel" than among women in "the upper ranks of society."[24] Divorce was an alternative, but many women could not afford it and even if they did secure one, they would still confront the problem of economic survival for themselves and their children. Therefore, Cobbe persuaded several prominent liberals to sponsor her bill, and in 1879, it sailed through the House of Commons without much opposition.

When Lucy Stone received a copy of Cobbe's article and the protection bill she published both in the *Woman's Journal*, pointing out that wife

---

resolved in 1871, when the Massachusetts Supreme Court ruled it a misdemeanor. The law held several advantages for women. A wife who left her husband because he beat her could apply for both a protection order requiring him to vacate her premises and forbidding him from forcing her to return, and an order requiring him to support her and her children. If a wife or her child was injured by a drunken husband, she could sue the saloonkeeper for damages. Finally, a husband convicted of assaulting his wife was required to post a bond for up to two years. Yet there were difficulties as well. A wife had to swear out a complaint against her husband, and, in some jurisdictions, police were instructed not to arrest a man unless they saw him commit a violent act. Then, too, if a husband claimed to have reformed and he demanded his wife's return, she was legally required to go back to him. Most important, the protection and maintenance orders required a lawyer to press the case before the state supreme court, and lawyers' fees were an expense only a few women could afford. On Massachusetts law regarding wife assault, see *Acts and Resolves Passed by the General Court of Massachusetts, 1874* (Boston: Wright & Potter, 1874), pp. 132–33; George A. O. Ernst, *The Legal Status of Married Women in Massachusetts* (Boston: Massachusetts Woman Suffrage Association, 1895), pp. 23, 24; *Massachusetts Laws, Statutes, Acts and Resolves Passed by the General Court of Massachusetts in the Year of 1879* (Boston: Rand, Avery & Co., 1879), p. 444.

24. Frances Power Cobbe, "Wife Torture in England," *Contemporary Review* (April 1878), p. 57.

beating occurred in every country and was increasing in the United States. She supplied statistics from the Boston police that indicated there were 500 arrests of wife beaters every year.

To remedy this situation, Stone and Blackwell introduced a protection bill that they believed offered distinct advantages. It granted the assaulted wife both custody of her children and economic support. By locating jurisdiction of these cases in neighborhood police courts, where decisions favoring the plaintiff were the rule, the bill almost ensured judgments in favor of the wife. But Massachusetts legislators raised several objections to the bill. Support orders, they claimed, were unenforceable because abusive husbands would flee the state. They also argued that assaulted wives would not make use of the law, and that legal separations granted by mundane police courts would become excessively easy to obtain. Ironically, Lucy Stone, the ardent opponent of divorce, was now accused of encouraging the dissolution of marriages.

After her protection bill had failed for the second time, Stone began to favor the punishment of wife beaters rather than the protection of their victims. She had long believed that criminals were punished too leniently; she favored capital punishment for rapists and believed that out of "maudlin sympathy" assailants of women received especially light sentences.[25] The rhetoric of extreme punishment was then in vogue, and some women in the social purity movement and the WCTU were advocating castration of rapists.[26] Influenced by English ideas, Maryland in 1882 became the first state to pass a bill to punish wife beaters with flogging at the whipping post. A similar bill was introduced in the Massachusetts legislature in 1885. Unlike male reformers who sought to introduce extreme punishments in the criminal law, Stone threw her support behind the bill because she believed a fine or imprisonment would merely deprive the wife beater's family of economic support. But the bill lost by a wide margin.[27] After this defeat, Stone tried one more time to pass her protection bill, but does not appear to have continued other legislative efforts.[28]

The failure to achieve passage of either bill only strengthened Stone and Blackwell's belief that women would never be protected from bru-

25. *Woman's Journal* (January 29, 1876) and (June 11, 1881).

26. Simeon E. Baldwin, "Whipping and Castration as Punishments for Crime," *Yale Law Journal* 8, no. 9 (June 1899): 381.

27. When this bill lost, its sponsor substituted another one to punish wife beaters with a three- to ten-year prison term. It also lost. See *Documents Printed by the Order of the House of Representatives of the Commonwealth of Massachusetts, 1884* (Boston: Wright & Potter, 1884).

28. Henry Blackwell opposed legislation designed to punish wife beaters at the whipping post. See *Woman's Journal* (February 11, 1905). Similarly, Matilda Gage viewed flogging as a "retributive punishment common among barbarians." She argued that the "remedy for crimes against women . . . does not lie in the punishment of offenders, but in different sentiments in regard to woman in both church and state" (Gage [n. 14 above], p. 145).

tality until they were considered equals under the law. Because women were unable to vote, they argued, penalties for wife beating were mild. Would battered wives "ever be adequately protected," Lucy Stone wondered, "until women would help make the laws?"[29] Enacting laws to ensure equality between the sexes would help to remove prejudice against women. Even the former wife beater would no longer regard his wife as his property, since he would realize the general esteem in which women were held.[30]

Stone and Blackwell contended that assaulted wives, recognizing they were protected under the law, would be more willing to complain to the police and press their cases in the courts. Judges, who had come to fear the wrath of the female electorate, would sentence wife beaters to long prison terms and governors would refuse to pardon wife murderers.[31]

Stone and Blackwell's arguments about the causes of crimes against women were virtually identical with those of Stanton and Anthony. Nonetheless, they attached the label "crimes against women" to a range of previously nameless acts, and they initiated legislation on behalf of assaulted wives. Stone and Blackwell differed from Stanton and Anthony primarily in their attitude toward divorce. In our own times, the battered women's movement is often sympathetic to and even encourages divorce and criticizes the mental health field for counseling women to remain in unhappy and violent marriages. It might seem, then, that the greater the tolerance for divorce, the more vigorous the efforts on behalf of assaulted wives. But in the late nineteenth century, it was extremely controversial to advocate divorce. Precisely because Stone opposed divorce, she could raise the issue of crimes against women without giving the appearance of threatening family stability. She did so primarily to demonstrate that solutions other than divorce—protective legislation and suffrage—would more truly aid assaulted wives.

The Women's Christian Temperance Union

The WCTU began as an organization solely interested in the question of temperance. After Frances Willard became president of the organization in 1879, the WCTU began to insist that drunkenness was not only the cause but also the effect of a variety of social problems. As the largest women's organization of its day, the WCTU favored a variety of social reforms from the introduction of police matrons to prison reform, to the eight-hour working day, and the kindergarten. Temperance

29. *Woman's Journal* (April 8, 1892).
30. Ibid. (January 11, 1879) and (January 18, 1879).
31. Ibid. (January 18, 1879).

workers also successfully campaigned for the passage of state laws designed to benefit abused wives of drunkards.

Because each spouse was immune to a tort brought by the other, wives did not have the legal right to sue an abusive husband for damages. Therefore, the WCTU championed special legislation that gave the drunkard's wife the highly unusual right to sue for damages. The laws did not hold the drunkard, a creature of his appetites, entirely responsible for his actions; rather, they held that the rum seller who had encouraged the man to drink should pay for the consequences of his customer's actions.

In 1873, the New York and Arkansas legislatures passed the first of these laws. In all, twenty states from Maine to New Mexico enacted such legislation, the last of them in 1891. The injured party could sue the saloonkeeper or the owner of the saloon for damages caused from injury inflicted by an intoxicated person. In some states, only the wife could sue for damages, although in others, several injured parties, including a husband, child, parent, or employer, were given the right to sue. In order to be awarded damages, the law generally required the wife to notify the saloonkeeper in advance that he should refuse to serve her husband.

Only a few drunkards' wives could afford to hire a lawyer to sue for damages, but in the few cases that reached the courts, wives generally won their suits and were awarded damages.[32] Ann J. Wilson of Genesee, Michigan, had informed the town saloonkeeper not to serve her husband. On the night in question, her husband had been served enough to make him drunk early in the evening and then served a second time later that night. When her husband finally came home, he attacked her in front of their children and struck her on the head with a chair. She was awarded damages, although the amount of the award was not stated.[33] Courts also upheld other legal transactions that favored the assaulted wife. One Illinois husband who pleaded with his wife not to separate from him signed a note promising to pay her six hundred dollars if he became drunk or abused her. He did, and she sued him for divorce. The Illinois Supreme Court upheld the validity of his promissory note.[34]

The WCTU also promoted the establishment of model facilities for dependent, neglected, and abused children. When there was no other society to protect children from cruelty, they ran their own. In the 1890s, the San Diego Union, an organization comprised of WCTU members from a range of social backgrounds, founded a home for dependent women and children. Although their major interest was in providing a

32. Henry Campbell Black, *A Treatise on the Laws Regulating the Manufacture and Sale of Intoxicating Liquors* (St. Paul, Minn.: West Publishing, 1892), pp. 277–377.

33. Wilson v. Booth, 57 Mich. 249.

34. *Woman's Journal* (April 19, 1877).

home for neglected and abused children and orphans, they also took in the children's poverty-stricken mothers, some of whom had been assaulted by their husbands. The San Diego Union also ran a day-care facility for the children of working mothers and a kindergarten. Their shelter continued well into the twentieth century.[35]

In all of these efforts, the WCTU marched forward under the banner of Christianity, motherhood, and the protection of innocent women and children. But they could not bring themselves to favor divorce as a solution for the sufferings of the drunkard's family. At first, articles in the *Union Signal*, the official publication of the WCTU, favored divorce only on grounds of adultery, although other articles argued that so long as saloons remained open, drunkenness was an acceptable grounds for divorce. They voiced no opinion on cruelty as a grounds for divorce, although from the general tone of conservatism, it appears that they would have favored a legal separation in cases of abuse rather than a divorce that permitted remarriage. They assumed that the legally separated wife did not require the right of remarriage because she was an asexual being and self-sacrificing mother who would be content to live modestly by respectable wage-earning.[36]

Although WCTU members regarded intemperance as the major cause of social ills, their increasing involvement in social purity campaigns suggests that they regarded male licentiousness if not as a twin evil, then at least as a secondary one. Therefore, they lobbied for legislation on behalf of assaulted wives, and unlike Stone, whose bill had been defeated because legislators perceived it as an attack on traditional marriage, the WCTU succeeded. The WCTU could claim to be alleviating misery, supporting women's traditional role, and protecting the family, rather than securing for women an independent existence.

Instead of attacking the traditional patriarchal family, women in temperance hoped to shore it up by forcing men to realize their responsibilities. They acknowledged that women as well as children were dependents, but they were not critical of female dependency, as were feminists. Instead they called for the protection of dependent women by decent men. Alcohol and lust had turned gentle men into brutes who had to be reformed. Indeed, the WCTU seemed more concerned with uplifting men than with raising the status of women.[37] In sum, they did

35. Ruth Bordin told me about the existence of this organization, which is described in her book, *Women and Temperance: The Quest for Power and Liberty, 1873–1900* (Philadelphia: Temple University Press, 1981), p. 103.

36. Barbara Leslie Epstein, *The Politics of Domesticity: Women, Evangelism, and Temperance in Nineteenth-Century America* (Middletown, Conn.: Wesleyan University Press, 1980), p. 134; Bordin, p. 14.

37. Janet Giele discovered that this concern with men's reform was present in many of the *Union Signal* articles—far more than in the *Woman's Journal*. But the *Union Signal* articles also expressed more hope for the ultimate redemption of men. See Janet Giele, "Social Change in the Feminine Role: A Comparison of Woman's Suffrage and Woman's Temperance, 1870–1920" (Ph.D. diss., Radcliffe College, 1961).

not believe in a marriage of equals, but in a marriage of respectables in which the protective husband remained the authority.

The Protective Agency for Women and Children

Nineteenth-century Americans established hundreds of societies for the protection of children, but only one, the Protective Agency for Women and Children, founded in Chicago in 1885, protected assaulted wives and rape victims. The first protective agency, organized by men, had opened in New York City in 1868; like those that followed in other eastern cities, it arose within the context of the urban charity movement of the post–Civil War decades. Similarly, the Women's Education and Industrial Union in Boston protected working women by investigating employee fraud, operating a lunchroom for employed women, conducting classes in labor law, and aiding victims of consumer fraud.[38] The Chicago agency carried protective work in a unique, new direction and became the most significant organizational effort to aid female victims of violence in nineteenth-century America.

Although the Chicago Woman's Club, sponsor of the protective agency, began as a literary society, by 1885 it had become deeply interested in a variety of reforms—lobbying the state legislature to pass compulsory school attendance laws and to abolish child labor; aiding in the establishment of a juvenile court; and demanding, with the WCTU, that city jails hire police matrons.[39] Edith Harbart of the Cook County Suffrage Association suggested that the club establish a separate department devoted to the protection of women and children. She believed that the club, which included so many wives of Chicago's elite men, would lend respectability to a protective agency. The Woman's Club agreed, and at the opening meeting of the Chicago agency, speakers denounced the "debauching" of women clericals and the extremely low age of sexual consent under Illinois law (at that time, only ten years). They called for a society that would hire its own agents, though it would be staffed primarily by women volunteers; its membership would be restricted to women.

The formal organization and daily operation of the agency were remarkable in other respects. Half of the officers were required to be members of the Woman's Club and the other half were from diverse city and suburban women's organizations. Most of the women were wealthy, with the possible exception of the representatives from the Swedish and Bohemian women's clubs. The governing board of the agency consisted of delegates from fifteen associations of women in Chicago, including

38. Annie Nathan Meyer, *Woman's Work in America* (New York: Henry Holt & Co., 1981), p. 289.

39. Dorothy Edward Powers, "The Chicago Woman's Club" (M.A. thesis, University of Chicago, 1939).

the WCTU, the Chicago Woman's Club, the Cook County Woman's Suffrage Association, and several social purity organizations. The agency established an office to offer legal aid, where women handled cases of sexual molestation, incest, rape, sexual harassment, wife beating, and consumer fraud. Other agencies referred women who were seeking legal assistance to them, and they in turn cooperated with these agencies. In a typical case, the protective agency handled the legal proceedings for a Russian immigrant who had been raped by her father. It cooperated with the Illinois Humane Society in terminating the father's right to custody and helped place the girl in an orphan asylum.[40]

The Chicago protective agency also sought out women believed to be rape victims, based on the reports of interested parties. Instead of waiting for the victim to come to their office, women went to her home, inquired as to the validity of her story, and asked her if she had enough money to hire her own lawyer. If she did not, they hired one for her and tried to provide her with a place to live and a job. These methods drew criticism from detractors who told the agency "that to go out in the highways and byways of life, and lift up those who are downtrodden, under the feet of wicked men, [was] very dirty business."[41] Agency members also appeared in court on behalf of rape victims, both because they believed that the presence of respectable women helped create a moral atmosphere and in order to encourage the victim to testify in a courtroom dominated by men. Rape victims, they believed, felt ashamed to testify and did not want to subject themselves to cross-examination, especially about their sexual history. But, the women claimed, "the shame and scandal of these crimes lies in the fact, not the telling of it." They went on to attack the double standard according to which a rape victim had to demonstrate to a jury "an unblemished reputation."[42]

The agency activists did not often discuss the ultimate solution to crimes against women. They did write of the economic dependency and exploitation of women and children, and they assumed that some mothers and older children would have to support themselves. But they seemed more interested in methods than in solutions; they believed in educating women about their legal and social status and viewed the sisterhood of women as a means of bringing about change. True virtue in marriage, child rearing, and personal relations was their ultimate goal.

The Chicago agency justified its work by arguing that women were the natural protectors of other women and children. Single females and

40. Unpublished Case Record, Illinois Humane Society (December 5, 1900), University of Illinois at Chicago Circle Archives.

41. "First Annual Report of the Protective Agency for Women and Children, 1887," p. 13, Chicago Historical Society. Mari Jo Buhle first alerted me to the existence of this organization.

42. Ibid., p. 11.

working women were in special need of protection because they were removed from their families and forced to fend for themselves in a world of men, while girls were especially vulnerable because they were sexually pure, young, and innocent. It was women's responsibility to protect these innocents from the "human brutes," or rapists, who preyed upon them. The protective agency defended itself against the charge that it was helping to break up the family by claiming that the marriages it helped to terminate were not "true marriages" but instead "a falsity and a sham" because of the violence, cruelty, or immorality that occurred within them.[43] In fact, however, helping abused women to gain separations enlarged the experience and deepened the feminist consciousness of agency members. By the third year of their work, they began to question the nature of marriage: "We come to ponder much more on these great questions—the sexual and financial relations of men and women, and often wonder what is wrong."[44] Within a few years they began to connect the victimization of women with the general inequality between the sexes.[45]

Eleven years after its founding, the protective agency merged with a larger, well-funded, and predominantly male organization, the Bureau of Justice, which furnished legal aid to indigent clients. In the agreement of consolidation, however, the women asked for and received sole jurisdiction over the cases affecting women and children, since they believed it "a self-evident truth that women can do better work for the wronged of their own sex than men can do."[46] As a result of the merger, their case load grew rapidly. They began to provide those assaulted wives with children legal aid to secure divorces, rather than just legal separations.[47] In 1905 the agency merged a second time, to form the Legal Aid Society of Chicago. The reason for this merger appears to have been the same as in the first—joining with a larger, better-funded organization that would provide the agency a necessary guarantee of autonomy.[48] The protective agency still maintained its separate identity and was represented on the Board of Legal Aid. By 1912, however, reports of its work disappeared from the annual report of Chicago Legal Aid. Among other ominous signs of change was the replacement of their old motto, "woman's work for women," with "men's and women's work for the wronged

43. Ibid., p. 10.

44. "Third Annual Report of the Protective Agency for Women and Children, 1889," p. 10, Chicago Historical Society.

45. "Sixth Annual Report of the Protective Agency for Women and Children, 1892," p. 10, Chicago Historical Society.

46. "Eleventh Annual Report of the Protective Agency for Women and Children, 1897," p. 14, Chicago Historical Society.

47. Reginald Heber Smith and John S. Bradway, *Growth of Legal-Aid Work in the United States*, Bulletin no. 67 (Washington, D.C.: U.S. Department of Labor, 1936), pp. 201, 207.

48. Legal Aid in Chicago appears to have been the only legal aid society to have emerged out of a woman's protective agency.

and helpless." By the 1920s, Chicago Legal Aid's official policy was to discourage divorce and urge reconciliation whenever possible. It is not known whether the organization continued to aid rape victims.

Reexamining the history of the protective agency reveals the problems that women reformers encountered when they worked on behalf of women victims. First, efforts on behalf of assulated wives led reformers to consider "the most embarrassing of all questions which come before us"—the issue of divorce.[49] They began cautiously by securing only legal separations for women. Later they began to help women secure divorces, but only on the grounds of extreme cruelty or drunkenness. The charge that aiding assaulted wives led to the breakup of the family had helped defeat Stone's protection bill. Opposition to divorce grew after a government report in the 1880s demonstrated that divorce was more common in the United States than in any other Western country. National magazines decried the prevalence of divorce, and even societies for the prevention of cruelty to children had to defend themselves against new charges that they were breaking up the family. Thus, women reformers tended to favor reforms that would force men to assume family responsibilities, such as child support and desertion laws, rather than those that would separate the family.

A second obstacle to the Chicago agency's work was the cultural attitude toward any discussion of rape, incest, or sexual molestation. The agency was forced to admit that "for obvious reasons, these cases cannot be told to the public."[50] The modesty of a virtuous woman was compromised by having to consider sordid incidents, and the virtue of the victim was further damaged by revealing the facts in her case. The agency was continually forced to challenge beliefs that the victim had provoked an attack or was of "blemished reputation." Ironically, because the prostitute's reputation had already been blemished, she could more readily become an object of pity and attention.

Why was the Chicago protective agency the only one of its kind when there were hundreds of societies established for the prevention of cruelty to animals and to children? Lucy Stone noted that there was more concern for beaten horses and dogs than for bruised and beaten wives.[51] She called for a society to prevent cruelty to wives, but she never organized one, and the protective agency in Chicago was the closest approximation of this goal in the nineteenth century. In fact, over the

49. "First Annual Report" (n. 41 above), p. 10.

50. Ibid., p. 14.

51. *Woman's Journal* (January 18, 1879). Even this obvious analogy was lost on many suffragists. The Boston Woman's Educational and Industrial Union offered quite a different one: "We form a Society for the Prevention of Cruelty to Children, and shall we forget the needless torture of women who must stand all day whether there is work to do or not?" Quoted in Karen J. Blair, *The Clubwoman as Feminist: True Womanhood Redefined, 1868–1914* (New York: Holmes & Meier, 1980), p. 46.

last three hundred years, concern for children (regardless of gender) has been much greater than for adult women, and the protective work on behalf of women that existed in the nineteenth century focused on intemperance and prostitution. Historians Linda Gordon and Ellen DuBois have recently argued that in the nineteenth century interest in social purity, and especially in prostitution, substituted for interest in crimes against women, especially rape.[52] They are quite correct that prostitution was the dominant metaphor for woman's victimization. But concern for social purity stimulated interest in crimes against women. It was not that crimes against women went unrecognized but rather that interest in the issue could not be sustained.

The Decline of Women's Interest

By the 1890s the feminist response to crimes against women began to diminish. Older leaders of the women's movement who had been interested in the issue died, while younger women and black women of all ages found it an unappealing, somewhat dated cause. Black suffragists, for example, who formed their own woman's clubs in this decade, associated crimes against women with the lynching of black males for alleged rape of white women.[53] They believed concern for the protection of women to be largely a subterfuge for racism. In the North the suffrage movement began to attract college-educated social reformers who were less interested in denouncing and punishing the brutishness of men than in eradicating the social conditions believed to cause crime. In addition, concern about crimes against women had flourished during the nadir of the suffrage movement, but as their movement gained momentum, suffragists began to shed the more controversial, less popular issues.

In contrast, English suffragists continued to debate divorce reform for assaulted wives as late as 1911. The English had been the first to respond to domestic violence, and English reformers from Mill to Cobbe had linked protection for assaulted wives with divorce reform. Furthermore, English suffragists continued to cling to social purity ideas with a vehemence that had disappeared elsewhere.[54]

52. Linda Gordon and Ellen DuBois, "Seeking Ecstasy on a Battlefield: Danger and Pleasure in Nineteenth Century Feminist Sexual Thought" (University of Massachusetts—Boston and State University of New York at Buffalo, Departments of History, April 1982).

53. Ida B. Wells, a black journalist who campaigned against lynching, claimed that most of these charges of rape were untrue, though her treatment of the issue did not fully explain the lynching of black men for beating or murdering their own wives. See Ida B. Wells, *A Red Record: Lynchings in the United States, 1892–1894* (Chicago: n.p., 1895), p. 13.

54. Margaret May, "Violence in the Family: An Historical Perspective," in *Violence and the Family*, ed. J. P. Martin (Chichester, West Sussex: John Wiley & Sons, 1978), pp. 149–50.

In the United States the response to crimes against women had depended as much on the social purity and temperance campaigns as it had on the movement for women's rights. The transformation of these movements by the 1890s diminished interest in what had always been a peripheral issue. The entire premise of social purity rested upon the protection of female sexual virtue from ruin. With the transition in sexual mores that occurred in the late nineteenth and early twentieth centuries, otherwise respectable women were giving away what had once been so zealously protected. As the value of female virtue began to decline, so did the elaborate lengths that were taken to defend it. Nonetheless, Progressive era reformers revived interest in prostitution not as an issue of social purity or individual sin, but rather as a social problem exacerbated by the anonymity of the modern metropolis. Instead of punishing male customers of prostitutes, these reformers concentrated on protecting health and hygiene. Their solution was to eliminate the cities' red-light districts. Even the temperance campaign, one of the last bastions of traditional moral categories, began to abandon its early rhetoric in favor of pamphlets concerning the effect of alcohol on health or the relation between saloons and prostitution. The monstrous drunkard became the pitiable alcoholic, who either suffered from a curable medical disease or, in more severe cases, was a genetic misfit. Control over such men passed to another set of reformers, the professional case workers and psychiatrists.

The earlier response to crimes against women had been moralistic, sexually prudish, and punitive in its attitude toward criminals. But these characteristics were not so much embarrassing excesses of belief as qualities essential to articulating women's position and waging a variety of reform campaigns. With the disappearance of rhetoric about "evil beasts" and social purity, the emotional outrage necessary to generate a public campaign was gone. Only after another eighty years would feminists renew their sisterhood with victims of crimes against women, to refute once again popular stereotypes and to challenge the conspiracy of silence.

Center for Research on Women
Wellesley College

Mary A. Hill

Charlotte Perkins Gilman

A FEMINIST'S STRUGGLE WITH WOMANHOOD

IN A LETTER written from Belmont, New Hampshire, September 2, 1897, Charlotte Perkins Stetson exclaimed, "Thirty-five hundred words I wrote this morning, in three hours!" A book's chapter in one sitting; a successive six-week dizzy pace of morning writing; elaborate consultations with her closest critic, Houghton Gilman, soon to be her second husband; and thus was *Women and Economics* dashed into print. Jane Addams, already emerging as one of America's foremost social reformers, expressed her gratitude to Charlotte, her "pleasure and satisfaction," her "greatest admiration" for the "Masterpiece." Florence Kelly, another pioneer of social settlement reform viewed it as "the first real, substantial contribution made by a woman to the science of economics." According to *The Nation*, "Since John Stuart Mill's essays on *The Subjection of Women*, there has been no book dealing with the whole position of women to approach it in originality of conception and brilliancy of exposition." [1]

Charlotte Gilman quite naturally felt increasingly elated as positive reviews rolled in, despite the societal distortions her book both reflected and described. A flamboyant speaker, a writer with a penetrating wit, she was rapidly emerging as a major theorist and popularizer for the woman's movement in turn-of-the-century America. Publicly she attempted to analyze and expose the ubiquitous effects of sex-based inequalities and the sources of female strength; and privately she acknowledged that many of her perceptions emerged as well from agonizing

[1] Quotations from private letters are made with the permission of The Arthur and Elizabeth Schlesinger Library on the History of Women in America, Radcliffe College, Cambridge, Massachusetts. Letters from Charlotte Stetson to Houghton Gilman, September 2, 1897; letter from Jane Addams to Charlotte Stetson, July 19, 1898; letter from Florence Kelley to Charlotte Stetson, July 26, 1898; *The Nation*, June 8, 1899.

conflicts of her life. "We ourselves," she publicly and sweepingly asserted, "have preserved in our own character the confusion and contradiction which is our greatest difficulty in life."[2] And privately she acknowledged the war between contending factions in herself. To Houghton Gilman she described a major challenge of her life: "To prove that a woman can love and work too. To resist this dragging weight of the old swollen woman-heart, and force it into place—the world's Life first—my own life next. Work first—love next. Perhaps this is simply the burden of our common womanhood which is weighing on me so."[3]

THE SEEDS OF CHARLOTTE'S RADICAL FEMINISM were rooted in an early struggle for independence, self-assertion, and self-respect. Raised primarily within a female kinship network necessitated by her father's absence, and deprived from early infancy of the motherly affection for which she yearned, Charlotte nonetheless disclosed in her diaries and notebooks a growing strength of character, a playful, lively, independent personality. Rebellious against the model of repressive discipline her unhappy mother, Mary Perkins, attempted to impose, she was active in physical fitness programs, lecture clubs, and language classes. Armed with books and reading lists provided by her librarian father, Frederick Perkins, Charlotte was well-read in contemporary philosophical, historical, and anthropological thought. She delighted in her physical as well as in her mental agility; her effort to control her body was maintained within her larger program to control her life. By the age of 21 she was self-supporting, busy from 6 AM to 10 PM, and thriving in the process.

---

[2] Charlotte Perkins Gilman, *Women and Economics: A study of the Economic Relation Between Men and Women as a Factor in Social Evolution* (New York: Harper ed., 1966), p. 331.

[3] Letter from Charlotte Stetson to Houghton Gilman, July 26, 1899. My focus here is on the relationships and experiences most richly documented in the Charlotte Perkins Gilman collection, particularly the relationships with Walter Stetson and Houghton Gilman. Charlotte's relationships with her parents, with female friends, and with many significant others will receive further attention in a forthcoming biography—Charlotte Perkins Gilman: *The Birth of a Radical Feminist, 1860–1896*. For an interim biographical and theoretical analysis of the life and writings of Charlotte Gilman see Mary A. Porter (Hill-Peters), "Charlotte Perkins Gilman: A Feminist Paradox," (Ph.D. dissertation, McGill University, 1975).

Despite the limitations imposed by her mother's prudish discipline, Charlotte constantly had calls, visitors, and stimulating friendships with males as well as females. She enjoyed hiking, sleighing, rowing, playing whist, and was exhilarated in her triumphs at the chess board. She enjoyed inspiring evening talks with Ada Blake and Augusta Gladding, and many long walks with Grace Channing, who became her lifelong friend. Also, she developed an intimate relationship with Martha Luther, a relationship of mutual trust and shared interests. They delighted in each other's company. "With Martha I knew perfect happiness," she later wrote. "Four years of satisfying happiness with Martha, then she married and moved away." [4]

Charlotte's friendship with Martha provided the kind of support, encouragement, and mutual affection historians currently believe was central to the experience of most nineteenth-century women. The reality of Charlotte's love was quite apparent, her grief at the impending separation was intense and disruptive. In 1881, Charlotte noted that "some swain" was threatening her relationship with Martha, that because of marriage she might lose her "most intimate friend." On November 5th she wrote: "Pleasant, to ring at the door where you've always been greeted with gladness; to be met by the smile that you value all others above—to see that smile flicker and vanish and change into sadness because she was met by *your* presence instead of her love." On November 16th she noted, "Walk in the dark streets for an hour or so in dumb misery." In December, she summarized: "A year of steady work. A quiet year, and a hard one. . . . A year in which I knew the sweetness of perfect friendship, and have lost it forever." [5]

---

[4] Charlotte Gilman, *The Living of Charlotte Perkins Gilman* (New York: Appleton-Century Company, 1935), pp. 78, 80. Diaries, 1879–1883.

[5] See particularly diary entries for October 12, October 30, November 5, November 16, December 16, 1881. Charlotte had many very close relationships with women during her lifetime, with Grace Channing, Adeline Knapp, Martha Luther, and Helen Campbell, for example. The data richly supports Carroll Smith-Rosenberg's suggestion that "women's sphere had an essential integrity and dignity that grew out of women's shared experiences and mutual affection." Carroll Smith-Rosenberg, "The Female World of Love and Ritual: Relations Between Women in Nineteenth-Century America," *Signs* 1, no. 1 (Autumn, 1975), 9–10. As historians increasingly appreciate the significance of female networks of support and companionship, we need also to consider the often painful feeling of rejection close female friends experienced with one another. Among Charlotte's most difficult emotional crises were the departure of Martha Luther and the disruption of the relationship with Adeline Knapp ("Dora" in *Living*, pp. 133, 141–144). See diary entries, 1892–93.

After a typical self-scourging, she became more stoic, striving to submerge her grief by helping others. But the vacuum left by Martha's absence heightened Charlotte's longings for affection, and may have paved the way for her acceptance of the comforting protection of a man.

On January 12, 1882, Charlotte met an aspiring artist, Walter Stetson. Within seventeen days of their first meeting he proposed. Her diary entry reads: "I have this day been asked the one great question in a womans [sic] life and have refused." Two days later she wrote:

> Now that my head is cool and clear, now before I give myself in any sense to another; let me write down my Reasons for living single.
>
> In the first place, I am fonder of freedom than anything else— . . .
>
> I like to be *able* and *free* to help any and everyone, as I never could be if my time and thoughts were taken up by that extended self—a family. . . .
>
> I am cool, fearless, and strong . . . .
>
> For reasons many and good, reasons of slow growth and careful consideration, more reasons that I now can remember; I decide to Live—Alone.
>
> God help me! [6]

For a time at least, Charlotte remained committed to her rationale for spinsterhood: "if I were to try the path you open to me I could never try my own," she wrote. "I knew of course that the time would come when I must choose between two lives, but never did I dream that it would come so soon, and that the struggle would be so terrible." It was, as she put it directly to Walter, "a trial which in very truth *does* try me like fire." [7]

---

[6] "An Anchor to Windward," Diary, January 31, 1882.

[7] Letters from Charlotte Perkins to Walter Stetson, February 20 and 21, 1882. According to the pre-1881 reading lists which Charlotte kept in her diaries, she was apparently unfamiliar with the rich feminist literature she might have drawn on. Moreover, it is striking that she did not mention her two successful great-aunts, Catharine Beecher and Harriet Beecher Stowe, as she described to Walter the seemingly irreconcilable conflict between marriage and career:

> I am beset by my childhood's conscientiousness . . . the voice of all the ages sounds in my ears, saying that this [marriage] is noble, natural, and right; that no woman yet has ever attempted to stand alone as I intend but that she had to submit or else. . . .

Despite her misgivings, Charlotte began to express increasing affection for Walter—"I am beginning to wonder how I ever lived through this winter, before you—; . . . You want to give me something! You are giving me back myself." By 1883, she was engaged to Walter and began to accept his sympathy, his comforting, his advice, even when it was constricting. For example, when a close friend gave her a new copy of Walt Whitman's *Leaves of Grass* she noted, "I am obliged to decline, as I had promised Walter I would not read it." She now resolved, first and foremost, to be "*Absolutely unselfish* . . . To find my happiness in the pleasurable sensations of others rather than in my own. To consider others, think of others, think first 'will he or she like it?' rather than shall I."[8]

As Charlotte's expressions of affection and self-sacrifice intensified, so also did her gloom. She experienced a loss of strength, discipline, and courage which she had worked so consciously to acquire. In December, 1883 she wrote: "Let me not forget to be grateful for what I have. Some strength, some purpose, some design, some progress, some esteem, respect—and affection. And some Love. Which I can neither feel, see, nor believe in when the darkness comes." She continued: "I mean this year to try hard for somewhat of my former poise and courage. As I remember it was got by practice." Nonetheless, a severe depression began to take its toll:

> I would more gladly die than ever yet; saving for the bitter agony I should leave in the heart of him who loves me. And mother's pain.
>
> But O! God knows I am tired, tired, tired of life!
>
> If I could only know that I was doing right.[9]

Charlotte's expressed attitudes toward marriage and motherhood were fiercely ambivalent. Rationally aware of possible conflicts between self-

---

> I have nothing to answer but the meek assertion that I am different from if not better than all these, and that my life is mine in spite of myriad lost sisters before me.
>
> (Letter to Walter Stetson, February 20, 1882.)

[8] Letter to Walter Stetson, March 6, 1882; Diary, April 5, 1883; "Thoughts and Fingerings," November 3, 1883. Charlotte's acceptance in 1883 of Walter's authority contrasts strikingly with her self-confident assertions of February 13, 1882: "You are the first man I have met whom I recognize as an equal; and that is saying a good deal for me. I would call you grandly superior, but that I am fighting just now against a heart-touched woman's passion of abnegation." Letter to Walter Stetson, February 13, 1882.

[9] Diary, December 31, 1883.

development and love, she was largely unprepared to meet the complex unconscious as well as deliberate patterns of socialization which forced most women to accept self-sacrificing love as natural, inevitable, and right. Drawing from conflicting signals of her mother, Mary Perkins, Charlotte knew that women could achieve a modicum of independence, but always at a price. Mary Perkins was a divorced and eventually self-supporting woman, nourished and sustained by a female network of friends and relatives; her nonconformity strengthened Charlotte's capacity for independence. But suffering from the stigma of divorce, from economic hardship, from the guilt and emotional insecurity her single life-style caused her, Mary quickened Charlotte's fear of spinsterhood. Both parents had also unwittingly encouraged Charlotte's independence by withholding their affection. Mary Perkins had denied caresses to her daughter: "I used to put away your little hand from my cheek when you were a nursing baby," Mary told Charlotte in her later years. "I did not want you to suffer as I had suffered." Likewise her librarian father, Frederick Perkins, kept his distance: "the word Father, in the sense of love, care, one to go to in trouble, means nothing to me," Charlotte wrote, "save indeed in advice about books and the care of them—which seems more the librarian than the father." [10]

A contemporary psychologist, Alexandra Symonds, discusses symptoms in her recent patients quite similar to those that Charlotte was beginning to exhibit. The women Symonds treated were active, vital, and self-assured before their marriages. Yet they were also often women who had to "grow up in a hurry." Denied experiences of warmth in childhood, they were encouraged to control their feelings and give the impression of strength and self-sufficiency. Symonds suggests a frequent pattern: "They repressed their healthy needs to be taken care of and repressed the child in them as well." Perhaps Charlotte's difficulties were rooted in the discipline and loneliness of youth, the loss of her friend Martha Luther serving only to exacerbate her thirst for love. Perhaps, as Symonds puts it, she desired "to put down a tremendous burden which she had been carrying all her life, and be the dependent little girl she had never been before." [11]

---

[10] *Living*, pp. 10, 5.

[11] "Phobias" emerge, according to the Symonds thesis, from a denial of self-expression that women often felt must be the price of love. "Marriage then becomes their 'declaration of dependence'. . . . [T]hey tend to become the paragons of Victorian femininity—helpless, housebound, and ineffectual." See Alexandra Symonds, M.D., "Phobias after Marriage: Women's Declara-

On May 2, 1884 Charles Walter Stetson and Charlotte Anna Perkins were married in Providence, Rhode Island. "O my God! I thank thee for this heavenly happiness!" she wrote in her diary the evening of the wedding.[12]

There were commonly expected roles of men and women in marriage that both Charlotte and Walter accepted. As a man, Walter was expected to provide for his family. He did not have to choose between marriage and his work. In fact, marriage lent further purpose to his artistic growth and creative efforts. Charlotte, by contrast, felt a momentous change occurring in her life. Formerly self-supporting, independent, and career-oriented, she found herself involved with time-consuming domestic chores which conflicted with the work she loved—painting and writing. Within a week, some spontaneous rebellion seemed to be occurring. She wrote in her diary, "I suggest he [Walter] pay me for my services; and he much dislikes the idea. I am grieved at offending him; mutual misery. Bed and cry." She was beginning to experience firsthand what later she would depict so trenchantly: "the home which is so far from beautiful, so wearing to the nerves and dulling to the heart, the home life that means care and labour and disappointment, the quiet, unnoticed whirlpool that sucks down youth and beauty and enthusiasm, man's long labour and woman's longer love." [13]

Although the personal dynamics of Charlotte's relationship with Walter must remain elusive, sexual experiences may have contributed to her growing discontent. At times Charlotte viewed sexuality with traditional Victorian prudery: "Purity," she wrote in 1883, "is that state in which no evil impulse, no base thought can come in; or if forced in dies of shame in the white light. Purity may be gained by persistent and long continued refusal to entertain low ideas." Yet it is also clear that she was by no means always cold or unapproachable in early marriage. On June 15, 1884 she noted: "Am sad: last night and this morning. Because I find myself too—affectionately expressive. I must keep more to myself and be asked—not borne with." And on June 25 the same year she wrote, "Get miserable over my old woe—conviction

---

tion of Dependence," in *Psychoanalysis and Women*, edited by Jean Baker Miller, M.D. (Middlesex, England: Penguin Books, 1973), pp. 288–303.

[12] Diary, May 2, 1884.

[13] Diary, May 9, 1884. Charlotte Gilman, *The Home: Its Work and Influence* (New York: McClure, Phillips and Company, 1903), p. 12.

of being too outwardly expressive of affection." [14]

Soon Charlotte was pregnant, a condition which lessened her physical and emotional stamina. Even after the birth of Katharine Stetson in 1885, Charlotte wrote in her diary, "Every morning the same hopeless waking . . . same weary drag." She appreciated her home, her healthy baby, the services of her mother and a competent domestic servant, yet was helpless and despondent: "and I lay all day on the lounge and cried." [15] A failure in her own eyes, she looked to Walter for protective love, and increasingly for pity. She was assuming what Carroll Smith-Rosenberg has referred to as those "character traits assigned women in Victorian society and the characteristic symptoms of the nineteenth-century hysteric: dependency, fragility, emotionality, narcissism." [16] Charlotte did not as yet attack the religion of maternity, the assumption that all mothers are "saintly givers." Instead, she resigned herself to misery. She wrote, Walter "would do everything in the world for me; but he cannot see how irrevocably bound I am, for life, for life. No, unless he die and the baby die, or he change or I change, there is no way out." She described her "hysteria" as follows:

> I could not read nor write nor paint nor sew nor talk nor listen to talking, nor anything. I lay on that lounge and wept all day. The tears ran down into my ears on either side. I went to bed crying, woke in the night crying, sat on the edge of the bed in the morning and cried—from sheer continuous pain. . . .
>
> I made a rag baby, hung it on a doorknob and played with it. I would crawl into remote closets and under beds—to hide from the grinding pressure of that profound distress. . . .[17]

In writing her autobiography, Charlotte described her "mental illness" as a disease beyond her understanding, an accidental misfortune. Suffering from recurrent depressions, she continued to believe that causes for her suffering lay not in the personal or political conflicts of her life, but in idiosyncratic weaknesses within herself. The price she paid for

---

[14] "Thoughts and Fingerings," November 3, 1883; Diary, June 15, June 25, 1884.

[15] Diary, August 30, 1885; *Living*, p. 89.

[16] Carroll Smith-Rosenburg, "The Hysterical Woman: Sex Roles and Role Conflict in 19th-Century America," *Social Research* 39, no. 4 (Winter, 1972), 671.

[17] Diary, August 30, 1885; *Living*, pp. 91, 96.

nonconformity was guilt, despite the fact that almost all of her feminist writings were inextricably related to her life, and despite the fact as well that her short story, "The Yellow Wall-paper" was itself a feminist-oriented autobiographical portrayal of insanity.

In "The Yellow Wall-paper," an "hysterical woman," overprotected by a loving husband, is taken to a summer home to recover from nervousness, and told to rest and sleep and try to use her "will and self-control" to overcome her miseries. The room her husband John assigns to her is covered with a yellow-patterned wallpaper. "The color is repellent, almost revolting; a smouldering unclean yellow, strangely faded by the slow-turning sunlight." Although the woman is quite ill, her husband, a physician, tells her that there is "no reason" for her suffering; she must dismiss those "silly fantasies." Of course, "it is only nervousness," she decides. But "it does weigh on me so not to do my duty in any way! . . . [and] such a dear baby! And yet I *cannot* be with him, it makes me so nervous." She tries to rest and do as she is told, but suffers doubly since her husband will not believe that she is ill. He "does not know how much I really suffer. He knows there is no *reason* to suffer, and that satisfies him." She thinks she should appreciate the protective love he offers. "He takes all care from me, and I feel so basely ungrateful not to value it more. . . . He took me in his arms and called me a blessed little goose." And yet it is impossible to talk to him "because he is so wise, and because he loves me so." Efforts to discuss the matter only bring a "stern reproachful look" and send her back to bed in shame.

John offers tender love, but enforces the inactivity which deepens her despair. I "am absolutely forbidden to 'work' until I am well again." Here he comes, "I must put this away,—he hates to have me write a word." Rest is what her physician husband says is right, so "he started the habit by making me lie down for an hour after each meal."

The first stage of the breakdown is one of self-blame. The woman follows the doctor's orders and tries to stop the fantasies that people tell her are unreal. When a physician of "high standing" assures "friends and relatives that there is really nothing the matter with one but temporary nervous depression—a slight hysterical tendency—what is one to do?" Gradually, however, the woman starts to believe in her fantasies. "There are things in that [wall-]paper that nobody knows but me, or ever will. Behind that outside pattern the dim shapes get clearer every day. . . . I didn't realize for a long time what the thing was that showed behind that dim sub-pattern, but now I am quite sure it is a woman." Dramatically she trusts her perceptions and acts wildly but assertively.

> I wasn't alone a bit! As soon as it was moonlight and that poor thing began to crawl and shake the pattern, I got up and ran to help her. I pulled and she shook, I shook and she pulled, and before morning we had peeled off yards of that paper.

The protagonist begins to creep and crawl within her madness. She separates herself from the perception of others, and when in a climactic scene her husband faints, she crawls over his body and says, "I've got out at last . . . in spite of you!"[18]

"The Yellow Wall-paper" stands in dramatic contrast to Charlotte's autobiography, *The Living of Charlotte Perkins Gilman*. There, the separation from Walter Stetson is portrayed as resulting from her individual weaknesses, or equally simplistically, from a mismatched marriage. She was not inclined publicly or explicitly to indict loved ones in her life. Yet in "The Yellow Wall-paper," she presented insanity as a form of rebellion, a crucial turning point toward independence. Only in a fictional version of her illness would she publicly express her anger: "I've got out at last . . . in spite of you." Anger is also apparent in her diary. On April 18, 1887, she wrote:

> I am very sick with nervous prostration, and I think some brain disease as well. No one can ever know what I have suffered in these last five years. Pain pain pain, til my mind has given way. . . . You found me—you remember what I leave you—O remember what, and learn to doubt your judgment before it seeks to mould another life as it has mine.
>
> I asked you a few days only before our marriage if you would take the responsibility entirely on yourself. You said yes. Bear it then.[19]

Although Charlotte often faced uncontrollable depressions during the bleak years of 1884–1887, fortunately a determination to trust her own

---

[18] Charlotte Perkins Gilman, "The Yellow Wall-paper," *New England Magazine* 5 (January, 1892), 647–656. I am taking the liberty of using "The Yellow Wall-paper" quite literally as autobiographical material. The names are different, the fantasies symbolic; but when asked to what extent "The Yellow Wall-paper" was based on fact, Charlotte replied, "I had been as far as one could go and get back." *Living*, p. 121.

[19] Diary, April 18, 1887.

abilities remained. In part, she benefited from a visit in California with Grace Channing and her family in the winter of 1885–86. In this supportive atmosphere she regained a measure of her former self-confidence. She felt more well, of gayer disposition, when she was separated from her family, a primary source of her guilt-induced anxiety. Moreover, the diaries indicate an emerging feminist consciousness during these same years; her reading, lecturing, and writing on women's issues predated and possibly contributed to her separation from Walter in 1888. For example, in 1883 she argued with a close friend, Jim Simmons, "till 11:45 nearly talking about Woman's Rights." He was a "man far from broad," she noted. In 1884 she read John Stuart Mill's *The Subjection of Women* (she also read it to her mother), and then began to lecture and to write on women's issues. She attended her first Woman's Suffrage Convention in 1886. In January, 1887, she read Margaret Fuller's *Woman in the Nineteenth Century* and "started a course of reading about women," although as she noted in her diary she stopped it temporarily to "oblige" Walter. By February she had accepted an offer from Alice Stone Blackwell to manage a suffrage column for a Providence weekly newspaper, *The People*.[20]

Many days Charlotte complained of weakness and exhaustion from domestic obligations yet found strength when she worked on articles or verse. Incensed by the situation of other women, she was depressed when she reflected on her own. On February 20, 1887 she had a "good talk" with a neighbor, Mrs. Smythe, who was "another victim" with a "sickly child" and an ignorant husband who was "using his marital rights at her vital expense." And a month later: "Getting back to the edge of insanity again . . . feel desperate. Write my 'column' though." She also returned to her physical fitness program. For example, on February 7, after getting "discouraged by Walter," she delighted in her "jolly time at the gym in the evening. I seem to slip into my old position of inspirer very easily. And the girls like it."[21]

What is most striking about Charlotte's life, particularly from 1884–1887, is that she had the energy to pursue any of the activities she found most satisfying. She was "ill," yet stubbornly ignored the admonitions of her family, refused their well-intentioned offers of "security," and proceeded to develop an independent plan of action. She rejected the

[20] See diary entries November 16, 1883; February 24, October 6, 1886; January 5, January 19, February 5, 1887.

[21] Diary entries, February 20, March 20, February 7, 1887.

advice of a nerve specialist, Dr. S. Weir Mitchell: "Live as domestic a life as possible. Have your child with you all the time. . . . And never touch pen, brush or pencil as long as you live."[22] Instead, she decided to try new alternatives. She believed that self-assertion, in her case the need to read, write, exercise, and enjoy the companionship of other women was crucial to her mental health. Lacking the support, or even the understanding of friends and relatives in Providence, Rhode Island, and with no income or well-defined plans for work, she determined to move herself and child to California in the fall of 1888. There, in Pasadena, the Channing family provided a brief respite of economic and emotional security.

Gradually, Charlotte began to meet other women like herself who were alone, without means of satisfying work, or without adequate income. Still personally distraught, she nonetheless moved toward a tactical involvement in the burgeoning feminist movement, began more seriously to analyze common problems women faced, and encouraged organizational and individual attacks on what she saw as pervasive social ills. Well-read in contemporary intellectual theory, and most particularly influenced by the writings of Lester Ward and Edward Bellamy, she became active in the lecture-writing circuit of the then highly politicized and often radical reform movements of the 1890's. Her expanding reputation brought her into close contact with socialist, nationalist, and Fabian thought. As a social theorist, she was eclectic rather than original. But in her partial adoption of socialist theory and in her continuing identification with oppressed groups, she was able to expand her feminist analysis beyond that of many of her contemporaries and to ground it in a broadly-based political perspective.

TURNING NOW TO THE FEMINIST ANALYSIS ITSELF, I suggest that there were four major forces which Charlotte Gilman isolated as having created and perpetuated female inequality, or the "artificial" feminine personality. The underlying premise of her environmentalist analysis was the innate similarity of human potentials of males and females. As she put it:

> That is masculine which belongs to the male sex as such; to any and all males *without regard to species*. . . . That is feminine which belongs to the female sex, as such, *without regard to*

[22] *Living*, p. 96.

> *species*. . . . That is human which belongs to the human species, as such, *without regard to sex*. . . . Every step of social development, every art, craft, and science . . . these have to do with humanity, as such, and have nothing to do with sex.[23]

The first of the major factors impinging on the lives of women, she perceived, was their economic dependence on men. Women had become in effect property of men. Women's work, she argued, had a use value but not an exchange value. She wrote, "whatever the economic value of the domestic industry of women is, they do not get it. The women who do the most work get the least money, and the women who have the most money do the least work." She insisted that economic dependence, wherever it occurred, necessarily resulted in a loss of integrity and self-respect. Encouraging women to view the political dimensions of their situation, she declared, "We have not as a class awakened to the fact that we have no money of our own." [24]

Charlotte Gilman's economic struggles as a separated and subsequently divorced woman, and earlier the child of a divorced woman, made her especially sensitive to woman's economic plight. She knew from experience that economic security in the home was a mirage, that if deprived of the support of a male protector, women would invariably confront extremely limited work opportunities, and often tragic impoverishment. Yet she recognized that it was the family itself, as a social and economic institution, which perpetuated female enslavement and denied women opportunity for economic independence. Consequently, she differed from many feminists who believed that no "fundamental economic change would be necessary in home relationships for women to achieve equality." [25] For Charlotte Gilman, women's most essential goal was the building of an economic power base.

The second significant factor leading to "artificial" femininity, Gilman believed, was non-voluntary alienating domestic servitude. She argued that inequality of women resulted from a division of labor along sex lines, further evidence of a causative relationship between the insti-

---

[23] Charlotte Gilman, "Masculine, Feminine, and Human," *Woman's Journal*, 35 (January 16, 1904), 18.

[24] *The Home*, p. 22; *Women and Economics*, pp. 14–15; Gilman, "Her Own Money: Is a Wife Entitled to the Money She Earns?" *Mother's Magazine*, 7 (February, 1912), 7.

[25] Aileen Kraditor, *Ideas of the Women's Suffrage Movement* (New York: Columbia University Press, 1965), p. 121.

tution of the family and women's low level of achievement. Cooking, sewing, nursing, washing, caring for children—"not only do we undertake to have all these labors performed in one house, but by one person." Just consider, she wrote, "what any human business would be in which there was no faintest possibility of choice, of exceptional ability, of division of labor." She decried the fact that domestic industry had become a "sex function, . . . supposed to pertain to women by nature." [26]

Third, Gilman examined the effects of women's psychological dependence on men. An eclectic popularizer as well as a theorist, she reiterated and reshaped the theoretical arguments of her predecessors, Mary Wollstonecraft and John Stuart Mill, for example; but in the process she also anticipated the direction of some of the most recent and perceptive feminist theorists: the concentration on the politics of the family, for example, the recognition that the personal is political, the understanding that only by examining the daily lives of women, and their experiences of submission to the demands of family life could an explanation of female "difference" ultimately be found.[27] Viewing women's powerlessness and dependence on men as both psychological and political phenomena, she argued that the female personality had become a slave personality. She wrote, "The position of women, after their long degradation, is in many ways analogous to that of the freed slave. He is refused justice on account of his inferiority. To reply that inferiority is largely due to previous injustice does not alter the fact." [28] The female personality was likewise conditioned to submission:

> Of women especially have been required the convenient virtues of a subject class: obedience, patience, endurance, contentment,

---

[26] Gilman, "Domestic Economy," *Independent*, 56 (June 16, 1904), 1359–1360; Gilman, "The Normal Social Group To-day," *The Forerunner*, 4 (July, 1913), 175; Gilman, *Women and Economics*, p. 226.

[27] See particularly Simone de Beauvoir, *The Second Sex*. Juliet Mitchell, *Woman's Estate* (Vintage ed.; New York: Random House, 1973). Juliet Mitchell, *Psychoanalysis and Feminism* (New York: Pantheon, 1974). Kate Millet, *Sexual Politics* (New York: Doubleday and Company, 1970). Shulamith Firestone, *The Dialectic of Sex: The Case for Feminist Revolution* (Bantam ed.; New York: William Morrow, 1970). Sheila Rowbotham, *Women, Resistance, and Revolution* (Vintage ed.; New York: Random House, 1974). Sheila Rowbotham, *Woman's Consciousness* (Middlesex, England: Penguin Books, Ltd., 1973). Maria Della Costa, *The Power of Women and the Subversion of the Community* (2nd ed.; Bristol, England: Falling Wall Press, Ltd., 1973).

[28] Gilman, "Educated Bodies," *Woman's Journal*, 35 (June, 1904), 178.

> humility, resignation, temperance, prudence, industry, kindness, cheerfulness, modesty, gratitude, thrift, and unselfishness.[29]

Although the conditions of women's lives had important variations, Gilman believed there existed a common institutional experience—the home—which affected women whether rich or poor. The politics of the family crossed class lines.

Fourth, finally, and least persuasively, Gilman ventured beyond many of her socialist contemporaries in exploring the unique effects of sexual oppression on women. She believed that the sexual relationship had become an economic relationship, marriage very often itself being merely a legally enshrined version of prostitution. Forced to emphasize sexuality at the expense of humanity, woman had necessarily to give the impression of weakness, frailty, timidity, and passivity—in short to prove her capacity for submission, the male's for dominance and control. Gilman wrote:

> We have been told so long that
>
> "Love is of man's life a thing apart,
> Tis woman's whole existence"
>
> That we have believed it. . . . [O]ur whole existence was carefully limited to this field; we were dressed and educated to grace it; we were bloomed out into a brief and glorious career while under inspection and selection before our final surrender, and then we pursued the rest of our lives with varying devotion and satisfaction in this one department of life.[30]

She advocated the distribution of information on birth control and sex-related matters, the development of physical fitness programs for women, and an end to man-made fashion dictates. She called for human fulfillment, for women's full control of their bodies as well as their lives.[31]

---

[29] Gilman, *His Religion and Hers: A Study of the Faith of Our Fathers and the Work of Our Mothers* (New York: The Century Company, 1923), p. 134.

[30] Gilman, "Love Stories and Life Stories," *Woman's Journal*, 35 (May 7, 1904), 146.

[31] Charlotte Gilman's support of Margaret Sanger's work in the birth control movement began roughly in 1915. Adopting the racist and ethnocentric attitudes all too common to her generation, however, Charlotte viewed birth

However, Gilman's understanding of the causes for sexual oppression was far more impressive than her theoretical projections. In short, she could *attack* the "feminine" woman, but not *envision* an alternative of equal womanhood. Her life and writings were always inextricably related. Where she had achieved certain of her feminist goals—economic independence, physical fitness, and considerable psychological strength as well, she believed in woman's capacity for excellence. But because she could not interpret the conflicting loyalties which seemed to occur, both within herself and other independent women when they entered love relationships with men (and wavering herself between both strength and deference, self-righteousness and self-sacrifice), Charlotte perhaps understandably concluded that certain stereotypes of "femininity" must somehow be innate.

THE PERSONAL ROOTS of Charlotte's theoretical contradictions are apparent in her early living, in her struggles with guilt as she faced her separation and divorce from Walter Stetson, and in her love relationship with Houghton Gilman, whom she married in 1900.[82] She wrote letters of passionate intensity to Houghton Gilman, but she seemed to fear him as a threat to her marginally-established independence. A sensuous woman, she was also a well-trained warrior in the feminist campaign. Unintentionally and tragically, she created sexual and psychological barriers against an intimate male-female relationship.

Charlotte had known Houghton as a child, as an affectionate first cousin eight years her junior, whose companionship she very much enjoyed. After a hiatus of some seventeen years, Charlotte visited Houghton in his law office to obtain legal advice concerning royalties on a publication. Erroneously, she assumed the relationship was "safe" from "complications" because of kinship, though she expressed her preference for even safer grounds than that: "I only wish I was your grandma or great aunt or I have it! an invalid sister that you simply *had* to have

---

control as an issue not only of personal importance for women; she also maintained that it could be used as a protection against the pressures of population expansion, particularly of the "unfit." See Gilman, "Birth Control, Religion, and the Unfit," *Nation*, 134 (January 27, 1932), 109; Gilman, "Birth Control," *The Forerunner*, 6 (July, 1915), 177–180.

[82] This discussion is limited to Charlotte's attitudes toward Houghton Gilman between 1897 and 1900 and is not intended as an interpretation of their marriage relationship from 1900 to 1934.

around you all the time!!!" She was delighted with his friendship: "You seem very near somehow—a background to most of my thinking when I'm not at work." Or again, "It's astonishing how many times a day I incline to write to you."[33] And write she did—twenty- or thirty-page letters, two or more times a week.

Nonetheless, expressions of increasing fondness for Houghton were interspersed with apologetic declarations of resistance:

> To most people . . . I can behave nicely. . . . But as soon as any one comes near me and takes hold, I wobble awfully. Now as you may have seen I am getting exceedingly fond of you. . . . And I don't like it. It makes me unreasonable. It makes me feel —where I don't want to feel; and think—where I don't want to think. It sort of wakes me up where I'm dead, or where, if I'm not dead I ought to be.
>
> Now I can't afford to be fond of anybody in that sort of way—man, woman, or child. I can't afford to want things . . . But [your] being here . . . and being, to your sorrow—my "entire family"—why it brings out all that is worst and weakest in me, instead of what is strongest and best. It makes me unreasonable—sensitive—disagreeable—absurd. It makes me want to be petted and cared for—me! And then all this makes me very mad; and I say "go to! I'll get out of this in short order!"[34]

Charlotte seemed to vacillate wildly between feelings of strength and insecurity. She was "rich in the tricks and shifts of an old campaigner weather-beaten and coarsened by long exposure." But also, she felt "bitterly depressed, often defeated, lonely, imprisoned, scared and wounded beyond recognition but not crippled past all usefulness. . . ." She seemed to need to ask for pity. She felt a "compelling desire . . . to complain and explain, to whimper . . . and seek for sympathy which don't do me any good if I get it." She extended her growing trust in Houghton with a "childish femininity":[35]

> I temporarily cuddle down and clutch you remorselessly. Later on I shall flop and wobble again. Later still soar off no doubt.

---

[33] Letter from Charlotte Stetson to Houghton Gilman, September 11, September 2, September 5, 1897.

[34] *Ibid.*, October 3, 1897.

[35] *Ibid.*, October 1, October 3, 1897; undated letter, October, 1897.

> But just for a little time—and with excellent reason that I can't help—behold me as it were a sleepy Newfoundland puppy in your overcoat pocket.[36]

Thus did a public advocate of woman's full equality privately reveal the anguish of her personal ambivalence. She wrote:

> I wish I could make a picture of the thing [herself] as I see it—sulky, frightened, discouraged, "rattled" to a degree; one foot forward and the other back; ready to rush forward in tumultuous devotion one minute, and run away shrieking the next—fingers in ears.[37]

However tentatively and indecisively, Charlotte began to break the barriers of her self-imposed lonely isolation. Insecurities sometimes re-emerged in the form of uncontrollable depressions, the "grey fog" she had faced since 1884. But increasingly she felt a passionate happy love for Houghton which, characteristically, she had to formulate in writing. She left, therefore, abundant documentation of her sensuous yearnings, as well as of her apprehensions:

> . . . I went to sleep with a smile on my lips and woke only to think again of the dear comfort that you are to me—of your unfailing loving kindness, your quiet strength, your patience and wisdom—and your tenderness. O it *does* feel so good! To have some one care for me enough to—well—to kiss me.[38]

She continued in December: "Everything is so different. I have a home now—in your heart." In February, 1898 she wrote: "Surely you can read it in my eyes—hear it in my voice, feel it in my arms about your neck—taste it on my lips that lean to you. You make me happy—so happy my darling. I love you—love you—love you!" And even more passionately for a supposedly "Victorian" lady, she wrote to him in May: "Sweetheart! You shall kiss me anywhere you want to and all you want to as soon as ever there is a chance. I will wait till you are exhausted and then begin operations on my own account." [39]

---

[36] *Ibid.*, November 4, 1897.

[37] *Ibid.*, November 7, 1897.

[38] *Ibid.*

[39] *Ibid.*, February 20, May 6, 1898. On a number of occasions Charlotte mentioned her desire to have a child with Houghton, but when she thought

Despite such passionate declarations, Charlotte also delighted in the image of herself as cared-for child: "And it will be the wholesomest thing in the world to . . . settle down to the definite and particular feeling of being your little girl." [40] Continuously she seemed to need protective reassurance; and when Houghton did not sufficiently comply, she responded angrily. So vulnerable did she feel, so intense was her level of hurt, that on one occasion in 1899, she threatened to break off the relationship entirely. She wrote: "When I think of what manner of letters I have written to you—of course I want to call them all back and burn them . . . and never think of love again lest I die of shame." [41] She insisted that Houghton be strong and more assertive, and that she, as woman, should wait more passively:

> If you don't love me more than to make dutiful responses to my advances it won't do to marry on . . .
>
> It is a woman's business to wait, not a man's.
>
> It is for a woman to be patient and still—not a man.
>
> If you are truly lover and husband—show it. If not—God bless you and good bye.[42]

Charlotte's outbursts were frequent but short-lived, her contests with self-hatred a recurring pattern of her life. She recovered from her anger, only to be tormented once again by uncontrollable anxiety. Back and

---

that she might be unable, she expressed delight: "Happy thought—take no precautions—take no treatment—all runs smoothly and nothing happens!!! There's an easy way out of the difficulty!!!" Sex without the fears of pregnancy seemed a grand relief. Letter from Charlotte Stetson to Houghton Gilman, May 16, 1900.

Carl Degler argues that many nineteenth-century women may not have been so fearful of or opposed to the sexual experience as was formerly assumed. Historians have too frequently relied on prescriptive data, he maintains, thus distorting the actual attitudes and experiences of women themselves. See Carl Degler, "What Ought to be and What Was: Women's Sexuality in the Nineteenth Century," *American Historical Review*, 79 (December, 1974), 1467–1490. See also Charles E. Rosenberg, "Sexuality, Class, and Role in Nineteenth Century America," *American Quarterly*, 25 (May, 1973), 131–153.

[40] Letter from Charlotte Stetson to Houghton Gilman, January 9, 1898. Also referring to a letter he had written, she responded, "This is the letter that says I'm your darling little girl, which remark I have kissed many times." *Ibid.*, November 14, 1899.

[41] *Ibid.*, January 22, 1899.

[42] *Ibid.*, January 25, 1899.

forth she went: "I don't wholly like to be held—and yet I do!" She wanted protective love, yet despised herself for needing it. "Makes me kind of angry too," she later wrote. "Seems a weakness. To be so tangled up in another person."[43] Torn between her feminist convictions and her feelings, she expressed discontent with what she thought she had become—a non-womanly woman:

> Don't you see dear how much at a disadvantage I am beside you? Try and feel like a woman for a moment—put yourself in their place. You know what a woman wants to bring a man —a boundless whole-souled love, absolutely and primarily his own—all his own.
>
> I haven't that . . . I can only give you a divided love—I love God—the world—my work as I love you. I have so little to offer—so pathetically little. . . .
>
> O my dear—do you not see what poignant grief and shame it is to a woman to have no woman's gifts to give![44]

Charlotte apologized for having achieved many of her goals: "I'm sorry," she wrote to Houghton, "that I can't add my life to yours—woman fashion . . . the usual style of immersion of the wife in the husband." Theoretically and practically she insisted on the right to satisfying work; emotionally she felt she should give it up to him. Come to my lectures, she had pleaded with Houghton in 1899. "Then you'd know—know me, know why I have felt as I do about marrying and all that. Why I so seriously fear lest the housekeeping part of it [marriage] should prove an injury to my health and a hindrance to my work." But hardly consistently for a radical feminist, she continued, "You see I am so afraid of my own long . . . instincts getting the better of me—and that, in my love for you and natural wish to make you comfortable I shall 'settle' too firmly."[45]

---

[43] *Ibid.*, June 2, November 6, 1898.

[44] *Ibid.*, November 14, 1899.

[45] *Ibid.*, March 14, 1900; February 28, 1899. On December 28, 1898 she wrote: "I quite envy those good women who really feel that the husband is their whole range of duty—it must be so sweet to have no call away from that dear love." In March she wrote, "Dear, it isn't fair! You ought to have a *whole* wife to give herself all to you." Although by November she more confidently asserted, "I want to carry out what I think is perfectly possible —a kind of married life that has both love and freedom. I see no need for the 'yoke.'" See letters, December 28, 1898; March 5, November 14, 1899.

Ambiguities expressed in Charlotte's letters to Houghton were also apparent in her public writings. An advocate of women's full equality, she inconsistently, ironically, contrasted masculine work-instincts with "feminine" instincts of nurturance and service, male adult-like strength and courage with female child-like insecurity and fear. Thus this "militant madonna" portrayed woman's "natural" yearning for a male's protective love.

If to a degree the "instincts" argument served to undermine Gilman's environmentalist analysis of the origins of sexual inequality, it also provided crucial leverage in her fight for female self-respect. Perhaps defensively, Gilman attempted to reverse traditionally-negative connotations of "femininity" by emphasizing the virtues of womanhood instead. Like most of her feminist contemporaries, proudly she proclaimed the primacy of womanhood: Woman's archetypal innocence was concomitant to her moral virtue; gentle kindness was a means of power, an antidote to assertive male combativeness. Woman's uniqueness was thus her strength and glory, her mother-love a countervailing force within the baneful androcentric culture.

The most explicit statement of Gilman's admiration and love for women was expressed in the novel *Herland* (1915). Utopia, she told her readers, was a land inhabited only by women and girl children, procreation occurring through parthenogenesis. Faithfully worshiping the "Goddess of mother love," and interacting cooperatively, respectfully, and affectionately, women demonstrated their capacity to build Utopia. Because they were not confined within the isolation of the private selfish home, women could use their nurturant capacities for social and community service. Trusting child care only to the "highest artists," they developed the *true* "womanly" virtues: "Beauty, Health, Strength, Intellect, Goodness. . . ." In *Herland*, the "essential distinction of motherhood was the dominant note of their whole culture." Motherhood was the "great, tender, limitless uplifting force." [46]

Theoretically as well as fictionally, Gilman asserted the natural superiority of the female sex. Enthusiastically endorsing the "scientifically based" Gynaecocentric Theory of the sociologist Lester Ward, she elaborated extensively on the civilizing capacities of women, the destructive combativeness of men. She wrote:

> The innate underlying difference [between the sexes] is one of principle. On the one hand, the principle of struggle, conflict,

---

[46] Gilman, *Herland*, in *The Forerunner*, 6 (May, 1915), 127–129; *Ibid.*, *Forerunner*, 6 (July, 1915), 186.

> and competition. . . . On the other, the principle of growth, of culture, of applying services and nourishment in order to produce improvement.[47]

Woman did not want to fight, to take, to oppress. Instead she exhibited "the growing altruism of work, founded in mother love, in the anti-selfish instinct of reproduction."[48] Fundamental to the evolutionary process was woman's inherent responsibility for the preservation of the race, the selection of a mate, and the nurturance of children.

CHARLOTTE GILMAN presents us with a paradox. Having developed a multi-dimensional feminist theory based on the idea of the natural equality of the sexes, having challenged patriarchal norms dividing males and females into their respective public-private spheres, she also enthusiastically maintained that women were the saintly givers, men the war-

---

[47] Gilman, *His Religion and Hers: A Study of the Faith of Our Fathers and the Work of Our Mothers* (New York: The Century Company, 1923), p. 271. Lester Ward projected a theory of sexual differentiation which he claimed proved "that in the economy of organic nature the female sex is the primary, and the male a secondary element." Clearly Darwinism could not be used as a justification for the subjection of the female sex, he argued, because in fact it was the female who was responsible for the preservation of the species. Since the first function of the male was simply to enable the female to reproduce, it was she who was the source of life and therefore of superior importance. Lester Ward, "Our Better Halves," *Forum*, 6 (November, 1888), 266. See also Lester Ward, *Dynamic Sociology* (New York: D. Appleton, 1883); Lester Ward, *Pure Sociology* (New York: Macmillan Co., 1903); Samuel Chugerman, *Lester F. Ward, The American Aristotle: A Summary and Interpretation of His Sociology* (Durham, NC: Duke University Press, 1939). Of Ward's Gynaecocentric Theory, Charlotte Gilman wrote, "nothing so important to humanity has been advanced since the Theory of Evolution, and nothing so important to women has ever been given to the world." Gilman, *The Man-Made World: Our Androcentric Culture* (New York: Charlton Company, 1911), Dedication.

Charlotte Gilman's support of the woman-as-superior argument, side by side with her environmentalist feminist position can also be interpreted as yet another manifestation of Social Darwinist and Lamarckian thought. Characteristically, turn-of-the-century thinkers blurred the distinction between inherited and acquired characteristics. Again, however, the emphasis of this paper is on the personal more than the philosophical roots of Charlotte Gilman's feminist paradox.

[48] Gilman, *Human Work* (New York: McClure, Phillips and Company, 1903), pp. 211, 207.

ring beasts. When she glorified female "instincts" of love and service, her radical theory of feminism dissolved into a sometimes sentimental worship of the status quo. Compromising her environmentalist analysis, she alternately emphasized not female powerlessness, but woman's natural passivity; not artificially-imposed dependence, but an innate desire to love and serve; not cowardice, but peacefulness and cooperation; not the oppressive restrictions of motherhood roles, but the glories of mother love. By proclaiming women's natural differences, Charlotte Gilman, like many of her contemporaries, "put to a test the entire ideology upon which arguments for the liberation of women had been based in the United States." [49]

Yet while claims to female nurturant superiority were ultimately dysfunctional, they were nonetheless, historically, a viable response to women's need for expanded decision-making power. A vital struggle for political autonomy lay beneath the mother-worship proclamations. Moreover, "the suffragists were not blushing Victorians but seasoned politicians who had learned how to beat the male at his own game." [50] Charlotte Gilman refused to treat women purely as the victims—incompetents within the world of men. Instead, she urged women to develop self-respect on their own terms, not those exclusively defined by men. Thus, when she emphasized woman's role as "the moral redeemer and culture bearer," she was acclaiming a philosophy which "actually permitted women to enhance their self-image as individuals and as a group and, ultimately to organize for action." [51] Whether tactically or ideologically, she seems to have understood that women might necessarily, if temporarily, expand their power by celebrating differences.

[49] Jill Conway, "The Woman's Peace Party and the First World War," *War and Society in North America*, edited by J. L. Granatstein and R. D. Cuff (Toronto: Thomas Nelson and Sons, 1971), p. 52. See also Jill Conway, "Women Reformers and American Culture, 1870–1930," *Journal of Social History*, 5 (Winter, 1971–72), 164–177; Susan Hartman, "The Paradox of Women's Progress: 1820–1920" (St. Charles, Missouri: Forum Press); Mary Ryan, *Womanhood in America* (New York: Franklin Watts, Inc., 1975), pp. 139–248.

[50] Mary Ryan, *Womanhood in America*, p. 246.

[51] Barbara Sicherman, "American History: Review Essay," *Signs*, 1, no. 2 (Winter, 1975), 470. Anthropologist Michell Zimbalist Rosaldo argues "that the very symbolic and social conceptions that appear to set women apart and to circumscribe their activities may be used by women as a basis for female solidarity and worth." Michelle Zimbalist Rosaldo, "Woman, Culture, and Society: A Theoretical Overview," in *Woman, Culture, and Society*, p. 39.

While Charlotte's dichotomous theories were in part an outgrowth of the intellectual and socio-economic forces of her era, my purpose here has been to illustrate instead some private sources for her feminist perspectives. The existence of contradiction in her theories, her fiction, and her living by no means lessens the significance of her historical contribution. Her theoretical analyses were themselves impressive, but so also was her constant testing of those theories in the experimental laboratory of her life. Since she kept voluminous accounts of her private struggles, she unintentionally preserved in the panorama of her eccentricity and genius, a wealth of historical data which will enrich our understanding of the underlying dynamics of feminist theory and practice at the turn of the century.

THE WOMEN'S TRADE UNION LEAGUE AND AMERICAN FEMINISM

Robin Miller Jacoby

The Women's Trade Union League provides an illuminating historical case study of the response of a certain group of women in the early twentieth century to the issues of feminism and class consciousness. As a mixed-class organization of women concerned about the problems of female workers during a period of an active male-dominated labor movement and a middle-class-dominated feminist movement, the WTUL was structurally in an extremely interesting position. As an organization it was not concerned with theoretical issues of feminism and class identity, but it did explicitly and consistently define itself as the women's branch of the labor movement and the industrial branch of the women's movement.

The League was founded in 1903 by a coalition of female trade unionists, settlement-house residents, and social reformers, and it remained in existence as a national organization with local branches in various cities in the East and Midwest until 1950, although its influence and activities declined significantly after the mid-1920s. The WTUL's membership consisted of female workers and "allies"—leisure-class women sympathetic to the general principles of the labor movement and to the special problems of female workers. The League's goals, which were carried out with varying degrees of success, were to improve the situation of female workers through organizing them into trade unions; lobbying for legislation controlling hours and work conditions; and educating female workers, trade-union men, and leisure-class women regarding the special problems of female workers and the value of organization and legislation on their behalf.

A comprehensive study of the League must take into account the various facets intrinsic to its dual identity as a women's labor organization.[1] There are four different aspects inherent in a thorough analysis of feminism in relation to the WTUL. One is the nature and content of WTUL members' views regarding the actual and potential roles of women. A second aspect concerns the extent to which the feminist ideal of sisterhood was achieved across class lines. A third aspect is to what extent feminist concerns were emphasized in the WTUL's relationship to the male labor movement; the fourth aspect concerns the nature of the League's relationship to feminist issues and organizations of the period.[2] This article will deal only with the fourth area—the WTUL in its self-defined role as the industrial branch of the women's movement—by examining the League's relationship to some of the issues and groups that comprised the American feminist movement in the first twenty years of the twentieth century.[3]

The primary phenomenon underlying the history of the WTUL and the feminist movement of the nineteenth and early twentieth centuries is the impact of industrialization on women. As Gerda Lerner has pointed out, the process of industrialization served to define more sharply class differences among women.[4] As production was physically separated from the home, the distinction between ladies of leisure and female workers became more pronounced. For women who entered the industrial labor force, the patterns that characterized their situation in the first part of the nineteenth century had not significantly altered by the early twentieth century. Female workers were predominantly young, single, unorganized, and clustered in the lowest paying, least skilled jobs. Cultural attitudes prescribing subordinate roles for women underlay and reinforced this constellation of economic conditions, and the combination of cultural and economic factors resulted in significant differences between the situation of women and men in the industrial labor force.

On the other hand, by increasing levels of wealth for the middle and upper classes and by removing so many productive functions from the home, industrialization brought women of these classes the possibility of a life of relative leisure. Intrinsically related to the economic changes of the first half of the nineteenth century was the codification of what has become known as the cult of true womanhood—the ideology that women belonged demurely and submissively in the home and that their primary function was to be the moral guardians of society through their maternal and wifely roles.[5] The development of the feminist movement and the working conditions faced by female workers are evidence that by the late nineteenth century industrialization had created an oppressive leisure life for many middle- and upper-class women and,an oppressive work life for most women in the industrial labor force. The membership and goals of the WTUL thus directly reflect the complex relationship between industrialization and the cult of true womanhood. In addition, the existence and activities of the League were part of the feminist attack on economic and cultural patterns that prescribed extremely restricted roles for women in the work force and in the home. Increasing awareness throughout the nineteenth century of the problematic consequences of industrialization led to a proliferation of reform organizations developing toward the end of the century. Middle-class women drawn to the WTUL shared the mentality of the rest of the progressive movement in many ways, and they tended to have been previously involved in other reform activities that had developed their awareness of the problems of female workers. Working-class women were interested in the League because it was the only organization in existence whose priority was reforming the working conditions of women in the industrial labor force and because it was also the only organization committed in principle to including female workers in this task.

Even though the members of the WTUL were not particularly interested in feminism and class consciousness per se, these concepts provide a useful and important analytic framework for discussing the League. Feminism and class consciousness are obviously complex notions in themselves, and very little serious theoretical attention has been paid to the relationship between them.[6] Feminism simultaneously complements and conflicts with the ideology of the primacy of class identity. It is complementary in that it implies equal rights and opportunities for women within sexually mixed, class-based settings such as labor unions; it is conflicting in that it also implies that gender identification creates solidarities transcending class divisions. Applying this general framework to the specific case of the WTUL and American feminism, it will be seen that for middle-class feminists outside the WTUL, class identity outweighed their rhetorical commitment to the ideal of cross-class female solidarity.

During the period under discussion, feminists based their actions on two somewhat contradictory premises: that women should have the same political, legal, educational, and economic rights as men; and that due to women's reproductive and maternal roles, they were physically, psychologically, and intellectually different from men in certain fundamental ways. Feminists held that the assumptions underlying these premises—that all women were oppressed and that all women were potential or actual mothers—created a bond of sisterhood between all women that theoretically transcended class, racial, and national differences.

It was precisely these assumptions that were behind the formation and subsequent history of the WTUL and that provided the rationale for its mixed-class membership. League members recognized that sexual inequalities were prevalent in the structure of the industrial labor force. Without fully analyzing the implications of the situation, League members also realized that a contributing factor to the condition of female workers was women's expectation, shared by their employers and male coworkers, that they were only temporary members of the labor force. In other words, most female workers regarded themselves as women first and as workers second; they expected to marry and become full-time housewives, and their identification with the personal, domestic sphere of life was one of several factors that impeded their serious, long-term commitment to the labor movement.[7] The relationship of female workers to the labor movement involves a complex set of factors that are more fully discussed in the accompanying articles by Alice Kessler-Harris and Nancy Schrom Dye. I mention this relationship merely to indicate that one of the reasons female workers were drawn into the feminist movement in this period was that they felt alienated from the labor movement and felt that the feminist movement, especially the suffrage movement, might be effective in helping them to improve their working conditions.

The struggle for suffrage was only one aspect of the feminist movement, but in 1903, when the WTUL was established, it was the dominant thrust of American feminism. Differences among the first generation of suffragists over whether the Fourteenth Amendment should be supported if it did not extend the franchise to women as well as to newly freed black men led to the establishment of two rival suffrage organizations in 1869—the National Woman Suffrage Association, which Eleanor Flexner has characterized as "aggressive and unorthodox," and the more socially and politically decorous American Woman Suffrage Association.[8] By the late 1880s changes in the social climate of the United States, changes in the attitudes of the leaders of the National Woman Suffrage Association, and the emergence of a new generation of suffrage leaders, who were, as Flexner gently describes them, "not, for the most part, distinguished by the breadth of their social views," led to the realization that significant differences no longer divided the two organizations.[9] The result was their merger in 1890 to become the National American Woman Suffrage Association. One indication of NAWSA's social composition is found in the composite biographical profile of leading suffragists compiled by Aileen Kraditor in an appendix to her important book, *The Ideas of the Woman Suffrage Movement, 1890-1920*.[10] Her analysis of twenty-six major figures associated with the movement reveals that they were all white, middle or upper class, Anglo-Saxon Protestants, except for one Irish Catholic, and were all considerably better educated than the average American woman of this period.

When the suffrage movement began in the 1850s, its primary argument was that women should have the vote on the grounds of natural rights. However, by 1890 the rhetoric of the movement had shifted to emphasize what Kraditor has termed arguments of expediency.[11] Sharing and capitalizing on prevailing racist and nativist prejudices, suffrage speeches and publications claimed that being excluded from a political right that was extended to black, immigrant, and working-class men was an insult to native-born, white middle-class women, and a danger to the nation at large. One example of this conviction was the following resolution, which was adopted unanimously at the 1893 NAWSA convention:

> We call attention to the significant facts that in every State there are more women who can read and write than the whole number of illiterate male voters; more white women who can read and write than all negro voters; more American women who can read and write than all foreign voters; so that the enfranchisement of such women would settle the vexed question of rule by illiteracy, whether of the home-grown or foreign-born production.[12]

Belle Kearney, a Southern suffragist, added a note of explicit racism in her address to the 1903 NAWSA convention. Reiterating the statistical argument on the proportion of white, native-born women to the rest of the population, she told the convention delegates, "The enfranchisement of women would insure immediate and durable white supremacy. . . . The South is slow to grasp the great fact that the enfranchisement of women would settle the race question in politics."[13]

While these attitudes never totally disappeared from the suffrage movement, by the early twentieth century other, more sympathetic views began to be expressed toward working-class people and immigrants, and there were various attempts on the part of suffrage groups to reach out to these segments of the population. (The same was not true regarding blacks; in order not to antagonize Southern congressmen and suffrage supporters, black women were consistently discouraged from participating in the suffrage movement.) This shift was partly due to the realization on the part of the suffragists that whether they liked it or not, these groups of men did have the vote, and it made more sense to have them as allies than as enemies of the women's cause. As Florence Kelley, head of the National Consumer's League, an organization dedicated to improving working conditions of women and children through the use of the boycott, told the 1906 NAWSA convention:

> I have rarely head a ringing suffrage speech which did not refer to the "ignorant and degraded" men, or the "ignorant immigrants" as our masters. This is habitually spoken with more or less bitterness. But this is what the workingmen are used to hear applied to themselves by their enemies in times of strike.

Rather we should recognize that, while for the moment they have power which we need, they have the same interest in the rising generation of citizens, so largely the children of working people.[14]

Another factor in the development of this perspective was the influence of social feminists such as Jane Addams and Florence Kelley, but even more significantly, the influence of Margaret Dreier Robins, the wealthy president of the WTUL, and other middle- and working-class members of the League. These women acted as liaisons between the women's movement and the working class, and their speeches, writings, and commitment to suffrage stressed the problems of female workers and their special needs for the vote.

One example of this broader outlook on the part of suffragists was the invitation in 1910 to Agnes Nestor, a glove worker from an Irish immigrant family and an active member of the Chicago WTUL, to join the delegation traveling on the Suffrage Special, a train headed for Springfield for a special suffrage session of the Illinois legislature. The train was scheduled to stop at various towns along the way so that the suffragists could speak to local groups, and Nestor was asked to be the main speaker in Joliet, an industrial town, where the suffragists expected the audience to be predominantly working class.

This broader perspective was even more clearly expressed in the constitution of the Illinois State Woman Suffrage Party, which was formed in 1911. According to Mary Gray Peck, a close associate of Carrie Chapman Catt:

The beginning of the Woman Suffrage Party of Illinois differs from that of any of the preceding organs. So, naturally and unobtrusively, a new intention in the struggle for suffrage was officially enunciated. It is true that from the first the N.Y. Party backed several measures looking to the betterment of women's working conditions, and in the platform adopted at the second convention formally endorsed them. But the Illinois Party was the first to link suffrage with women's industrial betterment in the keystone of its constitution. The older suffragists were a unit in fighting shy of "entangling alliances." The new generation boldly assume suffrage as a means to an end, valuable only as related to that end in the mind of every suffragist.[15]

Her view of the importance of this action was shared by the Political Equality Union of Chicago, an association of wage-earning women, who immediately endorsed the Illinois Woman Suffrage Party and applauded it for having the broadest platform of any major suffrage organization.[16]

In 1912 Rose Schneiderman, a Russian Jewish immigrant who had worked as a cap maker and then as an organizer for the New York WTUL, was hired by NAWSA to work as a temporary suffrage organizer in the Ohio campaign. Recognizing that her political views were not representative of most suffrage workers and not wanting to take the job under false pretenses, Schneiderman was straightforward in her interview with Anna Howard Shaw, telling Shaw that she was "a socialist and a trade unionist who looked upon the ballot as a tool in the hands of working women with which, through legislation, they could correct the terrible conditions existing in industry."[17] Delighted that she was given the job, since it came at a lull in her labor organizing work among female underwear makers in New York, the main theme of her suffrage speeches was that she did not expect any revolution when women got the ballot, but that it was imperative nonetheless that women be enfranchised because they needed protection through laws, and without the vote, lawmakers had no reason to pay serious attention to women.[18] Although other suffrage speakers predicted more fundamental social changes as a result of women being given the vote, Schneiderman's view on the legislative needs of women, especially working women, was shared by many middle-class suffragists.

In response to a letter from Schneiderman describing her work in Ohio, her close friend and sister WTUL member, Pauline Newman wrote:

> I knew that you would make good on the road. For the "cultured" ladies may be very sincere in their desire for the ballot, I don't doubt their sincerity, but because their views are narrow, and their knowledge of social conditions limited, they cannot do as well as some of us can. And as I come in contact with these women day after day, they are beginning to see the necessity of having a working girl tour a State rather than some professor.[19]

As Newman's letter indicates, suffragists were increasingly aware that while they may have supported the arguments Schneiderman was using in her speeches, she was better able than they to communicate effectively the special needs of working women to be enfranchised.

As far as Margaret Dreier Robins was concerned, the Ohio suffrage campaign was an example of NAWSA doing too little too late regarding the labor vote. It also indicated to her the necessity to expand the number of WTUL local leagues. Shortly after the Ohio vote, Robins wrote to Leonora O'Reilly, who had a long history of labor movement activity on behalf of women and was one of the most active working class suffragists in the WTUL:

> . . . the big break in Ohio in the suffrage fight was the fact that there was no converted working women's movement for suffrage. The few women unionists in the state had no way of expressing themselves collectively for the ballot, and had no way of protesting collectively against the action of the Cincinnati and Dayton Federations of Labor, which refused to endorse women's suffrage. It is such situations which make me realize how really important our League's Union Federations may be, and I was really distressed at the voicelessness of our working sisters in Ohio.[20]

Two years later, thinking back to that Ohio campaign in another letter to Leonora O'Reilly, Robins wrote, "You know one of the biggest reasons for the defeat of suffrage in Ohio was the inability of the suffragists to reach the mass of the working men. Rōschen, our Rōschen, was practically the only trade unionists they had. . . ."[21]

By 1915 the views of Ohio suffragists had been broadened to the extent that the Ohio Woman Suffrage Association issued a formal statement declaring its belief in the economic independence of women and affirming "the right of all wage-earning women to organize for the purpose of protecting their industrial interests."[22] The statement went on to deplore "the fact that the wage earning women of Ohio are not organized to the same degree as the wage earning men" and to express the support of the Woman Suffrage Association for "any movement looking towards such organization."[23] The statement also demanded "equal pay for equal work regardless of sex" and "the right of women to work in all trades and at all professions limited by no bound but that of their own capacity."[24]

By 1919 there was considerable interest in the situation of female workers. Clara Hyde, Carrie Chapman Catt's personal secretary, wrote to another leading suffragist regarding the NAWSA convention of that year, "The convention was a tremendous success. . . . The Industrial program under Mrs. Raymond Robins was the most satisfactory number of the whole convention, and to my mind the most popular."[25] Hyde went on to say that the presentations in this section of the convention program "roused a sponteneous demand for the printing in pamphlet form of their speeches. They are the only ones in the convention to whom this happened–which shows quite clearly how popular interest is centering on industrial and economic questions."[26]

Some of this interest represented a genuine broadening of the views of middle-class suffragists, but there is evidence that it also stemmed from pragmatic considerations of self-interest on the part of NAWSA leaders. Florence Kelley's remarks to the 1906 NAWSA convention (quoted earlier) on the need to conciliate working-class men, in part because they had the political power suffragists needed, is one indication of this double-edged basis to the shift on the part of suffragists. A letter in the NAWSA papers reveals that the offer of a NAWSA vice-presidency to Margaret Dreier Robins in 1917 was in fact "a bait for the labor vote."[27] (Robins declined, claiming her time was fully occupied with WTUL work.) An indication of how much this shift was based on tactical considerations rather than genuine changes in social attitudes comes from another private letter in the NAWSA papers where Carrie Chapman Catt revealed some of her feelings about workers and immigrants:

> I am a *good* democrat in theory but my faith weakens when it meets bad air, dirt . . . and horrid smells. I rather enjoy onions for instance when the odor pervades a clean home and is diluted with good air. To my nostrils it becomes a real aristocratic perfume, but when it is a democratic odor diluted with perfumes of beer and uncleanliness, the blood of my royal ancestors boils in protest. Of course I do not know positively that I had any royal ancestors, but if I had not why this shrinking from my fellow beings because of smells?[28]

Fully aware of the class bias of the suffrage movement, the WTUL nonetheless gave its whole-hearted support to the principle of women's suffrage and worked for it actively both in its own organization and in coalition with NAWSA groups. The consistent theme of WTUL suffrage activities directed at female workers and trade-union men was to stress that women's suffrage was relevant to their struggles for better working and living conditions. When dealing with NAWSA members and groups, the WTUL emphasized the special problems of female workers and their particular need for the vote; in addition, WTUL members urged that NAWSA organizations and publications broaden the scope and content of their activities and rhetoric to incorporate the views and participation of female workers.

The early leaders and members of the WTUL seem to have come to the League already committed to the principle of women's suffrage. The WTUL's earliest publications included news of the suffrage movement, and its first national convention in 1907 included "full citizenship for women" as one plank of its six-point platform. (The others were "equal pay for equal work, the organization of all workers into trade unions, the eight-hour day, a minimum wage scale, and all the principles embodied in the economic program of the American Federation of Labor.")[29] By 1908 a suffrage department had been established within the League, and work for suffrage was a significant aspect of WTUL activities until 1920. Although the suffrage movement had existed for half a century prior to the establishment of the WTUL, it was not until the early twentieth century that any kind of sustained interaction developed between working-class women and middle-class suffragists. There were never significant numbers of working-class activitists in the suffrage movement, but those who were tended to come from the WTUL. The reason for this is that the WTUL provided one of the few structures in which women's suffrage was discussed in the context of the needs and problems of female workers.

Some of the examples and incidents already mentioned indicate the basic thrust of WTUL arguments for suffrage. League members consistently put forward the view that while all women deserved the vote on the basis of equal justice, female workers especially needed it for the power it would give them in exerting some degree of control over their miserable working conditions. WTUL members never saw the vote as a total solution to the problems of working women, but they did feel that the legislative process was a crucial vehicle for ameliorating working conditions and that without the vote, female workers were severely hampered in their attempts to get legislation they favored passed at the state or federal level. A typical expression of this point of view is found in a speech given by Rose Schneidermen at a mass meeting in Cooper Union organized by the New York Wage Earners' Suffrage League in 1912. Replying to a recent public statement by an antisuffrage New York legislator, Schneiderman told the assembled crowd:

> I did some lobbying work last year for the 54-hour bill, and I can tell you how courteous our Senators and Assemblymen are when a disenfranchised citizen tries to convince them of the necessity of shorter hours for working women. . . .
>
> During the hearing at Albany our learned Senators listened to the opposition very carefully; . . . But when the Committee, who spoke for the working women came to plead for the bill, there was only one Senator left in the room—he was the chairman—he couldn't very well get out; . . . Mind you, we were pleading for a shorter work week for working women. We had evidence to show that physical exhaustion leads to moral exhaustion, and the physical and moral exhaustion of women will lead to the deterioration of the human species. What did these men care. We were voteless working women—no matter what we felt or thought we could not come back at them.[30]

The WTUL linked itself to NAWSA in many ways: from 1909 on there was an exchange of delegates between the two organizations to their national conventions; the WTUL encouraged and organized the participation of working women in NAWSA-sponsored rallies and parades; and *Life and Labor*, the WTUL's monthly journal, gave considerable publicity to NAWSA activities. But the WTUL also realized that working within NAWSA groups was not always easy or comfortable for working women. To meet this problem, the WTUL encouraged the formation of independent wage earner suffrage leagues as a way of bringing female workers into active involvement in the suffrage movement.

The first such league was formed in San Francisco in 1908 or 1909, and its establishment was the direct result of class conflict between working-class and middle-class suffragists in that city. The San Francisco délegate to the 1909 WTUL convention reported that the mixed-class suffrage organization in that city had fallen apart because the middle-class women had refused to support a strike of streetcar conductors. They had regarded the strike as ill-timed and as a personal inconvenience, and in discussions with the working-class suffragists had displayed no sympathy for or understanding of the labor cause. On the basis of this incident, the working-class women decided they could no longer work in the same group with the middle-class women, and they withdrew to form their own suffrage organization.[31]

Another example of this kind of class tension was expressed in a letter from Maggie Hinchey, a laundry worker, to Leonora O'Reilly. While attending a NAWSA conference in New York, Hinchey wrote:

> I feel as if I have butted in wher I was not wanted. Miss Hay gave me a badge was very nice to me but you know they had a school teacher represent the Industrial workers if you ever herd her it was like trying to fill a barrell with water that had not bottom not a word of labor spoken at this convention so far . . . I am not goying to wait for sunday meeting I am goying home satturday.[32]

Like the San Francisco women, Hinchey was not lost to the suffrage cause despite her experience, but rather shifted the focus of her work to the Industrial Section of the New York Suffrage Party, which was organized in 1914 and led by WTUL members.

An earlier and totally independent working-class suffrage organization in which WTUL members were involved was the New York Wage Earners' Suffrage League, which was founded in 1911 by Leonora O'Reilly. O'Reilly was the president of this group, and Clara Lemlich, known for her role in precipitating the 1909 shirtwaist strike, was its vice-president. The membership was confined to wage-earning women "to preserve harmony of purpose and propaganda and admit of greatest possible freedom of discussion at meetings."[33] O'Reilly was a very committed feminist, and she felt the WTUL had a crucial role to play in broadening the base and scope of the women's movement. Writing to Margaret Derier Robins in 1912, she said, "From my point of view, we have to build a woman's movement in this land on a Labor Foundation and ours are the only people who have had any training for this work."[34] Justifying her determination that the New York Wage Earners' Suffrage League be controlled entirely by working women, O'Reilly told Robins, "Really and truly the other women with the best intentions in the world rub the fur the wrong way, they really don't speak our language and so they use the w.w. [working women] and then throw them over."[35] Another passage in the same letter indicates how effective the activities of such working-class suffrage groups could be in winning support for women's suffrage among the working class. O'Reilly told Robins of the enormous amount of work the Wage Earners' Suffrage League had put into producing a vaudeville show with a suffrage theme for a working-class audience and how pleased she was to hear a murmur run through the theater at the end that she interpreted as indicating the collective sentiment of "Gee I never thought of Votes for Women as meaning anything like that before."[36]

In addition to organizing female workers into wage-earner suffrage leagues, the WTUL put considerable energy into working with trade-union men to gain their active support for the suffrage cause. National conventions of the WTUL passed resolutions directed at labor men in states where suffrage referenda were pending, and members of of local leagues visited union locals and state labor federation conventions to present their case. Through the Industrial Section of the New York State Suffrage Party, WTUL members wrote letters to labor papers, traveled throughout the state visiting union meetings, and made street speeches in industrial areas. One of the most effective workers in this arena was Maggie Hinchey, who according to a *New York Times* account, had her male audiences alternately shaking with laughter and moved to tears.[37] The Industrial Section also prepared a series of sixteen letters addressed to labor men explaining why wage-earning women and working-class housewives wanted and needed the vote.[38] According to Mary Dreier, chairperson of the Industrial Section, over two million copies were distributed throughout the state. She also noted that voting returns showed that labor areas played a key role in the 1917 suffrage victory in New York State.[39]

This examination of the relationship between the WTUL and the suffrage movement reveals two general tendencies. The first is that there was a broadening of the rhetoric and constituency of the suffrage movement in the last fifteen years of its existence, and I would contend that that achievement was directly due to the work and influence of the WTUL. However, it can also be seen that while the suffrage movement involved both middle-class and working-class women striving for a common goal, the evidence of social and political tensions, generated primarily by the class biases of the middle-class suffragists, indicates that it was at best a tenuous alliance. Thus, despite the increased commitment to suffrage on the part of working-class women in the early twentieth century, it cannot be said that the last phase of the woman suffrage movement represents an instance of the genuine achievement of sisterhood on a cross-class basis.

In addition to its work for suffrage, the WTUL directed a considerable amount of its energy toward public relations work with other women's groups. This work was done through letters, speeches, and the exchange of convention delegates with a variety of middle-class women's organizations. The aim of this activity was to educate middle-class women and to gain their support and sympathy for the struggles of working women. The WTUL discovered, however, that sensitivity and commitment to working-class women was even harder to achieve when a common goal such as suffrage was not present.

One of the first activities of the Chicago WTUL, established in 1904, was to take up the cause of a group of striking corset workers in Aurora, Illinois. After talking with the workers involved, the Chicago WTUL sent out letters to every women's club in Illinois telling them of the conditions under which these women worked, explaining their strike demands, and asking the club women to boycott the products of the Kabo Corset Company until the strike was settled. The company's attorney threatened the League with a suit for the boycott letters, and this was called to the attention of the delegates to an Illinois State Federation of Women's Clubs convention by Anna Nichols, a club woman and "ally" member of the Chicago League. Her action generated so much publicity that the company dropped its threat to sue. WTUL records do not indicate whether the boycott was effective, but there was enough interest in the League and sympathy for its work that the following convention of the Illinois State Federation of Women's Clubs voted to amend its constitution to allow an organization such as the WTUL to affiliate. However, as Agnes Nestor noted in her autobiography, not all the clubwomen supported this move, and one was overheard saying, "Isn't it dreadful! I suppose next year we'll have those corset workers here as members!"[40]

Another early activity of the Boston and New York Leagues was to send out circulars to women's clubs in Massachusetts and New York listing WTUL members and sympathizers who were prepared to speak to women's clubs on various topics related to women in industry. Some of the speakers and topics were Margaret Dreier on "The Objects of the Women's Trade Union League," Leonora O'Reilly on "The Song of the Shirt," Virginia Dock on "The Settlement and the Working Woman," Rose Schneiderman on "Why We Believe in Trade Unions," Mary Kenney O'Sullivan on "Women in Trade Unions," and Mabel Gillespie on "Club Women and Trade Union Women"[41] However, some of the working-class members of the WTUL who accepted invitations to speak to women's clubs encountered elitist reactions to their appearances before such groups.

Pushed by Mary McDowell, a settlement resident, WTUL ally, and chairperson of the Industrial Program Committee for the 1905 convention of the Illinois State Federation of Women's Clubs, the State Federation invited Agnes Nestor to speak to its 1905 convention. Nestor wrote in her autobiography that "it was a bold step" for the the clubwomen to consent to having a working woman speak to them on trade unionism and that she was anxious to present her case effectively. Wanting to look her best in the company of these women, she had a lovely silk blouse made for the occasion and described herself as looking as "gay as a butterfly." After the event, she was pleased to have her speech described as "stirring and informative," but terribly disappointed by a newspaper reference to her "dark and shabby appearance."[42] A sequel to this story is that Rheta Childe Dorr, a League ally and an active member of the General Federation of Women's Clubs, arranged for Agnes Nestor to speak the following year before the national convention of the GFWC. Nestor spoke of her experiences as a glove worker and a trade unionist and of working women's need for support in their legislative fight for an eight-hour day. After her talk, a clubwoman came up to Nestor, felt the material of her blouse—the same blouse she had worn to the Illinois meeting the year before—and said, "You're not a real working girl. Look at the good blouse you are wearing!"[43] Nestor was amused by the incident and wrote: "At least this time I had the satisfaction that the blouse was recognized for what it was. . . ."[44] These two incidents reveal how class-biased stereotypes influenced the response of middle-class women to the situation of female workers.

Probably the best known instance of the WTUL generating a constructive and positive response from leisured women was the supportive activities of what Rose Schneiderman called "The Mink Brigade" during the 1909-1910 strike of female garment workers in New York.[45] Prominent women such as Mrs. O. H. P. Belmont and Mrs. Henry Morgenthau staged fund-raising benefits and served as observers of police treatment of picketing strikers. Their involvement generated extensive publicity for the strike. However, as Theresa Malkiel, one of the strikers and a socialist, pointed out, the financial contributions of these women, while significant, were not as great as they could have been. In reference to the well-known Hippodrome rally sponsored by Mrs. Belmont, Malkiel wrote in her diary:

> Most of our girls had to walk both ways in order to save their car fare. Many came without dinner, but the collection baskets had more pennies than anything else in them—it was our girls themselves who helped to make it up, and yet there were so many rich women present. And I'm sure the speakers made it plain to them how badly the money was needed, then how comes it that out of the $300 collected there should be $70 in pennies?[46]

As part of the fund-raising effort during that strike, female strikers traveled throughout New York and New England to speak to local women's groups and ask for their support. A considerable amount of money was raised in this way, but the strikers did not uniformly meet with supportive responses in the towns they visited. Margaret Dreier Robins recalled one such instance in a letter on the relationship between the WTUL and the YWCA:

> One of our very fine young working women, a leader of one of the strikes in New York City, an English-American girl, was not permitted to stay overnight in the YWCA House in a small town in New York state because her name was so well known and the Matron said they would not accomodate any strikers. It was ten o'clock at night when this girl came in good faith to the YWCA for a night's lodging. This and some similar experiences naturally embittered the Trade Union girls against the YWCA. . . .[47]

Life and Labor acknowledged the significant help of the Woman Suffrage Party of Illinois during the 1911 Chicago garment workers' strike when it collected and contributed over $700 to the strike fund.[48] On the other hand, the experience with suffragists supporting the garment strike in Cleveland that same year was not so positive. Pauline Newman and Margaret Dreier Robins had arranged a mass meeting to publicize and explain the strike, and among the speakers were two prominent suffragists, both of whom were relatively wealthy women. The latter made stirring speeches in support of the striking workers, but then sent in bills to the League for a total of $40 for their services as speakers at the meeting. They also showed no further interest in the strike after their one appearance.[49] The energy expended by the WTUL in attempting to develop awareness of the problems of female workers among middle-class women and in soliciting their support for specific strikes thus met with limited success. The extent of generosity, sensitivity, and sustained commitment the WTUL was able to elicit from middle-class feminists was consistently disappointing to WTUL members who believed in the feminist ideal of cross-class sisterhood.

Although material on the relationship of the WTUL to the feminist movement tends to be impressionistic rather than quantifiable, the incidents and activities discussed here are representative evidence concerning the League's role as the industrial branch of the women's movement. The WTUL identified itself with the women's movement for two major reasons. One was that many of the leisure-class members of the League had social and cultural ties to the organizations (such as NAWSA and the General Federation of Women's Clubs) that comprised the women's movement, and these links greatly facilitated contacts between the League and other, more middle-class oriented, women's organizations of the period. Secondly, since the labor movement tended to be only superficially interested in the plight of female workers, the WTUL put increasing emphasis on legislative lobbying as a means of achieving its goals of improved working conditions for women. This shift in emphasis from organizing women into trade unions to legislative and educational activities was a further reason for League members to work for suffrage and seek support from leisure-class women. However, a study of the WTUL and American feminism in the years 1903 to 1920 reveals that while middle-class feminists were increasingly interested in allying with the WTUL over issues of common concern, they were not very active, sensitive, or supportive in joining female workers, as represented by the WTUL, in their struggles for better working conditions. Ironically, it was the middle-class feminists whose conscious and unconscious sense of class precluded the possibility of cross-class feminist solidarity. As a result, the WTUL did considerably more for the women's movement than the women's movement did for the WTUL and the cause of female workers.

NOTES

I would like to thank Eileen Epstein, Margaret Lourie, Elizabeth Pleck, and Marilyn Young for their help in the preparation of this paper.

[1]For a more comprehensive account of the WTUL, see Nancy Schrom Dye, "The Women's Trade Union League of New York, 1903-1920" (Ph.D. dissertation, University of Wisconsin, 1974), and my work in progress, "A Case Study of Feminism and Class Consciousness: The British and American Women's Trade Union Leagues, 1890-1925" (Ph.D. dissertation, Harvard University, expected completion date: June 1976.

[2]For discussion of some of these issues in relation to the New York League, see Dye, "The Women's Trade Union League," and Dye, "Creating a Feminist Alliance: Sisterhood and Class Conflict in the New York Women's Trade Union League," *Feminist Studies* 2, no. 2/3 (1975): 24-38

[3]1920 is an arbitrary cut-off date; it does not represent the end of the organized women's movement or of the WTUL. During the 1920s the League was primarily involved in legislative work, and it put considerable energy into mobilizing other women's groups to fight against the equal rights amendment advocated by the National Woman's Party. (The League was against the amendment because it felt it would cancel gains made in the legislative area that improved working conditions for women. The League attacked the Woman's Party for being selfish and elitist in not realizing or caring that the legislation it advocated would hurt many more women than it helped.)

[4]Gerda Lerner, "The Lady and the Mill Girl: Changes in the Status of Women in the Age of Jackson," *Mid-Continent American Studies Journal* 10 (Spring 1969): 5-15.

[5]See Barbara Welter, "The Cult of True Womanhood: 1820-1860," *American Quarterly* 18 (Summer 1966): 151-74.

[6]The classic nineteenth-century works on this subject are August Bebel, *Woman Under Socialism* trans., Daniel DeLeon (New York: Schocken Books, 1971) and Frederick Engels, *The Origin of the Family, Private Property, and the State* (London: Lawrence and Wishart, Ltd., 1940). The most important contemporary discussions are Juliet Mitchell, *Woman's Estate* (London: Penguin Books, 1971) and Sheila Rowbotham, *Women, Resistance and Revolution: A History of Women and Revo-*

lution in the Modern World (New York: Pantheon Books, 1972).

[7]The success of the British WTUL in organizing female workers suggests that the structure and attitudes of the American Federation of Labor, as contrasted with the Trades Union Congress, may have been the most decisive factor in the problems of getting American women organized and of sustaining their membership and participation in the labor movement.

[8]See Eleanor Flexner, *Century of Struggle* (New York: Atheneum, 1972), pp. 141-55, for further discussion of this split in the early suffrage movement.

[9]Ibid., p. 219. (See pp. 215-25 for a more comprehensive account of the reunification.)

[10]Aileen Kraditor, *The Ideas of the Woman Suffrage Movement, 1890-1920* (New York: Anchor Books, 1971).

[11]See ibid., and Aileen Kraditor, ed., *Up From the Pedestal: Sleected Writings in the History of American Feminism* (Chicago: Quadrangle Books, 1968).

[12]"Revolutions Adopted at a Convention," ibid., p. 260.

[13]Kraditor, "Belle Kearney, The South and Woman Suffrage," ibid., p. 264.

[14]Kraditor, *Ideas*, p. 115.

[15]This comment was made in a note by Mary Gray Peck on the back of a letter to her from Myra Straun Hartstrom, February 7, 1911, NAWSA papers, box 24, file Mary Gray Peck, Library of Congress.

[16]"Votes for Women," *Life and Labor* 2 (February 1911): 62.

[17]Rose Schneiderman, *All for One* (New York: Paul S. Eriksson, 1967), p. 121.

[18]Ibid., pp. 121-22.

[19]Pauline Newman to Rose Schneiderman, July 26, 1912, Schneiderman papers, Tamiment Library, New York University.

[20]Margaret Dreier Robins to Leonora O'Reilly, September 14, 1912, O'Reilly papers, box 6, folder 51, Schlesinger Library.

[21]Robins to O'Reilly, July 19, 1914, O'Reilly papers, box 6, folder 55.

[22]"Votes for Women," *Life and Labor* 5 (May 1915): 94.

[23]Ibid.

[24]Ibid.

[25]Clara Hyde to Mary Gray Peck, April 13, 1919, NAWSA papers, box 24, folder Mary Gray Peck.

[26]Ibid.

[27]Hyde to Peck, September 26, 1917, NAWSA papers, box 24, folder Mary Gray Peck.

[28]Carrie Chapman Catt to "Frances and Pan," October 15, 1910, Catt papers, box 7, folder Mary Gray Peck 1909-1910, Library of Congress.

[29]See "The Woman's Department," the WTUL's section in the *Union Labor Advocate*, 1904-1910 and notes from the 1907 WTUL convention in NWTUL papers, box 1, vol. 1, Library of Congress.

[30]Wage Earners' Suffrage League, New York, "Senators vs. Working Women: Miss Rose Schneiderman Replies to New York Senator," O'Reilly papers, box 6, folder 51.

[31]National American Women's Trade Union League, "Proceedings of the 1909 Convention," pp. 26-27, NWTUL papers, Library of Congress.

[32]Margaret Hinchey to Leonora O'Reilly, 1913(?), O'Reilly papers, box 6, folder 52.

[33]"The Woman Voter," *Life and Labor* 2 (November 1912): 344.

[34]O'Reilly to Robins, September 23, 1912, Robins papers, University of Florida.

[35]Ibid.

[36]Ibid.

[37]*The New York Times*, May 5, 1915, p. 6.

[38]A set of these letters is in the Schneiderman papers.

[39]Mary E. Dreier, "Building the Suffrage Victory," *Life and Labor* 7 (December 1917): 186.

[40]Agnes Nestor, *Woman's Labor Leader: An Autobiography* (Rockford, Illinois: Bellevue Books

Publishing Co., 1954), p. 66. See ibid., p. 65; "Minutes of the First National Executive Board Meeting," March 20, 1904, NWTUL papers, box 25, folder NWTUL Historical Data, Library of Congress; and Alice Henry, *Women and the Labor Movement* (New York: George H. Doran Co., 1923), p. 119 for accounts of this incident.

41"Club Programs of 1905-1906," NWTUL papers, box 1, vol. 1, Library of Congress.

42See Nestor, *Women's Labor Leader*, pp. 66-68, for a more complete account of this incident.

43Ibid., p. 74.

44Ibid.

45Schneiderman, *All for One*, p. 8.

46Theresa Malkiel, *The Diary of a Shirtwaist Striker* (New York: The Co-operative Press, 1910), pp. 40-41.

47Carbon of a letter from Margaret Dreier Robins to a Mr. Roberts, April 3, 1925, Robins papers.

48"Votes for Women," *Life and Labor* 1 (February 1911): 62.

49Pauline Newman to Margaret Dreier Robins, August 5, 1911, Robins papers.

CREATING A FEMINIST ALLIANCE: SISTERHOOD AND CLASS CONFLICT IN THE NEW YORK WOMEN'S TRADE UNION LEAGUE, 1903-1914

Nancy Schrom Dye

A "small band of enthusiasts who believed that the nonindustrial person could be of service to her industrial sister in helping her find her way through the chaos of industry"[1] formed the Women's Trade Union League of New York late in 1903. The organization's members—a unique coalition of women workers and wealthy women disenchanted with conventional philanthropic and social reform activities—dedicated themselves to improving female laborers' working conditions and their status in the labor movement.

The women who formed the core of the New York Women's Trade Union League's membership were both trade unionists and feminists. As unionists, they worked to integrate women into the mainstream of the American labor movement. As feminists, they tried to make the early twentieth-century women's movement relevant to working women's concerns. To these ends, the WTUL attempted to serve as a link between women workers and the labor movement and as a focal point for unorganized women interested in unionism. The League agitated among unorganized women workers in an effort to educate women to the importance of unionization. In addition, the organization made concerted efforts to change male trade unionists' negative attitudes toward women. The WTUL offered assistance to municipal labor organizations and often aided local unions during strikes. League members also worked as union organizers and helped establish several dozen unions of unskilled and semiskilled women workers in New York City. Most notably, the New York League played an important role in building the shirtwaist makers' union (International Ladies' Garment Workers' Union Local 25) and the white goods workers' union (International Ladies' Garment Workers' Union Local 62). In a later period of its history, particularly during the 1910s and 1920s, the New York League abandoned its singleminded emphasis on union organizing in order to concentrate most of its efforts on the campaigns for woman suffrage and women's protective labor legislation.[2]

Women came to the League from a variety of backgrounds. Many members were young working women who learned of the WTUL through their unions or through League publicity campaigns. Other members were wealthy women. Often college-educated, *allies*, as upper-class members were called, usually came to the League with experience in charity organizations, social reform societies, or social settlements. The New York City Consumers' League, the working girls' clubs, and the Workingwomen's Society were among the groups dedicated to improving women's position in the labor force. Such organizations as the Municipal League and the Young Women's Christian Association occasionally conducted investigations of women's working and living conditions. Residents of the city's settlements houses frequently took an interest in working women and in the rapidly growing trade union movement.

The WTUL, however, differed from these organizations in two important respects. First, the League stressed the importance of actual union organizing efforts rather than such customary reform activities as social investigations. Many women joined the League precisely because they were discouraged by the slow approach of social reform organizations or by the elitism of traditional charity work. As Gertrude Barnum, a leading upper-class member in the League's early years, explained,

> I myself have graduated from the Settlement into the trade union. As I became more familiar with the conditions around me, I began to feel that while the Settlement was undoubtedly doing a great deal to make the lives of working people less grim and hard, the work was not fundamental. It introduced into their lives books and flowers and music, and it gave them a place to meet and see their friends or leave their babies when they went out to work, but it did not raise their wages or shorten their hours. It began to dawn on me, therefore, that it would be more practical to turn our energies toward raising wages and shortening hours.[3]

Second, the Women's Trade Union League stressed the importance of cross-class cooperation between upper-class and working-class women, and it was the only early twentieth-century women's organization that attempted to build such an egalitarian, cross-class alliance into its organizational structure. New York League membership was open to any individual who professed her allegiance to the American Federation of Labor and who indicated her willingness to work to unionize New York's women workers. League members stressed that allies as well as workers could be dedicated trade unionists and effective labor organizers.

Examining the day-to-day relationships WTUL members established among themselves and studying the alignments on policy issues makes it possible to observe the dynamics of cross-class cooperation and conflict. Two questions are of particular importance: How successful was the League in establishing an egalitarian, cross-class alliance? What were the sources of conflict within the organization that undermined the alliance?

The success of the New York Women's Trade Union League depended upon maintaining harmony and a sense of purpose within its coalition of workers and allies. The individuals who founded the League did not expect the coalition's stability to be a problem. The first WTUL members—most of whom were settlement residents and social reformers—apparently anticipated few difficulties in relating to one another: women could, they believed, surmount social and ethnic differences and unite on the basis of their common femininity. In this respect, the Women's Trade Union League was typical of the early twentieth-century women's movement. A conviction that women could relate to one another across class lines in the spirit of sisterhood and an emphasis on the special qualities that women shared linked many League members to the larger feminist movement. One of the major ideological strains in American feminism at the turn of the century was that women were different, emotionally and culturally, from men. Unlike mid-nineteenth-century feminists who had inveighed against the notion of a separate sphere for women and who had argued that both sexes shared a common humanity, early twentieth-century feminists, suffragists, and social reformers stressed the importance of sex differences. As WTUL member Rheta Childe Dorr expressed this philosophy,

> Women now form a new social group, separate, and to a degree homogeneous. Already they have evolved a group opinion and a group ideal. . . . Society will soon be compelled to make a serious survey of the opinions and the ideals of women. As far as these have found collective expressions, it is evident that they differ very radically from the accepted opinions and ideals of men. . . . It is inevitable that this should be so.[4]

League members, like other feminists in the early twentieth century, were often vague when they tried to define women's sisterhood. They usually used the term to convey the idea that social class was less important than gender for understanding a woman's status. The primary social dichotomy was a sex distinction rooted in differences between women and men, not classes. Women, some League members argued, shared distinct emotional qualities: they were more gentle and moral than men, more sensitive and responsive to human needs. League members also argued that women, regardless of class, could empathize with one another because they belonged to an oppressed social group.[5] This belief in sisterhood provided the ideological impetus for the League's formation and helps explain why many women joined the organization.

In certain basic respects, members found that their ideal of sisterhood could be realized. As an organization in which both upper-class and working-class women played important roles, and in which working-class and upper-class women could gain knowledge and confidence from one another, the WTUL remained viable for several decades. And it is possible to document many examples of close personal and working relationships within the League that transcended class lines.

In many other respects, however, WTUL members discovered that it was considerably easier to make verbal assertions of sisterhood than it was to put the ideal into practice. In contrast to the League's public affirmation of sorority, the organization's internal affairs were rarely harmonious. Beyond a basic commitment to unionizing women workers and to the American Federation of Labor, there was little upon which women in the League could agree. Far from behaving in sisterly fashion in their day-to-day affairs, members were often at odds with one another over League objectives and policies: Who should be allowed to join the organization? How much money and energy should the League commit to labor organization, to educational activities, to suffrage agitation? Should the League support protective legislation for women? Personal animosity and rancor accompanied debates over WTUL priorities. Leading members frequently submitted resignations or threatened to resign. They wrote angry letters denouncing one another or defending themselves against others' attacks. In short, WTUL women were a contentious lot. "If we have failed in what might be our greatest usefulness to the workers," Leonora O'Reilly, a leading working-class member, concluded wearily in 1914, "it is just in proportion as we have exhausted the energy of our friends and ourselves . . . in periodical tiffs and skermishes [*sic*]."[6]

What accounted for the high level of animosity within the New York WTUL? It is tempting to single out class conflict as a blanket explanation for the League's factionalism, policy disputes, and difficult personal relationships. Without doubt, class conflict was a reality within the League and a factor which undercut members' attempts to create an egalitarian alliance. Allies and workers came to the organization with different conceptions of social class, different attitudes toward work, and, of course, radically different social, educational, and cultural backgrounds. The ideal of sisterhood notwithstanding, difficulties and misunderstandings between women from different social backgrounds were inevitable. Yet class conflict in and of itself is not an adequate explanation for the controversies that regularly shook the organization. Indeed, social relationships among League members sometimes tended to mitigate serious class conflict. More important, there were no simple class alignments on League issues. Clearly, factors in addition to class conflict were involved.

The women who made up the organization were never able to reconcile their dedication to women as an oppressed minority within the work force and their commitment to the labor movement as a whole. Belief in sisterhood, League members discovered, was not always compatible with a belief in the importance of class solidarity. In other words, League members were unable to develop a satisfactory solution to the problem of women's dual exploitation: were women workers oppressed because they were workers or because they were female? In effect, many controversies which characterized the organization were in large part a reflection of the League's struggle to synthesize feminism and unionism—a struggle that had personal as well as ideological ramifications for many WTUL members.[7]

Although differences in members' social backgrounds did not fully account for the conflicts within the League, they were an important contributing factor. In the organization's first years, from late 1903 through 1906, allies much more readily than working women joined the WTUL. During these years, when the League rarely had more than fifty members, upper-class women dominated the organization numerically. Although the League's first president was a working woman—Margaret Daly, a United Garment Workers organizer—she remained in the League for only a short time. She was succeeded by Margaret Dreier, an ally. With the exception of Daly, all of the WTUL's officers and a small majority of the executive board members were allies. References can be found to young working women who joined the League between 1903 and 1907, but their role in the organization was shadowy—few remained in the League for more than a year or took a vocal role in the organization's activities.[8]

To stem the tide of young college graduates and settlement residents who flocked to the League in its first years, Gertrude Barnum, an ally herself, suggested that the WTUL impose a quota system to limit the number of upper-class members and that prospective allies be required to endorse the principle of the closed shop as a measure of their commitment to the labor movement. The League did not implement either of these policies. The organization's major provision to guard against upper-class domination was contained in its constitution, which stipulated that working women were to hold the majority of executive board positions. In addition, positions of leadership on organizing committees were sometimes reserved for working women. Such safeguards, however, could not change the fact that in the first years allies dominated the organization numerically. Although no one questioned the desirability of large numbers of working-class members, the first members had difficulty recruiting them.

By 1907, the League had established itself and had begun to come to the attention of young working women through its organizing efforts and its support of labor activities. More workers joined the organization. Three of the League's five officers in 1907 were working women, as was a clear majority of the executive board. After the 1909 general shirtwaist strike, in which the WTUL played a central role, workers joined the League in greater numbers than at any time previously. The year after the strike, eight of the ten executive board members were working women. For the rest of the period under consideration, the League's total membership was several hundred individuals, and working women and allies were numerically balanced.[9]

Numerical equality, however, could not solve the more serious problem of upper-class cultural domination—a problem that was always with the WTUL. Most upper-class members were seemingly unconscious of the genteel atmosphere that permeated the League, despite its unpretentious headquarters in dingy Lower East Side flats. Allies apparently saw nothing incongruous about juxtaposing "interpretive dance recitals" with shop meetings or inviting women to stop by for an afternoon of "drinking tea and discussing unionism" For working women, however, the League had an aristocratic air about it. For example, Rose Schneiderman, a young Jewish capmaker who had grown up on the Lower East Side, recalled her amazement when she attended her first League meeting and watched the participants dance the Virginia Reel. She, like many workers, had to overcome initial reluctance to join an organization with so many wealthy, college-educated women. On a personal level, the League's gentility undermined workers' self-confidence and made them feel awkward; on an ideological level, the organization's aristocratic character was foreign and often suspect. "Contact with the Lady does harm in the long run," Leonora O'Reilly declared at one point. "It gives the wrong standard."[10]

Ideally, allies were to extirpate from themselves any trace of the "Lady with something to give to her sisters."[11] They were to make way for working-class members to take the initiative in labor affairs. In short, they were to learn about trade unionism, labor organizing, and working conditions from the women who had firsthand experience in such matters. Despite the emphasis on egalitarian relationships between working-class and upper-class members, however, allies often took the lead in day-to-day affairs. In part, this might be explained by the fact that upper-class members had the advantages of good education and financial independence. Then, too, allies were, on the average, ten years older than working-class members, and their age may have given them additional confidence and authority in the League.[12]

The patronizing attitudes of certain allies toward working-class members were evident in the WTUL's educational work. Upper-class members occasionally assumed the self-appointed task of discovering and developing natural leaders among New York City working women. As Mary Beard confided to another League member, "It has been my dream to develop young women to be a help in the awakening of their class. . . ."[13] One young WTUL organizer recorded in her monthly work report that her scheduled activities included writing lessons. ". . . Miss Scott felt that I ought to practice my writing as I would have to do a great deal of it in the future. I put in several days at nothing else but writing. I had two lessons with Mrs. Charles Beard."[14] Instead of working-class members teaching allies to relate to women workers and to be effective organizers, the opposite was sometimes the case.

Such attitudes did not go ignored or uncriticized. Leonora O'Reilly, a working woman with long experience as a garment trades organizer and labor speaker and one of the original members of the League, was particularly vocal in expressing her dislike of college women who came to the labor movement with lofty ideals of feminism and solidarity but who knew nothing about the realities of labor organizing or of working for a living. She was determined that working-class members should not be intimidated by upper-class women's academic and financial advantages. More specifically, she carried on a running campaign against Laura Elliot, an older ally who joined the League in 1910. Elliot offered League members courses in singing, elocution, and art history; she organized a League chorus and took groups of young women workers to museums and concerts. Most members apparently regarded Elliot as an eccentric but harmless individual and paid her little mind. O'Reilly, however, found her ideas pernicious enough to attack. She harangued Elliot about her condescending attempts to save working women by filling them with useless and pretentious notions of culture. Elliot was hurt and confused by O'Reilly's anger, but insisted that she had a contribution to make to the League.

> You cannot push me out and you cannot make me afraid of any working girl sisters or render me *self-conscious* before them, I refuse to be afraid to take them to the Metropolitan Museum and *teach* them and *help* them. . . . I feel no fear in putting my side of the proposition up to any working girl. I'm not *afraid* to tell her that I have something to bring her and I'm never afraid that she will misunderstand or resent what I say. She needs my present help just as the whole race needs her uprising. . . .[15]

Workers sometimes asserted that allies, despite good intentions, did not know how to appeal to working women: their experiences and backgrounds were simply too different from those of their constituents to bridge the gap. Pauline Newman, a young Jewish immigrant who joined the League during the 1909 shirtwaist strike, summarized her impressions of upper-class limitations in both the League and the suffrage campaign in her remark: "the 'cultured' ladies may be very sincere . . . I don't doubt their sincereity [*sic*] but because their views are narrow and their knowledge of social conditions limited, they cannot do as well as some of us can."[16]

Workers' frustration with the well-intentioned but sometimes inept efforts of their affluent colleagues was understandable. Allies, as the executive board admitted at one point, could be "trying."[17] Upper-class members were sometimes responsible for decisions which exasperated working women. On at least one occasion, for example, League officers scheduled a conference on Yom Kippur, despite Jewish members' protestations. In the League's book of English lessons, *New World Lessons for Old World People*, references to Jewish working girls going to church slipped by uncorrected. Only one League ally is known to have studied Yiddish. Some allies held stereotypic conceptions of immigrant women. Jewish women were often described as "dark-eyed," "studious," and "revolutionary" in League literature. Italians were usually "docile," "fun-loving," "submissive," and "superstitious."[18]

Overt class and ethnic conflict in the WTUL reached its peak during a 1914 presidential contest between Rose Schneiderman and Melinda Scott. At the time of the election, Rose Schneiderman was the WTUL's East Side or Jewish organizer. Scott, a skilled hat trimmer and president of an independent union in her trade, served as the League's organizer of American-born women in the neckwear and dressmaking industries. Although both candidates were workers, they represented widely divergent approaches to the problems of organizing women. Schneiderman had always emphasized the importance of reaching immigrant women. Scott was pessimistic about organizing immigrants and advocated a policy of concentrating on American-born workers. Thus, the election involved League attitudes and policies toward immigrants. Nevertheless, support for the two candidates divided along class lines: allies backed Scott while working women voted for Schneiderman.[19] When Scott won by four votes, Pauline Newman related the details to Schneiderman.

> Your vote, with the exception of three or four was a real trade Union vote. On the other hand, the vote for Linda was purely a vote of the social workers. People who have not been near the League for four or five years, came to vote . . . but they could not get the girls from the Unions to vote against you. . . . So you see, that nothing was left undone by them to line up a vote for Linda on the ground that you were a socialist, a Jewes [*sic*] and one interested in suffrage.[20]

Part of the difficulty underlying classes between allies and workers lay in the fact that the two groups had different conceptions of *class*. The importance of class differences was usually far more obvious to working women that it was to allies. Upper-class members were not as acutely aware of class antagonism within the League and often downplayed the importance of social background. Many were confused by the emphasis workers placed on class differences. As Laura Elliot wrote to Leonora O'Reilly, "Before I was unconscious about this class and that class and this stupid difference and that stupid difference. Girls were just girls to me, and now you people are putting all sorts of ideas in my head and making me timid and self-concsious."[21]

Many allies believed that with great effort an individual could transcend her social background. Social class was flexible, not immutable. When allies talked of transcending their backgrounds, they were referring to young women from wealthy families who became self-sufficient and who could relate to workers without self-consciousness. Helen Marot, an ally who came from a comfortably affluent Philadelphia family regarded herself as a worker because she worked as the League's secretary and supported herself on her earnings. In similar fashion, Violet Pike, a young woman who joined the League shortly after her graduation from Vassar in 1907, was included among the working women on the executive board because she performed some clerical duties and joined the Bookkeepers, Stenographers, and Accountants' union.[22] Maud Younger, a wealthy ally, was listed on the League's masthead as a representative of the Waitresses' Union because she conducted an investigation of waitresses' working conditions and attended meetings of the union. In a sense, these women were workers, and they were proud of being self-supporting and resisted being categorized in their fathers' class.

Allies and workers came to the League with different conceptions of work as well. Upper-class members frequently had romanticized views of poverty and often regarded self-sufficiency as a kind of luxury. Work meant liberation from the confines of proper femininity. This attitude contributed to allies' naivete concerning the role of work in the lives of female wage-earners. Because they idealized work and equated it with economic and emotional self-sufficiency, many allies never seemed to come to terms with the fact that most women were not independent laborers but part of a family economic unit in which work did not usually connote independent economic status.[23] "Thank God working girls have a chance to be themselves because they earn their own wage and nobody owns them," one typical League article began. "I am pretty sure you are somebody, because you are self-supporting."[24]

That the New York League was characterized by personal, cultural and political strife there can be no doubt. But Pauline Newman's 1914 depiction of an organization sharply divided between "social workers" and "trade unionists" was overdrawn and simplistic. Although it is easy to document class conflict, it is also possible to document experiences that mitigated serious, sustained conflict between upper-class and working-class women. There were cohesive factors as well as divisive tendencies that operated within the League and enabled the organization to function.

League members' personal relationships with one another constituted one factor that undercut the class conflict inherent in the organization. Sisterhood sometimes became a tangible reality in friendships. Mary Dreier, the WTUL's president from 1907 through 1914, and Leonora O'Reilly, for example, maintained a warm personal relationship for many years that survived numerous political and cultural differences between the two women. "You say you wonder whether I would always trust you," Breier wrote O'Reilly after some disagreement over League policy.

> There doesn't even seem to be such a word as trust necessary between thee and me. . . . I might not always understand, as you might not always understand my activities—but as to doubting your integrity of soul, or the assurance on which trust is built seems as impossible to me as walking on a sunbeam into the heart of the sun for any of us humans—a strange and beautiful mixture of personal and impersonal is my relationship to you and I love you.[25]

Such relationships were not uncommon among League women. Some, like that of Dreier and O'Reilly, cut across class lines. Other close friendships were established between women of the same social background.

It is not surprising that such relationships were common among League members. For many WTUL women, the organization was a full-time commitment, a way of life. Then, too, that League members should form their closest emotional ties with other women is not surprising in light of the social conventions that governed personal relationships in the pre-Freudian culture of the early twentieth century. Emotional attachments between individuals of the same sex were not viewed with the same suspicion that would characterize a later period. Intense relationships involving open expressions of tenderness and affection were accepted as natural.[26]

Then, too, the longer a working woman spent in the League, the more she had in common with an upper-class ally. Both groups of women were atypical in early twentieth-century American society: the majority were single at ages when most women were married, they prided themselves on being independent and self-supporting, and they lived in a gynaecentric environment in which other women were their closest companions, their working colleagues, and their sources of emotional support. Only an extremely mechanistic definition of social class could fail to take into account that these women shared many important life experiences.

Finally, class conflict is not an adequate explanation for the disagreements within the organization for the simple reason that a member's social background did not dictate her stand on League policies. On every important issue, alignments were unclear. Suffrage, traditionally regarded as a middle-class issue, was an important priority for many working-class members. Rose Schneiderman and Pauline Newman were the first members to devote themselves full-time to the suffrage campaign. Ally Helen Marot, on the other hand, resisted the League's growing emphasis on the importance of the vote. Protective labor legislation, an issue that was enormously important in the League's history during the 1910s and 1920s, was a more controversial issue than woman suffrage, but on that issue as well, there were no clear class alignments. Allies and workers could be found on both sides of the question. In short, one cannot argue that only upper-class League members supported such reform issues as protective legislation while only workers supported labor policies such as direct organizing. There is no evidence to support the view that working women saw the League as a labor union and allies viewed it as a social reform organization. Rather, it is clear that factors in addition to class conflict played a role in creating the controversies in which League members found themselves embroiled.[27]

League members, regardless of class background, viewed the WTUL both as a women's organization and as a labor organization. Therein lay the second and perhaps more pervasive source of discord. Members had difficulty reconciling their commitment to organized labor with their commitment to the women's movement. They could not agree on a solution to the problem of women workers' dual exploitation or find a way to reconcile their belief in sisterhood with their belief in the importance of working-class solidarity. If a woman dedicated herself to working for protective legislation or for suffrage, or if she advocated separate unions for women workers, she opened herself to the charge of dividing the working class. If, on the other hand, she stayed away from women's issues entirely, she was guilty of ignoring women's special problems in the work force. This dilemma was real, and neither the League nor the individuals in it fully resolved the question.

Some members felt strongly that dedication to the labor movement should override the League's feminist leanings. In their analysis, the problems of women workers were bound up inextricably with the problems of working men. Class, not gender, was the main concern. True, they said, women suffered discrimination in the labor movement, but such opposition was not insurmountable.

Other members found their primary orientation in the women's movement. Or, as happened more frequently, women first attempted to cooperate with organized labor but ultimately despaired of changing male unionists' attitudes. They dismissed the labor movement and turned to suffrage and protective legislation as ways to ameliorate women workers' conditions.

Helen Marot, the League's secretary and an organizer, epitomized the first, or "woman as worker" position. Although she was never an industrial worker, she never wavered from her conviction that the WTUL should be committed to organized labor as a whole and not to women as a separate group. Female workers, she emphasized, should be regarded as inseparable from male workers: to think otherwise was to impede class solidarity and to denigrate women's capabilities. Throughout her career in the League and in her book, *American Labor Unions*, Marot vigorously opposed any policy that smacked of caste-consciousness. She emphasized that women were difficult to organize because they were unskilled, not because they were female. She was vehement in her opposition to the minimum wage for women, despite the fact that the measure eventually won the approval of many working-class League members. "If women need state protection on the ground that they do not organize as men do," she told the New York State Factory Investigating Commission, "then also do the mass of unskilled, unorganized men who do not appreciate or take advantage of organization. . . . The reasons for trade unionists to oppose State interference in wage rates apply to women workers as they do to men."[28]

Harriot Stanton Blatch, a well-known suffragist, represented the other strain of the WTUL. Unlike Marot, her interest in women workers derived from her involvement in the women's movement, not from a concern with industrial problems. Unions for women were only one aspect of a multifaceted campaign for women's rights, not an end in themselves. For Blatch, any class-related issue was secondary to the vote. In part, expedient considerations motivated her participation in the League: she realized that working women's support was vital for the ultimate success of the suffrage movement, and the League offered an avenue by which to reach them. On another level, however, Blatch was convinced that political equality was a prerequisite for any other improvement in women's status. Thus, only when women could vote would they command the respect of the labor movement. And only with suffrage would women develop the confidence to fight for industrial equality. "I have . . . [been] working with the Women's Trade Union League and attending meetings of the women's locals on the E. Side," Blatch wrote Gompers in 1905. "Those young women need stirring up, need independence, and some fight instilled into them. . . . I am understanding of all that the vote would mean to them—[it] would help in the trade union work as nothing else could."[29]

Marot and Blatch were sure of their objectives and their ideological orientation. The problem of women's dual status was not so clearcut for the majority of League members, however. For working-class members, the problems posed by the WTUL's dual commitment to its constituents as women and as workers were particularly vexing. For them, the matter was not only a theoretical and political issue, but frequently a personal dilemma as well. On the one hand, workers identified with their class background. They came to the League with experience in organizing activities and committed to trade unionism. On the other hand, they, like allies, were also feminists. Although workers were less likely than allies to come to the WTUL with an interest in the women's movement and probably became acquainted with the ideas of organized feminism and with the goals of the women's movement through their relationships with allies, most became dedicated feminists. More important, by comparing their experiences in the League with their role in trade unions they often came to a realization that the WTUL offered more opportunities for women to fill autonomous, responsible positions than male-dominated unions did.

Leonora O'Reilly's career in the League provides a good example of working-women's difficulties. Her commitment to the League was always ambivalent. She was faced with what she regarded as a conflict between her class background and her work in a women's organization. This was aggravated by her conviction that any serious attempt to organize working women had to be a feminist as well as a labor effort. An outspoken feminist herself, she recognized the need for an organization such as the League to devote special attention to women. She knew from her own experience as a United Garment Workers' organizer that women could count on little assistance from male unions. For all that, O'Reilly never came to terms with her ambivalence. She vacillated between urging the League to refrain from interfering in union affairs and stressing that the League should implement its policies in an autonomous fashion.[30] Sometimes she exalted the ability of women to fend for themselves in the work force, independent of men. ". . . I want want to say to my sisters," she once declared to a WTUL convention, "for mercy's sake, let's be glad if the men don't help us!"[31] From her days in the Working-women's Society in the 1890s, O'Reilly had stressed the importance of sisterhood. She was a dedicated suffragist. On a number of occasions she spoke of "women's real togetherness." "Personally," she wrote, "I suffer torture dividing the woman's movement into the Industrial Group and all the other groups. Women real women anywhere and everywhere are what we must nourish and cherish."[32] Yet at other times, O'Reilly denounced the League as an elitist organization that had no real concern for working-class people. "The League ought to die," she reportedly said at one point, "the sooner the better."[33] Her two resignations from the WTUL in 1905 and in 1914 indicated her continual difficulty in resolving the conflict. In both instances she emphasized that working women would have to organize themselves.[34]

Rose Schneiderman and Pauline Newman exhibited similar confusion and ambivalence about their role as working women in the League. On the one hand, they identified with the East Side immigrant working-class community in which they had grown up. On the other, they regarded themselves as feminists devoted to women's issues. Like O'Reilly, they frequently experienced enough conflict to consider resigning from the League.[35]

Both women were torn between working in the WTUL and devoting themselves to the East Side Jewish labor movement. Yet to work as an organizer for a Jewish union or for the International Ladies' Garment Workers' union, as both women discovered, was an isolated and lonely experience. "Even as individuals they are not interesting, most of them are unintelligent and 'green' they have no manners and have no sence[*sic*]," Newman wrote to Schneiderman about her colleagues in the ILGWU. "I do not feel at home with them any more. . . . But the worst of it is that you cannot meet a person with whom you could sit down, and discuss something which is not or does not belong to Russia and because of this I often feel miserable."[36] If the WTUL was not sufficiently interested in the progress of the working class and did not sufficiently appreciate efforts and ability to reach immigrant women, the Jewish labor organizations ignored the special problems of women altogether and discriminated against the small number of women organizers. Newman, after several years of unhappy and unrewarding work as an ILGWU organizer concluded that League work was more desirable than she had thought originally. ". . . remember Rose that no matter how much you are with the Jewish people, you are still more with the people of the League and that is a relieff [*sic*]."[37] It seems clear, therefore, that working women could compare the League favorably with trade unions. The WTUL offered women organizers considerably more autonomy and responsibility than unions did. What was more, the League provided the company of women who shared interests and experiences.

Still, both Schneiderman and Newman continually had difficulty reconciling the women's movement and the labor movement. On occasion, both women denounced the superficial efforts of upper-class philanthropists and reformers to improve industrial conditions. Yet they were the first WTUL members to work as full-time suffrage agitators. Later in the League's history, both were vocal supporters of women's protective legislation, especially of minimum wage statutes and maternity insurance, despite the fact that the labor movement frowned upon the principle of protective legislation in general and upon the minimum wage in particular. During Rose Schneiderman's presidency in the 1920s, the WTUL devoted itself almost exclusively to legislative activity.[38]

The difficulties these women faced were not uncommon. Most League members experienced some conflict between feminism and unionsim. The organization's policies also reflected this: during the first decade of its history, from 1903 to 1914, the WTUL downplayed women's special problems in the work force and concentrated on integrating women into the labor movement as workers, while during a later period its members worked hard to implement demands that were relevant only to women workers: suffrage and protective legislation. For League members, explanations for the oppression of working women were always couched in "either/or" terms: either a working woman was exploited as a worker or she suffered as a woman. What the League needed was an analysis which came to terms with both facets of women workers' situation. That analysis was never realized, and the League remained split. Caught between two alternatives, League members frequently were unable to define their purpose or their role.

In short, the Women's Trade Union League had only limited success in achieving its goal of an egalitarian cross-class alliance. Although the League went further than any other women's organization in establishing sustained relations with working women and in grappling with the problems a feminist alliance posed, its internal affairs were reraly harmonious. In part, the organization's difficulties can be attributed to conflict between allies and workers. Both groups' problems in resolving the WTUL's dual commitment to the labor movement and the women's movement also contributed to the difficulties in establishing a cross-class alliance.

This paper was originally presented at the Conference on Class and Ethnicity in Women's History, SUNY–Binghamton, September 1974.

NOTES

1 Mary Dreier, "Expansion Through Agitation and Education," *Life and Labor* 11 (June 1921): 163.

2 The New York Women's Trade Union League was an autonomous organization, but it was closely related to a larger body, the National Women's Trade Union League of America. The same individuals founded both organizations in late 1903.

[3]*Weekly Bulletin of the Clothing Trades*, March 24, 1905, p. 2.

[4]Rheta Childe Dorr, *What Eight Million Women Want* (Boston: Small, Maynard, 1910), p. 5. For a good discussion of the changes in American feminist ideology from the mid-nineteenth century to the early twentieth century, see Aileen Kraditor, *The Ideas of the Woman Suffrage Movement* (New York: Columbia University Press, 1965), Chapter 3.

[5]See, for example, Gertrude Barnum, "The Modern Society Woman," *Ladies' Garment Worker* 2 (June 1911): 8. "All women before the laws of the country . . . are of equal rank or lack of rank, being classed without exception with children, idiots, and criminals. With a common sense of injustice, feminine descendents of Patrick Henry, Tom Paine, and Thomas Jefferson ignore social differences and march shoulder to shoulder in campaigns to secure their 'inalienable rights'—to secure the fullest possible social equality with man."

[6]Leonora O'Reilly to the executive board, Women's Trade Union League of New York, January 14, 1914, Women's Trade Union League of New York Papers, New York State Labor Library, New York, New York (hereafter cited as WTUL of NY papers).

[7]Some historians who have dealt briefly with the Women's Trade Union League have interpreted the discord within the organization and the shift from labor organizing to legislative activity as the result of class conflict between allies, or social reformers, and working women. William Chafe argues, for example, "Reformers viewed the WTUL's primary function as educational, and believed that the interests of the workers could best be served by investigating industrial conditions, securing legislative action, and building public support for the principle of trade unionism. Female unionists, on the other hand, insisted that organizing women and strengthening existing unions represented the League's principal purpose. One group perceived the WTUL as primarily an instrument of social uplift, the other as an agency for labor organization" (Chafe, *The American Woman, Her Changing Social, Economic, and Political Roles, 1920-1970* (New York: Oxford University Press, 1972), p. 71.

[8]The New York League was never a large organization. Although it counted several hundred women among its dues-paying members in the years after 1907, few of these individuals played active roles in the League's day-to-day work. In the years from 1903 to 1914, about twenty women formed a core group of members. These women made League policies, served as League officers, organizers, and speakers, and set League priorities. Although the composition of this core group changed from year to year, most of these members devoted most of of their time to the organization for at least several years. Using the lists of executive board members, officers, and committee members that are extant, it is possible to reach some conclusions about the changing class composition of the core membership group. This discussion on membership is based on a more complete treatment in my doctoral dissertation, "The Women's Trade Union League of New York, 1903-1920," (University of Wisconsin, Madison, Wisconsin, 1974).

[9]Women's Trade Union League of New York, *Annual Reports,* 1909-1910 to 1913-1914. For a more detailed discussion of membership, see Dye, "The Women's Trade Union League of New York, 1903-1920."

[10]Letter to Leonora O'Reilly, 1908. O'Reilly's statement is in the form of a note written to herself on the back of the letter. Leonora O'Reilly Papers, Schlesinger Library, Cambridge, Massachusetts (hereafter cited as Leonora O'Reilly Papers).

[11]William English Walling to Leonora O'Reilly, December 1903 (O'Reilly's handwritten note on the back of the letter), Leonora O'Reilly Papers.

[12]This statement is based on the compilation of biographical information on the WTUL's core membership group. For more complete information, see Dye, "The Women's Trade Union League of New York."

[13]Mary Beard to Leonora O'Reilly, July 21, 1912, Leonora O'Reilly Papers.

[14]Report of the Organizer, October, 1915, Women's Trade Union League of New York, WTUL of NY Papers.

[15]Laura Elliot to Leonora O'Reilly, March 1911, Leonora O'Reilly Papers.

[16]Pauline Newman to Rose Schneiderman, July 16, 1912, Rose Schneiderman Papers, Tamiment Institute, New York University, New York, N.Y. (hereafter cited as Rose Schneiderman Papers).

[17]Minutes, Executive Board, Women's Trade Union League of New York, January 25, 1906, WTUL of NY Papers.

[18]See, for example, Violet Pike, *New World Lessons for Old World People* (New York: Women's Trade Union League of New York, 1912); Gertrude Barnum, "A Story with a Moral," *Weekly Bulletin of the Clothing Trades,* November 20, 1908, p. 6; Gertrude Barnum, "At the Shirtwaist Factory, A Story," *Ladies' Garment Worker,* 1 (June 1910): 4.

[19]Pauline Newman recorded her impressions of the election in three letters to Rose Schneiderman. Pauline Newman to Rose Schneiderman, 1914, Rose Schneiderman Papers.

[20]Ibid.

[21]Laura Elliot to Leonora O'Reilly, March 1911, Leonora O'Reilly Papers.

[22]Women's Trade Union League of New York, *Annual Reports*, 1910-1911, 1911-1912. In both years, Pike is listed as a union representative for the Bookkeepers, Steographers, and Accountants' Union.

[23]U. S. Congress, Senate, *Report on Condition of Woman and Child Wage-Earners in the United States*, "Wage-Earning Women in Stores and Factories," S. Doc. 645, 61st Cong., 2d sess., 1910, 5: 18, 25, 144. Senate investigators pointed out that New York City had the smallest proportion of self-supporting women of all the major cities investigated.

[24]Gerturde Barnum, "Women Workers," *Weekly Bulletin of The Clothing Trades*, July 13, 1906, p. 8.

[25]Mary Dreier to Leonora O'Reilly, Jun 19, 1908, Leonora O'Reilly Papers.

[26]Other historical studies have touched upon this phenomenon. See, for example, Christopher Lasch and William Taylor, "Two Kindred Spirits," *New England Quarterly* 36 (Winter 1963): 23-41.

[27]This interpretation differs from brief accounts of the WTUL in other works. See, for, example, Kraditor, *Ideas of the Woman Suffrage Movement*, Chapter 6, and Chafe, *American Woman*, Chapter 3.

[28]New York, Factory Investigating Commission, *Fourth Report of the New York State Factory Investigating Commission, 1915* 1: 774; Helen Marot, *American Labor Unions, By a Member* (New York: Henry Holt, 1915), Chapter 5.

[29]Harriot Stanton Blatch to Samuel Gompers, December 30, 1905, American Federation of Labor Papers, Wisconsin State Historical Society, Madison,Wisconsin; Harriot Stanton Blatch, *Challenging Years* (New York: Putnam, 1940).

[30]See, for example, Leonora O'Reilly to executive board, Women's Trade Union League of New York, January 14, 1914, WTUL of NY Papers.

[31]National Women's Trade Union League, *Proceedings of the Second Biennial Convention, 1909*, p. 26.

[32]Leonora O'Reilly to Mary Hay, December 29, 1917, Leonora O'Reilly Papers.

[33]Leonora O'Reilly's statement was quoted in a letter from Pauline Newman to Rose Schneiderman, 1914, Rose Schneiderman Papers. Newman wrote, "Mrs. Robins wanted Nora [Leonora O'Reilly] to tell her what she thought of the candidats [*sic*] but Nora said that, 'this you will never know, but I can tell you what I think of the League, it ought to die, and the sooner the better."

[34]Minutes, Special Meeting, Executive Board, Women's Trade Union League of New York, November 19, 1915, WTUL of NY Papers.

[35]See, for example, Pauline Newman to Rose Schneiderman, February 22, 1912, Rose Schneiderman Papers.

[36]Pauline Newman to Rose Schneiderman, September 13, 1910, Rose Schneiderman Papers.

[37]Pauline Newman to Rose Schneiderman, April 17, 1911, Rose Schneiderman Papers.

Editor's note: The citing for footnote number 38 is missing from the original text.

FEMINISM AS LIFE-PROCESS: THE LIFE AND CAREER OF LUCY SPRAGUE MITCHELL

JOYCE ANTLER

Feminism, a word that did not become part of our general vocabulary until the close of the nineteenth century, has since that time acquired a variety of meanings. It seems apparent that, at present, there is no single framework—whether "women's culture," the more political "women's rights," or even the broad concept of "women's emancipation"—which can describe the multifaceted aspects of feminist theory and practice.[1] In this essay, I shall suggest yet another definition of feminism—feminism as life-process—a notion that I hope might complement existing concepts as well as provide a historical linkage between nineteenth- and early twentieth-century feminism and the contemporary women's movement. The variant of feminism I shall describe represents a single individual's struggle for autonomy, rather than a self-conscious, political strategy for altering the social order. It is a personal, rather than a collective, set of processes taking place over an individual's life course by which women have sought to mold their destinies in the world and confront, at each stage of their life cycle, the gender-defined issues that have traditionally limited female opportunities. Certain of these experiences might have marked paths for others and set the context for larger social change, but in any event, a rediscovery of the passion, pain, and vitality embodied in these individual struggles can help restore to our consciousness much of the humanistic quality of feminism that has sometimes frozen into the historical record.

The presentation of the life and career of Lucy Sprague Mitchell as a case study of feminism as a life-process also allows me to suggest some answers to a question that has long troubled historians—what happened to feminism after 1920. Although "public" feminism declined in the next decades, I shall suggest that at least in certain cases, women transferred the center of the struggle to their own lives during this period as they sought to work out the large

Feminist Studies 7, no. 1 (Spring 1981).

issues of feminism on an individual basis. In some instances—as for example, that of the Bank Street School, which Mitchell established in New York City for the "experimental" education of children and their teachers—institutions created by female professionals reflected and resolved certain of these issues. The existence of these structures suggests, furthermore, the survival of female institutions at a time when other feminist activities were dormant.[2] Although the kind of feminism which I am addressing—feminism as a life-process—must in the end remain a limited feminism, perhaps indeed, a "proto" feminism—because, focusing on the individual, it shies away from asserting the collective need of emancipation—recognition of this form might allow us at least to recover from the lost generation of feminist endeavor after 1920 some of the women whose lives might properly be called "feminist."

The central issue, I will argue, for many women of this lost generation was to devise a lifestyle that allowed them the opportunity to participate in the public sphere through their own professional, political, or other activities while at the same time to experience (for those who were heterosexual) marriage and family life. Suffragists and feminists in the nineteenth century had largely concentrated their attention on the public arena—the world of politics and work—to the exclusion of marriage and childrearing, a solution that was unacceptable to the younger women like Mitchell to whom I shall refer.[3] In their own lives, on an individual basis, these women now struggled to work out that balance of interests between the private and public (in this case, between marriage and career) that would allow them to achieve the self-determination and autonomy that they posited as their highest goals. Their struggles might in fact be seen as an essential backdrop to the feminism of the 1960s, the first feminist movement that has consistently dealt with women's private, as well as public lives. With Betty Friedan and her followers, and even with some of the more radical new feminists, issues that Mitchell and her contemporaries tried to confront on a personal level became political.

Writing in the 1890s, Charlotte Perkins Gilman in fact anticipated many of the concerns of Friedan and women today when she expressed in her theory and her fiction the grave necessity for the mediation of the public and private realms of experience. In presenting her theoretical framework for the employment of women in the larger world, Gilman attacked both the male opposition to paid female labor and the self-imposed domestic mythology that kept wives and mothers functional parasites in their own homes.[4] However, autonomy in the work sphere was not to be achieved at the expense of family life, for in Gilman's vision, the female work force was to be composed not of unmarried women, but of wives and mothers. Although in her two major nonfiction works, *Women and Economics* (1898) and *The Home* (1903), she does not base her argument for female economic independence on the needs of married women alone, it is clear that this is the group with which she is primarily concerned. Gilman makes the point explicitly in a 1916 article in the *Forerunner*. "The term 'woman,' " she writes, "should connote wifehood and motherhood. Until 'mothers' earn their livings, 'women' will not."[5]

The attempt to mediate between the private and public worlds of female experience became the fundamental struggle of Lucy Sprague Mitchell's life, as it was the central theme of Gilman's writing. In addition to founding and directing Bank Street, Mitchell was the author of numerous books and articles, particularly in the area of children's language and what she called "human geography" or ecology. What makes Mitchell especially important to American feminism, however, was not her educational achievements, which were significant, but the extent to which her experiences reflect feminism as a life-process. Mitchell's consciousness of the feminist element in the struggles for autonomy and the integration of private and public domain is revealed in her unpublished papers, and in her book *Two Lives: The Story of Wesley Clair Mitchell and Myself*, a literary tour de force that combined autobiography, biography (of her husband), and the story of a marriage. Published in 1953, fourteen years before Lucy Sprague Mitchell's death, the book has received little attention from historians or feminists, though it is classic study of female emancipation and provides a richly detailed social history of the modern period.

Born in 1878, Lucy Sprague Mitchell was eighteen years younger than Charlotte Perkins Gilman, but the social choices available to each woman—public/professional life versus the private world of domesticity—had changed little over time. The most obvious evidence of the fact that these options were mutually exclusive is provided by the life histories of educated women in the late nineteenth and early twentieth centuries. During this era, many educated women distinctly rejected marriage and the possibility of a conventional family life in favor of more worldly options. Female leaders of the Progressive Era such as Jane Addams and Lillian Wald are prime examples of this pattern. Of all the living graduates of the eight eastern women's colleges plus one coeducational university, Cornell, the average percentage of married graduates in 1914 was decidedly lower than that for male graduates or for those of the female population at large.[6] The more educated the woman, furthermore, the less likely she was to marry. Of all the women who received the Ph.D. degree between the years 1877 and 1924, 75 percent never married.[7] The proportion of unmarried women amongst those who defined themselves as professionals is even more striking: in 1920, for example, almost 90 percent of all professional women were unmarried.[8]

Lucy Sprague Mitchell was one of a small number of middle-class women who attempted to establish an alternative pattern, one that combined traditional family life—marriage and children—with full-time professional responsibilities. During the Progressive Era, many academic and professional women of this class chose different paths, establishing supportive homosocial or lesbian relationships, or, if they were married, determining not to have children.[9] Other married women combined family life with work, which, although it involved much thought and concern, was part-time and nonpaying. Mitchell's feminism differed from the most familiar model—the celibate, political kind—in that she demanded the "right" to merge a full, heterosexually female life with an active career. The implication is not that celibate women or lesbians did not have meaningful private lives, or that nonworking wives did not make significant contributions to civic life, only that a feminism that embraced marriage and work as essential components hoped to merge the private and public, the home and the world, in a rather different, and generally untried, fashion. In dedicating herself to achieving this goal, Mitchell took quite a different course than Jane Addams, a strong influence on her early life, and other women of the suffrage generation who had served her as role models (among them Lillian Wald and Florence Kelley). The distance between Mitchell and these women regarding the issue of marriage and career underscores, indeed, a significant change in the aspirations of educated women.

Mitchell did not write much about feminism or the particular dilemmas and opportunities of women's lives, nor was she especially active in the more political aspects of the women's movement. How to enrich the lives of children, rather than of women as a special group, became her particular focus. Nevertheless, in her effort to develop an identity for herself as an independent, professional woman—while not relinquishing the goal of maintaining a fulfilling family life as wife and mother—Mitchell may be said to have pioneered a mode of feminism that is of great relevance to contemporary women and men.

Although what I call Mitchell's alternative lifestyle set her apart from her middle-class contemporaries, the critical areas of choice confronting her at different stages of her life cycle do illuminate many of the vital emotional experiences of members of her generation. The dilemma of marriage or career, especially, was shared by many of her peers, as was the ambition to pursue some significant work outside the home at a time when social supports for women engaged in nontraditional occupations were desperately lacking. Under such inhospitable circumstances, female achievement in any professional or creative work was in fact a "miracle," as a recent biographer of Virginia Woolf has noted, so that the successes of exceptional women can indeed shed light on the struggles of less-favored contemporaries.[10] Mitchell's education, talents, and her considerable wealth—which undoubtedly diminished the hardships she encountered—could not eliminate the tensions and ambivalences that marked her unconventional career and the unification of public and private spheres which she sought, and which, had it been achieved, would also have been a "miracle." Mitchell's successes, and even more so, her failures, can tell us a great deal about the problem and conflicts of all the women who to some degree shared her aspirations. The search for autonomy which is dramatically reflected in Mitchell's life experiences can thus illustrate patterns of choice perceived by women of her era and can reveal to us much that is significant about the nature of feminism.

Lucy Sprague was born in Chicago in 1878 to Otho and Lucia Sprague, the fourth of their six children and third daughter.[11] Otho had come to Chicago from New England with his young bride several years earlier to join a small grocery business founded by his brother. By the time of Lucy's birth, Sprague Warner and Co. was well on its way to becoming one of the largest wholesale groceries in the world, an achievement due by all accounts to Lucy's father, one of an extraordinary group of businessmen whose pioneering spirit in the decades after the Civil War helped turn Chicago into a major urban metropolis. Charming, witty, and urbane, Lucy's father embodied the conventional New England virtues of thrift, ambition, and moral probity. Her mother, exceptionally musical and artistic in temperament, was, however, so shy and lacking in self-confidence that her children pitied as well as loved her.

Otho Sprague conscientiously undertook to bring up his family in the path of inexorable righteousness. At the Sprague household, duty dominated all living. Play, self-expression, indeed, any outward display of affection were considered symbols of laxity. Fear, humility, and a sense of guilt, Lucy explained in her memoirs, were symbols of grace—discipline and punishment the methods of achieving it. It is not surprising that in such an atmosphere the Spragues turned out to be a nervous group of children, with many illnesses. As a youngster, Lucy was lonely and introspective. Outwardly, her nervousness was manifested in her inability to attend school. Whenever she entered a classroom, she would "go to pieces," her face twitching uncontrollably and her legs remitting terrible pains. This malady, which Lucy attributed to her fear of failing in school, kept her out of it until she was sixteen. During these years, books became her chief hope of becoming educated, and she systematically read her way through her father's huge library.

In many respects, Lucy Sprague admired her father. A proud patron of the arts, he and his associates were responsible for the establishment of some of Chicago's most splendid cultural institutions, including the University of Chicago. At the new university, the Spragues grew to know such persons as novelist Robert Herrick, and especially important to Lucy, John and Alice Dewey and Alice Freeman Palmer, the former Wellesley College president who resided with the Spragues during her tenure as part-time dean of women at the University of Chicago.

Otho Sprague was also a leader in Chicago's struggle for clean government and a supporter of Jane Addams's settlement work at Hull House. When he broke with Addams during the Pullman strike, Lucy sided with Addams, creating a rift that was never to heal. Grasping the truth that her father's business interests dominated his attitudes toward people, she developed a sense of shame and guilt at being rich. "I felt I was a 'pampered darling,' " she realized, "bound by my father's wealth to a world of people whose standards I couldn't accept."[12] Jane Addams became for her a symbol of a human, non-material point of view, and thereafter every cause she stood for was to become Lucy's cause.

When Lucy Sprague was fifteen, the deteriorating state of her family's health forced them to leave Chicago for southern California. Her two youngest brothers had both died from contagious diseases, and one of her older sisters suffered a devastating mental collapse. This turn of affairs threw her mother into a profound depression. Her father, meanwhile, suffered recurrent hemorrhages from the tuberculosis he had contracted during the Civil War, which his wife was also to develop. With her siblings away at school, Lucy unhappily became the family nurse.

An invitation from Alice Freeman Palmer for Lucy to attend Radcliffe College and live with the Palmers in Cambridge, Massachusetts, changed her life. Over her father's initial objections, she entered Radcliffe in the fall of 1896 and majored in philosophy, taking courses with William James, George Santayana, Josiah Royce, and George Herbert Palmer, graduating magna cum laude with honors in philosophy. She was active in student affairs as well, president of her class, class historian, basketball team member, and chairman of the swimming pool committee. The only essentially upsetting event to befall her during her Radcliffe years was her love affair with a Harvard student named Joe, Mr. Palmer's cousin, who was arrested for selling pornographic photographs to students. Lucy Sprague was crestfallen.

After her graduation from Radcliffe, Sprague resumed her duties as family nurse. Although she recognized that "work was what she needed," she was "too listless to fight family opposition." Finally, however, she determined to get herself trained for something. "But what could I do without leaving home?"[13] she asked. She chose landscape gardening, but, unhappy at home and in her courses, she rapidly deteriorated.

Again she was rescued by the Palmers, who took her with them to Europe. While in Paris, however, Mrs. Palmer became suddenly ill, and, after an emergency operation, died. Sprague returned to Cambridge with the griefstricken widower and began to help with housekeeping. Although she felt that the sixty-year-old professor was turning to her with "alarming dependence," she decided to stay in Cambridge. "Or rather, I made no decision," she recalled, "I just stayed." She remained with Palmer for several years, taking some graduate courses at Harvard, and working as secretary to the dean of Radcliffe. "As the time passed," she wrote,

> I know I was caught in a vise stronger than Father ever forged for me. Mr. Palmer was subtle in his ways of limiting my life. . . . What is the matter with me, I wondered desperately, that I seem incapable of finding a satisfying normal life? Why do all my relations with people seem to rob me of my own soul? Am I always to lead a vicarious life?[14]

Finally, "the incredible happened," as had often occurred in her life. President Benjamin Wheeler of the University of California (whose only campus then was at Berkeley) invited her to become dean of women, a position she accepted on condition that she could also join the faculty. She in fact became the first regular woman faculty member. Coming from a "small man-scared woman's college" to a coeducational university, which had more than two thousand women students, Sprague felt ignorant, "on trial," and "scared of everything." Yet she felt a new world opening to her. "I came to realize," she wrote,

> the standards that our culture of that day held for women in education and

in the general management of their own lives. I had long been kicking against these standards in my personal life, but with no clear analysis of what so frustrated me.[15]

Now she began to understand that difficulties she had always interpreted as personal were in fact socially determined.

The congruence between the concerns of Sprague's job and her experiences as a woman strengthened her ambitions and fortified her attempt to find her "real self." As dean, she was innovative and dynamic, abandoning the traditional "motherly" conception of the role to focus instead on broadening the opportunities for students. She organized courses in sex education, attempted to improve housing conditions for women students, worked to strengthen women's organizations on campus, and urged students to examine social conditions in the San Francisco community. One of her activities at Berkeley was to conduct a survey which showed that 90 percent of female students intended to go into teaching, the only professional training the university offered women. It was a choice so limited that Sprague found it "preposterous." After the death of her father some years later (her mother had died previously), she resigned from her job and went to New York City to explore the variety of work opportunities available to women. She selected six different organizations, and in the cause of women's education—and not incidentally, her own vocational choices—asked each to allow her to work for them for a few weeks. After her trip, she returned briefly to Berkeley with a written report designed to improve the content of women's education.

Sprague worked first for Lillian Wald at the Henry Street Settlement on the Lower East Side. Next she worked for Florence Kelley at the Consumer's League, learning about labor legislation and hearing "tirades against capitalists and politicians." She then went to Mary Richmond at the Charity Organization Society, where she was placed in a department for homeless babies. After working with Richmond, she went to Pauline Goldmark of the Russell Sage Foundation, to assist in a social survey of a west side district. She then signed up with the Salvation Army to do field work in the same area. The last few weeks she spent with Julia Richman, principal of a public high school. Although she was much impressed by all these experiences, Sprague recalled the last placement to be of "tremendous" personal significance. "This is the work for me," she thought. Public education was "the synthesis of all my interests, all my hopes for humanity," she wrote. "I returned to Berkeley with a clear focus in my own life from which I have never since deviated."[16]

The New York apprenticeship indicated that at last she had begun to take steps toward directing her own life. Until that summer, the decisions of Sprague's life had been guided by drift, "incredible" happenings, and the suggestions of parents, surrogate family, or friends. Now, for the first time, she assumed control of her future. Her thoughtful movement away from passivity and toward active participation in defining her own development is shown in her letters during her four-month stay in New York to Wesley Clair Mitchell, the suitor she left behind in California. Mitchell was a young economist whom Sprague had first met in Chicago, where he was studying economics and philosophy with Veblen and Dewey. Later he joined the department of economics at the University of California, chaired by Lucy Sprague's brother-in-law, Adolph Miller. Mitchell fell in love with Sprague after watching her perform a spontaneous and passionate gypsy dance one evening at a Berkeley party, but she spurned his proposal of marriage, and their friendship quickly died. After a lapse of several years, the relationship was rekindled, blossoming into an ardent love affair. When Sprague left California for her New York trip, she went not only to consider her professional future, but also to ponder Mitchell's renewed offer of marriage. Sprague's letters to Mitchell demonstrate a steady growth in personal strength and a conviction that work—what she called her "vision"—would be her path to self-realization. At the same time, the letters expressed both her love for Mitchell and her ambivalence about marriage.

"The problem in many ways gets worse," she explained, "because the alternative life grows more and more rich in its possibilities. . . . Every day in New York is a new epoch to me." She wrote:

> A new current has surged over me. It is the creative impulse, the desire to embody myself—my thoughts, my ideals, my quivering sense, in a tangible form which will send others thinking, idealizing and questioning. . . . I find myself unconsciously thinking of this work as my next step in life—not marriage with you.[17]

Wesley Mitchell was sympathetic toward Sprague's desire to make work the center of her life. He wrote:

> Your need of work is to me one of your most splendid qualities. I not only admire but also sympathize keenly with it, because it answers my corresponding need. To stifle it would be to cut off the surest source of happiness to you and helpfulness to others. If marriage threatened such a result you certainly ought not to marry. . . .

Marriage need not mean the end of Sprague's plans, Mitchell continued:

> Your work would supplement and aid mine and mine would supplement and aid yours. You would not have to give up your plans, on the contrary you would realize them more effectively by marrying me.[18]

But Sprague was not readily persuaded. Her fluctuations about marrying Mitchell drove her to become confused to "the point of futility" until finally, she gave up trying to deal with the problem from an "intellectual" basis and acknowledged that the question "must be left ultimately to feeling."[19]

"It is the fear that I should be marrying you for the *sake of bonds* that keeps me undecided," she finally admitted. "It is the lurking fear that I am cowardly about my great freedom, the fear that I am running to shelter . . . because I am weary with the storm."[20] This fear kept Sprague ambivalent about marriage for many months. The autonomy she hoped to achieve was not only a challenge to her, but a burden. Freedom from the family claim and the restraints of gender left her to face an unknown future, without the help of traditional guideposts. If she "yielded" to Mitchell, as she put it, would she not be marrying him out of her own timidity, and ultimately, from the fear of the very independence she so desperately sought? Marriage signified a "refuge" from the world, and she feared that as a wife she might revert from actively participating in her own life to the passivity that plagued her early years. The models of professional women whom she deeply respected were either single women like Lillian Wald and Jane Addams, who had never married, or who, like Florence Kelley, were divorced. The married women who had most influenced her, on the other hand, were the childless Alice Freeman Palmer, who had renounced the presidency of Wellesley upon her husband's demand when they married, and of course, her own mother, a woman who lived her life soberly and cheerlessly in the shadow of her husband's personality.

Mitchell argued against her notion that marriage was a more cowardly choice than the "alternative life" that inspired her. "You are troubled by a lurking fear that you might marry because you are afraid of freedom," he wrote. But

> what is freedom but the opportunity to choose? Would you not be exercising freedom–making a splendid effort of your very own will against the pressure of environment by deciding that you want to marry me? . . . You would not be running to a shelter in which you would be free from the pressure of duties. I'd guard and cherish you certainly, but one of the things against which I'd

protect you, if that ever became necessary (wild thought!) would be the feeling that you could shift the burdens of life upon the soul of any one else. . . .

"You will find life not less full of opportunity for choosing, not less heavy with responsibilities," he wrote, "as a wife than as a spinster. It's not a refuge that I offer you, but a fighting mate."[21]

Lucy Sprague finally married Mitchell in 1912, when she was thirty-three and he was thirty-seven, some months after her return from New York and four years after Mitchell's first proposal of marriage. Throughout their correspondence, from which I have quoted only a small portion, she had remained reluctant to "surrender," as she expressed it, but on her return, a face-to-face meeting in the Sierra Mountains persuaded her at last.

The decision to marry Mitchell became the turning point of her professional as well as personal life. Without any secure professionsional identity, she had languished in the years after college, drifting in and out of various studies and employments until she had become severely depressed and physically ill. Restrained by a powerful family claim and "humiliated" by her lack of training, at Berkeley she at last came to see her problems as embodying the dilemma of all educated women. Conscious of this fact, it had become difficult to commit herself to marriage, which she understood as a threat to women's autonomy. When she finally decided to marry Wesley Mitchell, her struggle to develop her own identity and pursue her life goals took on a new form, for now, with the creation of her young family, her energies turned toward discovering ways to merge the demands of children, household, and husband with those of her intellectual and professional interests. The struggle was not without rewards, however, for indeed, it was not until Lucy Sprague Mitchell became a wife and mother that she discovered at last her true vocation: the education of young children.

Following their marriage, the couple moved to New York so that Wesley Mitchell could continue his research on business cycles at first hand. After her three-month sojourn in New York the previous year, Lucy Sprague Mitchell had also determined that the city offered the most career opportunities for her. During the next few years, she took courses with John Dewey and others at Teachers College and worked as a volunteer in a number of educational projects. (It was during this time also, that the Mitchells had their first two children, one of whom was adopted.) Then, in 1916, she launched the Bureau of Educational Experiments (later known as the Bank Street College of Education). (In the next two years, the Mitchells had two more children, again adopting one.) Lucy Sprague Mitchell remained chair of Bank Street's governing council for forty years, guiding its pioneering work in early childhood education and developing her own Dewey-inspired credo: the idea that learning must be an active adventure aimed at developing the whole child. After years of drift, her life now merged into a single personal and professional unity. "It was a highly focused life," she recalled, "with everything concentrated on children, each aspect of my work illuminating the others."[22]

Wesley Mitchell played a crucial role in the launching of his wife's career. He was a cofounder of the Bureau of Educational Experiments, contributing his enormous skills as an economist in establishing the institution on a sturdy financial course and in assuring that its research program was statistically sound. During the first frenetic years of the institution, Wesley Mitchell attended endless discussions about bureau goals and programs, met regularly with committees, wrote reports, and conducted numerous special assignments. For several years he would rush back from his classes at Columbia University or the New School for Social Research (of which he was a cofounder) to teach carpentry to the youngsters at City and Country School, affiliated with the bureau. He also performed janitorial and general handyman services at the bureau when needed.

Wesley Mitchell's involvement in the bureau reflected not only the fulfillment of his promise to support his wife's career—in effect, the courtship correspondence between the two served as a marriage contract, setting the terms of the couple's relationship to each other and to their work—but it also reflected the Mitchell's shared ideals: both believed that the Bureau of Educational Experiments could play a critical role in designing a new kind of education, one which took its cues from the scientific study of children to be conducted by interdisciplinary specialists, and which would create the optimal conditions for growth and creativity in children. This goal, which was the basis of Lucy Sprague Mitchell's lifelong "vision," corresponded nicely with the essentials of Wesley Mitchell's vision of economics. "From the beginning," Lucy Sprague Mitchell wrote,

> he and I had the same broad end in mind—the betterment of social organization. And we both believed in the same means of accomplishing that end—a scientific study of human beings and their behavior. . . . In details and in responsibilities, our work was separate. But our common aims and common methods made us share each other's work to a high degree and added a fullness and richness to our joint life.[23]

Wesley Mitchell also participated in the domestic management of the household. Although much of the childcare and housekeeping was done by a group of Irish maids who served the Mitchells while their four children were young, at least one parent was home for the children's meals and available for special activities. While neither parent devoted great amounts of time to the children, especially time that was spontaneous, their shared interest in the children is revealed in the detailed letters each wrote to the children's teachers and in Wesley Mitchell's daily diary entries concerning details of childrearing, family illnesses, outings, and so forth.

Mitchell's support of his wife's career and the presence of servants allowed Lucy Sprague Mitchell to merge career and family in an unusually productive synthesis. An additional contributory circumstance was the fact that her home and work occupied adjacent quarters. In 1921, she purchased six brownstone buildings on West Twelfth and Thirteenth Streets in Greenwich Village, which were used to house her family, the offices of the bureau, and the City and Country School. The Mitchells' backyard was shared with the school, which the children attended, and in which Lucy and Wesley Mitchell taught. Before the move to West Twelfth and Thirteenth streets, the bureau school and offices operated out of buildings owned by the Mitchells adjacent to their Washington Square home. When the children were infants, it was therefore an easy matter for her to nurse them at home without interrupting her vigorous work life.

Lucy Sprague Mitchell's sensitivity to questions of physical space is also evidenced in her design of the summer home in Greensboro, Vermont, where for more than thirty years the Mitchells did much of the bulk of their writing. The physical arrangement of the complex, consisting of rough, wooden buildings housing a nursery-dining area, children's sleeping quarters, Wesley Mitchell's study, and the master bedroom connected to Lucy Sprague Mitchell's study, allowed the couple to work more or less uninterrupted while the children played. Clearly, Lucy Sprague Mitchell grasped the notion, central to Gilman's work as well, that unless the home itself as well as its relation to the workplace was reconstituted in some fundamental fashion, unification of the separate spheres of women's lives would not be possible.[24]

Wesley Mitchell's commitment and his wife's fortunate economic circumstances—which allowed both for servants and for the special architectural features that integrated work and family life—were the primary reasons why the Mitchells' "marriage contract" never faltered. But also important was Lucy Sprague Mitchell's driving ambition and determination to see the thing through: she wrote her books on subways, buses, or anywhere she could find a moment; at bureau meetings she always brought some of the family clothing that needed darning or mending. Persons who encountered her outside her own educational circles often commented on her ceaseless energy, her iron will, and on what seemed to some a cold, impersonal brusqueness. To these individuals, though not to those with whom she worked closely, she was as much the driving, commanding "captain of industry" as her father had been. This personality configuration was a function of temperament, intellectuality, and early conditioning, perhaps, but also, I believe, of the social and cultural conditions that made it necessary for women in positions such as her's to adopt such characteristics in order to succeed.

And Mitchell did succeed. Not only did she establish a major educational institution and serve as chair of its governing board, she also founded a writers' laboratory for children's authors, started public school workshop programs, and wrote numerous articles and books on educational subjects. Although her work became the major interest of her life, the subject of this work was children, so that it could never be divorced from family life.

By the same token, Mitchell's public work, the education of children, benefited enormously from her family experiences. Her contribution to progressive education, which I have discussed elsewhere, sprang from several different sources (among them, her own childhood deprivations and her association with figures such as John Dewey), but the relevance of her own mothering to her educational innovations is clear.[25]

In Mitchell's case, there was thus a true mediation of life spheres: both the private and public aspects of her existence—her relationships within her family and her work in progressive education—were each acted upon, and changed, by the other. Gilman's feminist theory, I believe, ultimately called for a transcendence of sex roles and a mediation of life spheres in much the same fashion: women's very natures would be transformed as they shared in the world's work, but at the same time, their participation in the work force would change the basis of industry, politics, science, and education.[26]

Mitchell's work in early childhood education helped to redefine the public dimensions of women's private spheres, while her private life gave expression to the new patterns of sex role behavior beginning to emerge in the twentieth century. "I think my experience does represent a general trend of a breakdown in the old sharp separation of human society into two worlds—a woman's world in the home and a man's world outside the home," she wrote in her autobiography.[27] The role of women had changed, she believed, because women were entering public life in ever greater numbers—yet they were not rejecting marriage and childrearing. Perhaps even more significant was the fact that men's roles had also begun to change. "It might be said," explained Mitchell, "that 'men have entered the home' rather than that 'women have left it.' "[28] If Mitchell, writing this in the early 1950s, was overly optimistic in her perception of the tendency of husbands and fathers to assume a greater share of the burdens of home management and childrearing, recall, of course, that she was guided by her own successful marriage and the ever-present support of her husband.

Mitchell felt that the contribution of her husband had been critical to her development. In her life with him, she wrote, "I became a new person. I became happy, satisfied, secure. . . . I began to use what powers, what talents, what abilities I had instead of trying to ignore or suppress them."[29] His acceptance of her as a person "not merely in relation to him and our children" had helped her to overcome the guilt and self-doubt that were legacies of her childhood and had helped her to establish herself as a confident professional woman, wife, and mother. Clearly, Wesley Mitchell was exceptional in the depth of his support of his wife's amibtions, but of course, it was Lucy Sprague Mitchell's independent wealth that made it possible for both of them to fashion the kind of domestic lifestyle that fostered their professional productivity. Beyond this fact, though, Wesley Mitchell truly seems to have been the saintly individual his wife's portrayal summons up. Not only his wife, but colleagues, friends, and other relatives universally mention his qualities of gentleness, humility, humor, and his warmth and support.

Wesley Mitchell's death in 1948 left Lucy Sprague Mitchell without the anchor that had helped her establish her place in life. With the culmination of her active career some years later, her two main channels of fulfillment, her career and marriage, were suddenly closed off. Without these securities, she felt besieged by feelings of inadequacy, loneliness, and grief. During the next two decades, which she called her "fumbling years," she wrote scores of poems to her husband which commented frankly on her marriage, her present bewilderment and despair, and her quest for renewal. Eventually, she learned "to grow, to live in unaccustomed ways" in her widowhood. Old age became a "second adolescence" for her, a time of peace and creativity after the turbulent years of her busy middle life. In the poems she wrote throughout her seventies and eighties (until her death at eighty-nine), she was able to liberate the rich spirit of playfulness, which had been bottled up since childhood, and to express her deepest potentialities. Even the satisfactions of her professional work over the years did not compare with the sense of release she experienced through this poetry. Gradually her feelings of anxiety about living alone, without her husband or the work that had been so important to her, gave way to a new sense of self-worth and her own uniqueness. She was fond of explaining that in aging, she was not simply growing older, but "becoming more so," more her real self. Her old age is in fact one of the most interesting stages of her life, reflecting with great poignancy the search for fulfillment which shaped each phase of her development.

Lucy Sprague Mitchell's autobiography reveals a number of characteristics of feminism as a life-process. First of all is the fact that the search for autonomy, which I have described as at the core of feminist goals, is a continuing, lifelong struggle. During different phases of the life cycle, this struggle might be expressed in varying ways. In Lucy Sprague Mitchell's youth and early adulthood, for example, the drive for autonomy focused on breaking away from the filial role that limited her opportunities, while in her later life, developing an independent professional identity as a woman and establishing intimacy within her personal relationships became key goals. The creative feminism of her old age, finally, reversed earlier patterns, for in her last decades she sought a new sense of self by breaking the bonds of dependency created both by her marriage role and her attachment to her work identity.

The search for autonomy was not only a continuous and a changing process, it was also extremely difficult and painful. I have indicated that Mitchell was successful in unifying her private and public roles and in resolving the dilemmas of her last years, but I have not talked about all of the conflicts and ambivalences involved in these struggles. The cost of her life choices as a feminist become most difficult to assess when we examine her relationship with her children, a subject which will be more fully discussed in the larger work I am preparing on Lucy Sprague Mitchell's life. In brief, in spite of the measures she devised to merge her family interests with her career, her children wound up greatly resenting their mother's work (much less so their father's), although this was only one component in their attitudes toward her. She was saddened by the tribulations some of her children had to bear, but from her own tentative feminist perspective I think she concluded that the blend of family life and professional accomplishment which she had worked hard to develop was nevertheless effectively fashioned.

Finally, the struggle for autonomy is sharply defined by issues of gender in a way that makes women's search for self-definition fundamentally different from men's. Life cycle issues shaped by crises involving gender identity such as those I have delineated within Lucy Sprague Mitchell's life—the struggle of daughters to escape the family claim, the dilemma of choice between marriage and/or career, and the problems of widowhood—may play a large role in shaping women's professional as well as personal development (just as men may face similarly unique life cycle struggles).[30] In Mitchell's case, I believe these issues not only influenced her choice of career and the ways in which she organized her diverse activities, but also determined many distinctive aspects of her educational philosophy and style of leadership.

Through her conscious and deliberate creation of a world in which it was possible to live, work, and create in a manner that fulfilled her needs and aspirations, Lucy Sprague Mitchell's struggle for autonomy was successfully accomplished. It should be noted again, however, that her struggle was primarily a personal one, largely unconnected to the organized currents of feminism around her, and perhaps not even a fully conscious one, for she never carefully considered the implications of the fact that her own successes in bringing "unity" to her private and professional life were in some ways fortuitous—due to wealth, talent, and a sympathetic husband. Nevertheless at Bank Street, she did fashion some institutional structures and attitudes that changed things for other women in a small but potentially important way.

Thus, the long struggle preceding Lucy Sprague Mitchell's years of greatest generativity not only influenced her throughout her life, but also helped to mold the unusual character of Bank Street. Inspired by her, Bank Street became an organization distinctive not only in its contribution to the education of children, but also in the way in which it promoted growth and development of its faculty and students. In an important sense, Bank Street as an institution also exemplifies a mediation of public and private spheres, for it reflects the extension of a family model to a public organization, offering nurturance and support to its initiates in a personal manner reminiscent of Hull House under Jane Addams. The similarity is especially striking when we consider that the network of intimate relationships created at Hull House existed among unmarried women and was a cultural artifact of the fact that Hull House was a female institution. Bank Street, established a generation later than Hull House, was also a female world, although of a rather different kind, whose special patterns of mentoring and guidance I believe derived from Lucy Sprague Mitchell's own feminist experiences.[31] She reserved her personal life for her own family—and herein perhaps lies a significant difference from the settlement house pattern—yet the capacity for support and nurturance she brought to Bank Street helped shape the careers and lives of numerous women as they in turn mentored others. The sense in which Bank Street serves as a close-knit "family," bound by ties of emotional warmth and support, remains today, even though the size and scope of its activities have expanded substantially since her retirement.

Under Lucy Sprague Mitchell's leadership, Bank Street established a unique model of teacher training and curriculum development for young children that joined scientifically rigorous experimentation with knowledge derived from the environment and expressed creatively through the senses.[32] She shared with her economist husband a belief in the reliability of data gathering and other social science methodology, yet she was equally insistent that development of what she called the "whole" child and the "whole" teacher depended on the promotion of artistic as well as scientific impulses. At Bank Street, the boundaries of the traditional female interest in children were extended by tough-minded, rigorous professional analysis, but it was never the cold, impersonal analysis of children and methods of education that characterized many other child development institutions. Nurturance, the expression of feelings, and a model of education that sprang from the child's experiences and needs became central to Bank Street's program, but always in tandem with the strong emphasis on science and professionalism. Proud of its independence from foundations and universities, Bank Street might have borrowed methods from the outside (although more often it pioneered them), but it was never co-opted by the values, approaches, and associations of the general masculine world of institutions. In its commitment to children and especially young children (infants, preschoolers, and those in the primary grades), and the ways in which it dealt with children and their teachers, Bank Street took shape as a woman's institution. The women attracted to Mitchell in the 1930s and 40s, and to whom she gave tremendous encouragement, shared her strong desire to work as scientifically trained professionals, but they, too, allowed that their work ought to reflect the humanisti values of women's world.

Although they might not have articulated overt feminist goals, nevertheless, it can be argued that for some of these women the conscious choice of career and the articulation of approach sprang from values that had some feminist motivations. They argued, for example, not that women were superior childrearers, as did earlier generations of educators, but that it was critical to develop effective methods of education to provide each child, girl as well as boy, the chance to develop her or his capacities as a unique individual. At the same time, they searched to fashion career opportunities for themselves that were meaningful and possible. Some of these women had earlier experience working on behalf of women before becoming educators of children. Lucy Sprague Mitchell, as the first dean of women in any university of the far west, had labored to expand the parameters of women's higher education at Berkeley. Caroline Pratt, founder of the innovative Play School in Greenwich Village (later known as the City and Country School) and a significant influence on Mitchell, had previously been involved in investigations of the conditions of women working in the custom tailoring trade.[33] Pratt shared her life, home, and political sympathies with Helen Marot, a socialist activist who had been secretary for many years of the New York Women's Trade Union League, later becoming an editor of the *Masses* and the *Dial.* Because of their backgrounds, experience, and sympathies as women, the contributions of these women to early childhood education differed in important respects from that of many male experts who increasingly came to dominate university-sponsored research and practice in child development after 1920. I am not arguing that the majority of women who entered this profession were feminists, but that a number of the most significant educators were certainly influenced by a feminist perspective. At this time, the dilemma of marriage and career was resolved for most educated women through the advent of such movements as child study and parent education, which sanctioned full-time (but "educated") motherhood, guided by science. Lucy Sprague Mitchell and those of her colleagues who were married, with families, and who also established themselves in careers in education, represented a different solution to the same dilemma, different also from previous generations of unmarried women who entered traditional women's professions.[34]

Ultimately, Mitchell's pragmatic resolution of the conflict between career and marriage through the development of an environment that merged home and workplace, both physically and intellectually, was idiosyncratic (although a number of her Greenwich Village neighbors also sent their children to the Bank Street school, where they worked, or to City and Country, which adjoined it). But in a different respect, her resolution of the crisis of professional identity that plagued her until she settled on the education of children as her life work may indicate a larger trend involving the career paths of her contemporaries. It is possible that the experiences of women like Lucy Sprague Mitchell do help answer the question of what happened to feminists after 1920: while the paths of many women did reflect a retreat from the public arena into personal life, others took as their professional work those concerns that had been part of the private sphere of women's lives, focusing their energies not only on such activities as scientific housekeeping, but also on child development and preschool education.

The development of careers in these fields, furthermore, may not necessarily have been a "conservative trend," as Jill Conway argues was the case for an earlier generation of educated women.[35] Conway observes that women who founded the service professions in the Progressive Era accepted sex-typed roles predicated on the idea of a separate, nurturing female temperament. Thus, professions such as home economics and social work served to perpetuate traditional female domestic styles, rather than to channel women's energies into more creative, independent, and intellectually self-justifying endeavors. A generation later, however, Mitchell and her colleagues did not talk about a female temperament. Many of them selected early childhood education as a career not because of their belief in biological principles about gender, but because of its congruities with their own life cycles. In addition, although the institutions they characteristically developed were women-centered, as I have argued that Bank Street was, they shared interests, methodologies, and cooperative projects with male social scientists. The claim of an exclusive female sphere was rarely made. Finally, whether we talk about Caroline Pratt's Play School, or Lucy Sprague Mitchell's own *Here and Now Story Book*, acclaimed by reviewers in 1921 as "revolutionary" and "epoch making" in its focus on the child's direct world of experience (rather than the traditional fantasy world of fairy tales) as the springboard to learning, professional women in this field did find scope for their intellects, independence, and creativity, and were in fact responsible for a number of pioneering developments regarding issues that had long been of concern to male intellectuals such as John Dewey. What we need, I think, is to acknowledge the transformation, rather than betrayal, of the feminist impulse after 1920. Though, increasingly, educated women in large numbers settled down into domesticity, and although their representation in professions such as medicine and law declined, in some of the more traditional women's fields, the era ushered in one of the most fertile and creative periods in American history, as the progressive education wing of the child development movement under the leadership of Lucy Sprague Mitchell, Caroline Pratt, Elisabeth Irwin, and others exemplifies.

Although Mitchell's professional interests did not center around women as a special interest group, consciousness of women's plight became a formative influence in the resolution of her own problems and indeed, as I have suggested, in the shaping of the unique character of Bank Street. Because of the terrible agony of her own childhood loneliness and fears, she saw young children, not women, as the group most desperately needing liberation. But at the same time, Mitchell came to understand that her continuing life struggle had been dictated by issues of gender. "Every stage of life has its song," she wrote in the volume of poems she assembled shortly before her death. "My song has been a woman's song."

To understand the existential reality of women's past, it is crucial, I believe, to examine the histories of individuals such as Lucy Sprague Mitchell, for they reveal to us feminism not as theory but as a hard-fought life struggle. In an unpublished manuscript, anthropologist Ruth Benedict, a contemporary of Lucy Sprague Mitchell, wrote: "Feminism does not live by its logic. . . .

> One adventure through the life of one woman who has been profoundly stirred by a great restlessness and you will comprehend more than from a library of theorizings. The theory can only be the gloss and the addenda: the urge, the power of the woman's movement does not lie in the gift of logic. It comes from the bright stinging realm of [women's] dearest desires. . . . It is a passionate attitude toward their own lives. It is a cry to be awake in their life time, to hazard themselves and to risk the maiming, but somehow to attain to something that may conceivably be called living.[36]

It is in this sense—this passionate attitude toward life, the willingness to hazard oneself and risk the maiming—that Lucy Sprague Mitchell was surely a feminist. It is in this sense, too, that her feminism—a feminism that is embodied by life, not theory—can be instructive in illuminating the experiences of modern women and their relationship to the larger society.

NOTES

This is an expanded version of a paper presented at the annual meeting of the Organization of American Historians, New Orleans, April 12, 1979. I would like to thank Ellen Lagemann and Mari Jo Buhle for their comments on that essay.

[1] For further discussion of a conceptual framework for the study of feminism and women's history, see Ellen DuBois, Mari Jo Buhle, Temma Kaplan, Gerda Lerner, and Carroll Smith-Rosenberg, "Politics and Culture in Women's History: A Symposium," *Feminist Studies* 6, no. 1 (Spring 1980): 28-64.

[2] For a historical analysis of the role of female institutions in promoting feminist goals, see Estelle Freedman, "Separatism as Strategy: Female Institution Building and American Feminism, 1870-1930," *Feminist Studies* 5, no. 3 (Fall 1979): 512-29.

[3] The desire to merge home and career became a fundamental goal of feminists in the twenties. Elaine Showalter speaks of this drive in the introduction to her book, *These Modern Women: Autobiographical Essays from the Twenties* (Old Westbury: The Feminist Press, 1978), p. 4:

> The difference between modern women, and the suffragist or feminist of the nineteenth century, was her insistence on the right to self-fulfillment in both public life and in relationships with men. Where earlier feminist generations had renounced marriage in order to dedicate themselves to careers, the "truly modern" women . . . admitted that "a full life calls for marriage and children as well as a career." To be modern meant to want heterosexual love as well as work; neither was sufficient by itself.

Showalter believes, however, that the feminists whose *Nation* essays she reproduces were not very successful in this aim: most had erratic careers as writers, their achievements not affording them a place in history, and very few had children—on a broad societal scale as well, the results were discouraging.

[4] See Charlotte Perkins Gilman, *Women and Economics* (1898; reprint ed., New York: Harper and Row, 1966).

[5] Charlotte Perkins Gilman, "Maternity Benefits and Reformers," *The Forerunner* 7 (1916): 66.

[6] The average percentage of married graduates of the living graduates of eight women's colleges and Cornell, in 1914, was 39.1. The marriage rate at Harvard and Yale for those years (allowing ten years for a graduating class to marry) was 74 and 78 percent, respectively. Among the general population, census reports for 1910 showed that 79.1 percent of all women 25 to 34 years of age were married, and 88.6 percent of all those between 35 and 44 were married. The percentage of married women graduates at coeducational colleges, particularly in the West, was higher than at eastern women's colleges, but was still lower than that of the general female population. See Willystine Goodsell, *The Education of Women* (New York: Macmillan Co., 1924), pp. 34-60; Mabel Newcomer, *A Century of Higher Education for Women* (New York: Harper Bros., 1959), pp. 30-31; and Mary Van Kleeck, "A Census of College Women," *Journal of the Association of Collegiate Alumnae* 11 (May 1918): 557-91.

[7] Emilie J. Hutchinson, *Women and the Ph.D.* (Greensboro, North Carolina College for Women, Institute of Women's Professional Relations Bulletin, no. 2, 1930), pp. 178-79.

[8] Cited in William H. Chafe, *The American Woman: Her Changing Social, Economic and Political Role, 1920-1970* (New York: Oxford University Press, 1974), p. 100.

[9] On the development of communities of support among nineteenth- and early twentieth-century women, see Carroll Smith-Rosenberg, "The Female World of Love and Rituals: Relations Between Women in Nineteenth-Century America," *Signs* 1, no. 1 (Autumn 1975): 1-29; Blanche Wiesen Cook, "Female Support Networks and Political Activism: Lillian Wald, Crystal Eastman, Emma Goldman," *Chrysalis*, no. 3, (Fall 1977): 43-61; Patricia Ann Palmieri, "A Social Portrait of Academic Women at Wellesley College, 1890-1910," (unpublished paper, Harvard Graduate School of Education, 1978); and Ellen Lagemann, *A Generation of Women: Studies in Educational Biography* (Cambridge, Mass.: Harvard University Press, 1979).

[10]Phyllis Rose, *Woman of Letters: A Life of Virginia Woolf* (New York: Oxford University Press, 1978), p. xii.

[11]The biographical summary of Lucy Sprague Mitchell's life that follows has been developed from her book, *Two Lives: The Story of Wesley Clair Mitchell and Myself* (New York: Simon and Schuster, 1953); a fuller, more revealing unpublished autobiography, located in the Lucy Sprague Mitchell Papers at Columbia University; *Reminiscences*, Mrs. Mitchell's oral history, recorded at the University of California at Berkeley, in 1964; her correspondence and other manuscript materials at Columbia; the diaries of Wesley Clair Mitchell, loaned to me through the courtesy of Joseph Dorfman; interviews with Lucy Sprague Mitchell's children, grandchildren, friends, and colleagues; and materials in the Radcliffe College Archives and the Mitchell Papers at the University of California at Berkeley. See also my article, "Lucy Sprague Mitchell," in *Notable American Women: The Modern Period* (Cambridge, Mass.: The Belknap Press of Harvard University Press, 1980), pp. 484-87.

[12]Mitchell, *Two Lives*, p. 60.

[13]Ibid., pp. 127-28.

[14]Ibid., p. 133.

[15]Ibid., pp. 192-93.

[16]Ibid., p. 210.

[17]Lucy Sprague to Wesley Mitchell, 29 October, 13 November, 1911, Lucy Sprague Mitchell Papers, Columbia University, New York, N.Y.

[18]Mitchell to Sprague, 6 November 1911.

[19]Sprague to Mitchell, 30 November 1911.

[20]Sprague to Mitchell, 2 December 1911.

[21]Mitchell to Sprague, 7 December 1911.

[22]Lucy Sprague Mitchell's unpublished autobiography (written around 1946), Mitchell Papers.

[23]Mitchell, *Two Lives*, pp. xviii, xix.

[24]The connection between feminism and innovative architectural design is discussed by Dolores Hayden, in "Two Utopian Feminists and Their Campaign for Kitchenless Houses," *Signs* 4 (Winter 1978): 214-290.

[25]See my essay, "Progressive Education and the Scientific Study of the Child: An Analysis of New York's Bureau of Educational Experiments, 1916-1940," presented at a Conference on Needs and Opportunities for the Study of Educational History in New York City, sponsored by the Institute of Philosophy and Politics of Education, Teachers College, Columbia University, New York, N.Y., 1978.

[26]See, for example, Gilman's statement in *Women and Economics*, p. 313:

> as the private home becomes a private home indeed, and no longer the woman's social and industrial horizon; as the workshops of the world—woman's sphere as well as man's—become homelike and beautiful under her influence; and as men and women move freely together in the exercise of common racial functions—we shall have new channels for the flow of human life.

[27]Mitchell, *Two Lives*, p. 541. "Women's place in the home is as urgent as ever," she wrote. "Women who carry some work outside their homes want and need and love . . . their homes . . . and children as much as women who find full satisfaction with little or no contact with the world's problems. . . ."

[28]Ibid., p. 542.

[29]Ibid., p. 541.

[30]For further discussion of how the family bond acted to constrain daughters, see my article, "After College, What?: New Graduates and the Family Claim," *American Quarterly* 32 (Fall 1980): 409-34.

[31] As a child, Lucy Sprague Mitchell visited Hull House frequently. She was also familiar with Lillian Wald's settlement house and maintained a relationship with Wald. Harriet Johnson introduced Mitchell to the world of education in New York and worked closely with her as director of the Bank Street Nursery School until Johnson's death in 1934. Johnson and the woman she lived with, Harriet Forbes, a nurse, adopted a daughter, Polly Forbes-Johnson, who spent so much time with the Mitchells, along with "the Harriets," that she was considered a fifth Mitchell offspring. Although Johnson was Lucy Sprague Mitchell's primary mentor in the educational world, also vital to her development were Caroline Pratt and Elisabeth Irwin, the directors, respectively, of the City and Country School and the Little Red School House in New York. Both Pratt and Irwin, like Johnson, lived with women and were part of distinctly female circles.

Thus, although Lucy Sprague Mitchell was part of a "mixed" intellectual group in New York City, consisting of single men, single women, and married couples, she was familiar with, and influenced by, various female networks.

[32] My views on Bank Street are derived from analysis of its publications, archival material including Annual Reports and similar documents, and interviews with former colleagues of Lucy Sprague Mitchell. For further information, see my essay, "Progressive Education and the Scientific Study of the Child."

[33] For more information on Caroline Pratt, see her book, *I Learn From Children* (New York: Cornerstone Library, 1948); and Lawrence A. Cremin, *The Transformation of the School: Progressivism in American Education 1876-1957* (New York: Vintage Books, 1964), pp. 203-207.

[34] On the participation of women in child study and parent education movements, see Steven Schlossman's provocative article, "Philanthropy and the Gospel of Child Development," in *Private Philanthropy and Public Elementary and Secondary Education*, ed. Gerald Benjamin, Proceedings of the Rockefeller Archive Center Conference, 8 June 1979, pp. 29-30.

[35] Jill K. Conway, "Perspective on the History of Women's Education in the United States," *History of Education Quarterly* 14 (Spring 1974): 8-11.

[36] Ruth Benedict, notebook on "Adventures in Womanhood," Benedict Papers, Vassar College, Poughkeepsie, N.Y.

This research was undertaken at the Bunting Institute, Radcliffe College, under a grant from the Lilly Endowment, Inc.

Feminist Politics in the 1920s: The National Woman's Party

Nancy F. Cott

Some day the story of the working of the National Woman's Party machine will be told. It will be an interesting story, full of strange contradictions. It will tell of valiant self-sacrifice and magnificent defiance coupled with an incongruous willingness to appeal to the tradition of feminine weakness. It will be full of idealism and steadfast purpose and yet of a readiness to use any trick or pretense that might bring that purpose nearer to fulfillment. It will tell of independence and individual heroism existing side by side with obedience bordering on subservience. It will show sympathy and ruthlessness walking together.

—Freda Kirchwey

Alice Paul does not belong to the revolution, but her leadership has had a quality that only the revolution can understand.

—Crystal Eastman

The National Woman's Party (NWP) is not well known. For a long time it has stood under a pall, its history obscured by being recounted from its opponents' point of view when recounted at all. The minority faction among suffragists, it became an even more embattled minority among activist women in the 1920s because of its invention of the equal rights amendment. Insofar as it is known, the party has a paradoxical image. In histories of the suffrage movement in the 1910s, it appears as the militant, "left" wing; in histories of women's reform movements of the 1920s, it appears as a clique of prosperous business and professional women, repellent to the Left. The one organization of women that openly declared itself feminist, it has attracted most of historians' blame for the "demise" of feminism after woman suffrage was obtained. The whole story of feminism's fate after 1920 is more interesting than ever because of pos-

Nancy F. Cott is associate professor of history and American studies at Yale University. Research for this article was supported in part by a Rockefeller Foundation Humanities Fellowship and by a Radcliffe Research Scholarship, funded by the Andrew W. Mellon Foundation, at the Arthur and Elizabeth Schlesinger Library on the History of Women in America. The epigraphs are from Freda Kirchwey, "Alice Pulls the Strings," *Nation*, March 2, 1921, p. 332; and Crystal Eastman, "Alice Paul's Convention," *Liberator*, 4 (April 1921), 10.

sible parallels between the 1920s and the 1980s, and an internal examination of the NWP and a clearer interpretation of it are necessary if we are to begin to understand the earlier decade.[1]

The NWP grew from the Congressional Union, the suffrage organization Alice Paul and Lucy Burns founded when they broke with the leadership of the National American Woman Suffrage Association (NAWSA) early in 1913. Paul and Burns distinguished their approach from the mainstream in several ways that persisted as the Congressional Union evolved into the Woman's Party (1916) and the NWP (1917). A group of, by, and for women, it concentrated on the federal (rather than state) government and aimed to amend the United States Constitution to gain woman's rights; it used flamboyant publicity tactics, including street marches, open-air meetings, and eventually picketing of the White House and the Capitol; and it employed a "political" (rather than simply educative) strategy, attempting to marshal women's votes (in the states where women were enfranchised) to punish "the party in power," the Democratic party, until a woman suffrage amendment was passed. Between 1914 and 1919 the group took risks; it stood as "the party of youth" regardless of its members' chronological age; its leaders did not fear and did not fail to rankle the stalwarts of the mainstream suffrage association. The party appealed to working-class women and inadvertently or advertently to left-wing women with its militant tactics, opposition to the government during wartime, and sidestepping of gentility at the same time it appealed to wealthy socialites with its newsworthiness and its strategy of lobbying the president and national legislators in addition to exhorting the man on the street. In 1914 Alva Belmont (widow to Vanderbilt and Belmont millions) became the party's financial angel and an important voice.[2]

[1] Historians' neglect or distortion of the National Woman's Party (NWP) owes much to the fact that in compiling their massive documentary history of woman suffrage, leaders of the National American Woman Suffrage Association (NAWSA) systematically documented their own efforts and not those of other suffrage groups. See Ida Husted Harper, ed., *The History of Woman Suffrage*, vols. 5 and 6, *1900–1920* (New York, 1922). For information on the Congressional Union (CU) and the NWP, see Eleanor Flexner, *Century of Struggle: The Woman's Rights Movement in the United States* (Cambridge, Mass., 1959), 261–70, 275–77, 282–89. For NWP and NAWSA leaders, see Aileen S. Kraditor, *The Ideas of the Woman Suffrage Movement, 1890–1920* (New York, 1965), esp. 231–48. For the CU-NWP stance during the suffrage movement, see William P. O'Neill, *Everyone Was Brave: The Rise and Fall of Feminism in America* (Chicago, 1969), 126–30, 166–67, 201–04. For treatments of the NWP during the 1920s, see *ibid.*, 273–94; William Henry Chafe, *The American Woman: Her Changing Social, Economic, and Political Roles, 1920–1970* (New York, 1972), 112–26; and J. Stanley Lemons, *The Woman Citizen: Social Feminism in the 1920s* (Urbana, 1973), 49, 54, 118, 181–204. The most thorough study of the NWP after 1920 is Susan D. Becker, *The Origins of the Equal Rights Amendment: American Feminism between the Wars* (Westport, Conn., 1981). This is a work of useful scholarship but relies on the NWP newspaper *Equal Rights*, rather than on the archives, and thus inevitably overstates the approach of Edith Houghton Hooker, editor of *Equal Rights*, and underestimates the behind-the-scenes power of Alice Paul. The National Woman's Party Papers, now deposited at the Library of Congress, are available in two microfilm sets, "National Woman's Party Papers: The Suffrage Years, 1913–1920" (Microfilming Corporation of America, 1982); and "National Woman's Party Papers, 1913–1974" (Microfilming Corporation of America, 1979). The NWP correspondence appears in chronological order, without division into container or file, on the microfilm.

[2] For the CU-NWP history before 1920, see Loretta Ellen Zimmerman, "Alice Paul and the National Woman's Party, 1912–1920," (Ph.D. diss., Tulane University, 1964); Sidney Roderick

Only a fractional craft on the prosuffrage sea, the NWP made waves beyond its size because of the variety, devotion, and vigor of its organizers and members.[3] The organization charted a course with no contingencies, its orientation constantly toward a constitutional amendment for woman suffrage; and its heterogeneous membership worked toward that goal under control from above. "There is no difference of opinion in regard to Alice Paul in the Woman's Party," wrote Inez Haynes Irwin, the group's historian. "With one accord, they say 'She is the Party.' They regard her with an admiration which verges on awe." Paul seems never to have imagined any other than a tightly knit, ideologically pure, vanguard party. Though V. I. Lenin was probably far from her ken or sympathy, Paul's leadership style might be called "Leninist"; indeed, NWP organizer Doris Stevens thought in 1919 that Paul "must possess many of the same qualities that Lenin does, according to authentic portraits of him—cool, practical, rational, sitting quietly at a desk and counting the consequences." By virtually all accounts of the 1910s, Paul was charismatic. Sara Bard Field, a West Coast radical admired for oratory, addressed her not untypically as "dear, wonderful Alice Paul with your great, moist violets of eyes that always make me want to be good and with your high, daring soul that makes me want to achieve—not so much for my own sake as for the sake of the race"; and Stevens declared, "I have seen her very presence in headquarters change in the twinkling of an eye the mood of fifty people. It is not through their affections that she moves them, but through a naked force, a vital force which is indefinable but of which one simply cannot be unaware."[4]

Bland, "Techniques of Persuasion: The National Woman's Party and Woman Suffrage, 1913–1919" (Ph.D. diss., George Washington University, 1972); and Christine A. Lunardini, "From Equal Suffrage to Equal Rights: The National Woman's Party, 1913–1923" (Ph.D. diss., Princeton University, 1981). The major accounts by participants are Doris Stevens, *Jailed for Freedom* (New York, 1920); Inez Haynes Irwin, *The Story of the Woman's Party* (New York, 1921); and Caroline Katzenstein, *Lifting the Curtain: The State and National Woman Suffrage Campaigns in Pennsylvania as I Saw Them* (Philadelphia, 1955).

[3] Mabel Vernon agreed with the NAWSA claim to 98 percent of the suffrage army and stressed the vigor of NWP organizers. Mabel Vernon interview by Amelia R. Fry, 1976, "Mabel Vernon: Speaker for Suffrage and Petitioner for Peace," pp. 190–91, Suffragists Oral History Project (Bancroft Library, University of California, Berkeley). Paul claimed 5 percent for the CU and allowed NAWSA 95 percent. Alice Paul interview by Amelia R. Fry, 1976, "Conversations with Alice Paul: Woman Suffrage and the Equal Rights Amendment," p. 327, Suffragists Oral History Project. Loretta Ellen Zimmerman finds that the group had no more than 20,000 members in 1917, when Paul claimed 40,000. Zimmerman, "Alice Paul and the National Woman's Party," 243. The acting chairman of the NWP in 1921 said the national membership in 1919 stood at "about 40,000." Elsie Hill to Mrs. Dorothy C. Rice, March 30, 1921, reel 7, "National Woman's Party Papers, 1913–1974." Inez Haynes Irwin, official historian of the NWP, claimed no more than 50,000 for the NWP at the height of the suffrage fight when NAWSA had about 2 million members. Inez Haynes Irwin, *Angels and Amazons: A Hundred Years of American Women* (Garden City, N.Y., 1933), 392.

[4] Irwin, *Story of the Woman's Party*, 15; Stevens, *Jailed for Freedom*, 17, 10–11; Sara Bard Field to Alice Paul, Jan. 7, 1921, reel 5, "National Woman's Party Papers, 1913–1974." For another reference to the NWP as "Leninist," see Marjory Nelson, "Ladies in the Streets: A Sociological Analysis of the National Woman's Party, 1910–1930" (Ph.D. diss., State University of New York at Buffalo, 1976), 315, 320–21. The top-down control exercised early in the CU is emphasized in Bland, "Techniques of Persuasion," 78–79, 178. See also Lunardini, "From Equal Suffrage to Equal Rights," 118. Lavinia Dock referred tongue-in-cheek to "our Comrade Alice Paul Lenin." Lavinia Dock to Emma Wold, Jan. 1921, reel 6, series 1, "National Woman's Party Papers, 1913–1974."

Paul hewed to a narrow course with superb determination, letting other considerations fall aside. "The point is first, who is our enemy," she enunciated in August 1914, initiating the policy of "holding the party in power responsible," "and then, how shall that enemy be attacked?" "To count in an election you do not have to be the biggest Party; you have to be simply an independent Party that will stand for one object and that cannot be diverted from that object," she clarified two years later.[5] So long as Paul's object commanded as much fervor as the constitutional route to woman suffrage did, she was highly effective in inspiring and leading a vanguard party.

The NWP's 1917 strategy of picketing the White House (to persuade President Woodrow Wilson to lead the Congress to pass woman suffrage) and carrying the "strike" to jail when pickets were arrested was its most daring media ploy, but its decision in 1917 to decline any organizational declaration regarding the United States entry into the World War was equally indicative of its course. While the NAWSA pledged women's patriotism to the war effort, the NWP, in recognition of its members' varying points of view, refused commitment. In consequence of that negative policy and the party's persistent attacks on Wilson, the NWP became a haven for socialist and pacifist suffragists and a de facto proponent of civil liberties during the war and postwar years 1917–1919. Although the NWP's direct action remained nonviolent, defensible as a form of free speech, some NAWSA loyalists decried the NWP as "the I.W.W. of the suffrage movement"; the police who held back NWP demonstrators at Wilson's 1919 embarkation for Europe called them "cannibals" and "Bolsheviks." Despite the NAWSA leadership's conviction that NWP actions were traitorous and counterproductive, and despite NWP scorn for the NAWSA's distrust, the different approaches of the two organizations seem to have complemented one another. The NWP endowed woman suffrage with high drama, and the NAWSA insistently pursued its legislative plan to increase through state victories the number of states whose senators and congressmen would support a constitutional amendment for woman suffrage. If the NWP was wrong about Wilson's power over senators' votes, they were nonetheless convinced, more rightly, that their agitation had kept woman suffrage a national issue despite war and demobilization.[6]

The year 1920 was a crucial one for every woman suffrage organization, not only because the principal goal was attained, but also because that attainment was conditioned by world-historical events—the World War, the Russian Revolution, labor unrest on an unprecedented scale, the Red Scare, economic

[5] Irwin, *Story of the Woman's Party*, 75, 151.

[6] *New York Times*, Feb. 10, 1919, p. 4; Stevens, *Jailed for Freedom*, 332. For antiwar suffragists and woman suffrage, see Mari Jo Buhle, *Women and American Socialism, 1870–1920* (Urbana, 1981), 237–38. An excellent study revealing the NWP's joining with radical politics in 1917–1919 is Carole A. Nichols, "A New Force in Politics: The Suffragists' Experience in Connecticut" (M.A. essay, Sarah Lawrence College, May 1979), esp. 39–43. For conjunction of NWP and NAWSA strategies, see Stevens, *Jailed for Freedom*, 250–51; Bland, "Techniques of Persuasion," 134–38; Flexner, *Century of Struggle*, 290–92; David Morgan, *Suffragists and Democrats: The Politics of Woman Suffrage in America* (East Lansing, 1972), 121–23; and Anne F. Scott and Andrew M. Scott, *One Half the People: The Fight for Woman Suffrage* (Philadelphia, 1975), 40–42.

recession—that made contemporaries sense that one era had ended and another had begun. NWP members' opinions ranged from those who were "looking forward to the forming in this country of an historic feminist group—women who will go out to fight the forces of reaction as only they can fight them" to those who felt that "if the Woman's Party dissolves, it will be part of the general scheme—if it goes on, it will be a miracle."[7]

By July 1920, a month before the final ratification of the Nineteenth Amendment, Belmont was stressing the need for the NWP to continue as an organization to "obtain for women full equality with men in all phases of life and make them a power in the life of the state," and Paul had enunciated as a worthy goal some form of "blanket" legislation that would remove all legal discriminations against women.[8] From September 1920 through February 1921, the party's inner circle, the National Executive Committee, met monthly to hash out resolutions to present at the grand convention in February, where the future form and goals (if any) of the party were ostensibly to be decided by the delegates present. While Paul gave many of her followers the impression that she was too exhausted to go on leading them, her predilections guided preparations. In December she told the National Executive Committee that Sue Shelton White (a lawyer and vigorous party worker since 1917), who had been surveying sex discriminations in state legal codes, had drawn up a "blanket bill" that "could be introduced in Congress and each legislature to sweep away these discriminations" and "could be offered at the final convention as a possible piece of work for the future." Despite the contrary efforts of a few who wished for a broader-ranging program—especially Edith Houghton Hooker, a longtime social-hygiene proponent from Baltimore—the leadership moved undeviatingly toward the majority resolution offered at the convention: that the NWP disband but immediately regroup under the same name, with its "immediate work" being "the removal of the legal disabilities of women."[9]

Hundreds of women arrived at the February convention expecting to vent their opinions on the future of the organization. The minority report of the National Advisory Council (a second, broader tier of leadership below the National Executive Committee) produced the largest debate: it resolved that the party devote its efforts to disarmament. "Great masses of women do feel that the conservation of life, that the saving of the race from destruction is a feminist movement," asserted Belle LaFollette (wife of Robert LaFollette), a

[7] Mary Heaton Vorse to Florence Brewer Boeckel, May 5, 1920, reel 4, series 1, "National Woman's Party Papers, 1913–1974"; Harriet Brewer to Miss [Mabel] Vernon, Jan. 18, 1921, reel 5, *ibid. Cf.* Rebecca Hourwich Reyher interview by Amelia R. Fry and Fern Ingersoll, 1973, "Search and Struggle for Equality and Independence," p. 23, Suffragists Oral History Project; and Alice Park to *Suffragist*, Nov. 30, 1920, reel 5, series 1, "National Woman's Party Papers, 1913–1974."

[8] National Executive Committee, National Woman's Party, minutes, July 9, 1920, reel 114, part A, series 2, "National Woman's Party Papers, 1913–1974"; *New York Times*, July 18, 1920, sec. 6, p. 6; Peter Geidel, "The National Woman's Party and the Origins of the Equal Rights Amendment, 1920–23," *Historian*, 42 (Aug. 1980), 562.

[9] National Executive Committee, National Woman's Party, minutes, Sept. 10, Oct. 8, Nov. 16, Dec. 10, 1920, Jan. 22, Feb. 14, 1921, reel 114, part A, series 2, "National Woman's Party Papers, 1913–1974." The words "if desired" were added by hand after "introduced" and "offered" in the portions of the minutes quoted.

delegate from Wisconsin. Many—but not sufficient to prevent that goal from being quashed—agreed with her and subsequently left the NWP to form and join pacifist groups.[10] Next, Crystal Eastman, a feminist-pacifist-socialist lawyer and cultural radical who had been among the inner circle since CU days, presented her program: to remove legal and customary barriers to women's self-realization, to remake marriage laws and public opinion to eliminate the homemaker-childrearer's economic dependence, to end laws prohibiting birth control, and to renovate the laws of inheritance, divorce, child custody, and sexual morality on the basis of sexual equality. Eastman predicted that "nobody that has a thread of modern feminism will care a rap" for the NWP if it adopted the "old-fashioned" aim to remove legal disabilities. Her proposals were voted down, nonetheless, almost two to one.[11]

The convention had been planned to include both ceremonial and political features: the first, a parade of banner-waving, wreath-bearing representatives of more than a hundred women's organizations attendant on the installation of marble sculptures of Elizabeth Cady Stanton, Susan B. Anthony, and Lucretia Mott in the Capitol rotunda; next, the presentation of other women's organizations' legislative programs to inform and warm the NWP delegates' debate and decision about their own future. The ceremony became political, however, since the NAWSA's alienation from the NWP kept it and its successor, the League of Women Voters, from sending representatives to join in reverence for the suffrage pioneers.[12] And the political debate was ceremonial, at least in the eyes of disaffected delegates who saw it as a rubber stamp of the central leadership's decision.

The votes in support of the majority resolution—to disband, to regroup immediately under the same name, and to adopt the program of ending women's legal disabilities—were strong enough to suggest that the convention willingly supported Paul, although Eastman protested that the five hours left for actual discussion after all the speakers had had their turns were too short a time to allow the group to hammer out a program. Eastman, in the *Liberator*, and Freda Kirchwey, in the *Nation*, wrote acerbic articles characterizing the NWP leadership as a "steamroller" and a "machine." Party members who identified themselves with the political Left, as Eastman and Kirchwey did, were generally disappointed with the convention's outcome. Rebecca

[10] National Woman's Party Convention, transcript, Feb. 15–18, 1921, p. 117, folder 18, Alma Lutz Collection MC182 (Schlesinger Library, Cambridge, Mass.). For former suffragists' peace activism in the early 1920s, see Charles DeBenedetti, *Origins of the Modern American Peace Movement, 1915–1929* (Millwood, N.Y., 1978), 86–97; and Charles Chatfield, *For Peace and Justice: Pacifism in America, 1914–1941* (Knoxville, 1971), 147–50.

[11] National Woman's Party Convention, transcript, Feb. 15–18, 1921, pp. 129–34. The vote against Crystal Eastman's proposal was 170 to 95. Many years later Paul described Eastman's proposal as "a very involved feminist program . . . embracing everything that Russia was doing and taking in all kinds of things that we didn't expect to take in at all. . . . [W]e didn't give a second thought to it." Paul interview, 259.

[12] For invitees, arrangements, and charges for the ceremony, see correspondence Jan.-Feb. 1921, reel 6, series 1, "National Woman's Party Papers, 1913–1974"; National Executive Committee, National Woman's Party, minutes, Jan. 14, 1921, reel 114, part A, series 2, *ibid.*; and Geidel, "National Woman's Party and the Origins of the Equal Rights Amendment" [*Historian*], 563.

Hourwich of Chicago had "wanted the Woman's Party to do something more radical"; Agnes Leach of New York objected that legal disabilities were "felt chiefly by women of property," who could take care of themselves; Sylvie Thygeson of California "fail[ed] to see how women are to be liberated unless you get at the root of the matter."[13]

Once a new initiation fee of ten dollars and annual dues of ten dollars were set, more were alienated. Beulah Amidon of South Dakota refused to recruit members at so high a fee, which she felt made the party "at once a conservative, property-holding, upper-crust group" with whom she was "out of sympathy." Emma Bancroft of Delaware likewise did not want to belong to the new party if it was to be an "aristocratic affair." The temporary chairman of the new party, Elsie Hill of Connecticut, who had joined as an organizer in 1913, remonstrated that both the Socialist party and the Industrial Workers of the World (IWW) asked for one dollar per month, or twelve dollars per year, from their members, that the nominal membership fee required by the NWP during the suffrage campaign had made Paul and others into "beggars" of rich women, and that the organization now had to be self-supporting. "The work must be supported by those who feel the need, and direction of it must be in the hands of those who really care."[14]

Hill's response to a convention delegate displeased with the dismissal of disarmament shed additional light on the party's stance at that transitional moment. "The only peculiar merit of the NWP in the past" was "its unswerving concentration on its aim and the spiritual daring of its tactics," she believed, and all the competing resolutions at the convention would have diluted that. In Hill's view the "natural thing" for women was "always to be drawn hither and thither and give their feeble undominating support to many very appealing issues," but experience—she cited women's pacifism in 1914–1916—showed her "that women have got to be more powerful in society before they can aid conclusively the real issues which affect them vitally." Though antimilitarist, Hill felt strongly that "the greatest work" for the NWP was "to stick to the fight to increase the power of women, and their daring to use what power they have in securing immediate results, instead of merely announcing many beliefs." Having seen during her eight years as an organizer "the absorption of women in every interest excepting that of their own class," Hill was "not surprised that these interests still absorb them" but was "glad

[13] Crystal Eastman, "Alice Paul's Convention," *Liberator*, 4 (April 1921), 9–10; Freda Kirchwey, "Alice Paul Pulls the Strings," *Nation*, March 2, 1921, pp. 332–33. Rebecca Hourwich to Hill, May 6, 1921, reel 8, series 1, "National Woman's Party Papers, 1913–1974"; Agnes B. Leach to Paul, March 25, 1921, reel 7, *ibid.*; Leach to Mrs. [Elizabeth] Rogers, Feb. 25, 1921, reel 6, *ibid.*; Sylvie Thygeson to Hill, March 30, 1921, reel 7, *ibid.*

[14] Beulah Amidon to National Woman's Party, n.d. [April 1921], reel 7, series 1, "National Woman's Party Papers, 1913–1974"; Emma C. Bancroft to Hill, March 24, 1921, *ibid.*; Hill to Bancroft, March 26, 1921, *ibid.* The NWP was $12,000 in debt when the suffrage amendment was ratified. To raise money, Paul charged each women's organization the inflated sum of $25 for banners and wreaths at the convention ceremony. See Dock's complaints in LLD [Dock] to Miss [Emma] Wold, n.d. [Jan. 1921], reel 6, series 1, *ibid.*; LLD [Dock] to Alice [Paul], n.d. [Feb. 1921], *ibid.*

the National Woman's Party remains a workshop in which those women who wish to work for women can at any time come back to the fight."[15]

The machinations surrounding the convention made it clear that the NWP's single-issue politics and top-down control were intentional preferences of its leadership, not merely artifacts of the suffrage battle's intensity. In 1916 the party had determined to align women voters against Wilson purely because of the suffrage question, not weighing in the calculation potential benefit to the Republican candidate Charles Evans Hughes, who had endorsed the idea of a woman suffrage amendment but whose views on preparedness and social legislation were repulsive to many women. In 1917 the party had refused to take an organizational stand on the World War, to avoid committing its membership to anything but woman suffrage. In 1920–1921 the goal of woman suffrage having been won, the party's leadership moved to define a new single issue. To "remove all remaining forms of the subjection of women" became the party's new rallying cry; but since, in Paul's view, people needed "a simple, concrete object" to be mobilized, the removal of legal disabilities was to be the immediate work. Women who stayed with the party in the 1920s accepted the conditions that Paul's leadership imposed. As Josephine Bennett, a wealthy Connecticut woman with radical politics, aptly summarized in a post-convention letter to Paul, "the group gathered there . . . wanted you and no one else to lead them ultimately and under those circumstances it was only right that they should adopt your program." Though herself "not stirred over the removal of the 'legal disabilities' of women except as a part of a program of much larger scope," Bennett was "no obstructionist" and believed "it was the one program that they could all unite upon."[16]

The NWP's new priorities, and Paul's ruthlessness in paring away "diversions," were clarified in a little-known controversy over black women voters at the convention. Despite early links between the woman's rights and the antislavery movements, the suffrage movement after 1890 failed to take a stand against the oppression of blacks, knuckling under to the racism of the surrounding society, sacrificing principle and the interests or pride of black people, if that seemed advantageous to white women's obtaining the vote. Whether the NWP was more honorable on that score than was the NAWSA is debatable. The NWP's insistence on the constitutional route to woman suffrage seemed especially aimed against the South, where racist fears of the black vote combined with archaic notions of white womanhood and the concern of textile manufacturers for a manipulatable female labor force to stymie woman suffrage attempts at the state level. During its "militant" years the NWP sought and gained the support of some black women, including two outstanding leaders, Ida B. Wells-Barnett and Mary Church Terrell. Nonetheless, the NWP may have deserved the bitter assessment early in 1919 of

[15] Hill to Willystine Goodsell, April 1, 1921, reel 7, series 1, *ibid.*

[16] National Executive Committee, National Woman's Party, minutes, Jan. 22, 1921, reel 114, part A, series 2, *ibid.*; Josephine Bennett to Paul, Feb. 23, 1921, reel 6, series 1, *ibid.* For Josephine Bennett's role during the suffrage campaign in Connecticut, see Nichols, "New Force in Politics," 37–43.

Walter White, director of the National Association for the Advancement of Colored People (NAACP), following a wrangle with Paul, that "if they could get the Suffrage Amendment through without enfranchising colored women, they would do it in a moment."[17]

When the February 1921 convention was announced, Mary White Ovington, a white socialist, feminist, and founding member of the NAACP, wrote to all members of the NWP National Advisory Council wnom she knew personally, urging them to arrange for a black woman to address the group. Describing how prospective black voters in the South were being terrorized, Ovington stressed that black women would never vote unless their rights were upheld by all other women. She urged that the convention appoint a committee to investigate and take action on this issue. Although several National Advisory Council members endorsed Ovington's proposal, the response from the NWP headquarters was negative. Headquarters secretary Emma Wold, writing for Paul, explained that the convention could give the podium only to groups with legislative programs for women or with feminist aims. The point was to ensure that the NWP, in choosing its goals, did not duplicate another group's work. Since Mary C. Talbert of the National Association of Colored Women's Clubs, the speaker whom Ovington recommended, represented a group with a "racial," not "feminist," intent, she could not be featured. Wold emphasized that it was the definition of the convention program rather than lack of concern about blacks that caused this refusal. She encouraged the appointment of black women as delegates who could speak from the floor. Headquarters did make efforts to facilitate the inclusion of blacks in state delegations, and when a black woman from Virginia, probably fearing segregation, inquired "how will the arrangements be for the colord delegates in this convenchion," Wold replied for Paul that black delegates would have exactly the same arrangements as white delegates and would be seated with their state delegations. Paul also conferred with Hallie Brown, Terrell, and other black women leaders about representation of the National Association of Colored Women's Clubs at the ceremony unveiling the sculptures and reached agreement on a "representation of their race" satisfactory to the black women, according to Paul.[18]

[17] Kraditor, *Ideas of the Woman Suffrage Movement*, 163–218; Rosalyn Terborg-Penn, "Discrimination against Afro-American Women in the Woman's Movement, 1830–1920," in *The Afro-American Woman: Struggles and Images*, ed. Sharon Harley and Rosalyn Terborg-Penn (Port Washington, N.Y., 1978), 17–27; Angela Y. Davis, *Women, Race, and Class* (New York, 1981), 118. On the race issue in the CU, see Bland, "Techniques of Persuasion," 53–55. Regarding Ida B. Wells-Barnett's "picket pin," see Ida B. Wells-Barnett to Paul, March 21, 1921, reel 7, series 1, "National Woman's Party Papers, 1913–1974"; and Paul to Wells-Barnett, March 24, 1921, *ibid*. Though she mentioned the Alpha Suffrage Club, which she founded, Wells-Barnett did not record her NWP participation in her autobiography. Ida B. Wells-Barnett, *Crusade for Justice: The Autobiography of Ida B. Wells*, ed. Alfreda M. Duster (Chicago, 1970). Mary Church Terrell recalled joining the NWP pickets in Mary Church Terrell, *A Colored Woman in a White World* (Washington, 1940), 316–17. See also National Woman's Party headquarters to Mary Church Terrell, April 24, 1919, item 631, container 5, Mary Church Terrell Papers (Library of Congress); National Woman's Party headquarters to Terrell, [Jan. 1921], item 214, container 6, *ibid*.; and Walter White to Terrell, March 14, 1919, item 615, container 4, *ibid*.

[18] Mary White Ovington to Harriot Stanton Blatch, Dec. 3, 1920, "National Woman's Party 1920–21" folder, container 384, series C, National Association for the Advancement of Colored

Black women's formal presentation of their concerns at the convention was more significant, however, and here there was no satisfaction. Talbert, appreciating Ovington's efforts, confessed, "I do not believe that Alice Paul is at all sincere, I doubt her very much on the color line." Ovington herself, while trying to reverse the decision, judged that "Miss Paul unquestionably is more influenced by her southern white constituency than by those northerners who believe in working for the colored woman." When Florence Kelley, leader of the National Consumers' League and a member of the NWP National Executive Committee, intervened on behalf of Ovington's plea, Paul gave her a more complicated explanation. Next on the NWP's agenda, Paul said, and "by far the most important item of their immediate program" was to push for legislation "enforcing" woman suffrage by means of federal penal sanctions against any state registration or election official who discriminated against women. The proposed legislation was presumably aimed at southern states that disfranchised black women. Paul gave Kelley the impression that she feared Talbert's "inflaming" the southerners at the convention, once the enforcement bill became known. Kelley concluded that "Miss Paul, as a Quaker woman is of course entirely in sympathy with Mrs. Talbert and her work" but "as a tactician" denied the request for Talbert to speak from the podium. The NWP did in fact have an enforcement bill introduced to Congress, on December 30, 1920, by Wesley Jones, Republican senator from Washington.[19]

A group of black women subsequently took up the second part of Ovington's request, for an investigation of voting rights violations. Early in February a large delegation claiming to represent five million black women in fourteen

People Papers (Library of Congress); Ovington to National Woman's Party Advisory Council members, Dec. 6, Dec. 23, 1920, *ibid.*; Wold to Blatch, Dec. 29, 1920, with appended handwritten note by Blatch to Ovington, *ibid.*; Ovington to Lucy Burns, Dec. 17, 1920, with appended handwritten note by Burns to National Woman's Party headquarters, reel 5, series 1, "National Woman's Party Papers, 1913–1974"; Wold to Burns, Jan. 14, 1921, *ibid.*; Hallie Brown to Paul, Jan. 22, 1921, *ibid.*; Mrs. Lizzie McPherson to Paul, Feb. 2, 1921, reel 6, *ibid.*; [Wold] to Mrs. Sophie Meredith, Feb. 3, 1921, *ibid.*; [Wold] to McPherson, Feb. 4, 1921, *ibid.*; McPherson to Wold, Feb. 11, 1921, *ibid.*; Paul to Mrs. William Spencer Murray, Jan. 24, 1921, *ibid.*; Paul to Hallie Brown, Jan. 24, 1921, *ibid.*; Hallie Brown to Paul, Jan. 31, 1921, *ibid.*

[19] Mary Talbert to Ovington, Jan. 15, 1921, "National Woman's Party 1920–21" folder, container 384, series C, National Association for the Advancement of Colored People Papers; Ovington to Mrs. William Spencer Murray, Jan. 12, 1921, *ibid.* Vernon much later reported that Paul was prejudiced against blacks and Jews, though always polite to individuals of both groups. Vernon saw Paul's intimacy with Anita Pollitzer, a Jew, as an exception. Vernon interview, 157–58. Florence Kelley to Ovington, Dec. 22, 1920, "National Woman's Party 1920–21" folder, container 384, series C, National Association for the Advancement of Colored People Papers. For the enforcement bill, see *Congressional Record*, 66 Cong., 3 sess., Dec. 30, 1920, p. 808; Mary Winsor to Ovington, Dec. 31, 1920, "National Woman's Party 1920–21" folder, container 384, series C, National Association for the Advancement of Colored People Papers; clipping sent by Mary Talbert to Ovington, *ibid.*; Anna A. Clemons to Secretary of the National Woman's Party, Oct. 10, 1920, reel 5, series 1, "National Woman's Party Papers, 1913–1974"; Headquarters Secretary [Wold] to Miss Clemons, Oct. 20, 1920, *ibid.*; Clemons to Wold, Oct. 24, 1920, *ibid.*; Wold to Clemons, Oct. 28, 1920, *ibid.*; and Wold to Clemons, Nov. 2, 1920, *ibid.* Anna A. Clemons, a black woman from Southport, N.C., wished to register to vote.

states called on Paul to point out violations of black voting rights in 1920 and to ask for opportunity to call the NWP's attention to that travesty of the Nineteenth Amendment. Paul gave them only the same opportunity other individuals had—to speak as delegates from the convention floor. At the convention Ella Rush Murray, a white delegate from New York and member of the National Advisory Council, managed to present a minority resolution directing the NWP to form a committee to pressure Congress to investigate violations of the Nineteenth Amendment. (Mysteriously, her resolution, first moved at the National Advisory Council's meeting on January 28, was left out of that meeting's minutes and did not appear in the convention issue of the party's newspaper, the *Suffragist*.) The resolution was voted down. In the *Nation* Kirchwey asserted that "Miss Paul was indifferent to" the appeal of the black women and "resented the presence of the delegation." Kirchwey reported that black delegates were denied use of the elevator at the convention; moreover, she voiced a rumor that the NWP had agreed not to raise the race issue as a price for the ratification of woman suffrage in the South.[20]

Paul's view of the matter differed entirely. In a lengthy letter to the *Nation* (never printed and perhaps not even sent) and in letters to her intimates, Paul denied all of Kirchwey's damaging allegations. The elevator story was a mistake: black women had been asked by the elevator boy to use the stairs but so had all the white women, until someone complained, whereupon everyone was allowed to use the elevator. Paul asserted, more significantly, that the NWP had never made a "deal" to ignore the racial question in the South but always as a *general* policy ignored *all* issues outside the woman suffrage amendment. She maintained that she had made sure, after receiving the black delegation, that they had the same opportunity everyone else did to present their views from the convention floor, although she anticipated southern white delegates' hostility. Indeed, the entire white delegation from North Carolina at first refused to register, in protest against the black women's presence, and only with difficulty were persuaded to attend at all; they stayed away from the ceremonial dinner, where they would have had to eat with black women, and one member refused to receive her "picket pin" because Terrell was awarded one at the same ceremony.[21] In Paul's view no

[20] Inez Richardson to Paul, Feb. 2, 1921, reel 6, series 1, "National Woman's Party Papers, 1913-1974"; Paul to Mrs. Lawrence [Dora] Lewis, March 23, 1921, reel 7, *ibid.*; Paul to Mrs. John Rogers, March 24, 1921, *ibid.*; Ella Rush Murray, "The Woman's Party and the Violation of the 19th Amendment," *Crisis*, 21 (April 1921), 259-61; National Woman's Party Convention, transcript, Feb. 15-18, 1921, p. 61; Kirchwey, "Alice Paul Pulls the Strings," 333. NWP members, mostly unaware of the black delegation's visit to Paul, were shocked by Freda Kirchwey's snide and condemnatory tone; even Ella Rush Murray and Florence Kelley, who disapproved of what had happened, found Kirchwey's report too "flippant" and one-sided. Kelley to Mrs. [Dora] Lewis, Feb. 28, March 7, 1921, reel 6, series 1, "National Woman's Party Papers, 1913-1974"; Ella Rush Murray to editor, *Nation*, March 23, 1921, p. 434.

[21] Paul to Mrs. Lawrence [Dora] Lewis, March 23, 1921, reel 7, series 1, "National Woman's Party Papers, 1913-74"; Paul to Mrs. John Rogers, March 24, 1921, *ibid.*; Dora Lewis to Mrs. Brannon, March 9, 1921, *ibid.*; National Chairman [Elsie Hill] to Olympia Brown, March 8, 1921, *ibid.*; Dora Lewis to "Dearest Paulie" [Paul], April 11, 1921, *ibid.*

discrimination and no "machine" had operated. The convention had passed over black voting rights, as it had passed over disarmament and birth control, because its consensus genuinely formed around another goal, that of eliminating women's legal disabilities.[22]

Complaints surfaced from a few. Kelley expressed chagrin that the party had "welshed on the Negro question." Agnes Chase joined the reorganized party with the caustic protest that its circulars ought to have said "for white women" rather than "women." Murray declined to serve on the party's new National Advisory Council, "in view of certain phases of the recent convention," and ended her subscription to the party newspaper. After the convention the issue of the enforcement bill slipped from sight and was dropped entirely at a meeting of the National Executive Committee in May 1921 attended only by Hill and three southerners.[23]

It was a great credit to Paul and her immediate lieutenants that they asserted the ongoing need for an association dedicated to women's power, not to social service or to good government, but to "the removal of all remaining forms of subjection" of the female sex. The treatment of black women's concerns at the convention forewarned, however, that the party's interpretation of equal rights would narrow, rather than expand, its purview and its constituency. Paul presumed that equality of legal rights was, like woman suffrage, a "purely feminist" program on which women could unite regardless of their disagreements on other issues. Instead of encompassing the issue of black women's voting rights in the circle of women's legal equality, Paul regarded it as a diversion, and she regarded it as a diversion because black women were suffering an injustice imposed, not by sex, but by race—black men were similarly disfranchised. A diversion on which there might be controversy could not be taken up, for fear of compromising the goal on which presumably all women could agree. That Paul's outlook was at least as much due to her conception of the viability of single-issue politics as it was to racism is strongly suggested by her similar attitude at the convention toward birth control as a "diversion" from the principal route. The party's refusal to declare on any issue besides the woman suffrage amendment had been consistent with heterogeneity among its membership during the suffrage campaign, and Paul envisioned no difference in procedure for the future. But in the case of black

[22] Kirchwey also took Paul severely to task for hedging on granting the convention podium to birth control advocates. Kirchwey, "Alice Paul Pulls the Strings," 332, 333. Paul did try to suppress the appearance of both Margaret Sanger's American Birth Control League and Mary Ware Dennett's Voluntary Parenthood League because they were "too controversial," but under great pressure she allowed them limited time to present their aims. See Juliet Barrett Roublee to Paul, Feb. 5, 1921, reel 6, series 1, "National Woman's Party Papers, 1913–1974"; National Woman's Party headquarters secretary to Roublee, Feb. 8, 1921, *ibid.*; Mary Ware Dennett to Paul, Jan. 21, Feb. 3, 1921, *ibid.*; Mrs. Lawrence Lewis to Dennett, Feb. 4, 1921, *ibid.*; Marion May to Paul, Feb. 9, [1921], *ibid.*; Wold to Ethel McC. Adamson, Feb. 12, 1921, *ibid.*; Wold to Dennett, telegram, Feb. 14, 1921, *ibid.*

[23] Kelley to Mrs. Lawrence [Dora] Lewis, Feb. 28, 1921, *ibid.*; Agnes Chase to Hill, April 2, 1921, reel 7, *ibid.*; Ella Rush Murray to Temporary Secretary, April 7, 1921, *ibid.*; National Executive Committee, National Woman's Party, minutes, May 16, 1921, reel 114, part A, series 2, *ibid.*

women's voting rights, Paul's newly defined "simple, concrete object" excluded a group of women. The black women's question at the convention was the first clear indication that in claiming to make equal rights—intrinsically so much thornier to define and to pursue than suffrage was—stand for and speak to all women, the NWP would stand for and speak to fewer and fewer women.[24]

Besides those who did not join the reorganized NWP because their principal goal, suffrage, had been achieved, many women more strongly committed to black rights, pacifism, birth control, or social revolution departed. "I do not feel the interest in the new Woman's Party which seems to fill the hearts of some of the old group," wrote Jessie Hardy MacKaye, deserting to pacifism. Anne Martin, first president of the Woman's Party when it was formed in the western states in 1916, resigned from the National Advisory Council "with all good wishes"; Lilla Day Monroe, president of the Kansas Women Lawyers' Association, though "inordinately proud" of her past NWP involvement, could not consider herself "part and parcel of the new organization." "The old crowd has scattered never to gather in the same way again," a former organizer wrote presciently after a stay at headquarters in March. Two months after the convention, the new NWP had 151 paid members—as compared with a membership total between 35,000 and 60,000 at its height in 1919-1920. By dunning people for earlier pledges as small as $1, by selling whatever was salable from the old headquarters, by enlisting new "founders" at $1,000 apiece, and charging $10 for new members to join, the NWP paid off its $12,000 debt from the suffrage years in fairly short order, nonetheless. Small and large donations—the latter mainly from Belmont—kept the group solvent.[25] And membership grew, though it never exceeded—and probably fell far below—the party's claim of 10,000 during the 1920s. Recognizing the motivation toward feminism among women at work, especially in professional and semiprofessional fields, the NWP recruited members by structuring occupational councils: the Government Workers, Industrial Workers, Physicians, Homemakers councils, and so on, headed whenever possible by famous women such as Ruth Hale (Journalists), Zona Gale (Authors), Lavinia Dock (Nurses), and Ethel Barrymore (Actresses).[26]

[24] Marjory Nelson sees the resolution of the black women's issue as the NWP's first step toward elitism. Nelson, "Ladies in the Streets," 201-06. "Purely feminist" is Caroline Spencer's phrasing of Paul's intentions. Caroline Spencer to Paul, Oct. 10, 1920, reel 5, series 1, "National Woman's Party Papers, 1913-1974."

[25] Jessie Hardy MacKaye to Hill, March 21, 1921, reel 7, series 1, "National Woman's Party Papers, 1913-1974"; Anne Martin to Miss [Anita L.] Pollitzer, March 4, 1921, *ibid.*; Lilla Day Monroe to headquarters, March 30, 1921, *ibid.*; Katherine B. Day to Paul, March 22, 1921, *ibid.*; Pollitzer to Mrs. [Dora] Lewis, April 13, 1921, *ibid.* For April 1921 membership, see *ibid.* For 1919-1920 membership figures see Hill to Rice, March 30, 1921, *ibid.*; Irwin, *Angels and Amazons*, 392-93. For NWP debt, see Dora Lewis to Mrs. Alva Belmont, March 9, 1921, reel 7, series 1, "National Woman's Party Papers, 1913-1974"; and dunning letters to redeem pledges on reels 7 and 8, *ibid.* For detailed information on NWP finances in the 1920s, see Becker, *Origins of the Equal Rights Amendment*, 38-41.

[26] The *New York Times*, reporting that NWP membership had doubled during the three months preceding the dedication of a new headquarters in April 1922, stressed the New York society women who were enlisting as "founders." *New York Times*, May 29, 1922, p. 10. In the mid-

To translate "the removal of legal disabilities" into legislation was the prime task. Paul had been experimenting with forms for a constitutional amendment to end sex discrimination in law even before the convention gave its mandate. As a sequel to their strategy in the suffrage campaign, NWP leaders clearly preferred the "clean sweep" approach of amending the Constitution. (It should be noted, of course, that many reformers who did not support an equal rights amendment in the 1920s sought the route of constitutional amendment to accomplish other reforms, from the abolition of child labor to the outlawry of war.) Party leaders began surveying state legal codes for sex discriminations, conferring with lawyers, drumming up attendance for a delegation to President Warren G. Harding, and drafting numerous versions of equal rights legislation and amendments for the state as well as the federal level.[27]

When the issue of laws that protected women's hours, wages, and conditions of work came up, as it immediately did, NWP leaders at first made exceptions to their blanket legislation plans. For example, in March 1921 Paul advised the chairman of the Massachusetts NWP to

> be very certain that none of the legislation which you introduce in any way disturbs any protective legislation that may have been passed in your state for the welfare of women. I do not think we want to interfere in any way with the so called welfare legislation that has been passed at the instance of the Consumers League and other organizations for the purpose of protecting women from night work and from too long hours of labor, even though this legislation may not be equal for men and women. That is, it seems to me when there is an inequality in which the position of women is better than that of men, we do not want to bring the standard for women down to that of men, but want, on the contrary, to bring that of men up to the standard existing for women.

Early in 1921 NWP member Mabel Raef Putnam led a coalition in Wisconsin that succeeded in getting passed a state bill to grant women the same rights and privileges as men, exempting "the special protection and privileges which they now enjoy for the general welfare." Nonetheless, members of women's

1920s, the NWP claimed 10,000 members, but its opponents in the National Women's Trade Union League and the League of Women Voters thought such claims were exaggerated by a factor of ten. Ethel Smith to Belle Sherwin, May 10, 1926, folder 42, National Women's Trade Union League Papers (Schlesinger Library); Mary Anderson to Mary Mundt, Sept. 24, 1926, folder 11, Mary Anderson Papers (Schlesinger Library). Dora Ogle, business manager, reported in Dec. 1927 that the NWP newspaper *Equal Rights* had 1,425 subscribers, but this may have been in addition to members, for Ethel Adams Crosby wrote to Alma Lutz in 1936 that *Equal Rights* went to 739 "subscribers" in addition to 1,971 "members" and 179 "founders." National Council, National Woman's Party, minutes, Dec. 5, 1927, reel 114, part C, series 2, "National Woman's Party Papers, 1913–1974"; E. A. Crosby to Alma Lutz, May 23, 1936, folder 68, Lutz Collection. Lutz, who became national organization chairman for the NWP in 1930, concluded after a survey that "our 9000 members are a myth." "Report of Organization Chairman," draft, folder 23, Lutz Collection. Activities of the occupational councils can be followed in *Equal Rights*.

[27] Katherine Fisher to Paul, Nov. 8, 1920, reel 5, series 1, "National Woman's Party Papers, 1913–1974"; Paul to Hill, telegram, Jan. 4, 1921, reel 6, *ibid.*; Eva Epstein Shaw to Paul, Jan. 4, 1921, *ibid.*; Boeckel to Mr. Brigham, Jan. 28, 1921, *ibid.* For the deputation that met President Warren G. Harding and for state legislation, see correspondence of March 1921, reel 7, "National Woman's Party Papers, 1913–1974." For drafts of an equal rights amendment, see reel 116, part F, series 3, *ibid.*

groups who had led in creating sex-based protective legislation were becoming nervous and distrustful, suspecting that the NWP was less interested in preserving labor laws than in attaining "equal rights" and fearing that any blanket legislation, even with safeguarding clauses, would endanger welfare provisions for women and would throw the question of industrial protection into the reactionary courts.[28]

Meanwhile, differences of opinion within the NWP were surfacing. A few members had for some time seen sex-based protective legislation as only another form of sex discrimination and opposed it. One was Harriot Stanton Blatch (daughter of Elizabeth Cady Stanton), a New York State suffrage leader whose views had formed under the influence of Fabian socialists in England about 1900. Paul seems to have favored such legislation early on. Before the suffrage campaign she (like many other suffragists) had worked in settlement houses and with wage-earning women. Her letters of 1920–1921 affirming her desire to preserve labor legislation for women sound sincere. During 1921, however, Gail Laughlin, a prickly lawyer, NWP suffragist, and first president of the National Federation of Business and Professional Women's Clubs (1919–1920) who like Blatch opposed labor legislation restricted to women, seems to have exerted greater influence on Paul. Laughlin chaired the NWP Lawyers Committee that in the fall of 1921 drew up drafts of state bills and a federal amendment *lacking* the exempting clause. By late November the handwriting appeared on the wall as Paul explained to a New York member, Jane Norman Smith, "Personally, I do not believe in special protective labor legislation for women. It seems to me that protective labor legislation should be enacted for women and men alike in a trade or in a geographical district and not along sex lines. I think that enacting labor laws along sex lines is erecting another handicap for women in the economic struggle." The NWP was still trying to draft an amendment that would preserve special labor legislation, nonetheless, and continued to introduce state equal rights bills with safeguards through the following spring.[29]

At Kelley's behest, Paul and three other NWP members met in December 1921 with leaders of the League of Women Voters, the National Women's Trade Union League, the Woman's Christian Temperance Union, and the General Federation of Women's Clubs to discuss the amendment now proposed by the NWP: "No political, civil or legal disabilities or inequalities on account of sex, or on account of marriage unless applying alike to both sexes, shall exist within the United States or any place subject to their jurisdiction."

[28] Paul to Katherine Morey, March 20, 1921, reel 7, "National Woman's Party Papers, 1913-1974." Similar sentiments are in Hill to Kelley (early 1921), reel 6, *ibid.*; Hill to Mrs. Florence Kennedy [Kelley], March 21, 1921, reel 7, *ibid.*; Temporary Secretary to Shippen Lewis, April 1, 1921, *ibid.*; Hill to Shippen Lewis, April 7, 1921, *ibid.*; rough draft of Paul to Florence Sanville, April 2, 1921, reel 7, *ibid*. For the Wisconsin Equal Rights Bill, see Edwin E. Witte, "History and Purposes of the Wisconsin Equal Rights Law," typescript, Dec. 1929, Mabel Raef Putnam Collection (Schlesinger Library); and Peter Geidel, "The National Woman's Party and the Origins of the Equal Rights Amendment" (M.A. thesis, Columbia University, 1977), chapter 3.

[29] Paul to Jane Norman Smith, Nov. 29, 1921, folder 110, Jane Norman Smith Collection (Schlesinger Library). Paul much later recalled that Gail Laughlin had alerted her to the dangers of sex-based protective labor legislation. Paul interview, 476–78.

Kelley asked Paul to hold the amendment back until the safety of the labor laws could be assured; she proposed that "civil" and "legal" be removed from the wording. Having been betrayed on the "Negro question," Kelley seemed entirely distrustful of Paul. Kelley disapproved of blanket equal rights measures, regardless of safeguards, thinking they were "as dangerous as anything can possibly be" in the hands of the courts. At the meeting Paul was her one-issue self, asserting that pursuit of equal legal rights, not concern for other legislation, was her organization's mandate. The NWP had no particular intention to dislodge protective laws, she said, but had not (in twenty-six drafts) been able to arrive at language that would preserve such legislation without compromising the amendment's intent. Evading direct questions about her own opinions, Paul conceded that several members of the National Executive Committee, especially Laughlin, opposed labor or welfare laws based on sex. Two other NWP members present, however—Dora Lewis and Maud Younger—said they strongly supported the eight-hour day and minimum wage for women. (They, like many other NWP members, had devoted themselves to establishing such laws early in the century.) Paul refused Kelley's suggestion about wording because, she said, it would render the amendment worthless, but she welcomed others. Ethel Smith of the Women's Trade Union League and Maud Wood Park of the League of Women Voters left the meeting very worried about "a cleavage among women . . . which would be most deplorable and harmful to women's interests" though not at all willing themselves to temper their opposition to an equal rights amendment. Kelley was deeply distressed about the threat to welfare legislation. All felt that compromise was unlikely. By mid-1922 Kelley's, Ethel Smith's, and Park's organizations, and the American Federation of Labor (AFL) and the American Home Economics Association besides, had gone on record opposing blanket equal rights legislation.[30]

Already, each side on the question of an equal rights amendment thought the other intransigent, although debate within the NWP went on. At the February meeting of the National Advisory Council, Caroline Spencer of Colorado introduced an amendment worded, "Equality of the sexes shall not be denied or abridged on account of sex or marriage." She argued that the NWP should not be concerned with the fate of special labor legislation. Younger countered her, but the tide was turning. Younger was one of the last holdouts. How the lack of flexibility or cooperation shown by other women's organizations affected that (seemingly inevitable) evolution is impossible to judge. In April, Laughlin communicated her views, which became definitive. She

[30] "Conference on So-called 'Equal Rights' Amendment Proposed by the National Woman's Party (Dec. 4, 1921)," typescript, reel 2, National Women's Trade Union League Papers (Library of Congress); "Conference Held December 4, 1921," typescript, reel 116, part L, series 2, "National Woman's Party Papers, 1913–1974"; Kelley to Hill, March 23, 1921, reel 7, series 1, *ibid.* Ethel Smith reported that no consensus had been reached, and it was believed none could be, "largely because of the *known opposition of several members* of the Executive Board of the National Woman's Party *to the very laws we desire to protect.*" Ethel Smith to Members and Friends, Dec. 12, 1921, folder 378, Consumers League of Massachusetts Collection (Schlesinger Library). For NWP difficulty with safeguarding clauses, see Pollitzer to Jane Norman Smith, Jan. 5, 1922, folder 110, Jane Norman Smith Collection.

mollified those who still favored sex-based labor legislation by reasoning, lawyer-like, that the equal rights amendment declared women's freedom of contract no more strongly than did the Fifth and Fourteenth amendments, already on the books and more than once overridden in the name of the state's police power. Laughlin herself strongly opposed sex-based legislation. "If women can be segregated as a class for special legislation along any line," she asserted, "the same classification can be used for special restrictions along any other line which may, at any time, appeal to the caprice or prejudice of our legislatures." If sex-based laws were not abolished and prohibited, "the advancement of women in business and industry will be stopped and women relegated to the lowest, worst paid labor."[31]

The "clean sweep" approach seemed all the more appealing to NWP leaders as their lobbyists working on state legislatures made little headway between 1921 and 1923 in eliminating specific sex discriminations. By analogy with the suffrage struggle, frustration at the state level fueled the rationale for a constitutional amendment. At a grand conference staged in Seneca Falls, New York, in November 1923 to commemorate the seventy-fifth anniversary of Stanton's Declaration of Sentiments, the NWP introduced an equal rights amendment stating, "Men and women shall have equal rights throughout the United States and every place subject to its jurisdiction." The amendment was introduced into Congress on December 10, 1923.[32]

Forging ahead, the NWP cut its links with most women connected to the labor movement, who remained convinced of the need for sex-specific protection. The few NWP members with strong labor attachments, such as Blatch, insisted that trade union organizing, not special legislation, should protect women workers' interests. The NWP presented its opposition to sex-based legislation as a positive program of industrial equality, but only a handful of working-class activists agreed. Representatives of the AFL and of

[31] National Council, National Woman's Party, minutes, Feb. 14, 1921, reel 114, part C, series 2, "National Woman's Party Papers, 1913–1974." See also National Council, National Woman's Party, minutes, Dec. 17, 1921, *ibid.* (The National Council replaced the National Executive Committee as of March 1921.) For Maud Younger's eventual change of heart, see her unpublished autobiography, Maud Younger, "Along the Way" [c. 1936], reel 114, part I, series 1, *ibid.* Gail Laughlin to Fellow Members of National Council, April 7, 1921, National Council, National Woman's Party, minutes, April 11, 1921, reel 114, part C, series 2, "National Woman's Party Papers, 1913–1974." To NWP loyalists Laughlin's point was proved in 1923 by the Wisconsin attorney general's ruling that the state Equal Rights Bill did not invalidate a 1905 law prohibiting women from becoming legislative employees, since legislature service required "very long and often unreasonable hours," making the prohibition akin to an hours limitation law. Geidel, "National Woman's Party and the Origin of the Equal Rights Amendment" [*Historian*], 576–77. Paul read this case as "an extremely effective argument against including such a welfare provision" as the Wisconsin Equal Rights Bill had. Paul to Jane Norman Smith, Feb. 20, 1923, folder 111, Jane Norman Smith Collection.

[32] To emphasize the need for a federal equal rights amendment, *Equal Rights* contrasted thirty-nine equal rights bills passed by fourteen states with more than twice that number defeated. *Equal Rights*, July 21, 1923, p. 183; *ibid.*, Dec. 29, 1923, pp. 364–65; National Council, National Woman's Party, minutes, June 19, 1923, reel 114, part C, series 2, "National Woman's Party Papers, 1913–1974." Before 1923 the equal rights amendment went through scores of drafts. Reel 116, part F, series 3, *ibid.* Not until 1943 was the wording changed to "Equality of rights under the law shall not be denied or abridged by the United States or by any state on account of sex."

several international unions as well as a lengthy list of women's groups voiced opposition at the first Senate subcommittee hearings on the equal rights amendment. Mary Anderson, director of the Women's Bureau of the Department of Labor, fiercely opposed the NWP and threw the bureau's weight against the amendment.[33]

The arguments against the equal rights amendment offered by the various groups overlapped. They assumed that an amendment would invalidate sex-based labor laws or, at least, throw them (and welfare laws designed for mothers and widows) into the courts for protracted argument, during which time women would lose needed benefits. They argued that sex discriminations would be more efficiently and accurately removed from legal codes by attacking each case. Opponents of the amendment asserted that women workers, wary of employers' freedom to exploit them, valued sex-based labor legislation and that maximum-hour laws for women had benefited men, too, in factories where male workers could not continue operations once female employees had left for the day. If protective laws hampered job opportunities for some small minority of working women, then the proper tactic was to exempt some occupations, not to eliminate the laws altogether. They declared that only the elite who did not have to work at all or professional women whose conditions of work were entirely different could possibly denigrate the benefits of protective laws. They regularly accused the NWP of being the unwitting tool (at best) or the paid servant of rapacious business interests, although no proof was ever brought forward.[34]

In the NWP's view the equal rights amendment was the logical sequel to woman suffrage, the fulfillment of Susan B. Anthony's vision. The many

[33] *Equal Rights*, Dec. 22, 1923, p. 358; Mary Anderson, *Woman at Work: The Autobiography of Mary Anderson as Told to Mary N. Winslow* (Minneapolis, 1951), 159–72; Becker, *Origins of the Equal Rights Amendment*, 198–234; Judith Anne Sealander, "The Woman's Bureau, 1920–1950: Federal Reaction to Female Wage Earning" (Ph.D. diss., Duke University, 1977), 196–220. Blatch gave up her membership on the National Advisory Council in 1921 because she could not support the NWP's proposal to exempt protective labor legislation in the blanket bill for the District of Columbia. Blatch to Hill, March 22, 1921, reel 7, series 1, "National Woman's Party Papers, 1913–1974"; Blatch to Headquarters, April 8, 1921, *ibid.*

[34] The controversy over an equal rights amendment sparked an enormous outburst of writing, public and private. Sources for my summary of antiamendment opinion include Florence Kelley, "Shall Women Be Equal before the Law? No," *Nation*, April 12, 1922, p. 421; Florence Kelley, "The Equal Rights Amendment: Why Other Women Groups Oppose It," *Good Houskeeping*, 78 (March 1924), 19, 162–65; Kelley to Mrs. [Dora] Lewis, March 7, 1921, reel 6, series 1, "National Woman's Party Papers, 1913–1974"; Kelley to Freda Kirchwey, Jan. 16, 1922, "Equal Rights Amendment Correspondence" folder, box C4, National Consumers' League Papers (Library of Congress); Silas Bent, "The Women's War," *New York Times*, Jan. 14, 1923, sec. 4, pp. 4, 15; Ethel M. Smith, "Working Women's Case against 'Equal Rights,'" *New York Times*, Jan. 20, 1924, sec. 8, p. 12; Ethel M. Smith, "What Is Sex Equality and What Are the Feminists Trying to Accomplish," *Century Magazine*, 118 (May 1929), 96–106; Mary Van Kleeck, "Women and Machines," *Atlantic Monthly*, 127 (Feb. 1921), 250–60; Alice Hamilton, draft of letter to Mrs. [Edith Houghton] Hooker, Jan. 16, 1922, folder 19, Alice Hamilton Collection (Schlesinger Library); Alice Hamilton, "The Blanket Amendment—A Debate: II—Protection for Women Workers," *Forum*, 72 (Aug. 1924), 152–60; Elizabeth Glendower Evans, "The Woman's Party—Right or Wrong? I. The Woman's Party Is Wrong," *New Republic*, Sept. 26, 1923, p. 123; Mary Anderson, "Should There Be Labor Laws for Women? Yes," *Good Housekeeping*, 81 (Sept. 1925), 53, 166, 169–70, 173–74, 176, 179–80; Clara Mortenson Beyer, "Do Women Want Protection? What Is Equality?" *Nation*, Jan. 31, 1923, p. 116.

differences in state codes and practices in sex discriminations made a constitutional amendment the most direct route to equal rights. Protective laws that classed women with children as "the industrial and political wards of the state" only manifested women's long history of economic dependence and served to preserve the most lucrative and interesting jobs for men. (With reason the NWP accused the AFL of supporting sex-based protective legislation in order to keep women from competing for men's jobs.) By eliminating "anachronism" in the law, the amendment would encourage women to become self-respecting citizens, to slough off their history of subservience and their embedded psychology of the unpaid worker. Women workers' real interests lay in obtaining equal access to job opportunities and to trade union organization, the NWP maintained. The party became the champion of working women materially hurt by protective legislation, such as printers or railroad conductors or waitresses hampered by hours limitation, or cleaning women fired and replaced by men after the passage of minimum-wage laws. At the same time, the NWP expressed no opposition to protective labor legislation as such or to protection of motherhood, so long as neither legally treated women "as a class."[35]

This is not the place to analyze the controversy over the equal rights amendment in its full complexity, except to say that the opponents' attempts to portray the amendment as "class" legislation were simplistic, just as the proponents' attempts to portray it as legislation affecting only sex equality understated the case. Neither side acknowledged the real ambiguities and complications of the workings of sex-based protective legislation at the time. While the antiamendment side was right, in that protective laws had improved conditions for the great majority of women in industry, the proamendment side was also right, in that the laws had limited women's opportunities in the labor market and had helped to sustain the notion that women were dependent and secondary wage earners.[36] Supporters of protective legislation did not see that their expectations of women, rooted in biological and customary notions of women's place and purpose, helped to confirm women's second-class position in the economy. Nor did advocates of the equal rights amendment recognize the need protective legislation addressed or acknowledge that their program of equal rights would not in itself free women's economic opportunity from the stranglehold of the domestic stereotype.

[35] For NWP views, see Elsie Hill, "Shall Women Be Equal before the Law? Yes!" *Nation*, April 12, 1922, pp. 419–20; Doris Stevens, "The Blanket Amendment—A Debate: I—Suffrage Does Not Give Equality," *Forum*, 72 (Aug. 1924), 145–52; Harriot Stanton Blatch, "Do Women Want Protection? Wrapping Women in Cotton-Wool," *Nation*, Jan. 31, 1923, pp. 115–16. Secondary sources on the conflict include Lemons, *Woman Citizen*, 184–99; Chafe, *American Woman*, 112–32; O'Neill, *Everyone Was Brave*, 274–94; Becker, *Origins of the Equal Rights Amendment*, 121–51; Geidel, "The National Woman's Party and the Origins of the Equal Rights Amendment" (M.A. thesis); Sheila M. Rothman, *Woman's Proper Place: A History of Changing Ideals and Practices, 1870 to the Present* (New York, 1978), 153–65; Alice Kessler-Harris, *Out to Work: A History of Wage-Earning Women in the United States* (New York, 1982), 194–95, 205–12; Josephine Goldmark, *Impatient Crusader* (Urbana, 1953), 180–88.

[36] Kessler-Harris, *Out to Work*, 200–05, 212–14. For contemporary labor and management attitudes toward protective labor legislation in general, see also James Weinstein, *The Corporate Ideal in the Liberal State, 1900–1918* (Boston, 1968), 43–45; Elizabeth Faulkner Baker, "At the

When the Supreme Court in 1923 used reasoning consonant with the NWP's to invalidate the minimum-wage law covering women in the District of Columbia, the party's new newspaper, *Equal Rights*, applauded but deferred: "It is not within the province of the Woman's Party, as a purely feminist organization, to discuss the constitutional question involved or to discuss the merits of minimum wage legislation as a method of bettering labor conditions. On these points we express no opinion."[37] Just as black voting rights had been judged outside the "purely feminist," so was the betterment of labor conditions. That single-mindedness made the NWP virtually anathema to labor and the Left. In the 1920s context of Republican domination, with business in the saddle and with labor interests losing out in both trade union organization and state protection, to express no policy but equal rights for women was to affirm the status quo in every other respect. Although NWP members did not hold consistently laissez-faire views, the single-mindedness of their espousal of equal rights made them appear to. While the NWP was able to hold on through the 1920s to a few of its longtime members who had vital interests in changing conditions for the working masses, it could not recruit new ones with its insistence on "purely feminist" claims.

The NWP followed its exclusion-in-effect of blacks and of labor interests—though in the case of the latter the process was certainly not one-sided—with a decision in 1928 that alienated its adherents and potential adherents among Democrats. Standing on its head the earlier policy of "holding the party in power responsible" for failure to pass the desired amendment, the NWP formally endorsed the Republican ticket. Herbert Hoover's vice-presidential running mate, Charles Curtis, had been responsible for introducing the equal rights amendment in the Senate. The NWP had sent speakers to exhort equal rights planks to both the Republican and the Democratic conventions in the summer of 1928, with mixed results. The Democratic party adopted a straddling plank that linked women's welfare with children's; the Republican party endorsed the notion of women's equality but not the amendment. At a special conference at headquarters early in September, the NWP under the chairmanship of Jane Norman Smith decided to endorse Hoover and Curtis.

The rationale was that the Republican ticket, with Curtis on it, offered the best likelihood of success for the equal rights amendment. Alfred E. Smith, the Democratic candidate, had made clear his support for sex-based protective legislation. The Socialist candidate, Norman Thomas, had stated his opposition to the amendment. The Prohibitionist candidate endorsed the amendment, but he was not on the ballot in every state. NWP publicity

Crossroads in the Legal Protection of Women in Industry," *Annals of the American Academy of Political and Social Science*, 143 (May 1929), esp. 277. Recently historians have stressed the regressive potential of sex-based protective laws. See Rothman, *Woman's Proper Place*, 162–64; Nancy Schrom Dye, *As Equals and as Sisters: Feminism, the Labor Movement, and the Women's Trade Union League of New York* (Columbia, Mo., 1980), 159–60; Olive Banks, *Faces of Feminism: A Study of Feminism as a Social Movement* (New York, 1981), 115; and Judith A. Baer, *The Chains of Protection: The Judicial Response to Women's Labor Legislation* (Westport, Conn., 1978).

[37] *Equal Rights*, April 21, 1923, p. 76.

emphasized that solely the parties' positions relative to the amendment dictated its endorsement; its intent was to make the amendment an election issue. Formally and informally the NWP reminded all that it was following its characteristic mode of pressure on whatever party needed pressing: in 1916 it had thrown its weight against the Democrats; in 1920 it had picketed the Republican convention to speed ratification of the woman suffrage amendment by recalcitrant Republican-controlled state legislatures; in 1924 it had supported independent and third-party female candidates for Congress (all running against Republicans). The 1928 position was another instance of "remaining independent to use our votes in the way that we decide will be of greatest help to Equal Rights."[38]

That decision aroused immediate—and in some cases fatal—remonstrance from some leading members, both old and new. Lavinia Dock, one of the party's remaining socialists, most picturesquely objected, "I could no more cast a vote for the Republican Party than I could swallow a large, smooth, green caterpillar"; Sue Shelton White, a Tennessee Democrat, disavowed the party's choice and never came back to the fold; Emma C. Johnson, a founder six or seven years earlier, saw the decision as "a fair piece of 'railroading,'" judged that the organization had "grossly betrayed women," and tendered her resignation. Most objectors made the point that Curtis would not be president and that Hoover—who had appointed Margaret Dreier Robins, a National Women's Trade Union League leader and clear opponent of the equal rights amendment, head of his campaign among industrial working women—promised no brighter prospects for the amendment than did Alfred E. Smith. The basis for the endorsement seemed even flimsier when on October 26, 1928, Hoover made a statement opposing any change in protective labor laws applying to women. Ruby Black, a member who had never liked the endorsement, now protested that the NWP would be a laughingstock. Not as a Democrat, but as "a Feminist first of all, . . . not greatly interested in any other issue," she implored a change. A special meeting of seven members of the National Council led by Jane Norman Smith affirmed the decision a few days later, however.[39]

[38] *Equal Rights*, June 23, 1928, p. 155; *ibid.*, July 7, 1928, p. 171; *ibid.*, July 14, 1928, pp. 181-82; *ibid.*, Sept. 22, 1928, pp. 258-61; *ibid.*, Sept 29, 1928, p. 269; *ibid.*, Nov. 3, 1928, p. 306; National Council, National Woman's Party, minutes, Sept. 11, 1928, reel 114, part C, series 2, "National Woman's Party Papers, 1913-1974"; Jane Norman Smith to Member of the Woman's Party, Oct. 8, 1928, reel 40, series 1, *ibid.*; Vernon to Mrs. Rilla Nelson, Sept. 17, 1928, box 1, Lucia Voorhes Grimes Collection, Michigan Historical Collections (Bentley Historical Library, University of Michigan, Ann Arbor). Vernon's letter says that the decision was taken at a conference at headquarters, 34 to 8, with all except two of those "who take a really active part in our work" in favor. Susan D. Becker says the decision was made by a margin of 4 to 1. Becker, *Origins of the Equal Rights Amendment*, 94. However, when the issue was brought up and discussed favorably at the National Council meeting, Sept. 11, 1928, only ten people besides Jane Norman Smith were present, and no record remains in the NWP papers of another conference at headquarters before Sept. 17.

[39] Sue Shelton White to Member of the Woman's Party, Nov. 20, 1928, box 1, Grimes Collection; Sue S[helton] White to Miss Lucia V. Grimes, Dec. 28, 1929, *ibid.*; Sue Shelton White to Jane Norman Smith, Sept. 15, 1928, folder 35, Sue Shelton White Collection, (Schlesinger Library); Dock to Party, Oct. 2, [1928], reel 40, series 1, "National Woman's Party Papers,

Paul was not present during official moves toward the endorsement, but the action had her hallmarks: the decision was made at the top, the focus on the equal rights amendment was single-minded, and much more sympathy for the Republican than for the Democratic party was manifest. Although Paul usually avoided high office in the NWP during the 1920s, there is little question that her wishes determined major policy decisions. In 1928 Paul saw the opportunity to repeat the strategy of 1916, regardless that true parallels were lacking. Jane Norman Smith shared Paul's point of view on the Hoover candidacy and handily led the NWP's action. Jane Norman Smith, a longtime Republican and director of the NWP's "industrial equality" (that is, anti-protective legislation) activities, had behind her several years of head-to-head battling in New York State with proponents of sex-based labor legislation who were favored by the administration of Gov. Alfred E. Smith. She also believed entirely in Paul's "Leninist" structure. "The only reason the Woman's Party has been able to get anywhere is because it hasn't been hampered by an organization along the lines of the League of Women Voters, and hasn't been confronted with an endless amount of red tape when action was necessary," she wrote to Alma Lutz, a Boston member. In 1933 Jane Norman Smith came into direct conflict over this question with Edith Houghton Hooker, who had consistently advocated broadening the base and the compass of the NWP. Not only did Jane Norman Smith not want to move in the direction of democratization and decentralization advocated by Hooker, she even wanted to dissolve the occupational councils, lest the NWP become like the League of Women Voters or women's clubs, and "the tail will begin to wag the dog!"[40]

The authoritarian character of the NWP leadership became obvious to any who really participated in its work. As several women who were invited to serve on the National Advisory Council in 1921 commented, even that second-tier group had never been "advisory" nor been asked for "council."[41] In 1928 not only the endorsement of Hoover but also the NWP's turn toward international work for equal rights gave evidence that the ruling coterie ruled,

1913–1974"; Emma C. Johnson to NWP, Oct. 18, 1928, *ibid.*; Ruby Black to Mrs. [Jane Norman] Smith and Mabel [Vernon], Oct. 26, 1928, *ibid.*; National Council, National Woman's Party, minutes, Oct. 31, 1928, reel 114, part C, series 2, *ibid.* See also Florence Bayard Hilles to Hooker, Oct. 21, 1928, reel 40, series 1, *ibid.*; NWP Nebraska organization to Jane Norman Smith, Oct. 21, 1928, *ibid.*; and Becker, *Origins of the Equal Rights Amendment*, 93–96.

[40] NWP correspondence through the 1920s makes Paul's leadership clear. For Paul's thought about 1928, see Vernon interview, 87–88. Jane Norman Smith to Lutz, Feb. 6, 1932, folder 58, Lutz Collection; Jane Norman Smith to Lutz and Marguerite Smith, Dec. 9, 1933, folder 98, *ibid.* Jane Norman Smith's activities in New York in the 1920s can be followed in her correspondence in box 2, Jane Norman Smith Collection. For the New York network of antiamendment social reformers in the 1920s, see Susan Ware, *Beyond Suffrage: Women in the New Deal* (Cambridge, Mass., 1981), 33–38; and Clarke A. Chambers, *Seedtime of Reform: American Social Service and Social Action, 1918–1933* (Minneapolis, 1963), 260–61. There was reason for former suffragists to feel kindly toward the Republicans, for Republican state legislators and congressmen had overall better records than Democrats on votes for woman suffrage. Flyer [c. 1920], "Republican Party Record on Woman Suffrage," folder 12, Margaret S. Roberts Collection (Schlesinger Library); and Stevens, *Jailed for Freedom*, 250.

[41] Adamson to Hill, March 18, 1921, reel 7, series 1, "National Woman's Party Papers, 1913–1974"; MacKaye to Hill, March 21, [1921], *ibid.* Ethel McC. Adamson suggested "patroness" as a more appropriate designation for a member of the Advisory Council.

regardless of whether any mass base supported their aims. The NWP's international efforts had begun in 1926, when the League of Women Voters' successful endeavor to keep the NWP from membership in the International Woman Suffrage Alliance joined the battle between equal rights advocates and protective legislation supporters across the seas. The presence of women allies in Europe and South America (where also opinion was divided between pro- and antiprotectionists) encouraged the NWP's greater emphasis after 1928 on international treaties incorporating equal rights provisions, as did, too, a domestic political atmosphere hostile to NWP efforts once Franklin D. Roosevelt became governor of New York and then president of the United States. Paul, studying international law in the 1920s, framed her aims more and more abstractly and legalistically; her interest in international organization was spurred by Belmont's grandiose visions of an "International Parliament of Women." Belmont lived in France from 1920 until her death in 1933, and Paul constantly curried her favor to keep financial support flowing. Although the extent of Belmont's power over NWP decisions is not clear—some members regarded her as an old crank—she held the office of president for years and unquestionably had her greatest influence in fostering the party's international efforts. Here she not only goaded Paul but also kept Doris Stevens, a shrewd and effective activist, at her beck and call. At the Sixth Pan American Conference in Havana, Cuba, in January 1928, Stevens injected the NWP point of view into the discussions of the Inter-American Commission on Women and continued to serve vociferously on the commission for more than ten years.[42]

Hooker's dispute with Jane Norman Smith in 1933–1934 and an intraparty schism that shortly resulted manifested a crisis that had been building since 1928 because of such factors as action at the top, disregard for inviting or involving membership participation, and more distant and more legalistic application of the concept of equal rights. Those practices dimmed the beacon of the NWP's feminist ideas, beset anyway by the depression economy. Hooker noted early in 1934 that the treasury for the previous year showed five or six hundred paid members. But Hooker's attempts at that point to build up the state organizations and to collaborate with other women's groups on aims they shared were flattened by "the most spectacular exhibition of autocracy," Hooker herself said. "The steam roller plied back and forth." Another member who saw galvanizing more women as a priority also had "practically no hope that it will be given any serious thought by any considerable group of the leaders; for these leaders are too largely made up of pioneers who are gripped by conservatism. They will not face facts. . . . One's having been 'jailed for the CAUSE' seems to make one an oracle." In forming a vanguard party, Paul seems

[42] For the NWP's international work, see Becker, *Origins of the Equal Rights Amendment*, 161–86. For the NWP's difficulties under Franklin D. Roosevelt's administrations, see Jane Norman Smith to Paul, Feb. 26, 1933, folder 115, Jane Norman Smith Collection. For the National Council's positive and ingratiating response to Alva Belmont's query whether she was the head of international as well as domestic work of the NWP, see National Council, National Woman's Party, minutes, Oct. 9, 1928, Jan. 15, 1929, reel 114, part C, series 2, "National Woman's Party Papers, 1913–1974."

to have been oblivious to Lenin's warning, "Be it remembered that in order to become the vanguard, we must attract other classes." Or, as Hooker editorialized in not-so-veiled language in the throes of the 1934 crisis, "the leaders are powerless unless they have massed behind them ever-growing and evermore insistent followers. . . . If the rank and file of women do not realize their subjection, how can they be expected to struggle to free themselves?"[43]

Although it was not so obvious before 1928, the NWP neglected what had been, historically, a crucial element in building the woman movement: the *process* of grass-roots participation. That neglect was not fatal during the suffrage movement, since the party entered rather late and, as Carrie Chapman Catt later bitterly said, "played the cuckoo, and laid its eggs in nests that had cost much to build."[44] In the 1920s the NWP continued its reputation for working at the top, lobbying presidents and members of Congress; it staged brilliant events attended by notable people and carried out daring exploits for publicity; it attracted some individuals of artistic and professional renown, such as poet Edna St. Vincent Millay, artist Georgia O'Keeffe, and aviator Amelia Earhart. The ideas, researches, and perceptions of its small number of proponents were outstandingly acute: *Equal Rights* tracked instances of sex discrimination and of women's accomplishments around the world, editorialized about sex-role conditioning and the hypocrisies of gender hierarchy, published historical, autobiographical, and speculative essays on women's condition, and recorded the legislative progress of equal rights. Yet party leaders, who called themselves "Feminists," never recognized that cumulative grass-roots movement, as historian Ellen DuBois points out, was essential to the woman's rights legacy they saw themselves heir to.[45]

The significance of the suffrage movement, DuBois emphasizes, is that it was a *movement*, in which "increasing numbers of women would be transformed through the process of acting deliberately and collectively to achieve the equality and independence that enfranchisement seemed to promise." Sara Evans's history of the beginnings of the women's liberation movement in the late 1960s likewise emphasizes the importance of deliberative and collective *process* in the transformation of consciousness on an effective scale. DuBois's argument for the mid-nineteenth century applies to the much more recent period as well: that "it was women's involvement in the movement" itself that "created the basis for new social relations between men and women." The NWP, however, left out process entirely and focused single-mindedly on

[43] Hooker to Lutz, Jan. 5, 1934, folder 66, Lutz Collection; Mary Wilhelmine Williams to Lutz, April 22, 1934, folder 76, *ibid.*; Hooker to Stevens, Nov. 19, 1934, folder H, box IV, Stevens unprocessed adenda no. 76-246 (Schlesinger Library); James Weinstein, *Ambiguous Legacy: The Left in American Policitcs* (New York, 1975), 31; *Equal Rights*, June 23, 1934, p. 162. See also Hooker to Lutz, March 13, 1935, folder 67, Lutz Collection; Jane Norman Smith to Lutz, Feb. 6, 1932, folder 58, *ibid.*; Jane Norman Smith to Lutz and Marguerite Smith, Dec. 9, 1933, folder 98, *ibid.*

[44] Carrie Chapman Catt to Margaret Corbett Ashby, Oct. 20, 1925, "International Woman's Suffrage Alliance, 1925" folder, series 2, box 52, League of Women Voters Papers (Library of Congress).

[45] Ellen Carol DuBois, *Feminism and Suffrage: The Emergence of an Independent Women's Movement in America, 1848–1869* (Ithaca, 1978), 18, 24.

its *goal* of equal rights, conceived ever more abstractly. The equal rights amendment, supposed to be the first step in an agenda to end women's subjection, became itself the panacea. Stevens recognized this when in an acid critique of 1946 she wrote, "To my way of thinking the NWP in its direction since 1923 has lost more [and] more of that great feminist tradition handed on to our care from the 18th century. We are bogged down in legal formalism." The "dead hand" of Paul prevented anyone from "revitalizing the feminist climate": "the sad, bleak truth is that AP [Alice Paul] dislikes people . . . can't be bothered with members. . . . No sooner does a struggling state org[anization] show signs of life than, I am told, AP picks off their best workers for money and 'lobbying' . . . men on whom they have no claim. . . . One of our pioneers said lately, 'if AP had died 25 years ago, we'd now have the amendment.'"[46]

The failure to ratify the equal rights amendment in the 1980s indicates how obstacle-ridden the path of the amendment has been and thus how wrong, in one respect, that commentator on Paul was; yet Stevens's lament had a firm basis. Certainly a mix of historical factors in the 1920s conditioned the NWP's fate: the impasse over sex-based protective legislation was one; the defensive antisocialist trend of American politics was another; the panache of self-seeking in the younger generation was a third—not to speak of the deep-rootedness of gender hierarchy in the culture at large. But the NWP just as certainly had its dynamic, forged in the suffrage struggle and applied and misapplied obsessively after that. Though a full and fair treatment of the NWP would require richer detailing of its members, leaders, and activities, that dynamic is clear. It is not to dismiss the NWP's efforts—its carrying the banner of equal rights at state, federal, and international levels, its sustenance of a community of interest among its members, its serving as a resource for women seeking feminist affiliation—to acknowledge that after 1928 its once-envisioned vanguard role was no more. Considering its very small numbers and the odds against it, one can be amazed at what the NWP did in fact accomplish toward equal rights legislation in the interwar period, all the while it became less and less able or likely to lead a movement of women.

Initiated in a vision of inclusiveness, a stand for all women, the NWP campaign for equal rights devolved into a practice of exclusiveness and a defense of the status quo with regard to everything but the gender question. That devolution owed in great part to Paul's assumption that equal rights (like suffrage, in her view), a demand relevant to all women, was separable from all other issues. Paul posed women's political options in either-or, rather than both-and, terms: "work for women" (which meant equal rights) or something else. Within that framework NWP loyalists chose equal rights. Women who had any other priority were "followers of men, worms of the dust," in the vitriolic words of Caroline Spencer, "who cannot see that the tyranny of half

[46] *Ibid.*, 201; Sara Evans, *Personal Politics: The Roots of Women's Liberation in the Civil Rights Movement and the New Left* (New York, 1979); Doris [Stevens] to Betty [Gram Swing], Jan. 8, 1946, box IV, Stevens unprocessed adenda no. 76-246. This letter seems never to have been folded or mailed.

the race over the other half is the first wrong to be righted, and its overthrow, the greatest revolution conceivable."[47]

As a result of its construction of the gender imperative, the NWP made equal rights an abstract goal, because placing it in the context of social reality would have required stands on social and political issues that affected women but that were not strictly gender questions. (The suffrage battle might have provided a different lesson, regarding the separability of women's rights from politics in general, but perhaps only long retrospect allows us to see that feminist movements flourish best in the midst of other reforming politics and in alliance with other reforming aims.) With some justice Mary Anderson accused the NWP of putting the "woman question" first and of demanding that "the solution of all others should be determined solely by what is done with women's problems."[48] A tremendous irony lies here. The NWP set out to erase legislation that treated women "as a class" but predicated its feminism on construing women as a class, that "other half" of the human race. Its dilemma was the dilemma of twentieth-century feminism, that it required gender consciousness for its basis while it aimed for the dissolution of prescribed gender roles.

[47] Spencer to Pollitzer, April 30, 1921, reel 7, series 1, "National Woman's Party Papers, 1913–1974." Rebecca Hourwich Reyher, who admired the diversity among NWP members early on, recalled that "as time went on, there is no question but that the Woman's Party had a hard core of very conservative, very conventional women, and there is no doubt in my mind that Miss Paul was more comfortable with such women." Reyher interview, 221.

[48] Anderson, "Should There Be Labor Laws for Women?" 53.

The National Woman's Party and the Origins of the Equal Rights Amendment, 1920–1923

By
PETER GEIDEL*

WITH woman suffrage achieved in August 1920, feminists needed to decide on future activity. Suffrage had been a goal which easily united opinion, but in what areas should equality next be sought, and what methods should be used?

The two schools of feminists—the Social feminists and the Feminists—differed in approach.[1] The Social feminists, who held the numerical majority, considered feminism as only a part of their reform program.[2] They believed in woman's traditional roles as mother and reformer of society. They wanted to make women equal only in the political and civil areas and did not wish to forfeit protective labor legislation for women. They considered such measures as a minimum wage, limitation of hours, ban on night work, and exclusion of women from certain occupations beneficial. Social feminists argued that special protective labor laws would always be needed for women, regardless of what labor laws existed for men. Without such laws, women could contract diseases and either become sterile or give birth to inferior babies.[3]

*The author is a Ph.D. candidate at Columbia University. He gratefully acknowledges the guidance of Professor John A. Garraty in the preparation of this article.

[1]Feminists in the 1920s did not refer to themselves as "Social feminists" or "Feminists." William O'Neill originated the term "Social feminists" in his "Feminism as a Radical Ideology," in *Dissent: Explorations in the History of American Radicalism*, ed. Alfred F. Young (DeKalb: Northern Illinois University Press, 1968), 276. In the following pages, the capitalized "Social feminists" and "Feminists" will denote the two schools of feminism in the 1920s, and the uncapitalized "feminists" will stand for the entire movement, including both Feminists and Social feminists.

[2]See Elizabeth Tilton, "What Women Want," *Current History* 17 (November 1922): 282–87. To determine priorities among different issues, Tilton sent questionnaires to the major women's organizations. In responses from twenty-five states, there seemed to be most interest in Prohibition, disarmament, government corruption, and a child labor amendment.

[3]Social feminists used sociological and scientific studies to show that women were more subject to physical, mental, and moral harm than men in industry. In *Muller* v.

For their method, Social feminists wished to achieve political equality through state laws only, whereas they supported federal legislation in the areas of child labor and maternity health care. This was to ensure that equality did not extend into labor legislation. It was consistent with their presuffrage strategy, which had been to achieve suffrage through individual state referenda. Prominent among organizations involved in these efforts were the National American Woman Suffrage Association (which after suffrage became the National League of Women Voters), the National Women's Trade Union League, and the National Consumers' League (whose participation was due largely to its general secretary, Florence Kelley).[4]

The Feminists, represented mainly by the National Woman's party (NWP),[5] were constantly at odds with the Social feminists. During the

---

Oregon, 208 U.S. 412 (1908), Florence Kelley helped supply Louis Brandeis with scientific and sociological studies to support an Oregon law limiting women in industry to ten hours of work a day. After the Supreme Court had accepted this law and the logic behind it as legitimate, a "Brandeis Brief" was utilized in obtaining Court acceptance for many protective labor laws. Josephine Goldmark, *Impatient Crusader* (Urbana: University of Illinois Press, 1953), 155–58.

The Brandeis Brief in the *Muller* case deserves some attention. Citing specific studies to support his contention, Brandeis stated, "Physicians are agreed that women are fundamentally weaker than men in all that makes for endurance; in muscular strength, in nervous energy, in the powers of persistent attention and application. Overwork, therefore, which strains endurance to the utmost, is more disastrous to the health of women than to men, and entails upon them more lasting injury. . . .

"The effect of overwork on morals is closely related to the injury of health. Laxity of moral fibre follows physical debility. When the working day is so long that no time whatever is left for a minimum of leisure or home life, relief from the strain of work is sought in alcoholic stimulants and other excesses. . . .

". . . When the health of women has been injured by long hours, not only is the working efficiency of the community impaired, but the deterioration is handed down to succeeding generations." In Alfred Lief, ed., *The Social and Economic Views of Mr. Justice Brandeis* (New York: Vanguard Press, 1930), 342, 344.

[4]On November 22, 1920, the following Social feminist organizations formed the Women's Joint Congressional Committee, with Maud Wood Park as chairman: National League of Women Voters, General Federation of Women's Clubs, Women's Christian Temperance Union, National Mother and Parent Teachers Association, National Women's Trade Union League, National Council of Jewish Women, American Association of University Women, National Federation of Business and Professional Women's Clubs, American Home Economics Association, and National Consumers' League. By 1922, the committee had added the Daughters of the American Revolution, the Young Women's Christian Association, the Girls Friendly Society, and the Women's International League for Peace and Freedom. The coalition worked for the passage of social welfare legislation in Congress. J. Stanley Lemons, *The Woman Citizen: Social Feminism in the 1920's* (Urbana: University of Illinois Press, 1973), 55, 61n.; Charles A. Selden, "The Most Powerful Lobby in Washington," *Ladies Home Journal* 39 (April 1922): 5, 93, 95–96.

[5]Estimates of the size of the National Woman's party membership range from a high of one hundred thousand by Anne Herendeen, a contemporary journalist, to Anna

suffrage campaign, the NWP[6] concentrated on achieving suffrage through a federal amendment. Its methods, such as opposing the party in power as long as suffrage was not achieved, its refusal to cooperate with the government during World War I, and especially its civil disobedience campaign, were denounced by Social feminists.

At the close of the suffrage campaign, the National Woman's Party was composed of women of various political backgrounds: feminist writers such as Charlotte Perkins Gilman; Social feminists such as Florence Kelley and Madeline Doty; liberals and progressives such as Alison Hopkins and Mrs. Samuel Untermyer; laissez-faire capitalists such as Louisine Havemeyer; socialists such as Crystal Eastman and Harriot Stanton Blatch; labor activists such as Josephine Casey, Maud Younger, and Myrtle Cain; and women who were veterans of the women suffrage movement in Great Britain, such as Alice Paul, Lucy Burns, and Rheta Childe Dorr.[7]

Wiley's eight thousand. Perhaps the most realistic estimate was made by Inez Haynes Irwin, who had access to NWP records shortly after suffrage was achieved. Irwin maintained that the National Woman's party had over fifty thousand members just before suffrage. Alice Paul, one of the founders of the NWP, said that in the early 1920s the NWP reached a membership level of sixty thousand. Ruby A. Black, "The Congressional Hearings," *Equal Rights* 11 (14 February 1925): 7; Amelia R. Fry, *Conversations with Alice Paul: Woman Suffrage and the Equal Rights Amendment* (Suffragists Oral History Project, University of California, Berkeley, 1976), 434; Anne Herendeen, "What the Home Town Thinks of Alice Paul," *Everybody's Magazine* 41 (October 1919): 45: Inez Haynes Irwin, *Angels and Amazons* (Garden City, New York: Doubleday Doran, 1933), 358.

Article IX of the NWP constitution stated that at conventions there would be one delegate for every fifty branch members. At the February 1921 convention, one roll call showed 343 delegates present, representing a minimum of 17,150 members. *Stenographic Report, National Convention of the National Woman's Party* (1921), 123.

[6]The National Woman's party actually began in 1913 as the Congressional Committee of the National American Woman Suffrage Association (NAWSA). In February 1914, however, it split with NAWSA after changing its name to Congressional Union. In June 1916, the Congressional Union helped form the Woman's party for the twelve states where women could vote for president in order to campaign against President Woodrow Wilson. On March 2, 1917, the Congressional Union and the Woman's party united to form the National Woman's party.

See Eleanor Flexner, *Century of Struggle: The Woman's Rights Movement in the United States* (New York: Atheneum, 1974), 262–93, 306–324, and Aileen Kraditor, *The Ideas of the Woman Suffrage Movement, 1890–1920* (New York: Columbia University Press, 1965), for more information on the suffrage campaign and the conflicts between the NWP and the NAWSA.

[7]Charlotte Perkins Gilman, the leading feminist writer at the turn of the century, is perhaps best known for her book *Women and Economics*, first published in 1898. Florence Kelley's main activities during this period were with the National Consumers' League, of which she was general secretary; throughout the 1920s she pushed for her unsuccessful Child Labor Amendment. Madeline Doty was prominent in prison reform and other Social feminist causes. Alison Hopkins's husband, J. A. H. Hopkins, had been a leader of the Progressive party. Louisine Havemeyer's husband, Henry O. Havemeyer,

Many had been jailed for their militant efforts to achieve suffrage.[8]

After suffrage the sole objective of the Feminists was equality for women in all fields. Initially, the National Woman's party worked for state laws which would give women equal political and civil rights; they specifically excluded protective labor legislation. Social feminists rejected this approach, as well as any federal amendment, and refused to cooperate with the NWP even on bills both groups agreed upon. After a careful study of the laws of each state, the NWP introduced a federal equal rights amendment as the quickest, easiest, and perhaps the only way that women would ever achieve equality.

The National Woman's party has been perceived as a militant, dictatorial, uncompromising organization, used by employers in at-

---

is best known as the creator of the Sugar Trust. Crystal Eastman had actively supported socialism on both sides of the Atlantic. Harriot Stanton Blatch ran for controller of New York City on the Socialist party ticket in 1921. Gail Laughlin was the first president of the National Federation of Business and Professional Women's Clubs. Marie L. Obenauer had been the head of the Women's Division of the Bureau of Labor Statistics in the Department of Commerce. Josephine Casey had been involved with the General Federation of Women's Clubs and had been an organizer for the International Ladies' Garment Workers' Union and the National Women's Trade Union League. Maud Younger, a former vice-president of the National Consumers' League, had pushed successfully for an eight-hour law for women in California and had also helped form a waitresses' union. Myrtle Cain, who had been a president of the Minnesota Women's Trade Union League, was active with the Telephone Operators Union, the Working People's Nonpartisan Political League, and the Farmer-Labor party and was later elected to the Minnesota legislature in 1922. Even Alice Paul, who had worked with the militant suffragettes of Emmeline Pankhurst's Women's Social and Political Union in England, had organized a milliner's union on the lower East Side of New York City in 1904–5, just before she left for England. Blanche Wiesen Cook, ed., *Crystal Eastman on Women and Revolution* (New York: Oxford University Press, 1978); *New York Times*, 11 July 1921, 5; Harriot Stanton Blatch and Alma Lutz, *Challenging Years: Memoirs of Harriot Stanton Blatch* (New York: Putnam, 1940); Mary Anderson, *Woman at Work* (Minneapolis: University of Minnesota Press, 1951), 91, 159, 162; William L. O'Neill, *Everyone Was Brave: The Rise and Fall of Feminism in America* (Chicago: Quadrangle, 1971), 278–79, 281; William Chafe, *The American Woman: Her Changing Social, Economic, and Political Roles, 1920–1970* (New York: Oxford University Press, 1972), 116; Alice Paul to Jane Norman Smith, 29 November 1921, Jane Norman Smith Papers, Schlesinger Library, Radcliffe University, box 5, folder 110 (hereafter cited as Smith Papers); Barbara Stuhler and Gretchen Kreuter, eds., *Women of Minnesota: Selected Biographical Essays* (St. Paul: Minnesota Historical Society Press, 1977), 262–63; Fry, *Conversations with Alice Paul*, 432–33, 437.

[8]Among jailed NWP members were Alice Paul, Mary Winsor, Elizabeth Selden Rogers, Lucy Branham, Louisine Havemeyer, Elsie Hill, Agnes Morey, and Sue Shelton White. "Decorated for Service," *Suffragist* 8 (September 1920): 209. Alice Paul had been imprisoned and force-fed in both England and the United States and was once put in a psychopathic ward. For more on the NWP militancy campaign, see Flexner, *Century of Struggle*, 284–87; Inez Haynes Irwin, *The Story of the Woman's Party* (New York: Harcourt, 1921); Doris Stevens, *Jailed for Freedom* (New York: Liveright, 1920); Robin Morgan, "Alice Paul: Mother of the ERA," *Ms.* 6 (October 1977): 112.

tempts to nullify all protective legislation. Social feminists have been seen as rational, willing to compromise, and knowledgeable, due to the serious lobbying and industrial surveys undertaken by their different groups.[9]

The image of hysterical suffragists stayed with the National Woman's party even though its methods changed after 1920. During 1921 and 1922, the NWP had no official publication with which to present its position, and further, NWP leaders left few memoirs or other material. Only in contemporary newspapers did details of NWP activities appear: the state bills with safeguard clauses exempting protective legislation; the numerous lawyers who supported the NWP; and the state legal surveys. Only a few spectacular incidents have survived in historical accounts. Social feminists, on the other hand, have left a large amount of material—in organizational periodicals, memoirs, and other books—and so their viewpoint is well known. This essay seeks to redress the balance.[10]

The National Woman's party resumed publication of its magazine *Suffragist* in February 1920.[11] Along with suffrage news, it discussed issues facing the feminist movement, especially protective labor legislation for women. At first, editor Florence Brewer Boeckel was cautiously critical of protective legislation, but subsequent articles by National Advisory Council member Rheta Childe Dorr and a series, "Women in Industry," by Marie L. Obenauer sharply opposed such

[9]Lemons, *Woman Citizen*, 181–87, 188–89, 202, 204; O'Neill, *Everyone Was Brave*, 127-30, 230n., 281–86, 290–94; Chafe, *American Woman*, 114–16, 118, 123–24, 127; Clarke A. Chambers, *Seedtime of Reform: American Social Service and Social Action, 1918–1933* (Minneapolis: University of Minnesota Press, 1963), 77–79.

William L. O'Neill used the phrase "hard-core feminist" to describe the National Woman's party. This term has been accepted by J. Stanley Lemons in his study of the Social feminist movement in the 1920s and in theory by William Chafe. O'Neill, "Feminism as a Radical Ideology," 276; Lemons, *Woman Citizen*, viii; Chafe, *American Woman*, 113. Clarke A. Chambers referred to the NWP as "a stridently feminist group" in his chapter on the feminist movement in the 1920s. Chambers, *Seedtime of Reform*, 77.

O'Neill, in the 1971 edition of *Everyone Was Brave*, considered the National Organization for Women (the major organization supporting the Equal Rights Amendment today) to be the "true heir" of the National American Woman Suffrage Association (a Social feminist group whose successor, the National League of Women Voters, opposed the Equal Rights Amendment). At the same time, he saw a link between the National Woman's Party (which, while radical, engaged only in civil disobedience) and the Weathermen and Black Panthers. O'Neill, *Everyone Was Brave*, 361–63.

[10]For more information, see Peter Geidel, *The National Woman's Party and the Origins of the Equal Rights Amendment* (M.A. thesis, Columbia University, 1977).

[11]The *Suffragist* had begun publication in 1913; it was discontinued on September 20, 1919, when the NWP decided that since Congress had passed the Nineteenth Amendment, there was little Washington news worth reporting; also the NWP needed funds at that time for the individual state campaigns. "To the Readers of *The Suffragist*," *Suffragist* 7 (20 September 1919): 3.

measures. Protective legislation would prevent women from obtaining good jobs and good pay, equate women with children in ability, and keep married women dependent upon their husbands for support.[12]

The National Woman's party leadership also looked to the future. Party Chairman Alice Paul saw two aims for women: "the passage of a blanket enactment to remove all discriminations against women in existing legislation, and some form of endowment of motherhood or childhood."[13]

With the campaign for ratification of woman suffrage successfully concluded in August 1920, the National Executive Committee of the NWP convened on August 28, recommending that the NWP should continue in existence with the goal of achieving equality among the sexes and that a party convention be held to decide on specific issues.

This new stand was tested at a conference held on September 10, 1920, when the NWP's National Executive Committee, National Advisory Council, and state officers met at Alva Belmont's home in Port Washington, Long Island. Many options were presented. Belmont, a member of the National Executive Committee, urged women not to vote for parties dominated by men but to unite as a political bloc to achieve equality in all aspects of life. National Advisory Council members also had their say. Crystal Eastman favored a new group which would work for a sexually integrated socialist state where both men and women could be either self-reliant workers or homemakers. Harriot Stanton Blatch urged that the NWP work for equality internationally. Finally, Florence Kelley saw a Social feminist future, emphasizing nonfeminist reform, disarmament, and maternity health-care programs.[14]

The *Suffragist* noted that the consensus of the conference was that

[12]Florence Brewer Boeckel, "The Present Problem of Women in Industry," *Suffragist* 8 (February 1920): 14; Rheta Childe Dorr, "Women's Votes—A New Element in Politics," *ibid.* (April 1920): 36–37; Marie L. Obenauer, "Legislation for the Woman Wage-Earner," *ibid.* (March 1920): 15, 20; Marie L. Obenauer, "Women in Industry," *ibid.* (July 1920): 146–47.

[13]*New York Times,* 18 July 1920, sec. 6, p. 6. The concept of a blanket proposal for sexual equality was not new. The Feminist Alliance, founded in 1914, had proposed a federal amendment stating "that no civil or political right shall be denied to any person on account of sex." NWP National Executive Committee member Alva Belmont had been a member of this defunct organization. *New York Times,* 13 April 1914, 6.

[14]*New York Times,* 27 August 1920, 3; Florence Brewer Boeckel, "An Editorial," *Suffragist* 8 (September 1920): 191. The National Woman's Party hierarchy in 1920 consisted of a National Executive Committee of fifteen women, a National Advisory Council with over one hundred and fifty members, and the individual state chairmen. These were listed on the inside cover of each issue of the *Suffragist.* "What Next?" *Suffragist* 8 (October 1920): 234–37; *ibid.* (November 1920): 278–79; *New York Times,* 6 July 1920, 15. For changing NWP leadership, see also Geidel, *National Woman's Party,* appendix, part 1, #1–3; part 2, #6–7; part 4; and part 5, #3.

the party should continue to exist in order "to break down barriers opposed to their [women's] free activity on equal terms with men." Equality in industry and the professions was endorsed, and the NWP seemed to be uniting behind a goal.[15]

Social feminists, on the whole, were curiously silent during this period. Florence Kelley attended the Port Washington conference, but she did not speak out for protective legislation nor criticize the position of equality taken by the conference or by the *Suffragist.*[16] Mary Anderson, director of the Women's Bureau of the Department of Labor, wrote an article for the *Suffragist* endorsing NWP goals.[17]

Following these preliminaries, an NWP convention was held in February 1921 in Washington, D.C.[18] Regular events were preceded by a ceremony dedicating a sculpture that depicted early feminists. Over one hundred feminist organizations presented wreaths at the base of the statue. The show of unity was marred only by absence of representation from the National American Woman Suffrage Association, which had quarreled continually with the NWP during the suffrage campaign.[19]

Alice Paul[20] opened the convention on February 16 stating that the NWP must "decide whether this organization which has battled for eight years for the political freedom of women shall, now that this object is obtained, disband, or whether it shall take up some other program and continue the battle along other lines . . . [whether to] furl its banner forever, or whether it shall fling it forth on a new battle front."[21]

[15]"Woman's Party Leaders Confer on Present and Future Plans," *Suffragist* 8 (October 1920): 232–33; *New York Times,* 11 September 1920, 2.

[16]Kelley also did not stress protective legislation when she met with Democratic presidential nominee James Cox in October 1920. *New York Times,* 10 October 1920, sec. 2, p. 1.

[17]Mary Anderson, "Industrial Issues for the Woman Voter," *Suffragist* 8 (October 1920): 250.

[18]*New York Times,* 26 December 1920, 3; 15 January 1921, 7; and 29 January 1921, 7; "A Woman's Convention," *Suffragist* 9 (January–February 1921): 341. For a more detailed account of the convention, see Geidel, *National Woman's Party,* part 2, "The February 1921 Convention."

[19]Ironically, the National American Woman's Suffrage Association did send flowers for the ceremony, but these were inadvertantly left outside in the hall. Fry, *Conversations with Alice Paul,* 353–54. Many Social feminists participated. General Secretary Florence Kelley personally laid the wreath for the National Consumers' League, as did Legislative Secretary Ethel Smith for the National Women's Trade Union League. *Stenographic Report,* 5–6; *Washington Post,* 16 February 1921, 1, 4.

[20]Fry, *Conversations with Alice Paul,* 256; *New York Times,* 20 February 1921, 3. Paul left the party for a few months after the convention to work off the National Woman's party debt; she then accepted the position of vice-president.

[21]*Stenographic Report,* 6.

The first indication of the delegates' sentiments came in the afternoon session. When Research Secretary Sue Shelton White endorsed "absolute equality," she was met with applause.[22] The next day speakers from the National Executive Committee, the National Advisory Council, and the National Committee of State Chairmen all urged the party to continue its existence and to work for sexual equality. Only in the National Advisory Council was there even a minority opinion.[23]

The afternoon session was devoted to speeches by leaders of other feminist organizations. The delegates cheered Mary Stewart of the National Federation of Business and Professional Women's Clubs when she attacked protective legislation for women: "We have long known the burden and handicap called Privilege."[24]

Social feminists Julia Lathrop, chief of the Children's Bureau of the Department of Labor, Maud Wood Park, chairman of the National League of Women Voters, Ethel Smith, legislative secretary of the National Women's Trade Union League, and Mary Anderson did not stress protective legislation in their speeches. Only Florence Kelley did, arguing strongly that women should be protected "whether they demand it for themselves or not." Kelley's speech was met with silence. As the *New York Times* noted, "If there were those present who did not believe in the battle cry ['absolute equality for women'] they remained quiet, for they were in the minority."[25]

On February 18, the final day of the convention, Minnesota State Chairman Sarah T. Colvin presented the majority resolution, which advocated "that the immediate work of the new organization be the removal of the legal disabilities of women." The resolution also urged that the party work for equality in any new international organization of nations. It concluded without recommending any specific action, leaving the new NWP board "free to follow a program of its own choosing."[26]

An identical minority resolution was offered, differing from the majority resolution only in that its immediate object was "disarmament."[27] Eventually, in a voice vote, the majority resolution was approved.[28]

[22] *Ibid.*, 30.

[23] *Ibid.*, 58–62.

[24] *Ibid.*, 75–76.

[25] *Ibid.*, 75–85. *New York Times*, 17 February 1921, 11. A representative from the Women's Christian Temperance Union was scheduled to speak but was unable to do so because of illness.

[26] *Stenographic Report*, 106. For attempts by representatives of five political parties to induce the NWP to merge with them, and the applause which greeted Mabel Vernon when she stated that the NWP had done more than anyone else for suffrage, see *ibid.*, 90–104.

[27] *Ibid.*, 106. Speakers for disarmament, especially Mrs. Henry Villard, had been thunderously applauded by the delegates. *Ibid.*, 81, 83–84.

[28] *Ibid.*, 108–23.

As to the conclusion of the resolution allowing the NWP board to decide its own program, Crystal Eastman offered a specific four-point proposal in its place: (1) termination of all legal barriers preventing women from running for public office or entering a profession, business, or trade; (2) alteration of marriage laws and public opinion to make homemakers equal partners in marriage; (3) promotion of circulating birth control information; and (4) promotion of equal laws regarding divorce, inheritance, and sexual crimes.[29] In the resulting debate, there was agreement in principle, opponents of the proposal claiming only that it was unrealistic or that it limited the areas in which the organization could work. The proposal was rejected 170–95.[30]

Freda Kirchwey and Crystal Eastman, both minority delegates, and Florence Kelley lost no time in attacking the convention. Kirchwey felt that the National Woman's party leadership, "a veritable tank," had ignored the party membership and crushed all attempts to promote equality for black women, birth control, or a maternity endowment. Eastman denied that her proposal had been debated and indicated that the majority of delegates had supported her. Kelley said that the NWP had become a group of rich, professional women who ignored working women and were racist.[31]

Other members of the National Woman's party tried to counter this image of the convention, but were hampered by the lack of a party publication since the discontinuation of the *Suffragist.* Ella Rush Murray, in a letter to the *Nation,* denied that the NWP was racist, since she and many other delegates had spoken out for black women at the convention, urging a Southern campaign to give black women the vote. Sue Shelton White regarded the objective of equality as flexible, unlike a specific program: "I have not a doubt that the Convention intended . . . everything necessary to wipe out the practices that stamp women with inferiority."[32]

[29]*Ibid.*, 129; Crystal Eastman, "Alice Paul's Convention," *Liberator* 4 (April 1921): 9–10. In her article, Eastman added two other points to her resolution: "5) To legitimize all children" and "6) To establish a liberal endowment of motherhood."

[30]*Stenographic Report*, 130–35.

[31]Freda Kirchwey, "Alice Paul Pulls the Strings," *Nation* 112 (2 March 1921): 332–33; Eastman, "Alice Paul's Convention," 9–10; Florence Kelley, "The New Woman's Party," *Survey* 45 (5 March 1921): 827–28; Florence Kelley, "Questions for the Woman's Party," *Nation* 117 (5 September 1923): 241. Sarah T. Colvin, who had introduced the majority resolution at the convention, also complained that debate on the future of the party was not allowed. Fry, *Conversations with Alice Paul*, 407. The *Nation* had attacked the NWP as being racist even before the convention, using returned questionnaires that they had sent to members of the NWP National Advisory Council. "The White Woman's Burden," *Nation* 112 (16 February 1921): 257–58.

[32]Ella Rush Murray, letter, *Nation* 112 (23 March 1921): 434; Sue S. White, "The Future of the Woman's Party," *ibid.*; *Stenographic Report*, 61–62; 10; Fry, *Conversations with*

While debate had been limited on Eastman's proposal, five women (including Eastman) had spoken in favor of it.[33] No matter how long the debate had lasted, it is doubtful that it could have reversed the 170–95 vote. Florence Kelley's objection to a "new" National Woman's party is difficult to understand. The party leadership had united for equality as early as September 1920 at a conference which she had attended. Nor had the membership changed. All but two of the top NWP leaders attended the convention. In the National Advisory Council, which was formed again after the convention in June 1921, three-fourths of the old members from Connecticut, New Jersey, and New York (including Kelley and Eastman) remained on the council, and no new members were added.[34]

While events tend to support the majority National Woman's party version of the convention, many feminists (as well as historians) have accepted the validity of the arguments of the party's opponents.[35] The February 1921 convention was the last conference where Social feminists and Femmists met together and debated with some measure of freedom. The spirit and oneness of purpose shown at the dedication ceremony and the virtual unanimity among the speakers and delegates on continuing the feminist movement were never again to be achieved.

After the convention, the National Council of the NWP prepared for a federal campaign for sexual equality. New chairman Elsie Hill announced that a federal amendment and state bills granting blanket equality would be introduced as soon as NWP lawyers could draw them up. A party delegation met with President Warren G. Harding on April 6, 1921, and was encouraged by his endorsement of equality. In October 1921, the NWP purchased a new headquarters, or "Watch Tower," facing the Capitol Building in Washington.[36]

In April 1921, as a step in preparing state bills, the NWP sent the

---

Alice Paul, 261; Elsie Hill to Member of the Woman's Party, 21 March 1921, Smith Papers, box 2, folder 59.

[33]Crystal Eastman did not leave the NWP. At the convention she was chosen as a member of the new National Council; later she wrote for the NWP's *Equal Rights*.

[34]Fry, *Conversations with Alice Paul*, 257, 259. The two NWP leaders who did not attend the convention were Lucy Burns, who decided to retire from the movement, and the militant Feminist Alva Belmont, who was in Europe. *New York Times*, 20 June 1921, 2. For a comparison of the pre-February 1921 and June 1921 National Advisory Councils, see Geidel, *National Woman's Party*, appendix, part 3, #1.

[35]Lemons, *Woman Citizen*, 183–84; O'Neill, *Everyone Was Brave*, 275–76; June Sochen, *Movers and Shakers* (New York: Quadrangle, 1973), 117. All three expressed the view that the convention was decided for the delegates by the leadership.

[36]Elsie Hill to Member of the Woman's Party, 21 March 1921, Smith Papers, box 2, folder 59. Part of this letter is quoted in the *New York Times*, 21 March 1921, 15. *New York Times*, 4 April 1921, 17; *New York Times*, 7 April 1921, 15; *New York Times*, 9 May 1921, 1; *New York Times*, 3 June 1921, 3; *New York Times*, 11 June 1921, 7; *New York Times*, 2 October 1921, 1.

first draft of a federal amendment to all NWP state chairmen, so that they could rephrase the law to cover individual state requirements. The bill enumerated six areas in which unequal laws would be eliminated: "(1) freedom of contract, (2) choice of citizenship and residence, (3) guardianship or control of children, (4) jury service, (5) holding of public office or position through certification by the Civil Service, election or Court Order, and (6) control, disposition, or acquisition of property." In an obvious move to compromise with the Social feminists on their main concern, protective legislation, a "safeguard clause" was included in the draft: "This act shall not amend or affect any law relating to the labor of women or minimum wage for women."[37]

Mabel Raef Putnam, chairman of the Wisconsin National Woman's party, took this bill to Governor John H. Blaine and received his support. He referred her to Charles Crownhart, the Wisconsin revisor of statutes, who drew up a bill including only provisions for jury service and equal residence. Putnam was upset at this limitation and at a meeting on May 17, 1921, persuaded Crownhart to include all the original provisions: "Women shall have the same rights and privileges under the law as men in the exercise of suffrage, freedom of contract, choice of residence, holding office, holding and conveying property, care and custody of children, and in all other respects." The bill also included the safeguard clause, providing that equality would be the principle followed "unless such construction will deny to females the special protection and privileges which they now enjoy for the general welfare."[38]

Putnam then managed to obtain the support of Governor Blaine, both Wisconsin senators, and other leaders ranging from Catholics to Socialists. At the legislative hearings on the bill, she assembled supporting representatives from the National Woman's party, the Wisconsin Federation of Business and Professional Women, the Wisconsin League of Women Voters, the Federation of Women's Clubs, the Consumers' League, the Young Women's Christian Association, the Wisconsin Women's Progressive Association, and the Polish Housewives League. When the legislative chairman of the Milwaukee League of Women Voters began to lobby against the bill, Putnam sought and won the endorsement of Catherine Waugh McCullough, chairman of the National League of Women Voters' Committee on Legislation of Civil Laws.[39]

Putnam's efforts paid off. The Wisconsin Assembly easily passed

[37]The National League of Women Voters had voted to study the merits of a blanket amendment at its Cleveland convention. Mabel Raef Putnam, *The Winning of the First Bill of Rights for American Women* (Milwaukee: Frank Putnam, 1924), 9–10, 56.

[38]*Ibid.*, 22–25.

[39]*Ibid.*, 29, 47, 56.

the bill, and the Senate, which the year before had defeated a jury bill for women, passed it by one vote on June 21, 1921. (The only major change in the original bill was that jury service for women was made optional.) Bill 484-S, the Wisconsin Equal Rights Bill, became law on July 11, 1921; Governor Blaine signed it with a black quill pen provided by the NWP.[40]

The same day that the Wisconsin bill passed the Senate, the National Council of the National Woman's party endorsed a new draft of a federal amendment which was to be introduced in the United States Congress by Senator Charles Curtis and Representative Simeon Fess.[41] However, the party soon decided to postpone the latter action as premature. It was believed by many at that time that women were already substantially equal to men in most states and that, in any case, the state legislatures would surely pass equalizing laws if the women worked for that. To correct this view, and to show that it was more than a publicity-seeking organization, the NWP found thirteen women lawyers, led by Burnita Shelton Matthews,[42] to survey the legislation of all forty-eight states and to uncover unequal laws. Although the NWP continued to formulate new drafts of a federal amendment, action on introducing it into Congress was delayed while surveys were being conducted.[43]

Legal surveys of the disabilities of women in Florida, Mississippi,

[40] *Milwaukee Journal*, 11 July 1921, 1; *New York Times*, 12 July 1921, 1. J. Stanley Lemons maintains that the Wisconsin Equal Rights Bill was "unsolicited." Lemons, *Woman Citizen*, 187. It is true that this account of the bill's passage is based heavily on Putnam's own account. Nevertheless, the similarity in language of the two bills, Putnam's enlistment of support from other organizations, and Governor Blaine's acknowledgment of Putnam's role in the passage of the bill cannot be denied.

[41] *Washington Post*, 22 June 1921, 4; Alice Paul to Jane Norman Smith, 30 August 1921, Smith Papers, box 5, folder 110.

[42] Matthews would later become president of the National Association of Women Lawyers, and in 1950 was appointed by President Harry S Truman to be the first female District Court Judge in American history.

[43] "In Re: Burnita Shelton Matthews," Helen Hunt West Papers, Schlesinger Library, Radcliffe College, box 1, folder 25 (hereafter cited as West Papers). For example, Alice Paul, in a letter to John B. Dawson, general secretary of the Organized Charities Association of New Haven, wrote as follows on June 27, 1921: "We have not formed an opinion as yet concerning the advisability of introducing a federal amendment, and cannot form an opinion on this subject until we have completed our study of the discriminations against women in each of the states. When this investigation is completed we hope to be in a position to judge as to whether federal amendment or state action is the better way to succeed." John B. Dawson, "The Program of the National Woman's Party from the Point of View of Connecticut Social Workers," *Family* 3 (January 1923): 226. The National Woman's party was well aware of unequal laws even before the surveys began. Sue S. White, "Women and the Law," *Nation* 112 (16 March 1921): 402.

Alabama, and Louisiana, and the fewness of successes in the state legislative campaigns, convinced many NWP leaders that either a federal amendment or state blanket bills was the answer. In September 1921, new drafts for both bills and amendment were prepared by a lawyers' committee led by Gail Laughlin. Laughlin was personally opposed to protective legislation for women, and the draft federal amendment now lacked a safeguard clause: "No political, civil or legal disabilities or inequalities on account of sex, nor on account of marriage, unless applying equally to both sexes, shall exist within the United States or any territory subject to the jurisdiction thereof."[44]

The state bill also lacked a safeguard clause. It eliminated discriminations in fourteen specific areas, as well as "in all other respects." Section 4 further stated that "all acts and parts of acts in conflict with any of the provisions of this statute are hereby repealed."[45]

National Woman's party leaders claimed that these bills would not endanger protective legislation. Maud Younger, legislative chairman of the NWP, wrote that "as our measures now stand, it seems that they neither oppose nor disapprove such legislation—they do not touch it."

Most of the lawyers consulted by the National Woman's party agreed with Younger. Frank P. Walsh, former joint chairman of the War Labor Board, agreed to take any litigation to defend protective legislation after the amendment passed free of charge. He believed that "the political, civil and legal disabilities and inequalities leveled against women, . . . are so great in number and so deeply engrafted on our legal structure, by national and state statutes as well as by court decisions that I can see no way of approximating justice, as affecting the sexes, except by the passage of such an amendment as your organization has promised."[46]

[44] *New York Times*, 16 September 1921, 10.

[45] Putnam, *Winning of the First Bill of Rights*, 69; *New York Times*, 26 September 1921, 15.

[46] *New York Times*, 26 September 1921, 15; Alice Paul to Jane Norman Smith, 29 November 1921. Smith Papers, box 5, folder 110; *New York Times*, 19 March 1922, sec. 3, p. 27.

Other prominent lawyers and political leaders who maintained that a federal amendment would not further hurt the chances for protective legislation for women were George Gordon Battle, a prominent lawyer active in many causes; Shippen Lewis, secretary of the Legal Education Committee of the American Bar Association; Matthew Hale, national chairman of the Progressive Labor party; Henry A. Slattery; Charles W. Needham, solicitor for the Interstate Commerce Commission and a former president of George Washington University; Robert T. Scott, former assistant United States attorney general; James H. Webb, Democratic National Executive Committee of Alabama; and Walter B. Wilbur, chairman of the Child Welfare Commission in South Carolina and a national officer of the National Consumers' League. *New York Times*, 12 December 1921, 17; Zona Gale, "The Status of Wisconsin Women under the Equal Rights Law," *Proceedings of the Wisconsin State Bar Association* 14 (1922): 181.

Protective legislation now became the primary obstacle to an amendment and state blanket bills. Alice Paul explained the new NWP strategy:

> The reason that we have delayed about the introduction of the amendment in Congress is that we wanted to make certain that it would not touch upon the labor legislation for women. We have consulted the leaders of the movement for women's welfare legislation in order to secure their help in drafting the measure in a way that would not touch upon their legislation. They have not, however, given us any suggestions as to ways in which they thought the amendment could be improved.[47]

The National Woman's party opposed a safeguard clause in the federal amendment, not to nullify equal protective legislation, but because (1) it would put the NWP on record as supporting protective legislation (whereas the party at this time took no stand on the issue); (2) lawyers consulted on the safeguard clause said that it "would open the gate to many kinds of discriminations against women by allowing the court to interpret such discriminations as being legitimate"; and (3) "Protective legislation comes under the police power of the states; . . . such a clause has no place in a federal amendment."[48]

The National Woman's party tried to reach a solution with the Social feminists at a meeting at the Dodge Hotel in Washington, D.C., on December 4, 1921. Alice Paul met with Florence Kelley, Ethel Smith, Maud Wood Park, and other leading Social feminists on the merits of a blanket bill. The NWP argued that with an amendment the standards of protective legislation could be raised for men to equal those for women. The others believed that any blanket bill would nullify protective legislation. This first attempt to produce a workable bill satisfactory to all had failed.[49]

Despite this setback, the National Woman's party still sought to

---

In the southern states campaign, Sophie G. Meredith, NWP Virginia state chairman, assembled the following men for the state blanket bills: Robert Powell, Mississippi chairman of the Democratic State Committee and a former member of the National Democratic Executive Committee; James H. Webb; and Walter B. Wilbur. *New York Times*, 16 January 1922, 3.

[47]Alice Paul to Jane Norman Smith, 29 November 1921, Smith Papers, box 5, folder 110. Anita Pollitzer, NWP national legislative secretary, wrote as follows about the amendment: "We do not intend to have it introduced until we are as certain as possible that the form in which we have it introduced will remove all political, legal and civil discriminations against women and will not touch any other field of legislation. We are seeing lawyers constantly regarding the drafting, and are also in touch with the welfare workers. . . . We want to be quite sure that our amendment does not wipe away existing welfare legislation." Anita L. Pollitzer to Jane Norman Smith, 5 January 1922, Smith Papers, box 5, folder 110.

[48]Pollitzer to Smith, 5 January 1922, Smith Papers, box 5, folder 110; Gale, "Status of Wisconsin Women," 180; *New York Times*, 29 January 1922, sec. 7, p. 8.

[49]Fry, *Conversations with Alice Paul*, 410–12; Lemons, *Woman Citizen*, 187.

compromise.[50] In addition to obtaining the approval of lawyers for the federal amendment, the NWP also changed the language of the state bill to include the statement: "This act shall not affect laws regulating the employment of women in industry."[51]

The National Woman's party remained neutral on protective legislation. In an April 1922 debate with Florence Kelley, Maud Younger stated that the NWP did "not wish to touch the industrial field." In New York and New Jersey, while Florence Kelley and representatives from the Women's Trade Union League and other Social feminist groups spoke at legislative hearings in favor of new protective laws for women, the National Woman's party neither appeared nor spoke out against these bills. Alice Paul also advised the New York NWP to eliminate a section from a proposed law which would have negated every common-law disability, and the Massachusetts NWP remained neutral on protective legislation.[52]

Much attention was paid to the Wisconsin Equal Rights Bill, the only state blanket bill which ever passed. Florence Kelley, ever guarding the protective legislation for which she had worked for thirty years, opposed all blanket bills, including Wisconsin's: "No safeguarding clause or provision can give convincing assurance that, in the process of judicial interpretation, this amendment may not sweep out of existence all the measures for protecting women in industry which have been slowly developing during nearly seventy years, and have made more advances since 1900 than in the previous half century."

The National Woman's party tried to show that the law did not

[50]J. Stanley Lemons and Clarke A. Chambers viewed the conference as the final split. Immediately after the conference, Lemons wrote, "the NWP reversed itself, admitted that the amendment would eliminate protective laws, and said that the laws were holding back women and limiting their opportunities." Although neither Lemons nor Chambers offered a source for his contentions, the accounts are identical to Mary Anderson's. Lemons, *Woman Citizen*, 187; Chambers, *Seedtime of Reform*, 78; Anderson, *Woman at Work*, 161–62. Anderson, a bitter opponent of the NWP, wrote her memoirs thirty years after the event. As such, its section on the Equal Rights Amendment is of dubious historical value. For a critique of Anderson's account, see Geidel, *National Woman's Party*, part 4, "The National Scene: Attempts at Equal Rights Amendments," 7–8.

[51]For texts of the new bill, see *New York Times*, 19 December 1921, 17, and 16 January 1922, 1, 3; Elsie Hill, "Shall Women Be Equal before the Law? Yes!" *Nation* 114 (12 April 1922): 420. The proposed NWP blanket bill for New York State was even more explicit: "This section shall not affect laws regulating the employment of women in industry, trade or commerce, nor existing laws giving special protection to women, or extending privileges which women now enjoy for the general welfare." *New York Times*, 19 May 1922, 16.

[52]*New York Times*, 12 April 1922, 5; 31 January 1922, 4; and 23 February 1922, 11; Jane Norman Smith to Mrs. William Hutton Blauvelt, 6 March 1922, Smith Papers, box 2, folder 60; Chafe, *American Woman*, 117.

affect protective legislation, quoting the secretary of the Industrial Commission of Wisconsin to the effect that no "employers' association ever suggested that the effect of this Woman's Rights bill is to repeal the women's welfare laws"; it also quoted the chairman of the Industrial Commission of Wisconsin who said that the law had "no affect whatsoever" on protective legislation.[53]

The other main objection to the state blanket bill was that it gave the process of achieving equality to the courts instead of to the legislatures. Social feminists believed that a study should have been made of each state's laws and each inequality corrected specifically by legislation. The National Woman's party had tried this method in Massachusetts with no success. It therefore believed that the legal system should be given a principle of equality to follow, rather than the old common-law basis of judgment. As Zona Gale stated, "We know that it must be followed by specific legislation in those instances—and many may arise—in which the issues are not clear. But we hold that a foundation is necessary on which to build, for the guidance of future legislators."[54]

Social feminists did not accept this argument. Florence Kelley refused to allow a NWP representative to speak at the National Consumers' League National Convention, and in January 1922 its board of directors voted to oppose all blanket bills. On February 26, 1922, the National Women's Trade Union League assembled fifty representatives from the National Consumers' League, the National League of Women Voters, and the American Home Economics Association, all of whom agreed to oppose blanket bills regardless of whether they had a safeguard clause or not. The April 1922 convention of the National League of Women Voters overwhelmingly voted to oppose all blanket bills and to support protective legislation. In June, both the National Women's Trade Union League and the American Federation of Labor conventions went on record against blanket bills. Finally, a coalition of Social feminist groups organized a campaign against state blanket bills.[55]

[53]Florence Kelley, "The National Consumers' League," *Legal Aid Review* 20 (January 1922): 6; Florence Kelley and Carrie Chapman Catt, "Blanket Equality Bill," *Woman's Home Companion* 49 (August 1922): 89; Florence Kelley, "Shall Women Be Equal before the Law? No!" *Nation* 114 (12 April 1922): 421; Putnam, *Winning of the First Bill of Rights*, 76–77; Mabel Search, "Women's Rights in Wisconsin," *Marquette Law Review* 6 (June 1922): 165–66, 168–69; Gale, "Status of Wisconsin Women," 169, 179.

[54]Jennie McMullin Turner, "Women's Rights by Blanket Legislation," *Wisconsin Law Review* 2 (January 1923): 103–9; Zona Gale, "What Women Won in Wisconsin," *Nation* 115 (23 August 1922): 184. For an explanation of the Massachusetts bill, see "Five Types of Equal Rights Bills Suggested by the National Woman's Party," Bill Number 3, Smith Papers, box 10, folder 188.

[55]Alice Paul to Jane Norman Smith, 29 November 1921, Smith Papers, Box 5, folder 110; Kelly, "The National Consumers' League," 6; Lemons, *Woman Citizen*, 190–

The National Consumers' League began to raise money to defeat a federal blanket amendment in May 1922. However, the National Woman's party was still trying to draw up a final draft of an amendment acceptable to Social feminists and had no intention of introducing one in 1922.[56]

Social feminists believed that a bill which endangered protective legislation was unacceptable. They accepted without question that women were more susceptible to disease, mental illness, and loose morals than men in industrial work. Mary Anderson said, "Do you appreciate the significance of these figures in terms of health, of race? . . . this whole business of modern industry . . . is particularly dangerous where women and women's vital energies—that is to say, their race energies—are concerned." Hard work also hurt a woman's "nervous vitality," and these defects could be passed on to the next generation. To Anderson, if the United States did not pass more protective legislative laws for women, "presently we shall have our institutions overflowing with crazy, unbalanced, devitalized women, and children who are imbecile, defective, rickety or tubercular."[57]

Social feminists tried to downplay the extent of inequality. Carrie Chapman Catt claimed that women were virtually equal to men and castigated those who wanted to keep their own names after marriage, to be mothers out of wedlock, or to have both children and a career. Florence Kelley considered women workers to be better off than men due to protective legislation.[58] An amendment hardly seemed to be needed to achieve equality.

A vague amendment would open the way to endless court suits.

91; *New York Times*, 26 April 1922, 3, and 28 April 1922, 17; National Women's Trade Union League of America, "Declaration in Opposition to Proposed Equal Rights Amendment," *Proceedings of the National Women's Trade Union League of America* (1922), 92–94, 118; "Eighth Biennial Convention of the National Women's Trade-Union League of America," *Monthly Labor Review* 15 (August 1922), for August, pp. 193–94; for vol. 15, 423–24; American Federation of Labor, *Report of the Proceedings of the American Federation of Labor* (1922), 101. The text of the equal rights amendment quoted by Samuel Gompers had already been discarded by the NWP. "Resolution No. 109—By Delegate Julia O'Connor of Brotherhood of Electrical Workers," *ibid.*, 224, 476; *New York Times*, 16 June 1922, 19.

[56]*New York Times*, 16 May 1922, 19. The *New York Times*, due to this story, actually believed that a blanket amendment had already been introduced in Congress. Their misconception was corrected by Jane Norman Smith, legislative secretary of the New York NWP. *New York Times*, 17 May 1922, 18, and 19 May 1922, 16.

[57]Elizabeth Frazer, "Harnessing Industry with the Vote," *Ladies Home Journal* 39 (November 1922): 169. See also Kelley, "Shall Women Be Equal Before the Law? No!" 421.

[58]Carrie Chapman Catt, "Too Many Rights: Women Leaders Who Would Go beyond All Decent Limits," *Ladies Home Journal* 39 (November 1922): 31; Florence Kelley, "The Right to Differ," *Survey* 49 (15 December 1922): 375–76.

Individual state action was preferred. Florence Kelley was convinced that this could be done in an easier and safer way than by blanket bills. Catherine Waugh McCullough confidently asserted that if women worked hard for two more legislative sessions in each state "all existing civil disabilities would be removed."[59] Kelley, Catt, Anderson, and Ethel Smith also attacked the amendment as a threat to states' rights:

> a) Our Republic rests upon the right of local self-government, leaving to the states everything not expressly assigned by the Federal Constitution to the President and Congress.
> b) The proposed Federal amendment, on the contrary, makes it the duty of Congress to supplant the legislatures in innumerable matters, wherever the equality of women with men are concerned.[60]

As a result of this attitude, some members of the National Woman's party began to question the compromise strategy of their leadership. The state campaigns had largely failed, with only twenty-three bills in nine states passed during 1921 and 1922 (and most of these bills involved only minor changes in the law).[61] In many states women still did not have the right to sit on juries, sue for injuries to themselves, or have equal guardianship and property rights when married.[62]

The National Woman's party also organized professional councils to uncover discrimination, which was widespread. Civil Service positions were arbitrarily designated for men only. Only 40 of 482 general hospitals and 15 of 102 special hospitals accepted women as interns. Many law schools, including Columbia and Harvard, admitted only male students.[63]

59 *New York Times*, 16 May 1922, 19; Kelley, "National Consumers' League," 6; Search, "Women's Rights in Wisconsin," 166; *New York Times*, 26 April 1922, 3.

60 Kelley and Catt, "Blanket Equality Bill," 4, 89; Anderson, *Woman at Work*, 161–62. Florence Kelley, although a socialist, also supported a separate minimum-wage law for every state rather than one national statute. *New York Times*, 3 June 1923, sec. 8, p. 13. For an analysis of Kelley's ideology, which endorsed the traditional family concept, see Geidel, *National Woman's Party*, part 4, 8–10.

61 "What Has Been Won," *Equal Rights* 1 (17 November 1923): 318.

62 For examples of discrimination, see the following: *Washington Post*, 20 February 1921, 19; Sue S. White, "Women and the Law," *Nation* 112 (16 March 1921): 402; Hill, "Shall Women Be Equal before the Law?" 420; *New York Times*, 10 March 1922, 7, and 21 March 1922, 7; Anita Pollitzer to Jane Norman Smith, 5 January 1922, Smith Papers, box 5, folder 110; Gale, "Status of Wisconsin Women," 184; "Women as Members of the Jury," *Equal Rights* 1 (3 November 1923): 301; Mary Winsor, "The Freedom of Inequality," *ibid.* (24 February 1923): 13; *New York Times*, 10 December 1922, sec. 4, p. 12.

63 *Washington Post*, 5 November 1922, sec. 5, p. 2. For an example of the formation of a council, see the *Washington Post*, 29 October 1922, 7, on the Government Workers' Council. For other relevant material, see "National Woman's Party Forms Political Council," *Equal Rights* 1 (3 March 1923): 22; Mary Pittman, "Discriminations against

At the dedication of National Woman's party headquarters in Washington, D.C., in May 1922, Alva Belmont spoke of the party's "determination to come before the governing powers as dictators, not as beggars." Gail Laughlin, now vice-chairman of the National Council, called for equality of women in all fields in an indirect criticism of protective legislation. Only Maud Younger, the legislative chairman, still favored the compromise strategy.[64]

By mid-1922, most of the state legal surveys had been completed. They showed numerous discriminations in every state.[65] In October, the National Council unanimously approved a three-point program: (1) to prepare and introduce a federal equal rights amendment to do away with "all disabilities on the ground of sex"; (2) to continue the individual state campaigns for blanket bills and specific bills; and (3) to hold a convention in Seneca Falls, New York, in July 1923 to commemorate the seventy-fifth anniversary of the Seneca Falls meeting which had launched the suffrage movement.[66] On November 11, 179 delegates from thirty-two states endorsed the National Council's three-point program, as well as a Declaration of Principles drawn up by Alice Paul and Alva Belmont.

The Declaration of Principles covered three basic areas: (1) the husband-wife relationship; (2) family support; and (3) equal economic opportunity. It declared the National Woman's party to be in favor of equality between the sexes in all these areas. Protective legislation for women specifically was denounced: "Restrictions upon the laws, conditions and remuneration of labor shall apply alike to both sexes." The declaration concluded,

> IN SHORT—THAT WOMAN SHALL NO LONGER BE IN ANY FORM OF SUBJECTION TO MAN IN LAW OR IN CUSTOM, BUT SHALL IN EVERY WAY BE ON AN EQUAL PLANE IN RIGHTS, AS SHE HAS ALWAYS BEEN AND WILL CONTINUE TO BE IN RESPONSIBILITIES AND OBLIGATIONS.[67]

Women in Government Service," *ibid.* (2 June 1923): 123; "Are Taxes Paid by Men Only?" *ibid.* (2 June 1923): 124; "Speech of Miss Laura Berrien, Chairman of the Government Workers' Council," *ibid.* (4 August 1923): 200; "Discrimination against Women in Government Service," *ibid.* (8 December 1923): 339; Mary Pittman, "Government Workers Make Progress," *ibid.* (23 June 1923): 152; Carson C. Hathaway, "Woman's Demand for Man's Full Civil Rights," *Current History Magazine* 17 (January 1923): 645; *New York Times*, 10 December 1922, sec. 4, p. 12.

[64] *New York Times*, 22 May 1922, 1, 3. See also Mrs. O.H.P. Belmont, "Women as Dictators," *Ladies Home Journal* 39 (September 1922): 7, 43.

[65] *New York Times*, 23 June 1922, 9. For the New York report, see *The Legal Position of Women in New York—1922*, Smith Papers, box 10, folder 191.

[66] *New York Times*, 26 October 1922, 8.

[67] Original versions of the declaration may be found in Smith Papers, box 9, folder 167, and Fry, *Conversations with Alice Paul*, 657. A complete version with many paragraphs out of sequence appears in the *New York Times*, 10 December 1922, sec. 4, p. 12.

In addition to a federal amendment, the delegates also approved five state bills for use in the state legislative campaigns.[68]

Florence Kelley now immediately organized a conference of Social feminist groups, which denounced all blanket bills and "the threats of a sex war made by the National Woman's Party."[69] Nevertheless, there was still ground for cooperation between the National Woman's party and the Social feminists. Both groups had supported legislation such as the Cable Act and Civil Service reclassification.[70] Both sides also favored specific bills in many states. As Alice Paul wrote, "It seems to me that it is immaterial whether the bills which are passed are those which we have drawn up, or those which some other organization has drawn up. The only important thing is to see that they are passed and that these particular disabilities are removed."[71] However, Kelley and a Social feminist coalition rejected any offer of cooperation, and Kelley announced her intention to oppose even the specific bills introduced into state legislatures by the National Woman's party.[72] This decision ended all attempts at compromise on the national level.

The feminist split widened. In November 1922, an attempt to repeal a 1905 law prohibiting women from becoming legislative employees was defeated by the Wisconsin legislature. On January 15, 1923, Wisconsin Attorney General Herman L. Ekern ruled that the 1905 law was valid despite the 1921 Equal Rights Bill: "Employment in the legislative service necessitates work during very long and often unseasonable hours . . . it was not the intention of the legislature to change this practice, as would be required under the statutes relating

[68]For an account of the conference, see *Washington Post*, 11 November 1922, 2, and 12 November 1922, 3.

The five state bills prepared by Burnita Shelton Matthews and the NWP Legal Research Department were (1) a general blanket bill guaranteeing sexual equality in one sentence; (2) the Wisconsin bill, omitting the safeguard clause and voluntary jury service clause; (3) the Massachusetts Bill, containing every specific change which needed to be made; (4) a composite bill in which each section could be made into a specific bill if necessary; and (5) separate bills, each covering a separate topic. See "Five Types of Equal Rights Bills," Smith Papers, box 10, folder 188.

[69]*New York Times*, 30 October 1922, 17; *Washington Post*, 29 October 1922, 6; *New York Times*, 5 November 1922, sec. 2, p. 1; *Washington Post*, 10 November 1922, 3.

[70]The Cable Act was the first step toward allowing women who married foreign men to retain their American citizenship if they wished. Baroness Virginia Nugent, the niece of Maud Younger, had lost her American citizenship when she married an Austrian. She agreed to speak for the NWP on this issue. *New York Times*, 10 June 1922, 11, and 20 June 1922, 21; Irwin, *Angels*, 425. For Social feminists' involvement in these issues, see Lemons, *Woman Citizen*, 56–57, 66–67.

[71]Alice Paul to Jane Norman Smith, 17 January 1923, Smith Papers, box 5, folder 111.

[72]*New York Times*, 19 November 1922, 23; "Opposes Equality Bill," *Catholic Charities Review* 6 (December 1922): 361.

to the employment of women."[73] Social feminists were still unconvinced. Alice Paul, on the other hand, realized that because of the safeguard clause, many discriminations could be rationalized as protection: "It seems to me this is an extremely effective argument against including such a welfare provision in any state."[74]

At the Conference on Women in Industry in 1923, Mary Anderson refused to allow the National Woman's party and the Women's League for Equal Opportunity, two Feminist groups, to speak against protective legislation for women. Only three representatives of manufacturers' associations were allowed to do so. Alice Paul then refused to send an official delegation to the conference. On the final day of the conference, when Anderson read a letter from Paul stating why the NWP would not attend, an NWP member in the audience applauded. Ethel Smith then denounced the NWP and claimed it was trying to disrupt the conference.[75]

Feminists were denigrated by Social feminists in 1923. Clara Mortenson Beyer of the New York Consumers' League called the women in the NWP "society girls," unable to make a serious industrial survey. Felix Frankfurter accused Harriot Stanton Blatch of being, "like most laymen," ignorant of the law. Mary Anderson claimed that the NWP appealed to "prejudice and hysteria" rather than reason. The NWP was characterized as "militant suffragists, who, like the Irish, seem to have got the habit." Its tactics were denounced as "revolution by irritation, a coup d'etat by annoyance."[76]

The National Woman's party, now that its position on equality had been finalized, began to publish its own weekly paper, *Equal Rights*, on February 17, 1923. It gave news of individual state branches and national and international developments but dealt mainly with protective legislation. The NWP opposed protective legislation for women only and took no official stand except that labor

[73] *Opinions of the Attorney General of the State of Wisconsin* 12 (Madison, Wisconsin: 1923): 13.

[74] Alice Paul to Jane Norman Smith, 20 February 1923, Smith Papers, box 5, folder 111; "Women Barred from Employment in Wisconsin," *Equal Rights* 1 (24 March 1923): 43; "Special Privileges for Women," *ibid.*: 48; Putnam, *Winning of the First Bill*, 90.

[75] *New York Times*, 1 January 1923, 11; 11 January 1923, 16; and 14 January 1923, 8. J. Stanley Lemons concurred with the Social feminist viewpoint. In a section on the conference, he wrote about the "principal disruption-the attempt of the NWP to use the occasion as a forum for the discussion of the equal rights amendment." Lemons, *Woman Citizen*, 192.

[76] *New York Times*, 14 January 1923, sec. 4, p. 4; Florence Kelley, "Should Women Be Treated Identically with Men by the Law?" *American Review* 1 (May/June 1923): 277, 283–84; *idem*, "Questions for the Woman's Party," 241; *New York Times*, 23 December 1922, 12; Anderson, *Woman at Work*, 163; Mayme Ober Peak, "Women in Politics," *Outlook* 136 (23 January 1924): 147–48; *New York Times*, 10 December 1922, sec. 2, p. 6.

legislation be equal.[77] However, it did not consider that equal protective legislation was a Feminist issue. The *Equal Rights* writers, interestingly, did not exactly reflect this opinion; not one opposed equal protective legislation and many supported it. Anna Wiley, chairman of the Homemakers Council, stated that the National Woman's party wished "to secure protective legislation for men and women alike." Carol Rehfish wrote that the NWP wanted to create equality in protection, not to end protective legislation. Other articles endorsed a forty-hour week and an eight-hour day for all, and praised international women's conferences which had favored equal protection. Typical of the *Equal Rights* position was this editorial comment: "Dreadful, isn't it, to think of losing a minimum wage law that has already been declared unconstitutional for women only, or a ten-hour day, when in the union eight hours is the maximum, as it should be."[78] *Equal Rights* also urged women to form unions in order to earn higher wages.[79]

Alice Paul urged that the NWP try to amend the laws so that they would apply to all "persons": "Even though they [the amendments] are not passed and though we are not able to do much campaigning for them, the fact that we introduce them puts clearly before the world what our principle is on this matter."[80] This policy did win some support from labor and Social feminists, as in Michigan, Minnesota, and Ohio. However, in most states Social feminists refused to cooper-

[77] "Minimum Wage Laws for Women," *Equal Rights* 1 (31 March 1923): 56; "Longer Hours for Women?" *ibid.* (14 April 1923): 68; "Theory vs. Practise," *ibid.* (12 May 1923): 100; "The Woman's Party and the Minimum Wage for Women," *ibid.* (22 December 1923): 356.

[78] Mrs. Harvey Wiley, "The Work of the Woman's Party," *Equal Rights* 1 (3 March 1923): 21; "Seats for Working Women," *ibid.* (7 April 1923): 60; "I.C.W.W. on Special Labor Laws," *ibid.* (12 May 1923): 104; Carol Rehfisch, "The Woman's Party Is Right," *ibid.* (20 October 1923): 286; "Sops," *ibid.* (27 October 1923): 292; "Position of the Woman's Party on Laws Prohibiting Night Work for Women," *ibid.* (24 February 1923): 16; "The Minimum Wage Law for Women," *ibid.* (10 March 1923): 28; Emma Wold, "Teachers Council of Woman's Party," *ibid.* (10 March 1923): 30; "Notes of the Week," *ibid.* (16 June 1923): 138; "International Congress of Working Women and Special Labor Laws for Women," *ibid.* (23 June 1923): 147; "Getting down to Facts," *ibid.* (29 September 1923): 260; "Why the Argument," *ibid.* (6 October 1923): 268; "For the Amendment," *ibid.* (22 December 1923): 359.

[79] James L. O'Donnell, "Take Mary with You," *Equal Rights* 1 (12 May 1923), 101–2; "Reason Totters," *ibid.* (19 May 1923): 108; "Labor Speaks Truly," *ibid.* (7 July 1923): 164; Lavinia Egan, "Figures on Industrial Discrimination," *ibid.* (21 July 1923): 179; "The Right to Work," *ibid.* (21 July 1923): 180; "Common Sense," *ibid.* (3 November 1923): 300; "Woman's Place in Industry," *ibid.* (17 November 1923): 314; Lucy Branham, "Subtracting Women from Children in Labor Legislation," *ibid.* (15 December 1923): 347; *New York Times*, 25 March 1923, sec. 9, p. 3.

[80] Alice Paul to Jane Norman Smith, 26 December 1922, Smith Papers, box 5, folder 110; *New York Times*, 1 March 1923, 19.

ate with the NWP. In New York, the NWP tried to work with a Social feminist coalition on thirteen separate bills and consented to let them sponsor the bills; however, the Social feminists refused to cooperate unless the NWP ceased all attempts to amend protective laws or introduce any new laws. The result was a split in the New York movement.[81]

The 1923 state legislative campaign had been a failure. Of the bills sponsored by the National Woman's party, twenty-six lost in Connecticut and Rhode Island, over twenty in New York, fourteen in Ohio, nine in Oklahoma, five in Michigan, and one with thirty-two sections in Massachusetts. Numerous other bills failed elsewhere. Only forty-one NWP-endorsed bills in fifteen states had passed in three years. The NWP assistant secretary of the Legal Research Department had maintained that a successful state campaign would cancel the need for a federal amendment, but this lack of success made such an amendment necessary.[82]

On July 20, 1923, the National Council met and unanimously endorsed the federal amendment. At Seneca Falls, on July 21, 1923, Alice Paul presented her resolution to the gathering of NWP officials. The meeting unanimously passed the Equal Rights Amendment, subsequently called the Lucretia Mott Amendment: "Men and women shall have equal rights throughout the United States and every place subject to its jurisdiction."[83]

The NWP rationale in favor of the Lucretia Mott Amendment was as follows: (1) Suffrage had been achieved by way of a federal amendment, which the NWP had urged, and not by state referenda, as the Social feminists had advocated. Equality could be achieved in the same way. (2) The NWP believed all major issues should be considered in

[81]"Campaign over the Country," *Equal Rights* 1 (3 March 1923): 18–19; "News from the Field," *ibid.* (10 March 1923): 26; (31 March 1923): 52–54; and (7 April 1923): 62; Stuhler and Kreuter, eds., *Women of Minnesota*, 263; Jane Norman Smith to Alice Paul, 4 December 1922, Smith Papers, box 5, folder 110; Alice Paul to Jane Norman Smith, 8 December 1922, *ibid.*, box 5, folder 110; Jane Norman Smith to Elizabeth Fisher Read, 8 December 1922, *ibid.*, box 2, folder 60; Jane Norman Smith to Alice Paul, 16 December 1922, *ibid.*, box 5, folder 110; *New York Times*, 15 December 1922, 20; 14 January 1923, sec. 4, p. 4; and 28 February 1923, 6; "The Nation-wide Legislative Campaign," *Equal Rights* 1 (24 February 1923): 10–11; "News from the Field," *ibid.* (10 March 1923): 26; Jane Norman Smith to Mary Ertz Will, 8 March 1923, Smith Papers, box 2, folder 60.

[82]By 1925 the National Woman's party had drafted about five hundred state bills, few of which were ever passed. "Why a Federal Amendment?" *Equal Rights* 12 (12 September 1925): 244; F.L. Woodson, "The Washington End of the Equal Rights Campaign," *Equal Rights* 1 (24 February 1923): 14; "An Argument for a Federal Amendment," *ibid.* (29 December 1923): 364; "Equal Rights Bills That Failed in 1923," *ibid.* (5 January 1924): 374–75; "What Has Been Won," *ibid.* (17 November 1923): 318.

[83]Lavinia Egan, "The Seneca Fall Conference," *Equal Rights* 1 (4 August 1923): 195–97; *New York Times*, 21 July 1923, 8; Emma Bugbee, "Women Open Campaign for Equal Rights," *Equal Rights* 1 (28 July 1923): 189; *New York Times*, 22 July 1923, 1, 4.

a national way. Sexual equality should be a major issue. (3) An amendment was more permanent than state legislation. The Virginia legislature, which had given men and women equal guardianship of children, and the North Dakota legislature, which had made both parents equally responsible for illegitimate children, had both reversed themselves later. (4) An amendment would be less costly in time and money than individual state action. A Michigan woman justice of the peace was taken to court on the grounds that women were ineligible for the position. Although she eventually won her case, nationwide justice would be impossible if it meant carrying defense all the way to the supreme courts. (5) People would become more aware of inequalities against women if the issue were dealt with nationally. (6) Politicians would be forced to take a stand on woman's issues. (7) A federal amendment would be the only way to achieve equality in states which required a majority of registered voters to pass an amendment to the state constitution and in other states which required referenda in order to correct inequalities in the law.[84]

On December 10, 1923, Republican Senator Charles Curtis of Kansas introduced the Lucretia Mott Amendment (Senate Joint Resolution 21) in the Senate Judiciary Committee. On December 13, Republican Representative Daniel Read Anthony of Kansas introduced the amendment (House Joint Resolution 75) in the House of Representatives. The National Woman's party was encouraged by President Calvin Coolidge's response to a NWP delegation in November 1923. The Republicans controlled Congress and most state legislatures, and the NWP was confident that President Coolidge would use his power to help pass the amendment.[85]

Action on the amendment did not bear out this optimism. It was introduced every year, but only forty-nine years later, changed slightly and known as the Equal Rights Amendment, did it finally pass in Congress.

* * * *

Feminists and Social feminists have been in conflict throughout the twentieth century. During the suffrage campaign, they agreed as to the goal but differed as to tactics. After suffrage, both tactics and goals were in dispute. Feminists were for sexual equality, which conflicted

[84]"The Lucretia Mott Amendment," *Equal Rights* 1 (10 November 1923): 308; "Equal Rights Demand Is Taken to President Coolidge," *ibid.* (24 November 1923): 323; "A National Amendment Is the Permanent Way of Establishing Equal Rights," *ibid.* (15 December 1923): 348; Emma Fox, "The Need for a Federal Amendment," *ibid.* (7 July 1923): 166; "Why a Constitutional Amendment," *ibid.* (24 November 1923): 324; Burnita Shelton Matthews, "A Federal Amendment Avoids Referendum Campaigns," *ibid.* (29 December 1923): 365.

[85]"The President's Attitude," *Equal Rights* 1 (24 November 1923): 324; *New York Times*, 18 November 1923, 22.

with the predominantly nonfeminist concerns of the Social feminists.

Each side was partly to blame for the split, but Social feminists were the more uncompromising. The National Woman's party invited Social feminist groups to speak at its 1921 convention, but the Social feminists did not reciprocate. In the basic conflict over protective legislation, the NWP in 1921 and 1922 did not oppose protective laws and offered a state blanket bill with a safeguard clause for protective legislation. NWP lawyers maintained that even a federal equal rights amendment would not endanger protective legislation for women. Social feminists, however, would accept no solution except a specific state law for every sexual inequality in every state. After the NWP announced it would support a federal amendment and oppose protective legislation for women only, Social feminists refused to cooperate with the NWP or even work for NWP bills upon which both sides agreed.

Neither side realized that the feminist movement had to be united to some degree in order to achieve success. The National Woman's party was more desirous of cooperation, but it did not regard a split with Social feminists as fatal to the cause of equality. It believed that it had played the major part in obtaining suffrage. However, without the sheer mass of Social feminists, the relatively small National Woman's party stood little chance of implementing its program. On the other hand, Social feminists believed that they had been primarily responsible for achieving suffrage and that a small organization such as the NWP was no great loss in achieving their program. However, they lacked the NWP's ability to gain national publicity. Even in the Women's Joint Congressional Committee, Social feminist leaders quarreled bitterly among themselves as to who deserved credit for the passage of the Sheppard-Towner Bill.[86] Only in Wisconsin, where the NWP organized a coalition of Social feminist groups to push for the Equal Rights Bill, did women come near to obtaining equality.

The National Woman's party did make some decisions which hurt potential cooperation with Social feminists. The *Suffragist* came out against protective legislation in 1920. Although by 1921 the NWP had taken a neutral position on the issue, thereafter the Social feminists distrusted the NWP. When the NWP continued to refuse to endorse equal protective legislation on the ground that it was not a feminist issue, Social feminists could claim the NWP was trying to nullify all protective legislation. When the NWP finally opposed protective legislation for women, Social feminists regarded this as proof of their judgment.

The National Woman's party made mistakes. The lack of an official magazine from 1921 to 1923 was damaging because it was difficult to determine the NWP's official position during this critical period. The

[86]Lemons, *Woman Citizen*, 167–69.

pageants and ceremonies staged by the NWP, with tricolor banners and uniformed NWP members, tended to strengthen the myth that the NWP was an elite organization which was more interested in publicity stunts than in serious political activity. It can even be argued that since the Equal Rights Amendment did not stand a chance of passing in 1923, the NWP should have delayed its introduction so that it could cooperate with Social feminists. However, historical evidence does not tend to support this last contention. Social feminists, while supporting the unsuccessful Child Labor Amendment, believed the Equal Rights Amendment to be an infringement upon states' rights. Only individual state laws were acceptable to Social feminists. They were convinced that women, as future mothers, would always need more protective laws than men and that the courts would misinterpret any law not explicit in detail. This opinion did not change when the NWP state campaigns were shown to be largely unsuccessful. Even after World War II, when thousands of women were put out of work because of protective laws passed over twenty years before, Mary Anderson still supported protective legislation for women.[87]

The National Woman's party was faced with a series of decisions in the early 1920s. First, the need for equality had to be balanced with the need for cooperation with Social feminists. When the safeguard provision in the Wisconsin Equal Rights Bill was interpreted to keep women out of work, and when Social feminists rejected the Wisconsin bill as a solution, the NWP chose equality over the Social feminist position. When this decision had been made, the method of achieving equality remained. Despite Alva Belmont's desire to form a third political party, to attempt to do so was beyond the financial and physical means of women.[88] On the other hand, women could not be economically powerful until they were politically equal. Thus, in the NWP's opinion, the Equal Rights Amendment was the only possible solution; the party hoped for quick passage, but lack of success led to the decline of the NWP as an organization.

[87] *New York Times*, 14 October 1951, sec. 4, p. 8. Jean T. McKelvey covered the decisions of arbitrators for the National Labor Relations Board. She observed that in the period following World War II, most published decisions "would not uphold a woman's right to a job if the consequence would entail a violation of state protective legislation by the employer." Jean T. McKelvey, "Sex and the Single Arbitrator," *Industrial and Labor Relations Review* 24 (April 1971): 338.

[88] Ernestine Evans, "Women in the Washington Scene," *Century Magazine* 106 (August 1923): 508; Fry, *Conversations with Alice Paul*, 451–54.

Feminist Against Feminist: The First Phase of the Equal Rights Amendment Debate, 1923–1963

Judith Sealander

There have been few struggles for a constitutional amendment more dramatic than the fight for the Equal Rights Amendment. One of the most significant developments of a campaign that has spanned most of the twentieth century is the fact that the battle pitted not only feminists against antifeminists but also feminists against feminists. The Equal Rights Amendment became, as the Woman Suffrage Amendment had been until 1920, a focus for an intensely bitter dispute between two distinct groups of feminists, if feminist is a term used generically, rather than politically, to identify those people and organizations that advocate equal opportunity for women. The Equal Rights Amendment prompted a bitter forty-year dispute between people who correctly saw themselves as women's advocates, people agreed on an ultimate goal; a society which provided equal opportunity, equal treatment, and equal pay to women. These forty years, 1923–1963, form an identifiable first phase of the Equal Rights Amendment debate. This aspect of the debate, a prolonged, internal battle pitting the proposed amendment against protective labor legislation, illustrates the many problems feminists faced in the years between World War I and the Vietnam War.

Monomaniacal personalities and petty jealousies sometimes gave the ERA disputes an awkward, darkly comic tone. The underlying disagreements between feminists, however, began in serious differences of philosophy about how best to give American women the most advantageous environment in which to work and live. During decades of low pay, substandard working conditions, and little unionization among women, many women's advocates asked, "Would an ERA provide equal rights for only a

JUDITH SEALANDER *teaches at Wright State University and specializes in American social and labor history.*

The South Atlantic Quarterly, 81:2, Spring, 1982.

professional elite?" During years when in many states birth-control devices and information were illegal, some asked, "Would an ERA properly protect women's marriage and child-support rights?" Unlike the earlier constitutional struggle in which women argued over tactics but not over the final objective of a legal guarantee of woman suffrage, the early decades of the ERA debate stimulated violent disagreement about not only means, but ends as well. Until the 1960's many moderate feminists who wished for eventual equality between men and women, surveyed educational, occupational, and union barriers and concluded that American women needed additional temporary, protective legislation. More militant femininsts demanded immediate abolition of all legal distinctions in male and female citizens' rights and duties. Their demands for an Equal Rights Amendment, however, did not mean that they alone were interested in the advancement of women or angry about social inequity. The first phase of the debate, ERA vs. protective labor legislation, most significantly, was one which continued already established rivalries between people who disagreed about the value of cautious, gradual change, and the necessity of immediate, dramatic action.

The divisions had roots in the nineteenth-century suffrage campaign. At least the two major suffrage groups, the National-American Woman Suffrage Association, led by Carrie Chapman Catt, and the Congressional Union, headed by Alice Paul, agreed on a common goal: the passage of a constitutional amendment granting all adult women citizens the right to vote. Still under the leadership of Catt and Paul, each group's successor organization agreed that the battle for equal status for American women had just begun. The League of Women Voters sought to improve opportunities for women and tried to eliminate discriminatory laws and practices that hindered women's attempts to find fulfilling lives and work. It counted as allies such groups as the National Council of Women, the American Association of University Women, the General Federation of Women's Clubs, the National Consumer's League, the National Association of Business and Professional Women's Clubs, the YWCA, the Women's Christian Temperance Union, and the National Women's Trade Union League. These groups lobbied for the creation of a federal Women's Bureau in the Department of Labor. The Bureau, once created, worked closely with all of these prominent national women's groups, which in a sense remained for the next forty years its sponsors. The former Congressional Union, renamed the Woman's party, but still led by Paul, also wished to improve the position of women in American society. Their disagreements about techniques to accomplish these broadly shared goals divided these two groups of feminists into moderate and militant camps.

The bureau philosophy, which represented the official views of most government bodies until the early 1960's, was a moderate one. Women, especially working women, suffered an unfair burden of legal and social discrimination. However, laws, even a constitutional amendment, would not automatically erase social custom. Women, who left the labor force or worked erratically after marriage, were centered by their families, not jobs, and had at all stages of their lives commitments to care for family members. Women with additional family duties, even single women with responsibilities to aging parents or siblings, risked exhaustion working night shifts or long hours. A mandate of legal equality would not make the streets safer, guarantee fairness in event of divorce or abandonment, or protect poorly paid, unorganized women in the factories. The Woman's party, far more optimistic about the impact of legal change, demanded a militant approach: the immediate and absolute end to all legal distinctions based on sex through constitutional amendment.

These different judgments evaluating the utility of legal change are important. Interestingly both sides pointed to the plight of the woman worker to justify either their caution or their optimism. Women in the labor force remained single, poor, and a stable minority of one-in-four American workers until World War II. Educated, middle-class, married women discussed their problems and debated legal solutions but did not join them in significant numbers until the late 1940's. Educated middle-class women advocated or opposed the Equal Rights Amendment as either a boon or a harm to an economic class of women to which they did not belong. In each case the female elite which debated the value of the ERA argued that either victory or defeat would benefit all women, but especially working women.

Clearly self-interest played some role in the Equal Rights Amendment debate. The Women's Bureau, for decades, in effect defined its function and justified its bureaucratic existence by arguing that women needed benevolent federal supervision and protection. The Woman's party hierarchy included many professional women, eager to change interpretations of the status of women. Two of the most important leaders of the Party, Alice Paul and Doris Stevens, for instance, had gained reputations for brilliant legal argument. Most likely their self-image as constitutional pathbreakers included a certain desire for personal fame. However, what is striking about the Equal Rights Amendment controversy is not the unsurprising hints of self-aggrandizement. The debate provides an illustration of different philosophies about engineering social change among groups in both the public and private sector that broadly agreed that social change which granted women greater opportunity was necessary.

In 1922, with the Nineteenth Amendment finally a reality, the Woman's party announced that its next effort would be a campaign for another federal constitutional amendment, the "Lucretia Mott" amendment, which would guarantee absolute legal equality to American women, abolishing all laws which required different treatment of men and women. Introduced by two Kansas congressmen, it provided that "Men and women shall have equal rights throughout the United States and every place subject to its jurisdiction."[1] Moderate feminists almost immediately challenged it. The Women's Bureau of the United States Department of Labor assumed an unofficial leadership role, advising other moderates and organizing support for protective legislation. The Bureau under Director Mary Anderson and her immediate successor Frieda Miller steadfastly emphasized the theme of the woman worker as underdog. The idea that the federal government had a duty to concern itself with dangerous and unhealthy industrial conditions and the effect such conditions had on the lives of workers, especially those not capable of self-protection, was part of the progressive ethos. So was the belief that efficient and scientifically planned government fact-finding could help solve the problems of the poor. The establishment of a national women's bureau in the Labor Department was a small victory for progressives principally concerned about the plight of impoverished women workers. The efforts to establish a women's bureau buttressed a parallel campaign for a federal children's bureau. In both cases, these bureaus were to protect those who could not protect themselves. Although a few supporters of the idea of a women's bureau challenged the mistily romantic tones of those who wished to erect an agency to act as a wise and benevolent mother, most testimony in favor of a women's bureau emphasized the separate and special needs of a powerless group of laborers.

A majority of the earnest handful of progressive female professionals who came to Washington to staff the Women's Bureau remained loyal both to their agency and their agency's founding purpose, despite the bureaucratic odds which challenged such stability. With the striking exception of the agency director, Mary Anderson, a self-educated Swedish immigrant, most bureau investigators came from white, middle-class families. Their contact with poverty and poor working conditions for women was professional. In socioeconomic, if not ideological, terms they were similar to their opponents in the Woman's party who so strongly demanded the ERA. The first phase of the amendment struggle provides a fascinating study of two contrasting feminist solutions to problems which members of each group correctly conceded affected other women more than themselves. Nineteen sixty-three is a watershed both for the debate and for federal policy towards women workers. After that date both the federal government and moderate women's groups began publicly to reverse their long-standing opposition to the ERA. Before 1963, however, most moderates argued some temporary protective legislation had to remain until women gained more economic power. The wall of opposition to the ERA was not entirely solid. The Na-

1. The wording recommended to the Senate on May 23, 1943, which was finally passed in 1972 read differently: "Equality of rights under the law shall not be denied or abridged by the United States or by any State on account of sex."

tional Federation of Business and Professional Women endorsed it in 1937, and approval of the proposed amendment appeared in both the Democratic and Republican party platforms during the war-year national conventions of 1940 and 1944. During World War II the General Federation of Women's Clubs joined the NFBPW in endorsing the amendment. However these two major women's organizations wavered in their support of the ERA before the early 1960's. Support or withdrawal of support became matters for internal debate within both organizations. As late as 1963, the Business and Professional Women considered a motion to repeal their support for the ERA. Addressing a meeting of the Delaware Federation, Congresswoman Catherine May of Washington, a member of the NFBPW, urged yet another review. Noting that the Kennedy Commission on the Status of Women had repudiated the ERA, May declared, "I think it important that the BPW Federation give study and discussion to the alternative proposals (made by the president's commission) and then reach a decision on whether to maintain their support of the Equal Rights Amendment or modify their views."[2]

In general, however, feminists chose one of two ideological positions on the woman labor question. On the one side the Labor Department and its adherents in volunteer organizations argued that women should not be legally equal to men until they were socially equal. As long as society acquiesced in low pay scales for women and demanded that working women shoulder the burdens of housework and child care, society should also provide protective labor legislation. Eventually, adherents argued, the benefits of night work and hours restrictions, requirements about safety and weight-lifting limits, could also be extended to male workers. Nobody should have to work excessively long hours under unsafe conditions. However, given the special problems facing working women, laws protecting them should be advocated as a necessary half-loaf measure if legislatures were unwilling to regulate so thoroughly the workplace for both sexes. Opposing these arguments, members of the Woman's party declared that without full and total legal equality, guaranteed by constitutional amendment, social equality would forever remain elusive.

As early as 1922, Mary Anderson confided to Mary Dewson, then an officer of the National Consumer's League, that she was "having a time with the Woman's Party."[3] A conference on Women in Industry, in 1926 sponsored by the bureau, erupted chaotically when Woman's party delegates rose to their feet, shouting and marching down the aisles in support of an

2. Quoted in the Yakima, Washington, *Republic*, October 17, 1963, in "Press Clippings File," The Records of the President's Commission on the Status of Women, the John F. Kennedy Presidential Library, Boston, Mass. (hereafter PCSW, KL).

3. Anderson to Mary Dewson, December 20, 1922, "Correspondence—Organizations File," Bx 843, Records of the Women's Bureau, R.G. 86, The National Archives, Washington, D.C. (hereafter WB,NA).

Equal Rights Amendment and in opposition to protective legislation. Answering choruses of shouts and boos met the party members' demonstrations. Women jumped on chairs, screamed for recognition, pushed, shoved, and overturned furniture. When Mary Anderson finally gavelled the conference back to some semblance of order, she begged the delegates to debate protective labor laws in a "seemly manner" at a special night session. At the direction of this session, the conference urged the Bureau to make a comprehensive investigation of the effects of all special laws regulating the employment of women.

"The Effects of Labor Legislation," Women's Bureau *Bulletin #65*, published in 1928 and the result of the 1926 conference mandate, was one of the lengthiest and most extensively researched of all bureau bulletins. It was a policy statement used by moderate feminists for the next thirty years and concluded that labor laws did not constitute a significant handicap to women's economic advance and that any Equal Rights Amendment would most surely have disastrous consequences for working and nonworking women alike. Discrimination against women did not occcur because of the lack of a constitutional amendment but because of women's position in society. Protected by laws, women could have a chance to obtain slowly the economic rights and benefits already enjoyed by males. The Woman's party argued that the Bureau could not conduct an impartial investigation, and Alice Paul condemned the study as one done by women "sitting there with their nice big governmental salaries and all BREATHING incompetence." Mary Anderson, for her part, called Paul and her allies, "hysterical feminists."[4]

The domestic controversy over the need for an Equal Rights Amendment included a search for international allies. In 1925, Mary Anderson lobbied Lady Astor in England:

> May I say at the outset that those of us who oppose the Woman's Party Equal Rights Amendment are not against equal rights as a principle or equal rights in practice . . . but we disagree with the methods of the Woman's Party.[5]

Those methods included efforts to secure international approval of absolute equality for women. Doris Stevens, like Paul a former militant suffragette, directed the party's international campaign.

4. Mary Anderson, *Woman at Work: The Autobiography of Mary Anderson as Told to Mary Winslow* (Minneapolis; 1951) p. 168; Mary Anderson "Should There Be Labor Laws for Women—Yes" *Good Housekeeping*, 21, (September, 1935); The Alice Paul Oral History, typescript, pp. 476, 479, Regional Oral History Office, Bancroft Library, University of California, Berkeley, 1976, (interviewer, Amelia Fry; hereafter Alice Paul Oral History).

5. Mary Anderson to the Viscountess Astor, Mary Anderson Papers, March 27, 1925, Folder 17, Arthur and Elizabeth Schlesinger Library on the History of Women in America, Radcliffe College, Cambridge, Mass. (hereafter, SL).

In 1928, the Sixth Conference of Pan-American Republics met at Havana, Cuba, and Stevens, in charge of a delegation of women from some Latin American republics as well as the United States, arrived to lobby for the negotiation of a statement that supported legal equality of the sexes. She and her supporters marched through the streets, held rallies, and aggressively cornered individual delegates in hotel lobbies, restaurants, and meeting rooms. Although the conference refused to ratify a resolution supporting equal rights for women, Stevens won a partial victory: the conference voted to establish an inter-American commission of women to study the problems of women in the Western Hemisphere. Secretary of State Frank Kellogg sent Doris Stevens as unofficial United States member to the commission.[6]

The Seventh Pan-American conference, held in Montevideo in 1933, passed a resolution urging equal rights for all women in the Americas. The resolution, Stevens hoped, marked the beginnings of support for what the Woman's party hoped would be a world equal-rights treaty to be ratified by the League of Nations. However Stevens had no official role at the Montevideo conference. President Franklin Roosevelt had appointed social worker and protective legislation advocate Sophonisba Breckenridge rather than Stevens as the first official United States delegate to the conference, and Mary Anderson, an old friend, had written her:

> I was so happy when you were appointed.... And I know that you must have had a hectic time because as you know I know the ladies that you met down there ... Doris Stevens is back, and she is going to be here in Washington, and up on the Hill to lobby. We will hear much of them, and may have to counter-act some of their work.[7]

Anderson took plans for a counterattack seriously. She approached influential women in the Democratic party in an attempt to minimize the influence of the Woman's party at the next Pan-American conference to be held in Lima, in December, 1938. Mrs. Buston Musser, National Democratic Committeewoman from Utah, wrote Mary Dewson, head of the Women's Division of the Democratic party, that she worried about the party's "tremendous and powerful propaganda in Latin America." She urged that Dewson, a confidante of both Eleanor and Franklin Roosevelt,

6. Women's Bureau's records of the work of the Inter-American Commission of Women are curiously silent on certain historical points. Before 1950, two bureau employees, Mary Winslow and Mary Cannon, served as United States delegates to the commission. Bureau memos and releases praised their efforts on the commission. For the seminal and dominating role of Doris Stevens and the Woman's party in the formation and participation of the U.S. in the commission's affairs until the late thirties, see especially v. 1–39, "Inter-American Commission of Women," Report to the Seventh International Conference of American States, Doris Stevens Papers, SL.

7. Anderson to Breckinridge, January 26, 1934, "Correspondence—International File," WB, NA, Bx 829.

warn the president about Doris Stevens.[8] In 1939, under pressure from an obviously hostile administration, Doris Stevens resigned her position as head of the Inter-American Commission of Women. Secretary of State Cordell Hull, in an act beautifully symbolic of the rivalry, then appointed former Women's-Bureau member, Mary Winslow, to fill Stevens' seat.

The Inter-American Commission of Women was not the only international forum for the dispute between American organizations which differed on the Equal Rights Amendment. In 1935, the General Assembly of the League of Nations debated the question of the general status of women. In 1933, the International Conference of American States, held in Montevideo, had debated an equal-rights-for-women resolution. The resolution failed, despite the strenuous lobbying efforts of Doris Stevens. However, several of the Latin American member countries which had voted in its favor requested that the League consider the topic of equal rights for women.

The League dealt with this request by calling upon the International Labor Organization, one of its branches, to investigate the effects of an equal rights treaty upon labor legislation throughout the world. In turn, the Governing Board of the ILO asked members of its Advisory Committee on Women Workers to coordinate studies of the economic status of women. Mary Anderson agreed to organize a committee to prepare the United States report. In the process she and other members of the Women's Bureau became involved in an effort she would later describe as "completely unsuccessful."[9]

As Anderson met with the women economists, historians, business, government, and labor leaders she had recruited, the group gradually decided not to confine itself to a specific statement on the economic status of American women. Instead, they decided to draft a statement of objectives about which the women of the United States and Europe could cooperate with the women of India, Asia, Africa, and Latin America. All could benefit from such an international declaration of women's rights. The American originators of the charter idea, all of whom supported protective labor legisla-

8. Mrs. Buston Musser to Mary Dewson, Mary Dewson Papers, March 3, 1938, Bx 9, Franklin Roosevelt Presidential Library, Hyde Park, New York (hereafter, FDR Lib.); see also Dewson Papers, Bx 9, FDR Lib. for additional letters between Democratic National Committee women on the subject. The NLWV support is evident in a memo sent to Mary Winslow from Marguerite Wells, President of the NLWV: "Don't let people in Washington get discouraged. We had Doris on the run once. We can get her there again. I don't see why the whole thing can't be handled by clever administrative rulings and appointments. You must get the P.A.U. (Pan-American Union) to get over being intimidated by Doris. It's a bad habit people have. She is vulnerable in certain spots." Marguerite Wells, to Mary Winslow, February 13, 1939, Records of the National League of Women Voters (NLWV), Bx 418, Mss. Div., The Library of Congress, Washington, D.C. (hereafter LC).

9. Memo: "The Women's Charter," June 10, 1938, WB, NA, Bx 123; Anderson, *Woman at Work*, p. 210.

tion in the United States, saw a way not only to get an international statement attacking exploitation of women, but also to receive world support for their continuing battle with the Woman's party over the Equal Rights Amendment.[10]

After several months of meetings, the Women's Charter Committee presented a proposed draft of their document:

> Women shall have full political and civil rights; full opportunity for education, full opportunity for work according to their individual abilities, with safeguards against physically harmful conditions of employment and economic exploitation. They shall receive compensation, without discrimination because of sex. They shall be assured security of livelihood necessary for the establishment of these standards which shall be guaranteed by government; which shall insure also the right of united action towards the attainment of these aims. Where special exploitation of women workers exists, such as low wages which provide less than the living standards attainable, unhealthful working conditions or long hours of work which result in physical exhaustion and denial of the right to leisure, such conditions shall be corrected through social and labor legislation which the world's experience shows to be necessary.[11]

Mary Anderson did not wish the charter to be labeled as a proposal of the Federal government. However, she and Mary Pidgeon, of the Women's Bureau Research Division, sat on the charter planning committee. Moreover, the Women's Bureau had already offered to act as the United States coordinating center to collect material and to edit a comprehensive report for the ILO on the economic status of women in the United States.

Anderson, Mary Pidgeon, and Mary Robinson traveled widely giving speeches to promote the charter. It was an attempt, they would argue, to correct wide-spread misunderstandings about the causes for women's increased participation in affairs outside the home, including paid employment. It was an attempt to raise standards for both sexes that could provide a statement around which women could rally to oppose the rise of reactionary regimes that sought to deprive them of political and social rights; the world's women had an obligation to unite. They would otherwise become confused and swayed by the doctrines of fascism, like the women of Germany who had "betrayed themselves and played into the hands of Hitler." For a year, the idea of a women's center sparked widespread interest. But Charter Committee minutes reveal that only Women's Bureau representatives expressed real dedication to the charter idea. The movement lost

10. For a complete listing of members see "Minutes of Conference Group to Consider the Women's Charter: November 12, 1936," WB, NA.

11. Printed pamphlet, 1936, "The Women's Charter, What and Why" "Women's Charter—International conferences File," WB, NA.

momentum in a flurry of resolutions pledging careful study.[12]

The Woman's party vehemently denounced the charter as yet another bureau ploy to support its vested interest in protective labor legislation. Party members denounced the charter draft as the "Secret Mary Anderson Charter." Woman's party members in Washington visited their congressmen, charging that the Women's Bureau wished to put the stamp of United States governmental approval on a program of ill-thought out international advice. Mary Anderson worriedly tried to prod friendly organizations into action. "The sooner the better," she wrote Lucy Mason of the National Consumer's League. "I am so afraid that [the Woman's party] will come out with some more adverse publicity before we get into the field."[13]

Instead, the Charter Committee engaged in an embarrassing public wrangle. A feature article in the January 7, 1937, New York *World Telegram* titled, "Sponsor Spurns Charter for Women," heralded historian Mary Beard's disaffection with the project. In a series of letters to Mary Anderson, Mary Beard, a nominal member of the Woman's Party, had criticized the wording of the charter. When Mrs. Beard's name appeared on a newspaper list of charter sponsors, she publicly objected. Torn between the arguments for protection and the arguments for absolute equality Beard issued a statement saying she belonged to "neither camp."[14]

In the aftermath of this committee furor, Secretary of Labor Frances Perkins persuaded a reluctant Grace Abbott to present the Women's Charter at the international meetings of the ILO in 1937. The Chief of the Children's Bureau, already a delegate to the 1937 meetings, concluded that the evident lack of unity among members of the U.S. Committee weakened the usefulness of any statement the charter might make. She introduced a resolution paraphrasing the charter, but only as a member of the United States delegation, not as the spokeswoman of a united group of the world's women. The assembled delegates to the ILO conference passed the resolution, which stated that women should have full opportunity to work and should receive pay without discrimination because of sex, that women as well as men should be guaranteed freedom of association by governments and should be protected by social and labor legislation "which the world's experience has shown to be effective in abolishing special exploitation of women workers."[15] The disunity even among members of the committee

12. Mary Anderson, "The Significance of the Women's Charter," speech before the American Jewish Congress, New York City, March 30, 1937, "Speech File, unnumbered," WB, NA.

13. See Jane N. Smith to Alice Paul, March 7, 1937, Jane Norman Smith Papers, Folder 227, SL; Report of the Temporary Committee of Organization—Prepared for Submission at Meeting in Washington, D.C., January 30, 1937," Bx 81, WB, NA; Anderson to Lucy Mason, Records of the National Consumer's League, Bx C-16, December 10, 1936, Mss. Div., LC.

14. Beard to Anderson, November 8, 1936, "Women's Charter—International Conferences File," WB, NA; the *New York World Telegram*, January 7, 1937.

15. Anderson, *Woman at Work*, p. 213.

guaranteed that little international attention would be paid to this statement favoring protective labor legislation.

With de facto defeat of the Woman's Charter, open international wrangling between American opponents and supporters of the Equal Rights Amendment ceased. No truce existed, nor were both sides equally diverted by the Second World War and the changing status of American women in the 1950's. Mary Anderson, Alice Paul, and their organizations continued their strangely parallel courses. Anderson retired in 1944. When Dwight Eisenhower replaced her chosen successor, Freida Miller, with Republican Committeewoman Alice Leopold, she grumbled privately to friends about the Bureau's "decline." In truth Leopold did spend inordinate amounts of time fund-raising for the Republican party. She did however, reaffirm, though never in the same sort of passionate way, the Department of Labor's opposition to the Equal Rights Amendment.[16]

Alice Paul and the Woman's party were, in turn, by anyone's definition, in decline. By the mid-1940's a personal feud between Paul and Doris Stevens spawned by Stevens' jealousy of Paul exploded into destructive warfare. The fight, which culminated in 1947 in an unsuccessful court challenge of Paul's leadership by Stevens, was a bitter one from which the party never recovered.[17]

The Woman's party continued to exist, but its membership dwindled from a peak estimate of twelve thousand to several hundred diehards. These members as always, campaigned exclusively for the passage of an Equal Rights Amendment. The swan song of the long fight between the Women's Bureau and the Woman's party about the propriety of the Equal Rights Amendment occurred from 1961-1963. President John Kennedy received pressure from female trade unionists, the United States Department of Labor, prominent women leaders and others to consider formally women's status in America. Further, he expressed interest in government "white papers" issued by the bureaus of the Census and Labor Standards discussing the rise of the two-income middle-class family and projecting further economic and social change for American women. Esther Peterson, Kennedy's appointee as the new director of the Women's Bureau and a woman with White House entree, differed from her predecessor Alice Leopold and strongly urged the creation of a commission. Thus motivated, John Kennedy established in December, 1961, his President's Commission

16. Anderson to Mary Van Kleeck, April 12, 1959, Mary Van Kleeck Papers, Bx 9, Sophia Smith Collection, Smith College, Northampton, Mass. (hereafter SS); Alice Leopold, "Speech File" (typescripts), Bxs 1524-1526, WB, NA; Alice Leopold, "Statement: Determination of the Equal Rights Amendment," Secretary of Labor Mitchell Files, Bx 181, Records of the Secretaries of Labor, RG 174, NA.

17. For the Paul faction's side of the dispute see the 1945-1952 correspondence files of council member, Jane Norman Smith: Jane Norman Smith Papers, folders, 125, 126, 179, 180, SL; The Doris Stevens Papers, esp. Bx 23, SL, document the countercharges.

on the Status of Women. The twenty-six members of the commission received orders to submit a written report to the president by 1963 evaluating the economic, political, and social status of American women. Executive Order 10980 establishing the commission specifically required it to give detailed consideration of "differences in legal treatment between men and women."[18] The Woman's party requested and received permission to send representatives to commission hearings with formal statements of support for the Equal Rights Amendment. One of the Woman's party delegates to the commission was a woman named, ironically, Mary Anderson.[19] Chaired by Eleanor Roosevelt until her death, the commission's members represented organizations such as the Department of Labor, the AFL-CIO, the YWCA, the National Manpower Council, the National Federation of Business and Professional Women, and the National Council of Churches. Not too surprisingly, given the fact that during the decades of struggle with the Woman's party all of these organizations had issued statements challenging the need for an Equal Rights Amendment, the president's commission declared that such a constitutional change would not then be advantageous to women.

The commission's decision to oppose the ERA reflected the continuation of the old pro-protective legislation alliance coordinated by the Women's Bureau. However, the hostility that marked the long Equal Rights Amendment dispute had abated. Transcripts of commission meetings reveal efforts at compromise and accommodation of other points of view. While the president's commission ultimately argued that the Fifth and Fourteenth Amendments already assured legal equality for women, it agreed that federal courts might at some future point interpret these amendments in a way disadvantageous to women. The commission denied a need in 1963 for an Equal Rights Amendment. It did not state that such an amendment would never be necessary.[20]

Vice President Lyndon Johnson in 1962 delivered an address to the president's commission which emphasized these "special and different functions of the sexes." In fact he began, "It is a great pleasure for me to come before this group this morning and I dare say [it is] the only group

18. See "Materials: Minutes of Meetings, October 24, 1960—January 19, 1962," PCSW, KL; Cynthia Harrison, "A New Frontier For Women: The Public Policy of the Kennedy Administration," *The Journal of American History*, (December, 1980) pp. 630-46.

19. "Argument in Favor of the Equal Rights Amendment" made at the Request of the Woman's Party, to the President's Commission on the Status of Women, Miriam Holden, March 23, 1963, Bx 4, PCSW, KL; Esther Peterson to Mary F. Anderson, "Recommendations Concerning the Proposed Equal Rights Amendment," June 24, 1963, Bx 1, PCSW, KL.

20. See "The Purposes of the President's Commission on the Status of Women," March 15, 1963, Esther Peterson, (typescript) pp. 4-5, The Esther Peterson Papers, (unprocessd acquisition: author given access before cataloguing), SL; Interim Report of the Committee of Civil and Political Rights of the President's Commission on the Status of Women, April 11, 1963, PCSW, KL.

which can frankly and candidly and without any fear of criticism admit that the only thing on its mind is girls."[21] Despite continuing infelicities of phrase which incurred the wrath of some women, Lyndon Johnson presided over a series of watershed changes in federal perception of women's status. The Johnson years saw a series of antidiscrimination laws added to the books: the Equal Pay Act, Title VII of the Civil Rights Act, Title IX of the Education Acts Amendment, and Executive Order 11246 mandating the beginning of federal affirmative action programs. The sixties also witnessed the rebirth of an identifiable woman's movement, the establishment of new national women's organizations such as The National Organization for Women and the Women's Equity Action League which strongly supported the Equal Rights Amendment. Both moderate women's organizations and federal labor officials began to reverse their long-standing opposition to the measure. In 1970, the Women's Bureau itself finally endorsed the Equal Rights Amendment. Economics and the women's movement of the sixties proved more an impetus to this change in position than did the preachings of the Woman's party, by this time a bitterly divided and ineffective organization. Of equal importance was the fact that the cause of protective labor legislation became less compelling. Concessions granted labor during the New Deal and after meant that protective legislation for men became feasible. The forty-hour week became standard. Unions agitated for and won safety regulations for all workers. "Equal Rights," moderates began to concede, no longer had to mean dismantling basic protection for women workers.

Forty-nine years after its first introduction the Equal Rights Amendment finally received congressional endorsement in 1972. This victory owed little to the long years of internal feminist debate. Woman's place in society underwent rapid change in the sixties and early seventies. She could be married, middle class, and a member of the work force. The years of inflation after 1945 and increased consumer purchasing made a white, middle-class family combining the incomes of a male breadwinner and a female cake-winner socially acceptable. The vast majority of working women still labored long hours for low wages and won little prestige. Nonetheless, an important change of perception had occurred. The prosperity of the post-war period and the energy of the women's movement had given many moderate feminists a sense of great expectations. It was a similar sense of buoyantly optimistic great expectations in the face of far more ambiguous social realities that had led the militant Woman's party decades earlier to demand the Equal Rights Amendment. The ERA required faith that women would benefit and not suffer from complete

21. "Remarks of Vice President Lyndon Johnson," September 24, 1962, (typed transcript), Bx 4, PCSW, KL.

legal equality. The optimism of the social-protest movements of the sixties, with their visions of an egalitarian America implemented by a changed legal structure, proved infectious.

Society seemed to be changing rapidly; divorce rates skyrocketed, and so did remarriage rates. Formal employment and occupational barriers fell.[22] Fewer feminists publicly argued that they and their organizations had a major commitment to protect the downtrodden working woman. Following World War II and the retirement of Mary Anderson and many of her long-time coworkers, even the politics of the Women's bureau changed. Although statistically the average women worker was still a clerk, a secretary, or a member of a factory assembly line, the bureau publications increasingly addressed the woman professional. The public opponents of the Equal Rights Amendment after the early 1960's were more often those categorically against legal equality rather than people who argued, as did many feminists for decades, that a constitutional amendment was an improper and untimely method of seeking legal equality.

For forty years the Women's Bureau, its organizational allies, and the Woman's party all desired equal opportunities and equal rights for American women. But before the sixties the Woman's party almost alone championed the Equal Rights Amendment. Rather than a banner behind which to unite, the proposal, until the 1960's, was a feminist albatross.

Although the dispute became a heated one where personal hatreds flourished, the protective legislation vs. ERA debate was not rooted in problems caused by incompatible personalities. Until World War II a demographic profile of the typical woman worker remained stable. She was young, single, and poor. By the late 1950's it had changed. She was married, middle aged, and, when her income was combined with her husband's, middle class. The "average" woman no longer seemed in such need of protection, despite the fact that she remained overwhelmingly responsible for home and family care. Spurred by watershed changes in perception of who the woman worker was, long-time feminist advocates of protective legislation began to rethink their position. But economic and demographic change, not personality change, sped the process.

For years those people and groups organized and helped by the Woman's Bureau and rooted in the progressive traditions of "efficiency and uplift" lobbied for legal and special protection for the female worker. Woman's party members demanded no special quarter and no legal restrictions. Questions about self-interest became difficult to answer. Did the Women's Bureau have a vested interest in its perceived constituency of working

22. For discussion of the status of women during this period see: James Kenneally, *Women and American Trade Unions* (Quebec; 1978); Valerie Oppenheimer, *The Female Labor Force in the United States* (Westport, Conn., 1976); Milton Cantor and Bruce Laurie, *Class, Sex, and the Woman Worker*, (Westport Conn., 1977); William Chafe, *The American Woman: Her Changing Social, Economic, and Political Role, 1920-1970*, (New York; 1972).

women? Did Bureau members see advocacy of protective labor legislation as a way to get funding from a paternalistic Congress? What ulterior motivations might various moderate women's groups have had? Were the professionals and upper-class women in the Woman's party supporting the ERA because they wished to protect careers or inheritances? So many participants cannot have been completely selfless, to be sure. However, evidence of manipulation of the dispute for personal gain is difficult to uncover in the archives which house personal and organizational papers. Interviews with some participants reveal recollections of the battle as one of principle.[23] The militant feminists of the Woman's party believed all women would benefit from the Equal Rights Amendment. The moderates from many organizations, led by the bureaucrats in the U.S Women's Bureau, disagreed. An examination of the controversies generated by these early decades of the ERA campaign illustrates the complexity of the relations between American groups concerned with improving women's status. Federal bureaucratic disapproval certainly weakened the Equal Rights Amendment's chances of victory in Congress during these years. The disputes from 1923 to 1963 did not consitiute the sole reason for repeated legislative defeats of the Equal Rights Amendment. They did, however, form an element in the long congressional delay between first introduction and final passage of the ERA. Since they were disputes deeply rooted in major ideological differences about proper methods of engineering change, they were, in a sense, almost inevitable.

23. See: The Alice Paul Oral History, also interviews conducted by author in Washington, D.C., with Clara Beyer (January 19, 1976), Ethel Erickson (January 6, 1976), Mary Cannon (January 15, 1976).

ORGANIZED WOMEN IN MISSISSIPPI: THE CLASH OVER LEGAL DISABILITIES IN THE 1920'S

Martha H. Swain
Texas Woman's University

"No state has been more kindly disposed toward the women . . . in the passage of legislation beneficial to them than has Mississippi. It tops the list."[1] So wrote Senator Pat Harrison of Mississippi to Anita Pollitizer, a legislative field worker for the National Woman's Party in February 1922. There were notable exceptions to the senator's claim, particularly rejections by the state legislature of the Nineteenth Amendment in January of 1920 and of a woman suffrage amendment to the state constitution by the male voters of the state in November of that same year.[2] Nonetheless, the leaders of the National Woman's Party knew there was substance to Harrison's boast. In 1839 Mississippi had become the first state to secure property rights to "man's dearest idol"; in 1871 the legislature had defined wages as a part of a wife's separate estate; in 1880 it had abrogated women's common-law disabilities; and the Constitution of 1890 "fully emancipated women from all disability on account of coverture."[3] In 1884 the Mississippi Industrial Institute and College became the first state-supported college for women in the nation. Mississippi, Suzanne Lebsock has written, was "always ahead of the pack," at least among the southern states.[4]

Thus history warranted the Woman's Party optimism in 1921 that Mississippi would remove the last of its legal disabilities against women. Until a federal equal rights amendment could be drafted and introduced in Congress, Alice Paul, the party's founder and leader, determined that a "blanket bill" eliminating all remaining legal disabilities should be introduced legislature by legislature.[5] The proposed measure provided that "women shall have the same rights, privileges, and immunities under the law as men" in a broad field of rights including suffrage, office holding, jury service, choice of domicile and name, property rights, ownership and control of labor and

1. Harrison to Pollitizer, 18 February 1922, in National Woman's Party Papers, Reel #12. A microfilm of the NWP Papers in available in the library of Texas Woman's University. The original papers are in the Library of Congress.

2. See A. Elizabeth Taylor, "The Woman Suffrage Movement in Mississippi, 1890-1920," *Journal of Mississippi History*, 30 (February 1968), 29-33.

3. Lucie R. Bridgforth, "The Legal Status of Women in Mississippi, 1817-1920," paper delivered before the Mississippi Historical Society, 1980. Copy in possession of the author.

4. Suzanne D. Lebsock, "Radial Reconstruction and the Property Rights of Southern Women," *Journal of Southern History*, 43 (May 1977), 214.

5. Mimeographed letter to general membership, dated 21 March 1921, NWP Papers, Reel #7.

services, freedom of contract, custody and control of children equal to that of the father, equal grounds for divorce, and equal immunities or penalties for sex offenses.[6]

The Woman's Party joined with the League of Women Voters and other women's groups in support of the equal rights bill which was signed into law in Wisconsin in July 1921. This proved to be the only time that the Woman's Party and the League worked together on an extensive removal of legal disabilities. The Woman's Party soon dropped its acceptance of the clause exempting protective legislation for women in industry, and the League refused to endorse any blanket bill which retained the clause. As it turned out, the Wisconsin measure was the only blanket bill ever to pass in any state.[7] That such would be the fate of its proposed equal rights bill was something the Woman's Party was ideologically unprepared even to consider.

Mississippi did not have an effective branch of the Woman's party; the slight influence of the party during the suffrage campaign was due to its militancy in 1917.[8] After two women had resigned as chairman, Maud Younger, the legislative chairman of the Party, finally persuaded Mrs. Ellen P. Crump of Nitta Yuma to take the chairmanship. Mrs. Crump was the wife of a prominent doctor who was somewhat of a Warrick within the political faction in the state controlled by James K. Vardaman and Theodore G. Bilbo, two of the few men in the political power structure who had supported woman suffrage. In fact, Woman's Party organizers and lobbyists in the state first had met Mrs. Crump through their contacts with male politicians during the 1917-1919 suffrage campaign. Mrs. Crump, who would remain the nominal chairman of the Woman's Party in Mississippi for three decades, was never to be an effective leader. Ella C. Thompson, southern field secretary for the party, had written Alice Paul in 1917 that Mrs. Crump "physically . . . is not equal to accepting the State Chairmanship."[9] She was hard of hearing and plagued with various illnesses for which she sought cures out of the state, usually at the Greenbrier in West Virginia. But, if the party were to have any chairman in Mississippi, there seemed to be no one but Mrs. Crump, who demured, "I do not feel very confident of my abilities."[10]

Alice Paul's expectation that Mrs. Crump would organize Mississippi by

6. A copy of the proposed bill may be found in the Pat Harrison Papers, University of Mississippi Library, Box 5.

7. J. Stanley Lemons, *The Woman Citizen: Social Feminism in the 1920s* (Urbana, 1973), 189-90.

8. Taylor, "Woman Suffrage Movement in Mississippi," 24.

9. Thompson to Paul, 23 May 1917, NWP Papers, Reel #21.

10. Crump to Younger, 3, 12 August 1921, NWP Papers, Reel #9.

congressional and state legislative districts was totally unrealistic since few women in the state had even heard of the Woman's Party, there were no officers other than a nominal chairman, and there were less than ten members in the state in 1921. It was left to Anita Pollitizer and Elsie Hill, former suffrage campaign workers for the Woman's Party in the southern states, to lay the groundwork in Mississippi for the blanket bill to be introduced in January 1922. They soon learned what the national headquarters would have to contend with for the whole decade; Mrs. Crump's primary goal for the Mississippi branch was that it advance the programs and candidates of the Vardaman-Bilbo faction. Hill reported to Paul soon after her arrival in Mississippi in November 1921 that Mrs. Crump consulted with the Vardaman managers before scheduling any meetings. Hill wished that "they didn't have to always hear and think about the 'faction'."[11]

Hill was full of despair about her efforts to interest Mississippi women in the Woman's Party. "It is almost impossible to drag people's attention off the personal and local issues," she complained. She was disappointed that Henrietta Mitchell, the National Democratic Committeewoman for Mississippi, had become a director of the Woman's Foundation, an apolitical organization whose aims seemed "purposeless" to Hill. Mitchell was of the opinion that there were no legal disabilities remaining for women in Mississippi and she had no interest in either the Woman's Party or in the League of Women Voters.[12]

The League was well underway in Mississippi. By April 1921 an executive board was functioning. Mrs. B. F. Saunders, the former president of the General Federation of Women's Clubs, was the state president. Liba Peshakova, a league national organizer, reported to her headquarters in September and October of 1921 of local leagues initiated in Hattiesburg, Jackson, Greenwood, Laurel, Columbus, and Brookhaven in spite of a "prevalent feeling among women as well as men that the League was militant, aggressive, and a political party."[13] At the first annual statewide meeting, held in Hattiesburg in November, fifteen affiliated leagues and thirteen cooperative clubs reported a total membership of over one thousand women.[14] When Woman's Party organizers appeared in Jackson in November, Mrs. Henry Yerger, president of the local league, informed her that membership in the league was not compatible with membership in the Woman's Party, whose methods were "contrary to the traditions of the South." She reminded them that the league was committed to federal leg-

11. Hill to Paul, 14 November 1921, NWP Papers, Reel #1.
12. Ibid.
13. League of Women Voter Papers, Library of Congress, Series II, Box 1.
14. "Woman Suffrage" folder, Vertical Files, Mississippi State University, Special Collections; Memphis *Commercial Appeal*, 13 November 1921.

islation to protect the health of mothers and children, laws to protect women in industry, and child labor prohibition.[15]

When Hill and Pollitizer spoke to a group of thirty women at the Jackson Carnegie Library in late November 1921, many of them declined to comment on the blanket bill and the proposed federal equal rights amendment, news of which seemed to startle the audience. Some pointed out that Mississippi laws already gave women almost every right promised by the bill, while others protested that provision for equal choice of domicile would "break up family life."[16] Anita Pollitizer confided to Miss Paul, "This is the most tightly sot town we've yet struck and you have to speak and speak before anyone makes any motion of joining or approving."[17] Elsie Hill was weary of the apathy she encountered and the lack of commitment of most of the Jackson women to anything but social pleasure. "The leisureliness at times almost drives me crazy," she complained.[18]

A graver problem was the impasse existing between the two Woman's Party organizers and Mrs. Crump over the party's refusal to register women voters who could be expected to back Vardaman, Bilbo, and their protégé Lee M. Russell, the current governor. On the other hand, Mrs. Crump could not understand why the Woman's Party had earlier campaigned against Democratic candidates who opposed suffrage and now would not endorse candidates in Mississippi who had supported suffrage.[19] Since she herself was welcome among her husband's political friends, she could not understand why the Woman's Party was unwilling to form an alliance with male politicians. She wrote Alice Paul, "Individuals can do without the assistance of the members of the other sex but communities cannot unless they want to get off the face of the map entirely."[20] Pollitizer found the fervor of the politically active Mississippi women "depressing and ghastly." "The men they fall at the feet of are *such* terrible specimens," she wrote Paul.[21]

When Mrs. Crump left Jackson at Thanksgiving to return to her plantation, Hill and Pollitizer, apparently relieved to see her go, set about to "scout more freely for some good feminists" who could perceive of the Woman's Party as a "perpetually functioning group."[22] They met with no

15. Jackson *Daily Clarion-Ledger*, 15 November 1921.
16. Memphis *Commercial Appeal*, 25 November 1921.
17. Pollitizer to Paul, 29 November 1921, NWP Papers, Reel #11.
18. Hill to Paul 30 November 1921, NWP Papers, Reel #11.
19. The NWP in 1914 entered the campaign against Democratic candidates in the nine states where women could vote. William L. O'Neill, *Everyone Was Brave: The Rise and Fall of Feminism in America* (Chicago, 1969), 129.
20. Crump to Paul, 28 November 1921, NWP Papers, Reel #11.
21. Pollitizer to Paul, 4 December 1921, NWP Papers, Reel #11.
22. Hill to Paul, 24 November 1921, NWP Papers, Reel #11.

success at that but they were able to confer with prominent Jackson lawyers who apprised them of the chances that the blanket bill would have in the coming session of the legislature. They were not very promising. Pollitizer warned Paul that sections regarding jury service and the choice of domicile and name would be the stumbling blocks.[23]

When it became obvious that Mrs. Crump could not be relied upon to conduct the legislative campaign in 1922, Alice Paul turned to another Mississippian. Burnita Shelton Matthews, a Hazlehurst native, had gone to Washington to work as a clerk during World War I and had remained to obtain a law degree in 1919. In 1921 she began a long tenure as a legal research secretary (and later legal counsel) for the Woman's Party, analyzing state laws regarding women's rights and disabilities and drafting remedial legislation.[24] As the secretary of the Mississippi branch and its representative in Washington, Mrs. Matthews was the person through whom Alice Paul actually directed the Party's activities in the state. Mrs. Matthews, however, was unable to leave her legal practice and research duties to go to Jackson to conduct the legislative campaign.

Neither Pollitizer nor Hill could remain in Mississippi, and Mrs. Crump was both unwilling and unsuited to direct lobbying activities in Jackson. The two previous Woman's Party state chairmen no longer resided in the state. Consequently no one was on hand at the opening of the legislature, which had scarcely begun its work before other women's groups presented their legislative programs. On January 7 the Federated Women's Clubs convened at the Jackson public library to discuss its proposals to equalize appropriations for the state college for women with those for the Agricultural and Mechanical College at Starkville and also a bill to provide a public home for "fallen women." Chief spokeswomen for the GWFC were two prominent women leaders, Mrs. Julian Crisler, a former nominal member of the Woman's Party, and Mrs. Lizzie George Henderson, daughter of the revered former senator James Z. Geoerge.[25]

The Federated Women's Clubs were lightweights compared to the League of Women Voters which scored a coup when their national president, Maud Wood Park, addressed a joint session of the legislature on January 11. Mrs. Park, who had recently spoken in Florida and Georgia, brought her anti-blanket bill message to Mississippi.[26] She told the assem-

23. Pollitizer to Paul, 2 December 1921, NWP Papers, Reel #11.

24. In 1949 Burnita Shelton Matthews became the first women to be appointed to a federal district court judgeship. She remained on the bench until her retirement in 1979. For biographical material, see the Matthews Scrapbook, Vol. I, Department of Archives and History, Jackson, Mississippi.

25. Jackson *Daily Clarion-Ledger*, 10, 15 January 1922.

26. *The Woman Citizen*, 31 December 1921.

bled lawmakers that the league could not support an equal rights bill because it endangered existing protective legislation and would seriously upset civil procedure in the courts. Instead, she asked that the legislature endorse the federal Sheppard-Towner Act of 1921 through which Mississippi would receive ten thousand dollars during the first year for maternal and child care. The leading Jackson newspaper reported her address favorably, adding that she "made many friends for the League of Women Voters."[27] Two weeks later, LWV members throughout the state received a letter from Mrs. Park reminding them of the emphatic action taken at the two previous conventions in defense of protective legislation.[28]

The legislature had been in session for nearly a month before the Woman's Party finally placed a lobbyist in Jackson. Mrs. Isabelle Kendig Gill arrived from Washington during the second week in February and began a furious pace of lobbying among the legislators and speaking before women's club gatherings. Within a week she found sponsors for the Woman's Party bill, Senator Walton Shields of Greenville and Representative John A. Yeager of Lumberton. She wrote Alice Paul, "Now I have only to successfully lobby about 200 men," most of whom were holdovers from the same legislature that had defeated the suffrage amendment in ten minutes. She intended to promote Mrs. Matthews as the Party's "strongest card" because "the South doesn't relish outside dictation."[29]

Her days given to the legislature, Mrs. Gill spent her nights before the women's clubs. It was disheartening work and she was distressed to find Jackson the most "clannish community" she had ever seen and "infinitely worse than New England."[30] In talks before the Chaminade Club, the Arts Study Club, and the Research Club, she pointed out that Mississippi women still could not act as jurors, could not choose their legal residence, did not own their own services, were not equal guardians of their children, and did not have as liberal grounds for divorce as men. She was little more than politely received; after her appearance before the City Federation of Women's Clubs, the group tabled by a large majority the resolution to endorse the Women's Party bill.[31] The Shakespeare Club and the YWCA Business Girls League refused to give her an audience, but she found the Leagues of Women Voters to be her biggest opposition. She

27. Jackson *Daily Clarion-Ledger*, 12 January 1922; Memphis *Commercial Appeal*, 12 January 1922.

28. Park to Nannie Rice, 25 January 1922, "Woman Suffrage" folder, Mississippi State University Special Collections.

29. Gill to Paul, 19 February 1921, NWP Papers, Reel #12.

30. Ibid.

31. Jackson *Daily Clarion-Ledger*, 16, 22, 23 February 1922. The minutes of the Research Club, on deposit in the Mississippi Department of Archives and History, contain no comments on Mrs. Gill's presentation.

described the latter as a "loose confederation of intensely local clubs" which had been meeting monthly for two years. The league's greatest advantage was that its president, Mrs. Yerger, was a reporter for Jackson's leading newspaper and she had access to the Senate floor at any time. Furthermore, the postmistress of the House, a league member, was a widely known and respected woman. Mrs. Gill confided to Alice Paul that the league was "an effective political machine [with] a constructive moderate program." Its leadership, program, and support were local. On the other hand, legislators who assisted the Woman's Party would stand guilty of supporting a "vague, invisible, unpopular" organization.[32]

Mrs. Gill had to conduct her campaign alone. She dared not convene the few Woman's Party members in Jackson (among the mere fifteen in the entire state) because of the social ostracism invoked by the socially prominent league women against NWP members or their allies. She found that new recruits were too involved in club, social, and church work to take the party seriously. Whatever influence Mrs. Crump's faction may have exerted was shattered by a series of scandals involving Governor Russell, the most explosive being a suit filed against him in February 1922 by a young woman who alleged seduction.[33] Little wonder that Mrs. Crump did not care to come to Jackson!

On February 20 the equal rights blanket bill was introduced by Yeager and Shields and referred to the judiciary committees in each house.[34] While the bill was in limbo Mrs. Gill continued her conferences with club women. Mrs. Saunders, the state LWV president, informed her that the bill was "pernicious," and the state GFWC president promised only that her group would study it and it was unlikely that an endorsement could be expected at the executive committee meeting in April.[35] Mrs. Gill feared that all her work would be undone when Mrs. Hilda Pleasant of Louisiana arrived in Jackson the first week in March. Her vociferous opposition to the blanket bill had helped block its passage at a special session of the Louisiana legislature during the previous fall. Referring to the measure as a "home-wrecking and business-destroying bill," she found her attack against the "militants" good press copy for the city editors,[36] one of whom Mrs. Gill reported to her headquarters "will not touch us with a ten foot pole."[37]

32. Gill to Paul, 19 February 1922; Gill to Paul, February 1922, NWP Papers, Reel #13.
33. Albert D. Kirwan, *Revolt of the Rednecks: Mississippi Politics, 1876-1925* (New York, 1965), 297.
34. *Journal of the House of Representatives of the State of Mississippi*, 1922 Session, 853; *Journal of the Senate of the State of Mississippi*, 1922 Session, 550; Jackson *Daily Clarion-Ledger*, 22 February 1922.
35. Gill to Paul, 28 February 1922, NWP Papers, Reel #13.
36. Jackson *Daily Clarion-Ledger*, 4, 8 March 1922.
37. Gill to Paul, 12 March 1922, NWP Papers, Reel #13.

Mrs. Gill encountered continuing frustrations. The legislative delay created a family crisis at home. Her husband had fired the children's nurse because she had "over-fed and underbathed the baby!" The NWP headquarters solved that problem by securing another nurse, but it could not do anything about Mrs. Crump who refused to go to Jackson in spite of a personal plea from Mrs. Gill who made a trip to the Crump plantation at Nitta Yuma.[38]

When the Woman's Party bill was killed by the House Judiciary Committee, Mrs. Gill turned to a substitute bill sponsored by Senator William B. Roberts of Rosedale, an old friend of suffrage.[39] The Roberts bill deleted the blanket bill's provision for choice and name and domicile, two provisions especially anathema to conservatives in both the legislature and among organized women, and provided that jury service should be optional for women who might be called to duty. Mrs. Gill advised her headquarters that the bill held to the spirit of the Woman's Party, a majority of Mississippi women favored it, and the league had not announced its opposition. Moreover, the bill had been reported favorably by the Senate Judiciary Committee and was on the calendar for the evening of March 21.[40]

Mrs. Gill was correct in her report that there had been no organized league move against the bill. The league had only to rely upon Mrs. Yerger's quiet lobbying among the senators who had pledged their support to Mrs. Gill to undo her work. On the night of the debate the Senate gallery was filled with women but the few friends made by the Woman's Party offered myriad excuses for staying home. They had to stay with "their babies" or go to the Lenten service; they were "too tired" or "couldn't go out after dark." Mrs. Gill was disheartened to see Mrs. Yerger moving among the Senate opponents as they argued that the bill was too sweeping and that it conferred upon women "all the rights of a man but . . . none of the duties." Despite the fact that several senators spoke eloquently for the bill, a majority appeared to be swayed by the assertion that Mississippi women did not want the measure passed, an old argument that had once been effective against woman suffrage. In two hours it was all over; by a vote of twenty-one to fifteen the Senate postponed further action on women's rights. Mrs. Gill lamented, "We are not going to pass the bill until we get some women back of us." "If the Lord doesn't raise us up a real Mississippi leader" she feared that the party

38. Gill to Paul, 5, 12 March 1922, NWP Papers, Reel #13.

39. In 1920, following the defeat of the Nineteenth Amendment by the Mississippi legislature, Roberts had attempted to bring the matter to a second vote. Taylor, "Suffrage Movement in Mississippi," 31-32.

40. Gill to Paul, 12, 14, 18 March 1922, NWP Papers, Reel #13; Jackson *Daily Clarion-Ledger*, 17 March 1922.

would never make any gains.[41] Anita Pollitizer consoled her that the defeat was due to the "sickening performance" of the League of Women Voters.[42]

The 1922 legislature did not totally neglect the subject of women's disabilities. It passed an equal guardianship bill that extended to mothers equal rights with fathers to the custody, services, and earnings of their children.[43] Although there was no controversy between the league and the Woman's Party when the bill was passed, the two organizations later vied in the columns of their official publications to claim responsibility for the bill.[44] The Woman's Party clearly deserved little credit. The guardianship bill had been drafted by the national LWV office, introduced in Mississippi through Mrs. Yerger, lobbied by the Mississippi League, and passed without a dissenting vote.[45] The league also pointed to other successes with the 1922 legislature: the appropriation to implement the Sheppard-Towner Act and funding for the state college for women that exceeded that provided the state university at Oxford.[46]

The fact that the league was willing to endorse political candidates and the Woman's Party was not gave the league a further opportunity to assert its influence in Mississippi. In the 1922 summer campaign for United States senators, the league and *The Woman Voter*, its journal, urged women to register and vote for Belle Kearney, a former suffragist and prohibition lecturer, who was the first woman to seek a major office in Mississippi.[47] The campaign degenerated into the usual class conflict that marked most Mississippi elections. Alice Paul, despite the urging of Mrs. Crump, refused to endorse James K. Vardaman, who hoped to return to his old post, lost in 1918 to Pat Harrison. Vardaman had both voted for the woman suffrage amendment and as a candidate in 1922 had endorsed the blanket bill. "It is the present policy of the Woman's Party not to either support or oppose any candidate," NWP headquarters reminded the erstwhile Mississippi chairman.[48] When Miss Kearney was eliminated in the

41. Jackson *Daily Clarion-Ledger*, 22 March 1922; Jackson *Daily News*, 23 March 1922; Gill to Paul, 22 March 1922, NWP Papers, Reel #13.

42. Pollitizer to Gill, 22 March 1922, NWP Papers, Reel #13.

43. Mississippi was the second southern state to enact an equal guardianship law.

44. *Equal Rights*, 21 July 1923; *The Woman Voter*, 2 November 1922. The Federated Clubs credited the league for the equal guardianship bill. *Mississippi Club Woman*, November 1922, p. 19. Copy in Mississippi Department of Archives and History.

45. Jackson *Clarion-Ledger*, 9 March 1922.

46. Ibid, 9 April 1922.

47. Vinton O. Price, "Will Women Turn the Tide? Mississippi Women and the 1922 United States Senate Race," *Journal of Mississippi History*, 42 (August 1980), 212-20. For Kearney's campaign see Nancy C. Tipton, " 'It Is My Duty': The Public Career of Belle Kearney" (M.A. thesis, University of Mississippi, 1975), 83-108.

48. Crump to Matthews, 18 August 1922; Crump to Elsie Hill, 25 August 1922; Crump to Gill, 26 August 1922; Crump to Paul, 23, 26 August 1922; Eleanor Brannan to Crump, 2 September 1922, all in NWP Papers, Reel #17.

first primary, the league threw its support to Hubert D. Stephens, an opponent of suffrage who had refused to champion the blanket bill. Stephens defeated Vardaman in the runoff. Thwarted again in her attempts to promote her "faction" through the Woman's Party, Mrs. Crump gave little cooperation to the party's ongoing efforts to organize on a statewide basis prior to the 1924 legislature.

To extend its influence among Mississippi women outside of Jackson, the Woman's Party arranged in February 1923 that Mary Winsor, an enthusiastic member from Pennsylvania, speak in Columbus, Oxford, and Clarksdale. She was warned to avoid Jackson where "the League starts a big rumpus . . . everytime the Woman's Party has a speaker."[49] Through Minnie Brewer, editor of *The Woman Voter*, and Mrs. Saunders, the league arranged that Winsor be answered by Lucy Somerville, a recent honor graduate of the University of Mississippi Law School and the daughter of Nellie Nugent Somerville, the state's foremost suffrage leader.[50] The debate, presided over by Oscar Johnston, a prominent Delta planter and civic leader, turned into a media event. Well attended, it consisted of Winsor's advocacy of the NWP's equal rights program and Somerville's rebuttal that the party misrepresented the disabilities remaining against women, particularly those laws that held wives responsible for the debts of their husbands. Somerville warned that equal rights legislation would remove from women the right to demand support from husbands and lose for women the right to homesteads and alimony.[51] Despite the fact that Mary Winsor was politely received, the Woman's Party gained no members at the meeting.[52]

The party was correct that Mississippi laws and customs still perpetuated disabilities against women. Without an effective party organization, the NWP lowered its sights to specific legislation opening jury service to women. After learning that Mrs. Crump could (or would) not attend the 1924 legislative session, Mrs. Matthews gave up her attempts to send a bill for introduction by any of the few friends of equal rights that the Woman's Party had found in the legislature.[53] The League of Women Voters, which had endorsed a jury bill at its two previous annual conventions, managed to have its bill introduced in both houses but neither was reported favorably.[54] The Federated Women's Clubs had nothing in its leg-

49. Burnita S. Matthews to Vivian Cook, 17 February 1923, NWP Papers, Reel #20.

50. Vivian Cook to Matthews, 20 February 1923; Cook to Matthews, 21 February 1923; *The Woman Voter*, 23 February 1923.

51. *Clarksdale Daily Register*, 20 February 1923; Memphis *Commercial Appeal*, 4 March 1923; *Woman Voter*, 2, 9 March 1923.

52. Vivian Cook to Alice Paul, 8 March 1923, NWP Papers, Reel #21.

53. Matthews to Crump, 12, 24 January, 29 February 1924, NWP Papers, Reel #25.

54. *Woman Voter*, 9 November 1922; Jackson *Daily Clarion-Ledger*, 27 November 1923. Senators Wiley A. Blair of Tupelo and Edmund F. Noel of Lexington introduced the bills. Noel was a former governor of Mississippi.

islative program beyond the establishment of a protective home for prostitutes and an "equal guilt" law regarding sex offenses.[55] The mood of the Mississippi lawmakers was revealed by one who protested, "I don't object to my wife voting, but when it comes to neglecting household duties to sit on a jury . . . I am against that form of equal rights."[56]

The Woman's Party did not attempt to take any equal rights measures to the 1926 legislature. It still lacked an effective leader and an organization in Mississippi and was deeply involved in planning for its participation in the International Woman's Suffrage Alliance meeting to be held in Paris during the summer. In late 1927 Burnita Matthews once again tried to inspire Mrs. Crump to secure a legislative sponsor for the jury service bill but Mrs. Crump retreated from the field when she did not receive approval of her plan to have ex-governor Russell become a paid NWP lobbyist in Jackson.[57] When Mrs. Matthews learned after the session had begun that Mrs. Crump had left the state and was at the Greenbriar resort, Mrs. Matthews quickly forwarded a jury bill to Representative Hugh Barr Miller of Hazlehurst, who telegraphed that he would be "delighted" to introduce it. He moved so fast that there was no time for the Woman's Party to mobilize whatever support it had. The House Judiciary Committee killed it "gloriously." Miller wrote Mrs. Matthews that he was the only lawyer who voted for it and that "the rest of them seemed to take great pleasure in murdering it."[58]

Mississippi was not the only southern state in the 1920s in which the Woman's Party failed to outscore the League of Women Voters in the state legislatures and among other women's organizations. The pattern prevailed in Louisiana, Alabama, Georgia, and Florida where the NWP sent cadres of organizers and lobbyists.

The Woman's Party was too doctrinaire for Mississippi and it suffered the stigma that outsiders have traditionally faced in the state. There were a few emerging career and professional women in Mississippi, but they were too concerned about establishing themselves among their clients to become involved with an organization whose notions about woman's full equality would jeopardize advancement in their own professions. A vast majority of Mississippi women were homemakers who were not alienated by the league and the federated clubs whose emphases upon protection for mothers, children, and working women seemed far more appropriate for them than the NWP's militant careerism and total equality. Never able to

---

55. *Clarksdale Daily Register*, 7 March 1923.
56. *Woman Voter*, 29 February 1924.
57. Crump to Matthews, 1 December 1927; 21 January 1928; Matthews to Crump, 9, 21 December 1927, NWP Papers, Reel #38.
58. Miller to Matthews, 20 February 1928; Matthews to Miller, 23 February 1928, NWP Papers, Reel #38.

secure organizers and funding to reach beyond Jackson, the Woman's Party probably never understood the nature and extent of its opposition in Mississippi.

The experience of later groups which have expended their efforts to convert the Mississippi legislature to equal rights has been much the same as that of the Woman's Party. Protective legislation has not been invalidated in Mississippi, and it was not until 1968 that jury service was opened to women. By custom a married woman's name and domicile are still that of her husband; there is no law granting a woman the choice of either.[59] It is probably as true in Mississippi today as it was fifty years ago that many women are apathetic about equal rights, and there are still questions to raise about the men who represent them in the legislature. In the two most recent sessions of the legislature, ratification of the Nineteenth Amendment has been shunted into the constitution committees, languished for lack of a report, or otherwise choked.

Since the submission of this essay, the Mississippi legislature ratified the amendment in March, 1984 by a unanimous vote in both the House and the Senate, sixty-four years after its ratification nationwide. "What we're beginning to do is set the record straight for historical purposes in Mississippi," promised the freshman senator who sponsored the proposal. His statement is symbolic of a renaissance in the movement for women's political participation and equal rights in Mississippi (Jackson *Clarion-Ledger*, March 9, 1984).

---

59. Author's interview with Carolyn Ellis, University of Mississippi Law School, 3 July 1980. See M. Carolyn Ellis, "The Decline and Near Fall of Statutory Sexism in Mississippi," *Mississippi Law Journal*, 51 (June-September 1980), 191-234.

CHALLENGING "WOMAN'S PLACE": FEMINISM, THE LEFT, AND INDUSTRIAL UNIONISM IN THE 1930S

SHARON HARTMAN STROM

An important work which helped us see the history of women's work in a new way is Alice Kessler-Harris's 1975 article, "'Where Are the Organized Women Workers?'" Attacking the traditional question asked by organizers and historians, "Why don't women organize?" Kessler-Harris argued that the sexual segregation of women's jobs, their life cycles of work and marriage, and the overwhelming sexism of male unionists made the organization of any women workers remarkable. She suggested that a focus on women workers who had organized would be a more positive and instructive category in the new women's history.[1]

Historians have begun to look for more organized women workers, and, not surprisingly, have found them, particularly in the industrial sector.[2] The fact remains, however, that women have organized less frequently than men; by the mid 1970s 12 percent of working women were unionized while 29 percent of working men were. Some observers of women's work still see the relatively low level of organized female workers as evidence that women are inherently less organizable than men. Although acknowledging that women have had more difficulties to overcome in organizing, these observers still believe there is a psychological component in women's attitudes toward union organization that makes them less assertive, less willing to take risks, more willing to be victims of employer exploitation. For instance, in a recent book on women wage earners from 1900 to 1930 Leslie Tentler argues that women were more passive than men at work. Women saw themselves as powerless in the world outside the home, and they relinquished any notions of rebelling against male coworkers or bosses in order to inherit their tradi-

Feminist Studies 9, no. 2 (Summer 1983).

tional authority at home as wives and mothers.[3] On being presented with evidence of clerical organizing in the 1930s, one male sociologist who commented on a paper I gave at a convention several years ago was still not convinced. "Large numbers of male workers," he argued, "rose up and demanded industrial unions in the thirties. For whatever reason, large numbers of women didn't." Although the romantic content of this view is obvious, it is not enough, evidently, to show that women workers may have organized. We need to go beyond the question, "Where are the organized women workers?" and explain why women workers haven't been able to organize as effectively as men. In other words, what historical conditions needed to be present for women to perceive that protests against employers and sexist unions were worth risking their jobs? Why haven't such protests led to the forming of viable trade unions? What will make it possible for women to organize *en masse* in the primarily female occupations? When can women organize?

In this article I will explore depression-era organizing with these questions in mind. In so doing I will avoid attributing psychological motives to women workers. Instead I will try to show that economic, ideological, and political variables can explain why some women workers succeeded in organizing, but did not organize in as large numbers as men. The most important of these variables were women's occupational positions in the American economy, the discriminatory policies of the New Deal, prevailing cultural and ideological views of women's roles in the work force, the failure of industrial unionism to reach most women workers, the lack of community and family support networks for striking women workers, and the absence of a feminist critique within the progressive labor movement, especially the Communist party. I will argue that although women did engage in job actions and spontaneous labor protests in the thirties they were at an intrinsic disadvantage in getting the kind of wholehearted support men received. That support could not have been provided without a feminist ideology to justify changing the status of working women. As Ruth Milkman has argued, "minimally any successful struggle to organize women had first to challenge the ideology of 'women's place'—a problem that did not arise in organizing men."[4]

Unemployment, underemployment, and drastically reduced wages became a national experience during the 1930s. Under the banner of Franklin D. Roosevelt's New Deal, the federal government responded on a number of levels to ease the suffering of working people. Women did not receive equal assistance. The 1933 National Industrial Recovery Act (NIRA) minimum wage codes sanctioned lower pay rates for women workers than for men in the same occupations, and they excluded domestic and agricultural jobs—both major occupations for women, especially poor and minority women. Salaried workers and clerical workers in the insurance industry were also excluded. There was widespread evasion of maximum hour codes for clerical workers as employers changed titles, assigned salaries, increased duties, and then forced secretaries to work overtime with no extra pay. Women workers paid the same Social Security taxes as men, but received fewer benefits upon retirement. The domestic work, agricultural, and government sectors were not covered by Social Security; all three were employers of large numbers of women. The NIRA work relief section ignored women altogether, and the Civilian Conservation Corps camps were originally for men only. When camps for females were set up women received one-half of what men were paid. The Works Projects Administration (WPA) provided more jobs, but only one member of a family could earn relief, and that member had to be the main wage earner. Aid to Dependent Children (ADC) was widely seen in local communities as a way to get women off the WPA rolls and therefore out of the work force, although ADC payments were lower than WPA work rates. When the NIRA was found to be unconstitutional and was replaced by the Fair Labor Standards Act of 1938, clerks, seasonal employees, and domestic workers found themselves with no protection against substandard wages.[5]

National legislation lashed out at married women workers. Section 213 of the Economy Act of 1932 allowed the firing of one spouse if both husband and wife worked for the government, and of the fifteen hundred married persons fired within the next year, nearly all were women. A crop of proposed state laws tried to follow suit. Frances Perkins, secretary of labor and the first woman to hold a cabinet position, had, as state industrial commissioner of New York, called on women who did not need jobs to stay at home and deplored women who worked for "pin-money."[6]

Federal and state governments were in some ways merely expressing sentiments held by the public at large. Many people believed that working married women were partly responsible for unemployment, and there was widespread sentiment for the firing of married teachers and government workers. The president of the California Institute of Technology proposed that 75 percent of all jobs be reserved for men, and George Gallup, who repeatedly polled Americans on their attitudes toward working wives, claimed that he had never seen poll respondents "so solidly united in opposition" to an economic issue.[7]

Section 213 and other discriminatory policies against married women played a direct role in forcing women out of better jobs in the 1930s. Local and state employees had increased by 400 percent between 1900 and 1930, civilian employees of the federal government had tripled, and school workers had grown by two and one-half times. Women received many of these new jobs, and one-fifth of the women were married. The Women's Bureau found that Section 213 was usually applied to married typists and stenographers and rarely to married charwomen or elevator operators. These policies were repeated in private industry. In 1931, New England Telephone and Telegraph fired all its married women workers. Most large companies, and almost all banks and insurance firms, simply refused to hire married women as clericals. Numerous commentators observed that many workers lied about their married status in order to get or keep jobs. When Social Security cards were issued for the first time in 1937, regional offices were besieged by calls from women who feared their marriages would be revealed to their employers.[8]

Married women were not excluded from the labor force during the depression. In fact, the number of married women at work increased because families were forced to earn a living in any way they could. Overall, women's status in the job market declined in the thirties; men made gains in proportion to women in teaching, library work, social work, and nursing. Meanwhile, many women had to enter the lower-paid female occupations like domestic service, part-time work, canning, and farm labor. These were also job categories either not covered or only partially covered by Social Security, collective-bargaining legislation, NIRA, and the Fair Labor Standards Act. They were also the only job categories available to most black and minority women.[9]

The ramifications of attacks on married women workers were of grave import for all women workers, married or not. Because most women eventually married, the working woman was by default considered to be a young adult, or "working girl." She was not a permanent member of the work world, and therefore should not have the same say in government and union policy as the "working man." Every married working woman was an anomaly, present in the work force either through temporary financial necessity or personal selfishness. The implication for women was that work outside the home was a stage, not a right, and that the mature woman belonged at home.

Movies hammered home the same message. As Molly Haskell has observed, although many movies of the thirties portrayed an adventurous young working woman who could hold her own in a man's world, she usually capitulated to marriage and home by the film's end.[10] In any event, she worked because she had to; she was either a Jean Arthur, on her own and earning a living, as in *Mr. Smith Goes to Washington,* or a Barbara Stanwyck, supporting her brother and a widowed mother, as in *Meet John Doe.* Or if she didn't really need to work, she was a Katharine Hepburn, a silly, unfeeling snob who finally learned that suicide might be the consequence of taking a deserving young woman's job, as in *Stage Door.*

Thus, the makers of popular culture, government legislators, the general public, and private industry, while somewhat sympathetic to the plight of the working man, were ambivalent about the working woman. She was evidently a necessary evil but should remain confined to the lower-paying feminized occupations, which did not, for the most part, deserve the same benefits as male jobs. She faced a complicated range of problems in the work force, only one of which was union organization.

Women workers responded to Section 7 (a) of the NIRA in 1933. They were often given organizing help from Communist activists, many of them women, in the Trade Union Unity League (TUUL) and the Unemployed Councils. In Detroit, 6,000 workers, 2,000 of them women, went on strike at the Briggs Mack Avenue plant and won substantial wage gains for women. In Philadelphia, female and male workers at the Philadelphia Storage Battery Company (Philco) won an agreement which gave a 10 percent wage increase to men and a 15 percent increase to women aimed at narrowing the disparity between female and male wages. In May of 1933, 4,500 workers, mostly women, struck nonunion Philadelphia dress plants. A revitalized International Ladies Garment Workers' Union (ILGWU) was able to launch a general strike of dressmakers, mostly female, in New York, New Jersey, and Connecticut and won an agreement in four days. Similar strikes were conducted by the Amalgamated Clothing Workers in Pennsylvania, New York, and Connecticut. In St. Louis 1,400 women, mostly black, went on strike to protest a piece-rate reduction in the city's pecan-shelling factories. The strikers, who had gone out in 1927 as well, had the support of the TUUL and the Unemployed Councils. Husbands and children of the strikers joined them on the picket line, and sympathetic unionists and businesses in the black community provided food for meals. After the employers brought in scabs and strikebreakers, the local Jewish community and the American Civil Liberties Union provoked sympathy for the strikers in the press, and the mayor of the city helped to mediate negotiations.[11]

In 1934, textile workers went out on strike from Maine to Mississippi, and women, who made up 40 percent of all textile workers, were instrumental in the protracted and bloody strike which ensued. They fought state militias, participated in huge demonstrations, sat down on railroad tracks, and led "flying squadrons" from plant to plant to recruit new strikers and intimidate scabs. Thirty thousand women and men hotel workers struck fifty hotels in New York early in 1934 to gain union recognition. In December 1936, 4,000 female and male workers struck five of Philadelphia's six leading department stores. Warehouse workers, truckers, sales clerks, packers, porters, and waitresses were joined on the third day of the strike by seventy-five bookkeepers and office workers. Although the strike was hushed up in the newspapers and numerous arrests were made, workers achieved union recognition and a forty-eight-hour week.[12]

The entire labor movement entered a dynamic new phase in 1936 and 1937 when workers in basic production waged sit-down strikes. In both Akron, Ohio, and Flint, Michigan, despite the fact that they made up substantial numbers of workers in both the rubber and automobile industries, women workers—many of them young and single—were sent home by strike leaders and not allowed to sit-down. Women were discouraged from sitting in with men in factory strikes, for mixed groups of women and men might give employers a chance to charge sexual promiscuity or to provoke "unfit mother" cases in the courts.[13] Both men and married women, given the traditional allocation of childcare responsibilities in the thirties, probably feared that children would be neglected if mothers were not at home to care for them.

Sit-downs were perceived as men's affairs in the Congress of Industrial Organizations (CIO). One union official defined a sit-down in 1937 as "a cessation of work with the men remaining at work." But women workers throughout the country were quick to perceive that sit-downs might be of use to them. Jeremy Brecher found that both Chicago and Detroit experienced waves of sit-down strikes in stores and smaller factories following the great General Motors Strike in the spring of 1937. There were eighty-seven sit-downs involving 3,000 workers in Detroit alone, many of them in the auto parts and manufacturing firms which employed large numbers of women. Two hundred women, not allowed to participate in the Flint sit-down strike which led to a United Automobile Workers (UAW) contract with General Motors, sat down in a sewing room in the Fischer Body Plant No. 1 and were joined in sympathy an hour later by 280 additional women sewers. When sixty men in the shipping department also sat down, the entire plant was forced to close.[14] Clerks sat down in Detroit, Chicago, and New York department stores and five-and-tens, and women workers barricaded themselves in three tobacco plants in Detroit for several weeks. When 150 police attacked sit-downers at one of them, "hysterical cries echoed through the building as, by ones, and twos, the eighty-six women strikers, ranging from defiant girls to bewildered workers with gray hair, were herded into patrol wagons and sped away, while shattering glass and the yells of the street throng added to the din."[15] The UAW protested against such forced evictions, threatened to call 180,000 auto workers out on strike, and even raised the specter of a citywide general strike. The police stopped their raids. In Chicago there were sixty sit-downs in a two-week period in March of 1937, including 9,000 female and male Loop workers, ranging from peanut baggers to stenographers. Brecher reports that "1,800 workers, including 300 office workers, sat down at the Chicago Mail Order Company and won a ten percent pay increase; 450 employees at three deMet's tea rooms sat down as 'the girls laughed and talked at the tables they had served' until they went home that night with a twenty-five percent pay increase. . . ."[16]

We should also remember that women participated in strikes and job actions not only as workers, but also as wives or relatives of workers, mainly in women's auxiliaries. Male unionists at the time were more likely to respond to women who participated in women's auxiliaries than to women workers. The image of the woman standing behind her man and his job became a sentimental theme in union rhetoric, while the working woman was conspicuously absent. Women's auxiliaries often picketed and even fought the police, and they also provided meals for the duration of strikes, clearly an important key to their success.[17] There were obviously no "men's auxiliaries" to provide meals and childcare for striking women, although we need to know more about the ad hoc arrangements created by the friends, relatives, and communities of striking women. Working women and wives and relatives of working men all belonged to the auxiliaries; women workers who were sent out of plants in the Akron and Flint sit-downs of 1934 and 1937 participated by joining the UAW and United Rubber Workers (URW) auxiliaries.[18]

The auxiliaries did not lead to permanent union organizations which might have begun to articulate women workers' grievances. Although most male sit-downers were happy to have the support of women's emergency brigades during strikes, they expected that women would return to traditional roles once the emergencies were over. Some women resented this idea and saw the auxiliaries as a forum for discussion of women's concerns. Sometimes they were encouraged by Communist party (CP) organizers to address such issues as birth control, childcare, and who should do the housework, but the mere fact of organizing together as women was evidently a problematic idea for all concerned.

> In some cases the women through their activities won the respect of their striking husbands, and were given representation on strike committees. In other situations, the militancy of the CP-led auxiliaries enraged the male union leadership, who wanted women to stay home. Women in auxiliaries, as in the CP's women's units, developed some cooperative methods of child care, and occasionally forced their husbands to assume some of these responsibilities. These organizations did not equal liberation, of course, as tasks such as preparing food for the strikers still remained for the women. The CP often failed to push the auxiliaries and unions to go beyond sex-stereotyped roles.[19]

Yet some working-class women clearly articulated the larger issues their organizing as women had raised; one participant in the Flint Emergency Brigade said, "Just being a woman isn't enough anymore. I want to be a human being with the right to think for myself."[20] Beatrice Marcus reported in a December 1934 issue of the CP's *Working Woman* that women from coal miner families in Hillsboro, Illinois, had organized to demand adequate relief. They "held meetings, travelled through the countryside, raised money, and, in defiance of the male leadership of the Progressive Miners' Association, led demonstrations. As one march began on City Hall, the male demonstrators 'made vain efforts to keep their wives from the front ranks.'''[21] One of the most salient features of the thirties is the failure of any organized groups to develop this working-class womens' new consciousness and militance into a feminist position.

Middle-class feminist organizations were on the defensive in the thirties. In fact, because they had not recruited many younger women to join their ranks, older feminists found themselves increasingly talking to each other. Many of the goals they had been working toward since 1920 seemed to be under attack, particularly the right to combine marriage and work. In an attempt to gain some protection for the jobs of married women, feminists tended to emphasize that women workers did not usually compete with men and that most of them needed their wages to support families. Although useful in the short run, these arguments tended to reinforce popular notions of the thirties that women should work only when they had to and only when they did not take men's jobs.[22] Feminists in the thirties were also unable to establish any sustained point of view in the industrial union movement; they either ended up criticizing the role of Communists and other leftists, or they joined popular front alliances in which leftist women—most of whom were suspicious of traditional feminism—dominated. Although they had never been very successful in attracting working-class women to their groups, the failure of feminists to remain visible in the thirties meant that working-class women had no public sanction for articulating feminist ideas.

Feminist ideology might have survived if women on the Left had been interested in it. But although they often acted like feminists and addressed women's issues in their organizing efforts, most leftist women refused to associate themselves with the legacy of the movement for women's rights. While Trotskyists, Lovestoneites, Socialists, and A.J. Muste's Independent Labor party all made significant contributions to labor organizing in the thirties, Communist party members were clearly the most effective segment of the Left, and one of the most important in organizing women.

Communist party dogma officially viewed feminism as a bourgeois reform movement; women's problems would automatically be corrected with the arrival of true communism. Yet this view, as Robert Schaffer has recently argued, barely kept the lid on a smoldering debate within the party and in its publications on the "woman question." Party writers did discuss birth control, unequal pay, maternity insurance, and the role of men in housework. It was always clear, however, that industries dominated by male workers would be the target of vanguard organizing. Official writings also did not "admit to any conceivable antagonism between working-class men and women," and any struggle against male supremacy within the party had to be balanced against the party's desire to have its members live like ordinary workers and therefore accept ordinary workers' behavior—including the subordination of women to men.[23] These party lines, however, must be counterpointed by the actual experience of Communist women in the 1930s. There is no doubt that the experience of party membership, of organizing women's auxiliaries, consumer boycotts, and picket lines gave many a female Communist the organizing experience and self-respect she needed to become an independent woman. We must remember, however, that sometimes standing up for women, working with women, or becoming independent of men was not the same as possessing a feminist consciousness. One office worker organizer who was also in the CP in the thirties summed this up precisely: "My interest in the women's movement as such was quite peripheral if it was even conscious. It's not that I wasn't aware that women had problems, but I have always believed that . . . the basic problems of women will not be solved until we have socialism."[24] The consequence of this view was that women were always subject to having their grievances—whatever they were—superseded by the overall struggle of the working class, a struggle in which men and their families—not men and women—were participants.

The labor struggles of the Great Depression took on a new dimension after 1937 as the CIO rapidly expanded. The effects of increasing bureaucratization on women's organizing efforts were somewhat contradictory. Certainly the financial resources, institutional support, and power to impose a closed shop of the CIO made it possible to bring unionism to women who would otherwise have missed it. Any unionized shop was likely to raise women's wages significantly.[25] But there is also evidence to suggest that the early militancy of strikes and the wide-ranging scope of issues they raised in the early thirties began to disappear by 1937, as collective bargaining replaced confrontation and focused on the narrow range of issues laid out by contract negotiations.[26]

Frances Fox Piven and Richard A. Cloward have argued in their *Poor People's Movements* that legitimized workers' organizations like the CIO had a vested interest in discontinuing "unauthorized" job actions on the shop floor once they had large enough constituencies and had won agreements with employers. Communist organizers, now in their popular front phase, went along. The CP editor of the Flint *Auto Worker*, Henry Kraus, announced that the UAW's goal was "not to foster strikes and labor trouble. The union can only grow on the basis of established procedure and collective bargaining."[27] In a primer on how to organize an industrial union Clinton S. Golden and Harold J. Ruttenberg argued that "the written collective-bargaining contract is the means through which workers secure . . . a voice. This is one path to industrial peace that cannot be by-passed, either by managment or union officials. . . . Once wage earners successfully establish organization and collective bargaining at their point of actual employment, their relationship with management undergoes a transition from one of conflict in varying degrees to that of cooperation in some degree."[28] Both the General Motors (GM) and the U.S. Steel contracts signed by CIO unions in 1937 prohibited local strikes.[29] Unions called for grievances to be handled by shop stewards and union committees. In many unions women were denied access to this hierarchy, although they were a significant influence in locals of the United Electrical Workers (UE).[30]

These new developments probably prevented women from capitalizing on effective use of job actions to rectify their grievances. Complaints they had aplenty; Ruth Meyerowitz found that although the automobile industry was the biggest employer of women workers in Flint, it confined them to "women's jobs" like upholstery sewing and tedious assembly line work like spark plug manufacturing. Before the Flint strike they earned an average of ten to thirteen cents an hour while men made four or five times as much.[31] Although women in union plants did make gains in wages, the UAW abandoned a universal minimum wage in its contract with GM, which stipulated that wages could be determined by local plants in conjunction with local conditions. This was no different from the NIRA codes, which had allowed employers to maintain geographical, racial, and sexual differentials in wages. CIO unions continued the American Federation of Labor (AFL) tradition of setting lower wages for women's jobs than for men's jobs in their contracts.[32]

Although the CIO was more receptive to women workers than the AFL had been, women usually joined when they were present in industries with large numbers of men, as in, for example, the garment and electrical industries, or when they organized themselves. This was particularly true of minority women. When 400 black women stemmers in Richmond, Virginia, tobacco factories walked out in a spontaneous strike in 1937, they were told by the AFL that black workers couldn't be organized. The Southern Negro Youth Congress and the National Negro Congress, not the CIO, helped them form the Tobacco Stemmers and Laborers' Union. The ILGWU, which had a better record on helping southern workers than some other CIO unions, sent 500 women pickets to a Richmond tobacco strike in 1938, and the newly formed locals were passed on to the CIO in 1939. A similar strike by Mexican-American pecan shellers in San Antonio, Texas, in 1938 helped to establish the United Cannery, Agricultural, Packing and Allied Workers of America, a leftist union which was expelled from the CIO in 1950.[33] When women did organize, men saw little wrong with unequal pay; one male picket line protesting "girl's wages" dressed in drag and carried picket signs reading "Restore Our Manhood" to make its point.[34] When women did come into mixed CIO locals or tried to assume leadership roles they were often accused of being loose women and were asked to conduct union business in spaces like saloons, pool halls and union halls, where they were bound to feel uncomfortable.[35]

Only a "negligible proportion" of the 519 delegates to the first CIO convention were women (most of them from office worker unions); and by 1946 only 20 of the 600 delegates to the national convention were female. Only one woman, Eleanor Nelson of the United Federal Workers (UFW) was ever a president of any of the unions chartered by the CIO in the thirties. None of the 1938 constitutional convention's resolutions mentioned working women. The only specific reference to women thanked members of the women's auxiliaries, "the mothers, wives, sisters and daughters of industrial workers," thus ignoring entirely the contribution made by women workers to the auxiliaries. The *CIO News* either buried articles on women's strikes or failed to report them at all, and pictures of women workers in cheesecake poses were far more common than pictures of women on picket lines. Beauty contests for CIO women abounded in every affiliate, and mothers, wives, and girlfriends of unionists who "stood by their men" received the most praise. Wisconsin CIO members in 1938 thought "a good union girl" should only work to support herself or her family, be intelligent, a good housekeeper, and shorter than her boyfriend. She should use makeup moderately and keep her stocking seams straight. She should go out on the picket line "with her man," because having "girls come on the line . . . puts more pep in the gas." Although she should listen "with interest when a man wants to talk about his union," she mustn't ever "try to get bossy."[36]

Secretaries for labor unions complained that their employers did not pay them the minimum salary advocated by the CIO office workers' union, the United Office and Professional Workers of America (UOPWA). Joining the union itself was evidently seen as a threat to male unionists; a former secretary for the National Maritime Union (NMU) in Boston thought union men were "outraged, really in their hearts . . . when the secretaries of labor unions joined the UOPWA and dared to organize against them! There they were, the great champions of labor, (and) those ungrateful women sitting in those offices dared to organize a union to fight them. Disrupting the labor movement!" This same secretary, however, had taken the floor to explain police brutality to an enormous crowd in the Everett (Massachusetts) town hall after a bloody tear gas assault on an NMU picket line in 1937; the men were all too nervous to speak in public. Male unionists clearly had trouble maintaining the contradiction of the ornamental "union girl" that their ideology upheld with the militant union woman who they frequently encountered. One UFW member told a meeting of unionists that he wanted "to say a word in praise of this little girl of ours, Eleanor Nelson, who . . . has the tenacity of a bulldog and has been out there facing the guns for our union!"[37]

The narrow application of industrial unionism by the CIO to workers in basic production and manufacturing hurt women workers as well. Less than 22 percent of all working women worked in manufacturing by 1940, and more than 60 percent worked in other occupations, so the failure to reach out to service, domestic, sales, and clerical workers by the CIO played a crucial role in excluding women. Whether this failure was based on disinterest in nonindustrial occupations or on disinterest in women is not very important because it amounted to the same thing.[38]

Although it was not so obvious in the thirties, it is very clear now that the decision to ignore clerical workers was especially portentous. The census of 1940 indicated that more than 21 percent of all women workers were in clerical work, and the size of the occupation increased by nearly 85 percent from 1940 to 1944.[39] To ignore clerical workers was, then, to ignore a significant portion of women workers. Inevitably, however, clericals also caught the union spirit. Leftist clericals and office workers, both female and male, had begun by the mid thirties to agitate within long-dormant AFL locals for industrial unionism. In 1937 the CIO agreed to charter three office worker unions: the UFW, the State, County and Municipal Workers of America and the UOPWA. These unions grew substantially during the 1930s and 1940s, but were all purged by the CIO in 1950 and rapidly disappeared. Only the UOPWA could really follow the male industrial union model, because national state and local government employees were usually prohibited by law from going on strike.

The CIO never poured any effort into organizing assistance for the UOPWA and in fact repeatedly restricted its influence. Conceding to the protests of male industrial unions like the UAW and the URW, the CIO prohibited the UOPWA from organizing clerical workers in industries already represented by CIO nationals. Or, if such clericals did organize, their membership and dues would be handed, upon request, to the industrial union in question. The UOPWA was thus left with clericals in banks, insurance offices, small offices, social work agencies, paper work factories like the direct mail industry, and department stores. None of these workplaces had ever been strongholds of unionism, and especially not of industrial unionism.[40]

Office workers in the steel, mining, auto, rubber, and electrical industries were left to the whims of industry or of male unionists, none of whom made any significant attempt to organize clericals. In fact, many manufacturing unions tried to exclude office workers from their locals, a significant action because office workers made up 14.2 percent of all workers in manufacturing by 1938. The 1941 UAW contract with Ford Motors, for instance, specifically excluded most white collar workers. Sometimes industrial unions made gains explicitly at the expense of white collar workers. A UE contract with General Electric in 1937 cut salaries for office workers. In the late thirties, rubber workers in Jeanette, Pennsylvania, and Akron, Ohio, agreed to contracts which raised factory wages significantly, but cut or froze those of office workers.[41]

Not all office workers or blue collar workers wanted to be grouped with each other, and the National Labor Relations Board (NLRB) usually ruled that office workers should not be members of the same locals. One of the consequences of this bifurcation of the work force was that blue collar wages increased at a faster pace than white collar wages, with clerical workers increasingly earning lower wages than organized workers in manufacturing. Some office employees formed independent unions, but we don't know whether women clerical workers were in favor of this arrangement or not, or if they were even involved in the decisions to organize these. Certainly these independent unions were dominated by men, who had the better-paying and more responsible office jobs. The Federation of Westinghouse Independent Salaried Unions even tried to exclude married women from the Westinghouse offices.[42]

Although the CIO was indifferent at best and hostile at worst to the organizing of clericals, the office worker unions embodied important contradictions which helped prevent the widespread organizing of clericals. Young Communist women were particularly likely to be in a position to organize in the offices. The social character of the Communist party had changed dramatically since World War I, with many of the second-generation children of working-class parents receiving high school and even college educations by the 1930s. Many young leftist women with degrees in teaching could not find jobs and were forced to work as secretaries. By 1938 the CP estimated that 22 percent of its new recruits were technically "middle class." Young Communist women were working in business offices, social agencies, publishing houses, government offices, and trade union offices. As Communists they were expected to participate directly in the building of militant unions. They had received speaking, organizing, and protest experience in the CP, a vitally important ingredient for women workers, who often had trouble getting this experience elsewhere. They became the main leaders and organizers of the fledgling office worker unions which emerged in 1936 and 1937, an activity encouraged by the CP during the popular front.[43] Leftists helped break new ground in the organization of clericals in the thirties, but their antifeminist position and their class analysis of clericals hindered their effectiveness.

What class did clerical workers belong to in the thirties? Certainly many secretaries, especially older ones, came from the middle class, and some were college-educated women who had been pushed into lower-status jobs by the effects of the Depression. However, the new compulsory school laws and fewer industrial jobs for teenagers during the Depression meant that countless young working-class women were taking a "business curriculum" in high school and becoming clericals. Business had partly responded to hard times by reducing wages for office workers, instituting speedup, and increasing mechanization. This process involved a more clear-cut sexual division of labor with male office workers doing the managing and earning the best salaries and women performing the more tedious "assembly line" functions and earning the lowest wages. Most hard data on office workers indicated that female secretaries, typists, filing clerks, and other clericals were rapidly descending into the working class.[44] Nonetheless, most leftist observers continued to lump all female and male office workers together as though their interests and values were the same.

Two social scientists frequently quoted by leftists, Hans Speir, who wrote about German white collar workers, and the American economist Lewis Corey, both emphasized the increasing "proletarianization" of office work. Corey argued that most white collar workers were not "middle class in their relations to production and income: *they are economically and functionally a part of the working class: a 'new' proletariat.*" Speir acknowledged that "it is the man who typically has the principal authority, the girl who is typically the subordinate .... The majority of the subordinate employees in the large offices perform duties which are specialized and schematized down to the minutest detail." As his lengthy analysis continued, however, Speir left behind his reference to women as subordinates, giving the reader the impression that all this had little to do with sexual roles:

> In the case of the salaried workers who serve as subordinates in one of the many modern office machines, . . . the difference in the nature of the duties between such workers and the manual workers is completely wiped out .... Especially revealing with regard to the sinking of the social level of the white collar workers is, finally, the change in the social antecedents. The growing tendency to employ salaried workers of "proletarian origin" indicates that the number of untrained and poorly paid positions is increasing faster than the number of middle and principal positions. In other words, the salaried employees as a whole are being subjected to a process of decreasing social esteem.[45]

Speir's confusion rested on two traditional assumptions about clerical workers which most other analysts were unwilling to abandon: that the "social prestige" of office workers always made them identify with the middle class, and that female and male office workers' interests were necessarily inseparable. No one in the Left in the thirties was able to fully articulate the sexual division of office work or to grasp that women might prefer to be or even should be organized *as women* in an industrial clerical workers' movement. Organizers were also unable to discard the notion that because they were theoretically—if not actually—"middle class," office workers were a kind of parentheses to the main thrust of the industrial labor movement.[46]

In fact, the motives for organizing office workers sometimes bordered on the cynical. Communists routinely asserted in the thirties that fascism in Germany and Italy had relied on the support of the *petite bourgeoisie,* including white collar workers, for its political success. Fearful of the same social phenomenon in the United States, leftist theorists and organizers argued that the American middle class—especially the white collar sector—should be organized primarily to prevent it from supporting right-wing political causes and to facilitate the spread of unions in the industrial sector. According to Len DeCaux, editor of the *CIO News,* "if democracy and liberalism are to prevail over the menacing forces of fascism, unionization of white collar, office and professional workers is one of the most effective means of spreading labor sympathy and understanding among the middle classes."[47] This line of reasoning often obscured the actual grievances of working-class clericals and made them mere supporters of the struggle to help industrial workers. As one organizer told her UOPWA local: "It's important to you that all labor should be organized, stand together for legislation, better hours and wages, the right to organize, strike and picket. . . . Office workers if organized can help labor improve conditions and laws. . . . If manual workers in a shop strike, it would help them if the office workers were with them; the shop could be shut up tight. . . . Sometimes bosses take votes on who is for a strike or for a union, and count all the office workers against, even if they don't vote at all."[48]

Despite all these obstacles, thousands of female clerical workers joined the UOPWA in the thirties and hundreds went out on strike.[49] Some of these strikes were successful; others were not. A few examples should illustrate that female office workers could be militant, determined, and effective unionists and should also indicate the problems they might encounter.

In early 1936 machinists at the Margon Corporation, a small manufacturing firm in New York City, went on strike. The entire office staff of seven workers, all of them women and members of the leftist Bookkeepers, Stenographers, and Accountants Union

(BSAU), precursor of the UOPWA, refused to cross the machinists picket line. The strike was quickly won, and the factory workers went back to work with "increased wages, union recognition, and improved working conditions." On January 18, Sunny Grill, who had worked for Margon for six years, was fired and given her severance check. Officially told there was a slowdown in business, she was "privately told that she could no longer be 'trusted.'" Three days later union shop steward Claire Mitchell "interviewed the employers and told them that Miss Grill's discharge made them all feel insecure and that for the sake of efficiency and harmony in the office she should be reinstated, and if it were actually necessary to have any layoff, it be done on the basis of seniority." Mitchell was fired, and the remaining women were asked to sign pledges that "under no circumstances, especially in the case of a strike of the factory workers, would they go on strike or refuse to walk through the inside workers' picket lines." When they refused to sign, the women were fired, and the BSAU called a strike. Pickets were set up in front of Margon and the employers' homes. The company hired scabs and professional strikebreakers, and the police were called in to protect the scabs. Fifty-eight arrests were made in front of the Margon office in the next eight days, and eighteen members of BSAU were arrested in front of one of the owner's homes in Brooklyn. One picketer was beaten by a hired thug. Arrests finally halted after the intercession of Mayor La Guardia and the police commissioner. Two hundred factory workers, minus supervisors and skilled workers, did not honor the office workers' picket line until March 2, and by then the position of the owners was frozen. The strike continued into April, when the Margon owners moved their factory to Bayonne, New Jersey, where they had received "assurances that they would not be annoyed with labor disputes."[50]

Margon was the kind of small firm UOPWA often organized, and the 1936 strike typified some of the special dilemmas of organizing clericals. First, the clerical staff was far outnumbered by the industrial workers. That industrial workers, usually male, would honor clerical picket lines was not a foregone conclusion. One also senses here that employers were more threatened by the betrayal of their office staffs than they were by the militancy of factory workers; they were willing to move the factory rather than "tolerate the idea of their office girls belonging to a union and being as loyal to their fellow workers as they had been" to their bosses.[51] As for the factory workers, the message was crystal clear; saving jobs and union membership might necessitate throwing clerical workers overboard.

The advantages of penetrating a "clerical worker factory" were obvious in the wave of credit clearinghouse strikes in the Northeast in 1937-38. The 225 employees of the New York Credit Clearing House, the largest credit information bureau in the country, won union recognition and negotiated a contract under the leadership of office chair Lena de Pasquale. Salaries were as low as $11.88 a week, and employees were expected to work as much as two extra days a week without pay. An arbitrator set new minimum pay rates at $14 a week, but a strike ensued in 1940 over continued union recognition and new wage scales. Workers devised a new strike tactic—telephone picketing. New York Credit Clearing House had seventy-seven trunk lines, and unionists and their friends and relatives kept two thousand calls an hour coming in to jam the phones and stop business.[52] When the union's no-strike pledge prevented a strike in early 1942, UOPWA officials took workers' demands for a new contract to the U.S. Conciliation Service:

> The day before the UOPWA called upon the conciliation service, CCH workers tried their own hand at winning a settlement without a strike.
>
> With the boss directly behind her, little Lena de Pasquale, office chairman and leader of the 1940 strike, blew a signaling whistle. From every corner other whistles resounded. All employees left their desks and walked quietly over to one section of the office.
>
> A boss asked the cause. Lena bluntly told him it was a protest against the firm's stalling tactics. . . .
>
> Another boss told the workers "Whoever wants to go back to work, go right ahead." No one budged.[53]

Taking on a huge corporation, however, was far more difficult. At the New York office of L. Sonneborn Sons, Inc., an oil and paint company with widespread operations throughout the Northeast, Beatrice Limpson and six of her officemates organized and won a NLRB election for Local No. 16 in 1941. A strike in February ensued when contract negotiations broke down, and sympathetic picket lines were thrown up by UOPWA locals around Sonneborn operations all over the country. Longshoremen, seamen, teamsters, and painters all refused to cross picket lines, and names of scabs were advertised daily on picket signs. In an interesting reversal of family sympathies, Joseph Sonneborn, nephew of the company president, walked the picket line, while

Jack Gompers, nephew of AFL founder Samuel Gompers, went to work at Sonneborn as a scab. Picket captain Ruth Nettborn, "who once vowed she would never be seen on a picket line," was arrested while picketing Gompers's home. One observer reported that despite arrests, the strikers were "gay and lively," with one clerical worker teaching sister picketers the rumba to the music of a donated phonograph.[54]

UOPWA organizers realized early on they would have to reach Sonneborn's customers to make the strike effective. Accounts had to be visited, and if persuasion failed they were to be picketed or boycotted. The company's executives were hit with a barrage of telephone calls from strikers and their families; the "swanky Savoy Plaza," residence of the company president, was the target of a demonstration. Although Sonneborn eventually agreed to some of the union's demands, it refused to reinstate strikers, and rumor had it that new defense orders were making the company stronger than ever. Office workers at Sonneborn went back to work without a contract.[55]

The UOPWA had a better record than most CIO unions in organizing women workers, but it also reflected prevailing sexual attitudes of the period, despite its leftist leadership. The president of the national was always a man, and national organizers of the UOPWA frequently aired patronizing views of clerical workers in articles like the condescending weekly column signed by "Susie the Secretary." Susie said in 1937 that she didn't know if there were "any other girls in my department who have sense enough to stick together. They seem to be just out for themselves and not to care about how anyone else gets along. I used to be pretty dumb too, thinking that unions were just for common laborers and mechanics, so perhaps I can show them that organization is the thing."[56]

The UOPWA consistently allowed professional and higher-paid office workers, most of whom were men, to write contracts which excluded clerical workers or bargained away their contract rights. And in 1939 the union decided to launch a major campaign to organize insurance agents, almost all of whom were men. Although the insurance agents had suffered reduced salaries and worsened working conditions as a result of the Depression, they were not really devoted to industrial unionism, and routinely excluded clericals from their contracts and their locals. Clericals had to join separate locals of the UOPWA. The national accepted this sexism as the price it had to pay for attracting insurance agents to the union, but it meant that dues collected from clerical workers were sent to male locals with no intention of ever serving them.

The UOPWA had successfuly organized insurance agents at most of the major insurance corporations by the middle of World War II. In its desire to make these inroads, however, it essentially abandoned any attempt to include clerical workers in the insurance industry. Eventually the insurance workers bolted from the CIO and created independent craft unions or joined the AFL. Not surprisingly, these unions specifically excluded clericals. In 1952 striking AFL insurance agents set up a picket line outside a Prudential office building in Newark, New Jersey, hoping to convince clericals not to go to work; the clericals crossed the line. This episode was recorded as another example of how women workers, especially clerical workers, will not honor picket lines, but the story, as we have seen, was far more complicated.[57]

The arrival of the CIO in the 1930s must be viewed as a mixed blessing for women workers. Although many made gains in wages and working conditions, countless others were never offered industrial unions. The CIO acquiesced in the sexual division of labor and even actively sought to maintain it. And, whenever women were organized into unions without some sense of themselves as women, they tended to abrogate their rights. They usually became an adjunct to male unionism, paying in dues and receiving little else but a union card in return.

Women workers needed to challenge women's place to organize effectively in the thirties. They were not only establishing unions, but also the right to work, to have feminized occupations accorded equal treatment under federal statute, to earn comparable pay, and to win the support and cooperation of working-class men. In other words, women faced a complicated mesh of ideological, social, and economic obstacles in organizing that were peculiar to them. Where was this challenge to come from? To argue that working-class women could somehow have mounted a viable feminist movement on their own is to engage in the worst sort of wishful thinking. To perceive as an individual woman that one's exploitation as a wife, a mother, a daughter, an employee, and a unionist were all connected was one thing; to struggle collectively on occasion against one or more of these conditions was another; to band together in the face of women's economic dependence on men and attack them all at once was impossible. There were no existent forms of protest or organization along these lines, no popular symbols to evoke, no terms with which to identify the process of liberation, no audiences who would have taken such rhetoric seriously. Unions should have been the forum where the connections between women's problems as workers and as women were made; where the beginnings of a feminist consciousness should have emerged.

Leftist activists from both the working and middle classes were most likely to perceive these connections and to be able to act on them at the same time. Already in an antiestablishment posture, they might be able to see similarities between forms of patriarchy and forms of capitalism. As members of political groups or parties they would have alternative means of personal support other than traditional patriarchal families.[58] Socialist feminists had developed such connections earlier in the century. Women in the Socialist party articulated a far-reaching platform of goals for working women, including suffrage, birth control, and pay for housework. Anarchist Emma Goldman and socialist theorist Charlotte Perkins Gilman had attacked marriage as a capitalist institution ensuring male property rights. Their point of view was missing from leftist ideology in the thirties. The Communist party viewed women's issues as important but inferior to the issues of race and industrial unionism. When all three of these issues combined, as in the pecan sheller's strike in St. Louis in 1933, the Communists did some of their best work. But in organizng women they were prone to use them for the greater good of the party, not for engaging in an ongoing struggle to eliminate sexism. Yet Communist women were probably more engaged with women workers than were any other groups in American politics during the Depression. They helped women to articulate their own issues in a movement which would otherwise probably have ignored women as much as possible.

Whatever the failings of both feminists and leftists in the thirties, they did try to organize women workers and pioneered in the organization of clerical workers. Hundreds of clerical workers responded by joining CIO office worker unions, and their numbers grew larger during World War II. The contributions of leftist and feminist women during the thirties and during the war stand out in high relief when we look at women in unions in the fifties, a time when feminism was at its lowest point since the early nineteenth century. The Left was driven from the industrial union movement, and all three industrial unions for office workers were expelled from the CIO.

When can women organize? Women workers—whether they

are domestics, nurses, clericals, hairdressers, or seamstresses—must be given the impression by someone—male unionists, middle-class feminists, or leftist activists—that unions are appropriate for women, that unions are receptive to the elimination of sexism, and that taking the risks of losing jobs by striking will be worth the effort. The recent public attention paid to such sobering examples as Crystal Lee Jordan, on whom the film character Norma Rae was based, and the Willmar Eight may provoke more fear than courage, and it is easy to see why; women fighting for unions seem to get themselves fired.

It may also be true that years of experience with unresponsive male-dominated unions may account for the deep and abiding antiunion sentiment which many organizers find in women workers. Women may very well prefer dealing with one form of patriarchy—in the workplace—to adding another layer of patriarchy—the union—to their lives.

Women workers no longer have the vitality of a growing industrial union movement from which to draw inspiration. They do have a more consciously feminist atmosphere. There is considerable disagreement, however, over how strongly unions should be tied to the women's movement. Working Women has recently forged an alliance with Service Employees International Union to organize clerical workers for the AFL-CIO, and it will continue to maintain an independent existence as an organization representing women's interests. Yet workers as a group remain ambivalent about their feminism and its role in union organizing. Although they want to draw on some of the issues related to equal pay and equal representation raised by the feminist movement they are also reluctant to identify themselves as "women's libbers."[59] Recent strikes have shown that union women can use some aspects of feminist ideology to bolster their own self-esteem and create a rationale for the redressing of their grievances. "Feminist baiting," however, is also a tactic available to the opposition, and it will probably be increasingly used in the next decade.[60] Feminists who are also socialists will probably be particular targets of the corporations, hospitals, banks, and insurance companies, just as Communist women and men were particular targets in the McCarthy era. A unionist movement for women in this country will be successful to the extent that it acknowledges its past in radical industrial unionism and its future in militant feminism.

I would like to thank Susan Porter Benson, Kate Dunnigan, Ruth Milkman, and Bruce Laurie for reading an earlier draft of this paper and providing helpful suggestions.

1. Alice Kessler-Harris, "'Where Are the Organized Women Workers?'" *Feminist Studies* 3 (Fall 1975): 92-110.
2. Some recent sources include Rosalyn Baxandall, Linda Gordon, and Susan Reverby, eds. *America's Working Women: A Documentary History—1600 To the Present* (New York: Random House, 1976); Ellen Cantarow with Susan Gushee O'Malley and Sharon Hartman Strom, *Moving the Mountain: Women Working for Social Change* (Old Westbury, N.Y.: Feminist Press, 1980); Phillip S. Foner, *Women and the American Labor Movement,* 2 vols. (New York and London: Free Press, 1979-80); James J. Keneally, *Women and American Trade Unions* (St. Albans, Vt., and Montreal: Eden Press, 1978); Alice Kessler-Harris, *Out to Work: A History of Wage-Earning Women in the United States* (New York: Oxford University Press, 1982), Alice Lynd and Staughton Lynd, eds., *Rank and File: Personal Histories of Working-Class Organizers* (Boston: Beacon Press, 1973); Meredith Tax, *The Rising of the Women: Feminist Solidarity and Class Conflict, 1880-1917* (New York and London: Monthly Review Press, 1980); Barbara M. Wertheimer, *We Were There: The Story of Working Women in America* (New York: Pantheon, 1977).
3. Leslie Tentler, *Wage-Earning Women: Industrial Work and Family Life in the United States, 1900-1930* (New York: Oxford University Press, 1979).
4. Ruth Milkman, "Organizing the Sexual Division of Labor: Historical Perspectives on 'Women's Work' and the American Labor Movement," *Socialist Review* 10 (January-February 1980): 119.
5. Foner 2: 279-81; and Lois Scharf, *To Work and To Wed: Female Employment, Feminism, and the Great Depression* (Westport, Conn., and London: Greenwood Press, 1980), 110-33. Scharf provides the most thoroughgoing analysis to date of the New Deal's impact on women.
6. Scharf, 45-50; Foner 2: 278.
7. Foner 2: 257; Scharf, 50.
8. Scharf, 45, 104, 106-7; Grace Coyle, "Women in the Clerical Occupations," *Annals of the American Academy of Political and Social Science* 143 (May 1929): 183-84; U.S. Department of Labor, Women's Bureau, *The Employment of Women in Offices,* by Ethel Erickson, Bulletin no. 120 (Washington, D.C. 1934), 12-13.
9. For an overall analysis of the impact of the Depression on women's work see Ruth Milkman, "Women's Work and the Economic Crisis: Some Lessons from the Great Depression," *Review of Radical Political Economics* 8 (Spring 1976): 73-97; Scharf, 86-109.
10. Molly Haskell, *From Reverence to Rape: The Treatment of Women in the Movies* (New York: Holt, Rinehart & Winston, 1974), 141-52.
11. Keneally, 155; Foner, 2: 270, 272-73, 281-82, 285, 314-18.
12. Foner 2: 286-88; Keneally, 155-56; Irving Bernstein, *The Turbulent Years: A History of the American Labor Movement, 1933-1941* (Boston: Houghton Mifflin, 1970), 122-23; "Store Clerks Win Philadelphia Strike," *Ledger* 2 (December 1936): 1.
13. Sidney Fine, *Sit-down: The General Motors Strike of 1936-1937* (Ann Arbor: University of Michigan Press, 1969), 156; Robert Schaffer, "Women and the Communist Party, USA, 1930-1940," *Socialist Review* 45 (May-June 1979): 99.

14. Jeremy Brecher, *Strike!* (San Francisco: World Publishing, 1972), 203, 207-9; Foner 2: 311-12.
15. Foner 2: 312-13.
16. Brecher, 208-9.
17. For discussions of women's auxiliaries see Baxandall, Gordon, and Reverby, 264-65; Fine, 200-1, 279-80; Foner 2: 290-92, 302-12. One of the most important sources on the auxiliaries is the 1977 film, *With Babies and Banners: The Story of the Women's Emergency Brigade*, directed by Lorraine Gray, produced by Anne Bohlen, Lyn Goldfarb, and Lorraine Gray and distributed by New Day Films, P.O. Box 315, Franklin Lakes, N.J. 07417.
18. *With Babies and Banners;* Foner 2: 303-4. Ruth Meyerowitz found that working women were instrumental participants in the brigade ("Organizing the UAW: Wives, Workers, and Leaders, 1933-1974," Ph.D. diss. in progress).
19. Schaffer, 99-100. I have been influenced in this article by the views of Heidi Hartmann, who argues that working-class men actively tried to maintain traditional patriarchal controls over guilds and unions during the historical evolution of modern capitalism. They also convinced many capitalist employers to maintain the sexual division of labor, even when it was in the interest of capitalists to create a totally exchangeable labor market. See her "Capitalism, Patriarchy, and Job Segregation By Sex," in *Capitalist Patriarchy and the Case for Socialist Feminism*, ed. Zillah R. Eisenstein, (New York and London: Monthly Review Press, 1979), 206-47. Ruth Milkman argues persuasively that Hartmann ignores the extent to which working-class *families* (my emphasis), not just working men, used traditional patriarchal ideology to protect capitalist relations from totally encompassing the home and its members. Moreover, union men sometimes support equal rights and wages for women; the question is when and why. See Milkman, "Organizing the Sexual Division of Labor," 95-150, and her article "Redefining 'Women's Work': The Sexual Division of Labor in the Auto Industry During World War II," *Feminist Studies* 8 (Summer 1982): 337-72. Hartmann and Milkman both agree that working-class men have a vested interest in maintaining women's dependence on men in order to secure female childcare and housework services.
20. Fine, 201.
21. Beatrice Marcus, quoted by Shaffer, 89.
22. Scharf, 43-65.
23. Shaffer, 86-87.
24. Anne Prosten, interview with author, 5 February 1977, Brookline, Massachusetts. Vivian Gornick's recent book based on interviews with members of the CP, despite its judgmental style, does hint at the wide variety of sexual relationships within the party. The CP membership evidently encouraged some women to establish fuller and more assertive lives, but doomed others to horrible marriages in which they sacrificed themselves to the dual tyranny of their husbands and party discipline. One senses, however, that the activism of women in the party kept the "woman question" alive on a personal basis, whatever the official view. This ongoing struggle may explain the attraction of the current women's movement for many Old Left women. See Gornick's *The Romance of American Communism* (New York: Basic Books, 1977).
25. See Milkman, "Redefining 'Women's Work,'" 357, for an important discussion of this idea and its likely effect on women's militancy.
26. For a more detailed explanation of this argument see David A. Brody, *Workers in Industrial America: Essays on the Twentieth-Century Struggle* (New York: Oxford University Press, 1980), 127-35.
27. Henry Kraus, quoted in Frances Fox Piven and Richard A. Cloward, *Poor People's*

Movements: Why They Succeed, How They Fail (New York: Pantheon, 1977), 156. The authors do not consider sex as a variable in their analysis.
28. Clinton S. Golden and Harold J. Ruttenberg, *The Dynamics of Industrial Democracy* (New York and London: Harper & Brothers, 1942), 82, 310.
29. See Foner 2: 316-17 for a brief discussion of women in the UE; Piven and Cloward, 156.
30. Ruth Milkman, "The Reproduction of Job Segregation by Sex: A Study of the Changing Sexual Position of Labor in the Auto and Electrical Manufacturing Industries in the 1940's" (Ph.D. diss., University of California, Berkeley, 1981). Milkman argues persuasively that the greater numbers of women working in industry during World War II allowed them to exert more influence in the CIO and to raise women's issues more frequently.
31. Ruth Meyerowitz generously shared this information with me.
32. Fine, 324; Foner 2: 332; U.S. Department of Labor, Women's Bureau, *Women in the Economy of the United States of America* by Elizabeth Pidgeon, Bulletin no. 155 (Washington, D.C., 1937), 76-78.
33. Foner 2: 322, 324.
34. *CIO News* 2 (11 Sept. 1939): 7.
35. Genora Johnson Dollinger makes this point in *With Babies and Banners*. Also see the interview with Stella Nowicki in Lynd and Lynd, 83-84.
36. U.S. Department of Labor, Women's Bureau, *The Woman Wage Earner: Her Situation Today* by Elizabeth D. Benham, Bulletin no. 172 (Washington, D.C., 1939), 44; *Office and Professional News* 13 (December 1946): 4; Foner 2: 327, 329; "Stenos Strut," *CIO News* 2 (20 Feb. 1939): 3; and "Sweetheart of the CIO," *CIO News* 1 (6 Aug. 1938): 7.
37. Anne Prosten interview; "Regions Give 'All-Out' Aid to Organizing Drives," *Federal Record* 4 (3 Apr. 1941): 1.
38. Valerie Kincade Oppenheimer, *The Female Labor Force in the United States: Demographic and Economic Factors Governing its Growth and Changing Composition* (Westport, Conn.: Greenwood Press, 1976), 149.
39. Milkman, "Women's Work and the Economic Crisis," 530.
40. For a brief history of these unions see Sharon Hartman Strom, "Clerical Workers in the CIO, 1937-1950" (paper presented at the Society for the Study of Social Problems, San Francisco,3 Sept. 1978); and Jurgen Kocka, *White Collar Workers in America, 1890-1940: A Socio-Political History in International Perspective* (London and Beverly Hills: Sage Publications, 1980), 218-37.
41. Kocka, 20, 218-19, 226; Carl Dean Snyder, *White-Collar Workers and the UAW* (Urbana: University of Illinois Press, 1973); "Wage Cuts in Steel Offices Hit by Union," *Ledger* 4 (February 1938): 1, 8; "Union Grows in Rubber Company," *Office and Professional News* 6 (March-April 1940): 1; "Organizing the Unorganized White Collar Workers," *Career* 2 (15 Oct. 1949): 4.
42. Kocka, 224-25, 227, 230-31.
43. Nathan Glazer, *The Social Basis of American Communism* (New York: Harcourt, Brace & World, 1961), 116-17, 130. When Jessica Mitford worked in Washington for the Office of Price Administration during World War II, she assumed that joining the UFW would put her in touch with the CP (*A Fine Old Conflict* [New York: Knopf, 1977], 49). Len DeCaux, editor of the *CIO News*, said that the "new-type" leaders of white collar unions "differed little from the blue collars. Some college was common for all . . . many . . . were trained in the Communist movement as I knew it—a movement, that is, of militant unemployed; of Union pioneers before New Deal permitted or

CIO paid salaries; of rebels against corrupt inaction or reaction in AFL unions." See his *Labor Radical: From the Wobblies to CIO, A Personal History* (Boston: Beacon Press, 1970), 288-89.

44. For some sources that discuss the mechanization of clerical work, see Harvey Braverman, *Labor and Monopoly Capital: The Degradation of Work in the Twentieth Century* (New York and London: Monthly Review Press, 1974), 293-358; Coyle, "Women in the Clerical Occupations"; Erickson; C. Wright Mills, *White Collar: The American Middle Classes* (New York: Galaxy Paperback, 1956), 189-212; Orlie Pell, *The Office Worker—Labor's Side of the Ledger,* pamphlet published by the League for Industrial Democracy (New York, January 1937); and Strom, "Clerical Workers in the CIO."

45. Lewis Corey, *The Crisis of the Middle Class* (New York: Covici, Freide, 1935), 259; and Hans Speir, "The Salaried Employee in Modern Society," *Social Research* 1 (February 1934): 116-18. Also see J. Raymond Walsh, *C.I.O. Industrial Unionism in Action* (New York: W.W. Norton & Co., 1937), 148-155.

46. For instance, Joseph Starobin recalled that at a June 1945 meeting of the CP that a "Lew,"—certainly Lewis Merrill, president of the UOPWA—argued in favor of openly admitting membership in the party. However, as a representative of white collar workers party leaders felt his union was not among "the most crucial elements in the working class." See Starobin's *American Communism in Crisis, 1943-1957* (New York: Harvard University Press, 1972), 96-97.

47. Len DeCaux, "Unionizing the White Collared," *CIO News* 1 (21 May 1938): 4.

48. "Typewritten notes for speeches," circa 1936-40, Florence Luscomb Papers, Schlesinger Library, Cambridge, Massachusetts.

49. The UOPWA claimed 22,000 members and forty locals in 1937 out of an estimated white collar work force of four or five million. See "Merrill Article Shows White Collar Progress," *Ledger* 3 (November 1937): 5. By 1943 the UOPWA had 43,000 members and 118 locals. See Florence Peterson, *Handbook of Labor Unions* (Washington, D.C.: American Council on Public Affairs, 1934), 259.

50. Murray Nathan, "The Margon Strike," *Ledger* 2 (March 1936): 5-6; "Unity Pledged at Joint Rally," *Ledger* 2 (March 1936): 9; Murray Nathan, "The Margon Strike Continues," *Ledger* 3 (April 1936): 9.

51. Nathan, "Margon Strike."

52. "Union Recognized in Credit Firm. . . ," *Ledger* 3 (September 1937): 1; "Local 16 Pickets CCH by Telephone," *Office and Professional News* 6 (February 1940): 1, 3.

53. "Government Mediation Averts Credit House Strike," *Office and Professional News* 8 (11 Feb. 1942): 1.

54. "Local 16 Wins NLRB Poll in Oil Office by Two to One," *Office and Professional News* 7 (January 1941): 1; "Sonneborn Strikers Win Coast to Coast Support," and "Strikers Burned Up—Put Heat on Oil Company" 7 (February 1941): 1, 2, both in *Office and Professional News.*

55. "Strike Spirit Rises as Sonneborn Accounts Fall" (March 1941): 8; "Sonneborn Begins Talk in Strikes' 9th Week" (April 1941): 12; and "Local 16 Maps Changes in Sonneborn Strike" (May 1941): 8, all in *Office and Professional News.*

56. "Susie Steno Discovers the Union," *Ledger* 3 (June 1937): 6.

57. Harvey J. Clerment, *Organizing the Insurance Worker: A History of Labor Unions of Insurance Employees* (Washington, D.C.: Catholic University Press, 1966), 176; and Strom, "Clerical Workers in the CIO."

58. Ronald Schatz found that the women organizers of union locals at electrical plants in the thirties were even more likely than men to be children of radicals, socialists, or

union activists, although none had belonged to a union before joining the UE. They were also more likely than other female workers to come from female-headed households. See his "Union Pioneers: The Founders of Local Unions at General Electric and Westinghouse, 1933-37," *Journal of American History* 66 (December 1979): 586-602.

59. "Women's Group Set to Organize Office Workers," *New York Times*, 4 Mar. 1981: A12; "Women Clerical Workers and Trade Unionism," Interview with Karen Nussbaum, *Socialist Review* 10 (January-February 1980): 151-59.

60. See for instance, Gail Gregory Sansbury, "'Now, What's the Matter With You Girls?' Clerical Workers Organize," *Radical America* 14 (November-December 1980): 67-75; and the 1980 film *Willmar 8*, directed by Lee Grant, produced by Mary Beth Yarrow and Julie Thompson, and distributed by California Newsreel, 630 Natoma St., San Francisco, Calif. 94103.

HUMOR AND GENDER ROLES: THE "FUNNY" FEMINISM OF THE POST-WORLD WAR II SUBURBS

NANCY WALKER
Stephens College

BY NOW IT IS GENERALLY ACCEPTED THAT THE WOMEN'S MOVEMENT OF THE 1960s did not come into being overnight. The publication of *The Feminine Mystique* in 1963 provides a convenient watershed event, but Betty Friedan's book documents the fact that women's discontent with their narrowly prescribed roles had been brewing for some time, and a variety of studies has provided evidence that all was far from bucolic in the postwar suburbs to which middle-class women were consigned by societal expectations.[1] Although many women did not participate in the "back-to-the-kitchen" movement of the late 1940s and early 1950s, the prevailing ethic stressed woman's fulfillment as wife and mother. Resistance to this ethic found some overt expression in magazine articles,[2] but emerged more subtly in the popular art forms of the period, including film, fiction, and humor—particularly the humor created by popular women writers.

One study of the popular arts of the period is Brandon French's *On the Verge of Revolt* (1978), an analysis of the films of the 1950s. French points out that while the films of the World War II period reflected women's increased participation in

[1]See, among others, Molly Haskell, *From Reverence to Rape: The Treatment of Women in the Movies* (Baltimore: Penguin, 1974); Elizabeth Janeway, *Man's World, Woman's Place* (New York: Delta, 1971); Douglas T. Miller and Marion Nowak, *The Fifties: The Way We Really Were* (Garden City, N.Y.: Doubleday, 1977); Janice Radway, "The Utopian Impulse in Popular Literature; Gothic Romances and 'Feminist' Protest," *American Quarterly*, 33 (1981), 140–62.

[2]A fairly typical example is an article by Ann Leighton in a 1948 issue of *Harper's*, which begins:

> Kitchens, like wars, are planned around past crises, and men—never women—plan both. That men should plan wars, since they must be the first to go into them, is fair enough. Why they should also plan kitchens when they have no intention of entering them is not so clear. . . . Joy in a kitchen these days is as confined as the "matron" who cooks.

See "Back to *What* Kitchen?" *Harper's*, 196, April 1948, 356.

the work force, those of the 1950s reinforced the image of woman as the guardian of the domestic comfort and tranquility that Americans sought after the horrors of international conflict. Yet French stresses that an underlying theme of these films is women's uneasiness with this image:

> On the surface, fifties films promoted women's domesticity and inequality and sought easy, optimistic conclusions to any problems their fiction treated. But a significant number of movies simultaneously reflected, unconsciously or otherwise, the malaise of domesticity and the untenably narrow boundaries of the female role. By providing a double text, which contradicted itself without acknowledging any contradiction—that is, by imitating the culture's schizoid "double-think"—they documented the practical, sexual, and emotional transition women were undergoing beneath the threshold of the contemporary audience's conscious awareness.[3]

Another form of popular art that provides a contradictory "double text" for the postwar period is the domestic humor of American women. In popular humorous prose and light verse of the late 1940s and the 1950s, writers such as Phyllis McGinley, Jean Kerr, Margaret Halsey, Betty MacDonald, and Shirley Jackson made comic material of ordinary domestic life. These writers treated the subject of women as wives and mothers in a lighthearted way that conveyed an acceptance of the domestic role—even, as in the case of McGinley, celebrated its joys and mishaps. The exploits of children, pets, husbands; the chores of the domestic routine; interactions with neighbors and community groups—all are elevated by humorous treatment to a level of ideality that suggests a blissful, if not precisely peaceful, accommodation to the domestic role. Yet it would be wrong to take this image as a faithful depiction of the reality of women's lives. Below the surface of the humor are significant signs of restlessness and unease.

An immediate problem, of course, is the extent to which these writers could have hoped to present "reality." There seems to be a paradox, if not a duplicity, in accepting women such as McGinley, Jackson, and Kerr as representative of typical American housewives of the postwar period: their successful careers as writers make them by definition atypical. It is impossible to know how many readers of McGinley's light verse in *Good Housekeeping* realized that a woman who wrote regularly for a mass-circulation magazine was intricately involved in a world beyond the supermarket and the PTA, and was therefore not affected to the same extent as they by isolation and unfulfilled dreams; but Friedan, in *The Feminine Mystique*, is acutely aware of the paradox. Calling these humorists the "Housewife Writers," Friedman chides them for denying, in their *personae* as housewives, the "lives they lead, not as housewives, but as individuals." Even more important, Friedman says, is the way in which they mislead "real" housewives:

[3]Brandon French, *On the Verge of Revolt* (New York: Frederick Ungar, 1978), xxi.

> "Laugh," the Housewife Writers tell the real housewife, "if you are feeling desperate, empty, bored, trapped in the bed-making, chauffering [sic] and dishwashing details. Isn't it funny? We're all in the same trap." Do real housewives then dissipate in laughter their dreams and their sense of desperation? Do they think their frustrated abilities and their limited lives are a joke? Shirley Jackson makes the beds, loves and laughs at her son—and writes another book. Jean Kerr's plays are produced on Broadway. The joke is not on *them*.[4]

Though Friedan is correct in pointing out that the "Housewife Writers" could more easily afford to laugh than could their more restricted readers, she overlooks the fact that many of these writers struggled in both life and print with the tensions of career and home in ways that would have seemed quite familiar to many of their readers. Rather than telling the reader that her problems were not significant, these writers acknowledged them in both overt and covert ways in their humorous works. Perhaps the most succinct example of such acknowledgement in women's humor of the period occurs in Shirley Jackson's *Life Among the Savages* (1953). Entering the hospital for the birth of her third child, Jackson attempts to answer the receptionist's questions:

> "Age?" she asked. "Sex? Occupation?"
> "Writer," I said.
> "Housewife," she said.
> "Writer," I said.
> "I'll just put down housewife," she said.

At the end of the increasingly inane interrogation, the receptionist responds to Jackson's frustration by saying, "well, *really*, . . You're *only* having a baby."[5] This single conversation includes challenges to the significance of both Jackson's career and her motherhood; the receptionist represents a world unwilling accept the validity of woman's experience in either realm.

Just as women's experience has been frequently considered peripheral—even, often, by women themselves—so women's humor has seldom been studied for its underlying satiric intent. Scholars have acknowledged the sly, witty social satire of authors such as Jane Austen and Emily Dickinson, but the persistent distinction between "elite" and "popular" literature has precluded much study of social commentary in the work of writers whose apparent primary intention has been to amuse a mass audience of readers. In contrast to most of traditional (male) American humor, in which the central *persona* or narrator flaunts the standards of society—whether with ironic effect, like Huck Finn, or in fantasy, like the husband

[4]Betty Friedan, *The Feminine Mystique* (New York: Norton, 1963), 57.

[5]Shirley Jackson, *Life Among the Savages* (New York: Farrar, Straus and Young, 1953), 67–68. Subsequent references will appear in the text.

in Thurber's "The Unicorn in the Garden"—American women's humor commonly deals with the central (female) figure's attempt to meet or adhere to such standards. Whereas the male humorous figure, from Rip Van Winkle onward, seeks escape from the moral domination of women, the female figure in women's humor struggles vainly to live up to expectations for her behavior emanating from a culture dominated by men. Alfred Habegger, in *Gender, Fantasy, and Realism in American Literature* (1982), puts the matter plainly:

> The prevailing view of American humor is that it developed out of a kind of border warfare between two cultures, vernacular and refined. I am proposing an additional dialectic—between male and female. The social basis of American humor may have been the staggering difference in our ideal gender roles.[6]

The target or object in women's domestic humor of midcentury is usually the speaker (and, by autobiographical implication, the author) herself. The agent causing her sense of inferiority is suggested rather than named; the humor is directed inward at the self, not outward at a specific social evil. However, a sensitive reading of these works makes it clear that there are specific causes for these women's feelings of inferiority and uneasiness, located in social norms and attitudes that decreed woman's separate sphere. Even the editors of a 1934 anthology of women's humor speak in a tone of resignation about the origins of the humor they have collected: " . . . the angle of vision from which women see a lack of balance, wrong proportions, disharmonies, and incongruities in life is a thing of their world as it must be—a world always a little apart."[7] Because such humor deals with the day-to-day realities of women's lives rather than with large targets such as political corruption or human hypocrisy, it engages the reader at a more personal level and produces a response that is initially more emotional than intellectual.

The response to domestic humor may be said to occur in three stages: *recognition, sympathy,* and *assent*. Because the situations depicted in these works are familiar ones to most female readers, the reader first recognizes her own experience in the writer's account, however exaggerated or otherwise distorted for the purposes of humor. When, for example, Betty MacDonald bemoans her inability to accomplish more than cooking three meals a day, or Margaret Halsey describes the top of her husband's dresser as looking like "a plate of scrambled eggs,"

[6]Alfred Habegger, *Gender, Fantasy, and Realism in American Literature* (New York: Columbia Univ. Press, 1982), 125.

[7]Martha Bensley Bruère and Mary Ritter Beard, *Laughing Their Way: Women's Humor in America* (New York: Macmillan, 1934), viii. As an indication of the scant attention traditionally paid to women's humor, this anthology is the most recent to have as its specific purpose making available work by women rarely included in anthologies of humor.

the reader sees some aspect of her own experience reflected in the statement. Next, the humor itself invites sympathy: the writer's ability to make apparent fun of the situation engages the reader's respect and participation; humor becomes a strategy for coping with frustration, and the reader feels a bond with the writer who can simultaneously delineate and rise above a familiar, uncomfortable situation. Finally, and most important, the reader is subtly invited to agree with the writer about the source of the discomfort—to assent to the proposition that someone or something is at fault in a culture that isolates and trivializes women's experience. There is little way of knowing how actual readers of women's humor during the postwar period responded to either its overt or covert messages. It is safe to assume, however, that the primary readers were women rather than men—women who recognized the shape of their own daily lives in these accounts of domestic chaos and triviality. The apparent acceptance of such lives that is conveyed by the ability to laugh at their confusions lies thinly over a more meaningful subtext of protest. The necessity of the superficial geniality and the self-deprecation of such humor is illuminated by Martin Grotjahn in *Beyond Laughter*, written during this period:

> The woman of today is supposed to be warm, understanding, charming, attractive, passive, and accepting. She may show a sense of humor in her later years as a sign of maternal maturity; but she had better not show her wit too obviously if she is young and intelligent, for she will scare the contemporary male, who is easily frightened in his masculinity. She is permitted to have a sense of humor because it is an indication of her kindliness. Wit is decidedly not a sign of gentle love, but of undisguised hostility.[8]

The hostility in women's domestic humor is therefore muted, but it is undeniably present.

When we read women's humor of this era for both its explicit and implicit messages about women's role in society, we begin to see clearly the origins of some of the major themes of the women's movement of the 1960s. Despite their overt attempt to entertain the reader, women who wrote humor during this period made use of the various techniques of humor, including stereotype, hyperbole, deflation, and wit, to explore the problems of societal role definition. Underlying the cheerful surface of such popular works as MacDonald's *The Egg and I*, Kerr's *Please Don't Eat the Daisies*, and much of McGinley's verse is a contradictory current of uneasiness with the status quo—the isolation, the unrealistic expectations of women's lives, and male remoteness and domination.

The degree of the protest varies widely among these writers. MacDonald, in *The Egg and I*, openly deplores her situation as the wife of a would-be chicken rancher; at the other extreme is McGinley, whose *A Short Walk from the Station* is

[8]Martin Grotjahn, *Beyond Laughter* (New York: McGraw-Hill, 1957), 52.

announced as a defense of the suburban housewife's way of life. Yet the theme of isolation—even in what McGinley cheerfully describes as the "village of women"—the stereotypical image of the submissive woman who seems content and accomplished in her role, and an attitude toward men that combines awe and condescension are common to all the major female writers of humor from 1945 to 1960.

* * *

A discussion of isolation as a theme in the subtext of women's humor in the postwar period necessarily begins with Betty MacDonald's 1945 bestseller, *The Egg and I*. Not only was MacDonald one of the most accomplished and popular humorists of the era—*The Egg and I* also reveals the force of the social conditioning that caused women to be isolated not merely geographically, but also from any sense of real achievement. MacDonald's first comic novel thus prefigures the themes and techniques of that genre.[9] The narrator (a thin mask for MacDonald herself), following her mother's advice that "it is a wife's bounden duty to see that her husband is happy in his work," accompanies her chicken-rancher husband to "the Pacific Coast in the most untamed corner of the United States, with a ten-gallon keg of good whiskey, . . . and hundreds and hundreds of most uninteresting chickens."[10] The geographical remoteness of MacDonald's life is both a reminder of such nineteenth-century works as Caroline Kirkland's *A New Home*[11] and a precursor of the suburban sterility described by the writers of the 1950s. An example of the discomfort of MacDonald's isolation is "knowing that if I forgot to order matches I would darn well have to learn to rub two sticks together or walk four miles on the loneliest road in the world to a neighbor." She struggles to be self-sufficient, but finds that

> after nine months spent mostly in the company of the mountains, trees, the rain, Stove and the chickens, I would have swooned with anticipation at the prospect of a visit. . . . And if the clawing hands of civilization could only have run a few telephone and light wires in there they could have had my self-sufficient right arm to chop up for insulators (91–92).

[9] James D. Hart, in *The Popular Book* (Berkeley: Univ. of California Press, 1950), 267–68, attributes the overwhelming success of *The Egg and I* (more than a million copies were sold in the first two years) to a wave of late depression nostalgia for the rural life coupled with the book's reassuring message that "a return to nature could be even more irksome than an escape from it." This point is analogous to my contention that reading about the domestic trials of other women could make one's own complaints legitimate.

[10] Betty MacDonald, *The Egg and I* (Philadelphia: Lippincott, 1945), 11–12. Subsequent references will appear in the text.

[11] Caroline Kirkland, *A New Home–Who'll Follow? Glimpses of Western Life*, ed. William S. Osborne (1839; rpt. New Haven: College and University Press, 1965).

The isolation MacDonald describes is not only physical; more important is the emotional distance she feels from her husband, who has chosen this environment and who seems content with it. "He never seemed to be lonely, he enjoyed the work, he didn't make stupid blunders and then, of course, he wasn't pregnant" (93). The understatement of "he wasn't pregnant" both amuses us and reminds us of the separate realities of men's and women's lives. *The Egg and I* describes a classic pattern: the husband who enjoys the challenge of his work while the wife is left to cope with the routine tasks of household and children.

This contrast between husband and wife is at once a major source of the humor—in Habbeger's terms, the "staggering difference in . . . gender roles" —and an index of the female narrator's dissatisfaction with her position. The humor is often self-deprecatory, as when MacDonald describes the narrator's inability to take an egg from under a hen—a task her husband handles with ease—without becoming "a bundle of chittering hysteria with the hens in complete command." Self-deprecation is a major subversive device of the domestic humor of the 1940s and 1950s. By denigrating her own ability to live up to societal standards of domestic excellence, she appears to take the blame for her failure, and thus to accede to those standards; but the underlying message is that the standards—and those who seek to enforce them—are at fault. In the case of MacDonald's narrator, the agency of societal values has been transferred from her mother to her husband. In one passage in *The Egg and I* she describes the complete syndrome of the isolated wife. She begins with her excitement at her husband's return from town on Saturday afternoon, signaling the end of her lonely day. "How we reveled in those Saturday nights, smoking, eating, reading aloud and talking; unless, perhaps, as sometimes happened, I had forgotten to order kerosene." There follows the narrator's funny but frantic scramble to consolidate kerosene in one lamp and to coax light from the stubborn Stove (which is personified throughout to comic effect), but the scene ends on a sour note, thinly coated with wit:

> Bob was never one to scold, but he showed his disappointment in me by leaving the table still chewing his last bite and thrusting himself into bed, to dream, no doubt, of the good old days of wife beating (78).

The ultimate isolation is the silent disapproval, the mute renunciation of her efforts; and the hyperbole of "wife beating" at the end almost loses its comic force in the poignancy of the context.

In addition to the theme of isolation, *The Egg and I* also addresses the concept of woman's "proper role," both the subordination of female to male in the marital relationship and the gulf between the ideal of the perfect housewife and the frustrating reality of the individual woman's experience.[12] Surrounded by models of competence that she tries—and fails—to emulate, MacDonald's narrator is constantly aware that her being is defined by forces outside herself. The most immediate of these forces is her husband, whose exaggerated demands on her time and talents are treated with ironic humor. Early in their marriage, she realizes the limits of the role she is to play:

> "Who, me?" I asked when we were moving and Bob pointed casually to a large chest of drawers and said, "Carry that into the bedroom." "Who else?" he snapped and my lower lip began to tremble because I knew now that I was just a wife (50).

Yet instead of making the husband the object of the satire, MacDonald has her narrator respond to the realization that she is "just a wife" by attempting to become the perfect wife: "somewhere between a Grant Wood painting, an Old Dutch Cleanser advertisement and Mrs. Lincoln's cookbook" (71), but throughout *The Egg and I* MacDonald records the failure to live up to these ideals. The conditions of farm life are more primitive and rigorous than those of suburban existence, but in neither setting is there enough time to accomplish what seems required. Although Friedan stresses that housework expands to fill the time available for it, life on the farm, without suburban labor-saving devices, is truly demanding. Even so, MacDonald's narrator characteristically blames herself for never having enough time. "Obviously," she says, "something was wrong with my planning, for it took me sixteen hours a day to keep the stove going and three meals cooked." She continues:

> I leaped out of bed at 4 a.m., took two sips of coffee and it was eleven and time for lunch. I washed the lunch dishes and pulled a dead leaf off my kitchen geranium and it was five o'clock and time for dinner (68).

Though faced with tasks that would have given any pioneer woman pause, she locates the problem in her own inability to conform to the ideal of the "perfect wife."

The combination of isolation and frustrated ambition leads to the most telling

[12]This theme later became the source of much of the humor in television situation comedies, notably in "I Love Lucy." Though the use of female incompetence as a staple of popular comedy has long made feminists uncomfortable, the motives for using it may vary widely. Whereas in situation comedies—until recently written and produced almost exclusively by men—the woman who cannot cope is a stock slapstick character, in women's humorous fiction, such as *The Egg and I*, the depiction embodies a rejection of rigid standards of performance.

evidence of imminent rebellion in postwar domestic humor: resentment against men—typically husbands—who are not subject to the same restrictions. In *The Egg and I* this resentment is expressed more openly than it is in the humor of the 1950s, but it takes the same form: men are at once heroic and pitiable, capable of great feats and yet oddly childlike. The female narrator's distance from the actual lives of men—the rigid codifying of men's and women's separate responsibilities—causes her to regard her husband as an occasional visitor in her world: sometimes helpful, often merely annoying. Though Bob, the husband in *The Egg and I*, is not the absent and often nameless commuting businessman of suburban humor, his attitudes about "women's work" are similarly traditional in the extreme, and are exemplified by his insistence that she scrub the kitchen floor daily. "It was a badge of fine housekeeping," says the narrator with heavy irony, "a labor of love and a woman's duty to her husband" (75). Not only does Bob think in such clichés about housework; he is also incapable of helping with it. When the narrator, for example, announces on Monday morning that she plans to do a "HUGE ENORMOUS washing," he obligingly goes to the spring for water and brings back "about four tablespoonfuls in the bottom of each bucket" (69). The narrator's tone, here as elsewhere, is one of incredulity: Bob, in her view, becomes childishly inept when he enters her realm of household tasks.

By the end of *The Egg and I*, the serious rift between the narrator and her husband all but obscures the humor of their chicken-ranch experiences. They sit waiting for a babysitter, uneasy with their own silence, "like neighbors who suddenly find themselves in a hotel bedroom together" (285).[13] While this obvious marital tension is uncommon in domestic humor—precisely because its seriousness interferes with the light tone that such humor requires—MacDonald's acknowledgement of emotional distance, as well as her forthright complaints about the rigid role definition to which she is subject, provide more than a hint of dissatisfaction with being "just a wife." The feelings she expresses did not disappear as the postwar period continued; instead, they merely became more and more hidden beneath a humorous façade as the scene switched to the suburban version of the American Dream.

* * *

By the early 1950s, suburban existence had become an established fact of middle-class American life, and the voice of protest in women's humor became

[13]By the time of MacDonald's next book, *Anybody Can Do Anything* (Philadelphia: Lippincott, 1960), she is divorced from the "Bob" of *The Egg and I* and is making her way as a single woman with two children in Seattle. In this, an unfortunately neglected work by MacDonald, the latent feminist protest of *The Egg and I* becomes overt as she encounters sexist discrimination as a member of the work force.

more subtle as larger numbers of women were persuaded that suburban living held the promise of the "good life." Between 1950 and 1960, the population in the suburbs surrounding America's major cities increased forty-seven percent, and in one study, women asked for their "principal aspiration" in moving to a suburban area responded overwhelmingly (seventy-eight percent) that they wished to improve the quality of their home lives; as one woman put it, to better fulfill the "normal family role, being a homemaker."[14] In keeping with the prevailing values of the day, Phyllis McGinley's sixth book of light verse, *A Short Walk From the Station* (1951), is ostensibly a defense of life—particularly women's lives—in Westchester County. She acknowledges that suburbia has already become a cliché for many writers:

> I have yet to read a book in which the suburban life was pictured as the good life or the commuter as a sympathetic figure. He is usually as much a stock character as the old stage Irishman: the man who "spends his life riding to and from his wife," the eternal Babbit who knows all about Buicks and nothing about Picasso, whose sanctuary is the club locker room, whose ideas spring ready-made from the illiberal newspapers. His wife plays politics at the P.T.A. and keeps up with the Joneses. Or . . . [she is] a restless baggage given to too many cocktails in the afternoon.[15]

McGinley's declared intention is to defend her world against those who see it as a "congregation of mindless housewives and amoral go-getters," particularly by detailing the accomplishments of her neighboring women: one is a novelist, one teaches ballet, another paints portraits. The unhappy women described by the suburban clichés may exist here, too, McGinley acknowledges, but she dismisses them: "Let them. Our orbits need not cross" (18–20). At the same time, however, she describes the isolation of women's suburban life. "By day," she says, "it is a village of women. They trundle mobile baskets at the A & P, they sit under driers at the hairdressers, they sweep their porches and set out bulbs and stitch up slip-covers" (10). The high point of the day is meeting the train from the city, a moment that is "delightfully ritualistic": "The women move over from the driver's seat, surrender the keys, and receive an absent-minded kiss." Skipping briskly through this language of submissiveness, McGinley remarks coyly, "It is the sort of picture that wakes John Marquand screaming from his sleep" (21).

Yet many of the descriptions of women in *A Short Walk From the Station* depict satirically the pointlessness of women's isolated lives, and form a compelling subtext to McGinley's sturdy defense of the suburbs. In one poem after another she

[14]Sheila M. Rothman, *Woman's Proper Place* (New York: Basic Books, 1978), 224–25.

[15]Phyllis McGinley, *A Short Walk From the Station* (New York: Viking, 1951), 12–13. Subsequent references will appear in the text.

describes shallow, petty existences in the "village of women." In "Beauty Parlor," the women discuss operations, read movie magazines, and order sandwiches; the only decision one is confronted with is "whether to dapple/Her nails with Schoolhouse Red or Stolen Apple" (83). In "Lending Library" a woman selects bestsellers not for their literary merit, but so that she may "join in without arrears/The literary prattle of her peers" (87). The figure in "Hostess" is bent on keeping her guests busy with party games, lest "The scotched snake, Thought, should rear its venomed head" (98). The most sharply satiric portrait of the isolated, unhappy woman is "Executive's Wife," which, after sketching the woman's affluent setting, ends with the lines:

> She often says she might have been a painter,
> Or maybe writer; but she married young.
> She diets. And with Contract she delays
> The encroaching desolation of her days (79).[16]

These sketches prove the existence of those women whose "orbits" McGinley has chosen not to cross; however content she may seem in Westchester County, her verse makes clear that she perceives women's discontent in their suburban remoteness. That McGinley herself may have experienced some isolation in the suburban setting that she overtly glorifies is strongly suggested by the tone of "The 5:32," a poem celebrating the arrival of husbands from the city. At "This hour best of all the hours I knew," she describes "a man coming toward me, smiling, the evening paper/Under his arm" (88). It is clear that no matter how fulfilling McGinley would like to think the hours with hairdryers and slipcovers have been, only the eventual presence of men redeems the isolation of women in suburban settings.

If Phyllis McGinley reveals ambivalence about the suburbs as meaningful places for women to live, Margaret Halsey was far more convinced of their aridity. In the ironically titled *This Demi-Paradise: A Westchester Diary* (1960), Halsey uses the cover of humor to condemn the conformity and lack of purpose that she also treated seriously in several works of social criticism during the same period.[17] Halsey is the sort of neighbor McGinley would use as an example of the vital, engaged woman who disproves the suburban cliché; Halsey, in turn, feels remote from the women around her. At the supermarket she describes "the housewives of Suburbia . . . lined up like cows at milking time—patient, not visibly expectant,

[16]Perhaps significantly, the title of this poem was changed to the more general "Occupation: Housewife" in McGinley's selected poems. See *Times Three* (New York: Viking, 1961), 135.

[17]Margaret Halsey, *Some of My Best Friends are Soldiers* (New York: Simon and Schuster, 1944); Halsey, *Color Blind: A White Woman Looks at the Negro* (New York: Simon and Schuster, 1946); Halsey, *The Folks at Home* (New York: Simon and Schuster, 1952); and Halsey, *The Pseudo-Ethic* (New York: Simon and Schuster, 1963).

the carts with food piled in rounded pyramids suggesting udders upside down."[18] Intellectually and politically involved, she works with the PTA and the Brownies with more or less enthusiasm, but is always conscious of her difference from those around her. To the female members of the PTA program committee she is a "sort of 'clean' Vincent Van Gogh":

> Nobody entertains any serious apprehensions about my cutting off an ear; but the floors in my house are scuffed, stained and innocent of wax (they have carpets only in the center, and not always there) and I will tolerate anything on them except prostrate drunks. If that is not the sign of a mad genius, what is (65–66).

When visited by a pollster who represents all that is standardized and unimaginative in the middle-class world, Halsey "felt that twinge of loneliness I get when I again become aware that the world is full of nothing but engineers and electronics experts—whereas I want it to be full of people who majored in English" (25). Blandness extends even to the church she attends, a formerly "liberal" congregation now headed by a minister she calls "Dr. Aspirin," with a "low-calorie, salt-free, modern, liberal Sunday school" for her daughter. (11–13).

Halsey's stance as the remote, somewhat condescending intellectual living amidst dull mediocrity is quite different from McGinley's apparent defense of the suburban commitment to domesticity for women, and their differences place them at opposite ends of the spectrum of domestic humor. On a superficial level, McGinley endorses the majority view of women's "proper sphere": it is only in her satire that the spector of loneliness, of "desolation," emerges and the double message becomes clear.[19] Even in an apparently innocuous poem such as "P.T.A. Tea Party," McGinley describes a ritual that has become boring and meaningless. Instead of evincing an active concern for the education of their children, the women admire each others' hats and listen to listless reports. The teachers arrive apprehensively, expecting sharp questions, but find that the afternoon "droops/To smile and sip and talk of Hobby Groups" (77). Even the eagerly awaited husbands can be disappointing. In "Country Club Sunday" McGinley describes another ritual, one which shows the very image of suburban life she has overtly rejected. In the midst of a bucolic scene, for which McGinley alters Wordsworth's line to create the initial irony—"It is a beauteous morning, calm and free"—the reality of male-female relationships emerges:

[18]Margaret Halsey, *This Demi-Paradise: A Westchester Diary* (New York: Simon and Schuster, 1960), 2. Subsequent references will appear in the text.

[19]McGinley herself tired of the image of cozy domesticity her work so often conveyed. In a *Newsweek* interview in 1960, she said, "I'm so sick of this 'Phyllis McGinley, suburban housewife and mother of two.' . . . That's only an eighth or a tenth of my work. . . . There's a hell of a lot of straight social criticism." See "The Lady in Larchmont," *Newsweek*, 56, 26 Sept. 1960, 121.

Nothing remains of last night's Summer Formal
Save palms and streamers and the wifely glance,
Directed with more watchfulness than normal,
At listless mate who tugs his necktie loose,
Moans, shuns the light, and gulps tomato juice (75).

Although Halsey is the more obvious satirist, she and McGinley share a basic perception that women's existence in the suburbs is arid and unfulfilling.

Further uniting the two writers, and forming a continuous thread in women's domestic humor, is their resistance to the ideal of the perfect wife and mother. The ideal is promulgated in part by the media—for example, MacDonald's Old Dutch Cleanser advertisement—and in part by the examples of other women: neighbors in *The Egg and I* and the committee women who disapprove of Halsey's scuffed floors. While Friedan blamed women's magazines for endorsing the image of the "Happy Housewife Heroine,"[20] the humorists of the postwar period concentrated their subversive attack on the women who represented perfection in the domestic role: neighbors, friends, or acquaintances who managed households and children with ease and equanimity are presented as more potent forces affecting women's sense of their proper function.[21] Halsey's next-door neighbor in *This Demi-Paradise* is reminiscent of MacDonald's Mrs. Hicks. She wears so tight a girdle that, "seen from the rear, she looks like a tongue depressor," and is "the kind of housekeeper who washes the mailbox and scrubs the outside of the front door" (81). In Jean Kerr's *Please Don't Eat the Daisies* (1957), there is the woman "of unusually strong character who selected a college for her son in a single afternoon and who has always been able to plan a dinner for sixteen in five minutes."[22] These are the women against whom the domestic humorists measure themselves and find themselves wanting; they are regarded with envy and resentment because they embody the ideal of womanhood in the popular imagination.

Descriptions of the author's (or narrator's) own ineptitude in the domestic role constitute a substantial part of postwar domestic humor. It is here that the writer seeks identification with the reader, who feels reassured that one so famous as, say, Shirley Jackson occasionally makes a mess of things. Yet beneath the uproarious surface of domestic chaos—always stopping short of actual disaster or tragedy—is the suggestion that the repetition and trivialization of experience wear away at one's dignity. In *Life Among the Savages*, Shirley Jackson is openly defensive. Having detailed a morning spent washing diapers, cooking, and taking care of two small children, Jackson adds parenthetically, "and I don't care what *any*one says, that's a morning's work" (2). The "anyone" here is one who would call her "just a housewife," as the hospital receptionist does; more frequently, the

[20] Friedan, *The Feminine Mystique*.

[21] The choice of people rather than media as the target of satire depends also, of course, on their traditional potential for comic effect. We should not lose sight of the fact that Jackson, Kerr, and McGinley wrote for many of the major women's magazines during the period, and were unlikely to satirize their employers.

[22] Jean Kerr, *Please Don't Eat the Daisies* (Garden City, N.Y.: Doubleday, 1957), 54.

writer is comparing herself to the ideal housewife. In *The Snake Has All the Lines* (1960), Jean Kerr addresses this point hyperbolically when she cannot find anything suitable for her children's lunches:

> Another woman could make a tasty sandwich spread by mixing evaporated milk and mayonnaise with some curry powder. But I lack the dash for this kind of experimentation. For that matter I lack the curry powder, and—what is more to the point—I lack qualities of leadership. Yes, I do. I'm an unfit mother and a rotten housekeeper, as shiftless and improvident as a character out of *God's Little Acre*.[23]

Margaret Halsey, as "cookie chairman" of her daughter's Girl Scout troop, fantasizes about being unequal to the task and coming up short when the money is collected. "I could see the drumhead court-martial and the stern-faced women in field green. I could see the little back room where they left me with a revolver and a bottle of brandy" (57). Domestic humor is filled with spilled milk, dripping faucets, measles, empty refrigerators—and with women who cannot cope with it all, whose distance from perfection leads them to the hyperbole of failure.

Nor are husbands much help. The typical husband in domestic humor is a somewhat remote figure who is involved only minimally in the day-to-day operation of the household. He is seen getting off a commuter train, puttering in the garden on weekends, and occasionally attending social functions. Relationships between husbands and wives vary widely in these works—Betty MacDonald and her husband are on the brink of divorce, while Margaret Halsey's husband is sometimes pictured as warmly supportive—but men are characteristically viewed as either distant gods or curiously inept children. The humorists adhere to clear, stereotypical distinctions between the talents of male and female, as in the following quatrain by McGinley:

> A lady is smarter than a gentleman, maybe.
> She can sew a fine seam, she can have a baby.
> She can use her intuition instead of her brain.
> But she can't fold a paper on a crowded train.[24]

On the surface, the poem is a tribute to the digital aptitude of the male of the species, coupled with an acknowledgement that the man's world is the world of travel, movement, and news. Yet on another level the message is heavily ironic: the act of folding a newspaper is clearly trivial compared to having a child or making a garment, and the male accomplishment is thus diminished. When men are viewed as having exceptional prowess, as is sometimes the case when machinery is involved, their apparent mastery is another occasion for women to exercise self-deprecation. Usually, as in the following excerpt from *Life Among the Savages*, the writer's hyperbole betrays the fact that she is writing for this effect:

[23]Jean Kerr, *The Snake Has All the Lines* (Garden City, N.Y.: Doubleday, 1960), 89.
[24]McGinley, "Trial and Error," *A Short Walk From the Station*, 130.

> I am wholeheartedly afraid of fuses and motorcycles and floor plugs and lightning rods and electric drills and large animals and most particularly of furnaces. Laboriously, over the space of years of married life, my husband has taught me to use such hazardous appliances as a toaster and an electric coffee pot, but no one is ever going to get me to go down cellar and fool around with a furnace (148).

In "Apology for Husbands" McGinley says she is pleased that "He layeth rugs, he fixeth sockets,/He payeth bills from both his pockets."

Yet the true tone of McGinley's "Apology"—and the dominant attitude toward men in domestic humor—is revealed in the final stanza:

> What gadget's useful as a spouse?
> Considering that a minute,
> Confess that every proper house
> Should have a husband in it.[25]

The concept of the husband as an object, a "gadget," is condescending in the extreme. This excerpt from Kerr's *The Snake Has All the Lines* is perhaps the most blunt of all:

> But, charming as men are, we can't sit here and pretend they're perfect. It wouldn't be good for them and it wouldn't be true. Marrying a man is like buying something you've been admiring for a long time in a shop window. You may love it when you get it home, but it doesn't always go with everything else in the house (121).

Kerr goes on to note that a man seems incapable of filling a salt shaker or remembering "a simple fact like what size shirt he takes, or what grade Gilbert is in" (122). The husband's distance from the day-to-day operation of the household leads to his inability to be helpful or supportive in this realm. The wife must therefore take responsibility for all areas of household maintenance and child care, and her resentment at this burden often causes her to view her husband as one more child to be cared for. Even his accomplishments may be seen as those of a child. In "Volunteer Fireman," McGinley describes her husband as "A boy of forty who has skimmed the cream/From childhood's first and most enduring dream" (85).

This condescending attitude—similar, one must note, to the attitude toward women in much of male humor—seems almost certainly to be born of resentment. Isolated from much of the world and pressured to conform to ideal standards of domestic performance, the personae of postwar domestic humor adopt, for the purposes of humor, the stance of the cheerfully beleaguered. The overt message

[25]McGinley, *Times Three*, 261.

embodies acceptance of the role society has assigned; daily life is presented as an elaborate game with the woman as the perpetually amused loser—defeated, smiling, by a world that constantly demands more than she can handle. Yet beneath the façade of the humor is a serious challenge to societal expectations. The other half of the double text conveys severe discontent with the status quo, a discontent that emerges most clearly in the depiction of men. Men are not the enemy; the enemy, if there is one at all, is the woman who is apparently fulfilled by the domestic routine. Men are more nearly extraneous to the "real" lives of women; their experiences outside the home are so remote as to seem nonexistent, and their lives within the orbit of the home are trivial, insignificant, or mysterious. This complete separation of the lives of women and men might lead the writers to seek identity with other women, but when such closeness is effectively precluded by competition among women for societal sanction, the isolation is complete. In a telling passage in *This Demi-Paradise*, Margaret Halsey says:

> the thoughts of the housewife are long, long thoughts; and the lonely hours of cutting down bedspreads into cafe curtains or cooking up things for the freezer against company coming next week are often filled with fantasies and speculations. Some of these fantasies and speculations would cause the males of the society, could they know about them, considerable alarm in behalf of the status quo (179–80).

Although it would be far too strong to call the domestic humor of the 1950s a rallying cry for the feminist movement of the 1960s, it is safe to say that the female humorists of the period knew about—and often experienced—the sense of impotence and futility that pervaded women's lives. By treating these lives humorously, they were able to do two things. On a conscious level, they provided a safe, noncontroversial acknowledgment of the frustrations and limitations of the domestic experience for women, and thus provided readers with a safety valve for those feelings. Yet on a more important level, the humor expresses a hostility toward rigid role definition that prefigures the issues of the women's movement, and demonstrates once again that the movement was an inevitable part of a social continuum, with a broad base of support.

Despite the superficial approval that humor seems to bestow on its subject matter—in this case, the domestic lives of women in the postwar era—the principle of inversion on which humor works prompts us to consider the extent to which women's humor of this period provided an acceptable means of venting frustration for both writer and reader. Rather than, as Friedan suggests, offering merely a false panacea of laughter, women's domestic humor can be viewed as evidence of increasing hostility against societal expectations. Seen in this way, the humor is subversive—even if not consciously so—and provides a text for the actual concerns of middle-class women during this period.

The Women's Community in the National Woman's Party, 1945 to the 1960s

Leila J. Rupp

In the 1940s and 1950s, being a feminist in the United States could be an isolating experience. Postwar pleading for women's return to home and kitchen, an onslaught of advertising that sold women the feminine mystique, thunderous denunciations of feminists as neurotic and dangerous—all these factors conspired to keep women in their place. At the same time, however, women (even white, married, middle-class women) were moving steadily into the paid labor force; indeed, perhaps conservative admonitions came in response to this trend.[1] Yet while women's movement toward employment outside the home gradually undermined traditional notions of the proper societal division of labor, some women

Research for this essay was made possible by a research grant from the Ohio State University Graduate School for 1978–79; a one-quarter research leave from the Ohio State University College of Humanities in 1979; a fellowship from the Radcliffe Research Scholars Program for 1979–80; and a Basic Research Grant (RO-*0703-81) from the National Endowment for the Humanities awarded to me jointly with Verta Taylor for 1981–83. This essay is part of a larger collaborative study of the American women's movement from 1945 to the 1960s that Verta Taylor and I are currently completing. I am greatly indebted to her for many of the ideas developed here since this essay was written in the context of our collaborative work. Her contributions are so central that any acknowledgment is woefully inadequate. I would also like to thank all the women who participated in the Communities of Women conference for their comments and, more generally, for their inspiration and sense of community.

1. On labor force and demographic trends that created the context for feminist activity in this period, see Leila J. Rupp, "The Survival of American Feminism: The Women's Movement in the Postwar Period," in *Reshaping America: Society and Institutions, 1945–1960*, ed. Robert H. Bremner and Gary W. Reichard (Columbus: Ohio State University Press, 1982), pp. 33–65.

[*Signs: Journal of Women in Culture and Society* 1985, vol. 10, no. 4]

continued to attack directly the ideology of woman's place. Many of these women belonged to the National Woman's Party—the only nationwide self-proclaimed feminist organization in this period—within which they formed a community based on shared history, common beliefs, commitment to feminist goals, cooperative feminist activities, and friendship. This essay, based on the papers of individuals and those of organizations and on interviews with feminists from the period, explores the women's community within the National Woman's Party by describing and analyzing the factors that held the community together and by considering the impact of community building on feminist activism. It suggests that this community both enabled feminists to maintain their commitment in a hostile environment and limited the possibilities for recruitment to and growth of the organization. The relationship of community and activism—the tension between maintenance of and recruitment to an organization—remains an important issue for the women's movement, and thus this analysis of an earlier stage of the women's movement offers historical context for the contemporary movement.

Although historians assume that there was no feminist activism in the 1940s and 1950s, the National Woman's Party continued to devote itself exclusively to improving the status of women throughout this period. It fought for passage of the Equal Rights Amendment (ERA) by garnering support from other women's organizations, lobbying Congress and the president, and seeking publicity for the constitutional amendment. The National Woman's Party originated as the militant branch of the suffrage movement in the first decade of the twentieth century. Adopting the tactics of the British suffragettes, Woman's Party members picketed the White House, chained themselves to the White House fence, and protested U.S. involvement in the First World War, pointing out that Americans could not "make the world safe for democracy" while denying half of the population the vote.[2] Never popular with the mainstream suffragists of the National American Woman Suffrage Association, from whom the militants broke away, the Woman's Party set itself further apart from other groups in the women's movement in the years immediately after the suffrage victory. Rejecting all other proposals for a feminist program, the Woman's Party, under the firm direction of founder Alice Paul, launched a campaign for the ERA in 1923 and doggedly pursued the goal of legal

2. On the early years of the National Woman's Party, see Inez Haynes Irwin, *The Story of Alice Paul and the National Woman's Party* (1921; reprint, Fairfax, Va.: Denlinger's Publishers, 1977); and Doris Stevens, *Jailed for Freedom* (1920; reprint, New York: Schocken Books, 1976), both written by participants. See also Eleanor Flexner, *Century of Struggle*, rev. ed. (Cambridge, Mass.: Belknap Press, 1975); Amelia R. Fry, "The Divine Discontent: Alice Paul and Militancy in the Suffrage Campaign" (paper presented at the Berkshire Conference of Women Historians, Vassar College, 1981); and Aileen Kraditor, *The Ideas of the Woman Suffrage Movement, 1890–1920* (New York: Columbia University Press, 1965).

equality in the years that followed. This course of action guaranteed the isolation of the organization, for at first every other women's organization opposed the ERA out of the conviction that it would eliminate the protective legislation for women for which feminists and reformers had fought so hard.

The lines were drawn: on one side the Woman's Party, gradually joined by other women's organizations, insisting that protective laws in fact discriminated against women by keeping them out of desirable jobs; on the other, the vast majority of organized women who denounced the Woman's Party and its slowly growing list of allies as wealthy and privileged women with no concern for the oppressed working women who needed protection to survive. By the mid-1920s, the long-standing split between movement women who fought for women's rights as an inherently desirable goal and those who saw their fight as part of a struggle for general reform had widened into an irreconcilable conflict. Symbolic of the split, the National American Woman Suffrage Association transformed itself into a nonpartisan citizen education organization, the League of Women Voters, and aligned with other women's organizations in opposition to the ERA. Throughout the interwar years the conflict-ridden women's movement cooperated on some goals—such as guaranteeing independent citizenship for women married to citizens of other nations, eliminating discrimination against employed married women during the Depression, and opening jury service for women—but the various organizations spent more time fighting each other than joining forces.[3]

In this context, the National Woman's Party dwindled in size and effectiveness throughout the years. Both suffrage organizations lost a large percentage of membership after 1920, but the Woman's Party lost even some of its most active members when it turned its attention to the ERA. Socialists like Crystal Eastman and Florence Kelley left when Alice Paul set the organization's course in the 1920s. At the end of the Second

3. On the women's movement in the post-1920 years, see Susan D. Becker, *The Origins of the Equal Rights Amendment: American Feminism between the Wars* (Westport, Conn.: Greenwood Press, 1981); William H. Chafe, *The American Woman: Her Changing Social, Economic, and Political Roles, 1920–1970* (New York: Oxford University Press, 1972); Nancy F. Cott, "Feminist Politics in the 1920s," *Journal of American History* 71, no. 1 (1984): 43–68; Peter Geidel, "The National Woman's Party and the Origins of the Equal Rights Amendment, 1920–1923," *Historian* 42, no. 4 (1980): 557–82; Susan M. Hartmann, "Women's Organizations during World War II: The Interaction of Class, Race and Feminism," in *Woman's Being, Woman's Place*, ed. Mary Kelley (Boston: G. K. Hall & Co., 1979), pp. 313–28; J. Stanley Lemons, *The Woman Citizen: Social Feminism in the 1920s* (Urbana: University of Illinois Press, 1973); Marjory Nelson, "Ladies in the Streets: A Sociological Analysis of the National Woman's Party, 1910–1930" (Ph.D. diss., State University of New York at Buffalo, 1976); Lois Scharf, *To Work and to Wed: Female Employment, Feminism, and the Great Depression* (Westport, Conn.: Greenwood Press, 1980).

World War, the Woman's Party claimed about four thousand members, six hundred of whom paid annual dues; by the 1960s, the general membership had dropped to around fourteen hundred.[4] Although it is clear that the Woman's Party existed in a declining state throughout the years after 1945, the small membership never troubled Alice Paul, for she had always envisaged the organization as an elite vanguard that would show the way for other women's organizations rather than as a mass-membership group. As older members died, few young women replaced them in the ranks. But the Woman's Party leadership never lost confidence in its ability to pass the ERA, and the fact that Congress first voted on the measure in 1946 and considered the measure again in the 1950s served to confirm this view.[5]

I focus here on the post-1945 period for two reasons. First, the period from 1945 to the mid-1960s was especially inhospitable to feminism. The atmosphere of conformity, shaped by the Cold War and McCarthyism, meant for women the primacy of the "feminine mystique." The end of the Second World War brought an antifeminist backlash that labeled feminist protest a sign of emotional instability and neurosis.[6] Thus feminist survival, never easy in the best of times, presented particularly interesting challenges in this period. Second, although scholars have begun to explore the endurance of feminism in the years between the two world wars, the assumption that the women's movement was dead by 1945 has held. Therefore the persistence of a small and anachronistic band of feminists, who kept alive a commitment to women's rights and carried the ERA from the 1920s to the 1960s, takes on significance for our view of the movement's historical continuity.[7]

Who were these women who clung to their feminist beliefs in a period characterized, both then and now, as an era of contented domesticity?[8]

4. Membership Committee Report to Credentials Committee," August 1945, National Woman's Party Papers (NWP), reel 87; "Membership List," December 1947, NWP Papers, reel 92; "Active Memberships," December 15, 1947, NWP Papers, reel 126; "NWP Numerical State Membership List," [August 1964], NWP Papers, reel 126; "Members in Each State," [1965], NWP Papers, reel 126. The NWP Papers have been microfilmed and distributed by the Microfilming Corporation of America.

5. See Susan Louise Randall, "A Legislative History of the Equal Rights Amendment, 1923–1960" (Ph.D. diss., University of Utah, 1979).

6. On the antifeminist backlash, see Rupp, pp. 40–43; and Betty Friedan, *The Feminine Mystique* (New York: Dell Publishing Co., 1963).

7. On the continuity particularly of the British women's movement, see Olive Banks, *Faces of Feminism: A Study of Feminism as a Social Movement* (Oxford: Martin Robertson, 1981), and Dale Spender, *There's Always Been a Women's Movement This Century* (London: Pandora Press, 1983). The concept of continuity is one that will be explored more fully in the book Verta Taylor and I are writing together.

8. This general profile of the membership is based on a careful reading of the organization's papers, particularly correspondence, from 1945 on. Although it was not possible to determine the social characteristics of the majority of members, I recorded age; time of first

The most striking characteristic of the National Woman's Party membership in the period of the 1940s and 1950s was age. The most active women were those who had gotten involved in the women's movement in the early years of the twentieth century, particularly in the last years of the suffrage struggle. Few members were young, and women in their fifties, sixties, and seventies predominated.

Almost all the members were white. The only black member I have been able to identify was Mary Church Terrell, founder of the National Association of Colored Women, who fought to integrate the Washington, D.C., chapter of the American Association of University Women in the 1940s. Women of color in this period tended to organize in their own groups or in mixed-gender organizations like the National Association for the Advancement of Colored People in part because of racism in white women's organizations, manifested in outright exclusion as well as lack of concern for the issues of paramount importance to women of color.

Although it is impossible to be precise about the class composition of the membership, it is clear that most women were by birth, marriage, or occupation middle or upper class. A few working-class women did participate in the Woman's Party, but they were rare. Elitism, lack of concern with issues affecting working-class or poor women, and the need for sufficient funds to be active in the organization militated against the participation of working-class or low-income women. Most members were well educated, usually holding a college degree, and most were employed in professional positions. Many were unmarried or widowed. In a period during which a larger proportion of women than ever before was married, it was not at all uncommon for Woman's Party members, some of whom lived in couple relationships with other women, to be unmarried.

One final characteristic of the membership is important here. Members did not come predominantly from one political party, nor did they all share a common political outlook. Women prominent in both the Republican and the Democratic parties worked together without setting aside their own partisan commitments. Some women were liberals active in a variety of progressive causes, while others held right-wing views on everything from race relations to McCarthyism. In other words, membership in the Woman's Party had little relationship to an individual's general political views; women who agreed about little else put aside their differences to work together on women's issues.

---

involvement in the women's movement; and any information related to race, class, education, occupation, political affiliation, political views, marital status, and living situation for individual women wherever I encountered it. In addition, I took note of any comments members made about the nature of the membership. The profile that emerged from the NWP Papers matched that drawn by both Becker and Nelson.

The National Woman's Party membership constituted, then, a relatively homogeneous group, and this facilitated the creation of a community within the organization. The centrality of community does not mean, however, that the organization was free of conflict. On the contrary, in 1947 a major controversy escalated into a legal battle over the name, leadership, and resources of the party, contributing to the loss of membership and diverting members' time and energy away from feminist activities. What was at issue was Alice Paul's leadership—which the rebel group denounced as dictatorial—and the nature of the organization as an elite vanguard. The rebels wanted to oust Paul and expand membership, and they took to the courts to achieve their ends. Paul and her associates won the lawsuits, and the leaders of the rebel group resigned. The issues were raised again a few years later in a less dramatic way by the national chairman, who also lost her battle and resigned. The 1947 schism not only contributed to the decline in membership but also made the leadership suspicious and inclined to shut the door against new members. In this way, the conflict reinforced the centrality of community for the remaining members. For those who remained loyal to Alice Paul, the schism indicated how serious conflict could become in a close-knit community and confirmed how essential community was to feminist survival.

Despite the conflict, the Woman's Party functioned throughout the years after 1945 as much as a women's community as it did as a political organization lobbying for the ERA.[9] Community had always been central to women's political organizing. Thomas Dublin, for example, has shown how important the solidarity fostered by boardinghouse life was to labor protest in the Lowell mills in the early nineteenth century.[10] Blanche Cook argues for the significance of female support networks to the political activism of such women as settlement-house worker Lillian Wald, socialist Crystal Eastman, and anarchist Emma Goldman.[11] Susan Ware describes the friendship network that made political activity possible for women New Dealers in the 1930s.[12] Estelle Freedman has suggested that female institutions are central in keeping the women's movement alive; her argument about the necessity of separatism rests implicitly on the importance of women's communities in women's colleges, settlement houses,

9. In her sociological analysis of the early Woman's Party, Nelson emphasizes community, which she terms "subculture."

10. Thomas Dublin, *Women at Work: The Transformation of Work and Community in Lowell, Massachusetts, 1826–1860* (New York: Columbia University Press, 1979).

11. Blanche Wiesen Cook, "Female Support Networks and Political Activism: Lillian Wald, Crystal Eastman, Emma Goldman," *Chrysalis*, no. 3 (1977), pp. 43–61.

12. Susan Ware, *Beyond Suffrage: Women in the New Deal* (Cambridge, Mass.: Harvard University Press, 1981); on a different kind of network, see Mary P. Ryan, "The Power of Women's Networks: A Case Study of Female Moral Reform in Antebellum America," *Feminist Studies* 5, no. 1 (1979): 66–85.

unions, and women's organizations.[13] Although feminist scholars do not agree on the relationship between women's culture and politics, it is clear that community building has played a central role in women's activism throughout American history.[14] It is in this context that we must place the Woman's Party community.

To understand the consequences of community for the National Woman's Party in the post-1945 period, it is essential to explore the nature of the women's community within the organization. What follows is a description and analysis of five elements that defined the community and held it together: (1) a shared bond of participation in the suffrage struggle; (2) feminist identification in the face of hostility from the larger culture; (3) a high level of commitment to feminist activities; (4) shared activity at the Alva Belmont House—organization headquarters, feminist hotel, and surrogate home for some members; and (5) personal ties of friendship and love among Woman's Party members.

Suffrage Heritage

It should not be surprising that the bond of shared participation in the suffrage struggle could help to hold together a community of women across the years. Women who had demonstrated in front of the White House during the First World War and suffered imprisonment and forced feeding were not likely to forget the sacrifices they had made for "the Cause." (Before 1920 "the Cause" meant the vote; after 1920 it came to mean the ERA.) Having been a suffragist, and especially having been jailed for suffrage activism, gave one status within the Woman's Party. Anyone running for a Woman's Party office who had served a jail term for suffrage activities listed this proudly as a prized accomplishment. What publicity the Woman's Party attracted in the 1940s and 1950s invariably mentioned past struggles for suffrage, despite the organization's non-militance after 1920. Members too young to have been in the suffrage movement adopted a humble attitude toward the pioneers; one wrote, for example, "I was too young to enter the brilliant and successful campaign . . . but you must admit I tried to make up for it after I became a member of the National Woman's Party."[15] Lena Madesin Phillips, founder of the International Federation of Business and Professional

13. Estelle Freedman, "Separatism as Strategy: Female Institution Building and American Feminism, 1870–1930," *Feminist Studies* 5, no. 3 (1979): 512–29.

14. See "Politics and Culture in Women's History: A Symposium," *Feminist Studies* 6, no. 1 (1980): 26–64.

15. Mabel Van Dyke Baer to Anna Kelton Wiley, August 12, 1947, NWP Papers, reel 91.

Women's Clubs and a National Woman's Party member, confessed that she envied the jailed suffragists and felt shame that she had never gone to prison for her convictions.[16]

Nevertheless, even women who had not been suffragists could partake of the spirit of struggle through suffrage celebrations and the deliberate attempt by the Woman's Party leadership to connect the fight for the ERA to the movement for the vote. The Woman's Party regularly celebrated birthdays of suffragists and anniversaries of historic events such as the Seneca Falls convention and the ratification of the suffrage amendment. Today the National Woman's Party sells replicas of the prized jail-door pin designed by founder Alice Paul and worn by women who had been imprisoned. Such organizational tactics reinforced what one member described as "the warm glow that always comes when old Suffrage ties are renewed," and helped to foster a sense of community.[17]

Feminist Identification

Feminist identification was a second and particularly powerful element in holding together the women's community. By the 1920s, feminism had already begun to connote an anachronistic emphasis on women's rights that contrasted with the "modern woman's" interest in fitting in with the men.[18] The Woman's Party maintained a commitment to the word "feminist" as other women's organizations, most notably the League of Women Voters, increasingly disassociated themselves from feminism. In the 1940s and 1950s, National Woman's Party members, as part of the only national organization to identify itself publicly as feminist, regularly used the term "feminist" to describe themselves, their friends, and their organization. The group's journal, *Equal Rights*, carried a column entitled "A Feminist Thinks It Over" and reported women's achievements as "Feminist Firsts" and "Feminist Milestones." In private correspondence, members complimented other members and friends by describing them as "good feminists," "ardent feminists," "active feminists," "staunch feminists," "strong, articulate feminists," "real feminists," or "militant feminists."

Members were not, however, unaware of society's hostility to the label. Some avoided the term or used "equalitarian" as an alternative. But these were the exceptions. Despite the prevailing societal conviction that feminists were "kooks," "freaks," or "eccentrics," women in the Woman's

16. Quoted in Lisa Sergio, *A Measure Filled: The Life of Lena Madesin Phillips Drawn from Her Autobiography* (New York: Robert B. Luce, Inc., 1972), p. 135.

17. Caroline Babcock to Grace Cook Kurz, July 8, 1946, NWP Papers, reel 89.

18. Freedman; and Elaine Showalter, *These Modern Women* (Old Westbury, N.Y.: Feminist Press, 1978).

Party remained true to their feminist identity. Women who joined the Woman's Party found the comfort of community a support for their beliefs. One woman who came to the group in the 1940s as a relatively young woman recalled in an interview the excitement of finding other women who were feminists: "I had this marvelous feeling that I was no longer alone. . . . As soon as I became a member of the National Woman's Party, I felt this wonderful backing. I was not quite as peculiar as I thought I was. I was not the only one. . . . I said, 'Oh my God! . . . this is terrific, this is terrific.'"[19] Whatever women meant by the term "feminist"—and they meant different things despite a common recognition of gender-based inequality—the bond of common identity was important. One woman who came to feminist causes in the early 1960s recalled in an interview how carefully sympathetic women used the word "feminist" among themselves—she described it as an "in-house term"—which suggests how important the community could be to women who identified as feminists.[20]

Feminist Commitment

Feminist identification led to and reinforced a third element of the community, the high level of commitment that characterized active membership in the National Woman's Party. Although women might casually join some of the organizations that concerned themselves with women's issues, identification with feminism required commitment to an unpopular cause. The core of commitment to any cause or organization is the reciprocal relationship between the individual and the group, in which the individual benefits from the process of giving to the group.[21] In the National Woman's Party, members could devote their lives to the Cause and in return find the support of the community and the satisfaction of meaningful work.

The Woman's Party gained the reputation of fanatical devotion to the cause of the ERA. One woman active in other women's organizations and only peripherally involved with the Woman's Party reported that the group was "ingrown to the point of fanaticism," while another member apologized for her lack of activity, explaining, "I am interested but not with that dedicated drive I so admired."[22] Another member reported the

19. Interview no. 5, December 19, 1979. All interviews cited by number were conducted jointly with Verta Taylor.

20. Interview no. 3, October 15, 1979; also interview no. 4, October 15, 1979.

21. See Rosabeth Moss Kanter, *Commitment and Community: Communes and Utopias in Sociological Perspective* (Cambridge, Mass.: Harvard University Press, 1972).

22. Florence Kitchelt to Margaret Bruton, July 11, 1947, Kitchelt Papers, box 4 (93), Schlesinger Library, Cambridge, Massachusetts; Julia Pemberton to Alice Paul, [November 1955], NWP Papers, reel 101.

response of a former national chairman when the member returned from her first visit to national headquarters in Washington, D.C.: "Her eyes just beamed, and she said, 'Now you have done something,' and added, 'The rest of your life must be dedicated to the National Woman's Party.'"[23]

Many of the members did in fact devote their lives to feminist activity, speaking of their efforts as their "life work." One member who suffered an automobile accident that was eventually fatal could, according to the woman with whom she lived, "bear the broken bones but the breaking up of her life's work was far harder to take."[24] When Fannie Ackley, a working-class member described by a friend and coworker as a "zealot," died, her twin sister wrote that "EQUAL RIGHTS was Fannie's life work."[25] In response to this level of commitment, outsiders and newcomers to the Woman's Party found it "a revelation . . . to meet women who are working with such dedication"; they believed that "the secret of the ability of a small group to do so much in the face of such odds is that it can attract just such devotion and loyalty."[26]

The model for intense commitment to the Cause was Alice Paul. By 1945, Paul had already established an almost legendary reputation as a dedicated, iron-willed "super-feminist," a fanatic, and a martyr.[27] She continued to devote herself to the ERA—at times she seemed to direct the campaign single-handedly—into the 1970s. In 1965, for example, a Woman's Party member reported that Paul still worked from six in the morning until midnight. Other members approached the level of Paul's commitment. Fannie Ackley, the "zealot," was "a brave spirit faithful to the cause with her last breath."[28] Anna Kelton Wiley, one of the original members, wrote that she had given the "very best years of [her] life, the years when [she] could have been happy and carefree, to the cause."[29]

The commitment that bound such women to the organization involved strong belief in the cause; expenditure of time, energy, and financial resources; and the willingness or desire to shape personal relationships around political activities. Women attended meetings and

23. Lillian V. Hulse to Dora Ogle, April 14, 1952, NWP Papers, reel 98.

24. Elsie M. Wood to Alice Paul, February 1, 1955, NWP Papers, reel 101.

25. Mary Elizabeth Nye to Agnes Wells, March 1, 1950, NWP Papers, reel 96; Margaret Davis to Alice Paul, February 5, 1956, NWP Papers, reel 102.

26. Lorraine Bentley to Alice Paul, April 21, 1956, NWP Papers, reel 102; Mamie Sydney Mizen to Florence Armstrong, October 25, 1948, NWP Papers, reel 94.

27. See Irwin (n. 2 above); Stevens (n. 2 above); and Becker (n. 3 above). Amelia R. Fry, who interviewed Alice Paul for the Regional Oral History Office at the University of California, Berkeley, is currently working on a biography of Alice Paul, and I am grateful to her for sending me the drafts of several unpublished papers on Alice Paul.

28. Mary Elizabeth Nye to Amelia Himes Walker, October 20, 1955, NWP Papers, reel 101.

29. Anna Kelton Wiley to Caroline Babcock, October 21, 1945, Babcock-Hurlburt Papers, box 7 (96), Schlesinger Library, Cambridge, Massachusetts.

national conventions, wrote letters and articles, traveled to speak to existing groups or to organize new ones, and lobbied Congress. The National Woman's Party depended on the volunteer work of members at its national headquarters. A summons from Alice Paul or the national chairman often resulted in an extended visit in Washington devoted to office work or lobbying. Members often recognized how much time feminist activity demanded. "Since 1917 I have devoted all my spare time to feminism," one member wrote in 1952.[30] Another asked for a "cure for giving too much of one's time to one thing," although she continued to devote herself to the ERA.[31] Yet another, who described a week packed with meetings at lunchtime, in the evenings, and on weekends, noted: "I could not possibly be giving any more time to a cause if I were a cloistered nun!"[32] Women gave not only time and energy but money as well, even when this meant great sacrifices. Fannie Ackley, after her retirement, wrote and published booklets of pro-ERA doggerel that she sent to senators and representatives, spending in 1948 350 dollars of her own money on a single session of Congress—an enormous sum for a retired linotype operator if minuscule for a powerful lobby. Women sometimes sent money as a substitute for time. One member sent twenty dollars, noting, "I can do so little and I feel so grateful to those of you who are giving so much of your lives in my interest and the rest of the women of the world."[33] The national secretary in 1948 sold her car in order to raise the money to go to Washington and work at headquarters. The next year, the bookkeeper worried about the large sums that the national chairman, a retired woman of seventy-three, gave to the organization. Some women remembered the feminist cause in their wills.

The expenditure of resources, particularly time, on feminist work meant that commitment also required the desire or willingness to shape personal relationships around the cause. As we shall see later, women whose personal lives meshed with their feminist activity found it easier to commit themselves than women who felt a conflict between their organizational commitment and their personal lives. Not surprisingly, the intensity of commitment sometimes led to collapse and withdrawal. Workers at headquarters, in particular, periodically collapsed in illness or decided to take a vacation to prevent a breakdown. Of couse, not all Woman's Party members maintained such a strong commitment to the feminist cause. Aside from the question of individual psychology, structural conditions determined to a large extent whether women could act on their commitment. Obviously, women in good health without work or

30. Betty Gram Swing to Ethel Ernest Murrell, October 3, 1952, NWP Papers, reel 99.

31. Mary Kennedy to Agnes Wells, July 12, 1950, NWP Papers, reel 97.

32. Dorothy Shipley Granger to Caroline Babcock, December 1, 1946, Babcock-Hurlburt Papers, box 7 (98).

33. Esther Cloward to NWP, December 5, 1946, NWP Papers, reel 90.

family responsibilities that interfered with full-time commitment made ideal feminist activists. Advanced age and illness, the demands of employment, and time-consuming family responsibilities prevented many women, either temporarily or permanently, from committing themselves to the struggle for equality.

Women who were able to and did commit themselves completely to the cause of women, who gave of time and money sometimes beyond what they could afford, received something in exchange for their sacrifices. The Woman's Party did not achieve many concrete results in the 1940s and 1950s, so it was not a question of sacrificing for the gratification of a goal reached. It is clear that the work itself, quite apart from any results, had its own rewards. In part, these rewards consisted of the support of the community. In part, too, activity gave meaning to the lives of the women involved. Rose Arnold Powell, a Woman's Party member who devoted her life to winning recognition for the pioneers of the women's movement, saw feminist activity as meeting the same needs that other women satisfied through marriage and a family. Unhappy unless busy with her campaigns, Powell coped with discouragement because she enjoyed the struggle itself. Perle Mesta, the famous hostess and diplomat, described in her autobiography how she, as a wealthy, widowed socialite, found that work in the National Woman's Party filled her life and gave it meaning.[34] Of Fannie Ackley, a Woman's Party officer wrote, "What a noble soul [she] is! It seems such a pity to take money from her, yet I firmly believe that in that giving she is benefitted beyond what we can realize."[35]

The rewards of feminist activism were sometimes clear even to outsiders. Woman's Party members occasionally suffered from accusations that they did not want the ERA to pass since it constituted their "life work." One national chairman warned Alice Paul in the midst of an internal conflict that, if she were circumvented in her work for the ERA, she could only conclude "that there is truth in what has been said to me so often by those friends of ours on Capital [*sic*] Hill, and other friendly, if unkind, critics who laughed: 'those dear ladies do not want this Bill passed. It would take their reason for being alive away from them.'"[36]

Activity at Belmont House

Feminist work *was* a "reason for being alive" for many women in the Woman's Party. The high level of commitment, which may have been a response to societal indifference or hostility in the 1940s and 1950s,

34. Perle Mesta, *Perle: My Story* (New York: McGraw-Hill Book Co., 1960), pp. 77, 94.

35. [Mildred Palmer] to Amelia Himes Walker, August 21, 1950, NWP Papers, reel 97.

36. Ethel Ernest Murrell to Alice Paul, December 8, 1952, NWP Papers, reel 99; Ernestine Powell to Florence Armstrong, [October 1953], NWP Papers, reel 99; Ernestine Powell to Alice Paul, October 12, 1953, NWP Papers, reel 99.

helped to hold the women's community together. Commitment was expressed through a fourth element that united the community: activity at the Alva Belmont House, the national headquarters in Washington. Belmont House, named after and purchased and maintained with funds contributed by an early and extremely wealthy member, served not only as an office but also as a permanent residence, feminist hotel for visitors, and clubhouse. Belmont House created a female world for members of the Woman's Party when they came to Washington and served as a feminist space for all women who identified with the women's movement. The centrality of Belmont House in the Woman's Party community suggests the importance of class privilege—here represented by property ownership—to the group. A staff of servants maintained Belmont House and cooked and cleaned for the members, allowing them to devote their energies to feminist work.

A number of women lived at Belmont House and in two other Party-owned houses, and others stayed in them for periods ranging from a few days to several months while engaged in lobbying. Although some rooms in all three houses were rented to non-Party individuals, even men, Belmont House played an important role in maintaining the women's community. The environment of the house was so woman centered that one member wondered in 1945 if being married would prevent one's acceptance there.[37] Another member who traveled to Washington to serve as house manager emphasized the dwelling's "big contribution to the national and world woman-movement."[38] Some of the members made their home there; one woman wrote that she was "looking forward with joy to my return home, and *Home* to me now, means the dear Alva Belmont House."[39]

The women who lived and worked at Belmont House became, for some, the "Woman's Party family." Members occasionally created ties that they described as mother-daughter or sister-sister relationships. In fulfilling their functions as family members, women provided support of various kinds for each other. For example, Alice Paul, concerned about the loneliness of her old friend and fellow suffragist Nina Allender, gently encouraged her to come to Washington to live: "You would be surrounded by loving friends and by people who know and appreciate the very great gift you have made to our movement."[40] The daughter of another recently deceased member wrote to thank the members at Belmont House, whose kindness and consideration had made it possible for

37. Elizabeth Osgood to Caroline Babcock, September 4, 1945, NWP Papers, reel 87.

38. Martha Souder to Ethel Adamson, April 8, 1948, NWP Papers, reel 93.

39. Mary Alice Matthews to Alice Paul, March 24, 1945, NWP Papers, reel 85.

40. Alice Paul to Nina Allender, November 20, 1954, NWP Papers, reel 100; Kay Boyle to Alice Paul, December 5, 1954, NWP Papers, reel 100; Alice Paul to Nina Allender, December 6, 1954, NWP Papers, reel 100.

her mother to continue working as long as she did. Similarly, members sometimes provided financial support for other members in need; one woman, for example, started a fund to help another pay for dentures. Often members offered emotional support in times of stress, proffering sympathy, for example, upon the illness or death of a friend or a relative. In particular, members worried about Alice Paul's health, urging her to rest, telling her what to eat, and encouraging each other to take care of her. By the 1960s, one member recalled in an interview, the house had become a home for old women with problems. It was filled, she said, with women reminiscing about the past, talking about the wonderful golden-voiced women who had spellbound the crowds: "I used to think I was in fantasy land sometimes."[41]

If Belmont House served as a surrogate home for some Woman's Party members, it also functioned as a sort of feminist hotel. Visitors who stayed there—often women scholars engaged in research in Washington—sometimes ended up hard at work on the ERA at Alice Paul's urging. A staff member at the house, for example, wrote to another member that a woman staying there while researching seventeenth-century British actresses at the Folger Library had "always been a feminist, but only since living here . . . did she take an active part in what we are doing."[42] Bringing friends to Belmont House, in fact, seemed to be one of the ways that women recruited new members. The house manager brought to headquarters a friend who became so interested and appreciative of Alice Paul that she decided to try to help. Another member wrote about a friend who wanted to stay at Belmont House, adding, in what seems a hopeful vein, "She has *our* point of view and is a top news woman."[43] Party members today recall fondly how Alice Paul would immediately try to recruit any woman who visited Belmont House, often with success.[44]

For all National Woman's Party members, Belmont House served as a clubhouse and center of organizational activities. The party's main activities in the post-1945 period were lobbying Congress for the ERA and garnering support for the amendment from other organizations, especially women's organizations. As a result, much of the actual political work of the group took place at Belmont House or, since the house is located on Capitol Hill, with Belmont House as the base. National conventions were originally held in different locations throughout the country, but by the postwar period they were scheduled only sporadically and only in Washington at Belmont House. Organizational decisions were made

41. Interview no. 7, December 16, 1981.
42. [Mildred Palmer] to Lucy Rice Winkler, September 5, 1951, NWP Papers, reel 98.
43. Ruth Gage-Colby to Alice Paul, January 16, 1959, NWP Papers, reel 105.
44. Interview no. 7; Interview no. 11, November 16, 1982.

not at these conventions but by the national council, which met periodically at headquarters. Belmont House was also important as the site of feminist celebrations that were designed to win publicity for the organization and its cause: teas to honor women politicians or sponsors of the ERA, victory celebrations, and parties on Susan B. Anthony's birthday or on the anniversary of passage of the suffrage amendment.

The role of Belmont House underscores how important it was for members to be able to get to Washington, at least occasionally. Members who could not, because of job pressures, family responsibilities, or financial constraints, could not easily become part of the women's community even though they might work actively on behalf of the ERA. Fannie Ackley, for example, the working-class member mentioned above, never visited Belmont House. Living in Spokane, Washington, and retired from her linotype operator's job, she could not afford to travel across the country to meetings. Woman's Party members paid their own expenses, sometimes making great sacrifices, and this excluded many women from full participation. Ackley never seemed to get exasperated at suggestions that she come to headquarters for meetings but instead plugged away at her ERA work in Spokane. But she, like other women isolated by geography, family, job, or income, could never truly participate in the women's community.

The symbolic as well as practical importance of Belmont House became clear in the 1947 schism. One lawsuit filed by the rebels demanded the resources of the organization, including Belmont House, and the other asked for an injunction against the closing of the house to members. In fact, the height of the conflict came with an "invasion" of Belmont House by the dissident members, who were enraged that the Alice Paul group had posted a male detective at the door to keep the opposition away. In this conflict, as in later less serious ones, Belmont House figured as a major asset.

After the endowment had dwindled away, the house remained a prize worth fighting over not only because of its considerable monetary value but also because of its history and its association with the women's movement. Most recently, Sonia Johnson's Congressional Union, named after the suffrage group out of which the National Woman's Party grew, attempted to take over the organization by electing its own members to office at the 1981 national convention. Clearly the historic value of the name and the house still make the National Woman's Party vulnerable to takeover. Today the Woman's Party is as interested in the recently completed restoration of the house, which is a national historic landmark, as it is in its political battles. The current president put a great deal of effort into saving the house from the ravages of time and the threats of government appropriation; it is once again open to the public as a feminist museum, filled with portraits and busts of women, a living monument to Alice Paul and her feminist sisters.

Belmont House was an important material resource that helped to hold together the women's community in the National Woman's Party. But the most important factor for the existence of the community—in fact, the real essence of that community—lay in personal ties of love and friendship among members.

A great deal has been written about women's relationships in the nineteenth century.[45] We know that nineteenth-century American society, organized into homosocial worlds, encouraged intimate and lasting friendships between women. "Romantic friendships" and "Boston marriages" between women were relatively common and carried no taint of sexual or social deviance. What we know less about is the process of transition from this world to the heterosocial one of the twentieth century. The rise of feminism, the spread of Freudian ideas, and the new possibility of economic independence for women—all made Boston marriages and romantic friendships threatening to the established order.[46] But if we have some idea *why* the change occured, we still know very little about *how*. Popular adoption of historians' work on women's relationships has led to the assertion that women like Eleanor Roosevelt, who had a passionate and sensual relationship with journalist Lorena Hickok, lived "Victorian" lives even in the 1930s and beyond.[47] While it may be true that women in the mid-twentieth century lived in Boston marriages like those of their nineteenth-century sisters, the fact that lesbianism had been "discovered" and that a lesbian culture, however marginal, did exist made their experiences different from those of woman-committed women in the nineteenth century.[48] From this perspective, women's relationships

45. Carroll Smith-Rosenberg, "The Female World of Love and Ritual: Relations between Women in Nineteenth-Century America," *Signs: Journal of Women in Culture and Society* 1, no. 1 (1975): 1–29; Nancy F. Cott, *The Bonds of Womanhood: "Woman's Sphere" in New England, 1780–1835* (New Haven, Conn.: Yale University Press, 1977); Nancy Sahli, "Smashing: Women's Relationships before the Fall," *Chrysalis*, no. 8 (1979), pp. 17–27; Cook (n. 11 above), and "The Historical Denial of Lesbianism," *Radical History Review*, no. 20 (1979), pp. 60–65; Judith Schwarz, "*Yellow Clover*: Katharine Lee Bates and Katharine Coman," *Frontiers* 4 (Spring 1979): 59–67; the lesbian history issue of *Frontiers* (vol. 4 [Fall 1979]); Adrienne Rich, "Compulsory Heterosexuality and Lesbian Existence," *Signs* 5, no. 4 (1980): 631–60; and Lillian Faderman, *Surpassing the Love of Men: Romantic Friendship and Love between Women from the Renaissance to the Present* (New York: William Morrow & Co., 1981).

46. Sahli; Faderman; and Linda Gordon, *Woman's Body, Woman's Right: A Social History of Birth Control in America* (New York: Grossman Publishers, 1976).

47. See, e.g., Arthur Schlesinger, Jr., "Interesting Women," review of *The Life of Lorena Hickok: E. R.'s Friend*, by Doris Faber, *New York Times Book Review* (February 17, 1980), p. 31.

48. On lesbian culture in the 1950s, see Sasha Gregory Lewis, *Sunday's Women: A Report on Lesbian Life Today* (Boston: Beacon Press, 1979); Madeline Davis, Liz Kennedy, and Avra Michelson, "Aspects of the Buffalo Lesbian Community in the Fifties" (paper presented at

in the National Woman's Party seem anachronistic: women created a homosocial world within the boundaries of a political organization and maintained the kind of female public sphere that Estelle Freedman has argued was so essential to the survival of feminism.[49]

In this context, I shall focus here on three kinds of relationships in the National Woman's Party: close friendships, leader/follower relationships with Alice Paul, and couple relationships between women.

In the National Woman's Party, friendships grew out of and in turn supported the work for the ERA. Correspondence among members—and there was little separation between official and personal correspondence—rang with expressions of intimacy and friendship, indicating the intensely personal nature of the political work. Members wrote letters sprinkled with endearments such as "honey," "my dear," "darling," "dearest," and so on. That these were more than simple stylistic flourishes—that they expressed real love and affection—is indicated by the more direct statements in official correspondence. For example, a long-time member wrote of her cousin and coworker who had just died, "We were '*best friends*' for seventy-five years & her nobility of character & love were a sustaining joy and influence through all the years."[50] On the death of another member, her sister-in-law wrote, "I know what a sense of loss you feel in your organization, just as we feel here in the family circle. You, personally, loved her too, I know, just as she loved you."[51] Inez Haynes Irwin, the historian of the National Woman's Party, wrote of Maud Younger, an early suffragist who had died, "Outside of my two sisters, I have loved no woman as I loved her. . . . I think of her often and always with love, admiration and wonder."[52]

Friendships in the Woman's Party could be of long duration. Women who had been suffragists together often reminisced about the "warm glow" of old suffrage bonds. Two women who met at a convention in the 1930s became close friends and, even after leaving the organization during the schism, wrote each other twice a week into the 1980s. In fact, many of the rebels who left after 1947 maintained their close friendships. They gathered to celebrate the seventy-fifth birthday of one of their

---

the National Women's Studies Association Conference, Bloomington, Indiana, May 1980); and Joan Nestle, "Butch-Fem Relationships: Sexual Courage in the Fifties," *Heresies 12* 3, no. 4 (1981): 21–24.

49. Freedman (n. 13 above). On women's relationships in the twentieth century, see Leila J. Rupp, "'Imagine My Surprise': Women's Relationships in Historical Perspective," *Frontiers* 5 (Fall 1980): 61–70; Nancy Manahan, "Future Old Maids and Pacifist Agitators," *Women's Studies Quarterly* 10 (Spring 1982): 10–13; and Judith Schwarz, *Radical Feminists of Heterodoxy* (Lebanon, N.H.: New Victoria Publishers, 1982).

50. Elizabeth Kent to Agnes Wells, December 31, 1950, NWP Papers, reel 97.

51. Janet Griswold to Alice Paul, February 2, 1955, NWP Papers, reel 101.

52. Inez Haynes Irwin to Alice Paul, July 4, 1956, NWP Papers, reel 102.

number in 1952 and continued to reminisce about "the delightful times we used to have together slinking around corners to avoid running into the ubiquitous AP [Alice Paul]." For the majority, "most of the bitterness has disappeared and only the laughs and the priceless companionship remain alive."[53] Leaving the Woman's Party had raised the fear that friendships, too, would end: "Please," one woman wrote to former national secretary Caroline Babcock, "never lose touch with me. I would consider it one of the big losses in my life. . . . You are one of my most treasured friends."[54] Another member wrote to Babcock, "I love and admire you very much and the memory of your friendship and work together for a common cause, will always be very precious to me—always."[55] And yet another member wrote to Babcock: "Most of all thanks for your precious self—the very thought of you makes life better and sweeter and I look forward to and hope for the time when we will be together again."[56]

Close friendships sometimes helped to recruit women to the National Woman's Party, as in the cases where members brought their friends to Belmont House. More often, however, friendships grew out of and then came to support feminist work. Friendship tied the women's community together and in fact, as we have seen, provided a great deal of the reward for feminist work. But friendship could also aggravate conflicts, as is clear from the stormy history of the 1947 schism, in which political and personal conflict became hopelessly intertwined.

A second kind of relationship—intense devotion to Alice Paul—also had complex consequences for the organization.[57] Devotion to Alice Paul played a major role in holding together the women's community and the organization itself, but it also, on occasion, threatened to tear it apart. Paul inspired emotion that bordered on worship; one woman even addressed her as "My Beloved Deity."[58] Many Woman's Party members seemed to have joined because they had met Alice Paul and responded strongly to

53. Gaeta Boyer to Caroline Babcock, [1960], Babcock-Hurlburt Papers, box 9 (113).

54. Lorraine L. Blair to Caroline Babcock, December 19, 1946, Babcock-Hurlburt Papers, box 8 (101).

55. Nan [Anna Kelton] Wiley to Caroline Babcock, January 13, 1947, Babcock-Hurlburt Papers, box 8 (104).

56. Laura Berrien to Caroline Babcock, August 12, 1947, Babcock-Hurlburt Papers, box 8 (104).

57. Leaders of other women's organizations inspired the same kind of devotion. On the role of Anna Lord Strauss in the League of Women Voters, see Rupp, "'Imagine My Surprise'"; on Jessie Daniel Ames in the Association of Southern Women for the Prevention of Lynching, see Jacquelyn Dowd Hall, *Revolt against Chivalry: Jessie Daniel Ames and the Women's Campaign against Lynching* (New York: Columbia University Press, 1979). The papers of Mary Church Terrell in the Library of Congress suggest that Terrell played the same kind of role for the women in the National Association of Colored Women.

58. Lavinia Dock to Alice Paul, May 9, 1945, NWP Papers, reel 86.

her commitment to the cause. Her awe-struck followers offered her expressions of love, admiration, and devotion. Meanwhile, like a beloved but distant leader, Paul maintained an odd formality in her correspondence that contrasted strangely with the loving sentiments also found therein: "My warm love to you, dear Mrs. Smith"; "My deep and abiding love to you, dear Mrs. Rogers"; "My love & admiration, as always, dear Miss Dock." One woman who regularly wrote effusive letters commented, in a letter addressed "Dear lady": "I always *wish* I could say 'dear Alice,' but your addresses to 'dear Mrs. Vickers' freezes me!!"[59]

But this formality should not be taken to mean that Paul formed no close relationships. To the women whom she addressed so formally, she also expressed concern and love. She urged Jane Norman Smith, a co-worker from the suffrage struggle, "Please take care of yourself & do not undertake too much this summer. You are very precious to us all personally, as well as a great strength to our movement."[60] To Elizabeth Rogers, a wealthy New York woman with whom she stayed whenever she visited the city, she wrote, "I wanted so much to see you when I was in New York."[61] Rogers sent notes to Paul, saying that she did so "just so you will know I love you dearly."[62] Lavinia Dock, Paul's mentor from her settlement-house days and a woman who lived in the Henry Street settlement-house community for many years in an intimate relationship with Lillian Wald, maintained a warm relationship with Paul throughout the years. Dock and Paul—whose teacher-student relationship and age difference (Dock was 92 in 1950, Paul 65) probably compounded Paul's usual formality—found inspiration in one another. Paul wrote, in 1945, "You are a great inspiration to me when I feel too discouraged & too weary to take another step."[63] Dock, who could not believe that Paul ever wearied, saw her as superhuman, as indicated by her "Beloved Deity" salutation quoted above.

Paul does not seem to have formed an intimate relationship with any one woman, but she lived and worked within a close-knit female world. She lived, at least some of the time, at Belmont House; when she was away from Washington, she lived either alone or with her sister, Helen Paul, in Vermont and later in Connecticut. Although Paul herself did not form a couple relationship with another woman, she did maintain close friendships with a number of women who did. She had met Mabel Vernon, who had a long-term relationship with a woman, when they attended Swarthmore College together, and they maintained contact

59. Vicky Vickers to Alice Paul, [September 1954], NWP Papers, reel 100.
60. [Alice Paul] to Jane Norman Smith, May 2, 1945, NWP Papers, reel 86.
61. Alice Paul to Elizabeth Rogers, June 4, 1950, NWP Papers, reel 96.
62. Elizabeth Rogers to Alice Paul, July 4, 1945, NWP Papers, reel 87.
63. [Alice Paul] to Lavinia Dock, May 5, 1945, NWP Papers, reel 86.

throughout the years, despite Vernon's departure from the Woman's Party in the 1930s. When Paul first met Alice Morgan Wright, a sculptor and suffragist and companion of Edith Goode, she said that they "just became sisters right away."[64] Jeannette Marks, who had a life-long female companion and who was chairman of the New York state branch of the Woman's Party, regularly sent her love to "dear Alice" until the schism ruptured their relationship.

It is clear that Alice Paul's ties—whether to her sister or to close friends or to admirers—served as a bond that knit the Woman's Party together. But the women who worshiped Paul as a saint could also become disillusioned and begin to see her as the devil. One woman, who credited Paul with helping her "enter into a new life," left Woman's Party work because of disappointment in Paul, noting that many others had suffered the same "terrible experience." Several years after she withdrew she felt "like weeping with perplexity as to what went wrong," what made Paul hostile and implacable.[65] Women frequently left the group because of inability to get along with Paul; some described being "dropped" or "snubbed" by her. Doris Stevens, who had "affectionately" dedicated her 1920 book about the suffrage struggle to Paul, whose "brilliant and devoted leadership" she lauded, described Paul in 1946 as the "high priestess of the National Woman's Party" and a "venomous specimen of the snake pit."[66]

Ironically, both adoration and denunciation of Alice Paul tended to focus on the same qualities. Doris Stevens compared Paul to the alcoholic in *The Lost Week-End*, noting that the film "stripped naked . . . the moving force of one who is completely absorbed in one thing."[67] Stevens's criticism of Paul could be turned around, as it was by the members who lavished praise and admiration on her as "a thoroughly dedicated person," "an ideal to women all over the world," "the motive force behind the whole movement," or "the greatest woman living."[68] Paul's fanatic devotion must have seemed a reproach to many of her followers. Thinking of her as

64. Alice Paul, "Conversations with Alice Paul: Woman Suffrage and the Equal Rights Amendment" (an oral history conducted in 1972 and 1973 by Amelia R. Fry) (University of California, Berkeley, Bancroft Library, Regional Oral History Office, 1976), p. 197.

65. [Florence Armstrong], "What Alice Paul Has Done for ME," February 11, 1954, Armstrong Papers, box 1 (1), Schlesinger Library, Cambridge, Massachusetts, and notes on a telephone call from Ethel Johnson, May 20, 1957, Armstrong Papers, box 3 (42); Florence Armstrong to Alice Paul, August 28, 1959, NWP Papers, reel 105.

66. Stevens (n. 2 above); Doris Stevens to Westbrook Pegler, May 3, 1946, Stevens Papers, Schlesinger Library, Cambridge, Massachusetts.

67. Doris Stevens, diary entry, February 11, 1946, Stevens Papers.

68. Ethel R. Coombes to Alice Paul, November 24, 1952, NWP Papers, reel 99; Rosalind G. Bates to Alice Paul, June 27, 1957, NWP Papers, reel 103; Amelia Himes Walker to Alice Paul, January 31, 1958, NWP Papers, reel 104; Essie Newton to Alice Paul, February 22, 1965, NWP Papers, reel 109.

godlike, they did not expect weaknesses; faced with her perennial lack of gratitude, they saw her as a fallen angel. Because so many members sought her approval, some always suffered when she seemed to "play favorites." Unfortunately for the Woman's Party, rejection of Paul's leadership came to mean, for the most part, rejection of the organization.

If both close friendships and intense devotion to Alice Paul could tear the group asunder as well as bind it together, the same does not seem to be true for the third kind of relationship common among members, couple relationships between women. None of the women who lived in couple relationships and belonged to the National Woman's Party would, as far as can be determined, have identified as lesbians, but they did live together in long-term committed relationships accepted by their friends in the Woman's Party. The apparent openness, security, and confidence of women who lived together in couples, in a twentieth-century version of Boston marriages, is striking. An examination of two of these couples suggests that class privilege helped to protect them from the charges of deviance that were leveled against their contemporaries in the emerging lesbian culture of the time.

Jeannette Marks and Mary Woolley, subjects of a controversial biography, met at Wellesley College in 1895 when Marks began her college education and Woolley arrived as a history instructor. Less than five years later they made a "mutual declaration of ardent and exclusive love" and "exchanged tokens, a ring and a jeweled pin, with pledges of lifelong fidelity."[69] They spent the rest of their lives together, for many years at Mount Holyoke, where Woolley served as president and Marks taught English. Jeannette Marks committed herself to suffrage and later, through the National Woman's Party, to the ERA. Marks pressured Woolley, always more cautious, to join the Woman's Party, which she did in 1942. Marks served as chairman of the New York state branch in the 1940s and played a powerful role in the schism. It is quite clear from Marks's correspondence that her relationship with Woolley was accepted as a primary commitment by other members. Few letters to Marks in the 1940s fail to inquire about Woolley, whose serious illness clouded Marks's life and work. One married woman, who withdrew from Woman's Party work because of her husband's health, acknowledged the centrality of Marks's and Woolley's commitment when she compared her own reasons for "pulling out" to "those that have bound you to Westport," the town in which the two women lived.[70] After Woolley died, Marks spent several years writing her biography, and, when she finished, she sought sugges-

69. Anna Mary Wells, *Miss Marks and Miss Woolley* (Boston: Houghton Mifflin Co., 1978), p. 56.

70. Caroline Babcock to Jeannette Marks, February 12, 1947, Babcock-Hurlburt Papers, box 8 (105).

tions from her friends for promoting it "in the world of women," for she believed that women alone had the power to reach the goals that Woolley had set.[71]

The lifelong relationship between feminist biographer Alma Lutz and Marguerite Smith began when they roomed together at Vassar in the early years of the twentieth century. From 1918 to Smith's death in 1959, they shared a Boston apartment and a summer home, Highmeadow, in the Berkshires. Lutz worked both independently and with the National Woman's Party for the ERA and other feminist causes. Smith, a librarian, also worked in the Woman's Party. The two women traveled together, visiting Europe several times in the 1950s, and wrote to friends of their lives together: "We are very happy here in the country—each busy with her work and digging in the garden."[72] Letters to one of them about feminist work invariably included greetings and love to the other. When Smith died in 1959, Lutz struggled with her grief. She wrote to a friend: "I am at Highmeadow trying to get my bearings. . . . You will understand how hard it is. . . . It has been a very difficult anxious time for me."[73] She thanked another friend for her note and added, "It's a hard adjustment to make, but one we all have to face in one way or another and I am remembering that I have much to be grateful for."[74] Later she wrote to one of her regular correspondents to report that she was carrying on, although she was very lonely.

Lutz and Smith seemed to have had many friends who lived in couple relationships with other women, which suggests that the women's community provided a supportive atmosphere. One of the women who wrote to Lutz on Smith's death, for example, had herself suffered in 1943 through the death of the woman with whom she lived. Every year Mabel Vernon, a suffragist and worker for peace, and her friend and companion Consuelo Reyes, whom Vernon had met through her work with the Inter-American Commission on Women, spent the summer at Highmeadow. Two other women who also maintained a lifelong relationship, Alice Morgan Wright and Edith Goode, also kept in touch with Lutz, Smith, Vernon, and Reyes, sometimes visiting Highmeadow in the summer. Wright and Goode had met at Smith College and were described by one Woman's Party member as "always together," although they did not live together. They, like Lutz and Smith, worked with one another in the Woman's Party, traveled together, and looked after each other as old age began to take its toll.

71. Jeannette Marks to Emma Guffey Miller, June 6, 1955, Miller Papers, box 3 (44), Schlesinger Library, Cambridge, Massachusetts.

72. Alma Lutz to Florence Kitchelt, July 1, 1948, Kitchelt Papers, box 6 (177).

73. Alma Lutz to Florence Kitchelt, July 29, 1959, Kitchelt Papers, box 7 (178).

74. Alma Lutz to Florence Armstrong, August 26, 1959, Armstrong Papers, box 1 (17).

Being involved with a woman who shared a commitment to the National Woman's Party could help to facilitate feminist work because, as we have seen, the expenditure of resources, particularly time, required willingness to shape intimate relationships around the cause. Women whose personal lives meshed with their feminist activity found it easier to give themselves to such activity than did women who felt a conflict between party work and personal commitments. Some women felt that any personal life conflicted with the movement. One angry member who left even before the schism wrote to Doris Stevens, "I have been made to realize for a great many years that most of the best workers in the N.W.P. very definitely put the object of their organization ahead of any human relationship that might exist in the work."[75] But women like Jeannette Marks, Alma Lutz, and Marguerite Smith successfully combined a personal life and commitment to the cause. Living in a couple relationship with a woman who was also part of the women's community did not guarantee easy or pleasurable involvement, but it certainly eliminated some of the obstacles to participation that other women sometimes experienced.

Women in the National Woman's Party received support from the community for their relationships with other women, but in the world outside it was another story. Doris Stevens, who devoted herself to "red-baiting" after she left the Woman's Party, had her suspicions about some of her former friends. She recorded in her diary a conversation with a Woman's Party member about Jeannette Marks and Mary Woolley, noting that the member, who had attended Wellesley with Marks, "discreetly indicated that there was 'talk.' "[76] At another point she reported a conversation with a different member who had grown disillusioned about Alice Paul. Stevens noted that her informant related "weird goings on at Wash. hedquts. wherein it was clear she thought Paul a devotee of Lesbos & afflicted with Jeanne d'Arc identification."[77] Stevens's charges suggest that women's relationships within the context of women's organizations had the potential, particularly during the McCarthy years, to attract denunciation or ridicule. Stevens herself wrote to the viciously right-wing and anti-Semitic columnist Westbrook Pegler and thanked him "for knowing I'm not a queerie," despite the fact that she considered herself a feminist.[78] Stevens's homophobic views typified the connections McCarthyites made between Communist subversion and homosexual "perver-

75. Katherine Callery to Doris Stevens, October 11, 1944, Stevens Papers.
76. Doris Stevens, diary entry, February 4, 1946, Stevens Papers.
77. Doris Stevens, diary entry, December 1, 1945, Stevens Papers.
78. Doris Stevens to Westbrook Pegler, May 3, 1946, Stevens Papers.

sion." McCarthy himself attacked the "Communists and queers" in the State Department.[79]

Two cases of opposition to the appointment of women, described by India Edwards, highest-ranking woman in the Truman administration, give some idea of how important the acceptance of couple relationships must have been in the women's community. In 1948, opposition to tax court judge Marion Harron's reappointment to the bench arose from Harron's fellow judges on the basis of her lack of judicial temperament and from "unprovable charges of an ethical and moral nature." Harron, we know, wrote letters to Lorena Hickok that even Doris Faber—who wrote Hickok's biography attempting to deny the intimate relationship between her subject and Eleanor Roosevelt—admits were love letters.[80] The other case that Edwards described left no doubt about the nature of the charges. When Truman appointed Kathryn McHale, long-time executive director of the American Association of University Women, to the Subversive Activities Control Board, Senator Pat McCarran advised Truman to withdraw her name and threatened to hold public hearings during which "information would be brought out that she was a lesbian." Truman sent Edwards to talk to McHale and give her the chance to decide what she wanted to do, and McHale decided to stand for the appointment. "I will fight such a vicious lie with all the strength I have," Edwards quoted her as saying.[81] Whatever the reality of McHale's life, the attack forced her, in effect, to label lesbianism "vicious."

What all this suggests is that, in the world at large, women who lived in couple relationships with other women could be highly suspect. For woman-committed women, the acceptance and support of the women's community was thus all the more important. The Woman's Party members who lived in couples managed to do so "respectably," despite the emergence of a lesbian culture and the occasional charges of lesbianism, because they worked independently or in professional jobs, had the money to buy homes together, and enjoyed enough status to be beyond reproach in the world in which they lived. The woman-centered world of the women's community was made possible, that is, by class privilege. But, as the cases cited by India Edwards suggest, such privilege would not necessarily protect women who sought to enter powerful, mainstream institutions.

79. Richard Polenberg, *One Nation Divisible* (New York: Penguin Books, 1980), p. 124. John D'Emilio, "The Homosexual Menace: The Politics of Sexuality in Cold War America" (paper presented at the Organization of American Historians Conference, Philadelphia, April 1982), explores this connection; I am grateful to D'Emilio for sharing his work with me.

80. Doris Faber, *The Life of Lorena Hickok: E. R.'s Friend* (New York: William Morrow & Co., 1980).

81. India Edwards, *Pulling No Punches: Memoirs of a Woman in Politics* (New York: G. P. Putnam's Sons, 1977), pp. 180–90.

When we look at the women's community as a whole, we see, on the one hand, that the factors that held it together made it possible for feminists to maintain their commitment in the hostile environment of the 1940s and 1950s and yet, on the other hand, that those very factors contributed to the elitism and isolation of the National Woman's Party. The importance of suffrage history and the heroic stature of former suffragists who had been imprisoned meant that women too young to have participated in the suffrage struggle or women who came later to feminism never felt completely at home in the Woman's Party. It surely is revealing that even a young woman who found the support of like-minded women a glorious relief could ridicule her fellow members as "old fuddy-duddies."[82] The media played on the age and eccentricities of some of the members to create the image of little old ladies in tennis shoes hawking their anachronistic amendment on Capitol Hill. If even sympathetic women felt out of place, how must the group have appeared to women not already converted to the cause? Feminist identification was central in the National Woman's Party, and yet other women's organizations and individuals interested in the question of women's status in American society shied away from the term "feminism," which had, in the public view, become "as quaint as linen dusters and high button shoes."[83]

The high level of commitment expected of Woman's Party members made it difficult for women with work or family responsibilities to participate. Likewise, women who lacked the financial resources to travel to conventions or visit with other members could not easily become part of the community. The central role of Belmont House assured that women who lived there or visited regularly could become part of the "family," while others could not. And, finally, close friendships and devotion to Alice Paul could either unify the community or so infuse political conflicts with personal loyalties or hatreds that the community itself was endangered. The community created a world in which women's relationships, even couple relationships, were valued without thought to the label of lesbianism that the larger culture might attach. But the existence of such a world depended on class privilege.

Feminists in the long years between the Second World War and the resurgence of the women's movement in the 1960s created a community within the National Woman's Party that supported their commitment, but they failed to recruit younger women. They only halfheartedly tried, yet they regularly lamented the indifference of the majority of American

82. Interview no. 5.

83. Robert Coughlan, "Changing Roles in Modern Marriage," *Life* (December 24, 1956), pp. 108–18.

women. They hoped for a grand awakening of the women they perceived to be sleeping through the 1950s, but they failed to rouse their contemporaries. That, of course, was as much a consequence of Cold War society as it was any fault of their own. When Betty Friedan's *The Feminine Mystique* appeared in 1963, Woman's Party member Alma Lutz exclaimed joyfully, "It gives me a glimmer of hope that some of the younger generation are waking up."[84] When a strong women's movement began to grow in the mid-1960s, the older feminists were no longer at its center, although some of them made vital connections to the new movement and some of the younger feminists recognized the older women's "patient years of striving while most of the nation's women were asleep."[85] Although the resurgent women's movement in the 1960s had little use for the National Woman's Party, it has since come to revere Alice Paul and her organization, if only as a symbol of feminist survival.

From the perspective of the 1980s, the history of the Woman's Party community in the 1940s and 1950s has yet other lessons to offer. We can applaud the tenaciousness of the Woman's Party even while we deplore its elitism, conservatism, and racism, which violate the spirit of contemporary feminism. Yet we must understand that the very factors that tied the women's community together and made it possible for feminists to maintain their commitment also isolated the organization and made it difficult to recruit younger and less privileged women. Let this serve as a warning to the contemporary movement. We, too, need a supportive community that allows us to devote ourselves to our causes, but we must not pursue community at the cost of growth, or we, too, shall find ourselves isolated and ineffective, lamenting the apathy of women who do not hear our voices raised in protest.

Center for Women's Studies and
Department of History
Ohio State University

84. Alma Lutz to Emma Guffey Miller, February 23, 1963, NWP Papers, reel 108.

85. Jean Witter to Alice Paul, April 15, 1968, NWP Papers, reel 111. See Cynthia Ellen Harrison, "Prelude to Feminism: Women's Organizations, the Federal Government and the Rise of the Women's Movement, 1942 to 1968" (Ph.D. diss., Columbia University, 1982).

Women Activists, Southern Conservatives, and the Prohibition of Sex Discrimination in Title VII of the 1964 Civil Rights Act

By Carl M. Brauer

Title VII of the 1964 Civil Rights Act prohibited discrimination in employment on the basis of sex as well as on the bases of race, color, religion, and national origin. This prohibition was added to the civil rights bill through an amendment on the floor of the House of Representatives by Howard Worth Smith of Virginia, an ardent opponent of the legislation as a whole. Because his motives in proposing the amendment were questionable, because of the occasionally facetious tone of the debate on the amendment, and because women's rights were generally not taken seriously then, the prohibition of sex discrimination originally tended to be lightly regarded, even after it became law. The Equal Employment Opportunity Commission (EEOC), established by Title VII to administer the law against employment discrimination, initially treated the ban on sex discrimination as something of a joke. Others, however, did not. In the first two years of enforcement, over four thousand charges of sex discrimination were lodged, representing roughly one-quarter of all complaints. EEOC's languid record of enforcement precipitated formation of the National Organization for Women in 1966, an important institutional development in the birth of the women's rights movement. Pressure from this and other groups and individuals, along with a changing consciousness about sex roles, led in time to more rigorous enforcement and generally sympathetic court rulings. By 1975 legal experts on women's rights could aptly characterize Title VII "the most comprehensive and important of all federal and state laws prohibiting employment discrimination."[1]

[1] U. S. Equal Employment Opportunity Commission, *1st Annual Report* (Washington, [1967]), 58–64; U. S. Equal Employment Opportunity Commission, *Second Annual Report*

Mr. Brauer is research fellow at the Institute of Politics, Kennedy School of Government, Harvard University.

The Journal of Southern History
Vol. XLIX, No. 1, February 1983

Although the sex amendment eventually developed legal and practical significance that few, including its sponsor, seemed to anticipate in 1964, some people who played a critical, though generally unrecognized, role in its enactment relished the outcome. They were women—members of the National Woman's party (NWP) or members of Congress. Their advocacy of women's rights in 1963 and 1964 both foreshadowed the new women's rights movement and provided it with its most important legal tool to date. Able and committed though these pioneers were, they lacked numbers and power. Without a social movement behind them, they had to work for women's rights from marginal, rather than central, positions in politics, riding the forces unleashed by the powerful social movement of the time, the movement for black civil rights.[2]

The campaigns for civil rights for blacks and for women in America have long been intertwined, sometimes complementing one another, at other times clashing.[3] The fascinating story of the sex amendment's inclusion in the 1964 Civil Rights Act reflects a modern version of a historic ambiguity. In this recent instance the civil rights movement opened the door for women's rights, but it was the opponents, not the supporters, of federally mandated civil rights for blacks who escorted them across the threshold. Women's rights advocates requested and welcomed this act of chivalry; they

(Washington, [1968]), 52; Pauli Murray and Mary O. Eastwood, "Jane Crow and the Law: Sex Discrimination and Title VII," *George Washington Law Review*, XXXIV (December 1965), 232–56; Betty Friedan, *It Changed My Life*: *Writings on the Women's Movement* (New York, 1976), 76–86; and for the legal experts' view in 1975, Barbara Babcock *et al.*, *Sex Discrimination and the Law*: *Causes and Remedies* (Boston and Toronto, 1975), 229. The author gratefully acknowledges the assistance of many participants in this history who supplied vital information through interviews or letters. He also appreciates the criticism and advice of Catherine East, Cynthia Harrison, Jane DeHart Mathews, and Leila J. Rupp. Financial assistance for this article came from the National Endowment for the Humanities, the Charles Warren Center for Studies in American History, and the University of Virginia.

[2] The story of the inclusion of the prohibition of sex discrimination in employment in Title VII has been told before, but always on the basis of fairly limited sources and therefore only partially and sometimes inaccurately. See for example Robert S. Miller, Jr., "Sex Discrimination and Title VII of the Civil Rights Act of 1964," *Minnesota Law Review*, LI (April 1967), 877–97; Caruthers G. Berger, "Equal Pay, Equal Employment Opportunity and Equal Enforcement of the Law for Women," *Valparaiso University Law Review*, V (Symposium Issue, 1971), 326–73; Jo Freeman, *The Politics of Women's Liberation*: *A Case Study of an Emerging Social Movement and Its Relation to the Policy Process* (New York, 1975), 52–54; Donald A. Robinson, "Two Movements in Pursuit of Equal Employment Opportunity," *Signs*: *Journal of Women in Culture and Society*, IV (Spring 1979), 413–33. The tendency of women to operate on the margins of politics is treated in Marianne Githens and Jewel L. Prestage, eds., *A Portrait of Marginality*: *The Political Behavior of the American Woman* (New York, 1977).

[3] See for example Gerda Lerner, *The Grimké Sisters from South Carolina*: *Rebels Against Slavery* (Boston, 1967); Blanche G. Hersh, *The Slavery of Sex*: *Feminist-Abolitionists in America* (Urbana, Chicago, and London, 1978); Ellen C. DuBois, *Feminism and Suffrage*: *The Emergence of an Independent Women's Movement in America, 1848–1869* (Ithaca and London, 1978); Aileen S. Kraditor, *The Ideas of the Woman Suffrage Movement, 1890–1920* (New York and London, 1965); Sara Evans, *Personal Politics*: *The Roots of Women's Liberation in the Civil Rights Movement and the New Left* (New York, 1979).

were pragmatic, taking whatever assistance they could get. In doing so, they created an important legal basis for women in the future to claim equal rights with men, allowing them to become less dependent both upon men and chivalry.

With the burgeoning of the civil rights movement in the late 1950s and early 1960s some veteran women's rights advocates from the National Woman's party early saw a connection that might be forged between the rights of blacks and the rights of women. When Congress considered civil rights legislation in the late 1950s Alice Paul, the key figure in the National Woman's party since its founding in 1913, unsuccessfully promoted the idea of including women's rights. Shortly after President John Fitzgerald Kennedy asked Congress to enact sweeping new civil rights legislation in June 1963 some members of NWP again thought of connecting the two issues. "So much of the racial discussion, even that on the most elevated and inspired level," Mary F. Anderson wrote Alice Paul, "seems to assume that everybody but the Negro in this country has full equality." She hoped to see two birds, the "woman problem" and the "Negro problem," killed with one stone. An NWP loyalist from Richmond likewise was thrilled to hear Fulton Lewis, Jr., a conservative radio commentator, criticize Kennedy's omission of sex discrimination from his legislative proposals on civil rights.[4]

At this time most of the NWP's several hundred active members were elderly, middle- or upper-class women, many of them either former suffragists or relatives of suffragists. Very few NWP members came from working-class backgrounds, and the party accepted no men. Often party members were lawyers, businesswomen, or other professionals. Typically, they revered their leader Alice Paul, who had as a young woman led some of America's most militant suffragist demonstrations. The historic Alva Belmont House in Washington served as headquarters, gathering place, and hotel for NWP members. Although other women's organizations, such as the National Federation of Business and Professional Women's Clubs, supported women's rights, NWP members alone and with pride called themselves feminists. NWP had one overriding objective—passage of the Equal Rights Amendment (ERA) to the federal Constitution. In that objective and in its embrace of feminism NWP served as a link between the women's rights movement that preceded World War I and the one that came into being in the mid-

[4] "Conversations with Alice Paul: Woman Suffrage and the Equal Rights Amendment," interviews conducted by Amelia R. Fry, 1973 (Bancroft Library, University of California, Berkeley, Calif.), 617–19; Carl M. Brauer, *John F. Kennedy and the Second Reconstruction* (New York, 1977), especially 230–64; Anderson to Paul, June 16, 1963; Nina Avery to Paul, July 17, [1963], both in National Woman's Party Papers (Microfilming Corporation of America; hereinafter cited as NWP), reel 108.

1960s. In other respects, however, NWP tended to look backward rather than forward. Its overwhelmingly and perhaps exclusively white membership evinced little concern for racial or economic equality. More of its members appeared to be politically conservative or reactionary than liberal or radical. Yet their friendships with conservative politicians proved invaluable in 1964.[5]

The rise of the civil rights movement and the existence of a feminist organization with ties to conservative politicians constituted two essential ingredients in the story of the 1964 sex amendment, but the immediate precipitant came from the division that had existed among women activists over the Equal Rights Amendment ever since the National Woman's party had begun to promote it in the early 1920s. Proponents of ERA believed that it would eliminate all legally based barriers to women's advancement. Opponents feared its blanket effect. Though it would do some good, in their view, it would also do great harm by eliminating laws that favored women, such as those that set minimum wages and maximum hours, which they believed aided working-class women in particular. The debate over ERA had distinctly class, interest-group, and ideological overtones, pitting affluent, business-oriented, and politically conservative women against poor, union-oriented, and politically liberal women. The sources of congressional support for and opposition to ERA from the 1920s through the mid-1960s have not been systematically studied, but it is probably safe to say that most prounion congressmen were anti-ERA and most antiunion congressmen were pro-ERA.[6]

The long-standing division among women over ERA accounted in part for the creation of the President's Commission on the Status of Women in 1961. Like other presidential candidates before him, Kennedy endorsed ERA during his campaign. This troubled Esther

[5] On Alice Paul and the National Woman's party, the following sources are especially useful: "Conversations with Alice Paul"; Leila J. Rupp, "American Feminism in the Postwar Period," in Robert H. Bremner and Gary W. Reichard, eds., *Reshaping America: Society and Institutions, 1945–1960* (Columbus, Ohio, 1982); J. Stanley Lemons, *The Woman Citizen: Social Feminism in the 1920's* (Urbana, Chicago, and London, 1973), 182–204; Thomas C. Pardo, ed., *The National Woman's Party Papers, 1913–1974: A Guide to the Microfilm Edition* (Sanford, N. C., 1979).

[6] Lemons, *The Woman Citizen*, 182–204; Catherine East, author's interviews, August 6, 1979, and August 29, 1979; Esther Peterson, author's interview, July 30, 1979; Caruthers G. Berger, author's interview, November 10, 1979. These and all other author's interviews were conducted by telephone; in the case of several interviews "conversation" would probably be a more suitable description. Notes of these interviews are in the author's possession. East is a former vice-president of the National Woman's party; she was a friend of both Alice Paul and Esther Peterson. For thirteen years she was executive secretary of the Interdepartmental Committee on the Status of Women and the Citizens' Advisory Council on the Status of Women. Peterson was assistant secretary of labor in the Kennedy and Johnson administrations. Caruthers G. Berger was an attorney in the Labor Department and a member of the National Woman's party.

Peterson, an early Kennedy partisan and labor advocate, whom he appointed director of the Women's Bureau and assistant secretary of labor, and who was the most influential woman in his administration. Although she opposed ERA because it would void protective labor laws, Peterson had long advocated equal economic opportunities for women. For that reason she wanted a national commission to educate the public and promote legitimate change in this area. She hoped, too, that such a commission would focus attention on important, attainable objectives and divert it from agitation for ERA, which she regarded as misguided and futile.[7]

Peterson largely determined the composition of the President's Commission on the Status of Women, which Eleanor Roosevelt chaired until her death in 1962. Seeking a viable compromise between supporters and opponents of ERA, the commission declared that equality of rights under law was already embodied in the Fifth and Fourteenth amendments and urged appropriate test cases to vindicate this principle. The commission, therefore, concluded in its report on October 11, 1963, that "a constitutional amendment need not now be sought in order to establish this principle." Although the inclusion of the word "now" represented something of a concession, NWP's leaders were enraged. "Esther Peterson loaded the Commission against equality," Emma Guffey Miller, the eighty-nine-year-old president of NWP and a prominent Democrat, wrote an ally. "But instead of informing the public that some members were for the Equal Rights Amendment they issued what they term a compromise, but it is really what [Walter] Reuther and Peterson wanted."[8]

Had the commission endorsed ERA, Paul and the National Woman's party would probably have been content, at least for the moment, but the commission's refusal to do so angered and frustrated them, for what was the most prestigious national panel ever to report on the status of women had rejected their primary objective of the previous forty years. Including women in the coverage of the civil rights bill then pending thus presented a logical and available alternative. Perhaps, too, it was NWP's revenge. According to Paul's lieutenants, in her scheme to have sex added to the civil rights bill Paul hatched the idea either alone or in consultation with Emma Guffey Miller. The earliest documentary evidence are letters from her lieutenants to Howard W. Smith proposing the idea. On December 10, 1963, Butler Franklin wrote Smith that "This single word

[7] Cynthia E. Harrison, "A 'New Frontier' for Women: The Public Policy of the Kennedy Administration," *Journal of American History*, LXVII (December 1980), 630–38.

[8] *Ibid.*, 638–41 (first quotation, p. 640); Margaret Hickey, author's interview, August 6, 1979 (Hickey was a member of the commission); Catherine East, author's interview, November 21, 1978; Miller to Jane Grant, November 22, 1963, NWP, reel 108.

'sex' would divert some of the high pressure which is being used to force this Bill through without proper attention to all of the effects of it." Five days later Nina Horton Avery wrote Smith in similar terms.[9]

Paul called upon Franklin and Avery because they both knew Smith. Franklin, a constituent of Smith's, had worked successfully with him in establishing a national park in Fredericksburg, her hometown. The widow of a diplomat, Franklin had been encouraged by Paul to organize the wives of retired diplomats to lobby for improved widows' pensions. Avery, a former president of the Virginia Federation of Women's Business and Professional Clubs and a longtime member of NWP, had graduated from the University of North Carolina in 1917. Forty years later, after a career with a railroad where she encountered rank sexual discrimination, she became a lawyer. Both women were devoted to Paul, and neither appears to have had much sympathy for the civil rights bill. In the case of Avery one letter reveals blatant hostility to it. Paul herself, it should be noted, was probably not unsympathetic to black civil rights. Her Quaker background and her friendships with successful black women at least would so imply. Paul's only prejudice, one friend has noted, was the one she held against anyone opposed to ERA.[10]

The choice of Smith as sponsor made sense for several reasons. He was chairman of the House Committee on Rules, which was preparing to consider the civil rights bill for clearance to the floor. Even more important, he was one of the most influential southern conservatives and had a background of support and friendship for NWP, for Alice Paul herself, and for the Equal Rights Amendment. As far back as 1945 he had served as a sponsor of ERA. Probably not coincidentally, he had a long record of opposition to labor unions. Butler Franklin has also recalled that Paul fully expected Smith to welcome the opportunity to subject the civil rights bill to ridicule by adding sex to it.[11]

The National Woman's party did not confine its lobbying to

[9] Butler Franklin, author's interview, January 8, 1979; Nina Horton Avery, author's interview, January 31, 1979; Caruthers G. Berger, author's interview; Mrs. Lynn B. Franklin to Smith, December 10, 1963; Smith to Avery, December 26, 1963, NWP, reel 108. Butler Franklin's full name was Butler-Brayne Thornton Robinson Franklin. A letter in the papers of the National Woman's party (Frances Honour to Alice Paul, January 15, 1964, NWP, reel 108) attributes the idea to Butler Franklin and the letter's author, Frances Honour. Both Butler Franklin and Nina Horton Avery, however, dispute this attribution. Franklin explains that Honour only wrote as she did in order to please Alice Paul, who was, she says, extremely self-effacing. Unfortunately, Honour could not be located.

[10] Franklin, author's interview; Avery, author's interview; Catherine East, author's interview, August 29, 1979. East was the friend mentioned in the text.

[11] Catherine East, author's interview, October 31, 1979; *Congressional Record*, 79 Cong., 1 sess., 30–31 (January 3, 1945); Butler Franklin, author's interview.

Smith, however, nor did it refrain from framing its appeal in implicitly racist, anti-Semitic, and xenophobic terms. On December 16 NWP unanimously adopted a resolution calling for inclusion of sex in the civil rights bill. ". . . the Civil Rights Bill would not even give protection against discrimination because of 'race, color, religion, or national origins,' to a *White Woman*, a *Woman of the Christian Religion*, or a *Woman of United States Origin*, according to the construction that appears to have been placed on the words . . . in Orders and Statements by Government officials," the resolution declared.[12]

Privately, NWP members sometimes used stronger language. Nina Horton Avery wrote a Virginia congressman that the addition of sex to the civil rights bill was "from the standpoint of [the] National Woman's Party . . . merely a tool of strategy to take the pressure off the passage of any Civil Rights Bill albeit realistically we shall have to accept a Civil Rights Bill ultimately . . . ." She hoped, however, that provisions could be deleted from it which she believed to be unconstitutional and unacceptable to the American public. "Thank God for the Members of Congress who are from the South and for those Members from the East, North and West," she prayed, "who will use their brains and energies to prevent a mongrel race in the United States and who will fight for the rights of white citizens in order that discrimination against them may be stopped." In writing individual members of Congress Emma Guffey Miller did not speak of a "mongrel race," but she emphasized perceived threats to white, native-born Christian women in the civil rights bill.[13]

Smith did not adopt NWP's idea immediately, coming to it gradually instead. He wrote Avery in December that the Rules Committee did not have the privilege of amending a bill. He expected that an effort would be made to include sex when the bill reached the floor, but he did not promise to support it himself. On January 9, during the Rules Committee hearings, Smith noted that he had received a letter from the National Woman's party and asked Emanuel Celler, chairman of the Committee on the Judiciary, which had approved the civil rights bill, why sex was not included in it. Katharine Price Collier St. George, a Republican member of the Rules Committee from New York and an ally of NWP, interjected, referring to an earlier comment by Celler: "If I may be facetious, is that another dim memory, Mr. Celler?" Celler responded with an

[12] Resolution adopted by National Woman's party, December 16, 1963, NWP, reel 108. There is a copy of the resolution in Box 107, Howard W. Smith Papers (Alderman Library, University of Virginia, Charlottesville, Va.).

[13] Avery to J. Vaughan Gary, January 8, 1964, NWP, reel 108; and, for example, Miller to Julia Butler Hansen, January 20, 1964, *ibid.*

ethnic joke about presumed French sexual obsessiveness, which led Smith to observe that Celler had not answered the question. "This is a civil rights bill," Celler replied. "Don't women have civil rights?" Smith inquired. "They have lots of them," Celler answered. "They are supermen," alluding to George Bernard Shaw's play. In responding to a further question from Smith, Celler revealed that the Judiciary Committee had never considered adding sex to the bill. Dissatisfied, Smith said he still did not understand why it had not been added. "Do you want to put it in, Mr Chairman?" Celler asked, and Smith replied, "I think I will offer an amendment. The National Women's [*sic*] Party were serious about it."[14]

Several weeks later Smith made a rare appearance on a televised interview show, "Meet the Press," where one of his interrogators was Elisabeth May Craig, a veteran reporter from Maine and a member of NWP. "Judge," she addressed Smith, as was customary, "it was brought out before your Committee that the bill does not provide that women shall have equal rights. Would you try to get them for us in the bill?" "Would you like me to?" he asked. "Yes, sir," she responded. "Well, maybe I would. I am always strong for women, you know." "An amendment on the floor?" she wondered. "I might do that," he answered. Alice Paul promptly cabled her congratulations and appreciation to both Smith and Craig. Butler Franklin also expressed her thanks to Smith through his assistant on behalf of a "group of prominent women in Fredericksburg."[15]

The evidence on Smith's motives for deciding to offer a sex amendment is conflicting. On the one hand, he was adamantly opposed to the civil rights legislation and was a wily legislator. "I am a conservative and I have been scrambling and scratching around here for 32 years now," Smith told a reporter around this time, "and I have always found that when you are doing that you grasp any snickersnee you can get hold of and fight the best way you can." That the sex amendment was merely such a weapon in Smith's

[14] Smith to Avery, December 26, 1963, *ibid.*; Smith to Miller, January 6, 1963, Box 107, Smith Papers; *Civil Rights*: *Hearings Before the Committee on Rules, House of Representatives, Eighty-eighth Congress, Second Session* (Washington, 1964), 125. The Katharine Price Collier St. George Papers (Department of Manuscripts, University Archives, Cornell University Library, Ithaca, N. Y.) apparently contain no documentation on this legislative episode. Kathleen Jacklin to the author, July 5, 1979. The ethnic joke Celler told was as follows: "Mr. Chairman, it reminds me of the Frenchman who was going up the Empire State Building in New York. Somebody said, 'How do you like it?' He said, 'Well, it reminds me of sex.' 'Reminds you of sex? Why is that?' The answer was, 'Everything reminds me of sex.' "

[15] Transcript of "Meet the Press," January 26, 1964, Vol. 8, No. 2 (Microfiche, Millwood, N. Y., Kraus-Thomson Organization); Paul to Smith and Paul to Craig, January 27, 1964, NWP, reel 108; Franklin to Smith, January 29, 1964, Box 107, Smith Papers; Butler Franklin, author's interview.

hand was implied by the light tone of his comments on the House floor. Martha Wright Griffiths, who defended Smith's amendment in the floor debate, has recalled Smith's explicitly telling her that the amendment was a joke.[16]

On the other hand, Smith repeatedly claimed, during the debate and afterward, that he was sincere. Two of his former assistants have agreed, asserting that Smith fully expected the civil rights bill to become law and insisting that he simply did not sponsor or vote for things in which he did not believe. In an oral-history interview in 1973 Alice Paul recalled Smith's cautioning her that were he to sponsor the sex amendment, it would be handicapped since people would question his motives. Although no one will ever be able to say for sure, it is probably safe to guess that Smith's motives were mixed. He saw an opportunity to take a swipe at the civil rights bill, but as a chivalrous old southern gentleman he also believed that it was only fair that women, specifically white women, be granted the same legal protections that the government was preparing to afford black men.[17]

Several days after Smith's appearance on "Meet the Press" May Craig asked President Lyndon Baines Johnson whether he would support a sex amendment. In doing so, Craig quoted from the Democratic party's platform, which promised support for legislation guaranteeing to women equal rights under law. Johnson stood by his party, acknowledged the fact of discrimination against women in employment, and expressed his hope that substantial progress could soon be made in this area. But as Craig told Howard Smith, "The President could have said: 'Yes,' to me, if he really meant it." "We are not going to make much time with President Johnson on the principle of equal rights for women," Craig wrote an ally. "He evaded an answer to my question, just like all Presidents have."[18]

In fact, the Johnson administration did more than evade an answer; it opposed a sex amendment. It is probably impossible to

[16] Don Oberdorfer, " 'Judge' Smith Moves With Deliberate Drag," *New York Times Magazine*, January 12, 1964, p. 85; Martha Griffiths, author's interview, January 11, 1979.

[17] Miller, "Sex Discrimination and Title VII," 883; Mary Spencer, author's interview, November 9, 1978; Calvin Haley, author's interview, November 9, 1978; "Conversations with Alice Paul," 623-24; Phineas Indritz, author's interview, January 12, 1978. Spencer and Haley worked for Smith and knew him well. Phineas Indritz, a lawyer and close associate of Martha Griffiths, who was present during the debate, believes that chivalry was an important factor. The standard source on Smith is Bruce J. Dierenfield, "Congressman Howard W. Smith: A Political Biography" (unpublished Ph.D. dissertation, University of Virginia, 1981).

[18] Craig to Smith, n.d., Box 63, Smith Papers; Craig to [Jane] Grant, February 5, 1964, NWP, reel 108; *Public Papers of the Presidents of the United States: Lyndon B. Johnson, 1963-1964* (Washington, 1965), I, 259.

determine whether Johnson himself made this decision, but the reasons for it are fairly clear. From the day President Kennedy first proposed the legislation the strategy had been to hammer out a bill acceptable to a bipartisan majority of the House Judiciary Committee and to stick to that bill, not allowing the introduction on the House floor of amendments that might unravel the majority in favor of the legislation. In the past, opponents of civil rights legislation had used the amending process to kill or weaken legislation. The fact that no less a conservative leader than Howard Smith was taking an interest in a sex amendment made the administration all the more wary. Accordingly, the administration dissuaded Edith Green, a veteran Democratic congresswoman from Oregon, a member of the President's Commission on the Status of Women and the principal sponsor of recent legislation to require that women be given equal pay for equal work, from proposing her own sex amendments and even convinced her to oppose Smith's version.[19]

According to Nicholas deBelleville Katzenbach, deputy attorney general and the administration's principal manager of the legislation, the administration "believed, wrongly, that including sex might overburden the legislation." Although she was concerned about a sex amendment's possible effect on protective labor laws, Esther Peterson opposed an amendment primarily because she was worried that it might impede passage of the legislation. She believed that blacks, not women, faced the greatest discrimination, and she distrusted the amendment's proponents, Smith and the National Woman's party. Consequently, she wrote a letter to Emanuel Celler opposing any sex amendments, citing the recent report of the President's Commission on the Status of Women which had recommended against including "sex" in an executive order on discrimination in federal employment. " . . . discrimination based on sex, the Commission believes," Peterson quoted, "involves problems sufficiently different from discrimination based on the other factors listed to make separate treatment preferable."[20]

Although the administration succeeded in persuading Edith Green of its case, it failed to win over Martha Griffiths. A Democrat from East Lansing, Michigan, Griffiths was a shrewd, effective legislator and the first woman member of the powerful Ways and

[19] Nicholas deB. Katzenbach to the author, January 17, 1979; Burke Marshall, author's interview, March 15, 1979; *Congressional Quarterly Almanac, 88th Congress, 2nd Session . . . 1964*, XX (Washington, 1965), 343–45.

[20] Katzenbach to the author, January 17, 1979; *Cong. Record*, 88 Cong., 2 Sess., 2577 (February 8, 1964); Esther Peterson, author's interview; Margaret Hickey, author's interview; Peterson to Dorothy McDiarmid, January 9, 1973, Esther Peterson Papers (Schlesinger Library, Radcliffe College, Cambridge, Mass.).

Means Committee. Long aware of discrimination against women, Griffiths joined the National Woman's party in 1955 but came to regard it as an ineffectual organization on Capitol Hill. Contrary to an assertion by Alice Paul, Griffiths insists that she planned to introduce a sex amendment to the civil rights bill on the floor of the House if Smith did not. She has recalled that she deferred to Smith simply because he would command many more votes, probably over a hundred more than she could. In addition to being knowledgeable on the Hill, Griffiths was a skilled debater and was not reluctant to speak her mind. Interestingly, she was also attuned quite early to the white backlash against civil rights that was developing in the North. Just prior to the 1962 election her sharp warnings helped persuade President Kennedy to delay issuing his executive order against discrimination in federally assisted housing until after the election.[21]

Griffiths later recalled that prior to the floor debate she spoke of her plans only to Leonor Kretzer Sullivan and Edna Flannery Kelly, both friends and Democratic representatives. Women's networks have interested sociologists and historians of women, but if there was a women's network on Capitol Hill in 1964, it was of the loosest sort. There seems to have been relatively little communication among the women members of Congress. Yet, at the same time there was also a high consciousness of sex discrimination among them, irrespective of political party or ideology. Indeed, like the women of NWP, these professional politicians proved to be in the vanguard of the approaching women's movement. During and after the floor debate on the civil rights bill these elected women played a more important role than NWP, whose contribution to the passage of the bill had been to enlist Smith and other conservatives. For example, Emma Guffey Miller failed to get an appointment with the President to discuss the bill. NWP just did not possess enough influence or power.[22]

Having persuaded Edith Green not to introduce sex amendments

[21] Martha Griffiths, author's interview; Catherine East, author's interview, November 21, 1978; "Conversations with Alice Paul," 622–23; unsigned notes on sex amendment and notes by Hattie Milam Cook, February 1964, NWP, reel 108; Griffiths, "Women and Legislation," in Mary Lou Thompson, ed., *Voices of the New Feminism* (Boston, 1970), 103–14; Peggy Lamson, *Few Are Chosen: American Women in Political Life Today* (Boston, 1968), 88–98; Brauer, *John F. Kennedy and the Second Reconstruction*, 206–207. Griffiths' papers at the Bentley Historical Library in the Michigan Historical Collections, University of Michigan, are incomplete and revealed nothing about this legislative episode.

[22] Martha Griffiths, author's interview; Edna Kelley, author's interview, January 24, 1979; Paul to Elizabeth Carpenter, February 4, 1964, NWP, reel 108; "Conversations with Alice Paul," 621–22. The previous summer the National Woman's party had failed to get an appointment with President Kennedy to discuss ERA. See Nina Horton Avery to Emma Guffey Miller, July 13, 1963, NWP, reel 108.

and having alerted its forces, the administration apparently was not worried about Smith's amendment. Possibly, it was lulled by the defeat on February 5 and 6 of a series of amendments adding sex to different sections of the civil rights bill. Sponsored by John Vernard Dowdy, a Texas Democrat who opposed the bill as a whole, these amendments stimulated little debate and were defeated by hefty majorities. Late on February 8, however, a much more powerful sponsor rose, the venerable Howard Smith. Rather than attempt to amend the legislation in all places, he restricted his efforts to Title VII, the highly controversial employment section. His amendment, moreover, was vociferously defended by Martha Griffiths and four other women representatives.[23]

In his initial remarks Smith provoked considerable laughter on the floor by reading from a letter he had received from a woman in Omaha, Nebraska. She had facetiously proposed that he also offer an amendment correcting the imbalance between the number of men and women in the United States. "Just why the Creator would set up such an imbalance of spinsters, shutting off the 'right' of every female to have a husband of her own, is, of course, known only to nature. But I am sure you will agree that this is a grave injustice," Smith read to general amusement. Several times Smith insisted that he was serious about his amendment, but his comments appear to have been aimed at satirizing the logic behind the civil rights bill, which, in the view of Smith and many conservatives, was attempting to defy human nature. Smith did not dispute the perception of mock seriousness by presenting substantive arguments on behalf of his amendment. He did not, for example, cite data provided by the NWP of discrimination against women in employment.[24]

Emanuel Celler argued against his amendment in somewhat the same fashion. He protested that women were not in the minority in his own house, that although during nearly fifty years of happy marriage he usually had the last two words, those words were "Yes, dear." He quoted from Esther Peterson's letter and then questioned the notion of establishing blanket legal equality between the sexes. Celler, who long kept the Equal Rights Amendment bottled up in his committee, directed most of his fire at ERA, not against Smith's much more limited proposal: "Would male citizens be

[23] *Cong. Record*, 88 Cong., 2 Sess., 1978–79, 2264–65, 2280–81, 2297, 2577 (February 5, 6, 8, 1964).

[24] *Ibid.*, 2577 (February 8, 1964); Martha Griffiths, author's interview; Phineas Indritz, author's interview; Leila G. Whitney to Smith, January 26, 1964, Box 63, Smith Papers; "Employment Discrimination Omitted from the Civil Rights Bill and Fair Employment Practices Bill," January 1964, NWP, reel 108.

justified in insisting that women share with them the burdens of compulsory military service? What would become of traditional family relationships? What about alimony? Who would have the obligation of supporting whom? Would fathers rank equally with mothers in the right of custody to children? What would become of the crimes of rape and statutory rape? Would the Mann Act be invalidated? Would the many State and local provisions regulating working conditions and hours of employment for women be struck down?" Celler apparently regarded Smith's amendment merely as the entering wedge toward adoption of the Equal Rights Amendment.[25]

The two elderly chairmen then exchanged expressions of good-humored dismay at the other's position on the amendment and the bill, and they were soon joined by John Dowdy, Frances Payne Bolton of Ohio, a Republican and the senior woman in the House, and Ross Bass, a Democrat from Tennessee. They supported Smith's amendment, but in a light vein. The mood shifted, however, when Martha Griffiths spoke. " . . . I presume that if there had been any necessity to have pointed out that women were a second-class sex, the laughter would have proved it," she pointedly observed. " . . . I rise in support of the amendment," she declared, "primarily because I feel as a white woman when this bill has passed this House and the Senate and has been signed by the President that white women will be last at the hiring gate."[26]

Griffiths questioned Celler sharply, posing hypothetical cases to try to show that colored women would be protected by the legislation as written but that white women would not. In the abstract, it was a weak contention that Celler might have exposed through a hypothetical case of his own, such as one where a large trucking company that employed only white male drivers was sued for a job first by a qualified black man and then by an equally qualified black woman. If the company agreed to hire the black man but refused to hire the black woman it could have argued reasonably that it was not discriminating against her on the basis of race but on the basis of sex. Griffiths stood on firmer ground when she defended Smith's amendment on the practical grounds that without it black women would at least have some legal recourse, whereas white women would have none. Seeking victory, however, neither side confined its arguments to reason and practicality. Celler had raised the specter of the disintegration of the family and a revolution in sex roles. Griffiths now appealed to the emotions of opponents of the

[25] *Cong. Record.*, 88 Cong., 2 Sess., 2577–78 (February 8, 1964); quotations on p. 2577.
[26] *Ibid.*, 2578.

legislation as a whole. " . . . a vote against this amendment today by a white man is a vote against his wife, or his widow, or his daughter, or his sister," she warned.[27]

Three other congresswomen defended Smith's amendment, Katharine St. George, a Republican from New York, Catherine Dean May, a Republican from Washington, and Edna Kelly, a Democrat from Brooklyn. They emphasized the facts of job discrimination against women, called for equal treatment of women, and argued that the amendment would not rescind protective labor laws in the states. Nine southern men, including Smith, supported their cause on grounds of chivalry, equity, practicality, and emotion. Faced with a choice between hiring a white woman and a black woman of equal qualifications, Smith maintained, employers would choose the "colored woman" to prevent the government from suing them. "Some men in some areas of the country might support legislation which would discriminate against women," said James Russell Tuten of Georgia, "but never let it be said that a southern gentleman would vote for such legislation." "It is incredible to me that the authors of this monstrosity," Lucius Mendel Rivers, a senior South Carolinian, declared, ". . . would deprive the white woman of mostly Anglo-Saxon or Christian heritage equal opportunity before the employer."[28]

Edith Green led opposition to the amendment, questioning the motives of its southern defenders. She did not know whether she would be called an "uncle Tom" or an "aunt Jane" for her stand; in self-defense, she cited her past record as an advocate of women's rights. "For every discrimination that has been made against a woman in this country," she asserted, "there has been 10 times as much discrimination against the Negro of this country." The amendment, she said, would "clutter up the bill and it may later—very well—be used to help destroy this section of the bill by some of the very people who today support it," she warned. She also read a letter opposing the amendment from the legislative representative of the American Association of University Women. Green's position was supported by four leading members of the bipartisan coalition working for the civil rights bill, Frank Thompson, Jr., a Democrat from New Jersey, James Roosevelt, a Democrat from California, John Vliet Lindsay, a Republican from New York, and Charles McCurdy Mathias, Jr., a Republican from Maryland.[29]

[27] *Ibid.*, 2578–80; quotation on p. 2580.
[28] *Ibid.*, 2580–84; quotations on p. 2583.
[29] *Ibid.*, 2581–84; quotations on p. 2581.

When the vote was taken Martha Griffiths demanded tellers, and the amendment was approved 168 to 133. Reportedly, a woman in the gallery, which held a large representation from the NWP, cheered and was escorted out of the chamber. Unfortunately, no roll call was demanded, but Griffiths, who along with Celler was a teller, has recalled that most of the amendment's supporters were southerners and Republicans. Most nonsouthern Democrats voted against it. The amendment proved to be the only substantive change in the employment title made on the House floor. Interestingly, Smith's amendment inadvertently failed to insert "sex" in several places in Title VII, so two days later Frances Bolton offered a correcting amendment that the House accepted without objection, though Edith Green pointed out that the mistake illustrated that the original amendment had been ill-considered. Finally, Congressman Robert Paul Griffin, a Republican from Michigan, introduced an amendment that would have required that an individual filing a charge of sex discrimination certify that his or her spouse was unemployed and was unemployed at the time of the discriminatory act. This amendment provoked no debate and was defeated by a wide margin.[30]

The National Woman's party rejoiced in the victory, sealed on February 10 when the House approved the civil rights bill, and claimed sole credit for itself. The press gave the amendment only light-hearted treatment, if any at all. "Finally, the Southerners were wearing down—but not that other compulsively rhetorical segment of U. S. society: The Women," reported *Newsweek*, sarcastically noting the approval of the "May Craig Amendment (named for the frilly-bonneted Maine reporter seen so often on TV) . . . ." The result, the Washington *Post* commented lightly in an editorial, demonstrated "who's head of the house up there on the Hill."[31]

Some of the amendment's opponents, on the other hand, were dismayed. Griffiths has recalled that Jack Thomas Conway, a high-ranking official of the United Auto Workers, was furious at her. Esther Peterson reportedly said the amendment "might jeopardize the Civil Rights bill" and also had some harsh words for Griffiths, according to Griffiths. "This is the apples-and-bananas fallacy," Alexander Mordecai Bickel, the eminent constitutional lawyer from Yale, commented in the *New Republic*. "It is burdening with the

[30] *Ibid.*, 2584; Martha Griffiths, author's interview; New York *Times*, February 9, 1964, Sec. 1, pp. 1, 52; *Cong. Record*, 88 Cong., 2 Sess., 2718, 2720–21, 2728 (February 10, 1964); Legislative History and Scope of H.R. 7152, Title VII, Box 28, Burke Marshall Papers (John F. Kennedy Library, Boston, Mass.); *Congressional Quarterly Almanac*, XX, 348.

[31] Emma Guffey Miller to Fellow Members, February 14, 1964, NWP, reel 108; *Newsweek*, LXIII (February 17, 1964), 15; clipping, Washington *Post*, February 11, 1964, Scrapbook 8, Smith Papers.

regulation of bananas an agency already sufficiently overwhelmed with the problem of apples. That isn't the way to ensure adequate regulation of bananas; it is a way only to ensure less effective regulation of apples.'"[32]

Approval by the House was, of course, only the first of two critical steps the amendment needed to take, so the women who had fought for it in the House continued their efforts in the Senate. Martha Griffiths has written that she called Elizabeth Sutherland ("Liz") Carpenter, an assistant to President and Mrs. Johnson, "and asked her to tell the President that if that amendment came out of that bill, I would send my speech door to door in every member's district who had voted against it, and in my opinion, those who voted against it would never return to Congress." Members of NWP lobbied in the Senate, with both opponents and supporters of the civil rights bill as a whole. Emma Guffey Miller tried unsuccessfully to persuade James Oliver Eastland of Mississippi, chairman of the Committee on the Judiciary and a prominent opponent of the legislation, whom she regarded as "a great friend of Equal Rights for Women," to propose sex amendments to other parts of the civil rights bill.[33]

Liz Carpenter has no recollection of Griffiths' threat, but she has recalled that Johnson was always sympathetic to women's rights and that he had high regard for the women legislators with whom he had served. She has also said that at this point Esther Peterson lobbied hard for the amendment's retention. Peterson herself has explained her reversal simply by reflecting that once the amendment had cleared the House she could see no harm in leaving it in. Peterson's papers provide no additional evidence of her change in position, but Margaret A. Hickey, who knew Peterson well and who was head of the Citizens' Advisory Council on the Status of Women, has explained that Peterson believed in using every means available to help women. Peterson and Hickey opposed ERA because it threatened protective legislation, but it was unclear that adding sex to Title VII would also threaten protective legislation, contrary to Emanuel Celler's argument.[34]

[32] Quotation from Esther Peterson in clipping, Washington *Post*, February 10, 1964, Scrapbook 8, Smith Papers; Bickel, "Sleepers in the Civil Rights Bill," *New Republic*, CL (February 29, 1964), 16; Martha Griffiths, author's interview.

[33] Griffiths, "Women and Legislation," 113; Miller to Mrs. J. Alton Phillips, February 17, 1964 (second quotation); Miller to Ruth Gage-Colby and others, February 22, 1964, NWP, reel 108.

[34] Liz Carpenter, author's interview, June 21, 1979; Esther Peterson, author's interview; Margaret Hickey, author's interview; Catherine East, author's interview, August 6, 1979. East did not know that Peterson had reversed herself, though she imagined that she was in favor of the amendment.

Hobart Taylor, Jr., a black assistant to Johnson and a friend of Martha Griffiths', has recalled Johnson's asking him about the sex amendment and his recommending that it be retained. Johnson also received pleas from a number of women activists from his home state of Texas and elsewhere asking him to support women's rights in the civil rights bill. Responding to these petitioners on his behalf on March 27, Peterson wrote that it was not practical to add further amendments to the bill, implying that Johnson would not seek the elimination of the present one. A month later Johnson himself signed a letter explicitly accepting Title VII as amended.[35]

Given the positive support for the amendment as well as the lack of significant opposition to it, Johnson's decision to accept the work of the House is understandable, especially in light of the larger legislative struggle. The House bill was the strongest one Johnson might hope to have enacted. Most important, if the Senate approved a bill substantially the same as the House version, it would remove the necessity of sending the legislation to conference. A conference might well have effectively postponed action until the next Congress convened in 1965. Much of Johnson's efforts, therefore, as well as the efforts of his allies in the upper chamber, were directed at getting the Senate to keep the House bill substantially intact. They fully expected it to be subjected to an onslaught of weakening amendments there and did not want to encourage that process. In their eyes the sex amendment must have failed to warrant a potentially damaging fight. The prudent course was simply to let it be. When an aide to Hubert Horatio Humphrey, Jr., floor manager of the bill in the Senate, briefed him before an appearance on "Meet the Press" in early March, he noted that May Craig, who was "responsible for the women's equal rights provision . . . may ask about that." He suggested that Humphrey say, as he had said before, "I'm all for women," which is what Humphrey did. Peterson's reversal is, of course, also understandable in view of the larger legislative strategy. Thus, much as opposition to the civil rights bill proved decisive in adding the sex amendment in the House, the forces favoring the bill proved decisive in retaining the amendment in the Senate.[36]

[35] Martha Griffiths to the author, March 30, 1979; Hobart Taylor, author's interview, April 16, 1979; Peterson to Mrs. Cecil Norton Broy, March 27, 1964, and similar letters to others, Esther Peterson Papers; Lyndon B. Johnson to Mrs. Modell Scruggs, April 23, 1964, and attached letters and notes, Executive HU 3, Lyndon B. Johnson Papers (Lyndon B. Johnson Library, Austin, Texas).

[36] Bob Jensen to Humphrey, March 7, 1964, Box 241, Hubert H. Humphrey Papers (Minnesota Historical Society, St. Paul, Minn.); *Congressional Quarterly Almanac*, XX, 354–76; transcript of "Meet the Press," March 8, 1964, Vol. 18, No. 8. Robert Jensen served as Humphrey's aide.

One man stood in the way, though. Everett McKinley Dirksen of Illinois, the leader of the Republican minority in the Senate, held most of the cards on the civil rights bill. As the leader of a group of moderate and conservative Republicans, largely from the Midwest, he would decide whether cloture would be invoked and the southern filibuster broken. Hence, he had the power to extract some changes in the House bill and potentially to upset Johnson's legislative strategy. One of the changes he contemplated was the elimination of the sex amendment. In a working paper prepared in late February he questioned whether it would be wise to threaten the laws which protected women from the "heavy manual labor of the sort that falls to the lot of some men." "I suggest, therefore," he wrote, "that we look at this problem with compassion and care. We do not want women to be discriminated against, but we do not want, through inadvertence, to remove the protection which is appropriate." Although no documentary evidence has turned up in Dirksen's papers, it is possible, given his long record of support for business interests, that he was actually responding to the views of large employers of women, such as telephone companies, who worried about the sex amendment's financial implications. According to Esther Peterson, the telephone industry lobbied against the amendment in the Senate.[37]

Once again the National Woman's party and a woman legislator, particularly the latter, played critical roles. NWP alerted Republican senators whom they considered favorable to women's rights to the views of Dirksen. In Margaret Chase Smith of Maine, a highly respected middle-of-the-road veteran and one of only two women in the Senate (the other was Maureen Brown Neuberger, a Democrat from Oregon), it had a formidable ally. Smith, it should be noted, was a candidate for her party's presidential nomination in 1964. Although her candidacy attracted little support, primarily because most people would not take a woman's presidential candidacy seriously, it did suggest that Smith herself would not accept traditional notions of woman's place. It also provides another graphic example of a woman politician anticipating the women's rights movement by several years. Smith has recalled that Dirksen was quite irritated with her opposition to his position on the sex amendment but that she was supported in the Republican Conference by

[37] Working papers, Title VII, *ca.* February 26, 1964, f. 256, Everett M. Dirksen Papers (Dirksen Research Center, Pekin, Ill.); *Congressional Quarterly Almanac*, XX, 354–59; Esther Peterson, author's interview, July 30, 1979. I have encountered only one piece of documentary evidence of lobbying by the telephone industry. Herbert H. Butler to Eugene J. McCarthy, March 3, 1964, Box 121, Eugene McCarthy Papers (Minnesota Historical Society).

Clifford Philip Case of New Jersey, George David Aiken of Vermont (who had been a member of the President's Commission on the Status of Women), Gordon Llewellyn Allott of Colorado, and one other man whose name she could not recall. Several times the conference considered Dirksen's proposal that the sex amendment be deleted, but he repeatedly failed to obtain a majority and finally gave up, announcing that he did so "in order to avoid the wrath of the women."[38]

With the threat from Dirksen overcome, the sex amendment faced no further barriers, though the civil rights bill did. Private negotiations between Dirksen and the bill's sponsors, which resulted in largely minor changes (or at least changes that the House accepted without requiring a conference), however, eventually smoothed the way for breaking the southern filibuster on June 10, 1964. Before that occurred several southerners proposed sex amendments to other parts of the bill, but this time there was no Howard Smith and no Martha Griffiths. More important, though, the southern strategy was to filibuster, an all-or-nothing strategy, which, once Dirksen and the administration reached agreement, gave the southerners nothing. After the filibuster was broken, the Senate approved an amendment by Wallace Foster Bennett, a Republican from Utah, providing for employers to continue to differentiate in the payment of wages on the basis of sex if such differentiation was allowed under the Fair Labor Standards Act as amended by the Equal Pay Act. Soon thereafter, Ruth Gage-Colby, a liberal member of NWP, advised Alice Paul that "we had best not press too hard for a complete inclusion lest we lose the splendid gains we've made." In the end the 1964 Civil Rights Act prohibited discrimination on the basis of sex only in the area of employment.[39]

After President Johnson signed the legislation in July, Alice Paul wrote a comrade that it "would help us if you could get publicity . . . giving some credit to the National Woman's Party. We bore the entire burden of this battle and with absolutely no help of any kind from other women's organizations."[40] Although it was true

[38] Anita Pollitzer to Margaret Chase Smith, April 2, 1964; Miriam G. Holden to Alice Paul, April 8, 1964; Holden *et al.* to Kenneth Keating, April 8, 1964; Smith to Pollitzer, April 9, 1964; Emma Guffey Miller to Mary Kennedy, April 15, 1964; unsigned draft to Mary C. Kennedy [June 1964] (for Dirksen quotation), all in NWP, reel 109; Margaret Chase Smith to the author, December 20, 1978. Unfortunately, the Margaret Chase Smith Papers, which will be housed in a library bearing her name in Skowhegan, Maine, are not open for research.

[39] Gage-Colby to Paul, June 15, 1964; "Secretary" of National Woman's party to Anita Pollitzer, May 21, 1964, NWP, reel 109; *Congressional Quarterly Almanac*, XX, 354–76; *Cong. Record*, 88 Cong., 2 Sess., 12925 (June 8, 1964; an example of a sex amendment that died on the vine); *ibid.*, 13647 (June 12, 1964).

[40] Paul to unidentified [possibly May Craig or Mary Kennedy], July 10, 1964, NWP, reel 109.

that no other women's organizations had helped, certainly individual women politicians had, most especially Martha Griffiths, Margaret Chase Smith, and finally, even Esther Peterson.

The prohibition of sexual discrimination in employment, therefore, represented a convergence of conflicting, unrelated, and sometimes inherently ambiguous aims. It came about in the first place because of the rise of the civil rights movement, which led Presidents Kennedy and Johnson to seek legislation banning racially discriminatory practices. The ban on sex discrimination was merely an amendment to that legislation. Secondly, it resulted from the efforts of women activists, from both the feminist National Woman's party and from women in Congress, who sought the ban on its merits and who made the most out of the limited means they had available to them. Thirdly, it went through the House because of the support it received from southern opponents of the legislation as a whole, most notably from Howard Smith. Their motives are the hardest to determine precisely, but appear to have involved a combination of a desire to thwart or at least ridicule the legislation and a feeling of chivalry toward white women. Finally, the amendment also survived in the Senate because of legislative strategy, but this time the strategy of the legislation's supporters who wanted to get it approved as quickly and surely as possible, though here again women activists played an important role. Thus, the ban on sex discrimination came about because of both opposition to and support for the goals of the civil rights movement and because of the determination and skill of a relatively small number of women activists who anticipated the women's rights movement by several years.

The Origins of the Women's Liberation Movement

Sara M. Evans

According to Sheila Rowbotham:

> The emphasis on the importance of personal questions of liberation has not only recurred again and again whenever there is a high degree of participation of women, it has almost been a precondition for the mobilization of women in any significant numbers. (1)

While there is a crucial truth in her analysis, it is also a fact that previous feminist movements in the United States have generally failed to offer a thoroughgoing critique of personal life. Rather they have tended to use traditional definitions of woman as housewife to bolster their own arguments for political rights. Charlotte Perkins Gilman was quite alone in her critique of woman's role in the family and advocacy of socialised housework, and even she failed to make a frontal assault on sex-roles as such. (2) It is a new and striking characteristic of the contemporary women's movement that at the center of its existence is the assertion that "the personal is political." Such an assumption came first from the young women in the new left and has since penetrated the more conservative "women's rights" portions of the movement. As a result, contemporary feminism has focused not simply on legal or public inequities but on the broader questions of sex roles, socialization, and the economic function of women's work in the home.

The structural basis for this development lay in a process I shall call the "socialization of social production" which has created a widening gap between the myths and the realities of women's lives. Much of the work traditionally associated with the home has been brought into the public world of paid labor by the expansion of social services and white collar bureaucratic occupations since the second world war. While the analogous process in the nineteenth century offered men a clear role, wage-earner, these more recent developments have been clouded by the extension of a role associated with the private sphere of home into the public sphere. Women from educated, middle-income families in particular who drew their identities from the domestic social role of housewife lived in an ambiguous limbo as their roles were pulled out from under them.

Modern sex roles have been shaped by the sexual division of production which occurred when nineteenth century industrialization and urbanization removed most production of goods from the home to the factory. (3) The logic of this development forced men to work outside the home in order to "support" the family. Production within the home, social production, was now defined as "women's work." While women continued to prepare food and other necessities consumed within the home, their work focused increasingly on the socialization of children as the family became more child-centered and on the creation of a private haven from the competitive "outside" world. This growing division between the family and the outside workplace was experienced as a separation of public and private, and it permitted a radical polarization of traditional male and female images.

On the one hand the public realm, the sphere of men, came to represent rationality, competition, and political life. On the other hand the private realm, maintained by women, embodied emotion, cooperation, and personal life. Barbara Welter has described the crystallization of this female side of the polarization into the "cult of true womanhood" in the nineteenth century. (4) The same themes remained components of the female stereotype into the twentieth century. They appeared in the "cult of the home" at the turn of the century and the "feminine mystique" in the 1950's.

Despite their pervasive tenacity, however, the economic basis for sharply contrasting sexual images had seriously eroded by the mid-twentieth century. The changing life cycle of most women and the maturation of the corporate economy combined to produce radically new employment patterns for women. Women married younger, had fewer children, and lived longer. By the age of thirty-five a middle-class housewife faced the second half of her life with little to do in a house full of conveniences and emptied of children from nine a.m. to three p.m. (5)

Moreover, as women became available to work outside the home the American economy underwent changes which both encouraged and facilitated their doing so. Beginning with World War II and continuing through the 1950's and 1960's white collar clerical and service jobs boomed. Whole new industries emerged around mass media, advertising, and computer technology. From 1940 to 1965 government spending multiplied more than ten times. Corporations also consolidated, expanded, and diversified, creating their own gigantic bureaucracies. Increasingly their growth was dependent on the production of new technology and on new techniques of advertising and marketing.

Employment in the services grew 194% from 1947 to 1968, while employment in manufacturing grew only 31%. In 1947, 49% of the workforce was in services and 51% in manufacturing. By 1968, the ratio had shifted to 64% in services and 36% in manufacturing. (6) In effect the expansion of the social services removed into the sphere of paid work many of the social functions previously performed in the family or by female volunteers.

These changes constituted the socialization of social

production, a process similar to the socialization of goods production in the nineteenth century. The earlier economic revolution had brought men into the labor force in order to produce goods. This time, however, many of the jobs created in fields such as health care, education, child care, clerical work, social work, and advertising constituted extensions of the traditional social role of housewife, thus easing the transition for women from housewifery to paid employment. Educated women in middle income families already had the skills for the kinds of jobs which were opening up: technical and clerical jobs and social service work such as teaching, nursing, and social work. In 1966, 70% of all families in the $7,000 to $15,000 annual income range had at least two workers in the family, and the second was most often a woman. (7) Throughout the 1950's and 1960's the group entering the labor force at the greatest rate was married women from middle income families.

These same women, however, were thoroughly caught up in the resurgence of domestic ideology, the "feminine mystique." They constituted the sector of the female population who married early, had more children, and moved to suburbia. Yet the home as workplace was becoming increasingly alienating. The fantasy of total emotional and intellectual fulfillment in marriage and family frequently led to "colossal disappointment, guilt, and self-castigation" when it failed to be realized. (8) Growing suburbs isolated women and children farther and farther from the centers of public and community life. (9) The intensification of the family's function as a private enclave to which members escape from the outside world for warmth, nurture and support resulted in an inexhaustible stream of emotional demands placed on women. And finally, as the household technology developed, new standards of housework maintained the amount of work required at a high level. Consumption oriented, psychologically manipulative advertising reinforced and multiplied these new demands. For example, it used to be that soap would clean everything. By the 1950's the housewife was expected to choose and use a different cleanser for every surface in her home and on her body. And "clean" meant sootless, odorless, and antiseptic.

The women who found themselves simultaneously pushed out of the home and pulled back into it suffered an alienation at least as deep as the women who chose to stay at home. They may well have wanted to work, to escape loneliness and boredom. Yet a woman's work was likely to be threatening to her husband. It implied that he was not being a "good provider." Her guilt required that she avoid training, long-range planning, or high aspirations. As a result she could not resist discrimination when the only jobs open to her were repetitious and boring. This structural inability to take oneself seriously induced deep insecurity and a negative self-image. (10) In addition these women were shouldering two jobs. They continued to be the ones responsible for household work and they defined themselves as wives and mothers. Their bodies were at work but their psyches remained at home.

The oppression of those women revolved around their primary self-definition as "housewives" whether they worked inside the home or outside. Any revolt which drew on their discontent could neither accept a traditional stereotypic view of "female nature" as particularly suited to home and motherhood nor could it restrict itself simply to a critique of inequities in the public realm.

For this reason the emergence of NOW in 1966 did not initiate a massive feminist movement. NOW was the product of contradictions experienced by professional women. Professional women throughout the 1950's were the most unmistakably "deviant," and often harbored among themselves the few remnants of feminism left. Precisely because they perceived their work as important, they felt even more acutely the discrimination against them. Having openly admitted a certain level of drive and ambition, they were far more likely to see discriminatory hiring, training, promotion, and payrates as unfair. Other women could justify their unwillingness to fight against such barriers by saying "I wouldn't be here if I didn't have to" or "I am only doing this for my family, not for myself." Professional women could not do this. In addition, Jo Freeman has demonstrated that throughout the 1950's and 1960's the relative deprivation of professional women increased at a greater rate than for any other group. (11)

These women, in general, accepted the division between the public and the private. Betty Friedan's devastating critique of housewifery ends up with a prescription that women, like men, should be allowed to participate in both realms. In effect she urges women to do it all — to be super women — by assuming the dual roles of housewife and professional. She makes no serious assault on the division of labor within the home. For Friedan it was easier to imagine a professional woman hiring a professional "housewife" to take her place in the home than to challenge the whole range of sex roles or the division of social life into home/work, private/public, female/male domains. (12)

The catalyst for a more thoroughgoing critique and a mass mobilization of American women developed among young female participants in the social movements of the 1960's. These daughters of the middle class had received mixed, paradoxical messages about what it meant to grow up female. On the one hand the cultural ideal — held up by media, parents, and schools — informed them that their only true happiness lay in the twin roles of wife and mother. At the same time they could observe the reality that housewifery was distinctly unsatisfactory for millions of suburban women, and furthermore that despite the best efforts of the Ladies Home Journal, most American women could expect to work outside the home a substantial portion of their lives. Such contradictions left young, educated women in the 1960's dry tinder for the spark of revolt. The preconditions for that spark developed within the southern civil rights movement and portions of the new left.

Many former activists in the civil rights movement and the new left have attributed the rise of women's liberation to the discrepancy within the movement between the goal of equality and the actual subordination of women within it. I have found, however, that the preconditions for female revolt developed in those parts of the movement which offered women the greatest space in which to develop their own potential and discover their own strength. In the process they also accumulated many of the tools for movement building: a language to describe oppression and justify revolt, experience in the strategy and tactics of organizing, and a beginning sense of themselves collectively as objects of discrimination.

The two most important incubators of feminism within the new left were the Student Nonviolent Coordinating Committee (SNCC) and the community organizing projects of Students for a Democratic Society (the Economic and Research Action Projects: ERAP) which were modeled on SNCC. By late 1965 an interconnected group of experienced female organizers had articulated an analysis of women's oppression which focused squarely on the issues of sex roles. (13)

The most important source for new self-images within the movement lay in the nature of women's work. In contrast to the later mass mobilizations which placed a premium on public speaking and self-assertion in large groups, the vision of SNCC and of ERAP translated into daily realities of hard work and responsibility which admitted few sexual limitations. Young women's sense of purpose was reinforced by the knowledge that the work they did and the responsibilities they assumed were central to the movement.

In direct action demonstrations many women discovered untapped reservoirs of courage. Rarely did women expect or receive any special protection in demonstrations or jails. Frequently direct action teams were equally divided between women and men on the theory that the presence of women might lessen the violent reaction.

Working in local communities, organizing around voter registration, teaching in freedom schools, running libraries, creating block organizations or groups of welfare mothers, many women reached well beyond their previously assumed limits. One participant in the Mississippi "freedom summer" of 1964 wrote:

> I was overwhelmed at the idea of setting up a library all by myself.... Then can you imagine how I felt when at Oxford, while I was learning how to drop on the ground to protect my face, my ears, and my breasts, I was asked to coordinate the libraries in the entire project's community centers. I wanted to cry "HELP!" in a number of ways.... (14)

In SDS projects a few men were good organizers but most good organizers were women. The skills required by community organizing meshed with the social training of females: warmth, empathy, compassion, interpersonal radiation. Furthermore, community organizing tends to draw upon a largely female constituency. In northern communities, while male leaders futilely attempted to organize streetcorner youth, winos, and unemployed men, women successfully created welfare rights organizations, though their efforts received much less attention. (15)

Female community leadership in both the south and the north provided new role models as well. In 1962 SNCC staff member Charles Sherrod wrote the office that in every southwest Georgia county "there is always a 'mama.' She is usually a militant woman in the community, out-spoken, understanding, and willing to catch hell, having already caught her share." (16) The newsletters of ERAP were likewise filled with stories of courage in the face of hardship, of women who stood up for themselves against any and all authority. (17) For many middle-class white women in the new left these women were also "mamas" in the sense of being substitute mother-figures, new models of the meaning of womanhood. (18)

The opportunities to develop new strengths and a heightened sense of self were strengthened by the personal nature of new left politics. The new left consistently emphasized the importance of building new kinds of human relationships, and the political import of personal choice. Jane Stembridge, daughter of a Southern Baptist minister who left her studies at Union Seminary in New York to become the first paid staff member of SNCC, put it:

> ...finally it all boils down to human relationship. ...It is the question of...whether I shall go on living in isolation or whether there shall be a we. The student movement is not a cause...it is a collision between this one person and that one person. It is a I am going to sit beside you.... Love alone is radical. (19)

Three years later the SDS University Committee reported:

> The free university is not defined by a particular structural arrangement, but by the questions the participants ask.... The central question of the free university seems to be "what kind of interpersonal relations allow people to treat each other as human beings?" (20)

Within the student movement the intensely personal nature of social action and the commitment to equality resulted in a kind of anarchic democracy and a general questioning of all the socially accepted rules. "Let the people decide" and "participatory democracy" were the ideological passwords of SNCC and SDS. A spirit of moral idealism permeated the new left.

The ideas and ideals of students in the new left reflected the fact that they were in many ways engaged in a cultural revolt. The counter culture of the late 1960's grew from the perceptions of thousands of young people that suburban material "success" constituted a hollow promise and from their determination to build their lives around more meaningful goals. It was a natural extension for women to apply the same critique to sexual relationships: Casey Hayden and Mary King wrote in 1965:

> Having learned from the movement to think radically about the personal worth and abilities of people whose role in society had gone unchallenged before, a lot of women in the movement have begun trying to apply those lessons to their own relations with men. Each of us probably has her own story of the various results.... (21)

According to Casey and Mary, however, such ideas could be discussed seriously only among women. Despite their own cultural rebellions, men in the movement clung to traditional notions of sexual relationships. The effort to create a haven, a "beloved community" of equality either racially or sexually, foundered in a movement so deeply enmeshed in the very culture it set out to challenge. Feminism was born out of this contradiction: that the same movement which permitted women to grow and to develop self-esteem, new strength and skills, generally kept them out of public leadership roles and reinforced expectations based on woman's role as housewife: houseworker, nurturer, sex object, unintellectual.

In the years after 1965 the movement became increasingly alienating for women. Women were increasingly relegated to running the mimeograph machines, preparing and serving coffee, washing dishes, and being available for sex. Draft card burning, mass demonstrations, strident oratory left women more and more alienated and secondary. (22)

But women had developed along the way too much self-respect and too much organizing skill to acquiesce quietly. They rounded out the new left focus on the personal nature of political work by asserting that personal life was in itself political. They drew on the analogy with black oppression in defining a complex of discriminatory attitudes (sexism) comparable to racism which were backed by an infrastructure of discriminatory institutions and laws. They also understood quickly by analogy that women had internalized many of the negative things attributed to them and that mutual solidarity and support were necessary to wage a struggle that was at once internal and external.

When young women from middle-income families revolted against the replication of the housewife role within the new life, they did so with a sense of strength that allowed them to name and to politicize a dilemma experienced by millions of women. Where the public ideology of NOW had focused on legal inequities, the newer radical women's liberation movement made a critique of family and personal life the cornerstone of its existence. It created a medium, the consciousness-raising group, through which individual women could develop a sense of the social nature and political import of deeply ingrained attitudes, habits, and assumptions.

Without their critique, there could have been no mass movement, only a strong feminist lobby. For millions of American women only a movement which addressed their oppression as housewives — both in the home and in the outside workplace — could have generated the massive shift in consciousness which we can observe in the past six to eight years.

1. Sheila Rowbotham, WOMEN, RESISTANCE AND REVOLUTION (New York: Pantheon Books, 1972), 125.

2. Charlotte Perkins Gilman, WOMEN AND ECONOMICS (New York: Harper & Row, 1956); THE HOME: ITS WORK AND INFLUENCE (New York, 1910).

3. To my knowledge the term "sexual division of production" was first used in Kathryn Johnson and Peggy Somers, "The Political Economy of Sexism" (unpublished manuscript, mimeograph, June, 1972). While the process to which it refers has been analysed many times, I find their term useful because it focuses on the productive nature of women's work in the home and on the interrelation between the home and the outside workplace.

4. Barbara Welter, "The Cult of True Womanhood," AMERICAN QUARTERLY, LVIII (summer, 1966), 151-74.

5. See Robert W. Smuts, WOMEN AND WORK IN AMERICA (New York: Schocken Books, 1971), 24-37.

6. Daniel Bell, "Labor in the Post-Industrial Society," DISSENT, XIX (winter, 1972), 168; figures from THE U.S. ECONOMY IN 1970, U.S. Bureau of Labor Statistics Bulletin 1673 (Washington, D.C.: U.S. Government Printing Office, 1970); see also Victor Fuchs, THE SERVICE ECONOMY (New York: Columbia University Press, 1968).

7. Smuts, WOMEN AND WORK, 64; Ravenna Nelson, "The Changing Image of the Career Woman," JOURNAL OF SOCIAL ISSUES, 28 (1973), 34; William Henry Chafe, THE AMERICAN WOMAN: HER CHANGING SOCIAL, ECONOMIC, AND POLITICAL ROLES, 1920-1970 (New York: Oxford University Press, 1972), 190-191.

8. Ellen and Kenneth Kenniston, "An American Anachronism: The Image of Women and Work," AMERICAN SCHOLAR, 33 (summer, 1964), 355, 357.

9. Ibid., 371; Alva Reimar Myrdal and Viola Klein, WOMEN'S TWO ROLES: HOME AND WORK (London: Routledge and Paul, 1956), 136-53; David Reisman, Nathan Glazer, and Reuel Denney, THE LONELY CROWD: A STUDY OF THE CHANGING AMERICAN CHARACTER (New York: Doubleday, 1953), 332-33; Margaret Meade, "What Women Want," FORTUNE, 34 (December, 1946), 174-75; Betty Friedan, THE FEMININE MYSTIQUE (New York: Dell, 1963).

10. See Helen Hacker, "Women as a Minority Group," SOCIAL FORCES, 30 (October, 1951), 60-69.

11. Jo Freeman, "The Politics of Women's Liberation" (unpublished dissertation, University of Chicago, 1973).

12. Friedan, FEMININE MYSTIQUE.

13. See Casey Hayden and Mary King, "Sex and Caste," LIBERATION (April, 1966), 35-36; interviews with Mary King, July 24, 1973, Washington, D.C.; Dorothy Burlage, August 5, 1973, Cambridge, Massachusetts; Vivian Rothstein, July 10, 1973, Chicago, Illinois; Cathy Cade,

July 21, 1973, Berkeley, California; Leni Wildflower, July 18, 1973, San Jose, California; Jimmy Garrett, July 16, 1973, Washington, D.C.; and others.

14. Elizabeth Sutherland, LETTERS FROM MISSISSIPPI (New York: McGraw-Hill, 1965), 111-12.

15. This conclusion is a product of interviews with participants in most ERAP projects and of impressions gleaned from the papers of Students for a Democratic Society, State Historical Society of Wisconsin.

16. Quoted in James Forman, THE MAKING OF BLACK REVOLUTIONARIES: A PERSONAL ACCOUNT (New York: Macmillan, 1972), 276.

17. SDS Papers, State Historical Society of Wisconsin.

18. Interviews with Dorothy Burlage; Mimi Feingold, July 16, 1973, San Francisco, California; Mary King; Sue Thrasher, June 30, 1973, Atlanta, Georgia.

19. Quoted in Howard Zinn, S N C C: THE NEW ABOLITIONISTS (Boston: Beacon Press, 1965), 7.

20. "Report of the SDS University Committee," June 28-30, 1965, SDS Papers, Series 3, State Historical Society of Wisconsin.

21. Hayden and King, "Sex and Caste," 35.

22. This is a generalized impression drawn from primary and secondary sources and from interviews with participants. See James O'Brien, "The Development of the New Left in the United States, 1960-1965" (unpublished dissertation, University of Wisconsin, 1971); and Kirkpatrick Sale, SDS (New York: Vintage Books, 1974).

SARA M. EVANS has been active in the civil rights movement, the women's liberation movement, and the New American Movement (NAM). She is writing her Ph.D. thesis on the origins of the recent women's liberation movement.

RACE, CLASS, AND GENDER: PROSPECTS FOR AN ALL-INCLUSIVE SISTERHOOD

BONNIE THORNTON DILL

The concept of sisterhood has been an important unifying force in the contemporary women's movement. By stressing the similarities of women's secondary social and economic positions in all societies and in the family, this concept has been a binding force in the struggle against male chauvinism and patriarchy. However, as we review the past decade, it becomes apparent that the cry "Sisterhood is powerful!" has engaged only a few segments of the female population in the United States. Black, Hispanic, Native American, and Asian American women of all classes, as well as many working-class women, have not readily identified themselves as sisters of the white middle-class women who have been in the forefront of the movement.

This article examines the applications of the concept of sisterhood and some of the reasons for the limited participation of racially and ethnically distinct women in the women's movement, with particular reference to the experience and consciousness of Afro-American women. The first section presents a critique of sisterhood as a binding force for all women and examines the limitations of the concept for both theory and practice when applied to women who are neither white nor middle class. In the second section, the importance of women's perception of themselves and their place in society is explored as a way of understanding the differences and similarities between Black and white women. Data from two studies, one of college-educated Black women and the other of Black female household workers, are presented to illuminate both the ways in which the structures of race, gender, and class intersect in the lives of Black women and the women's perceptions of the impact of these structures on their lives. This article concludes with a discussion of the pros-

Feminist Studies 9, no. 1 (Spring 1983).

pects for sisterhood and suggests political strategies that may provide a first step toward a more inclusive women's movement.

THE LIMITATIONS OF SISTERHOOD

In a recent article, historian Elizabeth Fox-Genovese provided a political critique of the concept of sisterhood.[1] Her analysis identifies some of the current limitations of this concept as a rallying point for women across the boundaries of race and class. Sisterhood is generally understood as a nurturant, supportive feeling of attachment and loyalty to other women which grows out of a shared experience of oppression. A term reminiscent of familial relationships, it tends to focus upon the particular nurturant and reproductive roles of women and, more recently, upon commonalities of personal experience. Fox-Genovese suggests that sisterhood has taken two different political directions. In one, women have been treated as unique, and sisterhood was used as a basis for seeking to maintain a separation between the competitive values of the world of men (the public-political sphere) and the nurturant values of the world of women (the private-domestic sphere). A second, more recent and progressive expression of the concept views sisterhood as an element of the feminist movement which serves as a means for political and economic action based upon the shared needs and experiences of women. Both conceptualizations of sisterhood have limitations in encompassing the racial and class differences among women. These limitations have important implications for the prospects of an all-inclusive sisterhood.

Fox-Genovese argues that the former conceptualization, which she labels bourgeois individualism, resulted in "the passage of a few middle class women into the public sphere," but sharpened the class and racial divisions between them and lower-class minority women.[2] In the latter conceptualization, called the politics of personal experience, sisterhood is restricted by the experiential differences that result from the racial and class divisions of society.

> Sisterhood has helped us, as it helped so many of our predecessors, to forge ourselves as political beings. Sisterhood has mobilized our loyalty to each other and hence to ourselves. It has given form to a dream of genuine equality for women. But without a broader politics directed toward the kind of social transformation that will provide social justice for all human beings, it will, in a

poignant irony, result in our dropping each other by the wayside as we compete with rising desperation for crumbs.[3]

These two notions of sisterhood, as expressed in the current women's movement, offer some insights into the alienation many Black women have expressed about the movement itself.

The bourgeois individualistic theme present in the contemporary women's movement led many Black women to express the belief that the movement existed merely to satisfy needs for personal self-fulfillment on the part of white middle-class women.[4] The emphasis on participation in the paid labor force and escape from the confines of the home, seemed foreign to many Black women. After all, as a group they had had higher rates of paid labor force participation than their white counterparts for centuries, and many would have readily accepted what they saw as the "luxury" of being a housewife. At the same time, they expressed concern that white women's gains would be made at the expense of Blacks and/or that having achieved their personal goals, these so-called sisters would ignore or abandon the cause of racial discrimination. Finally, and perhaps most important, the experiences of racial oppression made Black women strongly aware of their group identity and consequently more suspicious of women who, initially at least, defined much of their feminism in personal and individualistic terms.

Angela Davis, in "Reflections on the Black Woman's Role in the Community of Slaves," stresses the importance of group identity for black women. "Under the impact of racism the black woman has been continually constrained to inject herself into the desperate struggle for existence. . . . As a result, black women have made significant contributions to struggles against racism and the dehumanizing exploitation of a wrongly organized society. In fact, it would appear that the intense levels of resistance historically maintained by black people and thus the historical function of the Black liberation struggle as harbinger of change throughout the society are due in part to the greater objective equality between the black man and the black woman."[5] The sense of being part of a collective movement toward liberation has been a continuing theme in the autobiographies of contemporary black women.

Ideas and experiences vary, but Shirley Chisholm, Gwendolyn Brooks, Angela Davis and other Black women who wrote autobiographies during the seventies offer similar . . . visions of the black woman's role in the struggle for

Black liberation. The idea of collective liberation . . . says that society is not a protective arena in which an individual black can work out her own destiny and gain a share of America's benefits by her own efforts. . . . Accordingly, survival, not to mention freedom, is dependent on the values and actions of the groups as a whole, and if indeed one succeeds or triumphs it is due less to individual talent than to the group's belief in and adherence to the idea that freedom from oppression must be acted out and shared by all.[6]

Sisterhood is not new to Black women. It has been institutionalized in churches. In many black churches, for example, membership in the church entitles one to address the women as "sisters" and the men as "brothers." Becoming a sister is an important rite of passage which permits young women full participation in certain church rituals and women's clubs where these nurturant relationships among women are reinforced.[7] Sisterhood was also a basis for organization in the club movements that began in the late 1800s.[8] Finally, it is clearly exemplified in Black extended family groupings that frequently place great importance on female kinship ties. Research on kinship patterns among urban Blacks identifies the nurturant and supportive feelings existing among female kin as a key element in family stability and survival.[9]

While Black women have fostered and encouraged sisterhood, we have not used it as the anvil to forge our political identities. This contrasts sharply with the experiences of many middle-class white women who have participated in the current women's movement. The political identities of Afro-American women have largely been formed around issues of race. National organizations of Black women, many of which were first organized on the heels of the nineteenth century movement for women's rights, "were (and still are) decidedly feminist in the values expressed in their literature and in many of the concerns which they addressed, yet they also always focused upon issues which resulted from the racial oppression affecting *all* black people."[10] This commitment to the improvement of the race has often led Black women to see feminist issues quite differently from their white sisters. And, racial animosity and mistrust have too often undermined the potential for coalition between Black and white women since the women's suffrage campaigns.

Many contemporary white feminists would like to believe that relations between black and white women in the early stages of the women's movement were characterized by the beliefs and actions of Susan B. Anthony, Angelina Grimke, and some others.

The historical record suggests however, that these women were more exceptional than normative. Rosalyn Terborg-Penn argues that "discrimination against Afro-American women reformers was the rule rather than the exception within the woman's rights movement from the 1830's to 1920."[11] Although it is beyond the scope of this article to provide a detailed discussion of the incidents that created mistrust and ill-feeling between black and white women, the historical record provides an important legacy that still haunts us.

The movement's early emphasis upon the oppression of women within the institution of marriage and the family, and upon educational and professional discrimination, reflected the concerns of middle-class white women. During that period, Black women were engaged in a struggle for survival and a fight for freedom. Among their immediate concerns were lynching and economic viability. Working-class white women were concerned about labor conditions, the length of the working day, wages, and so forth. The statements of early women's rights groups do not reflect these concerns, and "as a rigorous consummation of the consciousness of white middle-class women's dilemma, the (Seneca Falls) Declaration all but ignored the predicament of white working-class women, as it ignored the condition of Black women in the South and North alike."[12]

Political expendiency drove white feminists to accept principles that were directly opposed to the survival and well-being of blacks in order to seek to achieve more limited advances for women. "Besides the color bar which existed in many white women's organizations, black women were infuriated by white women's accommodation to the principle of lynch law in order to gain support in the South (Walker, 1973) and the attacks of well-known feminists against anti-lynching crusader, Ida Wells Barnett."[13]

The failure of the suffrage movement to sustain its commitment to the democratic ideal of enfranchisement for all citizens is one of the most frequently cited instances of white women's fragile commitment to racial equality. "After the Civil War, the suffrage movement was deeply impaired by the split over the issue of whether black males should receive the vote before white and black women . . . in the heated pressures over whether black men or white and black women should be enfranchised first, a classist, racist, and even xenophobic rhetoric crept in."[14] The historical and continued abandonment of universalistic principles in order to benefit a privileged few on the part of white women is, I think, one of the reasons why Black women today have been reluctant to see themselves as part of a sisterhood that does not extend beyond racial boundaries. Even for those Black women who are unaware of the specific history, there is the recognition that under pressure from the white men with whom they live and upon whom they are economically dependent, many white women will abandon their "sisters of color" in favor of self-preservation. The feeling that the movement would benefit white women and abandon Blacks, or benefit whites at the expense of Blacks, is a recurrent theme. Terborg-Penn concludes, "The black feminist movement in the United States during the mid 1970's is a continuation of a trend that began over 150 years ago. Institutionalized discrimination against black women by white women has traditionally led to the development of racially separate groups that address themselves to race determined problems as well as the common plight of women in America."[15]

Historically, as well as currently, Black women have felt called upon to choose between their commitments to feminism and to the struggle against racial injustice. Clearly they are victims of both forms of oppression and are most in need of encouragement and support in waging battles on both fronts. However, insistence on such a choice continues largely as a result of the tendency of groups of Blacks and groups of women to battle over the dubious distinction of being the "most" oppressed. The insistence of radical feminists upon the historical priority, universality, and overriding importance of patriarchy in effect necessitates acceptance of a concept of sisterhood that places one's womanhood over and above one's race. At the same time, Blacks are accustomed to labeling discriminatory treatment as racism and therefore may tend to view sexism only within the bounds of the Black community rather than see it as a systemic pattern.[16] On the one hand, the choice between identifying as black or female is a product of the "patriarchal strategy of divide-and-conquer"[17] and therefore, a false choice. Yet, the historical success of this strategy and the continued importance of class, patriarchal, and racial divisions, perpetuate such choices both within our consciousness and within the concrete realities of our daily lives.

Race, of course, is only one of the factors that differentiate women. It is the most salient in discussions of Black and white women, but it is perhaps no more important, even in discussions of race and gender, than is the factor of class. Inclusion of the concept of class permits a broader perspective on the similarities and differences between Black and white women than does a purely racial analysis. Marxist feminism has focused primarily upon the relationship between class exploitation and patriarchy. While this literature has yielded several useful frameworks for beginning to examine the dialectics of gender and class, the role of race, though acknowledged, is not explicated.

Just as the gender-class literature tends to omit race, the race-class literature gives little attention to women. Recently, this area of inquiry has been dominated by a debate over the relative importance of race or class in explaining the historical and contemporary status of Blacks in this country. A number of scholars writing on this issue have argued that the racial division of labor in the United States began as a form of class exploitation which was shrouded in an ideology of racial inferiority. Through the course of U.S. history, racial structures began to take on a life of their own and cannot now be considered merely reflections of class structure.[18] A theoretical understanding of the current conditions of Blacks in this country must therefore take account of both race and class factors. It is not my intention to enter into this debate, but instead to point out that any serious study of Black women must be informed by this growing theoretical discussion. Analysis of the interaction of race, gender, and class fall squarely between these two developing bodies of theoretical literature.

Black women experience class, race, and sex exploitation simultaneously, yet these structures must be separated analytically so that we may better understand the ways in which they shape and differentiate women's lives. Davis, in her previously cited article, provides one of the best analyses to date of the intersection of gender, race, and class under a plantation economy.[19] One of the reasons this analysis is so important is because she presents a model that can be expanded to other historical periods. However, we must be careful not to take the particular historical reality which she illuminated and read it into the present as if the experiences of Black women followed some sort of linear progression out of slavery. Instead, we must look carefully at the lives of Black women throughout history in order to define the peculiar interactions of race, class, and gender at particular historical moments.

In answer to the question: Where do Black women fit into the current analytical frameworks for race and class and gender and class? I would ask: How might these frameworks be revised if they took full account of black women's position in the home, family, and marketplace at various historical moments? In other words, the analysis of the interaction of race, gender, and class must not be stretched to fit the proscrustean bed of any other burgeoning set of theories. It is my contention that it must begin with an analysis of the ways in which Black people have been used in the process of capital accumulation in the United States. Within the contexts of class exploitation and racial oppression, women's lives and work are most clearly illuminated. Davis's article illustrates this. Increasingly, new research is being presented which grapples with the complex interconnectedness of these three issues in the lives of Black women and other women of color.[29]

PERCEPTIONS OF SELF IN SOCIETY

For Black women and other women of color an examination of the ways in which racial oppression, class exploitation, and patriarchy intersect in their lives must be studied in relation to their perceptions of the impact these structures have upon them. Through studying the lives of particular women and searching for patterns in the ways in which they describe themselves and their relationship to society, we will gain important insights into the differences and similarities between Black and white women.

The structures of race and class generate important economic, ideological, and experiential cleavages among women. These lead to differences in perception of self and their place in society. At the same time, commonalities of class or gender may cut across racial lines providing the conditions for shared understanding. Studying these interactions through an examination of women's self perceptions is complicated by the fact that most people view their lives as a whole and do not explain their daily experiences or world view in terms of the differential effects of their racial group, class position, or gender. Thus, we must examine on an analytical level the ways in which the structures of class, race, and gender intersect in any woman's or group of women's lives in order to grasp the concrete set of social relations that influence their behavior. At the same time, we must study individual and group perceptions, descriptions, and conceptualizations of their lives so that we may understand the ways in which different women perceive the same and different sets of social structural constraints.

Concretely, and from a research perspective, this suggests the importance of looking at both the structures which shape womens lives and their self-presentations. This would provide us, not only with a means of gaining insight into the ways in which racial, class, and gender oppression are viewed, but also with a means of generating conceptual categories that will aid us in extending our knowledge of their situation. At the same time, this new knowledge will broaden and even reform our conceptualization of women's situations.

For example, how would our notions of mothering, and particularly mother-daughter relationships, be revised if we considered the particular experiences and perceptions of Black women on this topic? Gloria I. Joseph argues for, and presents a distinctive approach to the study of black mother-daughter relationships, asserting that

> to engage in a discussion of Black mothers and daughters which focused on specific psychological mechanisms operating between the two, the dynamics of the crucial bond, and explanations for the explicit role of patriarchy, without also including the important relevancy of racial oppression . . . would necessitate forcing Black mother/daughter relationships into pigeonholes designed for understanding white models.
>
> In discussing Black mothers and daughters, it is more realistic, useful, and intellectually astute to speak in terms of their roles, positions, and functions within the Black society and that society's relationship to the broader (White) society in America.[21]

Unfortunately, there have been very few attempts in the social sciences to systematically investigate the relationship between social structure and self perceptions of Black women. The profiles of Black women that have been appearing in magazines like *Essence*, the historical studies of Black women, fiction and poetry by and about Black women, and some recent sociological and anthropological studies provide important data for beginning such an analysis. However, the question of how Black women perceive themselves with regard to the structures of race, gender, and class is still open for systematic investigation.

Elizabeth Higginbotham, in a study of Black women who graduated from college between 1968 and 1970, explored the impact of class origins upon strategies for educational attainment. She found that class differences within the Black community led not only to different sets of educational experiences, but also to different personal priorities and views of the Black experience.[22] According to Higginbotham, the Black women from middle-class backgrounds who participated in her study had access to better schools and more positive schooling experiences than did their working-class sisters. Because their parents did not have the economic resources to purchase the better educational opportunities offered in an integrated suburb or a private school, the working-class women credited their parents' willingness to struggle within the public school system as a key component in their own educational achievement. Social class also affected college selections and experience. Working-class women were primarily concerned with finances in selecting a college and spent most of their time adjusting to the work load and the new middle-class environment once they had arrived. Middle-class women, on the other hand, were freer to select a college that would meet their personal, as well as their academic, needs and abilities. Once there, they were better able to balance their work and social lives and to think about integrating future careers and family lives.

Among her sample, Higginbotham found that a larger proportion of women from working-class backgrounds were single. She explained this finding in terms of class differences in socialization and mobility strategies. She found that the parents of women from working-class backgrounds stressed educational achievement over and above other personal goals.[23] These women never viewed marriage as a means of mobility and focused primarily upon education, postponing interest in, and decisions about, marriage. In contrast, women from middle-class backgrounds were expected to marry and were encouraged to integrate family and educational goals throughout their schooling.

My own research on household workers demonstrates the ways in which class origins, racial discrimination, and social conceptions of women and women's work came together during the first half of the twentieth century to limit work options and affect family roles and the self perceptions of one group of Afro-American women born between 1896 and 1915.[24] Most of them were born in the South and migrated North between 1922 and 1955. Like the majority of black working women of this period, they worked as household workers in private homes. (During the first half of the twentieth century, labor force participation rates of Black women ranged from about 37 percent to 50 percent. Approximately 60 percent of black women workers were employed in private household work up until 1960.)[25]

The women who participated in this study came from working-class families. Their fathers were laborers and farmers, their mothers were housewives or did paid domestic work of some kind (cooking, cleaning, taking in washing, and so forth). As a result, the women not only had limited opportunities for education, but also often began working when they were quite young to help support their families. Jewell Prieleau (names are pseudonyms used to protect the identity of the subjects), one of eight children, described her entrance into work as follows: "When I was eight years old, I decided I wanted a job and I just got up early in the morning and I would go from house to house and ring doorbells and ask for jobs and I would get it. I think I really wanted to work because in a big family like that, they was able to feed you, but you had to earn your shoes. They couldn't buy shoes although shoes was very cheap at that time. I would rather my mother give it to the younger children and I would earn my way."

Queenie Watkins lived with her mother, aunt, and five cousins and began working in grammar school. She described her childhood jobs in detail.

> When I went to grammar school, the white ladies used to come down and say "Do you have a girl who can wash dishes?" That was how I got the job with the doctor and his wife. I would go up there at six o'clock in the morning and wash the breakfast dishes and bring in scuttles of coal to burn on the fireplace. I would go back in the afternoon and take the little girl down on the sidewalk and if there were any leaves to be raked on the yard, I'd rake the leaves up and burn them and sweep the sidewalk. I swept off the front porch and washed it off with the hose and washed dishes again—for one dollar a week.

While class position limited the economic resources and educational opportunities of most of these women, racial discrimination constricted work options for Black women in such a way as to seriously undercut the benefits of education. The comments of the following women are reflective of the feelings expressed by many of those in this sample:

> When I came out of school, the black man naturally had very few chances of doing certain things and even persons that I know myself who had finished four years of college were doing the same type of work because they couldn't get any other kind of work in New York.

> In my home in Virginia, education, I don't think was stressed. The best you could do was be a school teacher. It wasn't something people impressed upon you you could get. I had an aunt and cousin who were trained nurses and the

best they could do was nursing somebody at home or something. They couldn't get a job in a hospital. I didn't pay education any mind really until I came to New York. I'd gotten to a certain stage in domestic work in the country and I didn't see the need for it.

Years ago there was no such thing as a black typist. I remember girls who were taking typing when I was going to school. They were never able to get a job at it. In my day and time you could have been the greatest typist in the world but you would never have gotten a job. There was no such thing as getting a job as a bank teller. The blacks weren't even sweeping the banks.

For Black women in the United States, their high concentration in household work was a result of racial discrimination and a direct carry-over from slavery. Black women were in essence "a permanent service caste in nineteenth and twentieth century America."[26] Arnold Anderson and Mary Jean Bowman argue that the distinguishing feature of domestic service in the United States is that "the frequency of servants is correlated with the availability of Negroes in local populations."[27] By the time most of the women in this sample entered the occupation a racial caste pattern was firmly established. The occupation was dominated by foreign-born white women in the North, and Black freedwomen in the South, a pattern which was modified somewhat as southern Blacks migrated north. Nevertheless, most research indicates that Black women fared far worse than their white immigrant sisters, even in the North. "It is commonly asserted that the immigrant woman has been the northern substitute for the Negro servant. In 1930, when one can separate white servants by nativity, about twice as large a percentage of foreign as of native women were domestics. . . . As against this 2:1 ratio between immigrants and natives, the ratio of Negro to white servants ranged upward from 10:1 to 50:1. The immigrant was not the northerner's Negro."[28]

Two major differences distinguished the experiences of Black domestics from that of their immigrant sisters. First, Black women had few other employment options. Second, Black household workers were older and more likely to be married. Thus, while private household work cross-culturally, and for white women in the United States, was often used as a steppingstone to other working-class occupations, or as a way station before marriage, for Black American women it was neither. This pattern did not begin to change substantially until World War II.

Table 1. Percentage of Females of Each Nativity in U.S. Labor Force Who Were Servants, by Decades, 1900-1940

	1900	1910	1920	1930	1940
Native white	22.3	15.0	9.6	10.4	11.0
Foreign-born white	42.5	34.0	23.8	26.8	
Negro	41.9	39.5	44.4	54.9	54.4
Other	24.8	22.9	22.9	19.4	16.0
Total	30.5	24.0	17.9	19.8	17.2
(N, in thousands)	(1,439)	(1,761)	(1,386)	(1,906)	(1,931)
(Percent of all domestic servants)	(95.4)	(94.4)	(93.3)	(94.1)	(92.0)

Source: George J. Stigler, *Domestic Servants in the United States: 1900-1940*, Occasional Paper no. 24 (New York: National Bureau of Economic Research, 1946), p.7.

Table 1 indicates that between 1900 and 1940 the percentage of Black women in domestic service actually increased, relative to the percentage of immigrant women which decreased. The data support the contention that Black women were even more confined to the occupation than their immigrant sisters. At the turn of the century, large numbers of immigrants entered domestic service. Their children, however, were much less likely to become household workers. Similarly, many Black women entered domestic service at that time, but their children tended to remain in the occupation. It was the daughters and granddaughters of the women who participated in this study that were among the first generation of Black women to benefit from the relaxation of racial restrictions which began to occur after World War II.

Finally, Black women were household workers because they were women. Private household work is women's work. It is a working-class occupation, has low social status, low pay, and few guaranteed fringe benefits. Like the housewife who employs her, the private household worker's low social status and pay is tied to the work itself, to her class, gender, and the complex interaction of the three within the family. In other words, housework, both paid and unpaid, is structured around the particular place of women in the family. It is considered unskilled labor because it requires no training, degrees, or licenses, and because it has traditionally been assumed that any woman could or should be able to do housework.

The women themselves had a very clear sense that the social inequities which relegated them and many of their peers to household service labor were based upon their race, class, and gender. Yet different women, depending upon their jobs, family situations, and overall outlooks on life, handled this knowledge in different ways. One woman described the relationship between her family and her employer's as follows: "Well for *their* children, I imagine they wanted them to become like they were, educators or something that-like [sic]. But what they had in for my children, they saw in me that I wasn't able to make all of that mark but raised my children in the best method I could. Because I wouldn't have the means to put *my* children through like they could for their children." When asked what she liked most about her work, she answered, "Well what I like most about it, the things that I weren't able to go to school to do for my children. I could kinda pattern from the families that I worked for, so that I could give my children the best of my abilities." A second woman expressed much more anger and bitterness about the social differences which distinguished her life from that of her female employer. "They don't know nothing about a hard life. The only hard life will come if they getting a divorce or going through a problem with their children. But their husband has to provide for them because they're not soft. And if they leave and they separate for any reason or (are) divorced, they have to put the money down. But we have no luck like that. We have to leave our children; sometime leave the children alone. There's times when I have asked winos to look after my children. It was just a terrible life and I really thank God that the children grow up to be nice." Yet while she acknowledged her posisiton as an oppressed person, she used her knowledge of the anomalies in her employers' lives—particularly the woman and her female friends—to aid her in maintaining her sense of self-respect and determination and to overcome feelings of despair and immobilization. When asked if she would like to switch places with her employers, she replied, "I don't think I would want to change, but I would like to live differently. I would like to have my own nice little apartment with my husband and have my grandchildren for dinner and my daughter and just live comfortable. But I would always want to work. . . . But, if I was to change life with them, I would like to have just a little bit of they money, that's all." While the women who participated in this study adopted different personal styles of coping with these inequities, they were all clearly aware that being black, poor, and female placed them at the bottom of the social structure, and they used the resources at their disposal to make the best of what they recognized as a bad situation.

Contemporary scholarship on women of color suggests that the barriers to an all-inclusive sisterhood are deeply rooted in the histories of oppression and exploitation that Blacks and other groups encountered upon incorporation into the American political economy.[29] These histories affect the social positions of these groups today, and racial ethnic women[30] in every social class express anger and distress about the forms of discrimination and insensitivity which they encounter in their interactions with white feminists. Audre Lorde has argued that the inability of women to confront anger is one of the important forces dividing women of color from white women in the feminist movement. She cites several examples from her own experience which resonate loudly with the experiences of most women of color who have been engaged in the women's movement.[31]

> After fifteen years of a women's movement which professes to address the life concerns and possible futures of all women, I still hear, on campus after campus, "How can we address the issues of racism? No women of color attended." Or, the other side of that statement, "We have no one in our department equipped to teach their work." In other words, racism is a Black women's problem, a problem of women of color, and only we can discuss it.
>
> White women are beginning to examine their relationships to Black women, yet often I hear you wanting only to deal with the little colored children across the roads of childhood, the beloved nursemaid, the occasional second-grade classmate. . . . You avoid the childhood assumptions formed by the raucous laughter at Rastus and Oatmeal . . . the indelible and dehumanizing portraits of Amos and Andy and your daddy's humorous bedtime stories.

Bell Hooks points to both the racial and class myopia of white feminists as a major barrier to sisterhood.

> When white women's liberationists emphasized work as a path to liberation, they did not concentrate their attention on those women who are most exploited in the American labor force. Had they emphasized the plight of working class women, attention would have shifted away from the college-educated suburban housewife who wanted entrance into the middle and upper class work force. Had attention been focused on women who were already working and who were exploited as cheap surplus labor in American society, it would have de-romanticized the middle class white woman's quest for "meaningful" employment. While it does not in any way diminish the importance of women resisting sexist oppression by entering the labor force, work has not been a liberating force for masses of American women.[32]

As a beginning point for understanding the potential linkages and barriers to an all-inclusive sisterhood, Lorde concludes that "the strength of women lies in recognizing differences between us as creative, and in standing to those distortions which we inherited without blame but which are now ours to alter. The angers of women can transform differences through insight into power. For anger between peers births change, not destruction, and the discomfort and sense of loss it often causes is not fatal, but a sign of growth."[33]

PROSPECTS FOR AN ALL-INCLUSIVE SISTERHOOD

Given the differences in experiences among Black women, the differences between Black and white women, between working-class and middle-class women, between all of us, what then are the prospects for sisterhood? While this article has sought to emphasize the need to study and explicate these differences, it is based upon the assumption that the knowledge we gain in this process will also help enlighten us as to our similarities. Thus, I would argue for the abandonment of the concept of sisterhood as a global construct based on unexamined assumptions about our similarities, and I would substitute a more pluralistic approach that recognizes and accepts the objective differences between women. Such an approach requires that we concentrate our political energies on building coalitions around particular issues of shared interest. Through joint work on specific issues, we may come to a better understanding of one another's needs and perceptions and begin to overcome some of the suspicions and mistrust that continue to haunt us. The limitations of a sisterhood based on bourgeois individualism or on the politics of personal experience presently pose a very real threat to combined political action.

For example, in the field of household employment, interest in the needs of a growing number of middle-class women to participate in the work force and thus find adequate assistance with their domestic duties (a form of bourgeois individualism) could all too easily become support for a proposal such as the one made by writer Anne Colamosca in a recent article in the *New Republic*.[34] She proposed solving the problems of a limited supply of household help with a government training program for unemployed alien women to help them become "good household workers." While this may help middle-class women pursue their careers, it will do so while continuing to maintain and exploit a poorly paid, unprotected, lower class and will leave the problem of domestic responsibility virtually unaddressed for the majority of mothers in the work force who cannot afford to hire personal household help. A socialist feminist perspective requires an examination of the exploitation inherent in household labor as it is currently organized for both the paid and unpaid worker. The question is, what can we do to upgrade the status of domestic labor for ALL women, to facilitate the adjustment and productivity of immigrant women, and to insure that those who choose to engage in paid private household work do so because it represents a potentially interesting, viable and economically rewarding option for them?

At the same time, the women's movement may need to move beyond a limited focus on "women's issues" to ally with groups of women and men who are addressing other aspects of race and class oppression. One example is school desegregation, an issue which is engaging the time and energies of many urban Black women today. The struggles over school desegregation are rapidly moving beyond the issues of busing and racial balance. In many large cities, where school districts are between 60 percent and 85 percent Black, Hispanic, or Third World, racial balance is becoming less of a concern. Instead, questions are being raised about the overall quality of the educational experiences low-income children of all racial and ethnic groups are receiving in the public schools. This is an issue of vital concern to many racially and ethnically distinct women because they see their children's future ability to survive in this society as largely dependent upon the current direction of public education. In what ways should feminists involve themselves in this issue? First, by recognizing that feminist questions are only one group of questions among many others that are being raised about public education. To the extent that Blacks, Hispanics, Native Americans, and Asian Americans are miseducated, so are women. Feminist activists must work to expand their conceptualization of the problem beyond the narrow confines of sexism. For example, efforts to develop and include nonsexist literature in the school curriculum are important. Yet this work cannot exist in a vacuum, ignoring the fact that schoolchildren *observe* a gender-based division of labor in which authority and responsibility are held primarily by men while women are concentrated in nurturant roles; or that schools with middle-class students have more funds, better facilities, and better teachers than schools serving working-class populations. The problems of education must be addressed as structural ones. We must examine not only the kinds of discrimination that occur within institutions, but also the ways in which discrimination becomes a fundamental part of the institution's organization and implementation of its overall purpose. Such an analysis would make the linkages between different forms of structural inequality, like sexism and racism, more readily apparent.

While analytically we must carefully examine the structures that differentiate us, politically we must fight the segmentation of oppression into categories such as "racial issues," "feminist issues," and "class issues." This is, of course, a task of almost overwhelming magnitude, and yet it seems to me the only viable way to avoid the errors of the past and to move forward to make sisterhood a meaningful feminist concept for all women, across the boundaries of race and class. For it is through first seeking to understand struggles that are not particularly shaped by one's own immediate personal priorities that we will begin to experience and understand the needs and priorities of our sisters—be they black, brown, white, poor, or rich. When we have reached a point where the differences between us ENRICH our political and social action rather than divide it, we will have gone beyond the personal and will, in fact, be "political enough."

NOTES

The author wishes to acknowledge the comments of Lynn Weber Cannon and Elizabeth Higginbotham on an earlier version of this article.

1. Elizabeth Fox-Genovese, "The Personal is not Political Enough," *Marxist Perspectives* (Winter 1979-80): 94-113.
2. Ibid., 97-98.
3. Ibid., 112.
4. For discussions of black women's attitudes toward the women's movement see Linda LaRue, "The Black Movement and Women's Liberation," *Black Scholar* 1 (May 1970): 36-42; Renee Ferguson "Women's Liberation has a Different Meaning for Blacks," in *Black Women in White America: A Documentary History*, ed. Gerda Lerner (New York: Pantheon, 1972); Inez Smith Reid, *"Together" Black Women* (New York: Emerson-Hall, 1972); Cheryl Townsend Gilkes, "Black Women's Work as Deviance: Social Sources of Racial Antagonism within Contemporary Feminism" (Paper

presented at the Seventy-fourth Annual Meeting of the American Sociological Association, Boston, August 1979).

5. Angela Davis, "Reflections on the Black Woman's Role in the Community of Slaves," *Black Scholar* 2 (December 1971): 15.

6. Mary Burgher, "Images of Self and Race," in *Sturdy Black Bridges*, ed. Roseann P. Bell, Bettye J. Parker, and Beverly Guy-Sheftall (Garden City, N.Y.: Anchor Books, 1979), 118.

7. For a related discussion of black women's roles in the church, see Cheryl Townsend Gilkes, "Institutional Motherhood in Black Churches and Communities: Ambivalent Sexism or Fragmented Familyhood" (published paper).

8. For a discussion of the club movement among black women, see, in addition to Lerner's book, Alfreda Duster, ed., *Ida Barnett, Crusade for Justice: The Autobiography of Ida B. Wells* (Chicago: University of Chicago Press, 1970); Rackham Holt, *Mary McLeod Bethune: A Biography* (Garden City, N.Y.: Doubleday & Co., 1964); Jeanne L. Noble, *Beautiful, Also, Are the Souls of My Black Sisters: A History of the Black Woman in America* (Englewood Cliffs, N.J.: Prentice-Hall, 1978); Mary Church Terrell, *A Colored Woman in a White World* (Washington, D.C.: Ransdell Publishing Company, 1940).

9. Carol Stack, *All Our Kin* (New York: Harper & Row, 1970); and Elmer P. Martin and Joan Martin, *The Black Extended Family* (Chicago: University of Chicago Press, 1977).

10. Gilkes, "Black Women's Work as Deviance," 21.

11. Rosalyn Terborg-Penn, "Discrimination Against Afro-American Women in the Woman's Movement, 1830-1920," in *The Afro-American Woman: Struggles and Images*, ed. Sharon Harley and Rosalyn Terborg-Penn (Port Washington, N.Y.: Kennikat Press, 1978), 17.

12. Angela Davis, *Women, Race, and Class* (New York: Random House, 1981), 54.

13. Gilkes, "Black Women's Work as Deviance," 19. In this quotation Gilkes cites Jay S. Walker, "Frederick Douglass and Woman Suffrage," *Black Scholar* 4 (7 June 1973).

14. Adrienne Rich, "'Disloyal to Civilization': Feminism, Racism, and Gynephobia," *Chrysalis*, no. 7 (1978): 14.

15. Terborg-Penn, 27.

16. Elizabeth Higginbotham, "Issues in Contemporary Sociological Work on Black Women," *Humanity and Society* 4 (November 1980): 226-42.

17. Rich, 15.

18. This argument has been suggested by Robert Blauner in *Racial Oppression in America* (New York: Harper & Row, 1972); and William J. Wilson in *The Declining Significance of Race: Blacks and Changing American Institutions* (Chicago: University of Chicago Press, 1978).

19. Davis, "Reflections on the Black Woman's Role."

20. See Cheryl Townsend Gilkes, "Living and Working in a World of Trouble: The Emergent Career of the Black Woman Community Worker" (Ph.D. diss., Northeastern University, 1979); and Elizabeth Higginbotham, "Educated Black Women: An Exploration in Life Chances and Choices" (Ph.D. diss., Brandeis University, 1980).

21. Gloria I. Joseph and Jill Lewis, *Common Differences: Conflicts in Black and White Feminist Perspectives* (Garden City, N.Y.: Anchor Books, 1981), 75-76.

22. Higginbotham, "Educated Black Women."

23. Elizabeth Higginbotham, "Is Marriage a Priority? Class Differences in Marital Options of Educated Black Women" in *Single Life*, ed. Peter Stein (New York: St. Martin's Press, 1981), 262.

24. Bonnie Thornton Dill, "Across the Boundaries of Race and Class: An Exploration

of the Relationship between Work and Family among Black Female Domestic Servants," (Ph.D. diss., New York University, 1979).

25. For detailed data on the occupational distribution of black women during the twentieth century, see U.S. Bureau of the Census, *Historical Statistics of the United States: Colonial Times to 1970*. H. Doc. 83-78, (Washington, D.C.: GPO, 1973).

26. David Katzman, *Seven Days a Week: Women and Domestic Service in Industrializing America* (New York: Oxford University Press, 1978), 85.

27. Arnold Anderson and Mary Jean Bowman, "The Vanishing Servant and the Contemporary Status System of the American South," *American Journal of Sociology* 59 (November 1953): 216.

28. Ibid., 220.

29. Elizabeth Higginbotham, "Laid Bare by the System: Work and Survival for Black and Hispanic Women," forthcoming in Amy Swerdlow and Hannah Lessinger, *Race, Class, and Gender: The Dynamics of Control* (Boston: G.K. Hall); and Bonnie Thornton Dill, "Survival as a Form of Resistance: Minority Women and the Maintenance of Families" (Working Paper no. 7, Inter University Group on Gender and Race, Memphis State University, 1982).

30. The term "racial ethnic women" is meant as an alternative to either "minority," which is disparaging; "Third World," which has an international connotation; or "women of color," which lacks any sense of cultural identity. In contrast to "ethnic," which usually refers to groups that are culturally distinct but members of the dominant white society, "racial ethnic" refers to groups that are both culturally and racially distinct, and in the United States have historically shared certain common conditions as oppressed and internally colonized peoples.

31. Audre Lorde, "The Uses of Anger," *Women's Studies Quarterly* 9 (Fall 1981): 7.

32. Bell Hooks, *Ain't I a Woman: Black Women and Feminism* (Boston: South End Press, 1981), 146.

33. Lorde, 9.

34. Ann Colamosca, "Capitalism and Housework," *New Republic*, 29 March 1980, 18-20.

THE RISE AND FALL OF FEMINIST ORGANIZATIONS IN THE 1970s: DAYTON AS A CASE STUDY

JUDITH SEALANDER and DOROTHY SMITH

In 1972 the United States Congress passed the Equal Rights Amendment (ERA), *Ms.* magazine published its first issue, and women ran in the Boston marathon for the first time. A decade of federal congressional and executive decision making had created a new legal structure that seemed to nourish feminism. Who could doubt that the movement would continue to make gains when in less than a decade it had achieved the Equal Pay Act, affirmative action programs, Title VII and Title IX, the Equal Employment Opportunity Commission and other programs? Who could doubt, given the overwhelming majority favoring the amendment in the Washington vote, the state ratification for the ERA would take place quickly and easily? Who could doubt, given the continued flood of women into the work force, that wage disparities would soon begin to disappear? Who could doubt that by the 1980s the prospects for feminism would not seem even brighter?

What feminist would have thought that instead, in 1981, even such a staunch supporter of the women's movement as Barbara Ehrenreich would write that feminism had "peaked" and that forces of antifeminism were becoming ever more powerful?[1] What feminist in 1972 would have predicted a decade's bitter battle and final defeat for the ERA? What feminist would have predicted the overwhelming re-election in 1984 of a president who headed an administration that openly derided the need for affirmative action programs and lobbied for a constitutional amendment banning abortion?

Feminists, then, do not enjoy the luxury to wax proud over victories or to be nostalgic over past battles lost or won. Instead we need the kind of clear insight into the history of the movement

Feminist Studies 12, no. 2 (Summer 1986). © by Judith Sealander and Dorothy Smith

that derives from careful analysis and documented research. Yet such research is not readily available. In 1968 feminist protest at the annual Miss America Contest got front page coverage as American newspapers filled with stories of man-hating bra burners. Almost twenty years later, much of the analysis of contemporary feminism has remained on that condescending and inaccurate level. Although a few scholars have attempted to study gains and failures of contemporary feminism, their articles remain tentative and speculative, more concerned with the origins than the nature of the movement, and in need of the concrete detail a case study can provide.[2]

Why choose Dayton, Ohio, for such a case study? First, a wealth of evidence exists. Due to the aggressive collecting policies of a Wright State University archivist, the complete organizational files of three important feminist groups have been saved and inventoried. Membership lists in the files of each organization provided the names of many people to contact for interviews. The extensive nature of written and oral evidence about the history of feminist organizations in Dayton may, in fact, be unparalleled. To our knowledge, the records of contemporary feminist organizations in many other cities are still held in private hands or have been lost or destroyed.

Second, the fact that the records of Dayton's Women's Liberation, the Dayton Women's Center, and Dayton Women Working sit in cardboard boxes at a university archive rather than in cabinets in organizational offices suggests a second reason to choose Dayton, Ohio, for historical case study. The decade, 1970-80, exists as a meaningful and completed period in the history of contemporary Dayton feminism, for three major organizations began and ended within that period. A look at their rise and fall raises questions and suggests answers about the nature of contemporary feminism that would be more difficult to derive from an examination of existing organizations.

Third, since the early twentieth century, Dayton has shared with Muncie, Indiana, a reputation as a typical small American city. Pollsters in the 1970s continued to choose the city of roughly 200,000 citizens for random sampling with decidedly unrandom regularity. It was a frequent test market, and its population was given sneak previews of new movies, soaps, and underarm deodorants.[3] Pollster Richard Scammon claimed that the average

American voter was "a forty-seven-year-old housewife from the outskirts of Dayton, Ohio, whose husband is a machinist."[4]

Moreover, Dayton typified the problems of many American towns and communities trying to make the often painful shift from an industrial to a service economy. Although manufacturing in Dayton declined by over 20 percent during the 1970s, and one company alone laid off over 14,000 workers, Dayton achieved a net gain for the decade of 17,000 new jobs. Most of the jobs, however, were, "women's jobs"–jobs in the lower-paying service sectors. In 1950, Dayton, per capita, possessed the highest number of color televisions in the country. It was a city filled with people whose healthy paychecks, earned in the area's auto, tire, and printing factories, made the purchase of such luxuries possible. By 1970, Dayton no longer enjoyed that enviable image of a city of highly paid, skilled, union workers. Service sector work had filled the gaps caused by the closing of plants but had not fattened wallets. The new "typical" Dayton worker was a female bank teller, not a unionized auto worker. Therefore, a history of feminism in Dayton can provide an examination of organizational success and failure in a city widely viewed as far more typical than New York, Chicago, San Francisco, or Boston–the four "movement" cities which, to date, remain the focus of most journalistic comment about feminism. Such a history can also provide an examination of feminist organizations in a city which typified, sometimes even prophesied, changes in the national economy that had the most direct and important implications for female roles and status.

The women's movement arrived in Dayton in September 1969, via Ann Arbor, Michigan, not, as might have been expected, via nearby Antioch College in Yellow Springs, Ohio. Cheryl Radican, a University of Cincinnati student, had herself newly arrived in Dayton, accompanying her divinity school student husband. While commuting back and forth to Cincinnati to finish her degree, Radican also began to write for Dayton's recently established "underground" newspaper, the *Minority Report*, a Left-liberal newsletter staffed by volunteers who wrote the stories and then sold the issues on street corners and area college campuses. At a national underground newspaper conference in Ann Arbor in the summer of 1969, Radican met other women angry about their subordinate roles on their publications. As had happened at earlier meetings of student radicals, the women at the newspaper conference formed a separate caucus and told the men to stay away.[5]

Radican, "filled with the power of sisterhood," enthusiastically returned home and formed Dayton's first consciousness-raising (CR) group.[6] This first group grew rapidly by word of mouth. By January 1970 a new CR group formed every month, first in Dayton neighborhoods and then on nearby college campuses like Antioch and Wright State University in Dayton. The typical woman in these groups was not a radical even though Radican and many of her friends saw themselves as social activists, committed especially to protesting the war in Vietnam. A member of a CR group was likely to be white, "liberal Democrat," college-educated, married, and middle class. In 1969, she was far more likely to be in school or at home than she was to be at work full-time, though she was not necessarily at home with small children.[7] At least one-quarter of the women in the first CR groups were middle-aged, self-described "*Better Homes and Gardens* housewives. . .casualties of the 1950s."[8] Radican first organized her friends, and not surprisingly, these friends were often students, wives of ministers or divinity students, wives of teachers or college professors, or women active in the League of Women Voters and church children's education groups.[9]

The experience of joining CR groups, however, often proved radicalizing to these nonradical women. In the mid-sixties, hundreds of similarly earnest middle-class white women had gone south demanding civil rights for blacks. They expected opposition. They did not expect to be treated as inferiors and maids by their own coworkers and as "loose" women by the press. Similarly, in 1970 members of three CR groups in Dayton traveled to Columbus, Ohio, to take part in a large proabortion rally. They returned to find themselves described by the local media as "fourteen braless, make-up-less women." In fact, as one participant exclaimed, "We were all carefully dressed. One of us was in a mink coat and open-toed shoes. . . . They [reporters] just kept asking if the women were wearing bras."[10]

By mid-1970, these kinds of patronizing experiences convinced women in several CR groups that they had to unite, take their case to the public, and work with more than the ten to twelve women in their own groups. Dayton Women's Liberation emerged from these discussions. It quickly established a phone bank, staffed by members who answered questions about feminism. It set up a speakers' bureau; members traveled to high schools, police stations, and–on a regular basis–the television studio where Phil Donahue, still a local Dayton talk show host, filmed his programs. Although the organization issued a pamphlet denouncing the Vietnam War, Dayton Women's Liberation generally continued to emphasize small CR groups, rather than political activism. And most of these CR groups continued to explore personal issues, such as relationships with mothers, children, and husbands. By 1975, however, two other feminist organizations that were more concerned with programs to change politics and society–the Women's Center and Dayton Women Working–had joined Dayton Women's Liberation.

In 1973, the Dayton City Commission granted Dayton Women's Liberation funds to establish a "neighborhood Women's Center, focusing on the needs of women in the surrounding area. . .establishing a place for women to explore common concerns, to share and expand their knowledge." The proposal outlined several programs: self-help classes, a walk-in center and meeting place for women, an advocacy and referral service for women in need, political and personal counseling, a lending library, childcare for women using the center, and educational programs.[11]

Dayton Women Working initially was a product of one Dayton Women's Center member's efforts to engage in "political counseling and action."[12] In 1975, frustrated that her male colleagues in the Dayton chapter of the socialist New American Movement (NAM) did not take women's employment issues seriously, Sherrie Holmes organized the first Dayton chapter of the National Organization for Women (NOW) and drew up plans for a Women in the Work Force Task Force. Within months the NOW task force decided to establish itself as a separate organization, choosing in April 1975 the name, Dayton Women Working.

Dayton Women Working, begun in protest of her male colleagues' inattention by a woman who saw herself as a socialist and radical, linked the women's movement in Dayton to the New Left and linked Dayton to a national network of feminist groups interested in workplace problems. In fact, Dayton Women Working helped to create that network. In 1977, Dayton Women Working was a founding member of the National Women's Employment Project (NWEP), a consortium of six working women's organizations. The NWEP, launched with a $25,000 grant from the Rockefeller Family Fund, chose to emphasize the problems of office workers and to focus first on an employer "notorious" for discrimination against women clerical workers: the banking industry.[13] Dayton Women Working joined with the older and better established consortium members, especially Boston's 9 to 5, and adopted this emphasis.

What did these three groups accomplish? How did they fail? In what ways did their troubles illustrate problems faced by other feminist groups in other cities? What is their legacy? Examination of programs, finances, and membership can provide partial answers to these questions. Organized feminism in Dayton in the 1970s achieved communitywide visibility with well-planned campaigns and successful projects. Because it did not succeed, however, in anchoring itself to a stable base of committed dues-paying members, it suffered continual money and membership problems.

The Women's Center rented a two-story frame house on North Main Street near downtown Dayton in October 1973. Cleaning, painting, and floor-waxing parties generated enthusiasm and prepared the building for occupancy. Over 100 women attended a grand opening party in January 1974.[14] Within months the center had a full program of activities, including classes in self-defense, women's legal rights, careers, health, sexuality, auto mechanics, pottery, and yoga. Two therapy groups met weekly. There were regular community forums on topics of interest to women, such as daycare options and married women's property rights. Building on the Dayton Women's Liberation tradition, the staff compiled information for a referral service for women in need of community services.

Several women's groups met at the center, including a parent support group, a socialist-feminist discussion group, the Women on Rape Task Force, and a large lesbian organization called Sappho's Army. The center's four paid staff members, as well as members of its collective, accepted invitations to speak at local universities, church groups, Parent Teacher Association groups, social workers' associations, and women's clubs. The Women's Center began to issue a newsletter, and stories about the center appeared in eight local newspapers, and on two radio and two television stations. After the center had been open for two months, the collective reported that over 300 women had used the center's facilities.[15]

By 1975, the Women's Center programs had expanded significantly. Hundreds of women used its facilities for classes, counseling and feminist therapy, and activities and discussion groups. The center's referral service thrived, passing along the names of feminist doctors, lawyers, and welfare workers. It also provided advice to women about employment and legal rights and maintained regularly updated files on educational opportunities, as well as files of job listings and financial aid.[16] In 1975, the center opened an extremely popular Daycare Parents' Cooperative.[17] The Women's Center's many programs thus made feminism quite visible in Dayton. It "was a smorgasbord of services," and during its seven-year history approximately two thousand Dayton women a year helped themselves.[18]

Dayton Women Working also spread the feminist message in Dayton with initially successful, attention-getting projects. Member organizations of the National Women's Employment Project – Women Employed in Chicago, 9 to 5 in Boston, Dayton Women Working, Cleveland Women Working, Women Organized for Employment in San Francisco, and Women Office Workers in New York – agreed to monitor and investigate the effectiveness of post-1964 federal antidiscrimination laws and executive orders.[19] NWEP's own effectiveness suffered from serious internal disputes about equitable distribution of grant monies which led to the departure, by October 1977, of Women Employed in Chicago. Nevertheless, the five remaining organizations set to work on a national investigation of conditions for female clerical workers in banks.[20]

Dayton Women Working plunged enthusiastically into the project, which was designed to provide both a case study of employment discrimination against women and a study of the degree of employer compliance with antidiscrimination laws. The group's analysis of the banking industry of Dayton was to be its most important project and most significant success. It soon learned that three-quarters of the employees of the three major banks in Dayton were women, and more than 89 percent of these women worked in poorly paid office and clerical jobs. Using bank affirmative action reports, surveys and interviews with female bank employees, annual reports, banking directories, and other documents in the public record, Dayton Women Working printed a pamphlet that charged, among other things, that major Dayton banks were not seriously committed to equal employment opportunity. As one letter to a bank stated, banks limited affirmative action efforts to the creation of affirmative action plans that were "inadequate" and out of date.[21] Banks, as holders of federal deposits, had the status of federal contractors, and as such had to fulfill federal guidelines regarding affirmative action in employment. The Labor Department, as the agency charged with enforcement of contract compliance, agreed in 1978 to investigate Dayton Women Working's charges that Third National, First National, and Winters National Banks of Dayton practiced employment discrimination against women.[22]

The "banking study" generated much local publicity, and open meetings attracted large crowds.[23] Women employed in banks began to mail in anonymous testimonials. Citing fear of job reprisal, one woman (who, like most bank employees, asked that her name not be used in Dayton Women Working publicity) wrote: "I used to be a person who was hurt that I was paid so little. I thought there was something wrong with me, that I was being singled out. However, I recently learned that this is not the case, that many of the women in my department that have been with the bank a long time, make even less than I do."[24]

Barred from distributing materials within banking offices, members of Dayton Women Working stood on downtown street corners handing out over two thousand questionnaires to women office workers headed toward banks. Women who filled out the twenty-six-item questionnaires were to use a point system to rate their jobs: a "yes" equaled two points, a "not sure" one point, and a "no" zero points. Questions included "Are you permitted to discuss salaries with coworkers?" "Are there training programs available within your bank?" "Are women promoted at the same rate as men?" "Is there an effective grievance procedure to deal with discrimination?" Banks rating fewer than twenty points were "not good places to work. Watch out or call D.W.W."[25] In May of 1980, U.S. Department of Labor investigators charged Third National Bank with a "pattern of discrimination against its minority and women employees" and in initial review documents assessed nearly one million dollars in back pay for 110 employees who had "suffered the effects of past discrimination."[26]

However, by 1980 Dayton Women Working, on the verge of disbanding, was unable to capitalize on this victory. Despite its many programs and its contact with thousands of Dayton women who used its services, the Dayton Women's Center was equally unable to use the visibility and success of many of its projects to enter the next decade as a strong and growing feminist organization. As early as 1975 most Dayton Women's Liberation CR groups had ceased to meet. Personal and ideological conflicts, declining activism, and small membership, as well as recurrent financial crises, were all problems that plagued organized feminism in Dayton.

A staff of four paid workers ran the Women's Center and oversaw its programs. A Women's Center collective, with a rotating leadership, provided that staff with program and policy direction. Almost from the beginning, conflicts marred relationships between collective and staff. Even more importantly, the collective itself often divided into two warring camps. One group identified itself as socialist and saw women as an oppressed class to be organized as part of a larger movement to transform society. The other group defined itself as feminist, wanted an independent women's movement, saw women's issues as most important, and feared a close association with male-led politics. The conflict became bitter and open early in 1977, when some NAM members, including men, used the printing facilities at the Women's Center. Angry memos flew between the two factions, and collective meetings became battlegrounds.[27]

In retrospect Kathy Ellison, who judged herself to be a neutral collective member, felt that the fights were more personal than political. "From time to time these great political struggles would happen. I never thought the conflict was real, I felt it was more personality and power struggles. For whatever reasons, these strong-minded women didn't get along, and they had to imbue their interpersonal fights with issue overtones."[28] But Robin Suits, a longtime member of both the collective and the staff, perceived that in the women's movement the personal *was* political. "As your consciousness got raised, and you began to see things in more political ways, you got a sense that there was only one right way. Everybody had a slightly different way, and the groups became smaller and more splintered over the most ridiculous things."[29]

Both the Women's Center and Dayton Women's Liberation, each with at least some connections to student activism or the New Left, adopted the antihierarchical, antileader stances of these other movements. Members of Students for a Democratic Society (SDS), for instance, proclaimed: "Let the people decide." A rhetoric of shared decision making, however, did not prevent many New Left groups from following a strong leader. An emphasis on democracy, in fact, contributed to split many groups into competing factions. And Dayton feminist groups were not unique. With so many problems facing women demanding attention, disagreement readily surfaced about which problems were most important. By 1970, across the country, feminists debated priority lists for problems and challenged each other's analyses of the causes of sexism. Radical feminists, such as the New York Radical Feminists, the Feminists, and the Redstockings, emphasized the universality of male oppression. Socialist feminist groups like Bread and Roses considered class structure important too. Male domination could not be explained or countered in universalist terms. More moderate groups like NOW called for neither drastic changes in traditional marriage and childrearing patterns nor for an economic revolution. Instead, they urged legal, educational, and employment opportunity reforms; changes in states' property rights laws; the passage of the ERA; and equal access for women to schools and jobs.[30]

The emphasis on equality and democracy itself caused tension. In Dayton Women's Liberation, for instance, women selected CR groups by lot. The random choice procedure obviously emphasized common sisterhood and equality, but also it meant that groups were formed of women who sometimes had little in common. An early member of one such group, Carrie LaBriola recalled: "I actively disliked some of the people [in my group]." It meant, for some, that discussions of controversial topics, like abortion, were "too painful" and ceased. Here too the Dayton experiences echoed those in other cities. In New York one disgruntled member called the Feminists' emphasis on egalitarianism "an anti-individual mania." By 1970, the Feminists' lot system for division of tasks had become more elaborate; new rules sought to prevent the formation of cliques or the emergence of "stars." But the system, instead of bringing egalitarian harmony, contributed to conflicts that caused many members to resign.[31]

Painful discussions and memberships splintered into factions were not problems for Dayton Women Working, but apathy was. Noreen Willhelm and Sherrie Holmes, the two driving forces behind Dayton Women Working, were white political activists in their twenties. The average member of Dayton Women Working was also a young white woman.[32] Nevertheless, neither Willhelm nor Holmes led lives similar to those of their members. Neither had ever married; both had borne babies out of wedlock. Both lived in communal houses, had come of age in the late-sixties as anti-Vietnam War protestors, and had ties with leftist politics. In fact, to blur the differences between themselves and the more traditional members Willhelm and Holmes once discussed wearing phoney wedding rings to meetings.[33] Kathy Ellison, a friend of Holmes and a member of Dayton Women Working while a law student, remembered that Holmes and Willhelm made decisions to avoid certain feminist issues that might "alienate your average secretary or clerk." She recalled that abortion, socialism, and lesbianism, for instance, were not to be debated.

The leaders of Dayton Women Working staged many imaginative events that grabbed newspaper headlines. For instance, the group's Pettiest Boss awards earned the organization plenty of free local publicity. Contenders for one Petty Boss contest included the head of a jewelry firm who used clear nail polish on his fingernails and had his secretary paint the right hand nails, a boss who required an employee to go to his home to feed his dog, a physician who sent his bookkeeper downtown to buy a plunger to fix a clogged toilet, and a businessman who required his secretary to check him over carefully each day to see that he was properly dressed and that his socks matched. Charles Moody, the physician, received his award when several Dayton Women Working members showed up at his offices unannounced to deliver a toilet plunger, with a rose attached.[34]

Still, despite the efforts of Holmes and other "spokespersons"[35] who generated publicity and avoided controversial topics such as lesbianism, Dayton Women Working leaders failed to recruit an active membership. A memo Holmes sent to the national NAM program coordinating board illustrated a major problem. Rather than viewing her members as friends and compatriots, she seemed to see them as "the clerical sector." Unsuccessfully urging the national NAM leadership to support her efforts, she argued that "this (Dayton) project is important because (1) it is an important part of a nation-wide test of the organizing potential of clericals, (2) it is important for N.A.M. to build ties with this sector, (3) it is important to build ties with other clerical organizers."[36]

Of course, historical examples of successful movements in which leaders were not friends with their followers abound. Holmes did not have to be "your average secretary or clerk"; she did not have to marry and share her members' personal lives or moral values. But she did have to build ties. She did have to convince members that Dayton Women Working deserved their loyalty, support, and dedication; that the organization could be a vehicle for change in their lives.

In fact, Dayton Women Working leaders did build some ties with other clerical organizers, government officials, and private philanthropists. But ties with their own members, who became accustomed to having programs delivered to them ready-made, were the crucial, and neglected ones. Phrases in Holmes's letter echoed those used to justify projects such as the 1965 Economic Research and Action Projects (ERAP) of SDS, meant to build ties with the "urban poverty sector." The northern college student radicals who decamped to urban poverty in 1965 and 1966 were often genuinely committed to helping. They worked hard, received no salary, and lived on peanut butter. Some ERAP projects, such as those in Boston and Cleveland, succeeded in organizing welfare mothers, sowing the seeds for a national welfare rights movement. But many ERAP projects failed at least partially because their leaders were unable to communicate a sense of shared interest and mission with the often confused, sometimes hostile, residents of urban ghettoes.[37]

Holmes's rhetoric echoed that of some early twentieth-century American feminists. Alice Paul, for instance, had tried during the 1920s to make the Woman's Party a "vanguard" party, promoting absolute equality for women, including "industrial equality" for women workers. But few workers joined the Woman's Party; it remained a small organization of well-educated women, run in an authoritarian fashion by Paul and her coterie.[38] Sherrie Holmes was not another feminist generation's version of Alice Paul, however. She was no blue blood, sporting graduate degrees. She defined herself as a leftist but had no master plan for Dayton

Women Working to emerge as a vanguard party – still her attempts to forge links between leftist activists and women workers echoed Paul's. And like Paul, she seemed to possess greater skill in constructing phrases strategically calculated to appeal to leftists than to politically moderate women workers.

Of course, Dayton Women Working was part of a larger network and linked its work to that of the NWEP. In each of the NWEP chapters, Noreen Willhelm argued, one woman "*was*" the organization. If Sherrie Holmes "was" Dayton Women Working, Helen Williams "was" Cleveland Women Working, and Karen Nussbaum "was" Boston 9 to 5. In that respect, at least, the entire NWEP resembled the Woman's Party, in which "[Alice Paul] is the party."[39] These strong, intelligent women took on big challenges. But in many cases, not just that of Dayton Women Working, the romance of battles against American banking czars or federal power brokers wooed them away from the tedium of membership drives and they, with feminist leaders from past decades, reproduced organizations without sufficient grass roots strength. And women office workers, socialized already by job and family to be deferential and quiet, were often silent when they confronted their own organizations' authority figures. Unlike meetings at the Dayton Women's Center, which often boiled with charges, countercharges, and both good and bad feelings, Dayton Women Working held its meetings punctually at the end of workdays and followed Robert's Rules.

Thousands of women utilized the services of the Women's Center; only a small percentage joined the collective and worked hard to keep the center a vital force in the community. Over two hundred women filled out membership cards and joined Dayton Women Working, but far fewer came regularly to meetings. Many did not even pay the nominal $3.00 yearly dues. If these groups had focused on grass roots organization, would they have enjoyed greater success? A great influx of new members would not automatically have assured strength and stability. New Left organizing provides a cautionary example. In 1965, spurred by the escalation of the war in Vietnam, thousands of new members flooded into SDS, but such quick growth, Todd Gitlin has argued, did not really help the organization. All the new members and concomitant attention changed SDS into a mass movement too quickly, with leaders who increasingly became media stars, whose speeches were shaped by television and not constituency demands.[40]

Hundreds, even thousands, of active, committed members would not have ensured the longevity of Dayton Women Working, the Women's Center, or Dayton Women's Liberation. But such a membership could have provided a potential for strength. Through dues and donations it certainly could have provided funds. And lack of money became, along with membership recruitment and involvement, a serious problem for Dayton feminist groups, as well as their national umbrellas. On both a national and local level, leaders depended heavily on monies granted by the federal government or private philanthropies. When those funding sources disappeared so too did the organizations they fostered. In that sense feminist organizations in Dayton were not just outgrowths of 1960s' activism or products of the women's movement. They were also legacies of the national programs that had made federal monies available for local community action projects.

During the mid- and late-1960s, Dayton received large amounts of federal money under one of Lyndon Johnson's Great Society programs, Model Cities. Healthy Model Cities grants continued under the Nixon administration. In Dayton, locally elected Priority Boards made recommendations to the City Commission about projects in their neighborhoods to be funded by Model Cities.[41] In November 1973, the Dayton City Commission, using federal Model City monies, awarded the Women's Center $15,000.[42] Comprehensive Employment and Training Act (CETA) and Volunteers in Service to America (VISTA) money provided part-time staff positions and interns. At all times, between 1976 and 1980, the great bulk of monies available to Dayton Women Working were federal funds. CETA paid the salaries of its full-time director-organizer, its full-time program-organizer, and its part-time office manager.[43]

Between 1978 and 1979, the VISTA program provided funds for a VISTA worker, who was, ironically, installed at Dayton Women Working offices with federal money in order to "allow constituents to develop their leadership skills and make decisions" affecting Dayton Women Working. The paid VISTA worker was to "encourage members to volunteer their time."[44]

Dayton churches, like the Miami/Presbytery and the United

Church of Christ provided a few thousand dollars to Dayton Women Working and the Women's Center. By 1980, however, both organizations found that they "had worn out their welcome" at these private charities, which were inclined to give only one or two years of seed money.[45] In both organizations, membership dues provided only token support.

By 1980, Dayton Women's Liberation, Dayton Women Working, and Dayton Women's Center had died. A preliminary autopsy would suggest that causes of death included excessive dependence on federal funding and ambitious programs that eclipsed grass roots organizing. Such an autopsy would also note changes in political and economic climates. By 1980, Dayton organizations were certainly not the only feminist groups in the country to find funding sources less sympathetic and to experience a backlash against feminism. Finally, an autopsy would indicate that these three organizations died when subjected to the great stresses inherent in any social movement as it ages and moves from initial dreams and optimism to long-range realistic assessment. As Noreen Willhelm realized in retrospect, Dayton Women Working leaders "did get caught up in our myth before we had even created it."[46] Sherrie Holmes had "this initial fantasy about the Women's Center, that all we had to do was provide this place and women who wanted to change society would all come there and continue to build the movement."[47] Clearly, the slow building of a movement proved to be a harder task.

The task was complicated by the fact that organized feminism in Dayton, in common with organized feminism in other cities, failed to embrace working-class or minority women in any significant numbers, even though the Women's Center house was located in one of Dayton's few truly mixed-race neighborhoods. The leaders of the groups were white and overwhelmingly middle-class, women who sometimes seemed oblivious to a patronizing attitude when they tried to organize even white working-class women. Not surprisingly, meaningful contacts with the black community proved difficult. Moreover, as Cheryl Radican explained, "We [in feminist organizations] felt a lot of hesitation" about recruiting blacks. Radican and others who sympathized with the civil rights movement "did not want to drive a wedge into their black unity."[48] These white women, who had little direct contact with the black community and few friendships with blacks, seemed to feel that, for black women, issues of race superseded those of sex. The fact that many black women might have agreed with such an assessment did not negate the fact that few were consulted.

Also complicating the task of building a movement was the fact that neither Dayton Women Working nor the Women's Center achieved a clear focus and sense of purpose. Dayton Women Working did not see itself as a union for clerical workers; in fact, its leaders made little attempt to contact leaders of Dayton unions. The union leadership in Dayton, a town where traditional heavy industry unions like the Steel Workers and the United Auto Workers still dominated, returned the disdain. But Dayton Women Working did not really see itself as functioning as a women's center for women clerical workers, providing a place for women office workers to come to be together to talk about home lives, social relationships, and struggles at work.

Interestingly, the NWEP, which Dayton Women Working had helped create, did solve the dilemma of focus by forming a firm alliance with the union movement. NWEP, which ceased to exist formally in 1979, did not cease to exist in the same way that Dayton Women Working has ceased to exist. It became, under the new name Working Women, a project of the National Association of Office Workers. In 1981, Working Women and the Service Employees International Union formed District 925, specifically to organize office workers.[49]

The Women's Center, by 1977 torn by dissension, had its own problems setting an agenda. Frequent and bitter controversies erupted. Some collective members thought the center should be more openly socialist; others sought to downplay leftist politics. Some wanted a more visible role for lesbians; some did not. Even the wildly successful daycare co-op caused conflict as babies and children crowded into space formerly devoted to other programs. This disunity led to a Women's Center where angry resignations and statements of "exhaustion" were commonplace.[50] Many of the young, middle-class women who had given their energies to Dayton Women Working and the Women's Center began to direct their energies elsewhere. Many took full-time jobs; some went to graduate or law school; others started families.

This analysis chronicles the rise and fall of feminist organizations in Dayton. It does not, however, chronicle the rise and fall of feminism itself. Although none of the three organizations here examined survived, not all their ideas and programs disappeared. In that sense, their deaths were not a failure for feminism. Dayton Women Working played a central role in stirring interest among national unions in organizing office workers, and District 925 exists partly as Dayton Women Working's legacy. The feminist organizations here studied fell, but feminism itself survived. Although disillusioned with infighting or specific projects, no members of these Dayton feminist groups contacted for interviews were disillusioned with feminism itself. In fact they continued to live independent, self-confident lives centered by feminism. Some entered traditional male-only occupations – one, for instance, became a forester, another an engineer. Others continued to work long hours for feminist causes, staffing rape hot lines and battered women shelters.[51] Moreover, in important ways, feminism in Dayton itself became, as one Dayton Women's Center member put it, "mainstreamed" by the late-1970s.[52] Other groups, with fewer radical connections, began to offer some of the services first provided by Dayton Women's Liberation, Dayton Women Working, and the Women's Center. For instance, the Dayton YWCA opened a Career Development Center, offering seminars and workshops for women workers. A city-funded Victim-Witness Project offered advocacy and counseling for rape victims.[53]

But mainstreaming always imposes a price. In the mid-1980s, many of the objectives of organized feminism in Dayton during the 1970s remain goals and dreams. Most Dayton women clerical workers remain unorganized and poorly paid. Women still have problems with childcare, healthcare, and the host of other issues that concerned the Women's Center. And many federally funded programs meant to help women cope with those problems have disappeared. An organization called the Dayton Women's Center remains listed in the Dayton phonebook, but those calling its number hear the voices of members of a local chapter of a "Right to Life" group. In 1980, the Dayton Women's Center collective sent a letter to the women on its mailing list, announcing its "difficult decision" to close. "We need new strategies, new weapons, and new blood," the letter writers concluded.[54] In the 1980s, many

Dayton feminists were still seeking those visions, tools, and energies.

APPENDIX

Brief Biographical Sketches of Principal Informants

Egart, Katie: A 1972 graduate of the University of Dayton, Katie Egart worked for the Community Schools Project of the Dayton Model Cities Program during the time she was involved with Dayton Women's Liberation. She had been active in antiwar student politics in the 1960s. She is now an engineer.

Ellison, Kathy: A Smith College graduate, Kathy Ellison was a law student in her twenties when she became a member of the Women's Center Collective. She is now a Dayton attorney who started Dayton's first all-woman law firm.

Griesinger, Jan: A graduate of United Theological Seminary, Jan Griesinger became a civil rights activist in Dayton in the 1960s and was a self-described leftist. She was in her thirties when she became involved in the women's movement. She is still involved through her work in the peace movement and the United Church of Christ.

Holmes, Sherrie: A self-described social activist, Sherrie Holmes was in her early twenties when she became a central figure in the Dayton women's movement. She has since moved to California where she has worked as a grant administrator.

LaBriola, Carrie: In her early thirties when she attended Dayton Women's Liberation meetings, Carrie LaBriola was a full-time mother with two infants. She is now a newspaper reporter in Dayton.

Morgan, Mary: Active in Democratic party politics, Mary Morgan was in her mid-forties when she began attending CR groups. A school teacher, she was married and living in a Dayton suburb. She is now working to develop a rural women's community near Athens, Ohio.

Radican, Cheryl: A college student in her twenties when she was a key organizer of Dayton Women's Liberation, Cheryl Radican has since moved to Washington state where she works as a forester.

Rose, Joan Ruth: Joan Rose was in her forties and the divorced mother of two teenaged daughters at the time of her involvement in early Dayton Women's Liberation activities. She belonged to antiwar and civil rights organizations in Dayton, still considers herself a political activist, and now works as a counselor in a battered women's shelter in Springfield, Ohio.

Suits, Robin: A woman in her twenties when a member of the Women's Center, Robin Suits moved to Dayton from New York in 1968 to coordinate a church-funded project called Summer in the City, which sponsored street theater, workshops, and door-to-door canvassing, all meant to improve black-white relations and attack racism. She is now a public relations specialist.

Willhelm, Noreen: In her early twenties when she became a leader of Dayton Women Working, Noreen Willhelm had come to Dayton from Toledo, Ohio, to help organize protests against the municipal utilities corporation. She is now a newspaper reporter in Dayton.

Zurcher, Susan: A sculptor, working for the city of Dayton City Beautiful Project during the early 1970s, Susan Zurcher was a college graduate, in her late twenties at the time of her involvement in the women's movement in Dayton. Zurcher's work has since gained national recognition; she shows in major galleries, and is now an artist in New York City.

NOTES

1. Barbara Ehrenreich, "The Women's Movements: Feminist and Antifeminist," *Radical America* 15 (Spring, 1981): 101.
2. See for example, William Chafe, "Feminism of the 1970s," *Dissent* 21 (Fall, 1974): 508-17.
3. For a popularized summary of Dayton's history see, Bruce Ronald, *Dayton, the Gem City* (Tulsa, Okla.: Continental Heritage Press, 1981). Also, Judith Ezekiel is writing on the subject of the Dayton women's movement. Her dissertation – "Contribution à l'histoire du mouvement féministe américaine: l'étude de cas de Dayton, Ohio, 1969-1980" (in English; Ph.D. diss., University of Paris VIII, defense scheduled for fall 1986) – was unfortunately not completed in time to be available for our story.
4. Richard Scammon, quoted in *Dayton Daily News*, 20 July 1980.
5. Cheryl Radican, telephone interview from Richland, Washington, with Judith Sealander, 4 January 1985. For discussion of women in Students for a Democratic Society, see Sara Evans, *Personal Politics: The Roots of Women's Liberation in the Civil Rights Movement and the New Left* (New York: Vintage, 1979), esp. chaps. 6-7.
6. Ibid.
7. Carrie LaBriola, interview with Judith Sealander, Dayton, Ohio, 17 October 1984.
8. Tape-recorded group discussion with Jan Griesinger, Joan Ruth Rose, Mary Morgan, Katie Egart, Yellow Springs, Ohio, 17 October 1983.
9. *Dayton Women's Liberation Newsletter*, September 1970, the Records of Dayton Women's Liberation (hereafter cited as DWL), Department of Archives and Special Collections, Wright State University, Dayton, Ohio.
10. LaBriola interview.
11. Model Cities grant proposal submitted by Dayton Women's Liberation, 15 October 1973, box 1, #1, the records of the Dayton Women's Center (hereafter cited as DWC), Department of Archives and Special Collections, Wright State University, Dayton, Ohio.
12. Sherrie Holmes, interview with Dorothy Smith, San Rafael, California, 30 June 1983.

13. Minutes of National Women's Employment Project meeting, 8 October 1977, Chicago, "N.W.E.P. Memos and Correspondence," box 4, #1, the Records of Dayton Women Working (hereafter cited as DWW), Department of Archives and Special Collections, Wright State University Library, Dayton, Ohio.
14. Susan Zurcher, interview with Dorothy Smith, Dayton, Ohio, 17 February 1984; Robin Suits, interview with Dorothy Smith, Yellow Springs, Ohio, 25 February 1984; Minutes, Women's Center collective, 23 January 1974, box 1, #4, DWC.
15. Letter from Women's Center collective to Fair River Oaks Council Priority Board, 12 March 1974, box 1, #2, DWC.
16. Suits interview. See also "What's Happening at the Women's Center," printed newsletter, box 4, #3, DWC.
17. Holmes and Suits interviews.
18. Holmes interview.
19. Memo to National Women's Employment Project Board from Heleny Cook, 13 April 1977, "N.W.E.P. Memos and Correspondence," box 4, #2, DWW. Also Noreen Willhelm, interview with Judith Sealander, Dayton, Ohio, 18 July 1983.
20. Memo to National Women's Employment Project Board from Heleny Cook, 31 October 1977, "N.W.E.P. Memos and Correspondence," box 4, #2, DWW. Also Willhelm interview.
21. Noreen Willhelm to Mr. Marvin Michel, Vice-President, Personnel, First National Bank, Dayton, 13 February 1978, "Correspondence, Banking Study," box 3, #14, DWW.
22. Introduction, "Banks: Discrimination in Employment, a Dayton Working Women Study: Employment Discrimination in Dayton's Three Largest Commercial Banks," 10 July 1978, DWW.
23. Ibid.
24. Notes on Banking Industry Research, evidence compiled by Dayton Women Working and Cleveland Women Working, 1979, 15, box 3, #15, DWW.
25. Dayton Women Working, "Progress Report," January-July 1978, box 1, #8, DWW.
26. Banking Industry Research, 3.
27. Minutes of Women's Center collective, 26 January, 2, 9, and 23 February 1977, box 1, #4. See also letter from Roberta Fischer to Women's Caucus of New American Movement, 17 January 1977; letter from Women's Caucus of New American Movement to Women's Center collective, 27 January 1977, both in box 1, #3, DWC.
28. Kathy Ellison, interview with Judith Sealander, Dayton, Ohio, 10 August 1983.
29. Suits interview.
30. See, for example, Evans, chap. 9; William Chafe, "Feminism of the 1970's"; Wini Breines, *Community and Organization in the New Left, 1962-1968: The Great Refusal* (South Hadley, Mass.: Bergin & Garvey, 1982); Todd Gitlin, "The Dynamics of the New Left," *Motive* (November 1970): 45; Kirkpatrick Sale, *S.D.S.* (New York: Vintage Books, 1973); and Judith Hole and Ellen Levine, *Rebirth of Feminism* (New York: Quadrangle, 1971).
31. Hole and Levine, 145-49.
32. Dayton Women Working was made up primarily of white women. Membership cards do not list race, and although recollections about percentages of black members differ, all agreed that there were few black members. A rise in black members occurred after Deborah Walker, a black hospital worker, joined in 1979 and began actively to recruit members.
33. Holmes and Willhelm interviews.
34. See *Dayton Daily News* and *Dayton Journal Herald*, both for 5 May 1978.
35. Holmes interview.

36. Sherrie Holmes, typewritten memo [early 1977?], DWW.
37. See Evans, chap. 6; Sale, chaps. 2-4; and Mitchell Goodman, ed., *The Movement toward a New America* (Philadelphia: Pilgrim Press, Knopf, 1970).
38. Nancy Cott, "Feminist Politics in the 1920s: The National Woman's Party," *Journal of American History* 71 (June 1984): 43-61.
39. Inez Haynes Irwin, quoted in Cott, 45.
40. Todd Gitlin, *The Whole World Is Watching: Mass Media in the Making and Unmaking of the New Left* (Berkeley: University of California Press, 1980).
41. The Dayton City Managers's Office Special Projects Files: Model Cities Program, Department of Archives and Special Collections, WSU.
42. *Dayton Women's Liberation Newsletter*, November 1973, DWL.
43. See Financial Statements of Dayton Women Working, "Financial Records," box 1, #3, DWW.
44. Volunteers in Service to America Study, "Project Report," HQ02-390-3 (interviewer, Charles Hefner), 8 September 1978; "Fundraising–V.I.S.T.A.," both in box 1, #19, DWW.
45. Financial Statements of Dayton Women Working. See also letter to women on Women's Center mailing list, June 1974, October 1975, 8 November 1976, 25 July 1977, box 4, #3; Minutes, Women's Center collective, 9 March 1977, box 1, #4, DWC.
46. Willhelm interview.
47. Holmes interview.
48. Radican interview.
49. Memo, Ellen Cassedy to National Women's Employment Project Board, "Future of N.W.E.P.," 10 May 1979, box 4, #2, DWW; Steve Askin, "Female Rights Spell Trouble for Bosses," *In These Times*, July 27-August 9, 1983, 11.
50. Morgan interview.
51. See Appendix.
52. Ellison interview.
53. Letter to women on Women's Center mailing list, 31 December 1980, box 4, #3, DWC.
54. Ibid.

FEMINISM AND THE CONTEMPORARY FAMILY

Barbara Easton

MOST CONTEMPORARY American feminists see the nuclear family as patriarchal, based on male dominance and female subordination. Furthermore, feminists tend to see these family relations and the patriarchal system that they support as largely unchanging, impervious to political change and the rise and fall of social systems. Most feminist literature implies that patriarchy is static, by describing it as a uniform system, failing to point to any change within it. Some feminists make this point explicit by arguing that men have kept the realm of family life out of the arena of social struggle, acting upon a tacit agreement that whatever conflicts they engage in among themselves shall not be allowed to impinge upon the power of each man over his wife and children. If patriarchy were historically constant, then the task of feminism, the destruction of patriarchy, would also be fundamentally unchanging. Feminists might differ over the strategy to be employed in attacking patriarchy, or over the form that social relations should take after a feminist revolution, but these would be differences in approach rather than in fundamental aim.

But in fact the aims of feminism have shifted quite markedly, at least in the United States. The American women's movement of the nineteenth and early twentieth centuries took not the patriarchal family but the exclusion of women from public life as its main target. In this period of American feminism, women's oppression in the family was a subordinate theme of feminist discussion, and the term patriarchy was used little if at all. The critique of family relations has moved to the center of feminism only in the contemporary women's movement, in the 1960s and 1970s. Surely such a shift must point to some change in the structures that oppress women. Not that each new target necessarily represents what at the time constitutes the center of male power over women. In fact, I will argue, at each stage the women's movement has wisely chosen to attack the weakest, not the strongest, area of male dominance. The point is that the form of feminist activity, and the theoretical formulations accompanying that activity, have shifted in response to women's changing situation. When, in the mid-nineteenth century, the growth of capitalism and the emergence of an ideology of equality of rights and opportunity made it difficult to defend the exclusion of particular groups from the public realm, feminists demanded equal rights for women in public life. Now, as women's increased political and legal rights and their entry into the labor force begin to undermine traditional male power in the family, the critique of patriarchy comes to the fore.*

The central purpose of this article is to argue that the twentieth-century feminist attack on patriarchy has accompanied an actual weakening of patriarchy, and the emergence of new forms of male dominance. We do not yet have a name for these new forms, nor do we understand very much about them, but it is necessary to begin trying to identify them. It is always the first task of a movement to

*This article is about the history of white women and the white family in the United States. The discussion of the relationship of black women and the black family to feminism would require another article. I use the term "patriarchy" to mean male dominance and female dependence, based on men's ownership of property, ability to earn money, and legal rights over women. In this sense the American slave family was not patriarchal. The fact that since emancipation large numbers of black women have routinely worked outside the home places the issue of patriarchy in a different light in black than in white families. Because of these and other differences, it is necessary to discuss the histories of black and white women in the United State separately. Because American feminism has been shaped largely by white women, I restrict my discussion to their history.

attack oppressive institutions that are in decline. To the extent that they are anachronistic they can be shown to be illegitimate; it is possible to turn public sentiment against them with relative ease. But then it is necessary to begin to identify and attack forms of social control that are on the rise.

In the twentieth century, the virtually absolute economic and legal power that men once held over their families has been eroded; as men lose these formal rights it becomes easier to attack the ideas of female inferiority and the division of labor between the sexes that were shaped by patriarchy. But as men lose formal, socially recognized forms of control over women, they are likely, consciously or unconsciously, to turn to forms that are more subtle or less legitimate. If the women's movement and the left cannot address the new problems that women face in a post-patriarchal period, we will be in the position of those sections of the left that continue to describe capitalism as it appeared in the late nineteenth century, and so lose their audience and their relevance to popular concerns. One way to begin the task of identifying new forms of male dominance is to ask how feminist concerns have shifted in the past, and to look at the present women's movement with an eye to the places where significant concerns are not explained by present theory.

Nineteenth-Century Feminism

THE FEMINISTS OF THE mid-nineteenth century regarded the winning of equal rights for women as their central task. The first women's rights convention, held in Seneca Falls, New York, in 1848, issued a list of women's grievances that reflected this perspective. Women's disfranchisement was placed at the top of the list, in spite of some trepidation; the demand for suffrage had nearly been voted down as opponents argued that such a demand was too controversial and would discredit the movement. This grievance was followed by a list of women's legal and political disabilities: women's obligation to obey laws that they had no part in framing, the refusal of the courts to recognize the interests of married women apart from their husbands', the legal right of husbands to their wives' property and earnings, and women's legal disadvantages in case of divorce. Social issues such as women's exclusion from colleges and second-class status in the church, and the separate standards of morality for men and women, were lower on the list. At no point did the statement question marriage itself, the nuclear family, or the primary responsibility of women for children.[1]

In the years between Seneca Falls and the outbreak of the Civil War, women's rights conventions were held almost every year to discuss women's position, arrive at demands, and formulate strategies for achieving those demands. The protest against the inequality of power betwen men and women, and the demand for female autonomy, were at the heart of these discussions. Many feminists understood that the roots of this power imbalance and of women's dependence lay in the family, but the family itself was never the central issue for early feminism that it is for the contemporary women's movement. In the movement of the mid-nineteenth century, the topics of marriage and the family were more likely to come up in the context of discussions of women's legal rights or public role than to be raised as issues in themselves. For instance, Elizabeth Cady Stanton in her autobiography described a women's rights convention held in 1861 at which she argued that the movement should protest the legal biases against women in divorce proceedings. Wendell Phillips, an abolitionist who usually supported women's rights, opposed her motion. (Men who were sympathetic to feminism often attended these meetings.) Phillips proposed that the question of divorce be dropped, arguing that "as marriage concerned man and woman alike . . . woman had no special ground for complaint."

Susan B. Anthony rose to support Stanton's motion. She challenged the idea that men and women were equal in marriage:

> Marriage has always been a one-sided affair, resting most unequally upon the sexes. By it man gains all; woman loses all; tyrant law and lust reign supreme with him; meek submission and ready obedience alone befit her. Woman has never been consulted; her wish has never been taken into consideration as regards the terms of the marriage contract. By law, public sentiment, and religion . . . woman has never thought of other than as a piece of property, to be disposed of at the will and pleasure of man.[2]

The early feminists could use strong language when speaking of women's role in marriage and family; a critique of Victorian marriage was a sub-theme of the feminist discussion of women's status. Many feminists pointed out that it was unhealthy for women's activities to be confined to the home. Antoinette Brown Blackwell pointed out that no one would consider urging that men stay at their places of work twenty-four hours a day, and that the importance of fresh air, exercise, and change of scene to mental and physical health was common knowledge. The high incidence of illness among women confined to their homes should be no surprise, she wrote.[3]

Other feminists, in discussing women's position in the family, emphasized the deleterious moral effects of women's subordination. Susan B. Anthony wrote that though women were much less given to drunkenness and sexual licentiousness than men, women suffered most from these evils. She pointed out that women had little protection against the violence of a drunken husband or the corruption of a man who visited prostitutes. By virtue of men's power over women's subsistence, Anthony wrote, they were able to dictate to women a moral code much higher than the code to which men themselves adhered. At the same time, men deprived women of the power to insist on a higher standard of behavior from men.[4] Elizabeth Cady Stanton wrote of the damage this did to female self-respect. Women, she wrote, were "stripped of all . . . virtue, dignity and nobility" by pervasive female inequality. She asked, "How can women endure our present marriage relations, by which woman's life, health and happiness are held so cheap, that she herself feels . . . no individuality of her own?"[5]

These early feminist discussions of marriage and family give us a picture of virtually unlimited male power; lucky women were treated well by their husbands, but the unlucky ones had little recourse. In 1848 Emily Collins described a woman she had known as a child whose husband whipped her "because she scolded." She wrote,

> And pray, why should he not have chastised her? The laws made it his privilege—and the Bible, as interpreted, made it his duty. It is true, women repined at their hard lot; but it was thought to be fixed by a divine decree, for "The man shall rule over thee," and "Wives submit to your husbands," and "Wives, submit yourselves to your husbands as to the Lord," caused them to consider their fate inevitable.[6]

Though many early feminists condemned the subordination of women within marriage, no leader of the women's movement was willing to reject the institution of marriage itself. Many went out of their way to voice support for marriage, and for the sexual division of labor in the family, with women's responsibility for child rearing, and men's for economic support of the family. Harriet Stanton Blatch wrote that men had little paternal instinct and were therefore "undeveloped parents" and should not be blamed for their lack of interest in child care. Antoinette Brown Blackwell, after criticizing the confinement of women to domesticity, and arguing that both sexes would benefit if each worked outside the home part time, reversed herself by proclaiming her support of motherhood and wifely support:

> Still, I am ready to concede, most fully, that the mothers of young children ought not to be considered the breadwinners. . . . Our physiologists should teach her the laws of life in early girlhood, giving special heed to the maternal duty of being always fresh and vigorous, at whatever cost; not selfishly, but for the sake of her children, and in the interest of the peace and quietness of the home to which the husband should come as to a haven of comfort.[7]

Nineteenth-century women were trapped in domesticity not only because the economy was not open to them as it was to men, but also because in the nineteenth century marriage meant childbirth which meant domesticity, whereas failing to marry meant a lonely life. It was virtually impossible for a woman to choose not to have children once she married, not only because birth control information was relatively unavailable, but also because everyone, including the woman herself, expected that once she married she would have children. A woman who did not have children was pitied, and was likely to regard herself as a failure. And in a society in which men took no responsibility for child care and there was no provision for child care outside the home, continual childbirth meant that motherhood was a full-time job. Childcare had always been mainly women's responsibility, but in previous centuries it had been only one among many female tasks. In the nineteenth century motherhood was women's work, their main role in society; few women were able to carve out satisfying lives that did not involve having children.

Nineteenth-century American women were trapped into subservience to men within the family not only because they were largely excluded from the economy and, once they married, absorbed by childbirth and child care, but also because the power that men held over women in this situation was reinforced by the law. In the nineteenth century married women possessed few legal rights, and virtually none in relation to their husbands. In the rare event of divorce, custody of children was ordinarily granted to the father. Not only in divorce but in marriage as well women's rights were severely restricted; any inheritance or earnings that a woman might bring to a marriage or accrue once married were legally considered the property of the husband.[8]

Circumvention of these codes required elaborate legal work. As long as women did not have the vote, it was difficult for them to challenge such laws successfully. In the second half of the nineteenth century some progress was made, in some states, in women's legal position; this was in part due to feminist protest, but probably was more the result of pressure from wealthy and powerful families. Such reforms were only the first step towards any real weakening of men's power in the family. Through the nineteenth century, few cracks appeared in the patriarchal structure of the American family. Feminists would have been foolish to challenge men's power in the family head on.

IT WAS POSSIBLE for nineteenth-century feminists to challenge the exclusion of women from the public arena. It was not too difficult to stretch the definition of the domestic role to include nurturant, humanitarian activity outside the home; women could teach in Sunday Schools, raise money for missionaries, and even engage in campaigns for temperance or other reforms without stepping too far outside the accepted female role.[9] Some women stretched at least their own understanding of their role far enough to become involved in the abolitionist movement, and here they confronted the question of actual inequality in a society that proclaimed equality for all. Feminism first arose in the United States out of women's involvement in this movement, in part because abolitionist women began to extend their principles of human rights to themselves, and in part because in their activity on behalf of equal rights for blacks they were forced to confront their own lack of rights as women, especially the prohibitions against women engaging in public activity.

While activity in the abolitionist movement helped to shape the outlook of the early women's movement, in a larger sense the early feminist focus on women's exclusion from the public arena was determined by the shape of American society in the mid-nineteenth century. The traditional restrictions on women's activity were by this time in contradiction with the norm of equal opportunity that was held to govern public life; this blatant contradiction impelled nineteenth-century feminists to demand for women the rights that were promised to men. In the seventeenth and eighteenth centuries a movement for female equality would not have arisen because the promise of equal rights was not held out in any arena, for either sex. Outside the family as well as within it, people expected to defer to their superiors and be deferred to by their inferiors. In the nineteenth century, in the oldest and most populated areas of the country, the same areas in which feminism arose first, the competitive relations of the market were replacing the deferential relations of the earlier, more agrarian and less commercial society, and the ideology of competitive individualism was replacing the older ideology of hierarchical, corporate order.

The family, however, remained exempt from these developments. In the context of a society rapidly moving away from traditionalism, the patriarchal restrictions on women's activities appeared increasingly anachronistic. It was possible for women to demand equality in the public arena for the same reason that it was possible for freed black males to demand the vote: a capitalist system that promised equality of opportunity to all was vulnerable to protest from groups excluded from these opportunities.

Gilman and the Early Critique of the Family

OVER THE SECOND HALF of the nineteenth century, women gained confidence and some measure of power through their increasing activity in the public arena, not only in the feminist movement but also in the other reform and humanitarian movements of the time. It was on the basis of these gains that it began to be possible for a few women to raise the issue of power relations within the family. In the late nineteenth century Charlotte Perkins Gilman made an extended feminist analysis of the position of women in marriage and the family, criticizing sex roles for the first time without apologies. In *Women and Economics*, published in 1898, she described women's economic dependence upon men in marriage as the central problem facing women. Sexual attractiveness and childlike helplessness, Gilman wrote, were a woman's main assets in achieving marriage and the economic support that it brought; therefore women cultivated these qualities while their personal and intellectual growth were stunted. Gilman urged women to work outside the home, arguing that only economic independence could bring women a sense of integrity and true equality with men. She did not reject marriage or the family; she argued that in the long run they would be strengthened when women gained economic independence, for then women could marry without giving up the rest of their lives. But Gilman did believe that marriage would be tainted so long as within it men could buy sex with a promise of financial support.[10]

Gilman had a following within the women's movement, but the movement as a whole did not adopt her outlook or even consider her ideas to any great extent. This was partly because by the early twentieth century the struggle for suffrage was claiming most of the energies of the women's movement, and prospects of success were improving. A critique of marriage and the family would have been not only a distraction from that struggle but a real threat; raising such controversial issues might have lost the women's movement male support that it needed in order to win electoral victories.

Gilman's ideas were ignored primarily because for most women the situation that feminists had faced at mid-century still obtained. Opportunities for work outside the home, if slightly expanded by this time, were still limited, and women's power inside the home was still negligible. The main checks on men's power over women were men's own moral scruples, social pressure, and whatever leverage a woman could gain due to her husband's feelings for her. Physical abuse of wives took place, but it was not nearly as widespread as the damage done to women's self-respect by their dependency. Male power in the family was still too great for feminism to be able to confront it directly.[11]

GILMAN'S CONCERNS were given dramatic form in her short novel, *The Yellow Wallpaper,* a horrifying account of the emotional impact of male dominance on a woman. The woman narrator is driven to madness by being deprived of an adult life, of work or contact with the world outside her home. Her husband, in order to cure her of nervousness, forces her to rest and forbids her to leave her room or pursue her writing. He treats her as if she were a child, unable to make any decisions for herself. The woman at first tries to plot her escape, but she is increasingly drawn into fantasy: she sees a woman beckoning to her, moving through and beyond the wallpaper of her room. The narrator loses interest in the world that her husband moves in, the world that earlier she had so desperately wanted to join. She ends by crawling around the edges of the room, tearing at the wallpaper in an effort to escape into the world of her mind that lies beyond it.[12]

Gilman's story was not as far from reality as the twentieth-century reader might think: many Victorian women did seek refuge in physical or mental illness.[13] The significance of the story, however, lies not so much in either the husband's unconscious cruelty or the woman's escape into madness, but in the fact that for this woman the central issue was her husband's power and her own lack of autonomy. Gilman was seen as dangerously radical by most feminists of her time. In fact she was dealing with the same issues that other feminists were most concerned with. The difference was that most feminists attacked male dominance in the public sphere, where some progress could be made without threatening women's security. Gilman raised the questions of male dominance and female autonomy in the family, where the stakes were highest and the possible cost to women greatest.

The New Feminism of the 1960s

THE WOMEN'S MOVEMENT of the early twentieth century did not pursue the issues that Gilman had raised in *Women and Economics* and *The Yellow Wallpaper*. This issues remained the concerns of a small section of the movement, while the majority of feminists focused their attention upon the campaign for woman suffrage. When suffrage was won in 1920, the women's movement died. But over the four decades that followed it because increasingly evident that suffrage had been only the first step. When feminism ultimately re-emerged in the 1960s, the new movement was shaped by the fact that formal equality, having been at least partially achieved, was no longer as pressing an issue for women as it had once been, and also by the recognition that in any case equal rights in the public arena were not enough. The new feminists reversed the priorities of their predecessors: while they recognized the importance of continuing to fight for equality in the public arena, their central concern was the question of women's subordination within the family.

Like the early feminist movement, the feminism of the mid-sixties emerged out of women's experience in non-feminist political movements, and was shaped by that experience. In the early sixties young women were drawn to the civil rights and anti-war movements for much the same reasons as were their male contemporaries, out of outrage at a society that professed democratic and humanitarian principles while practicing racism and military aggression. Within these movements and the new left as a whole, it was men who took on leadership roles while women for the most part found themselves in the role of followers. At first this was tolerable: it was subtle, and it was no more than women expected. But as women's confidence and political awareness grew, so did authoritarianism within the movement. The seemingly unstoppable escalation of the war in Vietnam drove the left to increasing levels of desperation, a mood that allowed leaders to treat followers, especially women, in an increasingly high-handed manner. In the name of fighting for the liberation of black people at home and the Vietnamese abroad, women were now being asked to subordinate themselves to the authority of male leaders of their own movement.

Confronted with such hypocrisy, women began to leave the new left to form women's groups. The process was much the same as it had been over a century earlier, when abolitionist women had turned to feminism as obstacles to their activity in behalf of the abolition of slavery had made them aware of their own lack of rights as women. The difference was that while the abolitionist women had confronted the constraints on the public, political role of women, for the women of the new left, and primary issue was the discrepancy between the formal accordance of equality and the informal and private treatment of women as men's inferiors.

The feminism of the mid-sixties, again like early feminism, arose not only out of women's experience of discrimination within a movement for democracy, but also out of changes in the situation of women, especially those of the social strata that formed the base of the new left. In the fifties and sixties women of these strata were attending college in numbers greater than ever before. Like men, they were being trained for professional careers; unlike men, when they left college they were likely to face the choice between family life and no careers, or careers and no family life. There were few models for combining the two, and few men who were sympathetic to such an effort.

Because contradictions of this nature affected much larger numbers of women than those in the new left, a liberal feminist movement began to emerge at roughly the same time that new left women were forming the first women's groups. And the liberal wing of feminism quickly came to predominate in numbers. But it was the radical wing of feminism that gave the movement most of its impetus and direction, and that not only in the sixties but in the seventies as well has produced the main body of influential feminist literature.

The radical wing of feminism in the mid-sixties was united by its militant opposition to sexism, not by a coherent or shared analysis of the sources of sexism. And as such analyses began to be put forward, this wing of the women's movement began to spit into two camps. One, which came to be called radical feminism, was made up of women who saw the oppression of women by men as the basis for all forms of oppression. These women also believed that it was necessary to build a women's culture and women's institutions, to make it possible for women to live as far as possible in a female world. They argued that the women's movement should be autonomous of all other movements, and they tended to see that movement as holding out a new way of life for women rather than as a short-term strategy for overcoming women's oppression within a society that included men. Radical feminists, of all feminist tendencies, most sharply rejected marriage and the nuclear family. The theory that they produced criticized these institutions and their impact on women's lives, often without understanding the historical and social origins of these institutions. The most influential radical feminist writings linked family and society, but often described social roles outside the family as products of sex roles within the family rather than placing the family within a social context.[14]

The second tendency within the radical women's movement called itself anti-imperialist or Marxist feminist; part of this tendency evolved into socialist feminism. These women saw female oppression as one of many kinds of oppression, and sought to link the women's movement with others, especially the anti-war and black liberation movements. The Marxist feminists took issue with the radical feminist assertion that the oppression of women had formed the historical basis of class divisions, and that sex oppression continued to be of greater social significance than class oppression. Instead, the Marxist feminists placed the oppression of women within what they saw as the more basic framework of class relations.[15]

The third tendency in the women's movement was liberal feminism. In 1966, at the same time that radical women were leaving the new left, a group of women who had been involved in liberal and Democratic politics also came to the conclusion that there was a need for a women's movement, that mainstream liberal organizations would not take women's rights seriously. These women founded the National Organization for Women, which worked to complete the struggle for women's equality, especially in education, hiring, and the law. Since then a large number of women's organizations have emerged with the same goal of improving women's status; this is the largest section of the women's movement. But this section of the women's movement has been less interested in the origins of women's oppression than in practical activity, and has added relatively little to feminist theory.[16]

In the late sixties and early seventies, radical feminist writings dominated discussion in the radical wing of the women's movement and were influential in liberal feminist circles as well. The two most widely read statements of this outlook were Kate Millett's *Sexual Politics*, especially the chapter entitled "Theory of Sexual Politics," and Shulamith Firestone's *The Dialectic of Sex*. Both contributed to developing the theory, hinted at by so many early feminists, that the oppression of women had its origin in women's role in the family.

Kate Millett described both the family and society as patriarchal, characterized by men's domination of women and children. She distinguished between "traditional patriarchy," in which women had no legal standing or economic existence, as they could not own or earn in their own right, and "modern patriarchy," in which women are formally accorded equal or nearly equal rights with men, but in which most women do unpaid labor in the home rather than working for wages outside it.

Millett recognized that some women work outside the home in present-day America, but argued that these women have only a temporary relation to the labor force, constituting a reserve labor force "enlisted in times of war and expansion and discharged in times of peace and recession." She saw women's position as fundamentally defined by their dependence upon men rather than by their class position. "In general," she wrote, "the position of women in patriarchy is a continuous function of their economic dependence. Just as their social position is vicarious and achieved (often on a temporary or marginal basis) through males, their relation to the economy is also typically vicarious or tangential."[17]

Kate Millett described a male-dominated society based on a male-dominated family, but she did not discuss the workings of that family, or the link between it and society, in any detail. Shulamith Firestone, in *The Dialectic of Sex*, published the same year, developed these ideas further. She described the hierarchy of power in the nuclear family. Children, she wrote, are at the mercy of their parents, but ultimate authority rests with the father:

> In the prototypical patriarchal nuclear family . . . the father is the breadwinner; all other members of his family are his dependents. He agrees to support a wife in return for her services: housekeeping, sex, and reproduction. The children whom she bears for him are even more dependent. . . . His rights over them are complete. If he is not a kind master/father, tough luck. They cannot escape his clutches until they are grown, and by then the psychological molding has been accomplished: they are now ready to repeat his performance.[18]

Firestone argued that children of both sexes initially feel closest to the mother because she nurtures them and because they identify with her powerlessness. They fear the father and may secretly feel contempt for him. Firestone understood the oedipus complex as the father's intervention in this early mother-child relationship, his way of insuring that the nuclear family on which his power rests will be reproduced. He promises his son male status and power in return for the son's renunciation of loyalty to and identification with the mother. All the father holds out to his daughter, as a reward for shifting her love and loyalty from her mother to him, is that eventually she will marry and partake of male power through association with it. The daughter may envy her brother's privileges; she may even wish that she had a penis, out of a desire for the status associated with it. But eventually she must recognize that the male role is closed to her, and accept femininity and subordination to men.

Firestone saw male domination in the family as the historical origin of class systems, and the patriarchal family as the basic unit of societies—all historical societies—in which men hold power over women and a dominant class holds power over subordinate classes. She pointed out that the first division of labor was that between men and women, and was based on women's pregnancy and their responsibility for child care. She argued that a biological family in which women are dependent upon men creates a psychology that makes possible hierarchical relations throughout society. She wrote:

> Marxian analysis itself was insufficient: it did not dig deep enough to the psychosocial roots of class. Marx was onto something more profound than he knew when he observed that the family contained within itself in embryo all the antagonisms that later develop on a wide scale within the society and the state. For unless the revolution uproots the basic social organization, the biological family—the vinculum through which the psychology of power can always be smuggled—the tapeworm of exploitation will never be annihilated. We shall need a sexual revolution much larger than—inclusive of—a socialist one to truly eradicate all class systems.[19]

Firestone's rewriting of the Freudian account of the family was mechanical in its substitution of power relations for sexuality, and her social theory did not provide the basis for understanding the history of either women or the family, much less class relations in general. Firestone did not explain how hierarchies are transposed from family to society. Furthermore, women's mothering has thus far been a constant through history; in order to explain the changes in women's role in the family and in society it is necessary to look to economic and social forces outside the family and their impact upon it, not to an unchanging element of family structure.

The importance of Firestone's book lay not in her social theory or the specifics of her psychology, but in the fact that she linked sex roles with power relations in the family, and linked feminism with a protest not only against women's subordination, but against social hierarchies in general. Charlotte Perkins Gilman had said seventy years earlier that femininity was a product of women's economic dependence upon men; Firestone's presentation of this point was more psychologically sophisticated than Gilman's, but the main difference was that in 1970 the women's movement was ready to listen, while in 1898 it had not been.

WHY WAS THE WOMEN'S movement now ready to hear this message? In 1970 the radical wing of the women's movement—the section that was most responsive to these issues—was made up largely of college-educated young women, often from professional families. These women were able to criticize the family in a way that their feminist forebears could not because in the social milieu of the new feminists patriarchy was rapidly breaking down. Many of them were unmarried and quite able to support themselves; if they married, it was likely to be more out of choice than necessity, and they were likely to retain the ability to leave marriage if necessary. More importantly, these young women moved in a world in which the old patriarchal values were beginning to falter. A man whose education was in no way superior to his wife's, and whose work was, by his own standards, no more valuable than hers, might lack the old male self-confidence in proclaiming his superiority. A cultural vacuum had been created, and it was possible for the new feminism to walk into it and create a new set of values.

Although feminism appeared first among college-educated women who felt the changes in women's status most sharply, neither the changes nor the concerns were confined to this stratum. For about a century, an expanding American economy had been slowly drawing American women out of the domesticity of the nineteenth century and into increasingly full participation in the labor force.

At all times in American history some women had worked outside the home, and from the late nineteenth century on, the poorest women, blacks, and many immigrants had routinely worked outside the home when young, and often continued to work after marriage. But it was in the twenties and more dramatically in the forties and fifties that new groups of women began to join the labor force in large numbers: young white women who were needed to help support their families or who wanted the independence that their own incomes made possible, and, increasingly, white married women who needed to help support their families, and who may have wanted some life outside the home as well.[20]

Conveniently for capitalists, it was widely believed that women worked only temporarily, and that their work was not central to their lives in the way that men's was to theirs. Such ideas helped to keep women workers unorganized and highly exploited. Many unions excused their failure to organize women workers on grounds that they were marginal members of the work force, and many women failed to join unions out of the hope that they would stop working soon.[21] But though women's work has often been regarded as temporary and incidental, in fact in the middle decades of the twentieth century there has been a steady growth in the numbers of women who work outside the home, and in the number of years that women do such work. Furthermore, women are increasingly likely to work at points in their life cycles during which they once would have remained in the home. At the turn of the century, working women were almost invariably unmarried, and usually young. Now the majority of married women, and a large proportion of women with children, hold jobs. At the turn of the century, for most white women marriage involved the expectation that one would be supported by one's husband for the rest of one's life, and remain in the home raising children and doing housework. Now most American women can expect that they will work outside the home for much of their adult lives, including the period when their children are growing up.[22]

Women's increasing employment outside the home has increased women's options, in particular their ability to leave an unsatisfactory marriage, or to back up demands for improvement with the threat of leaving. A woman's ability to leave her marriage is of course affected by the wages that she can earn and the number of children that she would find herself supporting after a divorce. Clearly women of the poorer sections of the working class, who are likely to have less training, to marry earlier, and to have more children, have fewer options than women from more privileged sections of the working class, or the middle classes. But since the turn of the century there has been a general expansion of women's options that has affected women throughout American society, even though unequally. In the 1970s there are not only many more jobs available to women than there were at the turn of the century; the incomes that these jobs bring in have risen, making it much more likely that a working woman will be able to support not only herself, but perhaps children as well. At the turn of the century most women's jobs were so poorly paid that it took great ingenuity for a woman to support herself on her wages; prostitution constituted a major source of income to working women, who turned to it because it was the only alternative to starvation wages. There are no overall statistics on the relationship between men's and women's wages in this period, but it has been estimated that among factory workers, women generally earned less than fifty percent of what men earned.[23] In the economy as a whole the income of working women was probably an even lower percentage than this of the income of working men. Roughly a quarter of all working women were employed as domestics or servants at the turn of the century, and these women ordinarily earned even less than female factory workers, while the median income of working men was raised by the fact that men occupied the higher-paid clerical and white-collar jobs.

At the turn of the century, it was largely black, first-generation immigrant, and single women who worked outside the home. These women had little bargaining power: their desperate economic situation, their lack of organization and of political power forced them to accept virtually whatever wages were offered them. Thus it was possible for employers to pay women workers wages that were quite minimal. In the middle decades of the century employers faced the necessity of drawing new groups of women into the labor force, including women whose greater economic resources and social leverage enabled them to demand better wages. No doubt partly as a result, women's wages during these decades were slightly upgraded in relation to men's. In 1956, for instance, white women earned 63 percent of what white men earned. In the sixties and seventies this trend has again reversed, and the gap between men's and women's incomes has widened; in 1973, white women earned only 56.3 percent of what white men earned. Perhaps this shift reflects women's increasing need for jobs, and the fact that once women have been drawn into the labor force their labor can be treated as cheap and expendable.

But in spite of the current widening gap between men's and women's incomes, over the twentieth century as a whole women's ability to support themselves has improved. The United States is now considerably more prosperous than it was at the turn of the century. The growth of trade unionism, with union struggles for higher wages, has raised the standard of living not only of union members but to some extent of unorganized workers as well. A woman's 56 percent of a man's income in the 1970s brings her considerably closer to self-sufficiency than did her roughly 40 percent of her male counterpart's pittance at the turn of the century. Working women are still much more likely to be poor than working men. The difference is that now a woman is especially likely to fall below the poverty line if she is supporting a family by herself; seventy years ago virtually all working women in the United States were poor, and it was near-impossible for them to support families on their incomes alone. In 1973 the median income of a family headed by a woman who worked full-time was $8,795. While this is hardly a comfortable income, it does place self-sufficiency and the support of one or two children within the realm of possibility.[24]

Women's entry into the labor force and the overall rise in women's wages have increased women's chances for attaining economic independence, and increased their leverage within their families. The breakdown of patriarchy has been hastened by these changes, but it has also proceeded according to a rhythm of its own. As the social and economic basis for the old notions of male superiority has crumbled, new ideas have begun to take hold even in families in which women are still in fact economically dependent. In 1900 the vast majority of white American husbands, if asked, would have proudly announced that they would never allow their wives to work. In the 1970s, even in blue-collar families where women's economic dependence is most pronounced, husbands would be less likely to make such statements; those who did would be aware that they were going against the tide.[25]

Over the twentieth century women's legal and political gains and women's entry into the labor force have weakened the traditional sources of male power in the family, and it has become possible for the women's movement to make a direct attack upon patriarchy. Though it is the weakness of the institution that makes such an assault possible, the need to focus energies on this task has led feminism to emphasize the strength of patriarchy. But the women's movement is concerned with the immediate problems of women, especially those of the women closest to the movement itself, as well as with problems of theory. And the problems faced by women today, especially women of the professional families or milieus who are likely to be close to the women's movement, are more often those associated with the breakdown of traditional relations between men and women than those emanating from a strong and viable patriarchal structure. There is a discontinuity in feminist literature: while it presents a theory of patriarchy, it describes the problems associated with the breakdown of patriarchy. These problems cannot be fully understood in the context of that theory. In part, the theory of patriarchy is maintained because patriarchy tends to be seen as synonymous with male dominance, and it is clear that male dominance has not disappeared. But in fact patriarchy is only one possible form of male dominance. Feminist literature itself documents the emergence of a new form, one for which we do not yet have a name.

A central theme in contemporary feminist literature is that of the difficulties that women confront in trying to establish satisfying personal relations with men. Men are likely to be unable or unwilling to express deep emotions, to maintain the level of intimacy that women want in personal relations. Men are described as pulling away from such intimacy, either because they cannot tolerate it or because withdrawal itself can become a weapon in their struggles with women. In *The Dialectic of Sex,* Shulamith Firestone devotes several chapters to this theme. She quotes from the remarks of patients in clinical studies: women who complain of men who are emotionally distant or who withhold commitment, men who seem at pains to show how cool and cynical they are, how emotionally uninvolved. Firestone concludes that women need love and that men can't love; she writes, "love, perhaps, even more than childbearing, is the pivot of women's oppression today."[26]

Firestone's presentation of the contradiction between men's and women's emotional needs is extreme, but the theme itself is common in feminist literature, though much more in fiction and in discussions of women's experience than in theoretical pieces. Women's sharp awareness of emotional needs and men's emotional withdrawal is a central theme of Doris Lessing's writing, especially *The Golden Notebook,* a book that was widely read in the radical section of the American women's movement.[27] Lesbians point out that one of the advantages of loving women is that both partners are capable of emotional expressiveness;[28] Marge Piercy, in a discussion of sexism in the left, points to the ability of men to use sexual relationships for short-term gratification or political advantage, and the vulnerability of women, through their greater emotional involvement.[29] Firestone tries to explain the emotional contradictions between men and women in the framework of patriarchy: it is the imbalance of power that corrupts love, she writes, for in love both partners must be vulnerable, and man's greater power erases his consciousness of need. But this is inadequate. In *The Yellow Wallpaper* Gilman's narrator longed to escape male domination and lead an adult life; in *The Golden Notebook* Anna longs for a life that includes intimacy and emotional stability as well as freedom to define herself through writing and politics. The woman of *The Yellow Wallpaper* faces patriarchy; Anna faces something more complex.

The problem that Firestone and Lessing point to is a problem not of patriarchy but of its collapse. In the nineteenth century, women knew what marriage entailed and knew that there was no alternative. From everything that we know of marriage in this period, it seems that women were resigned to a certain emotional distance between themselves and their husbands, and that they routinely turned to other women, and perhaps to children, for the emotional contact that marriage so often lacked. What has changed over the twentieth century is less male behavior than women's expectations. As the traditional sources of male power in the family begin to slip away, men may be more prone to use emotional withdrawal as a weapon; but the unemotional male style itself is not new. What has changed is women's demands. With the geographical mobility and breakdown of communities of the twentieth century, women's support networks outside the family have weakened, and they are likely to turn to their husbands for intimacy that earlier generations would have found elsewhere. And increasingly women can back up these demands with the threat of leaving.

ANOTHER ISSUE OF contemporary feminism that is better understood in the context of the breakdown than the viability of patriarchy is that of women's difficulties in constructing new identities for themselves, finding a bridge between traditional domestic femininity and their new roles in work and social involvement outside the home. Most women, even if they work outside the home, are expected to take the main responsibility for children and housework. Like nineteenth-century women, women today are likely not to have families if they are not willing to do this. Women who work outside the home must do two jobs at once; this is alleviated only to the extent that they can induce their husbands to help them. Pat Mainardi's "The Politics of Housework"[30] was immensely popular in the women's movement of the late sixties because it outlined strategies for involving men in work in the home. Work outside the home often brings a new sense of independence, and it may bring greater leverage within the family, but it also entails new struggles.[31]

Women who work outside the home are under pressure not only to take on two sets of responsibilities, but also to behave according to two sets of standards. "Femininity" still means compliance, submission to men, and childlike helplessness, while women's work requires the competence and often the aggressive self-assertion that have been associated with masculinity. The transition from housewife to working woman involves finding a new way of looking at oneself and one's place in the world, often in the face of male resistance to what men understand as encroachment on their territory. Sheila Rowbotham, in *Woman's Consciousness, Man's World,* in discussing her entry into the left, wrote of the difficulties involved in being both a woman and an intellectual and political being, in merging two roles that men define as contradictory:

> We were allowed to play with their words, their ideas, their cultures as long as we pretended we were men. As soon as our cunts bobbed into the light of day, they stiffened, their lips tautened, they cut us down. It seemed better not to try. One part of ourselves mocked another. We joined in the ridicule of our own aspirations. Either you played their game or you didn't play at all. Part of us leapt over into their world, part of us stayed at home. . . . We were never all together in one place, we were always in transit, immigrants into alien territory. . . . Our immediate perceptions of ourselves were locked against our own social potential.[32]

The problems of establishing satisfying personal relations with men, of constructing a new female identity, may be emotionally wrenching, but at least they can be seen as part of a welcome process of reconstructing the roles of the sexes. But there are aspects of the decline of patriarchy that are much grimmer. As the old mechanisms of male control over women break down, the blatant efforts of some men to retain that control, through rape and other forms of violence, intensify. Recently, statistics indicate that rape has increased faster than any other violent crime. Over the past five years reported rapes have increased by 62 percent; other violent crimes, murder, aggravated assault, robbery, have together risen by 45 percent.[33]

It can be argued that this rise reflects nothing more than the impact of the women's movement, which by opening up public discussion of rape and beginning to remove the blame from the victim has enabled more women to report assaults.[34] But it seems likely that two other factors are also at work: women are readier to report rapes, and rape is also more widespread. Rape has been closely associated with period of social breakdown, such as war. Invading soldiers are likely to treat women of an enemy population in a manner in which they would not treat their countrywomen. In a stable society in which there are established notions of how women should behave, and women generally adhere to those standards, rape is not likely to be a major problem. Male control is asserted in more subtle, less disruptive ways, and men's anger at and contempt of women is for the most part kept within certain bounds.

In the United States of the 1970s, as women begin to take the freedom to carry themselves with new confidence, to behave in ways that many men consider outside the bounds of femininity, male anger can become volatile. Stretching the boundaries of acceptable female behavior is often described as inviting attack from men; but women who live alone, or walk alone at night, are doing no more than what would be taken for granted in a man. With the breakdown of patriarchy women who are without the old male protections become more vulnerable, and men, as they lose familiar avenues of control, may respond with violence.

THE EMPHASIS ON the strength of patriarchy and the parallel demand for female autonomy have had and continue to have a place in feminist strategy. Though the development of capitalism has drawn large numbers of women out of domesticity and enabled them to exert greater leverage within their families, as long as women are mainly responsible for children it remains possible for men to play a role in the family that contains some elements of patriarchal power. The sexual division of labor will not be overcome by the workings of capitalism but by the concerted efforts of people, especially women. And until there is real equality between the sexes in the family and elsewhere, patriarchy cannot be forgotten and demands for female autonomy cannot be entirely put aside.

But as patriarchy weakens, old demands begin to recede, old issues lose their force; new issues come to the fore. We are witnessing the emergence of a new form of male dominance, one that is much less clearly defined than patriarchy and that cannot claim the social acceptance that patriarchy once possessed. For these reasons it is more difficult for us to confront. Neither rape outside the home nor emotional blackmail within it are likely to be defended by anyone. Male violence toward women is regarded as deviant, male avoidance of commitment as neurotic. Both as usually seen as random or individual problems, or as problems that are historically constant, endemic to the relations between men and women. But in fact as the "legitimate" forms of male dominance are undermined, illegitimate forms become more prominent. Increasingly, women are confronted by forms of male control that lie outside the traditionally accepted definitions.

To the extent that the women's movement is unable to expand its understanding of women's oppression, it fails to speak to important concerns of its current constituency, and loses a much larger potential constituency. At a time when the divorce rate is very high, when roles within marriage are problematic and life outside marriage is likely to be lonely and difficult, many women feel the need to strengthen their marriages. For a period in the late sixties and early seventies the women's movement was to some extent able to provide the women in and around itself with a refuge from unsatisfactory or failed relationships with men. But increasingly women are likely to see this as an inadequate solution. If feminism cannot help them to deal with the problems that they face in their personal lives, they are likely to turn away from the organized women's movement, perhaps to psychotherapy, even while maintaining a commitment to feminism because of its relevance to other areas of their lives. For the great majority of women who are beyond the reaches of organized feminism the situation is more critical. If feminism does not address the question of the deterioration of family relations it is likely to appear irrelevant to their lives; if feminism seems to endorse this deterioration, they may regard it as hostile to their interests.

Feminism has at least by reputation often been associated with a female strategy of independence and with a rejection of the family, of marriage and monogamy. According to this popular view, a feminist would urge a woman who was unhappy with her marriage to leave it, and would probably regard the marriage as having been dishonorable in the first place. But most women want to establish and maintain relations with men, and want the security that marriage suggests.

It is a tricky business to construct a critique of marriage and the family that presents a vision of a future in which equality between the sexes makes possible new forms of personal life, and at the same time is responsive to the immediate interests of women in a male-dominated society. It is important that the women's movement avoid the trap of seeming to justify, through the rhetoric of liberation, male behavior that is in fact oppressive. When feminism seems to endorse such behavior the women's movement can become a target for anger that would be more appropriately directed at men. But there is also a sense of betrayal in this anger that is legitimate. A movement that proclaims its adherence to women's interests has a responsibility to live up to its words.

The responsibility of the women's movement, and of the left, is compounded by the increasing explosiveness of these issues. To dismiss concerns about family relations, or by lack of attention to them to collude in the construction of such an image of feminism and the left, is to hand these issues over to the right. Anita Bryant's attack on homosexuality as a threat to the family, or Marabel Morgan's Fascinating Womanhood movement which purports to teach women to hold onto their husbands through seduction, feed on fears of social isolation that have a basis in reality. The anti-abortion movement speaks to women's fears that motherhood is being devalued; this is a legitimate concern at a time when, for most women, there are no adequate alternatives to it.

The solutions that right-wing movements pose to these problems are not only anti-feminist but inadequate. Seducing one's husband will not alleviate the growing pressures on marriage, suppressing homosexuality will not hold families together, and preventing abortions will not improve the status of mothers. These movements attract women not because they point to any viable solutions, but because they bring into the open problems associated with the breakdown of traditional family structure and roles. They provide arenas in which women can voice real concerns. It is time for feminism and the left to address these questions.

REFERENCES

1 Elizabeth Cady Stanton, Susan B. Anthony, and Matilda Joslyn Gage, eds., *History of Woman Suffrage*, vol. 1 (New York, 1881), "Declaration of Sentiments," pp. 70–74.

2 Elizabeth Cady Stanton, *Eighty Years and More: Reminiscences*, 1815–1897 (New York: T. Fisher Unwin, 1898; Schocken, 1973).

3 Antoinette Blackwell Brown, "The Relation of Women's Work in the Household to the Work Outside," quoted in Aileen S. Kraditor, ed., *Up from the Pedestal: Selected Writings in the History of American Feminism* (Chicago: Quadrangle, 1970), pp. 150–59.

4 Ida Husted Harper, *The Life and Work of Susan B. Anthony* (Indianapolis, 1898), pp. 104–12, quoted in Kraditor, pp. 159–67.

5 Elizabeth Cady Stanton, in a letter to Lucy Stone, quoted in Leslie B. Tanner, ed., *Voices from Women's Liberation* (New York: Signet, 1970), p. 77.

6 *History of Woman Suffrage*, vol. 1, p. 88.

7 Antoinette Blackwell Brown, quoted in Kraditor, p. 156.

8 For a description of the legal status of women in nineteenth-century America, see Eleanor Flexner, *Century of Struggle* (Cambridge: Harvard University Press, 1959), ch. 4; and Leo Kanowitz, *Women and the Law: The Unfinished Revolution* (Albuquerque: University of New Mexico Press, 1969).

9 On the role of women in the abolitionist movement, see Gerda Lerner, *The Grimké Sisters from South Carolina: Rebels against Slavery* (Boston: Houghton Mifflin, 1969). On the impact of abolitionism on early feminism, see Flexner, ch. 3.

10 Charlotte Perkins Gilman, *Women and Economics* (Boston: Small, Maynard & Co., 1899; New York: Harper & Row, 1966).

11 The patriarchal father and husband, austere, emotionally distant from mother and children, and the ultimate power in the family, appears in biographies, autobiographies, and novels of the nineteenth century, as well as in guides to family life for women. See, for instance, Lucy Larcom, *A New England Girlhood* (Boston: 1889); Kathryn Kish Sklar, *Catharine Beecher: A Study in American Domesticity* (New Haven, Conn.: Yale University Press, 1973); Louisa May Alcott, *Little Women* (Boston: 1868). For an example of a nineteenth-century marriage guide, see William A. Alcott, *The Young Wife, or Duties of Woman in the Married Relation* (Boston: 1837).

12 Charlotte Perkins Gilman, *The Yellow Wallpaper* (reprinted, Old Westbury, N.Y.: Feminist Press, 1973).

13 See Carroll Smith-Rosenberg, "The Hysterical Woman: Sex Roles and Role Conflict in Nineteenth Century America," *Social Research*, vol. 39, no. 1 (Spring 1972), pp. 652–57, and Ann Douglas Wood, "The Fashionable Diseases: Women's Complaints and Their Treatment in Nineteenth Century America," *Journal of Interdisciplinary History*, vol. 4, no. 1 (Summer 1973), pp. 25–52.

14 Central pieces of radical feminist literature include the following: Kate Millett, *Sexual Politics* (New York: Avon, 1969); Shulamith Firestone, *The Dialectic of Sex: The Case for Feminist Revolution* (New York: Bantam, 1970); articles in Anne Koedt, Ellen Levine, and Anita Rapone, eds., *Radical Feminism* (New York: Quadrangle, 1972); and the journal *Notes*.

15 Central pieces of socialist-feminist literature include the following: Juliet Mitchell, "The Longest Revolution," *New Left Review* 40 (November–December 1966), pp. 11–37; Eli Zaretsky, "Capitalism, the Family, and Personal Life," *Socialist Revolution* 13/14, 15 (January–June 1973); Sheila Rowbotham, *Woman's Consciousness, Man's World* (London: Penguin, 1973); and articles in Leslie B. Tanner, ed., *Voices from Women's Liberation* (New York: Signet, 1970); in Robin Morgan, ed., *Sisterhood Is Powerful: An Anthology of Writings from the Women's Liberation Movement* (New York: Vintage, 1970); and from Edith Hoschino Altbach, *From Feminism to Liberation* (Cambridge, Mass.: Schenkman, 1971).

16 Judith Hole and Ellen Levine, *Rebirth of Feminism* (New York: Quadrangle, 1973) is a good history of the contemporary women's movement, with an emphasis on liberal feminism.

17 Millett, p. 38.

18 Firestone, p. 48.

19 Ibid., pp. 11–12.

20 William Chafe, *The American Woman: Her Changing Social, Economic, and Political Role*, 1920–1970 (New York: Oxford, 1972).

21 See Heidi Hartmann, "Capitalism, Patriarchy, and Job Segregation by Sex," *Signs*, vol. 1, no. 3, part 2 (Spring 1976), pp. 137–70, for an account of the

exclusion of women from unions and from higher-paying jobs, and an argument that this is the work of male trade unionists, acting in what they see as their own self-interest.

22 Chafe, pp. 144–46, 218–20.

23 Robert W. Smuts, *Women and Work in America* (New York: Schocken, 1971), p. 91.

24 These statistics are from the following sources: U.S. Dept. of Commerce, Bureau of the Census, *Historical Statistics of the United States, Colonial Times to the Present;* U.S. Dept. of Labor, Employment Standards Administration, Women's Bureau, *Bulletin* 297, 1975 *Handbook on Women Workers;* U.S. Dept. of Commerce, Bureau of the Census, *Statistical Abstract of the United States,* 1976.

25 See Lillian Rubin, *Worlds of Pain: Life in the Working-Class Family* (New York: Basic Books, 1976), ch. 9.

26 Firestone, p. 126.

27 Doris Lessing, *The Golden Notebook* (New York: McGraw-Hill, 1962).

28 "Loving Another Woman—Interview," in Koedt, Levine, and Rapone, pp. 85–94.

29 Marge Piercy, "The Grand Coolie Damn," in Morgan, pp. 421–38.

30 Pat Mainardi, "The Politics of Housework," in Morgan, pp. 447–54.

31 There is a large sociological literature on how marriage is affected when a woman works outside the home, most of it arguing that when women go to work their decision-making power within the family is enhanced. See Robert O. Blood and Donald M. Wolfe, *Husbands and Wives* (Glencoe, Ill.: Free Press, 1960), ch. 2; David Heer, "The Measurement and Bases of Family Power: An Overview," *Journal of Marriage and Family Living,* vol. 25, no. 2 (May, 1963), pp. 133–38; David Heer, "Dominance and the Working Wife," *Social Forces* 36 May 1958), pp. 341–47; and Janice Neipert Hedges and Jeanne K. Barnett, "Working Women and the Division of Household Tasks," *Monthly Labor Review* (April 1972), pp. 9–14. Dair Gillespie, in "Who Has the Power? The Marriage Struggle," *Journal of Marriage and the Family,* vol. 33, no. 3 (August 1971), pp. 445–58, criticizes this literature for failing to recognize the sources of male dominance that persist regardless of women's employment and income.

32 Rowbotham, pp. 30–31.

33 Susan Brownmiller, *Against Our Will: Men, Women and Rape* (New York: Bantam, 1975), pp. 190–91.

34 Brownmiller, for instance, makes this argument.

A Response to Inequality: Black Women, Racism, and Sexism

Diane K. Lewis

Introduction

The women's liberation movement has generated a number of theories about female inequality. Because the models usually focus exclusively upon the effects of sexism, they have been of limited applicability to minority women subjected to the constraints of both racism and sexism.[1] In addition, black women have tended both to see racism as a more powerful cause of their subordinate position than sexism and to view the women's liberation movement with considerable mistrust.[2]

Yet there are recent indications that a growing number of black women have become more responsive to the issue of women's rights.[3]

I am indebted to Oscar Berland and Naomi Katz for comments on an earlier draft of this paper.

1. For example, *Women, Culture and Society*, ed. Michelle Z. Rosaldo and Louise Lamphere (Stanford, Calif.: Stanford University Press, 1974), proposes several models of female subordination, but none considers fully the structural position and theoretical implications of women subject to both racism and sexism.

2. See Linda J. M. LaRue, "Black Liberation and Women's Lib," *Transaction* 8 (November–December 1970): 59–64; Nathan and Julia Hare, "Black Women 1970," ibid., pp. 68, 90; Jean Cooper, "Women's Liberation and the Black Woman," *Journal of Home Economics* 63 (October 1971): 521–23; Toni Cade, ed., *The Black Woman* (New York: New American Library, Signet Books, 1970); Mae C. King, "The Politics of Sexual Stereotypes," *Black Scholar* 4 (March–April 1973): 12; Inez Smith Reid, *"Together" Black Women* (New York: Third Press, 1972).

3. A 1972 poll showed that black women were more sympathetic than white women to efforts to upgrade women's status in society (62 percent to 45 percent, respectively) and that black women were also more supportive than white women of the attempts by women's liberation groups to do so (67 percent and 35 percent, respectively) (see Louis Harris & Associates, *The 1972 Virginia Slims American Women's Opinion Poll: A Survey of the Attitudes of Women on Their Roles in Politics and the Economy*, pp. 2, 4). Interestingly, Lucy Komisar notes that black organizations such as the Urban League and the National Association for the

[*Signs: Journal of Women in Culture and Society*, 1977, vol. 3, no. 2]

During the past few years black women's organizations have emerged whose specific aim is to combat both sexism and racism. In January 1973 fifteen women formed the San Francisco–based Black Women Organized for Action (BWOA). It now has between 300 and 400 members.[4] In December 1973 the first conference of the National Black Feminist Organization (NBFO) met on the east coast in New York. It attracted 400 women. Though its leadership acknowledged difficulties in organizing black women around feminist issues,[5] the group stressed that many goals central to the women's liberation movement—day care, abortions, maternity leaves—were of critical importance to black women. Indeed, some were of greater intrinsic concern to them than to white women because of their more severe economic disadvantage.

This paper attempts to explain the initial rejection and then more ˉ vorable reaction to the women's movement on the part of black women. To do so, it develops a model of inequality which may illuminate the situation of women in complex societies who experience discrimination because of race and sex. A trend toward a greater acceptance of feminism may be due to changes in black women's perception of oppression, which in turn reflects changes in the social order. In the 1960s the black liberation movement began to generate important structural shifts in the relationship between blacks and whites in America. Blacks began to participate more fully in public activities previously reserved for whites. In such domains they encountered patterns of sexual discrimination. As the bulk of the higher-status, authoritative positions meted to

---

Advancement of Colored People, which formerly had little interest in feminist issues, have, in recent years, worked jointly with the National Organization of Women to further both minority and women's rights (see Lucy Komisar, "Where Feminism Will Lead," *Civil Rights Digest* 6 [Spring 1974]: 9).

4. Patsy G. Fulcher, Aileen C. Hernandez, and Eleanor R. Spikes, "Sharing the Power and the Glory," *Contact* 4 (Fall, 1974): 52. Eleanor Spikes, a cofounder of the organization, gave the recent estimate of membership (personal communication, April 1976) (see also, *What It Is*, the BWOA Newsletter which can be obtained from P.O. Box 10572, San Francisco, California 94115). Other black women's groups recently organized to eliminate both racism and sexism are League of Black Women (in Chicago), Black Women Concerned (in Baltimore), National Black Women's Political Leadership Caucus (in Detroit), and Sisters Getting Ourselves Together (in Davis, Calif.). (List compiled by Hernandez Associates, 4444 Geary Boulevard, San Francisco, California 94118). The BWOA is dedicated to involving black women in the political process, to helping them get jobs, and to supporting them in business, the arts, and all areas where they face discrimination and exclusion.

5. For example, when Eleanor Holmes Norton, Commissioner of Human Rights for New York City and a NBFO board member stated, "Five years ago you couldn't have gotten five women to come here," a welfare mother said, "Five years ago! . . . We tried to start a consciousness raising group four months ago and nobody was interested" (see "Feminism: 'The Black Nuance,'" *Newsweek* [December 17, 1973], p. 89).

blacks went to black men, a number of black women, particularly in the middle class, became more sensitive to the obstacle of sexism and to the relevance of the women's movement.[6]

Structural Inequality and Black Americans

Michelle Rosaldo has offered a model of female inequality. It proposes that (*a*) women are universally subordinate to men, (*b*) men are dominant due to their participation in public life and their relegation of women to the domestic sphere, and (*c*) the differential participation of men and women in public life gives rise not only to universal male authority over women but to a higher valuation of male over female roles.[7] The point that female inequality is inseparable from differential male/female activity in the public sphere is well taken. Nevertheless, a careful look at the relationship between black men and women and between blacks and whites in this society casts doubt on the full validity of Rosaldo's model.

Historically, black men, like black women, have been excluded from participation in the dominant society's politico-jural sphere and denied access to authority. Moreover, special measures have been needed to reaffirm black male inferiority. Since slavery coexisted with male dominance in the wider society, black men, as men, constituted a potential threat to the established order of white superiority. Laws were formulated that specifically denied black men normal adult prerogatives.[8] Such covertly sanctioned acts as lynchings and the rape and sexual exploitation of black women further intensified black male powerlessness.

Stringent institutionalized barriers to male participation continued for almost 100 years after slavery. These included the refusal of membership in national trade unions, which effectively barred black men from the job market;[9] prejudicial welfare laws, which undermined the

6. Eudora Pettigrew concluded more bluntly: "The black man grapples to achieve social justice and parity with the white male—essentially to attain white male power, privilege and status—while black women are shoved to the back of the bus." Quoted in Geraldine Rickman, "A Natural Alliance: The New Role for Black Women," *Civil Rights Digest* 6 (Spring 1974): 62 (see also Pauli Murray, "The Liberation of Black Women," in *Women: A Feminist Perspective*, ed. Jo Freeman [Palo Alto, Calif.: Mayfield Publishing Co., 1975], p. 354).

7. Rosaldo, "Women, Culture and Society: A Theoretical Overview," in Rosaldo and Lamphere, pp. 17–42.

8. Even Moynihan notes that black exclusionary laws were aimed primarily at defining and keeping the black *man* in his place (see Daniel Moynihan, *The Negro Family: The Case for National Action* [Washington, D.C.: Department of Labor, 1965], p. 62; Lerone Bennett, Jr., *Before the Mayflower* [Baltimore: Pelican Books, 1968], pp. 70–71, 92–93).

9. Andrew Billingsley, *Black Families in White America* (Englewood Cliffs, N.J.: Prentice-Hall, Inc., 1968), pp. 85–90.

man's status as husband and father;[10] and vigorous tactics to block black participation in the political process.[11] The systematic exclusion of black men from the public sphere suggests that black sex-role relationships cannot be adequately explained by the notion of a structural opposition between the domestic and public spheres or the differential participation of men and women in the public sphere.[12]

Rosaldo also suggests that egalitarian sex relationships can only develop in a society at a time when both sexes share equal participation in the public and domestic spheres.[13] There is growing evidence of strong egalitarianism in black sex-role relationships.[14] However, black men and

10. For a discussion of how modern public welfare functions to replace the male in low-income families, a process which affects a still-sizable number of blacks on welfare, see Helen Icken Safa, "The Female-based Household in Public Housing," *Human Organization* 24 (Summer 1965): 135–39 (see also Johnnie Tillmon, "Welfare Is a Woman's Issue," in *Marriage and the Family: A Critical Analysis and Proposals for Change*, ed. Carolyn C. Perrucci and Dena B. Targ [New York: David McKay Co., 1974], p. 109).

11. In the past, this took the form of intimidation and poll tax laws in the South and gerrymandering and cooptation in the North. For an analysis of other establishment bars to effective black political participation, see Stokely Carmichael and Charles V. Hamilton, *Black Power: The Politics of Liberation in America* (New York: Random House, Vintage Books, 1967).

12. Among racially oppressed groups it is important to distinguish between the public life of the dominant and the dominated societies. Using this framework, we recognize a range of male participation from token admittance to the public life of the dominant society to its attempts to destroy the public life within a dominated society. Mexican-American men, for example, have played strong public roles in their own dominated society, and, in fact, as Mexican-Americans have become more assimilated to the dominant society, sex roles have become less hierarchical (see Leo Grebler, Joan W. Moore, and Ralph C. Guzman, *The Mexican American People: The Nation's Second Largest Minority* [New York: Free Press, 1970], pp. 361–72). On the other hand, Afro-American men historically faced attempts at exclusion, enforced by the dominant society, from participation in a public life even among their own people (see Bennett, pp. 70–71, 92–93, and also Robert Staples, "The Myth of the Impotent Black Male," *Black Scholar* 2 [June 1971]: 3).

13. Rosaldo, pp. 40–42.

14. Virginia Heyer Young, "Family and Childhood in a Southern Negro Community," *American Anthropologist* 72 (April 1970): 269–88; Peter Kunkel and Sara Sue Kennard, *Spout Spring: A Black Community* (New York: Holt, Rinehart & Winston, 1971); Diane K. Lewis, "The Black Family: Socialization and Sex Roles," *Phylon* 36 (September 1975): 221–37; Robert B. Hill, *The Strengths of Black Families* (New York: Emerson Hall, 1972), p. 18. It has been pointed out that the notion of women's universal inferiority may be a reflection of our own Western cultural bias (see Nancy Tanner, "Matrifocality in Indonesia and Africa and among Black Americans," in Rosaldo and Lamphere, pp. 129–56, and Ruby Rohrlich Leavitt, *Peaceable Primates and Gentle People: Anthropological Approaches to Women's Studies* [New York: Harper & Row, 1975]). After developing most of the ideas in this paper, I was interested to see further critiques of the thesis of worldwide female inequality by the contributors to *Women Cross-culturally: Change and Challenge*, ed. Ruby Rohrlich Leavitt (The Hague: Mouton & Co., 1975), particularly the articles "Women, Knowledge and Power," by Constance Sutton, Susan Makiesky, Daisy Dwyer, and Laura Klein (pp. 581–600), and "Class, Commodity, and the Status of Women," by Eleanor Leacock (pp. 601–16).

women shared equal exclusion from, rather than equal participation in, the public sphere. What the black experience suggests is that differential participation in the public sphere is a symptom rather than a cause of structural inequality. While inequality is *manifested* in the exclusion of a group from public life, it is actually *generated* in the group's unequal access to power and resources in a hierarchically arranged social order. Relationships of dominance and subordination, therefore, emerge from a basic structural opposition between groups which is reflected in exclusion of the subordinate group from public life. This process may be further accentuated by increasing differentiation between the public and domestic spheres.[15] Members of a subordinate group, moreover, constitute a potential common-interest group whose interests derive from their shared powerlessness.[16] Their interests remain latent, however, until the power relations between themselves and a dominant group begin to shift and the structural opposition between them erupts into conflict.

Black women, due to their membership in two subordinate groups that lack access to authority and resources in society, are in structural opposition with a dominant racial and a dominant sexual group. In each subordinate group they share potential common interests with group comembers, black men on the one hand and white women on the other. Ironically, each of these is a member of the dominant group: black men as men, white women as whites. Thus, the interests which bind black women together with and pull them into opposition against comembers crosscut one another in a manner which often obscures one set of interests over another. Historically, their interests as blacks have taken precedence over their interests as women. A shift in the power relations between the races had to come before changes in the structural relationship between the sexes.

It has been noted that the latent interests shared by members of a subordinate group become manifest when they have been formulated into a conscious ideology.[17] Ideology, I suggest, articulates increasing

15. See Louise Lamphere, "Strategies, Cooperation and Conflict among Women in Domestic Groups," in Rosaldo and Lamphere, p. 100; and Leacock, pp. 610–11. Lamphere notes the relationship between sex egalitarianism and the merging of public and private spheres, and Leacock suggests that it is the imposition of hierarchical social forms that give rise to a division between public and domestic domains.

16. This model derives from ideas in Ralf Dahrendorf, "Toward a Theory of Social Conflict" in *Social Change: Sources, Patterns, Consequences*, ed. Amitai Etzioni and Eva Etzioni (New York: Basic Books, 1964), pp. 98–111, and in Denton E. Morrison, "Some Notes toward Theory on Relative Deprivation, Social Movements, and Social Change," *American Behavioral Scientist* 14 (May 1971): 675–90. "Power" here refers to "having great influence or control over others" (*The American Heritage Dictionary* [New York: Houghton Mifflin Co., 1969], p. 1027); "interests" refers to common values, objectives, and definitions of a situation.

17. See Dahrendorf, p. 107.

discontent, which emerges as a group's members perceive that their legitimate expectations are being frustrated. Frustration arises as they experience a sense of relative deprivation vis-à-vis other groups, a process occurring when (1) members of a subordinate group perceive the possibility of their own improved, more equitable position in the social system by comparing themselves with another group of structurally equivalent status whose members are improving their positions, and (2) members of a dominant group continue to frustrate their legitimate expectations for improved position while granting privileges and resources to members of the other subordinate group. The set of potential interests most clearly perceived as illegitimately blocked will become manifest first through the process of structural conflict. The black women's reactions to the black liberation and feminist movements described below reflect, I feel, their changing interests as they have become manifest through shifts in power relations between the races and between the sexes. Their response suggests that, as a subordinate group's interests change, the lines of conflict and structural opposition between groups tend to shift correspondingly.

The Structural Position of Black Women and White Women in America

Both white and black women in America have been excluded from the politico-jural domain and from positions of authority and prestige which have been reserved mainly for white men. Their joint exclusion as women would place them structurally in the same subordinate group, sharing potential common interests. Yet, due to racism, black women have occupied a structural position subordinate to white women in society.[18] They have had less access to deference, power, and authority. Sanday, noting the difference between deference and power as a basis of women's position, finds that Western women may receive deference in their "often highly valued roles as helpmate, sex object, the 'driving force behind every successful man,' etc." She contrasts this with women

18. Class, a third mitigating factor, is purposely omitted from this section in order to highlight the contrasts between white and black women which stem from racism. That white women represent on the whole a far more privileged group than black women is shown in census data which reveal that 64 percent of employed white women but only 42 percent of black and other minority women hold professional, clerical, or sales jobs, while 19 percent of white women and 37 percent of black and other minority women work in low-paying service-related and domestic occupations (see U.S. Bureau of the Census, *The Social and Economic Status of the Black Population in the United States, 1974*, Current Population Reports, Series P-23, No. 54 [Washington, D.C.: Government Printing Office, 1975], table 49, p. 74). Thus, while poor white women occupy a subordinate position, a greater percentage of black women are poor, and their inequality is compounded by race as well as class and sex.

who, playing important economic roles in other societies, may have power over critical resources but who lack deference and may be resented and feared by their husbands.[19] Black women, on account of male exclusion from the job market, have been forced to share with black men marginal participation in the public work world of the dominant society through menial and ill-paying jobs. Their economic contributions have often been essential to their families. Their important economic role has assured them power over the limited resources available to a racially excluded group. On the basis of power over crucial resources, black women have held a relatively high position within a dominated society.[20] This contrasts with the deference accorded white women in the dominant society. For, unlike white women, black women have lacked deference in the dominant society principally because of the stigma of race. Within the dominated society, their source of power has become one basis of denial of deference. Black writers have noted that black men, unable to get and keep jobs, display resentment toward black women who assume the role of "provider."[21] Concomitantly, the roles played by white women which are highly valued, that is, "the driving force behind every successful man," the valued sex object, are frequently denied black women: the first because of the exclusion of black men from the public world, and the second because of the impossibility of attaining a white standard of beauty.

19. Peggy R. Sanday, "Female Status in the Public Domain," in Rosaldo and Lamphere (n. 1 above), p. 191.

20. See Clyde W. Franklin, Jr., and Laurel R. Walum, "Toward a Paradigm of Substructural Relations: An Application to Sex and Race in the United States," *Phylon* 33 (Fall 1972): 249.

21. For example, William A. Blakey, a black man who is Director of Congressional Liaison for the U.S. Commission on Civil Rights, writes that the attitude of many black men toward black women is one of disrespect and a desire to dominate. He suggests that black men feel they must persecute black women in order to repudiate the myth of the " 'castrating' black matriarch" (see William A. Blakey, "Everybody Makes the Revolution: Some Thoughts on Racism and Sexism," *Civil Rights Digest* 6 [Spring 1974]: 19). Alice Walker also noted the prevailing antogonism of black men when she stated: "Black women are called matriarchs, called castraters of the men, and all kinds of things by black men. . . . [However black women] don't [*sic*] realize that they were all these ugly things that people said they were. They thought they were just providing for their families, that they were just surviving" (see Alice Walker, quoted in "Women on Women," *American Scholar* 972 [Autumn 1972]: 601–2. See also Frances Beale, "Double Jeopardy: To Be Black and Female," in Cade (n. 2 above), p. 92; Toni Cade, "On the Issue of Roles," ibid., p. 106; W. H. Grier and Price M. Cobb, *Black Rage* (New York: Basic Books, 1968). The contrast between female power over resources and male attitudes toward women that vary from resentment to lack of deferential treatment, which is characteristic not only of black Americans but of a number of other societies as well (e.g., Nupe, Iroquois; see Sanday, p. 191), suggests the complex factors involved in assessing sex-role relationships. Thus, structural egalitarianism may or may not be paralleled by mutual respect and deference just as male dominance may coexist with female deference or with women's fear and resentment toward men.

White women have not only been given deference. They have also had some access to power and authority.[22] While they themselves lacked authority in the dominant society, they have had a route to power through their kinship and marital ties with men (e.g., fathers, husbands, and sons) who do exercise authority in the public sphere. Moreover, white women, as members of the dominant group, formerly held both considerable authority and power vis-á-vis the subordinate racial group.

The variance in deference and access to power and authority between black and white women have proven to be critical factors underlying the black woman's perception of common group interests with black men and distrust of white women. During the long period of male exclusion from the public sphere, black women shared the experience of racial oppression with black men. From their perspective as members of a subordinate and powerless racial group, white women wielded greater power and garnered more respect than black men and far more than black women. In fact, attributes of the white woman's status currently criticized by many feminists as examples of sexism were seen (and are still seen) by many black women as representative of the unique privileges of women of the dominant group. For example, women who were forced to take menial jobs (often, in the past, and still to some extent in the present, as domestics in white women's homes) and who were unable to care for their own children or to rely on men for economic support contrasted themselves with white women who were not required to work outside their own homes and who were well provided for by their husbands.

A Response to Inequality

During the protest political movements of the sixties, radical white women became discontented at the subordinate position assigned them by white male activists. They formulated an ideology of female liberation to express their common interests as members of a powerless group in conflict with men, whom they perceived as blocking their legitimate aspirations to authority and resources in society.[23] Significantly, their sense of deprivation grew as they saw black people demanding and acquiring an improved and more equitable position in the wider society. The women's liberation movement emerged, in part, to acquire for women the same

22. Authority can be defined as the legitimate right to make decisions and command obedience. It contrasts with power where influence and control over others are not institutionalized but rest informally with individuals or their roles (see Rosaldo, p. 21, n. 2).

23. Jo Freeman, "The Origins of the Women's Liberation Movement," in *Changing Women in a Changing Society*, ed. Joan Huber (Chicago: University of Chicago Press, 1973), pp. 37–39.

access to authority and resources that the civil rights movement was fighting to obtain for blacks.[24]

The reaction of white women to traditional female subordination did not go unnoticed by black women. They, however, initially began to crystallize their interests as women at the same time that they continued to perceive obstacles to their most legitimate interests primarily in racial terms. In the remarkable anthology edited by Toni Cade, black women warn that the patterning of sex roles in white society offers a dangerous and stultifying model for blacks.[25] They note the detrimental effect of the dominant society on black man-woman relations.[26] They clearly establish that their aim is not so much to demand rights as women as to clarify issues or to "demand rights as Blacks first, women second."[27] In fact, the shared interests of black women seem to have little in common with white women. Cade asks: "How relevant are the truths, the experiences, the findings of White women to Black women? I don't know that our priorities are the same, that our concerns and methods are the same."[28]

Three years after publication of the Cade anthology, however, black women began clearly to formulate their interests as women concomitantly with their interests as members of an oppressed racial group. At the NBFO conference in 1973 a participant stated: "While we share with our men a history of toil and dignity, it is categorically different to be Black and a woman in this society than it has been to be Black and male."[29] The emergence of a feminist movement among black women, signaled by formation of the NBFO, the BWOA, and other organizations concerned with the special problems of being female and black,[30] indicates that some contemporary black women have begun to perceive the way both sex inequality and race inequality affect their lives.

In order to understand the structural factors which account for the black women's growing responsiveness to feminism it is necessary to

24. Catharine Stimpson, " 'Thy Neighbor's Wife, Thy Neighbor's Servants': Women's Liberation and Black Civil Rights," in *Women in Sexist Society*, ed. Vivian Gornick and Barbara K. Moran (New York: New American Library, Signet Books, 1971), pp. 622–57.

25. E.g., Cade, "On the Issue of Roles," pp. 102–3.

26. Beale, pp. 90–92.

27. "Preface," in Cade, *The Black Woman*, p. 10.

28. Ibid., p. 9.

29. Eleanor H. Norton, quoted on p. 86 in Bernette Golden, "Black Women's Liberation," *Essence* 4 (February 1974): 35–36, 75–76, 86.

30. Patricia Bell Scott, "Black Female Liberation and Family Action Programs: Some Considerations" (unpublished paper, n.d., p. 4), suggests that most black women's organizations are now concerned with the issue of black feminism, that is, the plight of black women who are oppressed by both sexism and racism. Among groups she cites, in addition to the NBFO, are the National Welfare Rights Organization, the National Committee on Household Employment, Domestics United of North Carolina, and the Black Women's Community Development Foundation.

analyze the effect of the race struggle on the position of black women. The worldwide black struggle against oppression heightened the discontent of American blacks at their subordinate position. As African countries gained independence from European colonizers, Afro-Americans experienced a growing sense of relative deprivation and perceived the possibility of changing power relationships between whites and blacks in the United States. While for many years the conflict between black and white was waged at the covert level and expressed in an ideology of gradual "race" advancement, black Americans became increasingly impatient at obstacles to their legitimately perceived expectations. Their interests became manifest, their ideology "militant." Civil rights activity in the 1950s spawned the "Black Power" movement, aimed at direct black participation in the political process, and the "Black Is Beautiful" movement, focused on a legitimation of black standards of beauty and physical worth. While black women easily perceived their own interests expressed in these political and cultural ideologies, and while they played a critical role in civil rights activities,[31] these movements, significantly, were seen as primarily male inspired and male led. According to some, the black woman's alleged place was "a step behind" the man's, and her proper role was the bearing and rearing of warriors for the struggle. Many women activists interpreted this attitude as an understandable reaction by black men, who had been duped by proposed white models of black matriarchy and male castration. They counseled patience and conciliation at what they perceived as deliberate divisive tactics by the dominant society.[32] Consequently, Pauli Murray noted, in spite of the black women's broad participation in the civil rights movement ". . . the aspirations of the black community have been articulated almost exclusively by black males. There has been very little public discussion of the problems, objectives or concerns of black women."[33] The black liberation movement resulted in the passage of such federal laws as the Civil Rights Act of 1964 and the Voting Rights Act of 1965. They were to provide institutional support for the termination of black exclusion from the public sphere. The laws, which had a dominoes effect, began to knock down barriers in many American institutions. Edu-

31. For a discussion of some of the significant contributions of black women to the black liberation movement, see Phyl Garland, "Builders of a New South," *Ebony* 21 (August 1966): 27–30, 34–37.

32. See Beale, p. 93; Cade, "On the Issues of Roles," pp. 107–8; Jean Carey Bond and Patricia Perry, "Is the Black Male Castrated," in Cade, *The Black Woman*, pp. 113–18; and Gwen Patton, "Black People and the Victorian Ethos," ibid., pp. 143–48. Francis Beale in a 1970 newspaper interview noted: "Often, as a way of escape . . . black men have turned their hostility toward their women. But this is what we have to understand about him . . . as black women we have to have a conciliatory attitude" (see Charlayne Hunter, "Many Blacks Wary of Women's Liberation Movement in U.S.," *New York Times* [November 17, 1970], p. 47).

33. Murray (n. 6 above), p. 354.

cation, direct political participation, and jobs began to become more accessible to "upwardly mobile" blacks. However, as blacks began to participate in the wider society they moved into a public arena sharply characterized by sex inequality. This situation, together with male domination of the black movement, signaled a significant differentiation in the participation of black men and women in the public sphere. Observing this situation, another black women, corroborating Murray, notes: "It is clear that when translated into actual opportunities for employment and promotional and educational benefits the civil rights movement really meant rights for black men. . . ."[34]

This differentiation is apparent in a comparison of the relative educational levels of black men and women. Education for blacks appears to have shifted in favor of men during the past few years, preceding apace with greater black inclusion in institutions of higher learning. Formerly, sociological studies of black communities showed that black women had higher rates of literacy and more years of schooling than males.[35] They were expected to go into higher education more often than men and had different aspirations,[36] which were linked primarily to the job market for adult blacks in the past. For example, in the South in the 1940s black men aspired to some independence through working their own farms or learning a skilled trade like bricklaying, plastering, or painting, skills transmitted from father to son. Black women, however, were offered higher education so they could become schoolteachers in the segregated school systems of the South and thereby get "out of the white folk's kitchen," the only other job possibility for black females.[37]

In the past, black women were also given greater educational opportunities than men by their families because "educational achievement for black men did not mean the opening up of economic opportunities."[38] Census data show that black women have more median years of schooling and more often graduate from high school than black men. The median years of formal education for black women and men twenty-five years of age and older between 1940 and 1970 are given in table 1.

In 1966, for blacks between twenty-five and thirty-four years of age women more often had a college degree than men; 5.2 percent of the men and 6.1 percent of the women had completed four or more years of

34. Constance M. Carroll, "Three's a Crowd: The Dilemma of the Black Woman in Higher Education," in *Academic Women on the Move*, ed. Alice Rossi and Ann Calderwood (New York: Russell Sage Foundation, 1973), p. 177.

35. Charles Johnson, *Shadow of the Plantation* (Chicago: University of Chicago Press, 1969), pp. 129–30.

36. Hylan Lewis, *Blackways of Kent* (New Haven, Conn.: College and University Press, 1964), pp. 105–6.

37. Ibid.

38. Gerda Lerner, ed., *Black Women in White America: A Documentary History* (New York: Random House, Pantheon Books, 1972), p. 220.

college. However, by 1974 the situation had reversed, and 8.8 percent of the men and 7.6 percent of the women had achieved that level of education.[39] Recent figures also show a sharp rise in the numbers of black men currently enrolled in college. While in 1970 16 percent of black men and 15 percent of black women between eighteen and twenty-four years of age were enrolled in college, by 1974 the figures were 20 percent and 16 percent, respectively.[40] The data indicate a decided shift in favor of black men in higher education over the past few years.[41]

Even in the late 1960s, however, when black women were enrolled in college in somewhat greater proportions than black men, black men were more likely to obtain graduate degrees beyond the M.A. than black women.[42] Jackson's 1968 study of black institutions found that 91 percent of the professional degrees granted in the combined fields of medicine, dentistry, law, veterinary medicine, and theology went to black

Table 1

Median Years of Schooling for Ages 25 and Over

Year	Black Women	Black Men
1940	6.1	5.3
1960	8.5	7.9
1970	10.0	9.3

SOURCES.—Figures for 1940 are from U.S. Department of Commerce, Bureau of the Census, *Sixteenth Census of the United States: 1940. Population: Characteristics of the Nonwhite Population by Race* (Washington, D.C.: Government Printing Office, 1943), table 6, p. 34; for 1960 are for "nonwhite" and are from U.S. Bureau of the Census, *U.S. Census of Population: 1960. Educational Attainment of the Population of the United States: 1960.* Supplementary Reports PC (S1)-37. (Washington, D.C.: Government Printing Office, 1972), table 173, p. 6; for 1970 are from U.S. Bureau of the Census, *Census of Population: 1970. Subject Reports. Educational Attainment.* Final Report PC(2)-5B (Washington, D.C.: Government Printing Office, 1973), table 1, pp. 3, 6.

39. U.S. Bureau of the Census (n. 18 above), table 68, p. 97.

40. Ibid., table 65, p. 94.

41. See Cynthia Fuchs Epstein, "Positive Effects of the Multiple Negative: Explaining the Success of Black Professional Women," in Huber (n. 23 above), pp. 152–53. See also a study by Elias Blake, Linda Jackson Lambert, and Joseph L. Martin, "Degrees Granted and Enrollment Trends in Historically Black Colleges: An Eight Year Study" (Washington, D.C.: Institute for Services to Education, 1974), table 9a, p. 31, which shows that in black four-year colleges, as well, black male enrollment has gradually increased from 45.4 percent in 1966 to 47.8 percent in 1973.

42. Carroll, pp. 174–75.

men and only 9 percent to black women.[43] Two surveys of blacks with doctorates in all fields from all institutions in 1969 and 1970 suggest that black women hold roughly 21 percent of these advanced degrees.[44] Moreover, black men attend more prestigious institutions than black women, and this factor, along with their greater monopoly of advanced professional degrees, affects occupational patterns.[45]

For, according to figures of the U.S. Census Bureau, black women are the poorest paid in the occupational structure. Black men earn more than both black women and white women. The median earnings for year-round, full-time workers in 1963, 1970, and 1974 show an interesting trend over the eleven-year span (see table 2). Note that the wage differential between black women's and black men's salaries went from $1,739 in 1963 to $2,334 in 1974. Although the gap between the dollar earnings of black women and black men widened, there was some improvement in the ratio of female to male income, black women earning 57 percent of the income of black men in 1963 and 74 percent in 1974. In the past, the low pay of black women was related to their frequent employment as domestics. In 1963, as shown in table 3, one out of three black women was a private household worker, but by 1974 only 11 per-

Table 2

Median Earnings Year-round Full-Time Workers
($)

Group	1963	1970	1974
White males	6,245	9,447	12,434
Black males	4,019	6,435	8,705
White females	3,687	5,536	7,021
Black females	2,280	4,536	6,371

SOURCES.—Figures for 1963 are from U.S. Bureau of the Census, *Income of Families and Persons in the United States, 1963*, Current Population Reports, Series P-60, No. 43 (Washington, D.C.: Government Printing Office, 1964), table 18, p. 34 (the table compares whites and nonwhites; the latter are predominantly black); for 1970 are from U.S. Bureau of the Census, *Money Income in 1973 of Families and Persons in the United States*, Current Population Reports, Series P-60, No. 97 (Washington, D.C.: Government Printing Office, 1975), table F, p. 12; for 1974 are from U.S. Bureau of the Census, *Money Income in 1974 of Families and Persons in the United States*, Current Population Reports, Series P-60, No. 101 (Washington, D.C.: Government Printing Office, 1975), pp. 106–7.

43. Jacqueline J. Jackson, "Black Women and Higher Education" (unpublished paper, 1973), cited ibid., table 9.1, p. 174. Jackson's figures show that 62 percent of these professional degrees were in the fields of medicine and law and that 85.6 percent of the M.D.'s and 90.4 percent of the LL.B.'s were granted to black men.

44. See Kent G. Mommsen, "Career Patterns of Black American Doctorates" (Ph.D. diss., Florida State University, 1970), table 1, p. 41.

45. Jacqueline J. Jackson, "But Where Are the Men?" *Black Scholar* 3 (December 1971): 30–41.

Table 3

Occupation of Men and Women, 1963, 1970, 1974 (Annual Averages, in Percentages)

	1963				1970				1974			
	Women		Men		Women		Men		Women		Men	
	White	Negro and Other Races*	White	Negro and Other Races*	White	Negro and Other Races*	White	Negro and Other Races*	White	Negro and Other Races*	White	Negro and Other Races*
White-collar workers:	61	21	41	15	64	36	43	22	64	42	42	24
Professional and technical	14	8	13	5	15	11	15	8	15	12	15	9
Managers and administrators except farm	5	2	15	4	5	2	15	5	5	2	15	5
Sales workers	8	2	6	2	8	3	6	2	7	3	6	2
Clerical workers	34	10	7	5	36	21	7	7	36	25	6	7
Blue-collar workers:	17	15	46	57	16	19	46	60	15	20	46	57
Craft and kindred workers	1	0.5	20	11	1	1	21	14	2	1	21	16
Operatives, including transport	15	14	20	25	14	17	19	28	13	17	18	26
Non-farm laborers	0.3	0.7	6	21	...	1	6	18	1	1	7	15
Service workers	15	22	6	16	15	26	6	13	17	26	7	15
Private household workers	5	34	...	...	3	18	...	...	3	11	...	...
Farm workers	3	7	8	11	2	2	5	6	2	1	5	4

SOURCES.—Figures for 1963 taken from U.S. Bureau of the Census, *The Social and Economic Status of the Black Population in the United States, 1973*, Current Population Reports, Special Studies Series P-23, No. 48 (Washington, D.C.: Government Printing Office, 1974), table 38, p. 54 and table 39, p. 55; for 1970 and 1974 taken from U.S. Bureau of the Census, *The Social and Economic Status of the Black Population in the United States, 1974*, Current Population Reports, Series P-23, No. 54 (Washington, D.C.: Government Printing Office, 1975), table 48, p. 73, and table 49, p. 74.

*Nearly 90 percent are Negro.

cent of black women were domestics. However, a comparison of jobs held by black women with those held by black men in 1974 shows that while black women have been moving out of domestic work 37 percent or over one-third were still in low-paying service and household jobs not covered by the federal minimum wage, as compared with only 15 percent of black men. Moreover, while black women white-collar workers relative to black men have been highly represented in teaching, nursing, and social work—occupations which are extensions of their domestic roles and traditional careers for women—black men, as they have moved into the public sphere, have been more often found than women in the more prestigious and better-paid professions of medicine, law, science, and college teaching.[46]

Figures showing gradual black inclusion in the field of higher education clearly indicate that black women are either poorly represented or relegated to the lower-status and lower-paid jobs. For example, Carroll found that at the University of Pittsburgh in 1970 black and white women were disproportionately represented in nontenured academic positions and that black men, as well as white men, in relationship to their total numbers, monopolized the higher and tenured ranks (see table 4). Carroll notes that for the University of Pittsburgh, "Clearly, sex is more of a handicap than race . . . and the disproportion between the sexes is far greater for blacks than for whites."[47] Five years later, the occupational profile of the University of California, one of the largest educational complexes in the United States, shows that continued recruitment of blacks and other minorities has resulted in a marked sex inequality in high-level positions. The figures for April 1975 show employment in administration and in tenured and nontenured ladder-faculty positions for black men and women in the nine-campus system (see table 5).[48]

Table 4

Full-Time Professional Staff at University of Pittsburgh, 1970

Rank	White Men	White Women	Minority Men	Minority Women
Full professor	420	25	21	0
Associate professor	355	42	17	1
Nontenured	792	268	83	31

SOURCE.—Figures compiled from Constance M. Carroll, "Three's a Crowd: The Dilemma of the Black Woman in Higher Education," in *Academic Women on the Move*, ed. Alice Rossi and Ann Calderwood (New York: Russell Sage Foundation, 1973), table 9.3, p. 175.

NOTE.—"Minority" refers to predominantly black.

46. See Epstein, pp. 153–54, and Jackson, "But Where Are the Men?" p. 32.

47. Carroll, pp. 174–75 (see also William Moore, Jr., and Lonnie H. Wagstaff, *Black Educators in White Colleges* [San Francisco: Jossey-Bass, Inc., 1974], pp. 154–77).

48. It should be stressed that blacks and other minorities (Asian/Asian-Americans, American Indians and Mexican/Spanish-Americans) are still greatly underrepresented in

Information on black law-faculty members, nationwide, shows a similar skewing in favor of black men. The 1976 directory of minority law professors reveals that there are 226 blacks and thirty-eight nonwhite women out of a total of 282 minority professors. A check of the directory turned thirty-seven women who could be identified by name and judging by surname the majority of these were probably black (see table 6).

The situation in institutions of higher learning is paralleled in government jobs and in the business world generally. In 1974 black women were 19.8 percent of all women and 63.7 percent of all blacks working full time as GS-graded federal employees. While they were generally underrepresented among women in the higher-level jobs, among blacks they were both markedly overrepresented in the lower-ranking jobs and underrepresented in the higher-ranking jobs, as shown in table 7.

Similarly, the 1975 California State Personnel Board's report to the governor and legislature on state employees, which gave monthly salary by sex and race, showed that while the percentages of black men and women were approximately the same (i.e., 3.7 and 3.4 percent, respectively, of the total numbers employed) black men were more highly represented than black women at the higher salary ranges (see table 8). A recent survey of minorities in the mass-media industry indicates that 82 percent were males.[49] In the business-management training field as well, men, regardless of race, have been given a decided preference over women.[50]

---

higher education. The point here is that their gradual inclusion into the system has been proceeding along sex discriminatory lines. This was especially evident in the employment figures for April 1974 (see the table below for figures for April 1974). Comparison with table 5 shows that there has been some improvement for minority women over the ensuing eighteen months. A total of twelve additional black women were hired while seven "other minority" women were added.

	Black Men	Black Women	Other Minority Men	Other Minority Women
Deans and provosts	5	1	1	...
Tenured faculty	41	...	178	7
Nontenured ladder faculty	51	9	84	21

SOURCE.—University of California computer printout, PER 1096, "Summary of Ethnic and Sex Employment, as of April 30, 1974," pp. 1–3.

49. Abigail Jones Nash, Marilyn Jackson-Beeck, Leverne Tracy Regan, and Vernon A. Stone, "Minorities and Women in Broadcast News: Two National Surveys" (paper presented at the annual convention of the Association for Education in Journalism, San Diego, 1974), p. 7.

50. See Bird McCord, "Identifying and Developing Women for Management Positions," *Training and Development Journal* 25 (November 1971): 2.

Table 5

Total Minorities at the University of California, October 1975

Rank	Black Men	Black Women	Other Minority Men	Other Minority Women	Total Men	Total Women
Deans and provosts	6	1	1	2	155	16
Full professors	24	3	126	...	2,947	124
Associate professors	21	3	82	10	1,398	135
Nontenured ladder faculty	47	15	91	23	1,146	290

SOURCE.—University of California Computer printout, PER 1023, "Summary of Ethnic and Sex Employment, Academic Group/Rank, All Campuses, as of October 31, 1975," pp. 1–3.

Table 6

Minority Law-Faculty Members

Rank	Total Blacks	Minority Women
Professor	37	4
Associate professor	39	6
Assistant professor	51	8
Administrator	24	6
Teacher/administrator	22	5
Part time	49	6
Teaching fellow	4	2
Total	226	37

SOURCE.—*1976 Directory of Minority Law Faculty Members*, Section on Minority Groups, Association of American Law Schools, pp. 9, 25–48.

Table 7

Full-Time Federal Employment of Black Women

General Schedule Grade Grouping	Total Black	Black Women		
		N	All Blacks (%)	All Women (%)
GS-1–4	66,999	50,143	74.8	12.7
GS-5–8	67,316	45,147	67.1	19.5
GS-9–11	20,772	8,591	41.4	15.8
GS-12–15	11,429	2,206	19.3	12.2
GS-16–18	149	16	10.7	13.3
Total	166,665	106,103	63.7	19.8

SOURCE.—From U.S. Bureau of the Census, *The Social and Economic Status of the Black Population in the United States, 1974* (see table 3 above), table 53, p. 78.

Direct black participation in the political process through election to office has increased over the past five years. While blacks are still woefully underrepresented in government, they moved from 1,230 to 2,630 elected officials between 1969 and 1974. However, movement of blacks into politics, as into higher-paying jobs generally, replicates the wider societal pattern of unequal female inclusion in the politico-jural domain. In 1974, while 2,293 black men were elected officials only 337 black women held that position.[51] This is a significant shift toward disparity, given the tradition of egalitarianism between the sexes and the former importance of women in black public life.[52]

51. U.S. Bureau of the Census, *The Social and Economic Status of the Black Population in the United States, 1973*, Current Population Reports, Special Studies Series P-23, No. 48, (Washington, D.C.: Government Printing Office, 1974), table 74, p. 103. In 1974 blacks held 0.5 of 1 percent of the elective offices (see Herrington J. Bryce and Alan E. Warrick, "Black Women in Elective Offices," *Black Scholar* 6 [October 1974]: 17–20).

52. Lerner (n. 38 above), pp. 319–22, shows that in the past black women, although not holders of elective office, were active in politics.

Table 8

California State Employees: Percentage Distribution of Monthly Salary for Black Workers, March 1975

Monthly Salary Rate ($)	Black Men	Black Women
Under 500	3.6	12.5
500–699	2.6	7.9
700–899	5.2	5.3
900–1,099	5.7	2.8
1,100–1,299	2.9	1.1
1,300–1,599	2.4	0.9
1,600–2,099	2.4	0.7
Over 2,099	1.8	0.2

SOURCE.—"Minority Women: Triple Discrimination," *Affirmative Action in Progress* 2 (April 1976): 6.

If, as an aftermath of the 1960s, a number of black men were recruited into higher-paying, more authoritative, and prestigious positions, black women generally moved into the lower-status and lower-paying jobs traditionally reserved for women in the dominant society. During this process they made significant strides relative to white women. Although the difference in earnings between black men and women has widened, the income gap between black women and white women has tended to narrow (see table 9). Black women earned 62 percent of the median income of white women in 1963; this increased to 90 percent in 1974.[53] Similarly, recent census data indicate that the overall occupational distribution of black women has improved relative to white women. Since 1963 black women have moved out of domestic work and into clerical positions in greater numbers. Thus, in 1963, 34 percent of black women were domestics, and only 10 percent were clerical workers; in 1974, 11 percent were domestics and 25 percent were clerical workers. Since the percentages for white women clerical workers have remained relatively stable between 1963 and 1974 (34 percent and

Table 9

Wage Differential between Black Women, Black Men and White Women ($)

	1963	1970	1974
Between black women and black men	1,739	1,899	2,334
Between black women and white women	1,407	1,000	650

53. For a comparison of increases in the ratio of black to white median income from 1967 to 1973 for men and women, see U.S. Bureau of the Census, *Money Income in 1973 of Families and Persons in the United States*, Current Population Reports, Series P-60, No. 97 (Washington, D.C.: Government Printing Office, 1975), table F, p. 12.

36 percent, respectively), black women appear to be moving toward parity with white women in that occupation (see table 3). Although the position of black women has improved in relationship to white women, the data show that for women as a whole sexism continues to constitute a major barrier in the wider society. In fact, the ratio of white female to white male earnings has *decreased* slightly between 1963 and 1974, women earning 59 percent of the male's median income in 1963 and only 56 percent in 1975 (computed from table 3). The existence of sex bias in the wider society explains the observation that the civil rights movement elicited active efforts to provide career opportunities for black men, while little attention was paid to the employment needs of black women.[54]

Class and Sexism

The black liberation movement began to generate important structural changes in the relationship between blacks and whites in American society. For black women, these changes serve to heighten their perception of sexism, since they experience deep-seated sex discrimination as they engage in increased participation in the public sphere. Middle-class black women, in particular, are becoming more sensitive to the obstacle of sexism as racial barriers begin to fall and as the bulk of the higher-status, authoritative positions reserved for blacks have gone to black men. Nevertheless, if the leadership of black organizations recently formed to combat both racism and sexism appears to be middle class, the membership in these black women's groups seems to crosscut class lines. Thus the BWOA notes that its members include welfare recipients, maids, and the unemployed as well as high-income earners. In recognition of this diversity, the organization has adopted a flexible membership policy.[55] Similarly, the NBFO conference attracted domestic workers, welfare mothers, and other poor black women as well as students, housewives, and professionals. As one participant put it, "We were able to do what white feminists have failed to do: transcend class lines and eradicate labels."[56]

A further examination of the structural position of black women suggests why not only upwardly mobile black women but also poor black women will become more responsive to feminist issues. They, along with

54. See Pauli Murray, "Jim Crow and Jane Crow," in Lerner, p. 596.

55. Dues are computed on a sliding scale from $5.00 to $25.00 a year, but members pay when and what they can. Moreover, a woman can become a member *either* by paying dues *or* attending meetings *or* working on a committee (see Fulcher et al. [n. 4 above], pp. 52, 63).

56. Ashaki Habiba Taha, letter *MS* 3 (August 1974): 12 (see also Golden [n. 29 above], p. 36).

middle-class black women, are seriously affected by sex discrimination on the job. For example, Dietrich and Greiser in a study of black blue-collar workers found sexism to be an important factor in black poverty.[57] Furthermore, demographic and occupational trends, which affect all black women, should also elicit among them a sense of common interest which crosscuts class lines. There has been a steadily declining sex ratio from 95.0 in 1940 to 90.8 in 1970.[58] This probably contributes to the fact that black women are more often single than white women, more often work, and are more often heads of household. Thus, in 1974 about one half of minority women worked compared with 44 percent of white women.[59] In 1973, while 77 percent of white women who were fourteen years old and over and ever married were married and living with their husbands, only 54 percent of black women in the same category were married and residing with their spouses.[60] In 1975, while only 11 percent of white families were female headed, 35 percent of black families were supported by women.[61] Black women with preschool-aged children were also more likely to work than white mothers; in 1973, 49 percent of black women as compared with 32 percent of white women with small children were in the labor force.[62]

Black women, then, are more often self-supporting than white women and far more likely to carry single-handedly responsibilities for dependent children. These factors, together with their continued greater concentration in lower-paying service-related jobs than either white women or black men, cause poor black women, particularly, to be vitally affected by matters of inadequate income and child-care facilities, both major issues in the women's movement. For poor women, as a black welfare mother notes, women's liberation is "a matter of survival," a perception increasingly held by such groups devoted to removing obstacles to the legitimate interests of poor black women as the National Welfare Rights Organization.[63]

Since both poor and middle-class black women participate in and have been aware of some of the successes of the black liberation move-

57. Kathryn Dietrich and Lee Greiser, "The Influence of Sex on Wage-Income of Black, Blue-Collar Workers in Selected Non-metropolitan and Metropolitan Areas of Texas" (paper presented at the annual meeting of the Southern Association of Agricultural Scientists, Memphis, Tennessee, February 1974).

58. Jackson, "But Where Are the Men?" table 3, p. 39. The sex ratio among whites has also declined steadily but in 1970 was, at 95.3, far more favorable for whites.

59. U.S. Bureau of the Census, *The Social and Economic Status of the Black Population in the United States, 1973*, p. 93.

60. Ibid., table 64, p. 90.

61. U.S. Bureau of the Census, *The Social and Economic Status of the Black Population in the United States, 1974*, table 72, p. 107.

62. U.S. Bureau of the Census, *The Social and Economic Status of the Black Population in the United States, 1973*, table 68, p. 95.

63. Tillmon (n. 10 above), pp. 108, 109, 111.

ment, their expectations of greater access to resources have been raised. As these expectations have been frustrated, a sense of common interest is beginning to emerge which may increasingly include all classes of black women. A study of race and class factors affecting women's attitudes toward the women's liberation movement in Cleveland found that white working-class women were far less likely than white middle-class women to be interested in women's rights, while black working-class women were somewhat *more* receptive than black middle-class women to efforts to change women's status[64] (see table 10).

The shared experience of racism has also tended to blur class lines among blacks. This, too, probably will contribute to a greater tendency for both poor and middle-class black women to agree regarding women's rights. For example, middle-class black families are in a more precarious position than middle-class white families because of racism. Especially in times of economic recession and high unemployment, they may find themselves in economic straits similar to lower-class blacks.[65]

Whether black women develop a sense of common interests that is manifested more in opposition to sexism or to racism will depend upon the structural relationship between the sexes and between the races. With growing black participation in the wider society some black women, experiencing frustration of their interests primarily as women, now probably share the viewpoint a member of NBFO expressed. "White women are our natural allies; we can't take on the system alone."[66] Middle-class black women will increasingly feel their interests as women illegitimately frustrated if a combination of factors continues: (1) the

Table 10

Percentage of Black and White Women Manifesting a High or Low Degree of Interest in Women's Rights

	Black Women		White Women	
Degree of Interest	Middle Class	Working Class	Middle Class	Working Class
High	44	48	54	27
Low	56	52	46	73

SOURCE.—From Willa Mae Hemmons, "Toward an Understanding of Attitudes Held by Black Women on the Women's Liberation Movement" (Ph.D. diss., Case Western Reserve University, 1973), tables 7 and 8, p. 101.

64. Willa Mae Hemmons, "Toward an Understanding of Attitudes Held by Black Women on the Women's Liberation Movement" (Ph.D. diss., Case Western Reserve University, 1973). Her sample for this exploratory study was a purposive one, including eighty-three women, forty-five black and thirty-seven white. She notes that she sought women from different classes and residential and occupational areas; however the size of her sample makes her results more suggestive than conclusive (see her discussion of the sample, pp. 80–86).

65. Cf. Billingsley (n. 9 above), pp. 10–15.

66. Eleanor H. Norton, quoted in Golden, p. 86.

income gap between themselves and white women narrows even more, (2) the overall position of women remains low, and (3) the white male hierarchy persists in admitting minority males but excluding minority females from equitable participation in the wider society. Middle-class black women, even more than middle-class white women, occupy a structural position likely to generate a pervasive sense of relative deprivation and an ideology of discontent.

However, on the other hand, black women may see that racism still affects a considerable number of blacks, including black men. Jessie Bernard, analyzing occupations and earnings for black and white men and women for the period 1939–70, concluded: ". . . racism tends to be more serious for black men than black women . . . (and) sexism tends to be more serious for black women than racism."[67] While some middle-class black men have made significant advances, a careful inspection of the trends of the ratio of black to white earnings shows that black men, as a whole, are making much slower headway in closing the income gap between them and white men than are black women relative to white women. Black men earned 64 percent of the median income of white men in 1967; 67 percent of the income of white men in 1973.[68] This would appear to matter to black women. For example, if they marry, there will probably be more pressure on them to work in order to supplement the family income than on married white women. Indeed, now black married women are more likely to work outside the home than their white counterparts.[69]

Perpetuation of a situation in which all black men, irrespective of their socioeconomic status, are subject to racism, might well propel increasing numbers of black women, irrespective of their class backgrounds into overt opposition to both sexism and racism. Their way of doing so, however, might involve organizations concerned with women's rights, but limited to blacks and strongly racially oriented.[70] The concern with racism would preclude too exclusive a concern with sexism.

Department of Anthropology
University of California, Santa Cruz

67. Jessie Bernard, "The Impact of Sexism and Racism on Employment Status and Earnings, with Addendum," Module 25 (New York: MSS Modular Publications, Inc., 1974), p. 5.

68. U.S. Bureau of the Census, *Money Income in 1973 of Families and Persons in the United States*, table F, p. 12. This was similar to the rate of growth of black female income to the black male's, i.e., black women earned 67 percent of the income of black men in 1967 and 70 percent of the income of black men in 1973.

69. U.S. Bureau of of the Census, *The Social and Economic Status of the Black Population in the United States, 1973*, table 67, p. 95.

70. For an alternate thesis on the possible direction of change in the relationship between blacks and whites, males and females, see Franklin and Walum (n. 20 above), pp. 247–52. See also Rickman (n. 6 above), pp. 57–65, for an interesting discussion of the black professional woman's structural position which enables her to act as catalyst for change in the position of both women and blacks.

Copyright Information

Hewitt, Nancy A. "Feminist Friends: Agrarian Quakers and the Emergence of Woman's Rights in America." *Feminist Studies* 12:1 (Spring 1986): 27-49. ©1986 by Feminist Studies, Inc., Women's Studies Program, University of Maryland, College Park, Maryland, USA.

Basch, Françoise. "Women's Rights and the Wrongs of Marriage in Mid-Nineteenth-Century America." *History Workshop Journal* 22 (Autumn 1986): 18-40. ©Routledge, A Division of Routledge, Chapman & Hall, Ltd., International Thomson Publishing Services, London, England.

Levine, Susan. "Labor's True Woman: Domesticity and Equal Rights in the Knights of Labor." *The Journal of American History* 70:2 (September 1983): 323-339. ©Organization of American Historians, 1983, Indiana University, Bloomington, Indiana, USA.

Marti, Donald B. "Sisters of the Grange: Rural Feminism in the Late Nineteenth Century." *Agricultural History* 58 (July 1984): 247-261. ©Agricultural History Society, Washington D. C. and Davis, California, USA.

Brady, Marilyn Dell. "Populism and Feminism in a Newspaper by and for Women of the Kansas Farmers' Alliance, 1891-1894." *Kansas History* 7 (Winter 1984/85): 280-290. ©Kansas State Historical Society, Topeka, Kansas, USA.

Marsh, Margaret S. "The Anarchist-Feminist Response to the 'Woman Question' in Late Nineteenth-Century America." *American Quarterly* 30:4 (Fall 1978): 533-547. "©1981, 1978, 1986, 1984, 1971, 1970, 1976, 1985, American Studies Association, Washington, D.C., USA." Reprinted with permission of the Association and the author.

Pleck, Elizabeth. "Feminist Responses to 'Crimes against Women,' 1868-1896." *Signs: Journal of Women in Culture and Society* 8:3 (Spring 1983): 451-470. "©1983 by The University of Chicago. All rights reserved." Chicago, Illinois, USA.

Hill, Mary A. "Charlotte Perkins Gilman: A Feminist's Struggle with Womanhood." *Massachusetts Review* 21:3 (1980): 503-526. "Reprinted from *The Massachusetts Review* ©1980, The Massachusetts Review, Inc.," Amherst, MA, USA.

Jacoby, Robin Miller. "The Women's Trade Union League and American Feminism." *Feminist Studies* 3 (Fall 1975): 126-140. ©1975 by Feminist Studies, Inc., Women's Studies Program, University of Maryland, College Park, Maryland, USA.

Dye, Nancy Schrom. "Creating a Feminist Alliance: Sisterhood and Class Conflict in the New York Women's Trade Union League, 1903-1914." *Feminist Studies* 2:2/3 (1975): 24-39. ©1975 by Feminist Studies, Inc., Women's Studies Program, University of Maryland, College Park, Maryland, USA.

Antler, Joyce. "Feminism as Life-Process: The Life and Career of Lucy Sprague Mitchell." *Feminist Studies* 7:1 (Spring 1981): 134-157. ©1981 by Feminist Studies, Inc., Women's Studies Program, University of Maryland, College Park, Maryland, USA.

Cott, Nancy F. "Feminist Politics in the 1920s: The National Woman's Party." *The Journal of American History* 71:1 (June 1984): 43-68. ©Organization of American Historians, 1984, Indiana University, Bloomington, Indiana, USA.

Geidel, Peter. "The National Woman's Party and the Origins of the Equal Rights Amendment, 1920-1923." *The Historian* 42:4 (August 1980): 557-582. ©1980 by Phi Alpha Theta International Honor Society in History, Allentown, Pennsylvania, USA.

Sealander, Judith. "Feminist against Feminist: The First Phase of the Equal Rights Amendment Debate, 1923-1963." *The South Atlantic Quarterly* 81:2 (Spring 1982): 147-161. "Reprinted with permission from *The South Atlantic Quarterly*, vol. 81:2 (Spring 1982), pp. 147-161. ©1982 by Duke University Press, Durham, North Carolina, USA.

Swain, Martha H. "Organized Women in Mississippi: The Clash over Legal Disabilities in the 1920's." *Southern Studies* 23:1 (Spring 1984): 91-102. ©*Southern Studies*, Northwestern State University of Louisiana, Natchiotches, Louisiana, USA.

Strom, Sharon Hartman. "Challenging 'Woman's Place': Feminism, the Left, and Industrial Unionism in the 1930s." *Feminist Studies* 9:2 (Summer 1983): 359-386. ©1983 by Feminist Studies, Inc., Women's Studies Program, University of Maryland, College Park, Maryland, USA.

Walker, Nancy. "Humor and Gender Roles: The 'Funny' Feminism of the Post-World War II Suburbs." *American Quarterly* 37:1 (Spring 1985): 98-113. "©1981, 1978, 1986, 1984, 1971, 1970, 1976, 1985, American Studies Association, Washington, D.C., USA." Reprinted with permission of the Association and the author.

Rupp, Leila J. "The Women's Community in the National Woman's Party, 1945 to the 1960s." *Signs: Journal of Women in Culture and Society* 10:4 (1985): 715-740. "©1985 by The University of Chicago. All rights reserved." Chicago, Illinois, USA.

Brauer, Carl M. "Women Activists, Southern Conservatives, and the Prohibition of Sex Discrimination in Title VII of the 1964 Civil Rights Act." *The Journal of Southern History* 49:1 (February 1983): 37-56. ©The Southern Historical Association, Athens, Georgia, USA.

Evans, Sara M. "The Origins of the Women's Liberation Movement." *Radical America* 9:2 (March-April 1975): 1-12. ©*Radical America*, Somerville, Massachusetts, USA.

Dill, Bonnie Thornton. "Race, Class, and Gender: Prospects for an All-Inclusive Sisterhood." *Feminist Studies* 9:1 (Spring 1983): 131-150. ©1983 by Feminist Studies, Inc., Women's Studies Program, University of Maryland, College Park, Maryland, USA.

Sealander, Judith, and Dorothy Smith. "The Rise and Fall of Feminist Organizations in the 1970s: Dayton as a Case Study." *Feminist Studies* 12:2 (Summer 1986): 321-341. ©Judith Sealander, Dayton, Ohio, USA, and Dorothy Smith, Dayton, Ohio, USA.

Easton, Barbara. "Feminism and the Contemporary Family." *Socialist Review* 8:3 (May-June 1978): 11-36. ©*Socialist Review*, Center for Social Research and Education, Berkeley, California, USA.

Lewis, Diane K. "A Response to Inequality: Black Women, Racism, and Sexism." *Signs: Journal of Women in Culture and Society* 3:2 (Winter 1977)): 339-361. "©1977 by The University of Chicago. All rights reserved." Chicago, Illinois, USA.

Index

Abbott, Grace, 281
Abolitionists
former, late nineteenth century, 118
Garrisonian, 35
Hicksites, 19
Rochester (New York), 20
Ackley, Fannie, 352-54, 357
Act on Rights and Liabilities of Husband and Wife, 34
ADC. *See* Aid to Dependent Children
Addams, Jane. *See also* Hull House (New York City)
and Gilman, Charlotte Perkins, 142
influence of, 170
as model for single women, 205
and Progressive Era, 198-99
and Pullman strike, 201
and Stevens, Alzina, 62
Adultery, 128-29
African-American women
class relations and sisterhood, 401-420
Dayton (Ohio), race relations, 435-36
domestic service, 482, 486
in domestic service, 482
employment discrimination, 382
median income, 486
and National Woman's Party, 228-32, 347
and structural inequality, 470-73
tobacco industry, Richmond (Virginia), 310
white-collar jobs, 482
white women, structural position compared, 473-75
and women's liberation movement, 468-90
African-Americans. *See also* African-American women; Civil Rights Act of 1964
blue-collar workers, 481 (table), 488
Civil Rights Act of 1964, Title VII, 369-88
educational opportunities, 478-80, 482-83 n.48
employment discrimination, 381

faculty members, 482-83, 485 (table)
government jobs, 483, 485 (table)
median earnings, 480 (table)
militant movement, 477
occupations of, 481 (table)
oppression of, 227
poverty of, 480
suffrage
commitment of movement, 405
and The Grange, 79
poetry of, 94-96
and Socialist Party, 118
voting rights, 1920s, 228, 230-31, 235, 239
African countries, 477
Agricultural Packing and Allied Workers of America, 310
Aid to Dependent Children, 301
Aiken, George David, 387
Alcoholism
drunkenness as vice, 128
as grounds for divorce, 35, 42
Knights of Labor expulsion for, 56
Allen, Frances F., 104
Allender, Nina, 355
Allott, Gordon Lewellyn, 387
Alva Belmont House, 349, 354-68, 371
Amalgamated Clothing Workers, 303
American Association of University Women, 347
American Civil Liberties Union, 304
American Federation of Labor
and blanket equal rights legislation, 235-38
convention, 1922, 261
office workers, 312, 321
and President's Commission on the Status of Women, 283
wage-setting for men and women, 309
and Women's Trade Union League, New York, 1903-1914, 182-83
American Home Economics Association, 235, 261
American Indians, educational opportunities, 482-83 n.48, 484 (table)
American Labor Reform League, 119
American Revolution, ideals of, 29
American Woman's Suffrage Association, 34, 39
American Workers' Alliance, 67
Amidon, Beulah, 226

Amsterdam (New York), knit-goods industry, 59
Anarchist-feminists, late nineteenth century, 107-121
Anderson, Mary
on African-Americans' dilemma, 371
and Conference on Women in Industry, 266
and International Labor Organization, 279-80
and National Woman's Party, 237, 245, 252, 276
and President's Commission on the Status of Women, 283
and protective legislation, 253, 262-63
and protective legislation for women, 271, 277-78
retirement of, 285
and Women's Bureau, Department of Labor, 275, 281
and Women's Charter, National Woman's Party, 282
Andrews, Stephen Pearl, 37-38
Antebellum period, marriage, 26-48
Anthony, Daniel Read, 269
Anthony, Susan B.
birthday of, 357
and crimes against women, 1868-1896, 123-30
on divorce reform, 35
and Equal Rights Amendment, 237
and The Grange, 66, 79-80
on marriage, 29, 34, 445-46
men, opinion of, 42
race relations, influence on, 404
and Rose, Ernestine, 40
sculpture of, 225
on single women, 43
Anti-lynching movement, 405
Anti-Semitism, 375
Antifeminism, 1970s, 421
Apathy among women, 431
Arkansas, crimes against women, 1868-1896, 134
Arthur, Jean, 303
Arts and literature, gender roles, suburbs, post-World War II, 327-42
Asian-Americans, educational opportunities, 482-83 n.48, 484 (table)
Astor, Lady, 277
Atlanta, working-class women, 50
Auguste, Hector, 114
Aurora (Illinois), corset workers, 175
Austin, Jane, 329
Auto Worker, 309

Automobile industries, strikes, 304-305, 309
Avery, Nina Horton, 374-75

Babcock, Caroline, 360
Back-to-the-kitchen movement, 1940s and early 1950s, 327-42
Baird, Sarah E., 72
Bancroft, Emma, 226
Bank Street School (New York City), 197-98, 206-209, 212-15, 219 n.31
Banks (Dayton, Ohio), employment discrimination, 428
Barnum, Gertrude, 182, 185
Barry, Leonora M., 51, 57-61
Barry, William E., 58
Barrymore, Ethel, 232
Bass, Ross, 381
Battle, George Gordon, 258 n.46
Beard, Mary, 186, 281
Bebel, August, 53
Beecher, Catharine, 145 n.7
Beecher, Henry Ward, 128-29
Beecher-Tilton scandal, 128-29
Bellamy, Edward, 153
Belmont, Alva. *See also* Alva Belmont House
  fund-raising by, 176-77
  and National Woman's Party, 221, 224, 242, 251, 264
  and third political party, 271
Benedict, Ruth, 216
Bennett, Josephine, 227
Bennett, Wallace Foster, 387
Better Homes and Gardens, 424
Beyer, Clara Mortenson, 266
Bickel, Alexander Mordecai, 383
Bilbo, Theodore G., 288-90
Binghamton (New York), Knights of Labor, 52
Birth control, 231, 254
Black, Ruby, 240
Black is Beautiful movement, 477
Black Power movement, 477
Black Women Organized for Action (San Francisco), 469, 476, 487
Blackwell, Alice Stone, 152
Blackwell, The Reverend Antoinette Brown
  and divorce reform, 36
  on marriage, 445-47

men, opinion of, 41
and Rose, Ernestine, 40
Blackwell, Henry
and crimes against women, 1868-1896, 123, 129, 132-33
on drunkenness, 42
on marriage, 30
marriage of, 33-34
Blaine, John H., 256-57
Blake, Ada, 144
Blake, Lillie Devereux, 53
Blakely, William A., 474 n.21
Blatch, Harriot Stanton
and Frankfurter, Felix, 266
and legal protection for women, 234, 236
and National Woman's Party, 248, 251
on paternal instinct, 446
as Socialist, 249 n.7
and Women's Trade Union League, New York, 1903-1914, 191
Blue-collar workers, African-Americans, 481 (table), 488
Board of Legal Aid (Chicago), 138
Boarding houses and labor protest, nineteenth century, 348
Boeckel, Florence Brewer, 250
Bolton, Frances Payne, 381, 383
Bookkeepers, Stenographers and Accountants' Union (New York City), 188, 316
Boston
Communism, 109
crimes against women, 1868-1896, 125 n.7
Boston 9 to 5, 427, 433
The Boston Investigator, 116
Boston marriages, 358, 363
Branch, Julia, 37
Brandeis, Louis, 247 n.3
Branham, Lucy, 249 n.8
Bread and Roses, 430
Breckenridge, Sophonisba, 278
Brewer, Mary, 296
Brick Presbyterian Church (Rochester, New York), 16
British Fabian movement. *See* Fabian movement
Brooks, Gwendolyn, 403
Brown, The Reverend Antoinette. *See* Blackwell, The Reverend Antoinette Brown

Brown, Hallie, 228
Brown, Olympia, 34
Bruner, Mamie M., 105
Bryant, Anita, 465
BSAU. *See* Bookkeepers, Stenographers and Accountants' Union (New York City)
Bureau of Educational Experiments (New York City), 206-207
Burns, Lucy, 221, 248
Burtis, Sarah, 19
Bush, Abigail, 16-17
Bush, Henry, 16
Butler, Josephine, 126
BWOA. *See* Black Women Organized for Action (San Francisco)
Byron, Lord, 126-27, 129

Cable Act, 265
Cadwallader, Priscilla, 12
Cain, Myrtle, 248
California, University of, 482, 484 (table)
  Berkeley, 202-204
California Institute of Technology, 302
California State Personnel Board, 483, 486 (table)
Cameron, Hugh, 52
Canon law, 1868-96, 127
Career Development Center (Dayton, Ohio), 437
Carpenter, Liz, 384
Carpet weavers strike, 1884-1886, 51, 53, 56
Case, Clifford Phillip, 387
Casey, Josephine, 248, 249 n.7
Catholics, and woman suffrage movement, 169
Catt, Carrie Chapman
  on immigrants, 172
  and National American Woman Suffrage Association, 273
  and National Woman's Party, 243
  and protective legislation for women, 263
  secretary of, 171
  as Social feminist, 262
  and Woman Suffrage Party, 170
Celler, Emanuel, 375-76, 380-81, 383, 384
CETA. *See* Comprehensive Employment and Training Act
Channing, Grace, 144, 152-53
Charity Organization Society (New York City), 203

Chicago
Communism, 109
crimes against women, 1868-1896, 122
District Assembly No. 24, 57-58
factory strikes, 305
Knights of Labor, 54, 57
Local Assembly No. 1789, 57
Protective Agency for Women and Children, 136-40
Women's Trade Union League, 175
working-class women, 50
Chicago, University of, 201
Chicago Mail Order Company, 305
Chicago Woman's Club, 136-37
Child, Lydia Maria, 29
Child Labor Amendment, 271
Childrearing
and anarchist-feminists, 111
responsibility of women for, 446-47
Children. *See also* Childrearing
control of by women, 256, 263
education. *See* Education
Protective Agency for Women and Children (Chicago), 136-40
vulnerability of, 454

Chisholm, Shirley, 403
CIO. *See* Congress of Industrial Organizations
Citizens' Advisory Council on the Status of Women, 384
Citizenship, women's choice of, 256, 265 n.70
City and Country School (New York City), 214, 219 n.31
***City and Farm Record* (Topeka, Kansas)**, 86
Civil Rights Act of 1964, 477
Title VII, 284, 369-88, 421
Civil Service reclassification of women, 265
Civilian Conservation Corps, 301
Classes, social. *See* Social classes
Clerical workers. *See* Office workers
Cleveland (Ohio), women's liberation movement, 489
Cleveland Women Working, 427, 433
Cleyre, Voltairine de, 113-16
Clothed with the Sun, 120
Coal mining, Hillsboro (Illinois), 306
Cobbe, Frances Power, 131, 149

Cold War, 346, 368
Collins, Emily, 446
Colvin, Sarah T., 253
Communist Party
  dogma, 307
  headquarters, late nineteenth century, 109-110
  organizers, 306
  threat of, 1920's, 223
  and white collar workers, 315
  women in party, experiences of, 308, 313
Comprehensive Employment and Training Act, 434
Comstock Law, 128
Conference on Women in Industry, 266
Congregationalists, marriage, nineteenth century, 28
Congress of Industrial Organizations
  CIO News, 310, 315
  office workers union, 311-13, 318, 319, 321
  and President's Commission on the Status of Women, 283
  sit-down strikes, 304-305
  and tobacco strike of 1938, 310
  and unauthorized job actions, 309
Congressional Union, 221, 273, 357
Consumers' Leagues
  National
    convention, 1922, 261
    and labor legislation, 247
    leadership of, 229, 249 n.7
    officers of, 276
  New York City, 182, 203, 266
  Wisconsin, 256
Contagious Diseases Acts, 126
Contemporary Review, 131
Contract, women's freedom of, 236, 256
Conway, Jack Thomas, 383
Cook County Suffrage Association (Chicago), 136-37
Coolidge, Calvin, 269
Cornell University, 198
Corset workers, Aurora (Illinois), 175
Counter culture, 1960s, 397
County and Municipal Workers of America, 312
Couple relationships between women, 358-59, 363-66. *See also* Lesbian culture

Craig, Elisabeth May, 376-77, 383
Crimes against women, 1868-1896, 122-41. *See also* Rape
apathy of women, 140-41
and conservative feminists, 129-33
and liberal feminists, 123-29
Protective Agency for Women and Children (Chicago), 136-40
and Women's Christian Temperance Union, 133-36
Criminals, drunkenness, female victims of men, 42
Crownhart, Charles, 256
Crump, Ellen P., 288, 290-91, 293-94, 296-97
Cult of true womanhood, 391
Curtis, Charles, 239, 257
Curtis, Emma Ghent, 86, 94-95

Daly, Margaret, 184
Danville (Massachusetts), Knights of Labor, 52
Darwin, Charles, 53, 163 n.37
Davis, Andrew Jackson, 38
Davis, Paulina Wright, 39
Daycare Parents' Cooperation (Dayton, Ohio), 427
Dayton (Ohio)
Dayton Women Working, 422, 425-29, 431-37
Dayton Women's Center, 422, 425-27, 429-30, 434-37
Dayton's Women's Liberation, 422, 425-26, 429-30, 434-35
feminist organizations, 1970s, 421-41
De Claire, Harriet, 114
De Pasquale, Lena, 317
DeCaux, Len, 315
Declaration of Sentiments (Rochester, New York), 15
Delphi Grange, 72
Democratic Party
Mississippi, 290
and National Woman's Party, 1920s, 239-40
Demonstrations
coal miners, 306
Miss America Contest, protests at, 422
Vietnam War protests, 424
White House, 1920's, 221, 223
women's liberation movement, 395
Denver (Colorado), Communism, 110
Depressions and recessions, trade unions and woman's place concept, 1930's, 299-326

Deroin, Jeanne, 40
Detroit Labor Leaf, 56
Detroit (Michigan), factory strikes, 305
Dewey, Alice, 201
Dewey, John, 201, 206, 209, 215
Dewson, Mary, 278
Dial, 214
Dickinson, Emily, 329
Diggs, Annie L., 85 (photograph)
  on mental illness of farm women, 100-101
  national prominence of, 82
  as orator, 84
  and prohibition movement, 86-87
Dirksen, Everett McKinley, 386
District Assembly No. 24 (Chicago), 57-58
District Assembly No. 72 (Toledo, Ohio), 62
Divorce
  New York State, 124
  nineteenth century, 444
    abused wives, alternative for, 131-32
    liberalization of laws, 34-37
  post-World War II, divorce rate, 285
Dock, Lavinia, 232, 240, 361
Dock, Virginia, 176
Domestic service
  African-American women, 482, 486
  immigrants in, statistics, 413 (table)
Domesticity
  ideology of, 3
  and Knights of Labor, 49-65
Donahue, Phil, 424
Dorr, Rheta Childe, 176, 183, 248, 250
Doty, Madeline, 248
Douglass, Frederick, 5
Dowdy, John Vernard, 380-81
Dreier, Margaret. *See* Robins, Margaret Dreier
Dreier, Mary, 175, 188
Drunkenness. *See* Alcoholism

Earhart, Amelia, 243
Earnings Act, 34
Eastern European immigrants, as anarchist-feminists, 112

Eastland, James Oliver, 384
Eastman, Crystal
  and National Woman's Party, 251, 254-55
  quoted, 220
  as radical, 225
  as Socialist, 248, 249 n.7, 345, 348
Economic and Research Action Projects, 432
Economy Act of 1932, 301
Education. *See also* Education of women
  experimental, New York City, 197-98, 206-209, 212-15, 219 n.31
Education Acts Amendment, Title IX, 284, 421
Education of women, African-Americans, 478, 482-83 n.48, 484 (table)
Edwards, India, 366
EEOC. *See* Equal Employment Opportunity Commission
The Egg and I **(MacDonald)**, 331-35, 340
Egoist, 117, 120
Eisenhower, Dwight D., 282
Ekern, Herman L., 265
Eliot, George, 53
Elite. *See also* Elite women
  Chicago, 136
  industrialization, effect on, 167
Elite women, and Women's Trade Union League, 166-95
Elliot, Laura, 186, 188
Ellison, Kathy, 429, 431
Employment, women. *See* Wage-earning women
Employment discrimination
  and African-American women, 474
  Dayton (Ohio), 427-29
England woman suffrage, influence of, and National Woman's Party, 248, 249 n.7
Equal Employment Opportunity Commission, 369, 421
Equal Pay Act, 284, 387, 421
Equal Rights, 238, 266-67
Equal Rights Amendment
  debate over, 1923-1963, 272-86
  endorsement of, 373
  and National Woman's Party, 246-71, 371-72
    friendships of members, 359, 364
    Paul, Alice, leadership of, 344-46, 356-57
    strength of commitment of members, 351, 353-54
  opposition to, 384

passage of, 421, 430
support for, 374
Equal Rights Association (Rochester, New York), 20
ERA. *See* Equal Rights Amendment
ERAP. *See* Economic and Research Action Projects
Erie Canal, 4
Evangelical Protestantism, 4, 16
Executive Order 10980, 283
Executive Order 11246, 284

Faber, Doris, 366
Fabian movement, 234
Faculty members, African-Americans, 482-83, 485 (table)
Fair Labor Standards Act, 302, 387
Fall River (Massachusetts), working-class women, 50
Family
criticisms of, late nineteenth century, 108
feminism and the contemporary family, 442-67
Gilman, Charlotte Perkins critique on, 449-51, 456
1800s, 444-49
1960s, 451-65
Gilman, Charlotte Perkins on, 198, 389
The Grange, perception of place of men in household, 73-74
Knights of Labor view of, 56
male dominance, 454-55, 463-64
median income, 1973, 459
refuge, perceived as, 120
Farmer-Labor Party, 249 n.7
Farmers, Quakers and emergence of women's rights, 3-23
Farmer's Wife, 81-106
Fascinating Womanhood movement, 465
Federated Women's Clubs, Mississippi, 296
Federation of Westinghouse Independent Salaried Unions, 313
Female Anti-Slavery Society (Rochester, New York), 10
Female Charitable Society (Rochester, New York), 10
Female Moral Reform Society (Rochester, New York), 16
Feminine mystique, 346, 391-92
Feminism. *See* specific topics, such as Social Feminists, Liberal Feminism, Rural feminism
The Feminists, 430
Fern, Fannie. *See* Cleyre, Voltairine de
Fess, Simeon, 257

Fiction, gender roles in the suburbs, post-World War II, 328-42
Field, Sara Bard, 222
Fifteenth Amendment, 30
Fifth Amendment, 236
54-hour bill, 173
Film, gender roles, suburbs, post-World War II, 327-28
Finney, Charles Grandison, 4
Firestone, Shulamith, 454-56, 460-61
First International, 112
Fischer Body Plant No. I, 305
Fish, Sarah, 10, 16
Flint Emergency Brigade, 306
Folger Library, 356
Forbes, Harriet, 219 n.31
Forbes-Johnson, Polly, 219 n.31
Ford Motors, 312
Foremothers Day, 60
Forerunner, 198
40-hour week, 284
Foster, Stephen, 33, 37
Fourier, Charles, 6
Fourteenth Amendment, 129, 168, 236
Frankfurter, Felix, 266
Franklin, Butler, 373-74
Free love
  advocates of, 129
  nineteenth century, 37-39, 110-11
  and passivity of women, 117
  and secrecy, 124
Freedman, Estelle, 359
Freedom summer, Mississippi, 395
Freudian psychology, 358, 455
Friedan, Betty
  on domestic humor, 342
  The Feminine Mystique, 327-29, 368
  housewifery, critiques of, 394
  and Mitchell, Lucy Sprague, issues of, 197
Friendship
  in Alva Belmont House, 354-68
  in National Woman's Party, 354-68
  New Dealers, 1930s, 348
  and Women's Trade Union League, New York, 1903-1914, 189

Fuller, Margaret, 152
Woman in the Nineteenth Century, 53
Fundraising, Women's Trade Union League, 176

Gage, Frances, 42
Gage, Matilda Joslyn, 114, 123, 127
Gage-Colby, Ruth, 387
Gale, Zona, 232, 261
Gallup, George, 302
Garment workers
blacklisted, 1886, 52
strikes by
Chicago, 177
New York, 176
Garrison, William Lloyd, 20, 36
Garside, Frances, 100
Gender roles
of African-American women, 471, 476
home as woman's place, 3
self-perception and society, 401-420
and sisterhood, 401-420
suburbs, post-World War II, 327-42
and women's liberation movement, 389-400
General Electric, 312
General Federation of Women's Clubs, 177
and Equal Rights Amendment, 276
leadership of, 249 n.7
Mississippi, legal disabilities conflict, 1920's, 289, 291
and National Woman's Party, 234
General Motors, 305, 309
Genessee Yearly Meeting (Rochester, New York), 13, 15
German immigrants, white collar workers, 1920s, 314
Gifford, Eliza C., 66, 68, 77-79
Gill, Isabelle Kendig, 292-934
Gillespie, Mary, 176
Gilman, Charlotte Perkins
family, critique of, 108, 449-51, 456
feminist theory of, 209
as forerunner of contemporary feminism, 197-98
Herland, 162
life of, 142-65
on marriage, 320

and women's role in the family, 389
as writer, 248
"The Yellow Wallpaper," 150-51, 450, 451, 461
Gilman, Houghton, 142-43, 157-62
Gladding, Augusta, 144
Golden, Clinton S., 309
The Golden Notebook **(Lessing)**, 460-61
Goldman, Emma
as anarchist, 107, 113, 348
on marriage, 320
and *Mother Earth*, 120
Goldmark, Pauline, 203
Gompers, Jack, 318
Gompers, Samuel, 318
Good Housekeeping, 328
Good Templars, Michigan, 77
Good Will Assembly (Shawnee, Ohio), 54
Goode, Edith, 364
Goodell, Ella C., 75-77
Government jobs, African-Americans, 483, 485 (table)
The Grange, 66-80
Declaration of Purposes, 1874, 69-70
Indiana, 75
Maine, 73
Michigan, 77
Minnesota, 68, 72
New Hampshire, 73-74
New Jersey, 68
New York State, 66, 71, 72, 77-79
San Jose (California), 79
Texas, 72-73
Wisconsin, 74
Great Society, 434
Green, Edith, 378, 379, 382-83
Griffin, Robert Paul, 383
Griffiths, Martha Wright, 377-81, 383-84, 387-88
Grill, Sunny, 316
Grimké, Angelina, 404
Grimké, Sarah, 42, 43
Grosh, The Reverend Aaron, 70-71, 74, 80
Gynaecocentric Theory, 162

Hale, Ruth, 232
Hall, Caroline, 68, 71
Hallowell, Jeffries, 11
Hallowell, Mary, 15-16
Hallowell, William, 11
Halsey, Margaret, 328, 330, 337-40, 342
Harbart, Edith, 136
Harding, Warren G., 233, 255
Harman, Moses, 118
Harrison, Pat, 287, 295
Harron, Marion, 366
Havemeyer, Louisine, 248, 249 n.8
Haymarket riot of 1886, 109, 120
Helping Hand Assembly (Havervill, Massachusetts), 51
Henderson, Lizzie George, 291
Henry Street Settlement (New York), 203
Hepburn, Katherine, 303
Herendeen, Anne, 247 n.5
Herland (Gilman), 162
Herrick, Robert, 201
Hickey, Margaret A., 384
Hickok, Lorena, 358, 366
Hicks, Elias, 12
Hicks, Rachel, 12
Hicksites, Rochester (New York), 12-14, 19
Hill, Elsie, 226, 249 n.8, 255, 289-91
Hillsboro (Illinois), coal mining, 306
Hinchey, Maggie, 174-75
Holmes, Sherrie, 431-33, 435
Home Protection, and The Grange, late nineteenth century, 67, 76
Homemakers Council, 267
Homosexuality. *See also* Lesbian culture
  Bryant, Anita, attack on, 465
Hooker, Edith Houghton, 224, 241-43
Hoover, Herbert, 239-41
Hopkins, Alison, 248
Hourwich, Rebecca, 225-26
Housework
  arts, housewives in, post-World War II, 327-42
  The Grange, view of men's participation in, 73
  1950s, 392-94
  revolt against role of housewife, 398

self-perception and society, 411-12
Howland, Marie Stevens, 67-69
Hughes, Charles Evans, 227
Hull, Cordell, 279
Hull House (New York City)
Bank Street School compared to, 212
Mitchell, Lucy Sprague, visits by, 219 n.31
support for, 201
Humphrey, Hubert Horatio, Jr., 385
Hunt, Jane, 5
The Husbandman, 75, 76
Hyde, Clara, 171

ILGWU. *See* International Ladies' Garment Workers' Union
Illinois Humane Society, 137
Illinois State Federation of Women's Clubs, 175-76
Illinois State Woman Suffrage Party, 170
Illinois Women's Alliance, 92
ILO. *See* International Labor Organization
Immigrants
and anarchist-feminists, 112
crimes against women, 1868-1896, 130
discrimination against in woman suffrage movement, 172
in domestic service, 413 (table)
and Knights of Labor, 50
self-perception and society, 412-13
and Women's Trade Union League, New York, 1903-1914, 187
Incest, legal aid for victims, 1868-1896, 122, 127
Independent Labor Party, 307
Independent Order of Good Templars, 67
Indiana, The Grange, 75
Individualism, 402
Industrial Commission of Wisconsin, 261
Industrial Section of the New York State Suffrage Party, 174
Industrial unionism. *See* Trade unions
Industrial Workers of the World, 226
Industrialization, effect on middle and upper classes, 167
Ingersoll, Robert, 56
Insurance agents, 319
Inter-American Commission on Women, 364
Inter-American Conference of Women, 279
International Conference of American States, 279

International Federation of Business and Professional Women's Clubs, 349-50
International Labor Organization, 279, 281
International Ladies' Garment Workers' Union
leadership of, 249 n.7
Local 25, 181
Local 62, 181
revitalization of, 303
and tobacco industry, 310
International Woman's Suffrage Alliance, 297
Irish-Americans
Catholics and woman suffrage movement, 169
Knights of Labor, 58
Irwin, Elisabeth, 216
Irwin, Inez Haynes, 222
IWW. *See* Industrial Workers of the World

Jackson, Shirley, 328-29, 339
Jailed suffragists, 249, 349-50
James, William, 202
Jameson, Anna, 42
Jericho (New York), feminists, 6, 8
Jewish women
as anarchist-feminists, 112
marriage, nineteenth century, 29
and Women's Trade Union League, New York, 1903-1914, 187
Joan of Arc Assembly (Toledo, Ohio), 55, 62
John Swinton's Paper, 54
Johnson, Emma C., 240
Johnson, Harriet, 219 n.31
Johnson, Lyndon Baines
and Civil Rights Act of 1984, 377-78, 384-85, 387-88
Great Society program, 434
and President's Commission on the Status of Women, 283-84
Johnson, Oscar, 296
Johnson, Sonia, 357
Jones, Mary Harris ("Mother Jones"), 61
Jones, Walter, 229
Jordan, Crystal Lee, 321
Journal of United Labor, 56, 63
Jury duty for women, 256, 263

Kansas
Alliance Kindergarten, 92
Alliance Womens' Association, 92
City and Farm Record (Topeka), 86
Equal Suffrage Association, 97
Factory Girls' Union, 92
Farmers' Alliance, 1891-1894, 81-106
Farmer's Wife (Topeka), 81-106
Knights of Labor, 84
National Children's Home Kindergarten and Industrial Alliance, 102
Shawnee County Alliance, 91
Woman's Progressive Political Club (Topeka), 97
Woman's Progressive Political League, 97, 98
Women Wage Earners', 92
Womens' Labor Union, 92
Katzenbach, Nicholas deBelleville, 378
Kearney, Belle, 169, 295-96
Kelley, Abby, 13, 33
Kelley, Florence
and African-Americans, 235
Consumer's League (New York City), 203, 247
and labor legislation, 247
as model for single women, 205
and National American Woman Suffrage Association, 172
and National Woman's Party
African-American women, 229, 231, 235
convention of 1921, 254-55
labor legislation, 234-35
National Consumers' League Convention, 261
Social feminist future of, 251-52
and protective legislation for women, 253, 259-60, 262-63
as Social feminist, 265
as Socialist, 345
and working-class women, 169-70
as writer, 248
Kellogg, Frank, 278
Kelly, Edna Flannery, 379
Kelly, Florence Finch, 111, 116
Kelly, Oliver Hudson, 68
Kennedy, John Fitzgerald, 282, 371-72, 378-79, 388. *See also* President's Commission on the Status of Women
Kerr, Jean, 328-29, 331, 339-41

Kinship networks, Quakers, Rochester (New York), 7-11
Kirby, Amy. *See* Post, Amy (Kirby)
Kirby, Hannah, 8
Kirby, Sarah, 11
Kirchway, Freda, 220, 225, 230-31, 254
Kirkland, Caroline, 332
Knights of Labor, 49-65, 84
Knit-goods industry
  Amsterdam (New York), 59
  Mohawk Valley strike, 51
Kraus, Henry, 309

L. Sonneborn Sons, Inc., 317
La Guardia, Fiorello, 316
Labor, Department of, 282, 428. *See also* U. S. Children's Bureau; Women's Bureau, Department of Labor
Labor Book News Agency, 53
Labor laws
  and Paul, Alice, 233
  sex discrimination in, 233-38
  and Social feminists, 246-47
Laboring classes. *See* Working classes
LaBriola, Carrie, 430
Ladies' Christian Alliance (Sulphur Springs, Texas), 92
LaFollette, Belle, 224
LaFollette, Robert, 224
Lake, Obadiah Read, 61
Lamarckian thought, 163 n.37
LaSalle, Ferdinand, 53
Lathrop, Emily E., 102, 104
Lathrop, Julia, 253
Laughlin, Gail, 234-35, 249 n.7, 258, 264
Lawrence (Massachusetts), working-class women, 50
League of Nations, 278-79
Leagues of Women Voters
  Dayton (Ohio), 424
  and labor legislation, 247
  Milwaukee, 256
  Mississippi, 288, 292, 295-96
  National, 261
    Committee on Legislation of Civil Law, 256
  and National American Woman Suffrage Association, 345

and National Woman's Party, 234, 241-42, 350
Wisconsin, 256
Lease, Mary Elizabeth, 61-62, 82, 84, 96
Legal Aid Society of Chicago, 138-39
Legal disabilities, Mississippi, 1920s, 287-98
Lenin, V. I., 222, 243
Leopold, Alice, 282
Lesbian culture
Alva Belmont House, 358-59, 363, 365-66
1970's, 436, 460
Lessing, Doris, 460-61
Lewis, Dora, 235
Lewis, Fulton, Jr., 371
Lewis, Shippin, 258 n.46
Liberal feminism, 453-54
The Liberator, 225
Liberty, 111-12, 116-17
Life Among the Savages (Jackson), 329, 339
Life and Labor, 173, 177
Limpson, Beatrice, 317
Lindsay, John Vliet, 382
Little Red School House (New York City), 219 n.31
Livermore, Mary, 84
Louise, Marie, 112
Lowell mills, 50, 348
Lucifer, 112, 118, 120
Lucretia Mott Amendment. *See* Equal Rights Amendment
Lum, Deyer D., 113
Luther, Martha, 144-45, 147
Lutz, Alma, 241, 364-65, 368

MacDonald, Betty, 328, 330-35, 340
MacKay, John, 109
MacKaye, Jessie Hardy, 232
Mainardi, Pat, 461
Malkeil, Theresa, 176-88
Mann Act, 381
Marcus, Beatrice, 306
Margon Corporation (New York City), 315-16
Marks, Jeannette, 362-63, 365
Marot, Helen, 189-91, 214

Marriage
age factors, 391-92
child-support rights of women, 273
Mitchell, Lucy Sprague, view of, 205
nineteenth century, 26-48, 444-49
ideology, 39-44
and oppression, 29-33, 40
resistance of women to, 33-37
property, women as, nineteenth century, 32
property rights of women, 26, 31, 34, 263, 444
sexual intercourse, rights of women to refuse, 128
wife murders, 124-26
working wives, 303
Martha Washington Assembly, 52, 54
Marx, Karl, 53, 109
Marxist feminists, 453, 455
Mason, Lucy, 281
Massachusetts, crimes against women, 1868-1896, 130-31 n. 23
Masses, 214
Maternal Mystique, 108, 119
Mathias, Charles McCurdy, 382
Matthews, Burnita Shelton, 257, 265 n.68, 291-92, 296-97
May, Catherine Dean, 276, 382
Mayo, Mary Ann, 72, 74
Mays, Samuel J., 14
McCarthyism, 346, 347, 366
McClintock, Mary Ann, 5, 15
McClintock, Thomas, 15
McCormick, Fannie, 89 (photograph)
Fourth of July address by, 91
on housework, 101
and Kansas Knights of Labor, 84
and National Women's Alliance, 92, 96
McCullough, Catherine Waugh, 256, 263
McDowell, Mary, 176
McFarland, Albert, 124, 128
McFarland-Richardson Law, 128
McGinley, Phyllis, 328, 332, 336-38, 340-41
McHale, Kathryn, 366
Men
brutality of, perception of nineteenth century women, 41-42, 48 n.108
dominance, family life, 454-55, 463-64

The Grange, perception of place of men in household, 73-74
housework by, 461
Mental illness, farm women, 1891-1894, 100-101
Mesta, Perle, 354
Mexican-Americans
assimilation of, 471 n.12
educational opportunities, 482-83 n.48, 484 (table)
Michigan
The Grange, 77
Knights of Labor, 55
Middle class. *See also* Middle-class women
domination of feminist movement, 166
industrialization, effect on, 167
marriage, nineteenth century, 28, 33, 35
Middle-class women
employment, 392
and Equal Rights Amendment, 274
gender roles, suburbs, post-World War II, 327-42
self-perception and society, 410
and Women's Trade Union League, 166-95
and working-class women, class conflict, 173-74
working mothers, 457
Militant suffrage, jailed suffragists, 249
Mill, John Stuart, 39, 126-27, 140
Gilman, Charlotte Perkins, influence on, 142, 152, 155
Millay, Edna St. Vincent, 243
Miller, Adolph, 204
Miller, Emma Guffey, 373, 375, 379, 384
Miller, Frieda, 275, 282
Miller, Hugh Barr, 297
Millett, Kate, 454
Minnesota, The Grange, 68, 72
Minority Report, 423
Miss America Contest, 422
Mississippi
freedom summer, 395
legal disabilities conflict, 1920's, 287-98
Mitchell, Claire, 316
Mitchell, Henrietta, 289
Mitchell, Lucy Sprague, 196-219
Mitchell, S. Weir, 153
Mitchell, Wesley Clair, 204-210

Model Cities, 434
Modern Times (Long Island New York), 38
Mohawk Valley, knit-goods strike, 51
Monroe, Lilla Day, 232
Moody, Charles, 431
Morey, Agnes, 249 n.8
Morgan, Marabel, 465
Most, Johann, 118, 119
Mother Earth, 120
Motherhood
Farmer's Wife articles on, 102, 104-105
Maternal Mystique, 108, 119
mother-daughter relationships, 409
voluntary, legal rights of women, 129
Mott, Elizabeth, 7
Mott, Lucretia
domestic life of, 6
as Quaker, 12-13, 15, 18
sculpture of, 225
at Seneca Falls Convention, 1948, 5, 17
***Mr. Smith Goes to Washington* (film)**, 303
Ms. Magazine, 421
***Muller* case**, 247 n.3
Muncie (Indiana), voting polls, 422-23
Municipal League (New York City), 182
Murray, Ella Rush, 230-31, 254
Muste, A. J., 307

NAACP. *See* National Association for the Advancement of Colored People
NAM. *See* New American Movement
Nation, 230, 254
National Advisory Council
convention of 1921, 224, 253
and Equal Rights Amendment, 235
formation of, 255
investigations by, 230
leadership of, 231-32, 241
National American Woman Suffrage Association
Congressional Committee, 248 n.6
convention
1906, 172
1919, 172

goals of, 273
and The Grange, 80
and labor legislation, 247
and League of Women Voters, 345
and National Woman's Party, 221, 227, 252 n.18, 344
New York Conference, 174
Ohio campaign, 170-71
picketing of White House, 223
and Women's Trade Union League, 169, 173
National Association for the Advancement of Colored People, 228, 347
National Association of Colored Women, 347
National Association of Colored Women's Clubs, 228
National Association of Office Workers, 436
National Black Feminist Organization, 469, 476, 487, 489
National Committee of State Chairmen, 253
National Consumers' League. *See* Consumers' Leagues
National Council of Churches, 283
National Executive Committee, 253
National Farmers' Alliance, 93, 94
National Federation of Business and Professional Women, 234, 253, 275-76, 371
National Industrial Recovery Act, 301-302
National Labor Relations Board, 312, 317
National Liberal League (Rochester, New York), 20
National Manpower Council, 283
National Maritime Union, 311
National Negro Congress, 310
National Organization for Women
Dayton (Ohio), 425
formation of, 284, 369, 453
as moderate group, 430
public ideology of, 398
National Welfare Rights Organization, 488
National Woman Suffrage Association
officers, 127
Rochester (New York) members, 20
and Women's Trade Union League, 168
National Woman's Party
Alva Belmont House, 349, 354-68, 371
anti-Semitism in, 375
Charter Committee, 280-82
and Civil Rights Act of 1964, Title VII, 370-77, 379, 386-87

commitment to, 351-54
Declaration of Principles, 264
and Equal Rights Amendment, 178 n.3, 246-71
feminist identification, 350-51
Mississippi, legal disabilities conflict, 1920's, 287-98
National Advisory Council. *See* National Advisory Council
National American Woman Suffrage Association, 221, 227, 344
1945-1960s, 343-68
1920's, 220-45
race discrimination in, 375
suffrage heritage, 349-50
Wisconsin, 256
and Women's Bureau, Department of Labor, 277, 280-81
and women's community, 1945-1960s, 343-68
National Women's Alliance, 92-93, 96-97
National Women's Employment Project, 426, 427, 433, 436
National Women's Rights Convention, 1890, 29, 35-36
National Women's Trade Union League
leadership of, 240, 249 n.7
and National Consumers' League, 261
and National Woman's Party, 234
and protective legislation for women, 253
NAWSA. *See* National American Woman Suffrage Association
NBFO. *See* National Black Feminist Organization
Nebraska Woman Suffrage Association, 78
Needham, Charles W., 258 n.46
Nelson, Eleanor, 310, 311
Nestor, Agnes, 62, 170, 176
Nettborn, Ruth, 318
Neuberger, Maureen Brown, 386
New American Movement, Dayton (Ohio), 425, 429, 431
New Deal, 285, 300, 348
New England Telephone and Telegraph, 302
New Hampshire, The Grange, 73-74
New Jersey, The Grange, 68
New Left, 425, 429-30
New Republic, 383
New York City
Communism, 109-110
Knights of Labor, 55
schools, 197-98, 206-209, 212-15, 219 n.31
New York Credit Clearing House, 317

New York Radical Feminists, 430
New York State
crimes against women, 1868-1896, 134
divorce law, 124
The Grange, 66, 71, 72, 77-79
New York State Woman Suffrage Association, 79
New York Times
on free love, 37-38
and Hinchey, Maggie, 175
and protective legislation for women, 253
New York Wage Earners' Suffrage League, 173-74
New York Women's Trade Union League. *See* Women's Trade Union League
Newman, Pauline
and Chicago garment workers strike, 177
and Schneiderman, Rose, 171
and Women's Trade Union League, New York, 1903-1914, 187-89, 192
Newsweek, 383
NFBP. *See* National Federation of Business and Professional Women
Nichols, Anna, 175
Nichols, Clarina I. H., 38
Nineteenth Amendment, 224, 230, 274
NIRA. *See* National Industrial Recovery Act
NLRB. *See* National Labor Relations Board
NMU. *See* National Maritime Union
Noble and Holy Order of the Knights of Labor. *See* Knights of Labor
NOW. *See* National Organization for Women
Nugent, Virginia, 265 n.70
Nussbaum, Karen, 433
Nutt, Nettie S., 93, 105
NWA. *See* National Women's Alliance
NWEP. *See* National Women's Employment Project
NWP. *See* National Woman's Party

Obenaur, Marie L., 249 n.7, 250
Office workers
1930s, 311-21
1970s, 426-27, 486 (table)
Ohio Woman Suffrage Association, 171
O'Keeffe, Georgia, 243
O'Neill, William, 250 n.9
Open-air meetings, woman suffrage movement, 221

Order of the Patrons of Husbandry. *See* The Grange
O'Reilly, Leonora
and Knights of Labor, 62
and National American Woman Suffrage Association
New York Conference, 174
Ohio campaign, 171
speech by, 176
and Women's Trade Union League, New York, 1903-1914, 184, 186, 188-89, 191-92
O'Sullivan, Mary Kenney, 176
Otis, Bina, 97 (photograph)
articles by, 101, 102, 104
and *Farmer's Wife*, 84, 90
and Kansas Equal Suffrage Association, 97
and National Woman's Alliance, 92, 96
and Woman's Progressive Political League, 98
Otis, John, 84
Our Girls Co-op (Chicago), 52
Ovington, Mary White, 228-29
Owen, Robert Dale, 42
Owen, Sarah C., 16, 19

Pack, Emma D.
and *Farmer's Wife*, 84, 85-87
and Kansas Equal Suffrage Association, 97
and National Women's Alliance, 92, 96
and woman suffrage movement, 94, 96
Pack, Ira, 85-86
Pack, Maud E., 89-90
Paine, Thomas, 6
Palmer, Alice Freeman, 201-202, 205
Palmer, George Herbert, 202
Pankhurst, Emmeline, 249 n.7
Parent-teacher associations, Dayton (Ohio), 426
Park, Maud Wood
and labor laws, 235
Mississippi, legal disabilities conflict, 1920's, 291-92
and protective legislation for women, 259
as social feminist, 253
Patrons of Husbandry (Michigan), 77
Patterson, Mrs. E. C. Williams, 62-63

Paul, Alice
and African-Americans, 228-30, 235
and Allender, Nina, 355
and Alva Belmont House, 355-57
and Civil Rights Act of 1964, Title VII, 376-77, 379, 387
and Congressional Union, 273
and England woman suffrage, 248, 249 n.7
and Equal Rights Amendment, 241, 344
friendships of, 359-62, 365, 367
health of, 356
leadership of, 220
and legal protection for women, 233-34
and National Association for the Advancement of Colored People, 228
and National Woman's Party
African-American women members, 229, 231
aims for women, 251
civil rights movement, 371
convention of 1921, 224-26, 252
Equal Rights Amendment, 264-67, 274, 277, 346, 352-54, 373
industrial equality, 432-33
international law studies, 242
leadership controversy, 348
Mississippi, legal disabilities conflict, 1920's, 287-88, 290-93, 295
National American Woman Suffrage Association, break with, 221
relationship with other members, 222, 244
Socialist members, 345
and protective legislation for women, 259-60
Seneca Falls anniversary convention, 1923, 268
and Smith, Howard W., 374
and Women's Charter, National Woman's Party, 282
Paul, Helen, 361
Pecan shellers strike
San Antonio (Texas), 310
St. Louis (Missouri), 303-304, 320
Peck, Mary Gray, 170
Perkins, Charlotte. *See* Gilman, Charlotte Perkins
Perkins, Frances, 281, 301
Perkins, Frederick, 143, 147
Perkins, Mary, 143, 147
Peshakova, Liba, 289
Peterson, Esther
as politician, 388

Smith, Howard Worth, letter to, 380
and Title VII, 383, 386
as Women's Bureau director, 282, 372-73
Philadelphia
carpet weavers, 56
Communism, 109
crimes against women, 1868-1896, 124, 125 n.7
Knights of Labor, 52
working-class women, 50
Philadelphia Storage Battery Company (Philco), 303
Phillips, Lena Madesin, 349
Phillips, Wendell, 36, 445
Picketing, White House, 1920's, 221, 223
Pidgeon, Mary, 280
Piece-rate workers, St. Louis (Missouri), strikes, 303-304
Piercy, Marge, 460
Pike, Violet, 188
Pittsburgh, University of, 482
Pittsburgh (Pennsylvania), working-class women, 50
Play School in Greenwich Village (New York City), 214-15
Pleasant, Hilda, 293
Please Don't Eat the Daisies **(Kerr)**, 331, 339
Poetry
of abolitionists, 94-96
gender roles in the suburbs, post-World War II, 340-41
of labor movement, 52, 56
by Mitchell, Lucy Sprague, 210-11
Political protests, 1960s, 475-87
Poll tax laws, 471 n.11
Pollitzer, Anita, 287, 289-91, 295
Popular art, gender roles, suburbs, post-World War II, 327-42
Populist Party, Kansas, 1891-1894, 81-106
Post, Amy (Kirby), 7-11, 13-17, 19-20
Post, Isaac, 9, 11, 13, 15
Post, Mary, 10-11
Powderly, Terence V., 55, 57-58, 60-61
Powell, Rose Arnold, 354
Pratt, Caroline, 214-16, 219 n.31
Presbyterians, marriage, nineteenth century, 28
President's Commission on the Status of Women, 276, 282-83, 372-73, 387
Progressive Era
female leaders of, 198-99

prostitutes, reform of, 141
Progressive Miners' Association, 306
Prohibitionists
and *Farmer's Wife*, 86-87
and National Woman's Party, 1920s, 239
and Populist Party, 94
Property rights of women. *See* Marriage
Prostitution
reforms, 1868-1896, 122, 141
working mothers as prostitutes, 458
Protective Agency for Women and Children (Chicago), 123, 136-40
Protective legislation for women
and Anderson, Mary, 271
debate over, 276-81
and Kelley, Florence, 252 n.16, 253, 262-63
Mississippi, 298
and National Woman's Party, 233-38, 259
and Social feminists, 246-47
and Women's Trade Union League, 260
Protestants
and The Grange, 67
marriage, nineteenth century, 29
and woman suffrage movement, 169
Proudhon, Pierre Joseph, 119
Pullman strike, 201
Putnam, Mabel Raef, 233, 256

Quakers, agrarian states, 3-23

Race discrimination
African-American women, response to, 468-90
in National Woman's Party, 375
in woman suffrage movement, 169
Race relations and sisterhood, 401-420
Racism. *See* Race discrimination
Radcliffe College, 201-202
Radical feminists
1960s, 452-53
1970s, 430
Radican, Cheryl, 423-24, 435
Rape. *See also* Crimes against women, 1868-1896
of African-American women, 470

aid for victims, Chicago, 138
Boston, 1867-1874, 125 n.7
death penalty for, 124
legal aid for victims, 1868-1896, 122
marital, 42, 48 n.108, 127
and social breakdown, 463
statistics on, 462
Women on Rape Task Force (Dayton, Ohio), 426
Redstockings, 430
Rehfish, Carol, 267
Replogle, Georgia, 117
Republican Party
Kansas, 1891-1894, 100
and National Woman's Party, 1920s, 239-40
Reuther, Walter, 373
Revivalist movement, nineteenth century, 27
Reyes, Consuela, 364
Richman, Julia, 203
Richmond, Mary, 203
Richmond (Virginia), tobacco industry, 310
Rivers, Lucius Mendel, 382
Roberts, William B., 294
Robins, Margaret Dreier
as Hoover appointee, 240
and Woman's Trade Union League, 170-72, 174, 176-77, 184
Rochester (New York), women's rights, 3-23
Rochester Woman's Rights Convention (New York), 16, 19
Rockefeller Family Fund, 426
Rockford (Illinois), Foremothers Day, 60
Rodgers, Elizabeth, 57-60
Rogers, Elizabeth, 361
Rogers, Elizabeth Selden, 249 n.8
Roland, Pauline, 40
Roosevelt, Eleanor
and Dewson, Mary, 278
and Hickok, Lorena, 358, 366
and President's Commission on the Status of Women, 283, 373
Roosevelt, Franklin D., 242, 278, 300
Roosevelt, James, 382
Rose, Ernestine, 26 (photograph)
on divorce reform, 35-36
on free love, 37

on natural rights theory, 39
on oppression of women, 30-31, 40
origins of, 29, 45 n.7
on single women, 43
Rowbotham, Sheila, 462
Royce, Josiah, 202
Rubber industries, strikes, 304-305
Rural feminism, late nineteenth century, 66-80
Ruskin, John, 76-77
Russell, Lee M., 290, 293
Russian immigrants as anarchist-feminists, 112
Russian Revolution, 223
Ruttenberg, Harold J., 309

Salaries. *See* Wages
Salvation Army (New York City), 203
San Antonio (Texas), pecan shellers strike, 310
San Diego (California), crimes against women, 1868-1896, 122, 137
San Diego Union (California), 134-35
San Francisco
Black Women Organized for Action, 469
Local Assembly No. 2999, 62
San Jose (California), The Grange, 79
Sanderson, Jeremiah, 14
Santayana, George, 202
Saunders, William, 67
Schneiderman, Rose
Cooper Union meeting, 173
and National American Woman Suffrage Association, Ohio campaign, 170-71
support for by elite, 176
and Women's Trade Union League, New York, 1903-1914, 185, 192
Scott, Melinda, 186, 187
Scott, Robert T., 258 n.46
SDS. *See* Students for a Democratic Society
Section 213, 302
Seduction as crime, 124
Self-perception and society, 408-416
Seneca Falls Convention, 1848
anniversary convention, 1923, 264, 268, 350
grievance list of women, 444-45
and race relations, 405

Rochester (New York) attendees, 5, 16-17
Servants. *See* Domestic service
Service Employees International Union, 321, 436
Service professions, 391
Settlement residents, New York City, 1903-1914, 182
Seventh Pan-American Conference, 278
Sex discrimination
African-American women, response to, 468-90
Civil Rights Act of 1964, Title VII, 369-88
legal protection for women, 233-38
and social class, 487-90
Sex reform, rural areas, late nineteenth century, 67
Sexism. *See* Sex discrimination
Sexual relationships. *See also* Free love; Homosexuality; Lesbian culture
varietism, 111
Shakers, marriage, nineteenth century, 27
Shaw, Anna Howard, 170
Shaw, George Bernard, 376
Shawnee (Ohio), Knights of Labor, 54
Sheppard-Towner Act of 1921, 270, 292
Sheridan, A. M., 56
Sherrod, Charles, 396
Shields, Walton, 292
Shirtwaist makers
strike, 1909, 185, 187
trade unions, 181
A Short Walk From the Station **(McGinley)**, 336-38, 340-41
Simmons, Jim, 152
Single women
and aging parents, 274
nineteenth century, 43
protection against crime, 137-38
Sisterhood
all-inclusive, prospects for, 416-18
limitations of, 402-408
race, class and gender and, 401-420
self-perception and society, 408-416
and Women's Trade Union League, New York, 1903-1914, 182-83
Sixth Pan American Conference (Havana, Cuba), 242, 278
Slattery, Henry A., 258 n.46
Smith, Alfred E., 239, 241

Smith, Ethel
National Woman's Party, denunciation of, 266
and protective legislation, 253, 259, 263
and Women's Trade Union League, 235
Smith, Howard Worth, and Civil Rights Act of 1964, 369, 373-78, 380, 387-88
Smith, Jane Norman, 234, 240-42, 361
Smith, Margaret Chase, 386, 388
Smith, Marguerite, 364-65
***The Snake Has All the Lines* (Kerr)**, 340-41
SNCC. *See* Student Nonviolent Coordinating Committee
Social classes
class conflict, working-class and middle-class women, Women's Trade Union League, 173-74, 181-95
class consciousness and trade unions, 166
relations between
self-perception and society, 408-416
and sisterhood, 401-420
and sex discrimination, 487-90
Social feminists
on class structure, 430
conflict with feminists, 269-70
and protective legislation, 246-53, 259, 261-62, 265-67
Social Party, late nineteenth century, 108, 118
Social production, 390
Social purity, 126-27
Social Security, 302
Social structure
and African-American women
inequality, 470-73
white women, structural position compared, 473-75
self-perception and society, 408-409
Social workers, and Women's Trade Union League, New York, 1903-1914, 188
Socialist Party, and National Woman's Party, 1920s, 239
Society of Friends. *See* Quakers
Somerville, Lucy, 296
Somerville, Nellie Nugent, 296
Sonneborn, Joseph, 317
Southern Negro Youth Congress, 310
Spencer, Caroline, 235, 244
Spiritualists, nineteenth century, 27, 44
Sprague, Lucia, 200

Sprague, Lucy. *See* Mitchell, Lucy Sprague
Sprague, Otho, 200-201
Sprague Warner and Co., 200
St. George, Katharine Price Collier, 375, 382
St. Louis (Missouri), piece-rate workers, strikes, 303-304
***Stage Door* (film)**, 303
Stanton, Elizabeth Cady
and American Labor Reform League, 119
autobiography, 445-46
and crimes against women, 1868-1896, 123-30
Declaration of Sentiments, 236
on divorce reform, 35-37
on family relationships, 108
on free love, 38-39
on marriage, 29-32, 34
men, opinion of, 41-42
on motherhood, 43
and Rose, Ernestine, 40
sculpture of, 225
and Seneca Falls Convention, 1948, 5
at Seneca Falls Convention, 1948, 17
Stanwyck, Barbara, 303
Steel Workers (Dayton, Ohio), 436
Stembridge, Jane, 396
Stephens, Hubert D., 296
Stereotypes, class-biased, 176
Stetson, Charlotte Perkins. *See* Gilman, Charlotte Perkins
Stetson, Katharine, 149
Stetson, Walter, 143 n. 3, 145-46, 148-50, 152, 157
Stevens, Alzina P., 62
Stevens, Doris
and Belmont, Alva, 242
and Equal Rights Amendment, 244, 274, 277-79
homophobic views, 365
and Paul, Alice, 282, 362
Stewart, Mary, 253
Stone, Lucy
and crimes against women, 1868-1896, 123, 129-33, 139
on divorce reform, 35-36
on drunkenness, 42
on marriage, 30-31
marriage of, 33-34

Stowe, Harriet Beecher, 126-27, 129, 145 n.7
Strikes
automobile industries, 304-305, 309
carpet weavers, 1884-1886, 51, 53, 56
garment workers
Chicago, 177
New York, 176
knit-goods workers, Mohawk Valley, 51
pecan shellers strikes
San Antonio (Texas), 310
St. Louis (Missouri), 303-304, 320
Pullman strike, 201
shirtwaist makers, 185, 187
and tobacco strike of 1938, 310
Student movement, women's liberation, 395-97
Student Nonviolent Coordinating Committee, 395-97
Students for a Democratic Society, 395-97, 429, 432, 433
Suburbs
and gender roles, post-World War II, 327-42
growth of, 392
Suffragist, 250-52, 254
Sugar Trust, 249 n.7
Suicide, 130
Sullivan, Leonor Kretzer, 379
Support networks, 348
Sutherland, Elizabeth, 384
Swinton, John, 53, 54

Talbert, Mary C., 228-29
Taylor, Hobart, Jr., 385
Taylor, Samuel, 53
Telephone Operators Union, 249 n.7
Temperance movement
and Knights of Labor, 64
and male cruelty, 42
Terrell, Mary Church, 227-28, 347
Texas
crimes against women, 1868-1896, 122
The Grange, 72-73
This Demi Paradise: A Westchester Diary **(Halsey)**, 337-40, 342
Thomas, Norman, 239
Thompson, Elizabeth, 67

Thompson, Ella C., 288
Thompson, Frank, 382
Thurber, James, 330
Title IX. *See* Education Acts Amendment
Title VII. *See* Civil Rights Act of 1964
Tobacco industry, Richmond (Virginia), 310
Tobacco Stemmers and Laborers' Union, 310
Toledo (Ohio), Joan of Arc Assembly, 55, 62
Trade unions. *See also* Strikes; Women's Trade Union League
  growth of unionism, 459
  Knights of Labor, 49-65
  shirtwaist makers, 181, 185, 187
  white goods workers', 181
  and woman's place concept, 1930's, 299-326
Truman, Harry, 366
Tucker, Benjamin, 117
Tuten, James Russell, 382

UAW. *See* United Automobile Workers
UFW. *See* United Federal Workers
Unemployment, 1930s, 300
Union Seminary, 396
Union Signal, 135
United Automobile Workers, 305-306, 383, 436
United Cannery, 310
United Electrical Workers, 309
United Federal Workers, 310-12
United Garment Workers, New York City, 184, 191
United Office and Professional Workers of America, 311-312, 315-19
United Rubber Workers, 306
Universalists, marriage, nineteenth century, 28
UOPWA. *See* United Office and Professional Workers of America
Upper classes. *See* Elite
URW. *See* United Rubber Workers
U.S. Children's Bureau of Labor, 253, 281
U.S. Commission on Civil Rights, 474 n.21
U.S. Commissioner of Agriculture, 69
U.S. Conciliation Service, 317
U.S. Steel, 309
Utopian Socialists, nineteenth century, 27, 37, 44

Vardaman, James K., 288-90, 295-96

Vaughn, Hester, 124
Venereal disease, 128
Vernon, Mabel, 222 n.3, 361-62, 364
Victims of crime, women as, 122-41
apathy of women, 140-41
and conservative feminists, 129-33
and liberal feminists, 123-29
Protective Agency for Women and Children (Chicago), 136-40
and Women's Christian Temperance Union, 133-36
Victorian attitudes
on marriage, 445
patriarchy, 44
toward sexuality, 148
Victory Assembly (Amsterdam, New York), 59
Vietnam War protests, 424-25, 433, 451-52
Villa Range: Ladies' Home Journal, 86
Virginia Federation of Women's Business and Professional Clubs, 374
Volunteers in Service to America (VISTA), 434
Voting Rights Act of 1965, 477

Wage-earning women. *See also* Office workers; White-collar jobs; Working conditions; Working mothers
clubs, 182
demographic profile of, pre-World War II, 285
and Equal Rights Amendment, 274
legal protection for, sex discrimination in, 233-38
professionals, 393-94
protection against crime, 137-38
Rochester (New York), 19
wives, working, 303
woman's place concept and trade unions, 1930's, 299-326
and Women's Trade Union League, 166-95
Wages
and American Federation of Labor, 309
and Knights of Labor, 50
legal protection for women, 233
minimum wage law, 235, 301, 372
office workers, 1930's, 317
working mothers, contemporary families, 458
Waitresses' Union (New York City), 188
Wald, Lillian
Henry Street Settlement, 203, 219 n.31

as model for single women, 205
and Paul, Alice, 361
and Progressive Era, 198
as Socialist, 348
Walker, Mary, 79
Walsh, Frank P., 258
Ward, Lester, 153, 162
Wayne County Grange Council, 76
Ways and Means Committee, 378-79
WCTU. *See* Women's Christian Temperance Movement
Webb, James H., 258 n.46
Welfare rights organizations, 396
Wellesley College, 201, 204, 363
Wells-Barnett, Ida B., 227, 405
Western New York Anti-Slavery Society, 13-14, 16
Wheeler, Benjamin, 202
White, Sue Shelton, 224, 240, 249 n.8, 253-54
White, Walter, 228
White-collar jobs. *See also* Office workers
African-American women, 482
post-World War II, 391
White goods workers, trade unions, 181
Whitman, Walt, 146
Widows, property rights of, nineteenth century, 31
Wife abuse. *See also* Rape
divorce as alternative, nineteenth century, 131-32
Knights of Labor expulsion, 56
legal aid for victims, 1868-1896, 122-23, 129, 130-31 n. 23, 133
Wilbert, Walter B., 258 n.46
Wiley, Anna Kelton, 247-48 n.5, 267, 352
Willard, Frances, 95 (photograph)
and domestic imagery, 49
Farmer's Wife contributions, 84
and The Grange, 67, 77
Home Protection, 76
and Knights of Labor, 58, 64
and Populist Party, 94
and Rodgers, Elizabeth, 58
and victims of crimes against women, 1868-1896, 133
and Women's Christian Temperance Union, 74
Willhelm, Noreen, 431, 435
Williams, Helen, 433

Willis, Amy, 8
Willis, Phebe Post, 13
Willmar Eight, 321
Wilson, Woodrow
voters against, 227
and woman suffrage movement, picketing of White House, 223
Winslow, Mary, 278 n.6, 279
Winsor, Mary, 249 n.8, 296
Wisconsin
The Grange, 74
working conditions, legal protection for women, 233
Wisconsin Equal Rights Bill, 257, 260, 270
Wisconsin Federation of Business and Professional Women, 256
WNYASS. *See* Western New York Anti-Slavery Society
Wold, Emma, 228
Wollstonecraft, Mary, 6, 116, 155
Woman question controversy, and anarchist-feminists, late nineteenth century, 107-121
Woman Suffrage Alliance, and National Woman's Party, 242
Woman suffrage movement. *See also* specific organization
and The Grange, 70, 77
image of, 250
Kansas, 1891-1894, 94, 96
Woman Suffrage Party, Illinois, 170, 177
Woman's Convention, New York, 1853, 38
Woman's Journal
crimes against women, 1868-1896, stories on, 130-32
editorship, 129
Woman's National Liberal Union, 114
Woman's Party. *See* National Woman's Party
Woman's place concept, 1930's, 299-326
Women in Amsterdam (New York), 59
Women in Industry Conference, 1926, 276
Women in the Work Force Task Force, 425
Women Office Workers (New York City), 427
Women on Rape Task Force (Dayton, Ohio), 426
The Women Voter, 295-96
Women's Bureau, Department of Labor
allies of, 285
director of, 373
endorsement of Equal Rights Amendment, 284
and Equal Rights Amendment, 273-75, 277

and National Woman's Party, 237, 252
Research Division, 280
and Section 213, 302
Women's Catholic Order of Foresters, 61
Women's Charter Committee, 279-82
Women's Christian Temperance Union
and differences between men and women, 108
and domestic imagery, 49
and The Grange, 67
and National Woman's Party, 234
and victims of crimes against women, 1868-1896, 123, 133-36
and woman suffrage movement, 79
Women's cooperatives, 52
Women's Education and Industrial Union (Boston), 136
Women's Equity Action League, 284
Women's Joint Congressional Committee, 270
Women's League for Equal Opportunity, 266
Women's liberation movement, 389-400
Women's rights, Quakers and emergence of women's rights, 3-23
Women's Trade Union League, 166-80
and labor legislation, 247
New York, 181-95, 214
and protective legislation for women, 260
and working conditions for women, 235
Woodhull, Victoria, 39, 45 n.8, 128-29
Woolf, Virginia, 100
Woolley, Mary, 363, 365
Working-class women
crimes against women, 1868-1896, 131
and Knights of Labor, 49-65
and middle-class women, class conflict, 173-74
minimum wages for, 372
National Woman's Party members, 347
self-perception and society, 409-410
and Women's Trade Union League, 166-95
Working classes. *See also* Working-class women
Rochester (New York), 17
Working conditions
54-hour bill, 173
40-hour week, 284
protective legislation for women. *See* Protective legislation for women

Working mothers. *See also* Motherhood; Wage-earning women
  contemporary families, 457-58, 462
Working People's Nonpartisan Political League, 249 n.7
Working Woman, 306
Working Woman's Protective Union (Rochester, New York), 19-20
Working Women, 321
Working women. *See* Wage-earning women
Workingwomen's Society (New York City), 182
Works Projects Administration, 301
World Anti-Slavery Convention, 1840, 15
World Telegram, 281
World War I
  National Woman's Party during, 248
  War Labor Board, 258
World War II
  employment following, 391
  office workers unions during, 320
WPA. *See* Works Projects Administration
Wright, Alice Morgan, 362, 364
Wright, Martha, 5, 15
Wright State University, 422, 424
WTUL. *See* Women's Trade Union League

Yarros, Victor, 117
Yeager, John A., 292
"The Yellow Wallpaper" (Gilman), 150-51, 450, 451, 461
Yerger, Mrs. Henry, 289, 293-95
Yonkers (New York), carpet weavers strike, 53
Young Women's Christian Association
  Dayton (Ohio), 437
  discrimination against working women, 177
  Mississippi, Business Girls League, 292
  New York, 182
  and President's Commission on the Status of Women, 283
  Wisconsin, 256
Younger, Maud
  and labor laws, 235
  and National Consumers' League, 249 n.7
  and National Woman's Party, 248, 258, 264, 288, 359
  and protective legislation for women, 260
  and Women's Trade Union League, New York, 1903-1914, 188

Zanesville (Ohio), Ladies of Labor, 51

Bei Fragen zur Produktsicherheit wenden Sie sich bitte an:
If you have any questions regarding product safety,
please contact:

Walter de Gruyter GmbH
Genthiner Straße 13
10785 Berlin
productsafety@degruyterbrill.com